TABLE 2
PRESENT VALUE OF ANNUITY

Interest Rate

Period	0.01	0.02	0.03	0.04	0.05	0.06	0.07	0.08	0.09	0.10	0.11	0.12
1	0.99010	0.98039	0.97087	0.96154	0.95238	0.94340	0.93458	0.92593	0.91743	0.90909	0.90090	0.89286
2	1.97040	1.94156	1.91347	1.88609	1.85941	1.83339	1.80802	1.78326	1.75911	1.73554	1.71252	1.69005
3	2.94099	2.88388	2.82861	2.77509	2.72325	2.67301	2.62432	2.57710	2.53129	2.48685	2.44371	2.40183
4	3.90197	3.80773	3.71710	3.62990	3.54595	3.46511	3.38721	3.31213	3.23972	3.16987	3.10245	3.03735
5	4.85343	4.71346	4.57971	4.45182	4.32948	4.21236	4.10020	3.99271	3.88965	3.79079	3.69590	3.60478
6	5.79548	5.60143	5.41719	5.24214	5.07569	4.91732	4.76654	4.62288	4.48592	4.35526	4.23054	4.11141
7	6.72819	6.47199	6.23028	6.00205	5.78637	5.58238	5.38929	5.20637	5.03295	4.86842	4.71220	4.56376
8	7.65168	7.32548	7.01969	6.73274	6.46321	6.20979	5.97130	5.74664	5.53482	5.33493	5.14612	4.96764
9	8.56602	8.16224	7.78611	7.43533	7.10782	6.80169	6.51523	6.24689	5.99525	5.75902	5.53705	5.32825
10	9.47130	8.98259	8.53020	8.11090	7.72173	7.36009	7.02358	6.71008	6.41766	6.14457	5.88923	5.65022
11	10.36763	9.78685	9.25262	8.76048	8.30641	7.88687	7.49867	7.13896	6.80519	6.49506	6.20652	5.93770
12	11.25508	10.57534	9.95400	9.38507	8.86325	8.38384	7.94269	7.53608	7.16073	6.81369	6.49236	6.19437
13	12.13374	11.34837	10.63496	9.98565	9.39357	8.85268	8.35765	7.90378	7.48690	7.10336	6.74987	6.42355
14	13.00370	12.10625	11.29607	10.56312	9.89864	9.29498	8.74547	8.24424	7.78615	7.36669	6.98187	6.62817
15	13.86505	12.84926	11.93794	11.11839	10.37966	9.71225	9.10791	8.55948	8.06069	7.60608	7.19087	6.81086
16	14.71787	13.57771	12.56110	11.65230	10.83777	10.10590	9.44665	8.85137	8.31256	7.82371	7.37916	6.97399
17	15.56225	14.29187	13.16612	12.16567	11.27407	10.47726	9.76322	9.12164	8.54363	8.02155	7.54879	7.11963
18	16.39827	14.99203	13.75351	12.65930	11.68959	10.82760	10.05909	9.37189	8.75563	8.20141	7.70162	7.24967
19	17.22601	15.67846	14.32380	13.13394	12.08532	11.15812	10.33560	9.60360	8.95011	8.36492	7.83929	7.36578
20	18.04555	16.35143	14.87747	13.59033	12.46221	11.46992	10.59401	9.81815	9.12855	8.51356	7.96333	7.46944
21	18.85698	17.01121	15.41502	14.02916	12.82115	11.76408	10.83553	10.01680	9.29224	8.64869	8.07507	7.56200
22	19.66038	17.65805	15.93692	14.45112	13.16300	12.04158	11.06124	10.20074	9.44243	8.77154	8.17574	7.64465
23	20.45582	18.29220	16.44361	14.85684	13.48857	12.30338	11.27219	10.37106	9.58021	8.88322	8.26643	7.71843
24	21.24339	18.91393	16.93554	15.24696	13.79864	12.55036	11.46933	10.52876	9.70661	8.98474	8.34814	7.78432
25	22.02316	19.52346	17.41315	15.62208	14.09394	12.78336	11.65358	10.67478	9.82258	9.07704	8.42174	7.84314

MANAGERIAL

INFORMATION *for* DECISIONS

ACCOUNTING

Robert W. Ingram
University of Alabama

Thomas L. Albright
University of Alabama

John W. Hill
Indiana University

SOUTH-WESTERN College Publishing

An International Thomson Publishing Company

Sponsoring Editor: Steven W. Hazelwood
Developmental Editor: Sara E. Bates
Production Editor: Peggy A. Williams
Production House: Matrix Productions Inc.
Cover Design: Tin Box Studio
Cover Illustration: John Bleck
Internal Design: Joseph M. Devine and Michael H. Stratton
Exhibit Illustrations: Rick Moore
Exhibit Diagram Illustrations: Mohammad Monsoor
Photo Researcher: Jennifer Mayhall
Marketing Manager: Matthew Filimonov

ISBN: 0-538-86717-5

2 3 4 5 6 7 8 9 VH 4 3 2 1 0 9 8 7

Printed in the United States of America

Library of Congress Cataloging-in-Publication Data

Ingram, Robert W.
    Managerial accounting : information for decisions / Robert W. Ingram,
    Thomas L. Albright, John W. Hill.
        p.   cm.
    Includes index.
    ISBN 0-538-86717-5
    1. Managerial accounting.   I. Albright, Thomas L.,   II. Hill, John W.,
    III. Title.
    HF5657.4.I57   1997
    658.15'11 --dc21   96-39474
                                                                            CIP

International Thomson Publishing
South-Western College Publishing is an ITP Company. The ITP trademark is used under
license.

Dedication

We dedicate this book to our families whose love and support have been essential to our success.

Preface

How to Make an A in this Course
(For Students Only)

We are going to let you in on some trade secrets instructors seldom tell students. That's why this section is labeled, "For Students Only." If instructors find out we have revealed these secrets, we'll probably get a lot of mail.

Getting good grades is not a matter of luck. That's not the secret. Also, it is no secret that doing assignments (on time), going to class (regularly), getting enough sleep and exercise, eating properly, and studying throughout the semester (instead of just at exam time), will improve your grades. But, this is hard work. So, what you want is a way to get good grades and not work so hard, right? Well, pay attention— the secret is to work smarter! That's not the same as being smarter, which is a matter of luck. Here's how you work smarter.

Step 1: Determine why this course is important for you. First, figure out why you're taking this class. What are your goals for the class? Do you care about this course? Do you have a strong motivation to learn about accounting? Perhaps being an accountant comes pretty far down on your list of career options. Maybe your goal is to make lots of money. Or, maybe you're just in college to have a good time until you inherit the family fortune. In any case, this course is designed for you. One of the surest ways to have a million dollars is to start with ten million and not know anything about accounting and business management. If you don't inherit wealth, you're not likely to get it without speaking the language of business. Accounting is the language! Maybe you just want to get a good job, but you're pretty sure you don't want to be an accountant. Fine! This course isn't going to make an accountant out of you. It will help you understand some of the "mystical rituals" of accounting that non-accountants often find confusing. Whatever type of management position you have in any organization, you can be pretty sure you're going to have to work with accountants and with accounting information. You should know they can have a major effect on your life. Many organizations use accounting information to evaluate their employees for salary and promotion decisions. You should understand how to interpret this information. You may even learn accounting isn't what you think.

Whether you grow to love or hate accounting, decide what you can get out of this course that will be useful to you.

Step 2: Find out what your instructor expects of you in the course. Next, check out your instructor. If you're lucky, your instructor is sensitive, warm, caring, has a good sense of humor, is witty, loves teaching, and wants you to do well in the course. If instead, your instructor is more normal (and less perfect), remember, I'm OK, you're OK, and the instructor is still the instructor. And, as the instructor she/he has power over your life. So, find out what she/he expects from you. What are her/his goals for the course? What does she/he want you to know or be able to do once you complete the course? Perhaps, she/he will tell you (good sign), but if not, ask. You should say: "Professor _____ (it would be wise to use the right name) what's the lowdown on the layout for this course?" This is education jargon for "what are your goals for this course?" This may catch her/him off guard, so give her/him a minute or two to think. You may even have to wait until the next class meeting to get your answer. Make sure you and your instructor understand each other's goals. Some accounting instructors expect all their students to become accountants. If you have one of these, make it clear. Tell your instructor: "I don't plan to be an accountant." Find out what's in this course for you.

Step 3: Find out how you will be graded. Now, find out how you will be graded. How does the instructor test? Is she/he one of the picky types: "What is the third word on the fifth line of page 211?" Or, does she/he go in for the broader, thought questions: "Explain how accounting was instrumental in negotiating the third treaty of Versailles in 1623." Does she/he go in for multiple guess, or are short answers her/his cup of tea? We expect our students to be able to interpret financial information. If students come to the exam expecting picky questions from the text, they're likely to be very disappointed. Whatever the method, you need to know what is expected of you and how these expectations translate into grades. Occasionally, you'll find an instructor whose stated expectations don't agree with how she/he tests and grades. That's why you need to find out about both expectations and grades. If they don't seem to be consistent, you'll have to determine what the instructor really expects.

Step 4: Emphasize learning what's important. Figure out what you need to do to accomplish your goals and meet the instructor's (real) expectations. A major lesson you should learn, if you haven't already, is "what you take from a course (and almost anything else) depends on what you bring to it." Your attitude is important. If you decide something is worth learning, you'll probably find a way to learn it. Not because you're supposed to learn it, but because you want to. "Wanting to" is the biggest part of working smarter. Wanting to learn will go a long way toward helping you get a good grade. Unfortunately, it may not be enough unless what you want to learn is also what your instructor wants you to learn. Therefore, you need to make sure you and your instructor are on the same wave length. If you're not, talk it over. Find out why the instructor has a different outlook. You may change your opinion about what's important. Determine how to focus your efforts. Not everything in this book or course is equally important. Focus on what's most important to you and to your instructor.

Step 5: Communicate with your instructor. Try to remember your instructor is a person. Even the authors of this book are people. There are a few instructors around who enjoy treating students like peasants. Luckily, most of us really want to see you do well, but we need your help. Instructors don't know everything. In particular, we can't read your mind. You need to let your instructor know if you're having problems understanding the material you're expected to learn, figuring out what the instructor expects of you, or figuring out how to prepare for tests and other assignments. Talk with your instructor about problems you're having with the class. Remember, your instructor really is human.

This is your class. You paid for it. OK, maybe it was your parents, or somebody else who put out hard, cold cash for you to take this course. Don't let anybody keep you from getting your money's worth. Working smarter means determining what's important and focusing your attention and efforts on these things. Then, don't be distracted from your goals. If you run into problems, deal with them. If you don't understand something in class or in the book, ask questions. If you're afraid of asking dumb questions in class, remember: looking dumb in class is better than looking dumb on an exam. If you think you may be missing key points, talk with your instructor. If you want to learn, you can.

That's it. Give it a try. We think you'll find the course more enjoyable and the experience more rewarding. Of course, you might also try doing assignments, going to class, getting enough sleep and exercise, eating properly, and studying throughout the semester. They usually help, even though they are hard work. Finally, there's no guarantee you'll make an A in this course. But remember, what you take from class depends on what you bring to it.

Best wishes to you, not only in this course, but throughout life.

Rob Ingram
Tom Albright
John Hill

A side note:

To aid you in the learning process, basic concepts are indicated by margin icons. The concepts and their respective icons are shown below.

Transformation Process		Control of Accounting Systems	
Decisions, Decision Making, Analysis, Understanding, Strategy		Time, Accrual Accounting	
Organizations, Management, Professionals		International	
Accounting Information Systems		Stockholders	
Accounting, Processing Accounting Information		Obligations, Valuation, Contracts, Service Organizations	

Effect of Business Activities (Risk and Return, Efficiency and Effectiveness, Business Results)

Costs

New Business Environment

Comparison between methods, pros and cons of a method

Traditional Approach to Management Accounting

An Example

One more icon ⟩ON⟨ THE INTERNET lets you know there's a related Internet hotlink connected to the text's World Wide Web site. Visit our site and follow the directions.

Preface

To the Instructor

PURPOSE AND OBJECTIVES

This introduction to managerial accounting presents basic accounting concepts that are important to management decisions in the modern business environment. The purpose of the book is to help students learn how to use accounting information. Thus, the emphasis is on analyzing and interpreting information rather than on information preparation. While procedures that are important for understanding the information are explained, an effort has been made to keep those explanations brief and simple.

This book views managerial accounting within the context of multidisciplinary management. In modern organizations, management accountants work with managers from other areas, particularly marketing and operations. Accountants are part of a team, and the members of that team use accounting information to resolve questions about costing, pricing, and production. Therefore, we believe that it is critical that accounting be viewed from the perspective of management decision making. The book examines the types of internal decisions that rely on accounting information. The tools and information that are important are described within the decision framework. For example, make or buy and sell-now or process-further decisions are considered part of cost behavior since they are applications of cost behavior concepts, not isolated accounting procedures. Certain topics that are becoming less important in modern organizations but often are included in introductory managerial accounting texts are omitted. Examples include fixed overhead variances and FIFO process costing.

PEDAGOGY

A pedagogical technique used frequently in this book is to bring students into the management decision process. Students "sit in" on managers' discussions about business problems, such as transfer pricing decisions. An attempt is made to help students understand how managers think about problems and the reasoning that underlies the accounting tools and information they use. These discussions and the examples used throughout the text are based on the authors' experiences with actual companies. The problems are real, and the approaches to solving the problems are those actually applied by real people.

Other pedagogical techniques are used to provide structure, coherence, and consistency to the material so that students can follow the flow of content from chapter to chapter. A decision wheel at the beginning of each chapter links the chapter content to management decisions and helps the students follow the flow of content from chapter to chapter. Students are reminded in each chapter of the importance of accounting information for decisions. Each chapter begins with a brief overview of major topics. Learning objectives are provided at the beginning of each chapter and are repeated within the chapter as the relevant material for each objective is presented. The learning objectives to which end-of-chapter exercises and problems relate are also identified.

Each chapter contains three self-study problems, along with answers, to reinforce major topics and help students test their understanding of the material as they read the chapters. Also, the chapters contain Learning Notes that identify issues that frequently are troublesome to students. These notes highlight the issues and draw students' attention to them. Cases in Point are included in the chapters to identify real-world examples of companies that are dealing with the problems and issues discussed in the chapter. Many exhibits are used to present concepts visually and to underscore major relationships that are important for understanding the concepts. Key terms are highlighted in the chapter and listed at the end of each chapter to assist students in developing their management vocabulary. A glossary at the end of the book provides a readily accessible source of definitions when students find they need to refresh their memories. A review of important concepts at the end of each chapter outlines key topics and relationships among the topics. End-of-chapter exercises, problems, cases, and projects emphasize the use of accounting information in decisions. Students frequently are asked to apply their knowledge to management problems, to analyze how they would approach and solve problems, and to communicate their solutions in short memos or reports. Thinking and communication skills are emphasized along with computational and technical accounting skills.

Throughout the text a World Wide Web icon appears in the margin. This icon indicates to the student that more information can be obtained from the Internet by first going to the Ingram site. From that site the viewer can hotlink to the appropriate topic highlighted in the chapter.

CONTENT

This book integrates the new management environment throughout rather than separating such topics in isolated or add-on sections. The theory of constraints, advanced manufacturing technology, just-in-time manufacturing, cellular manufacturing, statistical process control, and nonfinancial performance measures are introduced as common concepts or approaches to decision making in the modern organization. Activity-based costing is considered as an approach to product mix and pricing decisions in a multiproduct environment. Application of these approaches to decisions, rather than computational mechanics, is emphasized. Traditional and new business environment approaches are compared and contrasted when appropriate to draw attention to changes in concepts and their effects on management decisions.

This book includes topics that are not considered in detail in most managerial accounting texts. Internal control is presented as a major concern of managerial accounting. Students are introduced to basic internal control concepts and reasons for the importance of these concepts in modern business organizations. Japanese cost management techniques are described because of their growing importance. These approaches are being adapted in many organizations, and some are likely to be common in the business environment today's students will experience during their careers. Throughout the book, emphasis is placed on accounting decisions in both manufacturing and service companies. A separate chapter also is included to describe those accounting issues that are especially relevant for service organizations.

Chapter 1, **Accounting and Management Decisions,** introduces the role of managerial accounting in making business decisions. After describing the traditional view of managerial accounting as a planning and control tool, it summarizes the implications for managerial accounting of the new business environment and the emerging global economy. This discussion explains why managerial accounting is changing in response to the demands of the new environment. A major aspect of this change is the increasing interaction between accounting and other areas, particularly marketing and operations, where accounting information is important for many business decisions. The chapter also introduces activity-based costing because of its important role in strategic cost management.

Chapter 2, **Cost Categorization, Cost Flow, and Measurement Decisions,** uses the manufacturing process of a typical company to illustrate manufacturing cost flows and classifications. Students are introduced to the relationship between costs and volume and the importance of this relationship for decisions. Target costing, make or buy decisions, and sell-now or process-further decisions are integrated with the cost behavior discussion.

Chapter 3, **Unit Costs for Decision Making,** explains the importance of unit costs in decisions within manufacturing and service companies. It examines the costs that should be included in unit costs, how to measure these costs, and appropriate methods for assigning unit costs. Job-order and process costing are considered in a conceptual, rather than procedural, manner.

Chapter 4, **Cost Measurement for Management,** examines cost behavior further. Variable costing is discussed in the context of cost-volume-profit analysis and in comparison to absorption costing. Differences between variable and absorption costing are explained. The advantages and disadvantages of each approach are considered for decision making, including decision making in service organizations.

Chapter 5, **Cost Allocation and Business Strategy,** describes how important marketing and production decisions can be supported by a well-designed cost management system. Activity-based costing principles are illustrated using two competing manufacturing companies. One is a single-product company, and the other is a multiproduct company. Students "tour" the factories to better understand the production environment. Cooper's hierarchy of overhead costs is explained.

Chapter 6, **The Role of Budgets in Decision Making,** describes how budgets are used and how a master budget is developed. The chapter discusses the basic analysis of budget data and the difference between static and flexible budgets. The effects of inflation and foreign operations on budgets are covered. The chapter emphasizes the elements of effective budgeting and the need for a sound budget culture. Special consideration is given to behavioral aspects of budgeting and how budgets influence strategic decisions.

Chapter 7, **Evaluating Performance Within an Organization,** uses a factory that prints designs on containers to illustrate concepts of variance analysis, statistical process control, and quality costs. A team made up of an accountant, an engineer, a purchasing manager, a personnel manager, and a plant manager discusses behavioral problems caused by an emphasis on variances. The team searches for nontraditional performance measures to drive its quality initiative.

Chapter 8, **Management Accounting in a Global Business Environment,** explores the manufacturing process of a rotary mower manufacturer to illustrate the concepts of total quality management, just-in-time manufacturing, and the theory of constraints. Students are guided through the development of nonfinancial performance measures, such as cycle time, lead time, and throughput. Also, they learn to identify bottlenecks in a manufacturing process. The chapter focuses on decisions for process improvement and how these decisions are important to corporate strategy.

Chapter 9, **Controlling Decisions in Decentralized Organizations,** uses the pulp and paper divisions of a paper company to illustrate the concepts of decentralized organizations. The manager of each division is evaluated using return on investment. The pulp division supplies raw materials to the paper division, providing a test case for evaluating the effect of financial performance measures on behavior. In addition, dialogue among division managers and a corporate representative examines the pros and cons of various transfer pricing models.

Chapter 10, **Decisions About Capital Investments,** describes traditional tools for capital investment analysis, such as net present value and internal rate of return. It also identifies the limitations of these tools in the new business environment. The importance of capital investments in supporting a company's strategy is emphasized. The discussion includes extensive treatment of the behavioral aspects of budgeting. The chapter also examines the common problem of continuing to fund unsuccessful projects and ways to prevent this problem.

Chapter 11, **Internal Control,** introduces internal control concepts and procedures. Internal control is an important accounting and management issue that often is omitted from business education, especially for nonaccounting majors. This chapter presents a simple, applied overview of the purpose of internal control. Examples of internal control problems are used to introduce methods that are commonly used to detect and prevent these problems.

Chapter 12, **A Closer Look at Service Companies,** uses a medical center as an example of a service organization. A team-based management approach is illustrated through dialogue among clinical and financial managers who are responsible for restructuring the hospital's care delivery system. Topics include allocating service department costs to revenue-producing departments and tracing costs to a patient. The chapter underscores the national debate over escalating health care costs while illustrating how a cost management system is part of a strategic plan to reduce costs, restructure operations, and improve quality.

Chapter 13, **The Japanese Perspective,** examines Japanese cost management systems, relying largely on the work of Robin Cooper. A sports clothing manufacturer provides an example of introducing a new garment in a highly competitive market. Employees who have returned recently from a Japanese exchange program discuss whether Japanese cost management techniques would be useful for their company. Topics include strategic positioning of a new product, target costing, value engineering, and micro-profit centers.

STYLE

The style of the text includes features to capture, maintain, and focus student interest. A full-color, visual format is used to stimulate and hold students' attention. Primary headings include icons to identify the section's primary content. A reader-friendly writing style, including dialogue and real-world stories, assists with comprehension. Students are encouraged to apply what they are learning to issues with which they are familiar. Photos at the beginning of each chapter help students visualize the business environment to which each chapter is related. Additional photos in the chapters identify products and company settings for topics and self-study problem materials. End-of-chapter materials include exercises, problems, cases, and projects that are suitable for cooperative and group-oriented learning approaches. Extreme care has been used in proofing text, problem, and solution materials to avoid errors and misstatements. All of these features are intended to make the text user-friendly and to encourage student reading and comprehension.

An important goal in writing this book has been to help students view accounting as an essential tool that is relevant to them as future managers. We want them to view accounting not as a set of technical procedures or as a separate discipline, but as a way of viewing business problems that is applicable to them, regardless of their intended major.

ANCILLARIES

Accompanying this text are several helpful ancillaries.

For the Student:

Study Guide: This guide reinforces and enhances student understanding of the topics covered in the text. It is a thorough, value-adding book that has been carefully prepared by Stephen Senge and George Sanders, both of Western Washington University. (0-538-86720-5)

PowerNotes and Forms: Contained in this book are copies of the key PowerPoint slides with space for note taking. In addition, working paper forms have been included to assist students in preparing selected homework assignments. (0-538-86932-1)

BusinessLink Video Workbook: Enrich student understanding of the BusinessLink Video through questions and activities presented in this student workbook. (0-538-87053-2)

For the Instructor:

Solutions Manual: Carefully verified solutions to all exercises, problems, and cases are presented in this manual. Because of the open-ended nature of the projects, it is not possible to provide solutions to them. (0-538-86721-3)

Test Bank: A thorough, carefully prepared and verified test bank provides testing materials for key points covered in each chapter. (0-538-86722-1)

MicroExam: This microcomputer test-generation package, which contains the test bank, allows for random selection of questions and, if desired, generation of multiple tests. Instructor-created items may be imported in ASCII format for more customized testing. MicroExam can be used on the IBM PC and compatible machines. (0-538-86846-5)

Cooperative Learning Techniques and Instructor's Guide: Contained in this supporting item are chapters explaining cooperative learning techniques for use in the classroom and matrices that suggest application of techniques to specific end-of-chapter items. Philip Cottell, Jr., of Miami University and Barbara Millis of the Air Force Academy have prepared this information. In addition, there are outlines of each chapter and teaching notes to assist in class preparation. (0-538-86723-X)

PowerPoint Presentations: Creatively prepared by Paul Juras of Wake Forest University, these colorful, lively PowerPoint slides present the key topics of each chapter. This product has a built-in PowerPoint viewer program. (0-538-86848-1)

Solution Transparencies: Where appropriate, solutions to the end-of-chapter assignments have been printed in large type on easy to read acetate transparencies for use in classroom coverage. (0-538-86849-X)

Cooperative Learning Workshop Video: This workshop video presents Philip Cottell, Jr., of Miami University, who explains a number of cooperative learning techniques for use in the teaching of accounting. (0-538-86498-2)

BusinessLink Video: Five video segments cover activity-based costing, performance evaluation, just-in-time manufacturing, quality, and differential/incremental analysis. Real companies are featured. (0-538-87052-4)

BusinessLink Video Instructor's Manual: This manual assists instructors in the use of the BusinessLink Video and student workbook. (0-538-87054-0)

Acknowledgments

The authors gratefully acknowledge the suggestions of those who have assisted in reviewing this text.

Deborah F. Beard   *Southeast Missouri State University*
Douglas Blocher   *Indiana University*
Louann Hofheins Cummings   *Siena Heights College*
Todd DeZoort   *University of South Carolina*
Sheila D. Foster   *The Citadel*
Lou Fowler   *Missouri Western State College*
Larry Hegstad   *Pacific Lutheran University*
Robert G. Held   *William Rainey Harper Community College*
Dan A. Hulett   *Anoka-Ramsey Community College*
Debra Kirby   *Truman State University*
Charles R. Lacey   *Henry Ford Community College*
Stan Locknar   *McHenry County College*
Alexander J. Sannella   *Rutgers University*
Nancy L. Saltz   *Lynchburg College*
Ronald P. Stephenson   *Indiana University*
Mary Tharp   *Kirkwood Community College*
Scott H. Wang   *Detroit College of Business*

The authors are particularly indebted to Kevin Smith of Indiana University for his assistance in preparing end-of-chapter materials.

The authors also acknowledge the professional assistance of the South-Western College Publishing Accounting Team, which has been instrumental in creating this book.

About the Authors

ROBERT W. INGRAM

Robert W. Ingram is the Ross-Culverhouse Chair in the Culverhouse School of Accountancy at the University of Alabama. He teaches courses in financial accounting and has been actively involved in course curriculum development. He has served as Director of Education for the American Accounting Association, as a member of the Accounting Education Change Commission, and as editor of *Issues in Accounting Education,* a journal dedicated to accounting education research.

Professor Ingram is a Certified Public Accountant and holds a Ph.D. from Texas Tech University. Prior to joining the faculty at the University of Alabama, he held positions at the University of South Carolina and the University of Iowa, and a visiting appointment at the University of Chicago. His research, which examines financial reporting and accounting education, has been published widely in accounting and business journals. He is the recipient of the National Alumni Association Outstanding Commitment of Teaching Award and the Burlington Northern Foundation Faculty Achievement in Research Award at the University of Alabama. He has also received the Notable Contribution to Literature Award of the Government and Nonprofit Section of the American Accounting Association and the Award for Excellence and Professional Contributions of the Alabama Association for Higher Education in Business.

Professor Ingram is married and has two children. He and his family enjoy sports, travel, reading, music, and art. They live contentedly in Tuscaloosa, Alabama.

THOMAS L. ALBRIGHT

Thomas L. Albright is an associate professor of accounting in the Culverhouse School of Accountancy at the University of Alabama. He teaches undergraduate cost accounting and the management accounting component in the MBA and Executive MBA curriculum.

Professor Albright is a Certified Public Accountant (California) and holds a Ph.D. from the University of Tennessee. His research and consulting activities have spanned various industries including paper, farm equipment manufacturing, iron casting, telecommunications, glass production, metal decorating, and health care. Dr. Albright is a frequent contributor to academic and applied accounting journals in the area of cost system design and performance measurement. He has been the recipient of the Faculty Excellence Award on three occasions in relation to his work with MBA and Executive MBA students. In 1993 he received the Certificate of Merit from the Institute of Management Accountants.

Professor Albright lives with his wife, Debby, and their two children, Michael and Jenny. He enjoys scuba diving and underwater photography.

JOHN W. HILL

John W. Hill is Chairman, Accounting Graduate Programs and Price Waterhouse Faculty Fellow at Indiana University. He teaches courses in management accounting and financial statement analysis and has developed courses at the undergraduate and MBA levels in both topics. He serves on the editorial boards of four journals including the *Journal of Accounting Education* and *Accounting Education: A Journal of Theory, Practice & Research*. He has published articles about accounting education in academic and practice journals.

Professor Hill is a member of the Georgia Bar Association and holds a Ph.D. from the University of Iowa. Prior to becoming an academic, he was the chief financial officer of a bank. His research, which focuses on auditor litigation and turnover, financial institutions and management accounting, has been published in numerous journals. He is the recipient of eleven teaching awards and recognitions including the President's Award for Distinguished Teaching at Indiana University. He has won the Deloitte & Touche/American Accounting Association Wildman Medal for research that has made the greatest contribution to the practice of accounting. He has also received the Silver and Bronze Lybrand Medals and three Certificates of Merit from the Institute of Management Accountants for excellence in contributing to the management accounting literature.

Professor Hill is married and has three grown children. He and his wife live in Bloomington, Indiana with their cat and four dogs. In his spare time, he is a major general in the U.S. Marine Corps Reserve and enjoys caving, weight lifting, and jogging with Jack, his faithful canine companion of many years.

Brief Contents

Contents

4 Cost Measurement for Management   110

5 Cost Allocation and Business Strategy   146

SECTION 2
CONTROL, MEASUREMENT, AND EVALUATION   183

6 The Role of Budgets in Decision Making   184

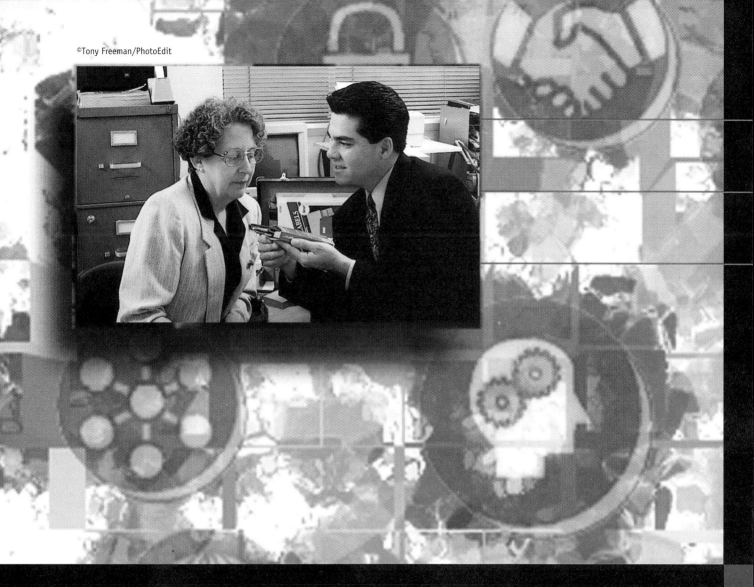

Section 1

Product Costing and Decision Making

Accounting and Management Decisions

Accounting and Management Decisions

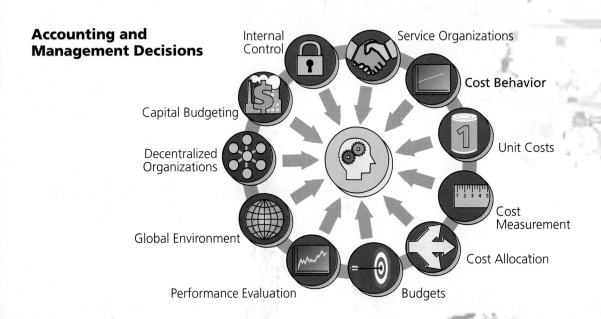

Internal Control

Service Organizations

Cost Behavior

Unit Costs

Cost Measurement

Cost Allocation

Budgets

Performance Evaluation

Global Environment

Decentralized Organizations

Capital Budgeting

Overview

Accounting information used by *external* decision makers is **financial accounting information,** whereas accounting information used by *internal* decision makers is **managerial (or management) accounting information.** Managerial accounting historically has been viewed as a tool for planning and control. Recently, however, it has been suggested that this view is too narrow and sometimes leads to poor decisions. This chapter discusses criticisms of the traditional view of managerial accounting. It also describes how managerial accounting is changing to meet the needs of businesses in complex, dynamic, and global markets.

A main question in this text is, "How can accounting information assist managers who make marketing and operations decisions?" Many critical marketing and operations decisions depend on accounting information. Other users of managerial accounting information may be connected to marketing and operations. This text emphasizes the marketing and operations uses of accounting information and identifies many internal decisions that rely on this information.

This chapter introduces managerial accounting and provides an overview of its role in decision making. It provides a foundation for discussing the topics shown in the above graphic, which will appear at the beginning of each subsequent chapter with the topic of the chapter highlighted. These topics are important for understanding managerial accounting. Each topic will be explained in more detail in a future chapter.

©Walter Hodges/Tony Stone Images

Objectives

Once you have completed this chapter, you should be able to:

1. Explain the purpose of managerial accounting and why it is important.
2. Distinguish managerial from financial accounting.
3. Explain how changes in the business environment are affecting managerial accounting.
4. Discuss how the quality of managerial accounting information affects decision making.
5. Explain the role of managerial accounting in planning and control decisions.
6. Discuss how strategic and operational planning use accounting information.
7. Identify governance and measurement aspects of control that rely on accounting information.
8. Discuss ways in which managerial accounting interacts with marketing and operations in the new business environment.
9. Describe major changes in management philosophy resulting from the new business environment.
10. Identify weaknesses of traditional managerial accounting techniques.
11. Identify managerial accounting techniques that have been developed to meet information needs in the new business environment.
12. Identify ways managerial accounting assists service companies.

Major topics covered in this chapter include:
- The importance of managerial accounting information for decision making in a company.
- The traditional view of managerial accounting, focusing on planning and control.
- The implications that a growing global economy has for managerial accounting.
- Relationships among managerial accounting and marketing and operations decisions.
- Changes needed in managerial accounting in response to the global economy.

INTRODUCTION TO MANAGERIAL ACCOUNTING

Objective 1
Explain the purpose of managerial accounting and why it is important.

Different activities within a company, such as marketing and operations, require different types of accounting information for decision making. For example, marketing managers consider the cost per unit of a product when they determine a price for that product. On the other hand, operations managers may be interested in the cost of the labor, materials, and overhead required to make the product. Thus, the needs for managerial accounting information differ depending on the types of decisions being made.

Also, new demands for information arise as the business environment changes. For instance, as the profit earned on a line of products begins to shrink, accurate information about the cost of manufacturing the product becomes critical if the product is to remain profitable. A shrinking profit may indicate a shift in consumer preferences and a need to change the way a company competes. In that instance, the company may need to become a low-cost producer rather than competing on the basis of product features or quality.

Changes in companies' strategies have taken place in recent years because of intense foreign competition and the growing complexity of business. These changes have increased demand for accurate, high-quality managerial accounting information. However, systems that produce high-quality information often are expensive. The more detailed and accurate the information, the more it costs to produce. This cost includes the cost of the accounting systems that produce information and the cost of the services of the employees who design and manage these systems. Therefore, companies must balance the level of detail and accuracy they demand from their accounting systems in order to make good business decisions with what is affordable.

Corporate Structure and Accounting Information Needs

As companies grow, they divide managerial responsibilities among a larger number of people. Businesses frequently are organized according to functions to assist in decision making and control. For example, a company might be structured around the functions of accounting, finance, information systems, marketing, and production. Middle managers report to the company's top managers. Top managers develop company goals and the plans to achieve these goals. Top management also is responsible for reporting to stockholders, creditors, and other external decision makers. As illustrated in Exhibit 1, the types of information that different decision makers need depend on their positions in an organization's structure. Those at the top of the structure require less detailed and timely information about the ongoing operations of a company than those at the bottom of the structure.

Each function in a business usually has subdivisions, resulting in an organization with several layers of management. Typically, the higher managers are in the structure, the more responsibility they have for results and the more authority they have to make decisions. These decisions often require information that is more timely and detailed than the information required by external decision makers. Therefore, in markets where the prices and costs of products change frequently, marketing managers may need continuous information about product costs to make profitable sales.

Some of the accounting information used for internal decision making is the same as that reported to external decision makers. For example, the product cost information used for internal decisions also may be used in valuing inventories for a company's financial statements. Top managers often examine financial accounting information to evaluate a company's overall performance. However, the managerial accounting information provided to decision makers within the organization differs in many respects from the information reported externally. These differences will be considered in this and future chapters.

Exhibit 1   Types of Users and Information Needs

Users	Accounting Information Needs
External Users	Summary information about performance for a period of time (financial accounting)
Stockholders, creditors	
Top Management	Information for evaluating performance, for establishing goals, and for devising plans to meet goals (financial and managerial accounting)
Board of directors	
Chief executive officer	
Functional and Division Managers	Timely and detailed information for evaluating performance and implementing plans (primarily managerial accounting)
Accounting	
Finance	
Information systems	
Marketing	
Operations	
Product and territory sales managers	
Plant managers	
Middle Managers	Very timely and detailed information for day-to-day decisions to achieve company goals (managerial accounting)
Sales representatives	
Production managers	
Purchasing managers	
Service managers	

Objective 2
Distinguish managerial from financial accounting.

Financial accounting provides information that conforms with generally accepted accounting principles (GAAP). GAAP help to ensure that information is consistent from period to period and is comparable across companies. This information is valuable particularly to stakeholders, such as stockholders and creditors, who have limited access to information about companies.

An accountant who produces managerial accounting information for a specific company is referred to as a *management accountant*. Because managerial accounting information is used only within a company, it does not have to conform to GAAP. Rather, it is produced in a variety of formats that meet the particular information needs of a company's managers. Thus, the type, format, amount of detail, and timeliness of the information differ between financial and managerial accounting.

The Changing Needs of Business

Objective 3
Explain how changes in the business environment are affecting managerial accounting.

Prior to World War II, the United States produced about one-fourth of the world's total goods and services. After World War II, all of the world's major economies except that of the United States had been severely damaged by the war. In contrast, the United States emerged with a huge productive capacity, greatly increased by the war effort, and a labor force swollen by returning veterans. As a result, following the war, the United States produced about one-half of the world's total goods and services. Most products consumed in the United States were produced in this country. In this type of environment, U.S. businesses could survive using less than optimal business practices. The situation began to change, however, with the growth of economies in Western Europe and Asia during the 1960s and 1970s. Foreign competitors seriously challenged U.S. companies with high-quality, technologically sophisticated products. U.S. companies had to change if they were to remain competitive in a global economy.

In recent years, changes in the ways companies market and produce their goods and services have led to changes in managers' needs for accounting information. For example, increased foreign competition has led U.S. firms to place more emphasis on the quality of the goods and services they produce. This emphasis on quality and the increasing complexity of business have increased the demand for timely and accurate information, thereby changing the role of managerial accounting.

Competition is driving many manufacturing and service companies to redesign their marketing and operations to better meet the demands of a changing marketplace. Examples of such changes are just-in-time manufacturing, time-based management, and total quality management, which are described later in this chapter. Managerial accounting systems are being redesigned to meet the changing information needs caused by these changes in the way products and services are created and delivered.

Today, many U.S. businesses are changing their management philosophies to become more competitive. These changes frequently involve:

- New marketing strategies directed at global markets
- Emphasis on customer satisfaction, including a focus on product quality and variety
- Large investments in new production technologies, including increased reliance on robotics and computerized manufacturing
- New relationships between management and labor that emphasize a greater role for labor in many decisions
- Creation of management teams with representatives from the various functional areas of business, including accounting
- Development of real-time (immediate) business information systems

As visualized in Exhibit 2, these changes have created a "new business environment," which has brought a high degree of product and service complexity, a greater number of parts that go into products, and new types of business transactions.

Exhibit 2   The New Business Environment

Managerial accounting must change in two ways if businesses are to compete successfully in this new competitive environment. First, management accountants must become involved in making decisions about a company's products and the processes used to create, market, and deliver these products. Through this involvement, management accountants can identify the critical accounting information needs of other decision makers. Second, decision makers throughout a company must be able to use accounting information properly. This means that decision makers must have a knowledge of managerial accounting concepts and techniques. It also means that they must be aware of the potential inaccuracies in accounting information. Companies that fail to make these changes in their managerial accounting systems are likely to receive inadequate information that leads to poor decisions.

The Quality of Accounting Information

Objective 4
Discuss how the quality of managerial accounting information affects decision making.

The quality of information must be weighed against its cost. To be useful, information must have the potential to affect decisions and influence behavior. If a company is to perform well, information must be accurate enough to lead to the right decisions and behaviors. Accounting information often is not as accurate as many decision makers believe, however.

Accountants have some choice regarding the methods used to produce accounting information. GAAP permit choice in methods of measuring certain activities and reporting them to external decision makers, such as the choice of inventory and depreciation methods. Estimation also is used in preparing accounting information, such as estimation of the expected useful lives of depreciable assets. When accounting information is prepared for *internal purposes,* a company is not restricted to any particular accounting methods. Nevertheless, companies often use the same accounting methods for internal purposes that they use for external purposes. Unfortunately, accounting systems and methods designed for external reporting are not always well suited for internal use. An example of this is accounting for plant assets on the basis of historical cost which is required by GAAP. Using historical costs in plant replacement decisions, however, may lead to poor decisions.

The decision about using financial accounting systems for internal purposes usually involves weighing the increased accuracy that comes from separate systems against the costs of maintaining two systems. Greater accuracy in accounting information is costly, because greater accuracy frequently involves more extensive data collection. Thus, a company must decide how much accuracy it needs and how much it is willing to pay for this accuracy. Further, **a particular accounting system that is adequate for one company may be inadequate for another because of differences in strategies, markets, production and delivery systems, and controls.**

All accounting systems rely on assumptions and choices, such as the choice of LIFO or FIFO to estimate inventory and cost of goods sold. The usefulness of an accounting system depends largely on how well these assumptions fit the intended purpose of the information. For example, if products are sold separately, accurate costs for each individual product are needed, but the accuracy of individual product costs may not be as important if products are sold only as a bundle. Therefore, the following are important questions when assessing the adequacy of managerial accounting systems:

- What is the intended use of the information produced by a system?
- How accurate does the information need to be?
- Is greater accuracy worth the cost?

SELF-STUDY PROBLEM 1

Charles Robert Carpets, Inc., (CRC) is a manufacturer of commercial carpet for use in vehicles and boats. Though sales of automobile carpet represent most of CRC's business, the recreational vehicle (RV) and boat (marine) markets have been growing in recent years. CRC's automobile carpet products are sold to companies, called finishers, that cut and bind the carpet to fit into a vehicle. Most of these finishers are divisions of major automobile manufacturers. In the nonautomobile markets, CRC sells to independent finishing companies that concentrate on those markets. The vehicle and boat markets tend to change with the economy. During periods when the economy is growing and unemployment is low, vehicle and boat sales are higher than during slow periods, when unemployment is high. CRC's management has considered manufacturing carpet for the housing market, but senior management has rejected this idea, believing that it is better for the company to compete solely in the vehicle and boat markets.

Required

What does CRC's business suggest to you about its need for accurate cost accounting information to aid in marketing and production planning? CRC earns a profit of about 10% on its sales. Is the accuracy of accounting information more important to CRC than to a grocery store chain that has a profit of 4% on its sales? Explain your answer.

The solution to Self-Study Problem 1 appears at the end of the chapter.

THE ROLE OF MANAGERIAL ACCOUNTING IN PLANNING AND CONTROL

Objective 5
Explain the role of managerial accounting in planning and control decisions.

Managerial accounting traditionally has been viewed as providing the "numbers" needed for two management functions, planning and control. Planning and control are important for business success. Managerial accounting information is very important to planning and control.

Exhibit 3 illustrates the planning and control process. Managers **(a) develop goals,** such as a target return on assets, which are major outcomes desired by top management. Next, managers **(b) set specific objectives,** such as target income for each division of the company, and **(c) make plans** for achieving these objectives. Then management **(d) implements the plans and controls the actions** of employees to ensure proper execution of the plans. Managers **(e) evaluate the performance of products, services, activities, and people** who are responsible for them. As feedback about how well plans are being met is received, adjustments are made. This means that management **(f) modifies its goals** or changes its plans or procedures for meeting these goals. The process then is repeated. Managerial accounting provides financial numbers used in making these planning and control decisions.

As an illustration, consider the process of purchasing various types of synthetic fiber used to make carpet at Charles Robert Carpets, a manufacturer of carpet for

Exhibit 3 The Planning and Control Process

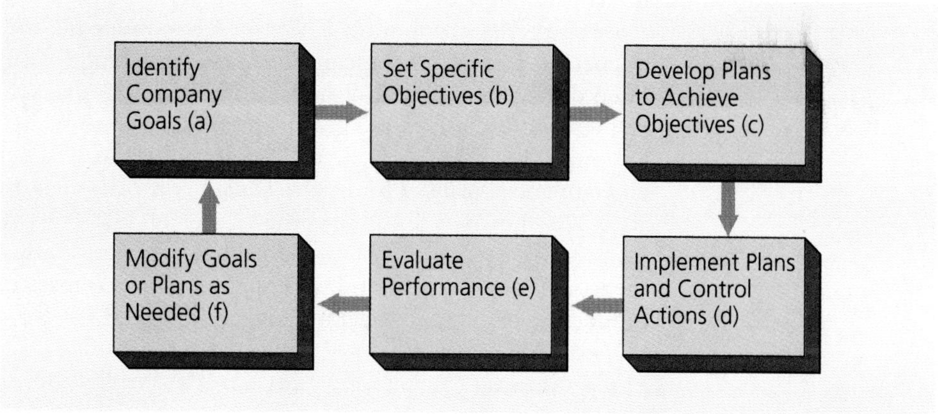

automobiles, recreational vehicles, and boats. Before the beginning of the year, management sets a goal to maintain production costs at a specific level (a). It establishes a specific objective by identifying a planned cost for each type of synthetic fiber used in its products (b). The purchasing department, which is responsible for purchasing all raw materials used in production, is held accountable for meeting this objective. It creates a plan to meet the objective by identifying sources of materials and negotiating costs with suppliers (c). The purchasing department buys the materials at the agreed-upon costs (d). After the year begins, the vice president of operations, who is responsible for the purchasing department, receives periodic reports identifying the actual cost of various types of fiber and comparing these costs to planned costs (e). If the actual costs exceed the planned costs, the differences are investigated to determine their cause. The production cost goal may have to be adjusted, or a new source of materials may be sought in order to achieve the existing goal (f).

Planning

Objective 6
Discuss how strategic and operational planning use accounting information.

Planning involves creating a map for achieving corporate goals and objectives. Planning can be strategic or operational. *Strategic planning* **involves identifying a company's long-run goals and developing plans for achieving these goals.** Strategic plans often involve large investments. Strategic decisions include starting a new line of products, building a new plant, or entering a foreign market for the first time.

An example of strategic planning at CRC would be a long-term plan for financing a new line of boat carpets. Strategic planning almost always involves top management because of its importance to a company's long-run success. CRC's chief executive, marketing, operations, and financial officers probably would participate in a decision to expand into a new product line.

Operational planning **involves identifying objectives for day-to-day activities.** For example, CRC would need to plan the types and amounts of carpet to be produced each day to meet sales requirements for the boat line. Except in small companies, operational plans often are made by middle management with input from top management. In planning CRC's daily production requirements, the production manager would work with managers in marketing, purchasing, and accounting to plan production and to ensure that sufficient materials were available to meet production goals.

Operational planning also involves setting *performance objectives,* **which are standards for the desired performance of various divisions of a company.** Every department is expected to meet specific performance objectives. The marketing department has sales quotas, and the production department has production quantity and quality expectations. Performance standards are a major part of operational planning and are used to evaluate performance.

Managerial accounting is important in strategic and operational planning. An important part of strategic planning is long-range financial planning. Companies often develop strategic, long-range financial plans that set target financial results several years into the future. These plans are supported by operational plans that forecast the monthly or quarterly financial results necessary to achieve the company's long-range financial plans. **The** *master budget* **is a one-year financial plan for a company.** As shown in Exhibit 4, the master budget ties together long-range financial plans and day-to-day financial objectives for the company's divisions and departments. It is developed from other operational plans for specific activities, such as sales, production costs, and operating expenses. The master budget identifies required investment in new plant assets and expected cash flows. It also describes expected profits for a company's product lines and major divisions.

Exhibit 4 Levels of Planning

Type of Plan	Planning Time Horizon	Nature of Planning
Strategic financial plan	Several years in the future	Sets major financial goals, such as long-range profitability, targeted stock price, and shares of major markets.
Master budget	Annual	Provides a one-year financial master plan linking long-range planning with operational planning. Developed from operational budgets such as projected sales, production, operating expenses, and cash flows.
Operational budgets	Monthly to quarterly	Provide specific inputs to the master budget. Often developed at the divisional and departmental levels as well as for the company as a whole.

Operational planning often involves departmental budgeting, analysis of budgeted versus actual revenues and costs, and evaluation of departmental performance. Inadequate and inaccurate data can result in budgets that provide poor plans. Imagine what would happen if CRC's budget greatly overstated the profits that could be generated by a new product line. CRC would invest in new plant assets and market its new line, only to discover that its profits were much lower than expected.

Decision making during the planning process often involves choosing among alternatives. For example, management may need to decide whether to use cash (1) to offer a new line of products or (2) to invest in new equipment that will improve the quality of existing products. Once a plan is adopted, however, management must continue to make decisions in order to implement the plan. Management accountants become involved in several types of ongoing decisions. Examples include decisions

- to continue producing a product or to drop it from a product line,
- to retain or close a branch or plant facility,
- to accept or reject a special product order from a customer,
- to complete a product or sell it partially completed at a lower price,
- to produce more of one product or more of another, and
- to keep, reduce, or eliminate certain costs.

Control

O b j e c t i v e   7
Identify governance and
measurement aspects of
control that rely on
accounting information.

Once a plan is in place, it is necessary to monitor the performance of a company and its members. In all but the smallest companies, monitoring usually means assigning the responsibility for achieving certain objectives to specific managers and evaluating their success. **Control involves identifying and rewarding behavior that encourages desired outcomes and detecting and correcting behavior that does not.** It is concerned with controlling people's behavior so that desired outcomes are achieved. A company identifies performance characteristics useful for evaluating results. Measurement of these characteristics can be objective or subjective, formal or informal, but in any case it is tied to some form of incentive system. Identification and detection can be accomplished using three methods:

- Directly observing behavior to assess the quantity and quality of effort
- Measuring the outcomes of behavior
- Establishing informal work environment habits (corporate culture) that guide behavior

Many businesses use some combination of all three methods of control. For example, **Schofield Electronic Instruments, Inc.,** uses direct **observation of behavior** by office managers to control the quality and efficiency of clerical personnel in the telephone sales department. These employees perform tasks such as answering incoming calls, returning customers' calls, taking orders, and processing order forms. Their work is observable by the department manager, who can control behavior and take corrective action. For example, if telephones are unanswered after several rings, an office manager can temporarily reassign people to telephone duty to correct the situation. In this environment, performance measurement tends to be subjective and is based on effort.

Control of outside sales personnel is a different matter. Because outside sales representatives frequently travel alone, their behavior is not directly observable. Therefore, Schofield **measures** sales **outcomes** to control behavior. Representatives are assigned sales dollar quotas and are evaluated on whether they meet these quotas. A large portion of a sales representative's compensation is determined by sales outcomes.

Laboratory workers responsible for the research and development (R&D) of new products are governed in the short run mainly by yet another form of control. Because of the highly creative nature of their work, and their tendency to work in informal teams, R&D workers' behavior is not easy to observe directly. Schofield does not use short-term outcome measures, such as the number of new products developed, to evaluate R&D personnel because it is better to develop one outstanding new product than several poor ones. Instead, Schofield uses **cultural controls** for R&D personnel. Its culture emphasizes using R&D time and funds carefully to improve upon competitors' products and to develop ways to manufacture similar products at a lower cost than competitors. Researchers are guided by Schofield's culture, which defines the type and extent of risks the company is willing to run in the R&D area.

Incentives are important to the control process. **Incentives** are the rewards, monetary and nonmonetary, used to encourage decision makers to make decisions that are consistent with company goals. Examples of incentives are salaries, bonuses, special benefits, such as the use of a company car, and awards, such as recognition for outstanding performance.

Exhibit 5 shows the role of incentives in the corporate planning and control process. Planning influences measurement because plans establish measurable performance targets. Measurement aids in controlling performance. Measures provide a means of comparing planned performance results (expected behavior) with actual results. Measurement, in turn, is linked to financial and nonfinancial incentives. These incentives are based on achievement of planned results (meeting goals) and motivate the company's members to accomplish corporate objectives. How effective the control process is in causing members to meet company performance targets is one of the things planners consider when they revise plans to achieve future performance objectives.

Exhibit 5   Role of Incentives and Measurement in Corporate Planning and Control

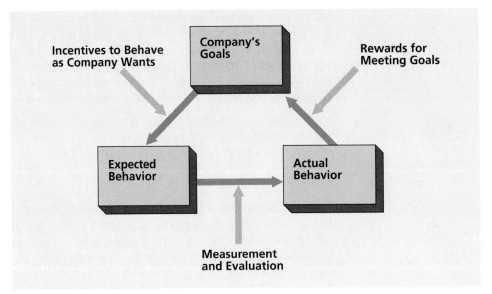

Accounting usually is important when outcomes are measured and evaluated. Some accounting measures are collected specifically for the purpose of measuring performance. Other measures are collected for other reasons and are used to measure performance as a matter of convenience. Incentives and measurement do not always lead to the desired behavior or outcomes, however, as explained in the following section.

Ethics and Control

http://www.swcollege.com/ingram.html

Learn more about the IMA and the CMA certification.

Ethics involves standards of conduct for members of organizations. Well-designed managerial accounting systems encourage ethical behavior on the part of employees. Management should try to eliminate features of managerial accounting systems that inadvertently encourage unethical behavior. For example, many companies consider it improper for an employee to record transactions associated with one period in another period in order to make performance appear better than it really is. Senior management should make it clear that this type of behavior is considered unethical. Senior management should also be careful to design managerial accounting systems with safeguards that limit employees' ability to engage in this kind of behavior.

The Institute of Management Accountants (IMA) has created ethical standards for management accounting. Certified Management Accountants (CMAs) are accountants who have received professional certification by the IMA. CMAs are expected to adhere to the ethical standards set forth by the IMA.

INTERACTIONS AMONG ACCOUNTING, MARKETING, AND OPERATIONS

Marketing and operations managers use accounting information extensively in day-to-day decisions. Pricing and production activities depend heavily on accounting measurement. Consequently, as shown in Exhibit 6, a close relationship among accounting, marketing, and operations managers is needed in most companies, both to facilitate day-to-day decisions and to formulate marketing and production strategy.

Exhibit 6   Examples of Ways Accounting, Marketing, and Operations Work Together

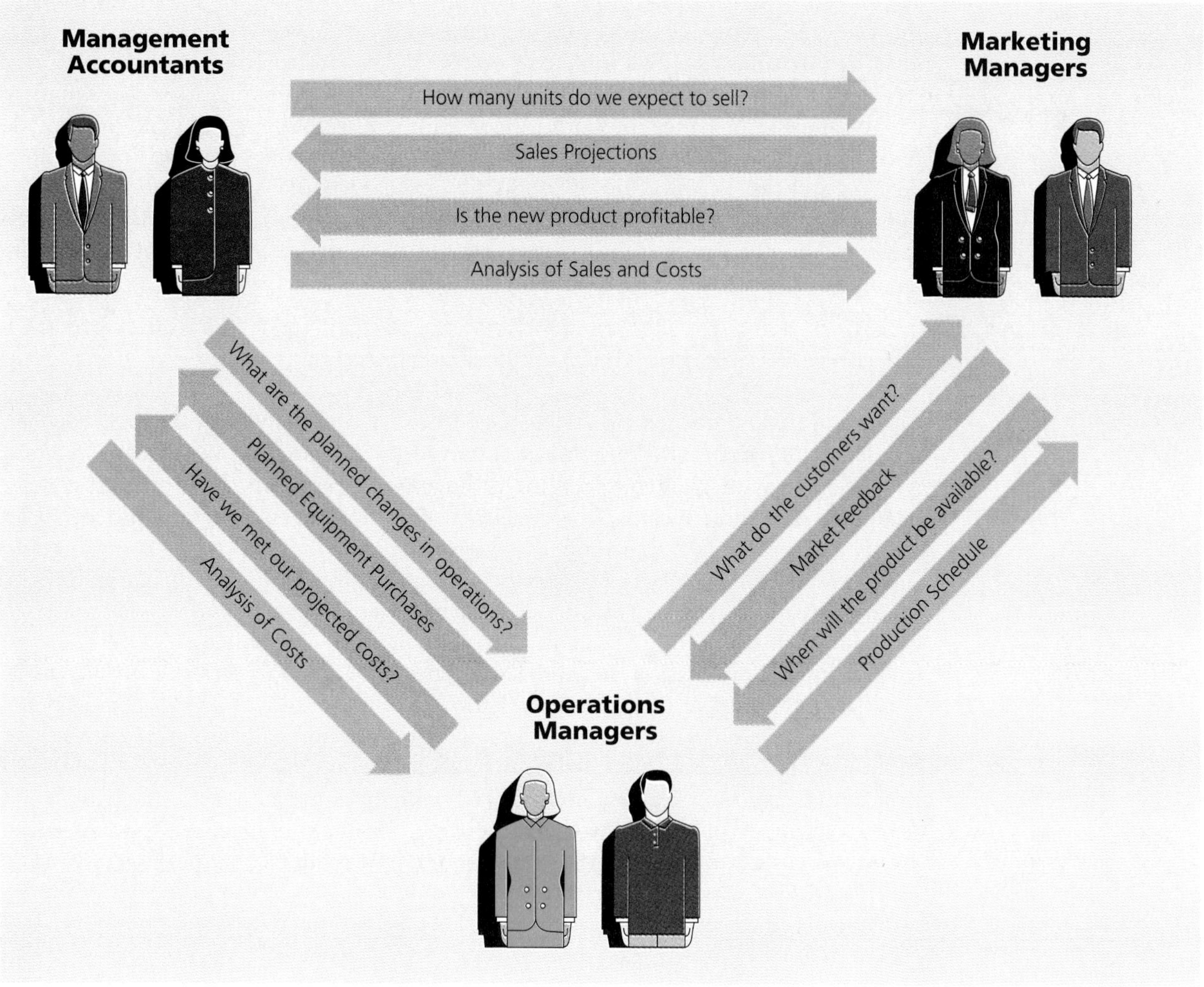

Managerial Accounting and Marketing

O b j e c t i v e   8
Discuss ways in which managerial accounting interacts with marketing and operations in the new business environment.

Why is accounting information so important in marketing decisions? The marketing function involves the activities required in order to advertise, promote, and sell products. Marketing is essential for the success of a company because it drives sales revenue. If a company cannot market its products, it has little need for other functions such as production and accounting. Marketing strategy also affects a company's plant investment and manufacturing strategies.

For companies to be competitive in the new business environment, they require accurate and timely information to support their marketing efforts. As customers have demanded faster response times, companies have given their sales forces more authority to make decisions. The sales forces, in turn, rely on up-to-date accounting information to monitor and control sales activity. A company must price its products competitively and meet profit objectives. Manufacturing cost per unit of product frequently affects the product price. For example, a manufacturer may set the price of a product at some percentage above cost to achieve a target profit. Using inaccurate unit costs to set prices can have serious adverse consequences. Further, many companies allocate resources to divisions based on their profitability. If profit data are inaccurate, poor resource allocation decisions can result. These decisions, in turn, can lead to reduced profits and lower company value.

As noted earlier, sales representatives are often compensated on the basis of sales results. The commissions they are paid may be based on profits rather than on unit or dollar sales. Accounting information can help representatives negotiate prices with customers. Also, it can help them to identify products that produce high profits so that they can encourage sales of these products.

Organizations usually compete as either (1) low-cost producers of products and services or (2) providers of products and services that are differentiated in terms of quality and performance, or both. A company's accounting system should provide information that is consistent with the company's marketing strategy. For example, detailed and timely reporting of production costs to marketing is likely to be more important for success with a low-cost strategy than with a product-differentiation strategy. Thus, accounting information should meet the needs of a company's marketing managers.

Managerial Accounting and Operations

Operations refers to the actions necessary to create and deliver products or services. Operations decisions also rely on accounting information. For example, production is concerned with manufacturing or acquiring the products that a company sells, including obtaining the raw materials necessary for the production process. This means that production managers need information about the costs of production, such as labor and materials. Production managers often compare the actual cost of production to costs that were forecast during the company's budgeting process to determine whether production costs are being properly controlled.

Traditional production methods sometimes have failed to produce quality products that can compete in a global market. As a result, production managers in many companies have changed to new manufacturing methods, such as just-in-time and flexible manufacturing. Just-in-time manufacturing improves product quality and speeds up delivery times. Flexible manufacturing helps meet customer demands for a wider variety of products. At the same time, production managers have reduced inventory costs and reduced the time required to manufacture products by using automated processes. This need for faster production has led to efforts to compress product-development and production cycles. These changes affect production managers' information needs and require adjustments in managerial accounting systems.

Other Effects on Marketing and Operations

Developing a marketing plan is one area in which marketing and accounting interact at the strategic level. In addition to being concerned about unit costs, marketing personnel are concerned about such strategic issues as competitors' costs and marketing strategies, and the cost and profit implications of changes in product mix. At the operational planning level, accounting and marketing managers work together to make decisions about pricing individual products and monitoring competitors' responses to this pricing, tracking sales force time and costs, accounting for advertising and promotion costs for individual products, and monitoring marketing and distribution expenditures. For example, at the operational level, financial measures of quality, such as warranty cost, can be linked to nonfinancial measures of quality, such as defective parts per million. This linkage provides information about which parts generate the most warranty costs and helps focus management's attention on those areas where quality improvement can be most effective in reducing costs.

At the strategic planning level of operations, accounting can play an important role in providing information about the costs and benefits of alternative strategies to improve quality, delivery, and service. For example, information about a company's share of the market for a product line and about the profitability of that product line can be combined. This allows the company to weigh lowering prices to increase sales against maintaining prices in order to make a higher profit on each unit of product sold.

Though manufacturing companies have been the focus of much of this discussion, service companies face similar issues. In these companies, pricing and resource allocation decisions are sometimes more troublesome than in manufacturing companies because measuring service costs and profits is more difficult. Consider the difficulties a bank faces in determining the cost of checking accounts. Transactions involving checking accounts are performed by many different departments within the bank. Examples are check cashing, done by tellers, check processing, performed by departments within the bank, electronic funds transfers, performed by the data processing department, and telephone inquiries, handled by the customer service department. Because these departments handle many other types of transactions as well as checking, it is difficult to determine the portion of each department's costs that is associated with checking accounts. In some service businesses, a lack of accurate cost data has led to poor decisions because managers have little guidance as to which services are profitable and which are not.

Because of the role that product cost data play in strategic marketing and production decisions, it is difficult to overestimate the importance of accounting to business strategy. Companies often focus on the operational aspects of accounting information and forget the strategic aspects. However, they ignore the strategic implications of managerial accounting information at their peril. There are numerous examples of businesses that made poor strategic decisions, or even failed, because of inaccurate accounting data.

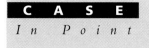
C A S E
In Point

Managerial accounting information showed a division of a major manufacturer to be losing money. The company decided to put the division up for sale. A group of employees in the division got together and raised the money to buy it. Under the new ownership, the division immediately became profitable. A major reason was that when the division was part of the major manufacturer, it was charged for costs incurred by the manufacturer's other divisions. When it became a separate company, it was no longer charged for these costs. The errors in the managerial accounting system led the manufacturer's management to believe that the division was unprofitable when, in fact, it was profitable. The result was a bad business decision.

SELF-STUDY PROBLEM 2

The president of a small remanufacturer of used automobile parts was concerned about his company's poor financial performance, high warranty costs, and complaints from customers about poor delivery of orders. To boost sales, the company gave price discounts to several large customers. It also began a quality improvement program and adopted as its slogan, "The Quality Remanufacturer," in an attempt to emphasize to its customers its claim to have improved the quality of its products and service. Despite the creation of a quality assurance department, however, the firm continued to

have product quality problems and to experience poor financial results.

Consultants found that the remanufacturer's accounting system was designed primarily along financial accounting lines. The system did not provide reliable information about customer profitability, product profitability, or quality performance. Consequently, the remanufacturer often sold its products at a loss. Low-volume, high-cost products were sold at too low a price. Marketing, lacking proper product cost data, sometimes emphasized the low-profit products, believing them to be more profitable than they were.

The consultants found that there was little communication between sales and production. The sales department took so many rush orders from customers that production could not always fill orders on a timely basis. As a result, customers turned to other manufacturers for their needs. Accounting provided production with no information about product quality. The manufacturer's facilities were poorly designed, so that changing its equipment from producing one product to producing another was difficult. This design problem, combined with the tendency of the cost accounting system to encourage greater production volume, led production managers to pay little attention to the shipping dates promised by sales or to product quality. Instead, production filled all available orders for the type of products it was set up to produce before changing to another product. The results were too much inventory of some products and not enough of others, and high defect rates. These results led to higher inventory and warranty costs and even more customer dissatisfaction.

Required

Identify how the lack of good information affected this company. Provide examples of information that might prevent the problems the company experienced.

The solution to Self-Study Problem 2 appears at the end of the chapter.

RESPONDING TO THE NEW BUSINESS ENVIRONMENT

Objective 9
Describe major changes in management philosophy resulting from the new business environment.

Traditional managerial accounting systems often have been criticized for not meeting decision makers' information needs. Much of this criticism comes about because of the rapidly changing business environment. Increased foreign competition and business complexity have reduced the ability of many companies' managerial accounting systems to support business decisions. In this new business environment, management needs to focus on strategic as well as operational decisions. As major changes affect a company's marketing and production activities, accounting systems that provide information different from that provided by traditional accounting systems are needed. Many companies are responding to the new business environment by making major changes in their business philosophies. These changes influence the need for managerial accounting information. This section describes some of these changes. The relationship of these changes is shown in Exhibit 7. Each has some characteristics in common with the others. For example, the elimination of non-value-adding activities is common to both total quality management and just-in-time manufacturing. Note also that just-in-time manufacturing, time-based competition, and flexible manufacturing are just three of several approaches making up total quality management.

Total Quality Management

One of the most important trends in many companies is *total quality management (TQM)*. **TQM is a *management philosophy* that attempts to eliminate all waste, defects, and activities that do not add value to a company's prod-**

ucts. Supporters of TQM argue that, in the long run, profits will be greatest if a company provides high-quality products and excellent service. Therefore, TQM emphasizes customer satisfaction and focuses management attention on meeting customer requirements.

Exhibit 7   The Relation of Total Quality Management, Just-in-Time Manufacturing, Time-Based Competition and Flexible Manufacturing

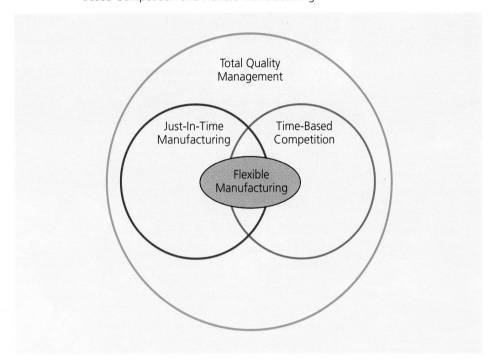

TQM requires many marketing and operations changes in most companies and affects a company's information needs. For TQM to be successful, accounting systems must provide management with information that traditional managerial accounting systems have not provided. An important example is information about the cost of quality, which can include the cost of inspecting products, warranty and return costs, the cost of reworking flawed products, and even the cost associated with sales lost because of poor quality. Accounting systems also must be redesigned to encourage behavior that is consistent with TQM.

To illustrate, assume that Charles Robert Carpets expects to manufacture 1,000 rolls of carpet during January. To meet its plan, the production department produces the rolls without carefully monitoring the quality of the product. The company may meet its production plan, but it may also have a large number of rolls of carpet that it cannot sell because of poor workmanship.

Just-in-Time Manufacturing

Another major trend that influences a company's need for accounting information is just-in-time manufacturing. *Just-in-time (JIT)* **is a** *manufacturing philosophy* **that attempts to eliminate activities that do not add value by reducing inventory levels.** Under JIT, no product or component is manufactured until it is needed. JIT seeks to reduce the amount of time spent creating products, to minimize inventories, to improve quality, and to reduce costs. Inventories of raw materials, component parts, and finished products held just in case they might be needed are eliminated.

JIT and TQM are philosophies with much in common. Managerial accounting can support JIT by supplying information that identifies sources of delay, error, and waste in the manufacturing system. This requires measures such as defect rates, production and delivery times, order accuracy percentages, and the percentage of planned production that was actually produced.

Time-Based Competition

A third major trend that has important implications for accounting is time-based competition. *Time-based competition* **reduces the length of time it takes to develop, manufacture, and deliver a product.** It applies the principles of JIT to important business functions other than manufacturing. The goal of time-based competition is to eliminate idle time wherever it exists, to process work in small batches, and to maximize time spent adding value to products. Examples of time-based activities include:

- Reducing the time required to respond to customer demands such as cashing checks at banks
- Moving finished products faster to reduce inventory
- Reducing distribution time once products leave the factory

Like TQM and JIT, time-based competition has implications for accounting, as well as for marketing and operations. It requires changes in such activities as product development, manufacturing, and distribution, and the accounting systems that support these activities. Accounting measures are needed in order to evaluate a company's success in time-based competition. An example of such a measure is the time required to redesign a product line to meet new product specifications and deliver the first unit of product. Another measure is the time required to move a specific type of product through a production process.

Flexible Manufacturing

Flexible manufacturing **refers to the ability to change from manufacturing one product to manufacturing a different product without incurring significant delays or costs.** Flexible manufacturing permits companies to offer a wider range of products, to be more responsive to customers' needs for rapid delivery, and to reduce the costs associated with changing from production of one product to production of another. Flexible manufacturing sometimes involves reorganizing production into small manufacturing cells (sometimes called cellular manufacturing) that are capable of producing a variety of products. It frequently involves highly automated processes. Flexible manufacturing has implications for marketing strategies because it means that companies are able to offer a wider variety of products, often at a lower cost than the competition, and are better able to provide timely delivery.

Reorganization of manufacturing into cells has implications for how manufacturing performance is measured. Managerial accounting systems may adapt to flexible manufacturing by providing measures of the speed and cost of converting cells from making one product to making another. Flexible manufacturing often involves the purchase of new capital equipment to better automate processes. Managerial accounting plays a role in providing information about the costs and benefits of these capital investments. For example, the Plastics Division of **Monsanto Company** may consider installing a new flexible manufacturing system that will enable it to greatly reduce the time and cost of changing from producing one color plastic to producing another. Managers will want information that will help them assess the costs and benefits of the new system. Traditionally information, such as the operating cost of the new system and any reduction in the cost of scrap plastic created in changing from one product to another, is helpful. Nontraditional information about improvements in quality that might lead to increased sales also may be important.

Exhibit 8 summarizes the key changes that are taking place in the new business environment and what each emphasizes. Note that a given company may make more than one or even all of these changes, often at the same time. Further, the changes often support each other. For example, reducing non–value-adding activities with just-in-time systems may improve the total quality of products and services by focusing more attention on the critical activities that do add value. Without the distraction of non–value-adding activities, workers can give more time to making products and delivering services correctly.

Exhibit 8   Changes in the New Business Environment

Change	Emphasis
Total quality management	Emphasizes making products and delivering services with no defects or errors and the reduction of non-value-adding activities
Just-in-time manufacturing	Emphasizes the elimination of all non-value-adding activities and inventories and the identification and elimination of defects and errors by line workers
Time-based competition	Emphasizes reduction in the amount of time required to manufacture a product or deliver a service
Flexible manufacturing	Emphasizes the ability to shift from the manufacture of one product to the manufacture of another without significant costs or delays

EFFECTS OF THE NEW BUSINESS ENVIRONMENT ON MANAGERIAL ACCOUNTING

Objective 10
Identify weaknesses of traditional managerial accounting techniques in the new business environment.

Companies need information systems that support marketing and operations strategies. This requirement has expanded in the new business environment of global competition and increased demands for quality. Old managerial accounting systems often do not support new business strategies very well. For example, their failure to integrate marketing and operations concerns into accounting information can lead to poor decisions. Poor decisions, in turn, lead to customer dissatisfaction and lost sales. Consequently, a new philosophy of managerial accounting is emerging. In this view, managerial accounting systems support strategic approaches such as JIT and TQM. This new philosophy uses new tools for decision making, which are described in this section.

A very important change in this new philosophy is that more attention is being given to the **activities that create costs, called** *cost drivers*. One shortcoming of traditional managerial accounting systems is that they do not focus enough on cost drivers. Many companies have been criticized for spending too much time focusing on reducing costs without dealing with the activities that actually create the costs. This sometimes has led managers who are held responsible for costs to try to change the way the costs appear in managerial accounting reports without actually reducing the costs. For example, managers may try to lower repair and maintenance costs by postponing necessary maintenance instead of addressing the causes of high maintenance costs, such as old, worn-out equipment. The result is that the equipment breaks down even more often, and, in the long run, repair costs are even higher.

Traditional Managerial Accounting Systems

Changes in the business environment have had a strong effect on traditional managerial accounting systems in terms of aiding planning and control. The traditional approach was to treat managerial accounting as a separate, technical function, distinct from other business functions. Management accountants often were considered "number crunchers" who were not part of the management team. In their traditional role, management accountants provided information for marketing and operations decisions, but did not participate in these decisions. Managers who are not accountants sometimes are unaware of the dangers of misusing accounting information.

From a **planning perspective,** managerial accounting traditionally has focused on operational decision making. Traditional managerial accounting systems were not designed to provide the kind of information and the degree of accuracy most useful for strategic planning. The information that these systems produced often did not identify whether the company's planned marketing costs were consistent with its strategic marketing goals. For example, a company might be spending money for new research on a product that is near the end of its economic life. Most traditional managerial accounting systems have not highlighted such inconsistencies.

From a **control perspective,** traditional managerial accounting systems sometimes produce inaccurate information that can lead to poor marketing and operations decisions. For example, managerial accounting often is too focused on dollar figures and does not consider enough the nonfinancial measures of business performance that should affect decisions. Information about the quality of products may explain lost sales. Another reason managerial accounting can lead to poor decisions is that the accounting measures used to evaluate management performance usually are short-run. These measures encourage managers to focus on short-run costs and profits, instead of on success in achieving the company's long-run goals. For example, managerial accounting reports often compare the actual costs of manufacturing to planned costs. These reports may encourage employees to achieve planned costs instead of continuously improving product quality in ways that will lead to long-run profits.

Planning and control are essential for effective business management. The challenge is to provide accurate and timely information that aids planning and control at both the strategic and the operational levels of decision making, not just at the operational level. As noted earlier, this is particularly important to marketing and operations strategy. In order to meet this need, companies are resorting to several new tools that directly involve managerial accounting in strategic decisions.

New Decision-Making Tools

Several new managerial accounting tools have gained considerable acceptance in the new business environment. These are value chain analysis, strategic positioning analysis, and activity-based management (including cost driver analysis and activity-based costing). These tools sometimes are lumped together under an umbrella called strategic cost management. *Strategic cost management (SCM)* **is the development**

Objective 11
Identify managerial accounting techniques that have been developed to meet information needs in the new business environment.

of a sustainable competitive advantage through understanding a company's costs.

The *value chain* is the set of value-creating activities that extends from the production of raw materials to the sale and servicing of finished goods. The value chain includes activities both inside and outside a company. Managing the value chain requires the company to look beyond its own operations to those of its customers and suppliers. For example, to eliminate or reduce cost-creating activities, companies develop close relationships with customers and suppliers to reduce costs of excess inventories of raw materials and finished products. Exhibit 9 provides an example of a value chain.

Exhibit 9   Value Chain for Vehicle Carpet

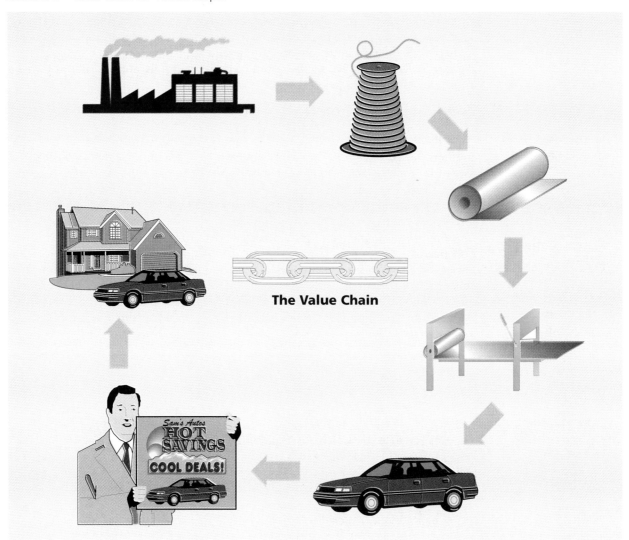

The Value Chain

Value chain analysis permits management to identify when a company has a competitive advantage by understanding the value added at each stage in the chain. When value chain analysis is applied at an operational level, non-value-adding activities within a company's production and delivery processes are eliminated or reduced. At the strategic level, the focus of value chain analysis is on finding those places in the value chain where a company can exploit comparative advantages over competitors to earn high returns.

To illustrate, consider the value chain presented in Exhibit 9. Charles Robert Carpet's management is considering whether CRC should expand into the yarn portion of the value chain by purchasing a supplier of yarn. CRC's vice president of production believes that if CRC owned and operated its own yarn mill, it could better ensure the quality of the yarn it uses for carpet manufacture. Further, he argues that CRC could better plan for deliveries of yarn and reduce inventories by ordering smaller amounts more frequently. He also argues that CRC's knowledge of the carpet industry would give it a comparative advantage in operating yarn mills.

The chief financial officer questions this position and provides the following information about yarn companies:

- Yarn companies are typically small firms that use mostly nonunion labor. CRC is unionized and has a higher wage scale.
- Yarn companies buy their synthetic fiber from very large petroleum companies that sell these fibers to a wide variety of manufacturers for many uses. Yarn companies are only a small portion of the market for synthetic fiber, and consequently have little leverage in negotiating prices with their suppliers.
- Yarn mills typically have a lower profit than carpet mills and are subject to many of the same business risks.

By evaluating its value chain, CRC can assess the pros and cons of owning its own yarn mills.

CRC might negotiate with mills to supply yarn more frequently but in smaller amounts so that there is no need to invest in a large amount of raw materials inventory or in storage facilities. The value chain also shows that CRC's customers are finishing firms that cut the carpet CRC makes to fit automobiles. CRC might negotiate with these customers to set delivery schedules for carpet in advance so that CRC does not have to keep a large finished goods inventory.

Strategic positioning analysis **considers the information needs of different competitive strategies.** Companies can compete in two basic ways—by offering lower-cost (cost leadership strategy) or higher-quality (product differentiation strategy) products than their competitors. The importance of various types of accounting information depends on a company's competitive strategy. Exhibit 10 illustrates how the need for accounting information differs under product differentiation and cost leadership strategies.

Exhibit 10   Accounting Information and Corporate Strategy

Type of Information	Cost Leadership Requirements	Product Differentiation Requirements
Costs for performance assessment	High—cost control is paramount in maintaining margins	Low—emphasis is on innovation, not cost control
Perceived importance of meeting budgets	High to very high—budgets are a primary means of monitoring costs	Moderate to low—to allow for product improvements, budgets are not set tight
Product or service cost as an input to pricing decisions	High—pricing decisions are critical to customers' buying decisions	Low—customers are buying the highest quality, not the lowest price
Marketing cost analysis	Low—marketing expenditures are not as critical where little differentiation is required	High—appropriate marketing emphasis is critical
Analysis of competitors' costs	High—it is important to know competitors' costs in order to meet or beat their prices and maintain acceptable profits	Low—competition is not based on cost; it is competitors' product and service improvements, not their costs, that are important

Activity-based management (ABM) **emphasizes a company's ability to measure activities that create costs as the key to performance improvement.** Its goal is to eliminate activities that do not add value and to perform more efficiently those activities that do add value. Examples of non-value-adding activities include storage, moving, and handling. For ABM to be most effective, management should first focus on major activities that create costs in a product or service's value chain.

ABM also focuses on lead time. *Lead time* **refers to the amount of time it takes to process, move, store, and inspect inventory.** Lead time includes both value-adding and non-value-adding activities. Generally, the longer the lead time, the more expensive products are to make. Longer lead times often are associated with inefficient production and delivery processes. Reducing lead times forces managers to eliminate non-value-adding activities and to reduce the time consumed by value-adding activities. For example, CRC's efforts to reduce its lead time might result in:

- Reorganization of its production process so that products travel less distance or so that the process occupies less space
- Elimination of several material handling steps to save money on forklifts
- Reaching an agreement with suppliers to guarantee yarn quality to reduce the need for costly inspections
- Investment in new equipment that reduces the number of defects in manufacturing finished carpet and the need for costly inspections

ABM includes cost driver analysis and activity-based costing. *Cost driver analysis* **considers that costs are created or driven by many interrelated factors.** Understanding cost behavior means understanding the activities that create costs in any given situation. This understanding requires an accounting system that identifies cost drivers and traces costs to these activities. *Activity-based costing (ABC)* **links the activities performed to create products with the costs of these activities.** ABC measures resource costs and assigns these costs to cost drivers. These costs then are assigned to **cost objects,** which are goods, services, or customers that benefit from the activities. Strategic cost management relies on ABC. ABC will be examined in detail in a future chapter.

Exhibit 11 summarizes the roles of the new decision-making tools in the new business environment. Recall that these tools all fall under the umbrella of strategic cost management. These tools provide companies with the ability to understand where their competitive advantages lie (value chain analysis), how to best position products and services (strategic positioning analysis), which cost drivers create costs (ABM), and how those activities are linked to the costs reported in the managerial accounting system (ABC).

Exhibit 11   New Decision-Making Tools for the New Business Environment

Tool	Role in Strategic Cost Management
Value chain analysis	Focuses on the set of value-creating activities that extends from the production of raw materials to the sale and servicing of finished goods
Strategic positioning analysis	Considers information needs under different competitive strategies—whether a product or service is low-cost or differentiated
Activity-based management	Emphasizes a company's ability to measure activities that create costs as the key to performance improvement
Activity-based costing	Links the activities performed to create products with the costs of these activities to better control cost drivers

MANAGERIAL ACCOUNTING IN SERVICE COMPANIES

Objective 12
Identify ways managerial accounting assists service companies.

http://www.swcollege.
com/ingram.html

Visit Coopers & Lybrand's information page to learn more about activity-based costing in service organizations.

As the United States economy has matured, it has changed from being principally a manufacturing economy to being a service economy. This means that more companies are providing services than goods. This change has implications for the use of managerial accounting. The production of tangible products makes tracing costs to products somewhat different in manufacturing companies and in service companies. For example, manufacturing companies have inventories of raw material and finished goods, whereas service companies do not.

Like manufacturing companies, service companies require relevant, timely, and accurate accounting information in order to make sound decisions. However, service companies have often been slower to use managerial accounting than manufacturing companies, perhaps partly because many service companies, such as airlines, railroads, and banks, have been regulated. Regulation may have made service companies less cost conscious than manufacturing companies because it often limited the services that companies could provide and fixed the prices that they could charge.

In recent years, many service industries have been deregulated. Examples are the airline and banking industries. Deregulation means that these companies will be operating in a more competitive environment. As competition increases, so does the need for better accounting information. Companies need to know the costs of their services with more accuracy. They need to be able to better predict the financial results of changes in marketing and operations. Without relevant, timely, and accurate managerial accounting information, it is unlikely that service companies can prosper.

SELF-STUDY PROBLEM 3

A division of a major corporation that manufactures transmissions for trucks and other heavy vehicles installed a new manufacturing system. Parts made by many departments must be assembled to form the transmission. Under the new manufacturing system, the parts should arrive at the point in production where they are ready at the time they are needed. The division spent a great deal of time training its production personnel in the new system. Despite these efforts, however, the results were disappointing. Departments continued to manufacture more parts than were needed, and quality did not improve as much as had been expected.

Management was disappointed. The firm had spent a great deal of time and effort implementing the new manufacturing system, with poor results. They began to look at the managerial accounting system that was used to measure departmental performance and discovered some problems. The division had long used an accounting system that emphasized producing as many parts as possible as fast as possible. Because labor was paid by the hour, the more component parts a department could make in a day, the lower its labor cost per unit. Consequently, department managers pressed for higher production volume despite the change in production philosophy.

Required

Why did the information provided by the accounting system lead to the wrong results? What types of information might the accounting system provide that would be useful for achieving management's objectives?

The solution to Self-Study Problem 3 appears at the end of the chapter.

R E V I E W   *Summary of Important Concepts*

1. Managerial accounting refers to accounting information developed for use by decision makers inside the company.
    a. Managerial accounting is different from financial accounting.
    b. Managerial accounting is not governed by GAAP.
    c. The information produced by managerial accounting systems is important to many business decisions, especially marketing and operations decisions.

2. Managerial accounting interacts with decisions by other functions, notably marketing and operations.
    a. Marketing decisions often are based on the cost of manufacturing a product.
    b. Operations decisions frequently require cost and other accounting data for purposes of cost control and quality assurance.

3. Businesses' needs for accounting information are changing.
    a. Global competition and the need for higher quality are driving U.S. businesses to control costs and produce higher-quality products, creating new accounting information needs.
    b. Management accountants need to become involved in business functions like marketing and operations to ensure that the information they produce is timely and accurate enough and appropriate to the decisions being made.

4. The traditional view of managerial accounting needs to be changed to fit the new business environment.
    a. Managerial accounting has been traditionally viewed in the context of planning and control at the operational level.
    b. This view needs to be expanded to include a more strategic focus and the demands made by the new business environment.

5. Many companies are responding to the new business environment in ways that profoundly affect their needs for accounting information.
    a. Approaches such as total quality management, just-in-time manufacturing, time-based competition, and flexible manufacturing are among the changes being adopted.
    b. Business employs tools such as value chain analysis, strategic positioning, and activity-based management.
        1. These tools are part of a strategic cost management focus.
        2. Cost driver analysis and activity-based costing are important to activity-based management.

6. Service companies as well as manufacturing companies need managerial accounting information.
    a. Service companies differ from manufacturing companies in that they do not make a tangible product.
    b. Many service companies are realizing that knowing the cost of providing services is critical to their success in the new business environment.

D E F I N E   *Terms and Concepts Defined in This Chapter*

activity-based costing (ABC)   (23)   lead time   (23)   strategic planning   (9)
activity-based management   management accountant   (5)   strategic positioning analysis   (22)
   (ABM)   (23)   master budget   (10)   time-based competition   (18)
cost driver analysis   (23)   operational planning   (9)   total quality management
cost drivers   (19)   performance objectives   (9)   (TQM)   (16)
flexible manufacturing   (18)   strategic cost management   value chain   (21)
just-in-time (JIT)   (17)   (SCM)   (20)

S O L U T I O N S

SELF-STUDY PROBLEM 1

CRC's business has several key features that affect its need for accounting information to aid in sound marketing and production decisions. CRC is expanding into new product lines (RV and marine carpet) while maintaining its position in the automobile carpet market. As production of these new product lines grows, CRC's management will want to evaluate their profitability relative to that of the automobile line to determine where to place its marketing emphasis for future growth. Having accurate product cost data is important to developing accurate product profitability information. Accurate information about product costs will assist CRC's marketing managers in pricing their products. This product cost information also will assist CRC's management in controlling the costs of manufacturing and deciding how to allocate scarce product research and production resources.

CRC's business fluctuates with the national economy. This is due to the fact that consumers on the whole tend to buy vehicles and boats in greater quantities when the economy is growing and unemployment is lower. This means that CRC is likely to be faced with too much production capacity when the economy is slow and too little capacity to meet demand when the economy is growing. Cost control will become very important during slow phases because CRC will need to be very cost-conscious to maintain profitability when sales are slack.

CRC's profit of 10% on every dollar of sales is considerably higher than that of a grocery store chain. This means that based on this consideration alone, having accurate information about product costs will be somewhat less critical to CRC than to the grocery store chain. As profit margins shrink, the need for cost information becomes more critical because the firm has to be more cost-conscious to maintain profitability. In the case of CRC, however, the cyclical nature of its business increases its need for accurate cost information. The grocery business tends to have more stable sales throughout economic swings than the carpet industry because demand for food is not as sensitive to economic conditions. Consumers can postpone automobile purchases but not food purchases. This means that prices will be generally more stable in the grocery business. Therefore, it is difficult to say whether CRC or the grocery chain will have a greater need for accurate cost information. Both have characteristics that make accurate cost accounting information important to their business decisions.

SELF-STUDY PROBLEM 2

The small automobile parts remanufacturer in this real example suffered greatly because of inadequate and inaccurate accounting information. Because its accounting system did not provide reliable information about customer profitability, the firm sold more and more units of products to its largest customer, believing that these sales were profitable. It was ultimately determined that, because of the excessive demands made by this customer, the relationship was unprofitable. The firm also accepted a large number of orders for small batches of hard-to-find products. However, because it did not have accurate cost information, it underpriced these products. The lack of communication between marketing and production resulted in the production of too many units of some products and not enough of others. Continually having to insert rush orders into the production schedule disrupted this schedule, resulting in delays in getting products to customers and causing the purchasing of materials needed to make the products to be chaotic. Production often lacked some necessary parts. The accounting system provided no information about the costs associated with orders canceled because of late delivery, revenue lost because orders were incompletely filled and warranty costs associated with poor workmanship resulting from hurried production.

The information breakdown between marketing, operations, and accounting also resulted in the accumulation of excess inventory, as orders sometimes were canceled because of lack of timely delivery. Also, in an attempt to make the production of infrequently ordered products more efficient, the firm made more of these products than the order called for and kept the excess in inventory. This excess inventory occupied floor space in the warehouse, increased the firm's insurance costs, and tied up badly needed working capital. The poor production layout increased the costs of moving and handling products in production and made inventory tracking more difficult. This, in turn, complicated inventory costing.

This example demonstrates how a lack of information in general and cost accounting information in particular can seriously affect a firm's ability to price its products appropriately and serve its customers profitably. It also shows the interdependencies that exist between marketing and production decisions and accounting information. Making sound decisions about product pricing and production scheduling requires good cost accounting information. The absence of well-organized marketing and production activities complicates efforts to account for costs. Perhaps the most important lesson to take away from this situation is that a company's long-term success often depends upon its management's understanding the need to plan marketing, production, and accounting efforts in a way that recognizes their interdependencies.

SELF-STUDY PROBLEM 3

The basic problem in this situation was that division management failed to take its management accounting system into consideration when it implemented a new manufacturing system. This new manufacturing system had many of the characteristics of just-in-time manufacturing. The division wanted to minimize the costs associated with the inventory of component parts used to manufacture the transmissions, in the belief that this would lower the overall costs of production. Parts were not to arrive at the place where they were needed until just before they were actually used in production. Only the exact number of parts that were needed at the time were to be manufactured.

Problems arose when the division attempted to operate the new manufacturing system in conjunction with the old managerial accounting system. The old accounting system was ill suited to the new manufacturing system because the way in which it measured departmental performance was not aligned with the desired performance under the new manufacturing system.

The old accounting system had measured the efficiency of each individual department in making the individual parts of the transmissions, not the overall cost of making the transmissions. Efficiency was defined as the number of parts made per labor hour used. Under the old system, departments were evaluated in terms of cost per component manufactured, with lower being considered better. The way to accomplish this was to manufacture as many parts per labor hour as possible. Each department therefore had an incentive to make as many parts as possible during a given period of time. The result was that some departments made parts faster than they could be used in manufacturing. Thus, excess parts often accumulated at various stages in the production process. This resulted in a costly buildup of inventory awaiting further processing.

Despite the training on the goals of the new manufacturing system, the department managers continued to act as they had under the old system, making as many parts as possible. This meant that the expected savings in inventory costs were not realized. Only after management recognized the problem and changed the managerial accounting system to one that recognized the reduction in inventory cost achieved by making only what was needed at the time did the managers' behavior become aligned with the division's goals. Perhaps the most important lesson to learn from this situation is that human beings respond to the way they are measured. Even though the department managers knew that they were supposed to reduce production to the level required for current needs, they continued to produce as much as possible to make their accounting reports look better. It is important to ensure that accounting systems used to measure human performance are aligned with corporate goals and objectives.

EXERCISES

1-1. Write a short definition for each of the terms listed in the *Terms and Concepts Defined in This Chapter* section.

Obj. 1   **1-2.** Managerial accounting is useful only to profit-oriented manufacturing companies. Do you agree? Why or why not?

Obj. 1   **1-3.** Rita Patterson went into the marketing field because she "hated accounting." Rita has been working for a large multinational company and is being promoted to assistant product manager. In her new job, Rita will prepare sales quotes for various large clients. Should Rita expect to use managerial accounting techniques in her new job? Why or why not?

Obj. 2   **1-4.** James and Hanna are senior accounting students at the state university. James plans to find a job in financial accounting, whereas Hanna wants to work in managerial accounting. What is the difference between these two types of accounting?

Objs. 1, 2, 3   **1-5.** Why does the accounting system used for financial statement preparation not always provide the information that managers need for decision-making purposes?

Objs. 1, 3, 4   **1-6.** Why must managers have accounting information to make decisions?

Objs. 4, 5   **1-7.** Tri-States Manufacturing produces a line of electric fans. Over the past several years, the company has seen its profit margin on fans decline from 12% to 8%. How has the decrease in profit margin affected the company's need for managerial accounting information?

Obj. 5   **1-8.** In order to meet increasing demand for its product, Hathaway Industries is considering an expansion of its manufacturing facilities. What sort of planning does this decision represent, strategic or operational? Explain your answer.

Obj. 5, 6   **1-9.**   Webco Products manufactures a line of small ice chests. The production department has experienced problems working with some of the raw materials used in the production process. The company is considering a change in materials that would increase the cost of an ice chest by 5%. What sort of planning does this decision represent, strategic or operational? Explain your answer.

Obj. 5, 6, 7   **1-10.**   Advent Technologies, Inc., has developed a detailed planning and budgeting program that involves almost every layer of management. Tina Riser, plant manager, made this comment: "I don't know why we put so much effort into these budgets; after we complete them, we never see them again until the end of the year." If it is true that managers are not held accountable to budgets, would this represent a weakness in planning or in control? Explain your answer.

Obj. 8   **1-11.**   If marketing and operations managers need information for decision making, why don't they collect and keep the information themselves instead of relying on the accounting department to provide the needed information?

Obj. 9   **1-12.**   Cheyenne Industries produces air filtration systems. Because of increased competition from foreign manufacturers, Cheyenne has implemented a total quality control program that includes elements of just-in-time inventory management and flexible manufacturing. What impact would these changes in the business environment and Cheyenne's new program have on the need for managerial accounting information?

Obj. 11   **1-13.**   Martin Incorporated has analyzed its production process and has identified each element of the product value chain. What should the company do with non-value-added activities identified in the value chain?

Obj. 11, 12   **1-14.**   Virgil Cartwright is a medical doctor with a small family practice. Each time a patient visits the doctor, certain medical and administrative costs are incurred. Would you agree that patients are a cost driver for the doctor? Explain your answer.

Obj. 11   **1-15.**   Starco Incorporated manufactures scientific testing equipment used in research laboratories. The company has seen a decline in its business because a competitor is providing similar equipment with higher quality at a lower price. How would the use of activity-based management assist Starco in meeting the challenge posed by this competitor?

PROBLEMS

PROBLEM 1-1   Terminology

Complete each of the following sentences with the proper term or terms.

1. Managerial accounting information is used primarily by ___*internal*___ decision makers.

2. An accountant who produces information for a specific company is referred to as a(n) ___*managerial Accountant*___

3. ___*Strategic Planning*___ involves the identification of long-run goals and plans to achieve these goals.

4. ___*Operational Planning*___ involves the identification of objectives for day-to-day activities.

5. A financial plan that summarizes operational activities for the coming year is known as the ___*Master Budget*___

6. Managerial accounting exists primarily to assist in the management functions of
   _____ and _____.

7. A managerial philosophy that attempts to eliminate defects and improve quality is
   referred to as _____TQM_____.

8. A management philosophy that focuses on reduction of inventory at all levels of operation is referred to as _____JIT_____.

9. The ability to change from one manufacturing process to another without significant
   delays or costs is referred to as _Flexible MFG_.

10. A two-stage approach that links costs to activities by measuring costs and assigning them
    to objects is known as _Activity based Costing_

PROBLEM 1-2   Financial versus Managerial Accounting

Obj. 2

Alberta Enterprises is being audited by a local public accounting firm. The management of Alberta hired an independent accountant to prepare financial statements in
good form for presentation to the board of directors. The financial statements will
contain an auditor's report stating that the financial statements have been prepared in
accordance with generally accepted accounting principles.

Brent Haskill, production manager at Alberta, reviewed the financial statements
prepared by the independent accountant and noted that the reported inventory value
was higher than that contained in the company's monthly operating report. Brent
asked the company's accountant to explain the difference. The accountant explained
that the auditors adjusted inventory to a LIFO basis in accordance with GAAP,
whereas the company does not reflect LIFO calculations in the monthly operating
report.

Required

a. Does managerial accounting prescribe specific methods that must be followed? Since the
   inventory value was adjusted by the independent accountant, would the company's
   inventory valuation be worthless to its managers? Why or why not?
b. Must accounting information be calculated in accordance with generally accepted
   accounting principles to be useful to managers? Why or why not?

PROBLEM 1-3   Strategic and Operational Planning

Objs. 5, 6

Isaac Lieberman owns several successful coffeehouses. Each one has its own manager
and is operated independently of the others. Isaac meets with the manager of each
location each month to review operating results. During this meeting, the manager
must present a projection of operations for the coming month. Isaac reviews the sales
projections and any promotional campaigns and entertainment that the manager is
planning to use.

Based on the success of his current coffeehouses, Isaac is considering opening
two new facilities. He has found two locations where long-term leases can be
obtained. Both locations are in high traffic areas near a mall or shopping center. Isaac
has determined the cost to furnish the shops with equipment and has obtained
approval from a bank that will assist in the required financing.

Required

a. In what ways do the coffeehouses utilize managerial accounting in the operational planning process?
b. Explain how Isaac utilizes strategic planning.

PROBLEM 1-4 **Managerial Accounting and Performance Measures**

Objs. 1, 4, 6

An-Hour Foto provides film processing at a single store location. The store has a policy that film will be developed in 24 hours, or the processing is free. It also has a policy that it will refund customers' money for any pictures that were poorly developed.

In order to improve income without raising prices, the company must find ways to reduce costs. To this end, the company has experimented with a new chemical used in its film processing. Management has determined that the new chemical takes longer to process film and is more sensitive to improper handling than the old chemical. While the new chemical is less expensive than the old chemical, the amount of free processing and photo returns have increased since the company switched to this chemical. Accordingly, management must decide whether to continue using the new chemical or return to the old chemical.

Required

a. How can managerial accounting be used to assist the company in determining whether to continue using the new chemical?
b. What are some of the nonfinancial measures provided by managerial accounting to assist managers in the decision-making process?

PROBLEM 1-5 **Managerial Accounting, Value Chain**

Obj. 11

Unisco Products manufactures a line of children's toys that are painted in bright, colorful tones. One of the most popular toy colors is yellow oxide. The company has become aware, however, that the yellow oxide paint it is using is possibly toxic. Accordingly, the company has sought a replacement paint of the same color that is guaranteed safe. The only feasible replacement it has found will cost three times as much as the paint currently being used. Switching to this paint would require a substantial increase in the toy's sales price to cover the added cost.

Rosemary Terry, marketing manager, insists that sales of this toy will decline significantly if the price is increased to cover the additional paint cost.

Required

a. What role does paint have in a toy's value chain? Does paint add value to the product? Why or why not?
b. How does managerial accounting create an ethical concern for managers at Unisco? Explain your answer.

PROBLEM 1-6 **Multiple-Choice Overview of the Chapter**

1. Management accounting is concerned primarily with providing:
   a. information in accordance with generally accepted accounting principles.
   b. information to stockholders, creditors, and others outside the organization.
   c. information to managers inside the organization.
   d. information to regulatory agencies.

2. The managerial functions of planning, control, and decision making typically are:
   a. approached in precisely the same way in every organization.
   b. carried out simultaneously, with decision making being an inseparable part of the other functions.
   c. carried out independently of one another, so that a function may be omitted without negative effects.
   d. conducted only by the managers of manufacturing entities.

3. In decision making, a manager uses:
   a. financial accounting information exclusively.
   b. information from his or her department only, ignoring other departments' costs and
       activities.
   c. information that must conform to generally accepted accounting principles.
   d. information that is relevant to the decision even if the information does not con-
       form to generally accepted accounting principles.

4. Daley is a stockholder of Public Company, Inc. In his role as a stockholder, Daley would
   most likely use:
   a. managerial accounting information developed by the organization.
   b. financial information contained in Public's annual report.
   c. accounting information obtained directly from Public's computer system.
   d. no accounting information about Public, since it is not available to outsiders.

5. Budgets:
   a. are a form of planning for an organization's operating and financial matters.
   b. are concerned only with the company's cash position.
   c. are typically not prepared on an annual basis.
   d. are usually prepared for an organization as a whole, not for individual departments.

6. Management accounting in the 1990s would be most accurately described as:
   a. a branch of financial accounting.
   b. a form of accounting that is concerned mainly with production-related managerial
       decisions.
   c. a form of accounting that is necessary if a business is to successfully compete in a
       global business environment.
   d. a branch of industrial technology.

7. The value chain for a given product or service:
   a. reflects all activities associated with providing the particular product or service.
   b. identifies non-value-adding activities that should be eliminated or reduced.
   c. includes activities both inside and outside the company.
   d. All of the above are correct.

8. The management tool that measures activities that create costs in order to improve performance is referred to as:
   a. value chain analysis.
   b. cost driver analysis.
   c. activity-based management.
   d. just-in-time manufacturing.

9. The management tool that links activities performed to create products in order to control cost drivers is referred to as:
   a. activity-based costing.
   b. cost driver analysis.
   c. activity-based management.
   d. value chain analysis.

10. The use of managerial accounting in service organizations
    a. is pointless, since service organizations produce no tangible product.
    b. provides timely, relevant, and accurate information to managers.
    c. occurs more than the use of managerial accounting in manufacturing companies.
    d. is required by regulatory agencies.

PROJECTS

PROJECT 1-1   **Managerial Accounting Information**

Objs. 4,5,6,12

Interview a manager who works in either a manufacturing or a service industry. Inquire about the nature of managerial accounting information that the manager needs for decision-making purposes. Write a short account of your interview and present your findings to your class.

PROJECT 1-2   **Value Chain**

Obj. 11

Select a common item for which the value chain is obvious. Document the value chain and the costs that would be incurred at each activity in the chain. Write a short narrative on the item and present your findings to your class.

PROJECT 1-3   **Management Accounting and Decision Making**

Objs. 1,4,5,6

Find an article in *The Wall Street Journal* or another business periodical that discusses a particular company or industry decision that required managerial accounting. Write a short narrative explaining the decision that was made and the role managerial accounting played in assisting in the decision-making process.

Cost Categorization, Cost Flow, and Measurement Decisions

Accounting and Management Decisions

Internal Control

Service Organizations

Cost Behavior

Capital Budgeting

Unit Costs

Decentralized Organizations

Cost Measurement

Global Environment

Cost Allocation

Performance Evaluation

Budgets

Overview

This chapter explores how the costs of materials, labor, and overhead are accumulated to produce values shown on a company's financial statements. It examines the flow of costs through an organization's accounting system and the ways managers classify and use product cost information to make decisions. Like most managerial accounting textbooks, this one uses manufacturing companies as examples to illustrate how product costs change in relation to output levels. However, principles discussed in this chapter also apply to service organizations—hospitals and banks, for example—that must understand how costs change in relation to changes in the volume of services they provide to their customers.

Managers use their knowledge of cost behavior to help them make decisions. The text describes three types of cost-related decisions: new-product introductions, outsourcing, and further processing. To determine if a new product can be introduced profitably, managers often use target costing, a process that helps managers meet customers' demands for functionality, quality, and price. Outsourcing decisions—to buy a product or component instead of manufacturing it—also rely on an analysis of costs. Finally, an understanding of cost behavior helps managers understand the economic consequences of selling products at various stages of completion.

Major topics covered in this chapter include:
- How an accounting system tracks the flow of costs through an organization
- The form and behavior of manufacturing costs
- How cost information is used to make common business decisions

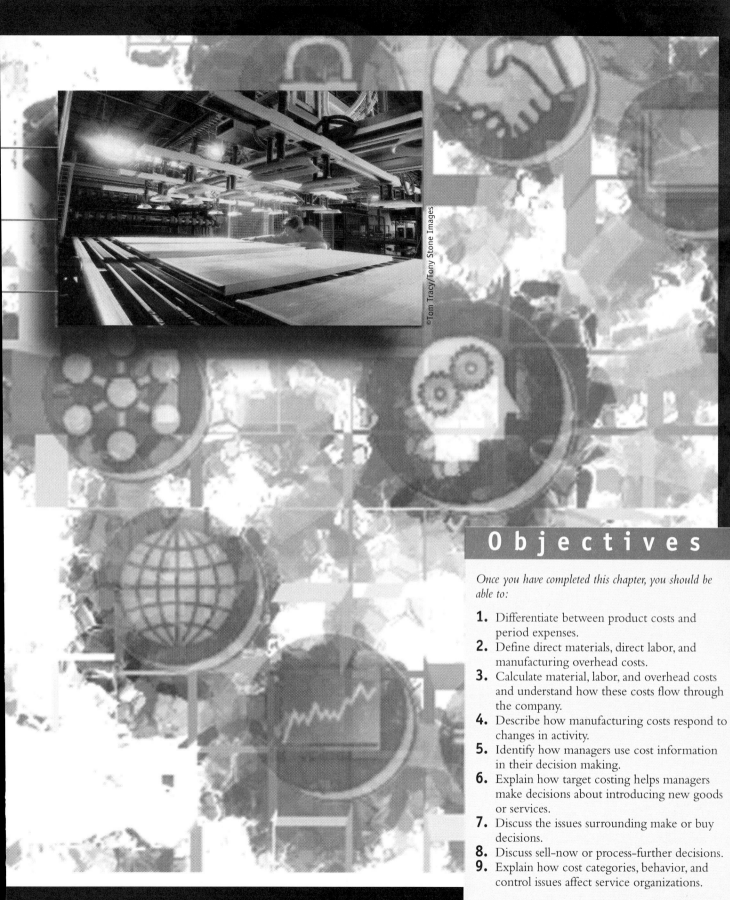

©Tom Tracy/Tony Stone Images

THE PRODUCTION PROCESS: AN ILLUSTRATION

All business organizations produce a product. Whether that product is a good or service, all business organizations incur costs in the production process. Because it's easier to understand the nature of production costs, and the ways those costs behave when the product is a good—a car, a computer disk, a chest of drawers—the text follows the production process in a manufacturing plant. Remember that the process of producing a service also incurs costs and that an understanding of those costs is as important to the managers of service organizations as it is to decision making in manufacturing companies.

Our discussion of cost measurement and managerial decision making begins with a look at Pine Belt Furniture Company.

Products and Market

Pine Belt manufactures and sells mid-priced pine furniture to retailers. The company's product line consists primarily of bedroom sets and is targeted at cost-conscious buyers who want quality but cannot afford furniture constructed of expensive wood, such as maple, oak, or mahogany. Marketing studies indicate that the company's typical customer is under 30 years old, is often recently married, and has a family income of less than $40,000 a year. Pine Belt recognizes the needs of cost-conscious buyers and has developed marketing and manufacturing strategies to meet those needs. For example, the company offers its products at three price levels: budget, economy, and deluxe.

Budget. Budget-priced furniture is targeted at buyers who are willing to assemble and finish a piece of furniture sold in kit form. The kits come with lumber components cut to specifications and all the hardware required for assembly.

Economy. Economy-priced furniture is assembled but unfinished. These pieces require light sanding, staining, and finishing.

Deluxe. Deluxe-priced furniture is assembled and finished and is ready for immediate use.

Pine Belt's kits typically are sold at discount chain stores; its unfinished and finished furniture is available at specialty furniture stores.

Product Design and Manufacturing

The designs for new products at Pine Belt begin with the engineering department. There the product and the manufacturing process are designed at the same time, minimizing manufacturing costs.

Once product design and manufacturing processes are complete, raw materials (lumber and hardware) are ordered from suppliers and placed into raw materials inventory. Pine Belt works closely with its suppliers to minimize variation in the quality of the materials it buys. In addition, as materials are delivered and placed into inventory, quality control engineers select random samples for inspection and testing.

Working with customers' orders, production schedulers at Pine Belt try to group similar products so that they can be manufactured at the same time. The manufacturing process involves three departments:

- Cutting
- Assembly
- Finishing

Exhibit 1 illustrates the flow of materials within the Pine Belt plant.

Exhibit 1   Pine Belt Furniture Company: The Flow of Raw Materials, Labor and Overhead Costs

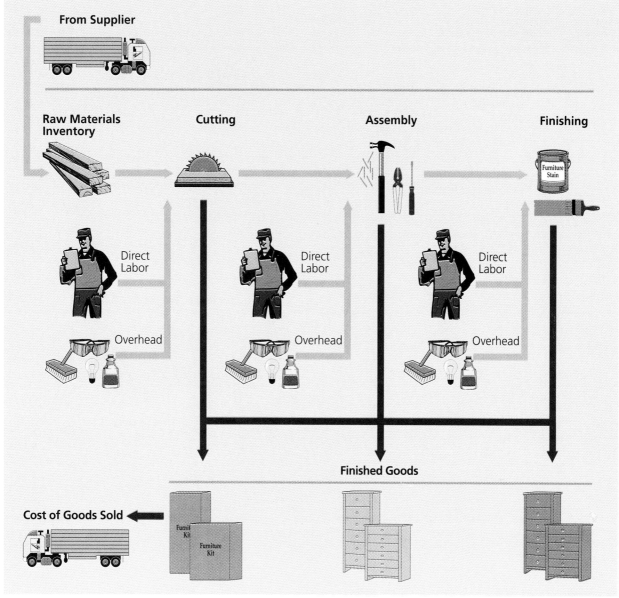

Cutting. When an order is received on the manufacturing floor, an equipment operator moves raw materials from the storage area and places them into production. Processing steps involve cutting lumber to meet specifications, cutting square edges of the lumber at appropriate points to produce curves or other geometric designs, cutting dovetail joints where two pieces of lumber will be attached, and drilling holes to accommodate hardware. Panel A of Exhibit 2 shows the activities that go on in the cutting department. At the completion of this stage, some of the processed materials are boxed and shipped in kit form to retail stores while the rest are transferred to the assembly area.

Assembly. In the assembly department, the wooden components transferred-in from the cutting department are assembled and hardware is attached. Here the pieces of lumber are glued, clamped, and screwed together (Panel B of Exhibit 2). Some of the unfinished furniture is boxed and shipped to retail stores; the rest moves on to the finishing department.

Exhibit 2   Pine Belt Furniture Company: The Production Process

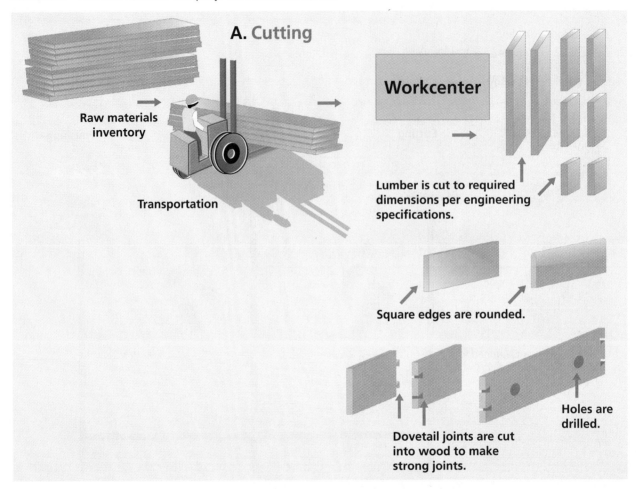

Finishing. In the finishing stage, the assembled products are sanded and stained to darken the wood and to accent the grain. Next a polyurethane finish is applied to the surface to protect against scratching and other damage during use. Pine Belt gives each piece of furniture five coats of polyurethane. Workers lightly buff the surface with steel wool between each coat. When the last coat of polyurethane has dried, the product is boxed and shipped to retail furniture stores. Panel C of Exhibit 2 shows the activities of the finishing department.

PRODUCT COSTS VERSUS PERIOD EXPENSE

Objective 1
Differentiate between product costs and period expenses.

Before managers can use cost accounting information to make decisions, they have to understand how that information is gathered. In your study of financial accounting you learned that most expenses are classified as either *cost of goods (or services) sold* or *operating expenses*. For a manufacturing company, *cost of goods sold* **is the dollar amount of materials, labor, and other resources consumed directly in producing the goods sold during a fiscal period.** *Operating expenses* **are the cost of resources consumed as part of administrative and selling activities during a fiscal period.**

Learning Note   Merchandising (retail) firms have product costs that appear on the income statement as inventory or cost of goods sold. However, such firms do not manufacture their own products. Rather, they purchase the goods ready to sell to customers.

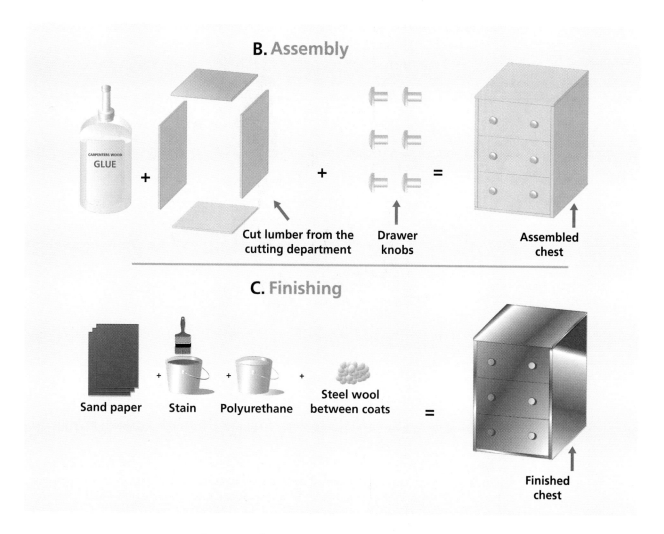

B. Assembly

GLUE + Cut lumber from the cutting department + Drawer knobs = Assembled chest

C. Finishing

Sand paper + Stain + Polyurethane + Steel wool between coats = Finished chest

The cost of goods sold and operating expenses stem from product costs and period expenses (Exhibit 3). *Product costs* **are the costs of manufacturing a company's products.** They are reported as either inventory (before the units are sold) or cost of goods sold (after the units are sold). Thus, product costs don't become expenses until the products are sold. (Remember that units in inventory are assets.) *Period expenses* **are the costs of selling and administrative activities.** These costs are recognized on the income statement during the fiscal period in which they are incurred.

Learning Note Accountants must adhere to GAAP (generally accepted accounting principles) or tax regulations when deciding whether to capitalize a cost as inventory or treat it as a period expense for financial reporting purposes. However, for internal purposes, cost information may be classified according to the needs of management.

Product Costs

Objective 2
Define direct materials, direct labor, and manufacturing overhead costs.

Accountants use three categories to classify the costs of manufacturing: direct materials, direct labor, and manufacturing overhead.

Direct Material Costs. The costs of the significant raw materials from which a product is manufactured are classified as *direct material costs.* For example, Pine Belt uses pine lumber to construct its product line. The cost of that lumber is a direct material cost. The company also classifies the costs of the wooden

Exhibit 3   Pine Belt Furniture Company: Product Costs and Period Expenses

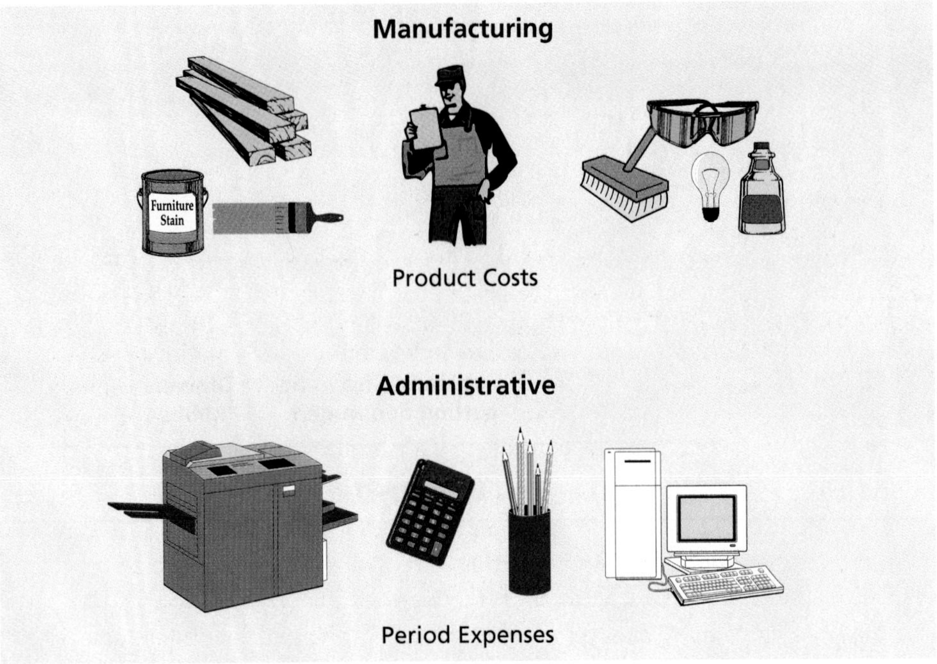

knobs or brass drawer pulls that workers attach to assembled pieces of furniture as direct material costs.

Direct Labor Costs. *Direct labor costs* **are the costs of workers who add value to a product through their direct involvement in the production process.** Pine Belt's direct labor costs include wages of the saw operators who cut parts from the lumber. Wages of those who assemble the parts and apply the stain and polyurethane finish also are classified as direct labor costs.

Manufacturing Overhead Costs. As a general rule, manufacturing overhead costs are not as easily associated with products as are direct materials and direct labor costs. *Manufacturing overhead costs* **usually are produced by activities that support a process but often are not directly related to any specific product.** Thus, overhead costs often are classified as indirect manufacturing costs. While examples of direct materials and direct labor at Pine Belt have been identified, certain types of materials and labor are classified as *indirect*. For instance, the salary of the quality inspector and wages of workers who maintain equipment and clean the manufacturing area are considered *indirect labor costs*.

   The cost of *indirect materials* is a manufacturing overhead cost. At Pine Belt, those costs include the costs of saw blades in the cutting department, glue and screws in the assembly department, and steel wool in the finishing department. How do accountants decide whether to treat glue and screws as direct materials or indirect materials? Generally they use a *cost/benefit rule*. **If the cost of tracking an item exceeds the benefit or value of that information, the cost of the item should be assigned to an overhead category and later allocated to products in a logical manner.** For example, the cost of glue—about $0.03 a unit—is not worth measuring separately as a direct material cost.

   In addition to indirect labor and indirect materials, Pine Belt incurs other overhead costs in the production process:

- Electricity for the manufacturing equipment
- Fire insurance on factory assets

- Supplies (cleaning rags, solvents, brooms, safety glasses, ear plugs and dust masks) for equipment operators
- Depreciation on factory buildings and manufacturing equipment

COST FLOWS THROUGH AN ORGANIZATION

Objective 3
Calculate material, labor, and overhead costs and understand how these costs flow through the company.

With an understanding of how manufacturing organizations classify production costs, we can begin to visualize how materials, labor, and manufacturing overhead costs flow through an organization and its accounting system. In this section the methods used by manufacturing organizations to accumulate, process, and summarize manufacturing costs are discussed. First, the section explains how each type of product requires different amounts of direct materials, direct labor, and overhead. Next, cost flows through an accounting system are illustrated.

To continue the example, let's assume that the following activities took place at Pine Belt during the month of January:

January 4. Raw materials—pine lumber (cost $2,000), pine drawer knobs (cost $500), and polyurethane (cost $100)—were received to produce 100 units of BR-001, a five-drawer chest.

January 5. 100 units of BR-001 were placed into production.

January 31. 80 units of BR-001 were shipped: 35 in kit form, 25 assembled but unfinished, and 20 in finished form. The remaining units, all to be sold in finished form, consisted of 15 work in process (WIP) units that had been cut but not assembled, and 5 units that had been assembled but not finished.

Manufacturing Costs

Exhibit 4 lists the direct material costs of production at Pine Belt in January. For each unit (kit, assembled, or finished) the company used lumber that cost $20 and knobs that cost $5. Polyurethane was used only for the products that were finished. Notice the $80 charge for the 20 finished units.

Exhibit 4 Pine Belt Furniture Company: Direct Materials Costs for January

	Lumber	Knobs	Polyurethane
35 kits	$ 700[1]	$175[2]	$ 0[3]
25 assembled units	500	125	0
20 finished units	400	100	80
15 WIP units awaiting assembly	300	75	0
5 WIP units awaiting finishing	100	25	0
100 units	$2,000	$500	$80

[1] *$2,000 total lumber costs ÷ 100 units = $20 per unit; $20 per unit × 35 kits = $700.*
[2] *$500 total knob costs ÷ 100 units = $5 per unit; $5 per unit × 35 kits = $175.*
[3] *Kits and assembled units do not receive polyurethane finish; therefore, their cost is listed as 0.*

Exhibit 5 identifies the direct labor costs associated with each unit as it progresses from cutting through finishing. Because of different wage rates and production times, direct labor costs vary by department. For example, each unit incurs $25 in direct labor costs within the cutting department; units that are assembled and finished incur additional labor charges of $20 and $15, respectively. Charges within the assembly and finishing departments do not apply to units that are sold in kit form.

Exhibit 5   Pine Belt Furniture Company: Direct Labor Costs for January

	Cutting	Assembly	Finishing
35 kits	$ 875[1]	$ 0	$ 0
25 assembled units	625	500[2]	0
20 finished units	500	400	300[3]
15 WIP units awaiting assembly	375	0	0
5 WIP units awaiting finishing	125	100	0
	$2,500	$1,000	$300

[1] $25 per unit × 35 units = $875
[2] $20 per unit × 25 units = $500
[3] $15 per unit × 20 units = $300

The third category of manufacturing costs is manufacturing overhead. Each department incurs costs that are not classified as direct materials or direct labor. Exhibit 6 lists several types of overhead costs and the total costs incurred by each department. (For simplicity, the exhibit does not list individual cost amounts, but simply indicates whether the department incurred a specific cost.) Notice that the costs of indirect materials are assigned to individual departments: for example, saw blades to the cutting department and steel wool to the finishing department. Indirect costs common to all departments include electricity, fire insurance, supplies, safety equipment, and depreciation. Because different amounts of manufacturing overhead are consumed by each department, the overhead cost per unit varies across the three departments. Each unit that passes through the cutting department consumes $15 in manufacturing overhead costs. The same unit consumes $36 in overhead costs in

Exhibit 6   Pine Belt Furniture Company: Manufacturing Overhead Cost for January

	Cutting	Assembly	Finishing
Indirect labor	Yes	Yes	Yes
Direct material:			
Saw blades	Yes	No	No
Glue	No	Yes	No
Screws	No	Yes	No
Steel wool	No	No	Yes
Electricity	Yes	Yes	Yes
Fire insurance	Yes	Yes	Yes
Supplies	Yes	Yes	Yes
Safety glasses, etc.	Yes	Yes	Yes
Depreciation	Yes	Yes	Yes
Total cost	$1,500	$1,800	$460
Units processed	100[1]	50[2]	20[3]
Cost per unit (Total cost ÷ units processed)	$15	$36	$23

[1] The cutting department processes all units, whether they are sold as kits, unfinished furniture, or finished furniture. Thus, the cutting department processed 100 units: 35 kits were sent to finished goods inventory, and the remaining 65 were transferred to the assembly department.

[2] The assembly department processed 50 of the 65 units transferred in from the cutting department. Thus, 15 units (65 − 50) remain in the assembly WIP inventory. Twenty-five assembled units were transferred to finished goods inventory, and 25 were transferred to the finishing department.

[3] The finishing department received 25 units from the assembly department and processed 20 of them. Thus, 5 units (25 − 20) remain in the finishing department as ending WIP inventory.

passing through the assembly department and $23 in overhead costs in the finishing department.

Exhibit 7 summarizes the direct material, direct labor, and manufacturing overhead costs for each form of BR-001 that Pine Belt manufactures. Notice that each unit, whatever its final form (kit, assembled, or finished), consumes $20 in lumber and $5 in knobs. Direct labor costs are different across the product line: Kits require no assembly or finishing labor; chests that are finished, on the other hand, consume direct labor costs in all three departments. Also, overhead costs (from Exhibit 6) are added at each stage of manufacturing.

Exhibit 7   Pine Belt Furniture Company: Unit Manufacturing Cost for BR-001 in Kit, Assembled, and Finished Form

	Kit	Assembled	Finished
Direct materials			
Pine lumber	$20	$ 20	$ 20
Knobs	5	5	5
Stain/polyurethane	0	0	4
Direct labor			
Cutting	25	25	25
Assembly	0	20	20
Finishing	0	0	15
Manufacturing overhead			
Cutting	15	15	15
Assembly	0	36	36
Finishing	0	0	23
Unit manufacturing cost	$65	$121	$163

Manufacturing Cost Flow

This chapter has explained how various types of manufacturing costs, such as direct materials, direct labor, and manufacturing overhead, are classified. It has shown how manufacturing costs are summarized to help managers understand cost differences in products across a product line. Next, consider how direct material, direct labor, and manufacturing overhead costs flow through the accounting system at Pine Belt. Exhibit 8 shows the factory layout with accounts added to illustrate cost flows.

The lumber ($2,000), wooden pine knobs ($500), and polyurethane ($100) received on January 4 are placed in raw materials inventory. The balance in the Raw Materials Inventory account increases $2,600 **(a)**. On January 5, when the lumber and knobs are removed from raw materials storage and are placed into production, their costs are transferred to the Work in Process Inventory account **(b).** Next, direct labor ($2,500) **(c)** and overhead ($1,500) **(d)** are added in the cutting department to convert the lumber into components for the BR-001 chest. Once the workers in the cutting department complete their part of the manufacturing process, the components are transferred to finished goods inventory (to be sold as kits) or to the assembly department. Here 35 kits, with a cost of $65 each ($2,275) **(e)** are transferred to finished goods inventory. The components for 65 chests (65 × $65 = $4,225) **(f)** are transferred to assembly.

In the assembly department, direct labor ($1,000) **(g)** and overhead ($1,800) **(h)** are added. Of the 65 chests transferred from the cutting department, 25 assembled chests are moved to finished goods inventory (25 × $121 = $3,025) **(i)** to be sold as unfinished furniture, and 25 assembled chests are transferred to the finishing department ($3,025) **(j).** The other 15 units remain in the assembly department in WIP inventory (15 × $65 = $975) **(k).**

Exhibit 8   Pine Belt Furniture Company: Manufacturing Cost Flows

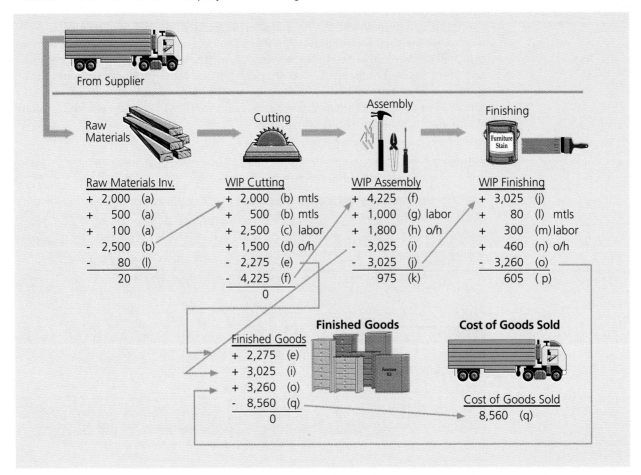

The finishing department receives 25 chests from the assembly department ($3,025) **(j).** To complete 20 chests, finishing department workers add direct materials ($80 for polyurethane) **(l),** direct labor ($300) **(m),** and manufacturing overhead costs (20 × $23 = $460) **(n).** The finishing department transfers the 20 chests (20 × $163 = $3,260) **(o)** to finished goods inventory. The remaining 5 chests (25 transferred in—20 completed and transferred out) represent work in process cost of $605 **(p)** (5 chests × $121 transferred-in cost from the cutting department).

Pine Belt does not keep completed goods in inventory. That means that all units transferred to finished goods inventory are shipped during the month and are recorded as cost of goods sold. The total cost of inventory completed and shipped is $8,560 **(q).** When Pine Belt's controller (chief accountant) prepares the balance sheet and income statement at the end of January, she includes inventory and cost of goods sold as follows:

	Inventory	Cost of Goods Sold
Raw Materials	$ 20	
WIP Cutting	0	
WIP Assembly	975	
WIP Finishing	605	
	$1,600	$8,560

Here are several key points to remember about the way costs flow through a manufacturing facility. First, when materials are placed into production, their costs become part of the Work in Process Inventory account. In addition, direct labor and overhead costs become part of the Work in Process Inventory account as labor and overhead are used to convert raw materials to products. Accountants often call direct labor and overhead costs *conversion costs*. *Conversion costs* **are the costs required to convert materials into products.** Imagine a product with hooks on it. As it moves through the factory, direct labor and overhead costs are attached to the hooks. When the product is finished, all of the costs that have "hooked on" to the product during manufacturing become part of finished goods inventory and, ultimately, the cost of goods sold.

SELF-STUDY PROBLEM 1

© Bob Daemmrich

Greencut Manufacturing produces energy-efficient lawn mowers for homeowners. Workers at Greencut manufacture the mower bodies from steel sheets and then attach a gasoline-powered engine, a blade, a handle, and four wheels to each unit.

The following events took place during the month of January:

1. Greencut bought steel sheets (cost $5,000) for constructing mower bodies.
2. Steel sheets (cost $2,000) were removed from raw materials inventory and delivered by fork lift operators (total monthly wages $5,000) to a metal-press machine operator (total monthly wages $3,000), who pressed the flat sheets of steel into mower housings. Fork-lift operators delivered the mower housings to an automated painting booth. There, workers (total monthly wages $2,000) placed the housings onto overhead conveyor hooks that moved through a booth containing robotic paint sprayers. All surfaces of the mower housing were sprayed with paint (total paint cost $1,000). The painted housings moved along the conveyor belt into a dryer that was heated with propane gas (total monthly gas cost $1,000).
3. After drying, forklift operators transported the painted housings to the assembly area. At the same time, engines, blades, handles, and wheels were removed from the inventory of "purchased parts" (total cost $20,000) and delivered by forklift to the assembly area. Finally, workers installed a motor, a blade, a handle, and four wheels to each housing (total monthly wages of assemblers $6,000).
4. Greencut estimates depreciation costs on plant equipment to be $24,000 for the month of January.
5. Following assembly, the completed mowers were crated and shipped to retail stores throughout the world.
6. Greencut does not carry WIP or finished goods inventory. All units are completed and sold during the month. Sales people earned commissions of $10,000 in January.

Required

1. Draw a simple diagram that shows the flow of costs through Greencut's factory.
2. Prepare an exhibit similar to the one presented in Exhibit 8 to show the effects of January's activities on the company's Raw Materials Inventory, Purchased

Parts Inventory, Work in Process Inventory, Finished Goods Inventory, and Cost of Goods Sold accounts. Assume that all beginning balances on January 1 were zero, except for the Purchased Parts Inventory account that had a beginning balance of $25,000.

3. What was the company's cost of goods sold for January?
4. What was the value of Greencut's raw materials and purchased parts inventories at the end of January?

The solution to Self-Study Problem 1 appears at the end of the chapter.

TRADITIONAL COST CATEGORIES

Objective 4
Describe how manufacturing costs respond to changes in activity.

Direct materials, direct labor, and manufacturing overhead are categories of product costs. In this section we look at the behavior of those costs. First, consider how costs respond to changes in activity levels.

Cost Behavior in Relation to Changes in Activity Levels

Managers often make decisions about pricing, production levels, product mix, and external purchases after considering cost information. Later in this chapter, we examine the types of decisions managers commonly face. First, it is important to understand which costs are relevant to certain types of decisions. Often, whether a cost is relevant depends on how costs change (or do not change) when volume changes. The following paragraphs explore the impact of volume on manufacturing costs and identify examples of costs that typically are classified as variable, fixed, semivariable, and step-pattern.

Variable Costs. *Variable costs* **are costs that change in total with volume but remain fixed on a per unit basis.** For example, the cost of lumber Pine Belt uses in its manufacturing process is a variable cost because the total cost of lumber varies in relation to the number of products manufactured. Remember that the cost of lumber for each BR-001 chest produced is $20. If a single chest is produced, the total cost of lumber is $20. However, if 100 chests are manufactured, the total cost of lumber would be $2,000.

Exhibit 9 Behavior Pattern: Variable Costs

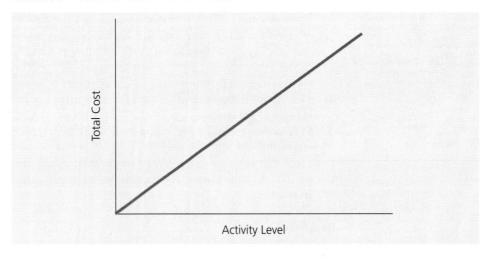

Variable costs go up as the level of activity (volume) rises. Exhibit 9 illustrates that behavior pattern. Managers can predict the total cost of a direct material at any level of production by multiplying the cost per unit times the number of units produced:

Total variable cost	=	cost per unit × number of units produced
$20	=	$20 × 1 unit produced
$60	=	$20 × 3 units produced
$2,000	=	$20 × 100 units produced

Fixed Costs. *Fixed costs* **are costs that do not change in total with volume but vary on a per-unit basis.** Generally, depreciation is a fixed cost. A company's *total* depreciation cost does not change whether it produces 2,500 units or 5,000 units in a year (Exhibit 10). However, the cost *per unit* does vary with output because fixed depreciation costs are spread over a greater or lesser number of units.

Suppose, for example, that a company has $50,000 in depreciation expense this year. The total cost is fixed, but the cost per unit depends on the number of units produced:

Cost per unit	=	total fixed cost ÷ number of units produced
$20	=	$50,000 ÷ 2,500 units produced
$10	=	$50,000 ÷ 5,000 units produced

Notice that fixed costs per unit fall as the number of units produced rises.

Exhibit 10   Behavior Pattern: Fixed Costs

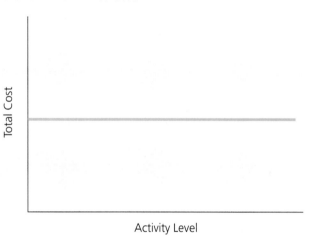

Semivariable or Mixed Costs. *Semivariable* **or** *mixed costs* **are a combination of variable and fixed costs.** For example, total electricity consumption at Pine Belt changes with production levels as the number of machine hours varies.

CASE
In Point

http://www.swcollege.com/ingram.html

Visit WCI Steel's home page and learn more about the world of automotive steels.

Companies that use large amounts of equipment often have high fixed costs in relation to their total manufacturing costs. Examples of capital-intensive industries—those with a large amount of resources invested in long-term assets—include steel, paper, and chemical manufacturing. Profits in those industries are very sensitive to fluctuations in production volume and sales. For example, the following information relates to **WCI Steel:** "In the first quarter, a $32 million increase in revenues brought a $16 million boost to gross profit, showing the big impact a higher production rate can have on a company with high fixed costs and substantial assets." Clearly, an understanding of how costs respond to volume is important for managers who want to make informed decisions about production and pricing.

Source: "WCI Steel," **Barron's,** *May 2, 1994, p. 45.*

Machinery consumes most of the electrical energy used in the plant. However, even if production falls to zero, electricity would be used for lighting and heating or cooling of plant facilities. Exhibit 11 shows how mixed costs react to changes in amount of output. The key point: Total cost is a function of both variable and fixed costs; costs vary with output but cannot drop to zero as long as a company is in business.

Exhibit 11   Behavior Pattern: Semivariable Costs

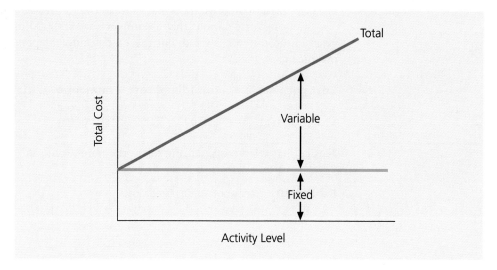

Step-Pattern Costs. *Step-pattern costs* **are costs that increase or decrease in total over a wide range of activity levels. However, these costs remain fixed over a narrow range of activity levels.** The relationship between variable costs and volume is linear (Exhibit 9): Every unit produced increases total costs by the same amount. Step-pattern costs also vary with respect to volume but not in a linear pattern (Exhibit 12).

For example, assume that one quality control engineer can inspect up to 1,000 units a month. If Pine Belt increases its production to 1,500 units, it must hire another quality control engineer. The company cannot hire a portion of a quality control engineer; it has to hire the entire person. If production levels go up to more than 2,000 units a month, Pine Belt is going to have to hire a third quality engineer. Quality inspection costs move in a step pattern with respect to volume.

Exhibit 12   Behavior Pattern: Step-Pattern Costs

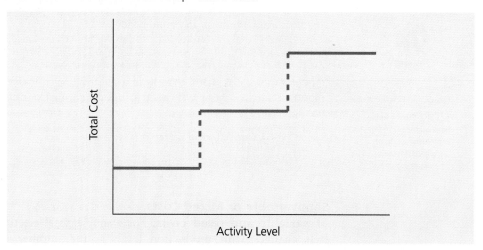

Exhibit 13 categorizes by activity the overhead costs illustrated in Exhibit 6. Most of those costs—saw blades, supplies, glue, screws, steel wool, and safety equipment—are variable. Total costs go up with each unit produced. The company's depreciation cost is fixed because depreciation typically does not vary in total with the level of output. The costs of electricity and fire insurance are mixed because each has a component that varies with the level of production as well as a fixed component. Finally, the costs of indirect labor are stepped because workers are not hired in fractional increments as production levels rise. The costs of indirect labor vary as the number of workers who support the manufacturing process changes, as those workers are hired, let go, or retire.

Exhibit 13 Pine Belt Furniture Company: Cost Behavior

	Variable	**Fixed**	**Semivariable**	**Step**
Indirect labor				X
Indirect materials:				
Saw blades	X			
Glue	X			
Screws	X			
Steel wool	X			
Electricity			X	
Fire insurance			X	
Supplies	X			
Safety glasses, etc.	X			
Depreciation		X		

Other Behavior Considerations: Management Policies and Time

Some management accounting experts argue that costs are not inherently variable or fixed, that their behavior is a function of the way in which costs are contracted.[1] Workers in an assembly department, for example, could be paid by the piece: the higher the level of production, the larger their paychecks. Here the terms of the contract tie the worker's wages to output; wages are a variable cost. On the other hand, if the company contracts with the same workers to pay them a fixed amount every week, whatever their output, their wages are fixed. You should be careful when you classify costs by behavior because costs that appear variable may in fact be fixed. An example: Assume a factory worker is being paid on an hourly basis. Are these wages variable or fixed? Most people would say that the wages are variable because the total wage costs vary according to the number of hours worked. Suppose you have one more bit of information: workers in this factory are never told to go home, even during times when the factory is producing below expected volume. In other words, each employee works 40 hours a week. In this case, management's policy has changed what is traditionally a variable cost—the wages of hourly employees—into a fixed cost. Here the total hours worked do not vary with the level of production.

Another important factor in understanding the effect of volume on costs is time. For example, the cost of raw material generally is thought to be variable; however, if raw materials have been purchased and are available in the warehouse, one could argue that their costs are fixed. In the short run, raw material costs do not vary because the materials have been paid for and are available. There are times when fixed costs respond more like variable costs. Depreciation on plant assets generally is considered a fixed cost. However, in the long run, as assets are acquired or sold in

[1] Cooper, R. and R. Kaplan. 1992. *Activity-Based Systems: Measuring the Cost of Resource Usage,* Accounting Horizons *(September): 1–13.*

response to changes in demand, plant depreciation behaves like a variable cost. Thus, general patterns of cost behavior exist; however, most costs can be affected by management actions.

SELF-STUDY PROBLEM 2

To solve this problem, use the information in Self Study Problem 1.

Required

Classify each of Greencut's costs in January as variable, fixed, semivariable, or step-pattern. Explain your classifications.

The solution to Self-Study Problem 2 appears at the end of the chapter.

© Ted Horowitz/The Stock Market

COST-BASED DECISION MAKING

O b j e c t i v e   5
Identify how managers use cost information in their decision making.

Throughout this chapter, you have worked with manufacturing costs to understand how costs accumulate, how they flow through the organization, and how they behave. This next section describes how managers use cost information to make the following types of decisions:

- Target costing
- Make or buy
- Sell now or process further.

Target-Costing Decisions

Assume that the managers at Pine Belt have made the strategic decision to expand the product line to offer a product that can compete with those offered by high-quality furniture manufacturers. The first piece in the new line is a bedroom chest of drawers, BR-1000, constructed from clear (knot-free) pine and solid brass drawer pulls.

Pine Belt's managers have invested resources in engineering drawings, product prototypes, and studies of manufacturing processes before implementing full-scale production of the BR-1000. Naturally they want to recover that investment and earn a profit on the sale of the new product. To determine the price of the BR-1000, the managers estimate the per-unit costs of producing the chest and the behavior of those costs (Exhibit 14).

Pine Belt's management offered the following explanation of the unit costs:

Direct materials. The BR-1000 chest differs from other products in the line because expensive, knot-free wood and solid brass are used in its construction. Management expects direct material costs to vary with the number of units produced.

Direct labor. Managers predict that the direct labor costs of the BR-1000 in the cutting department will be identical to that of other products in the line. However, they expect direct labor costs to go up in the assembly and finishing departments because the process of assembling and finishing the BR-1000 chest is more complicated and time-consuming than for other products in the line. Management thinks labor is a fixed cost because workers are not asked to go home when production stops for any reason.

Exhibit 14 Pine Belt Furniture Company: Estimated Total Manufacturing Cost for the BR-1000

	Unit Cost	Cost Behavior
Direct materials		
Pine lumber	$100	variable
Brass drawer pulls	55	variable
Stain/polyurethane	4	variable
Direct labor		
Cutting	25	fixed
Assembly	40	fixed
Finishing	30	fixed
Manufacturing overhead		
Cutting	30	semivariable
Assembly	90	semivariable
Finishing	76	semivariable
Total manufacturing cost	$450	
Estimated selling and administrative expenses	$ 25	semivariable
Total cost per unit	$475	

Manufacturing overhead. The increase in the manufacturing costs per unit of the BR-1000 chest is in large part due to additional engineering time and new equipment purchased solely to assemble and finish the new chest. Pine Belt managers understand that overhead costs contain both variable and fixed elements.

Estimated selling and administrative expenses. The managers at Pine Belt want to associate selling and administrative expenses directly with the BR-1000 to understand the full cost of manufacturing and delivering a unit of product. These direct costs include salesperson's commissions and various administrative expenses.

To ensure the highest quality assembly and finishing, management decides to market the BR-1000 exclusively in finished form through specialty furniture stores. The total estimated cost of the BR-1000 is $475. Pine Belt generally adds a 30% markup to the unit cost when it quotes prices to customers. For our purposes, *markup* **is the difference between the unit cost and the selling price of a product.** The managers at Pine Belt calculate the wholesale selling price to a furniture store as follows:

(Unit manufacturing cost + selling and administrative expenses) × markup percentage = markup in dollars
($450.00 + $25.00) × .30 = $142.50

Unit manufacturing cost + selling and administrative expenses + markup in dollars = wholesale selling price
$450.00 + $25.00 + $142.50 = $617.50

Using costs to help them determine a selling price, Pine Belt's managers set the wholesale price of the chest at $618. After applying their own markup, retailers must sell the chest for approximately $1,000. Unfortunately, after producing a new catalog and price list, as well as floor models of the BR-1000 for display in retailers' showrooms, the managers at Pine Belt hear some disappointing news. Retailers are not interested in carrying the line because consumers are not willing to pay $1,000 retail for pine furniture, even when that furniture is constructed of knot-free lumber and solid brass pulls. How could this happen? The management of Pine Belt carefully studied the details of cost behavior when it calculated product costs, yet found the flagship of its product line, the BR-1000, sank! What went wrong?

This situation illustrates a traditional cost-based pricing policy in which the following steps occur:

1. A product and manufacturing process are designed.
2. The product is manufactured.
3. Manufacturing costs are accumulated.
4. The unit cost plus markup determines the selling price.
5. The company tries to sell the product.

Objective 6
Explain how target costing
helps managers make
decisions about introducing
new goods or services.

What's missing here is an analysis of the market and an understanding of what consumers want. Although the new chest seemed to meet consumer's demands for quality and functionality, it did not meet their price demands. By starting the pricing process with their costs, Pine Belt's managers priced the BR-1000 out of its market.

Target costing changes the focus of the pricing decision: Instead of cost determining the selling price, the selling price determines costs. *Target costing* **relies on market information to determine the quality, functionality, and price consumers are looking for in a new product and the feasibility of meeting consumers' demands.** The target here isn't the selling price; it's the cost at which a product of a certain quality and functionality can be produced.

The process is simple:

1. Determine the quality and functionality consumers want in a new product and the price they are willing to pay for that product.
2. Subtract the retailer's markup from the retail price to determine the wholesale price.
3. Subtract the manufacturer's markup from the wholesale price to determine what the manufacturer can spend to produce the product.
4. Study the feasibility of the new product. Can the company produce a product consumers want at a price the market will accept?

The target-cost calculation involves an understanding of the relationships among three variables: the selling price, the targeted manufacturing cost (cost), and the markup on the manufacturing cost (markup). The relationship among the variables is defined as follows:

Selling price − markup = cost
Markup   = cost × markup percentage

Suppose that market research sets the wholesale price of the BR-1000 at $400. Remember that Pine Belt's required markup is 30%. Now we can substitute cost × 0.30 for markup and solve for cost:

Selling price − (cost × 30%) = cost
Selling price   = cost + (cost × 30%)
Selling price   = cost × 1.3
Selling price ÷ 1.3   = cost

The company's target cost and markup are calculated as follows:

Target cost $400 ÷ 1.3 = $308
Markup $308 × 30% = $92

The target-cost information for Pine Belt can be summarized as follows:

Selling price (wholesale) $400
Less required markup on cost   92
Target cost $308

Determining the cost at which Pine Belt must deliver the BR-1000 is the first step in using target costing for strategic purposes. Clearly the managers at Pine Belt have a problem: To market the new chest successfully, they have to reduce the unit cost of producing the chest from $475 to $308.

One way companies begin to address a cost problem is by forming a multidisciplinary team, a team whose members are drawn from different functions—marketing, accounting, finance, production, purchasing, and engineering, for example. The team looks for ways to save costs and to eliminate inefficiencies. An understanding of cost behavior is key to understanding the cost-effectiveness of design changes in products and manufacturing processes.

Pine Belt's team would evaluate the major cost categories listed in Exhibit 14. Its managers would discuss redesigning the manufacturing process, reconsidering the types of materials used and ways to reduce suppliers' costs. They would study the sources of overhead costs and methods of reducing those costs. Based on the team's recommendations, Pine Belt's top management may decide to manufacture the BR-1000. However, if it determines that it cannot produce the chest for $308, it should not produce the product.

C A S E

In Point

Nissan Motor Company, Ltd. uses target costing to sell quality automobiles that meet the company's target profit. Nissan subtracts its required markup from the anticipated selling price of a new vehicle. If the resulting target cost is too low, the company redesigns the product until the target cost can be met. Target costing helps Nissan control manufacturing costs by identifying costs in the design phase, when product and process changes can be made, rather than in the production phase, after product and process designs are committed.

Source: R. Cooper, Nissan Motor Company—Teaching Note 195-063. (Boston: Harvard Business School Publishing, 1995), p. 3.

Make or Buy Decisions

Objective 7
Discuss the issues surrounding make or buy decisions.

http://www.swcollege.
com/ingram.html

Find out more about outsourcing.

A company that has to decide between manufacturing a component or buying that component from an outside source (outsourcing) is facing a make or buy decision. Typically managers evaluate many factors, including costs, before choosing to make or buy a component.

Currently, Pine Belt is buying from an outside supplier the wooden knobs it uses for drawer pulls. The company's management wants to know if it should continue to outsource the knobs or manufacture them internally. Which costs are relevant to a make or buy decision? *Relevant costs* **are the costs that change under two or more decision alternatives.** Plant depreciation costs are not relevant to a make or buy decision because depreciation costs are fixed; they will not change regardless of the decision. However, if a worker has to be hired to produce the knobs, the additional cost of direct labor is a relevant cost.

Let's evaluate the costs of outsourcing the knobs versus manufacturing them. According to Exhibit 4, the knobs cost $500 per 100 chests, or $5 per chest. The $5 unit cost is relevant to the make or buy decision because if Pine Belt manufactures the knobs internally, it does not incur that $5 cost. The relevant costs of manufacturing the knobs internally include the costs of additional lumber, machinery (a new lathe), labor (one worker has agreed to work an extra half day each month to manufacture all the knobs needed for a month's production), and overhead.

Exhibit 15 summarizes the costs relevant to the make or buy decision. All of those costs are variable costs, with one exception. Depreciation usually is a fixed cost. However, depreciation costs are relevant to the decision here because the equipment has not yet been purchased.

The cost analysis suggests that Pine Belt should make the knobs internally and save $1 per chest. Cost isn't the only factor in the make or buy decision. By manufacturing the knobs internally, the company controls both the quality of the knobs and

Exhibit 15 Pine Belt Furniture Company: Make or Buy Cost Analysis per Unit

	Make	Buy
Outsource cost		$5.00
Direct materials:		
Lumber	$1.00	
Direct labor	2.00	
Overhead:		
Electricity	.15	
Supplies	.10	
Steel wool	.05	
Lathe depreciation	.70	
Total cost per unit	$4.00	$5.00

the reliability of delivery. Availability is especially important if a labor dispute, a flood, or a fire could stop production at a supplier's facilities.

Companies often seek bids from outside suppliers for components that are made internally in an attempt to reduce costs by outsourcing. Sometimes external firms make very low bids in an attempt to attract customers. Companies must be careful when deciding to discontinue production of a component in favor of purchasing. Cost savings that initially appear attractive may disappear just as quickly if suppliers later increase prices.

Sell-Now or Process-Further Decisions

Objective 8
Discuss sell-now or process-further decisions.

Pine Belt's managers analyzed the company's market and made the strategic decision to produce products in three forms: kit, assembled, and finished. To determine an appropriate selling price for each form of product, managers have to understand the costs of producing each form and how they differ. Managers also have to understand the dynamics of the marketplace. How do the sales of one type of product affect the sales of another type? What factors differentiate people who buy kits from the people who buy assembled or finished pieces of furniture? Again, remember that cost information is only one piece of data for managerial decision making.

In determining whether to sell a product at an intermediate stage or after further processing, managers compare the cost of production at the intermediate stage with that at the more completed stage. If the difference in selling prices between the intermediate stage and the completed stage is more than the cost of further processing, generally managers choose to process the units further. For example, let's assume that Pine Belt manufactures only kits and assembled units and that only now is the company considering the financial impact of marketing finished pieces. Exhibit 7 shows the incremental per-unit costs incurred by the finishing department:

Stain/polyurethane	$ 4
Labor	15
Overhead	23
	$42

Remember that in this example, Pine Belt does not have a finishing department at the time of this analysis. To produce finished products, management would have to incur materials, labor, and overhead costs. That means all of the $42 in incremental costs per unit are relevant to the decision.

Assume Pine Belt sells the assembled products for $170 each and expects to sell the same item in finished form for $250. The incremental revenue per unit would be $80

($250 − $170). As shown in Exhibit 16, subtracting the incremental cost per unit of further processing ($42) from that incremental revenue results in a net increase in gross profit of $38. The management at Pine Belt has obtained one piece of information suggesting further processing is a sound business decision.

Exhibit 16   Pine Belt Furniture Company: Sell-Now or Process-Further Cost Analysis per Unit

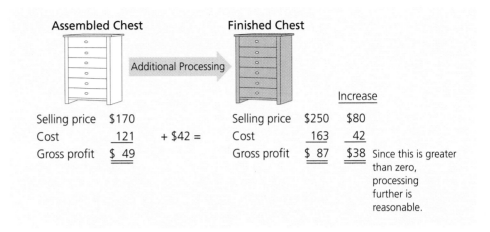

What commonality do you see among the analysis of target-costing, sell-now or process-further, and make or buy decisions? All use the concept of relevant costs for decision-making. Thus, gaining an understanding of cost behavior with respect to changes in activity level can assist managers in making many types of operational and marketing decisions. Later in this text you will revisit the topic of cost behavior when the concepts of activity-based management are explored.

COST INFORMATION FOR SERVICE ORGANIZATIONS

O b j e c t i v e   9
Explain how cost categories, behavior, and control issues affect service organizations.

In service organizations, costs attach to products *(cost objects)* in much the same way as they do in manufacturing organizations; only the nature of the product is different. A hospital doesn't produce a chest of drawers. Its product is patient health care. When a patient leaves the health-care system, the costs of providing care become part of the cost of services provided, the service organization's equivalent to cost of goods sold. This section describes three aspects of cost measurement for health-care providers—cost categorization, cost behavior, and cost control—and relates them to costs in a manufacturing environment. As you will see, many similarities exist.

Cost Categories

Hospitals, like manufacturers, classify costs as direct and indirect. The costs of nurses' salaries, drugs, and X-rays are all direct costs of delivering care to patients. Like direct costs in manufacturing, direct costs in a hospital are easily associated with a patient. Hospitals and most other service organizations generally have a large proportion of indirect costs that must be assigned to individual patients or customer services in some manner. Among a hospital's indirect costs are salaries of administrators, admission and discharge personnel, and insurance specialists.

Cost Behavior

Costs in service organizations can behave much like those in manufacturing organizations. For example, in a hospital, daily costs of linen and food generally are variable costs. Because linen is changed daily and meals are provided three times a day, those costs clearly vary with the length of a patient's stay.

Health-care costs also vary with the severity of a patient's condition. A patient who is recovering from open-heart surgery requires highly skilled nursing care and access to more sophisticated equipment than a patient who has had a tonsillectomy. It is not surprising, then, that hospitals often charge more to patients who consume more clinical care.

In the new health care environment, cost control is more important than ever. Therefore, health care providers are taking steps to control costs. This is particularly important since payments from insurers are decreasing. The next section considers similarities between service and manufacturing organizations in their actions to control costs.

Cost Control

In today's economy, all businesses are taking steps to control production costs. Health-care providers face a special challenge. At one time hospitals were reimbursed by insurance companies (or the federal government in the case of Medicare) based on their costs of treating patients. Today, insurance companies are applying pressure by limiting the fees they pay for each type of treatment. Because their revenue is fixed (and determined by insurance providers), hospitals can operate profitably only if they manage costs effectively.

Manufacturing companies use target costing to help them design products and processes that reduce costs. Hospitals use a technique called *critical path*. They identify the steps necessary for each procedure from preadmission to discharge. By standardizing procedures, heath-care providers often find ways to reduce inefficiency and costs. The critical path helps service organizations control costs in a similar way that target costing helps manufacturing companies control costs.

SELF-STUDY PROBLEM 3

Part 1

Greencut is considering adding a mulching lawn mower to its product line. The new mower cuts grass clippings into fine particles, eliminating raking, bagging, and disposing of lawn wastes. The new product is intended to meet the needs of urban and environmentally-conscious homeowners.

Greencut wants to conduct a target-costing exercise to determine the cost at which the new product must be produced. Market surveys indicate that retailers typically pay $300 and sell for $500 products with similar features. Thus, the company expects the wholesale price for the new mower to be $300. Greencut's standard markup is 35% of the manufacturing cost.

© Don Smetzer/Tony Stone Images

Part 2

A team of design engineers, accountants, manufacturing engineers, and finance professionals has determined the target manufacturing cost for producing the mulching mower. To meet that cost, the team must find ways to reduce costs without compromising quality. Someone on the team recommends outsourcing some components instead of manufacturing them. After studying the recommendation, the team concludes that the target cost can be met if those components are outsourced.

Required

Part 1

1. Calculate the target cost of the new mower and Greencut's required markup.

Part 2

2. Discuss the *types* of costs that are relevant to the make or buy decision.
3. Discuss nonfinancial issues that the management team should consider before it recommends outsourcing the components.

The solution to Self-Study Problem 3 appears at the end of the chapter.

R E V I E W   *Summary of Important Concepts*

1. Costs may be classified according to a number of categories including:
   a. Product cost versus period expense.
   b. Direct materials, direct labor, or overhead.

2. Manufacturing costs flow through an accounting system as products physically move through the factory.
   a. When raw materials are acquired, their value is added to the Raw Materials Inventory account.
   b. When raw materials are placed into production, their costs, along with the costs of labor and overhead, are added to the Work in Process Inventory account.
   c. The cost of completed goods is transferred to the Finished Goods Inventory account.
   d. The costs in the Finished Goods Inventory account are transferred to the Cost of Goods Sold account when the units are sold.

3. Manufacturing costs may be classified according to their behavior with respect to changes in production volume as follows:
   a. Variable costs change in total with volume but are fixed per unit.
   b. Fixed costs do not change in total with volume but vary per unit.
   c. Semivariable or mixed costs combine variable and fixed costs.
   d. Step-pattern costs vary over a wide range of activities.

4. Managers use cost information to help them make better decisions.
   a. Target costing helps managers in the introduction of new products.
   b. Costs are one factor in the decision to make or buy the components of a product.
   c. Costs also are a factor in the decision to sell now or process a product further.

5. Organizations that produce services instead of tangible products also incur production costs.
   a. The costs of services are classified as direct or indirect.
   b. The costs within service organizations can respond to changes in the level of activity.
   c. Service organizations often implement cost control procedures to identify and eliminate waste.

D E F I N E   *Terms and Concepts Defined in This Chapter*

conversion costs   (45)
cost/benefit rule   (40)
cost of goods sold   (38)
direct labor costs   (40)
direct material costs   (39)
fixed costs   (47)

manufacturing overhead costs   (40)
markup   (51)
mixed costs   (47)
operating expenses   (38)
period expenses   (39)
product costs   (39)

relevant costs   (53)
semivariable costs   (47)
step-pattern costs   (48)
target costing   (52)
variable costs   (46)

S O L U T I O N S

SELF-STUDY PROBLEM 1

1.

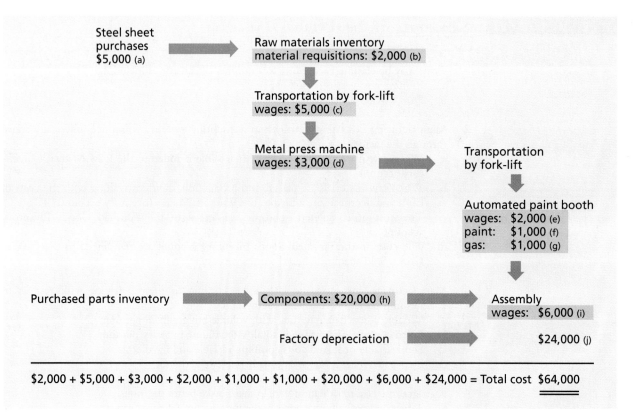

$2,000 + $5,000 + $3,000 + $2,000 + $1,000 + $1,000 + $20,000 + $6,000 + $24,000 = Total cost $64,000

2.

Raw Materials Inventory	Purchased Parts Inventory	WIP Inventory	Finished Goods Inventory	Cost of Goods Sold
Beg $ 0	Beg $25,000	Beg $ 0	Beg $ 0	Beg $ 0
+ 5,000(a)	− 20,000(h)	+ 2,000(b)	+ 64,000(k)	+ 64,000(l)
− 2,000(b)	End $ 5,000	+ 5,000(c)	− 64,000(l)	End $64,000
End $3,000		+ 3,000(d)	End $ 0	
		+ 2,000(e)		
		+ 1,000(f)		
		+ 1,000(g)		
		+20,000(h)		
		+ 6,000(i)		
		+24,000(j)		
		−64,000(k)		
		End $ 0		

Key to cost flows:

(a) Greencut purchased steel sheets that were placed into raw materials inventory.
(b) Steel was removed from inventory and placed into production as WIP inventory.
(c) Overhead for the fork-lift operators' wages was incurred.
(d) Direct labor costs of $3,000 for the press operator were incurred.
(e) Direct labor wages for paint booth / conveyor operators were incurred.
(f) Direct materials cost of $1,000 for paint was incurred.
(g) Overhead cost (indirect materials) for the propane gas was consumed.
(h) Purchased parts (direct materials) were transferred from inventory to production.
(i) Direct labor costs ($6,000) for workers in the assembly area were incurred.
(j) Depreciation on manufacturing assets was estimated to be $24,000 during the month.
(k) Completed mowers were transferred to the finished goods inventory.
(l) Finished mowers costing $64,000 were sold.

Note: Sales commissions are not part of product costs or the cost of goods sold. Sales commissions are a period expense and are reported on the income statement below gross profit.

3. Cost of goods sold in January was $64,000.

4. The balance in the Raw Materials Inventory account was $3,000, and the balance in the Purchased Parts Inventory account was $5,000.

SELF-STUDY PROBLEM 2

The costs identified by Greencut included the following:

Direct materials
Steel
Paint
Wheels, motors, handles, and blades
The cost behavior of all direct materials is variable with respect to the number of units produced. The cost per unit is fixed; however, the *total* cost of paint, steel, wheels, motors, handles, and blades varies with production levels.

Direct labor
   Metal-press machine operator
   Spray-booth workers
   Assembly area workers
Assuming that Greencut guarantees each employee 40 hours of work a week, the company's direct labor costs are fixed in the short run. However, in the long run those costs may vary. For example, if production levels rise beyond the capabilities of the existing workforce, the company is going to have to hire more workers. In the long run, then, the costs of direct labor may resemble a step-pattern.

Overhead
   Indirect materials
      Propane gas
   Indirect labor
      Fork-lift operators' wages
   Other manufacturing overhead costs
      Depreciation on the plant equipment
Because the amount of propane gas varies with the level of output, the cost of the gas is a variable cost.

   Indirect labor costs typically are fixed in relation to changes in volume in the short run. In the long run, the company can let some support workers go or can hire more. Since the actions of management can affect the level of overhead costs, those costs are not necessarily fixed in terms of volume.

   Depreciation on plant assets generally is treated as a fixed cost of manufacturing.

SELF-STUDY PROBLEM 3

1.

   Selling price − markup   = cost
   markup   = cost × 35%

   thus,

   Selling price − (cost × 35%)   = cost
   Selling price   = cost + (cost × 35%)
   Selling price   = cost × 1.35
   Selling price ÷ 1.35   = cost

   The target cost is $222 ($300 ÷ 1.35) and the markup is $78 ($222 × 35%). The target cost information for Greencut may be summarized as follows:

Selling price (wholesale)	$300
Less required markup on cost	78
Target cost	$222

2. The multifunctional team should examine the varying costs the company would incur if it (1) manufactures the components or (2) outsources them. Those costs that change between the two alternatives are relevant to the make or buy decision. The costs that do not change should not affect the decision because the company is going to incur those costs whether a component is outsourced or not.

   Certain fixed costs also may be relevant to the make or buy decision. If Greencut has to buy new equipment to produce the mulching mower, depreciation costs of the new equipment are relevant to the decision to make or buy. Why? If Greencut chooses to outsource the components, it will not purchase new equipment. If, on the other hand, the company chooses to make the components, management must acquire new equipment. Thus, *before* equipment is purchased, its cost is relevant to the outsourcing decision.

3. Manufacturers generally produce a final product by assembling a number of smaller components. Some of those components are manufactured in the plant, while others may be acquired from outside sources. Cost certainly is a key factor in the make or buy decision. The dependability of the suppliers and the quality of the components should be considered, as well.

EXERCISES

2-1. Write a short definition of each of the terms listed in the *Terms and Concepts Defined in This Chapter* section.

Obj. 1

2-2. Classify each of the following costs as either a *product cost* or a *period expense*. Briefly justify your answers.

pc	a.	Wages for factory maintenance workers	pc	h.	Indirect materials
pc	b.	Direct materials	pe	i.	Accounting fees
pe	c.	Sales salaries and commissions	pe	j.	Warehousing costs for finished goods
pe	d.	Depreciation expense, office equipment			
pc	e.	Machinery repairs and maintenance	pc	k.	Production Supervisor's salary
pe	f.	Advertising	pc	l.	Utilities for plant
pc	g.	Property taxes, factory building	pc	m.	Rent on factory buildings

Obj. 2

2-3. Manufacturing overhead costs are considered *indirect costs*. Why?

Objs. 2, 3

2-4. You recently attended a meeting of your school's accounting club. The guest speaker at the meeting was Joan Smead, the controller of a local corporation, who talked about inventory control. During her presentation, Joan made the comment that a large portion of her company's assets is manufacturing overhead cost. Your friend was confused by this statement and later asked you to explain how manufacturing overhead costs can be assets of a company. What would be your response?

Objs. 2, 3

2-5. Carlton Industries manufactures orthopedic devices, such as hips and joints, from specialty metals. Each device is produced individually based on the dimensions of a specific patient. The company ships the devices to surgeons as soon as production is completed. Define and explain the different types of inventory accounts that Carlton would use in its manufacturing environment. What costs are associated with each of these accounts?

Obj. 3

2-6. The Exact Company is a distributor of industrial products such as tools, solvents, and factory supplies. Exact purchases products from a large number of manufacturers and sells those products directly to plants and factories. What costs should be included in the cost of goods sold section of Exact's income statement? Why?

Obj. 3

2-7. The Wendell Fromm Company manufactures hand tools that are used in many factory applications and sells its product through industrial distributors. The company manufactures tools from metal alloys and incurs labor and overhead costs during the manufacturing process. What costs should Wendell Fromm include in the cost of goods sold section of its income statement. Why?

Obj. 4

2-8. Tonkle Industries produces a wide variety of pet supply products. These products include various sizes of pet collars made from leather and synthetic materials. Due to recent losses incurred on the pet collar product line, the president of Tonkle has called a meeting to discuss the manufacturing costs. In particular, the president wants to discuss both variable and fixed costs related to the production of those products. The company's cost accountant, Art Fitch, has prepared and distributed a report for the meeting. The report shows the variable and fixed unit costs of each of the products. Chuck Noble, the production manager, has reviewed Art's report and is confused about the difference between variable costs and fixed costs. Specifically, he does not understand why fixed costs differ between products. Briefly explain to Chuck the difference between fixed costs and variable costs on a per unit basis.

Obj. 4 **2-9.** You decide to study for an upcoming accounting exam with a friend. Your friend says that fixed costs are considered fixed because they remain constant, or "fixed," for each unit produced. Do you agree? Explain your answer.

Obj. 4 **2-10.** Use (a) variable costs, (b) fixed costs, (c) semivariable costs and (d) step-pattern costs to classify each of the following costs based on its cost behavior. Provide a brief explanation of your answer.
- a. Direct materials
- b. Direct labor
- c. Depreciation
- d. Salary of production supervisor
- e. Telephone expense
- f. Machine repairs
- g. Factory janitor wages
- h. Property taxes
- i. Sales commissions
- j. Material handling

Obj. 4 **2-11.** Pagoda Company manufactures metal picture-framing materials. Part of the manufacturing process is the coating and painting of the metal with finishes. Management of Pagoda believes the painting process is a variable cost that is incurred evenly for each unit that passes through the painting operation. An analysis of several recent production runs revealed, however, that costs differ on a per-unit basis when the run sizes differ. Is the cost of painting a variable cost? What explanation could you provide for the cost behavior of the painting operation?

Objs. 4, 5 **2-12.** Explain the importance of cost behavior as it relates to various levels of production activity. Why is information about cost behavior important to managers? Identify some decisions that managers make that require information about cost behavior.

Obj. 5 **2-13.** Sue Mitchell is the President of Embassy Manufacturing, a company that produces key chains. In an effort to control costs, she wants to form a multidisciplinary team to review the costs the company has incurred over the past year. What areas of the company should be represented on the team? How would each member of the team contribute to the cost analysis?

Obj. 6 **2-14.** Kalida Incorporated manufactures a single product that sells for $150 per unit. The unit cost of the product includes direct materials ($60), direct labor ($40), and manufacturing overhead ($25). What is the markup percentage on this product?

Obj. 6 **2-15.** Refer to the information in Exercise 14. If Kalida requires a markup of 25%, how much cost must be eliminated from the product to reach this markup level if there is no change in the sales price? If cost cannot be eliminated from the product, how much must the item sell for to achieve the 25 percent markup?

Obj. 7 **2-16.** Dentco manufactures electrical extension cords. One of the cords it produces is a six-outlet cord with surge protection, designed to be used with computer equipment. One component of that cord is a special fuse connector that Dentco can make internally or can buy from an outside supplier. What are the relevant costs that the company should consider in its decision to make or buy the connector?

Obj. 7 **2-17.** Which of the following costs are relevant to a decision to make or buy a part? Briefly explain your answers.
- a. Direct materials costs
- b. Variable manufacturing overhead costs
- c. Depreciation expense on factory building
- d. Advertising expense
- e. Rental income from excess warehouse space created by buying the part outside
- f. Income generated from another product produced internally if the part is bought from an outside supplier
- g. Fixed manufacturing overhead costs

Objs. 5, 8   **2-18.**   The Hydromix Company makes a line of iced-tea drinks in a variety of flavors. The company is considering a new line of drinks that would use the basic iced-tea mix. What costs are relevant to Hydromix's decision to sell its tea as is or to process the tea further? Why are relevant costs important in a sell-now or process-further decision?

Objs. 3, 9   **2-19.**   Your older brother, Moe, started a yard maintenance company. The business has grown. Moe has hired several workers and services a number of homeowners as well as several large companies. The company bills its clients periodically for services, charging for labor on an hourly basis plus any out-of-pocket expenses Moe incurs. Your brother has asked you to help him set up accounting records for his growing business. He wants to be able to prepare monthly financial statements. Explain how a Work in Process account would be used in a service environment such as Moe's. Why is the use of work in process accounting necessary in such a service environment?

Obj. 9   **2-20.**   The nurses on the fourth floor of Western Medical Center care for and administer drugs to patients who have undergone orthopedic surgery. Also located on the fourth floor is a mobile X-ray station that Western recently purchased for $250,000. How do the costs of the nursing care and the drugs behave with respect to patient care compared with the cost of the X-ray machine? Explain your answer.

PROBLEMS

PROBLEM 2-1   Cost Flows in an Accounting System

Objs. 2, 3

Skarloey Company showed the following balances in its inventory accounts as of January 1, 1997:

Raw Materials Inventory	$12,000
Work In Process Inventory	15,000
Finished Goods Inventory	10,000

The following transactions took place during 1997:

1. Manufactured overhead costs of $147,000 were incurred.
2. Raw material purchases totaled $32,000.
3. Direct labor charges in the amount of $171,000 were paid.
4. The cost of goods sold was determined to be $225,000.
5. Raw materials in the amount of $36,000 were placed into production.
6. The ending finished goods inventory balance was $14,000.

Required   Prepare a schedule that shows the raw materials, work in process, finished goods, and cost of goods sold accounts. Determine the year-end balance of each account.

PROBLEM 2-2   Accumulating Manufacturing Costs

Obj. 3

The partial information that follows pertains to the operations of Missing Data Company in 1997:

Raw Materials Inventory, January 1, 1997	$ 5,000
Raw Materials Inventory, December 31, 1997	2,000
Direct labor charged to production during 1997	20,000
Factory overhead costs incurred during 1997	10,000
Cost of goods manufactured, for the year 1997	35,000
Work in Process Inventory, December 31, 1997	15,000
Work in Process Inventory, January 1, 1997	5,000
Finished Goods Inventory, January 1, 1997	15,000

Sales were $100,000, which produced a markup on cost of 150%.

Required   Determine the cost of materials purchased, raw materials used during the year, and the balance in the Finished Goods Inventory account on December 31, 1997.

PROBLEM 2-3   **Costs and Volume**

Objs. 1, 4

Great Industries recently expanded its production line. The new product has the following costs: direct materials, $20 per unit; direct labor $18 per unit; production supervision, $1,500 per month; warehouse rental for finished goods storage, $1,000 per month; advertising, $1,200 per month; sales commissions, $8 per unit sold; and monthly depreciation on new factory equipment needed for the new product, $500.

Required

a.   Classify each of the new-product costs as a product cost or a period expense. Identify the behavior of each cost as variable, fixed, or semivariable.

b.   Determine the total of product costs and period expenses that would be incurred to manufacture and sell 1,000 units per month.

PROBLEM 2-4   **Cost Behavior**

Objs. 1, 2, 4

Westco, Inc., has the following costs:

Cost	Variable or Fixed	Period Cost	Product Cost Direct	Indirect
a. Factory depreciation	F			X
b. Packaging materials				
c. President's salary				
d. Sales commissions				
e. Machine lubricants				
f. Magazine subscriptions, factory breakroom				
g. Insurance on finished goods				
h. Workers' wages in assembly department				
i. Salary of payroll clerk				
j. Grounds upkeep				
k. Shop rags				
l. Training program, factory workers				
m. Ink used in textbook production				
n. Health insurance, factory workers				
o. Glue used in production of wooden chairs				
p. Life insurance on executives				
q. Raw steel, tool box production				
r. Gas for salesperson's car				
s. Sales travel expenses				
t. Disposal of machine coolants				

Required   Complete the schedule provided. Indicate the cost behavior and classification of each of the costs listed. The first one is done for you.

PROBLEM 2-5   **Cost Behavior**

Objs. 1, 2, 4

Tim Ricker lives in Atlanta. He is a toolmaker for Georgia Industries, a manufacturer of heavy equipment such as backhoes, graders, and earth moving equipment. Tim makes specialty tools and jigs that are used on different machines in the plant. His annual salary is $35,000. Ann Thompson also works for Georgia Industries. She is an independent sales representative who lives in El Paso, Texas. She is paid a straight salary of $25,000 but also earns a 5% commission on sales. Ann is responsible for accounts in the west Texas area, works out of an office in her home, and is reimbursed by Georgia Industries for her travel expenses.

Required

a. Is Tim's salary a manufacturing or non-manufacturing expense? If manufacturing, would it be classified as direct labor? Explain your answer.
b. Is Ann's salary a manufacturing or non-manufacturing expense? Are the commissions she earns manufacturing or non-manufacturing? Explain your answer.
c. Classify Tim and Ann's income as fixed, variable, or mixed expenses.
d. Classify Ann's travel expenses as fixed, variable, or mixed. What considerations are important in arriving at your answer?

PROBLEM 2-6 Cost Behavior

Obj. 4

The data for costs A, B, and C are as follows:

	Number of Units Produced	Unit Cost	Total Cost
Cost A	1	?	$ 15
	10	?	150
	100	?	1,500
	1,000	?	15,000
Cost B	1	$6,000	?
	10	600	?
	100	60	?
	1,000	6	?
Cost C	1	?	$ 4,025
	10	?	4,250
	100	?	6,500
	1,000	?	29,000

Required

a. Determine the cost behavior (variable, fixed, or semivariable) of Cost A, Cost B and Cost C.
b. Prepare a graph depicting the cost behavior of each of the three costs, using total cost as the vertical axis and production volume as the horizontal axis.

PROBLEM 2-7 Cost, Margin, and Markup

Obj. 6

Calico has the following products:

	Item Description	Target Unit Cost	Target Markup	Target Markup %	Selling Price
Example:	Item A	$15	$ 5	33%	$20
	Item B	?	$24	10%	?
	Item C	$72	?	?	$84
	Item D	?	?	15%	$69
	Item E	$42	$ 6	?	?
	Item F	?	$12	?	$96
	Item G	?	$20	8%	?
	Item H	$50	?	12%	?

Required Complete the schedule above. The first one has been done for you.

PROBLEM 2-8 Make or Buy Decisions

Obj. 7

Each year, Dobb Incorporated manufactures and uses 15,000 units of a particular component part used in production. An outside supplier is willing to produce the component for $35 per unit. Currently, Dobb's cost per unit to produce this part is as follows:

Direct materials	$14
Direct labor	10
Variable manufacturing overhead	11
Fixed manufacturing overhead	4
Total	$39

Required

a. Should Dobb continue to produce the part internally or accept the offer to purchase it from the outside source?

b. Assume that Dobb would be able to rent the unused warehouse space to another company if it outsources the component. Rental income would be $1,500 per month. Would this change Dobb's decision to make or buy this part? Explain your answer.

PROBLEM 2-9 Make or Buy Decisions

Obj. 7

Bravo Company manufactures 27,000 components of a particular product each year. The costs per unit of this part are as follows:

Direct materials	$ 4.20
Direct labor	12.00
Variable factory overhead	5.80
Fixed factory overhead	6.50

Bravo has received an offer to purchase the 27,000 parts from an outside supplier at $25 per unit.

Required

a. Assume that there are no other uses for the facilities. If Bravo makes the component internally, how much higher or lower would income be than if the part were purchased from the outside supplier?

b. Assume that by purchasing the part from the outside supplier $35,100 of fixed factory overhead cost per year could be avoided. Suppose the manufacturing facilities now being used to produce the component could be rented to another company for $64,800 per year. If Bravo purchases the parts from the outside supplier under these circumstances, what would be the difference in net income due to accepting this offer?

c. Given the circumstances in requirement b, at what price from the outside vendor would Bravo be indifferent to making the part or buying it from the outside vendor?

PROBLEM 2-10 Sell-Now or Process-Further Decisions

Obj. 8

The Marvel Meat Market sells 16 ounce T-bone steaks for $5.25 each. Mike Marvel, the owner of the meat market, has asked for your assistance in making a decision concerning the processing of steaks. Mike indicates that a T-bone steak can be processed further. One 8 ounce strip steak and one 6 ounce filet can be obtained from one T-bone steak. A strip steak will sell for $4.25 and a filet will sell for $4.75. It currently costs Mike $4.65 to process a T-bone steak. Additional costs of $3.25 would be incurred if the steaks were processed further. Mike believes that all steaks will be sold regardless of whether they are T-bone, strips or filets.

Required

a. What would be the additional income or loss per steak if the additional processing is done?

b. Would you advise Mike to process the steaks further?

PROBLEM 2-11 Multiple-Choice Overview of the Chapter

1. During May, 1997, Bennett Manufacturing Company purchased $43,000 of raw materials. The company's manufacturing overhead for the month totaled $27,000 and the total

manufacturing costs were $106,000. Assuming a beginning inventory of raw materials of $8,000 and an ending inventory of raw materials of $6,000, direct labor must have totaled

a. $34,000.
b. $38,000.
c. $36,000.
d. $45,000.

2. All of the following are variable costs except
   a. direct labor.
   b. sales commissions.
   c. utilities.
   d. plant manager's salary.

3. The wages of the maintenance personnel in a manufacturing plant would be an example of:

	Indirect Labor Costs	Manufacturing Overhead Costs
a.	No	Yes
b.	Yes	No
c.	Yes	Yes
d.	No	No

4. As the number of units produced by a manufacturer increases,
   a. the variable costs per unit remains the same.
   b. total fixed costs remain the same.
   c. total variable costs increase.
   d. all of the above

5. The distinction between indirect and direct costs depends on
   a. whether the costs are product costs or period expenses.
   b. whether the costs are variable or fixed.
   c. whether the costs can be easily traced to specific units of production.
   d. the manager responsible for controlling the cost.

6. As a general rule, in relevant cost analysis:
   a. variable costs are always relevant.
   b. fixed costs are always relevant.
   c. future costs and revenues which differ between alternatives are always relevant.
   d. depreciation is always a relevant cost.

7. A sell–now or process–further decision should be based on:
   a. costs incurred before the new product is manufactured.
   b. incremental revenue that would be earned by further processing.
   c. incremental costs that would be incurred by further processing.
   d. additional revenue less the additional processing costs.

8. Alamo Company produces products A, B, and C from a single raw material. Each of those products can be sold at an intermediate point or processed further. The data on the products are as follows:

	Product A	B	C
Units produced	2,500	3,000	4,000
Sales value at intermediate sales point	$20	$22	$25
Added costs to process further	$ 8	$ 9	$ 9
Sales value if processed further	$30	$30	$35

If the cost of raw materials is $200,000, Alamo should continue the processing of:

	A	B	C
a.	no	yes	no
b.	no	yes	yes
c.	yes	no	yes
d.	yes	yes	no

9. The Rockin Roller Company manufactures rocking chairs. The following costs have been identified relating to the production of rocking chairs for the current month:
   1. $100,000 of springs was purchased. Each chair requires 2 springs at a cost of $10 per spring.

2. $1,700 of glue was used from one gallon containers.
3. $500 of stain was used to touch up spots on the chairs.
    The total cost that should be assigned to indirect materials for the month would be:
    a. $102,200
    b. $500
    c. $2,200
    d. $1,700

10. Product costs appear on the balance sheet only
    a. if goods are partially complete at the end of the period.
    b. if goods are unsold at the end of the period.
    c. in merchandising firms.
    d. if goods are partially complete, are unsold at the end of the period, or both.

C A S E S

CASE 2-1 Cost Behavior and the Income Statement
Objs. 1, 2, 4

Leesa Sordelet owns Willie's Restaurant which sells hamburgers for carry out or drive through only. Each hamburger sells for $2. Leesa employs several part time employees and a full-time manager. She leases the building and hires a cleaning company to provide services on a weekly basis. The manager, who is paid a monthly salary, carries out all administrative functions such as hiring, scheduling, and counting cash.

The following expenses were incurred in November.

Ground meat	$2,000	Manager's salary	2,200
Lettuce	250	Utilities	500
Tomatoes	300	Depreciation, grill	400
Buns	350	Depreciation, signs	150
Condiments	50	Advertising	100
Part-time labor, cooks	2,320	Rent	750
Part-time labor, servers	2,150	Cleaning service	320
Wrapping paper and bags	40		

The restaurant sold 10,000 hamburgers during the month, and there is no WIP inventory at the end of the month.

Required

a. Classify each cost as one of the following: direct materials cost, direct labor cost, overhead cost, or period expense.
b. Prepare an income statement for November.

CASE 2-2 Cost Behavior and Sell-Now or Process-Further Decisions
Objs. 4, 5, 8

Clean Up Company produces a line of cleaning products for both industrial and household use. While most of the company's products are processed independently, a few are related such as Abrase-All and Wink Silver Polish.

Abrase-All is an abrasive cleaner used in industrial applications. It costs $1.60 per pound to produce and sells for $2.40 per pound. A small portion of Abrase-All each year is combined with other ingredients to form Wink Silver Polish. Wink sells for $5.00 per jar.

Each jar of Wink uses ¼ pound of Abrase-All. The other costs of ingredients and labor required for further processing are as follows:

Additional ingredients	$1.00
Additional direct labor	1.48
Total added cost	$2.48

The additional overhead costs required each month for further processing are:

Variable overhead   50% of additional labor costs
Fixed overhead $3,000, related mainly to depreciation

Advertising costs for Wink total $5,000 per month; the variable selling costs related to Wink are 10% of sales.

Because of a recent drop in demand for silver polish, the management of Clean Up is thinking about stopping production of Wink. The sales manager believes it would be more profitable to just sell Abrase-All.

Required

a. What is the additional revenue less the additional processing costs, per jar, from further processing Abrase-All into Wink?

b. What is the minimum number of jars of Wink that must be sold each month to justify the continued processing of Abrase-All into Wink?

c. Assume that marketing projections indicate the company can sell 5,000 jars of Wink each month. What advice would you give to the Clean Up management? Support your advice with a calculation.

PROJECTS

PROJECT 2-1 Examining Inventory Costs
Obj. 2

http://www.swcollege.
com/ingram.html

Visit the SEC's on-line site. Request the 10-K form for the company you want. Scroll down through the company's form until you find the financial statements.

Obtain published financial statements for each of five manufacturing companies from the Internet or your library. Review each company's statements for total inventory costs. What components of inventory are reported? What differences do you see between the types of inventory classifications? Which classification has the largest balance? The smallest? What costs would you expect to find included in each of the classifications? Write a short report on the companies you reviewed, the product or products the companies manufacture, and the costs you would expect to find in the inventory accounts.

PROJECT 2-2 Comparing Inventory Costing Methods
Objs. 2, 5

Obtain published financial statements of three manufacturing companies and three merchandising companies from the Internet or your library. Compare the inventory sections of the balance sheets and related notes to the financial statements. What differences do you notice? What are the differences in the amount of cost goods sold among the companies? What costs do the manufacturing companies include that the merchandising companies do not? Summarize your findings in a short report.

PROJECT 2-3 Recognizing Fixed and Variable Cost Behavior
Obj. 4

Review your own checking account or cash activity for the past three months. Make a list of your expenses and then categorize the behavior of each as a variable, a fixed, or a semivariable cost. For each variable cost identify the activity that produced it and determine the amount of activity that resulted in the expense. Identify those expenses you incur that are semivariable in behavior. Separate the semivariable cost items into variable and fixed components. Prepare a schedule of your personal spending showing your expenses as either variable or fixed.

PROJECT 2-4   **Business Failure and Expense Categorization**

Objs. 1, 2, 5

Look through business periodicals or *The Wall Street Journal* to identify a manufacturing company that recently filed for bankruptcy. Using published financial reports or other accounting information, review the company's inventory balances and period costs for the past three years. Based on your review, what cost problems do you think led to the business failure? Were inventory balances increasing before the failure? What patterns of nonmanufacturing expenses did you see? Summarize your findings in a short report.

PROJECT 2-5   **Managerial Decision Making in Current Events**

Objs. 5, 6, 7, 8

Review the marketing section of *The Wall Street Journal*. Look for examples of managerial decision making in areas discussed in the chapter: target costing, make or buy decisions, or sell-now or process-further decisions. Write a short report of your findings.

Unit Costs for Decision Making

Accounting and Management Decisions

- Internal Control
- Service Organizations
- Cost Behavior
- **Unit Costs**
- Cost Measurement
- Cost Allocation
- Budgets
- Performance Evaluation
- Global Environment
- Decentralized Organizations
- Capital Budgeting

Overview

Unit costs are necessary for valuing and reporting inventory and cost of goods sold on a company's financial statements. Unit costs also play an important role in the strategic and operational decisions of marketing and operations managers. For example, at the strategic level, the costs of different products in a company's product line often are combined in estimating the profitability of the product line. These estimates may be used to determine how the product line should be marketed or whether a company should discontinue a product. At the operational level, estimates of individual product unit costs are commonly used by marketing managers in pricing products. Production managers are concerned about unit costs of product lines and individual products in order to control those costs and to support a company's marketing strategy. Service organizations also

use unit costs to determine the cost of services provided to customers and to analyze whether costs are in line with strategic plans. Because unit costs are used extensively in managerial decisions in both manufacturing and service organizations, it is important to know how to develop those costs and how to assess their accuracy.

To develop unit costs, a company has to measure costs and then assign those costs to individual units. This chapter describes two methods for measuring costs: actual costing and normal costing. Most companies use one of those methods. The chapter also describes two common methods for assigning costs to units: job-order costing and process costing. In choosing methods for measuring and assigning costs, managers are concerned with appropriateness for their company. Often one method is more appropri-

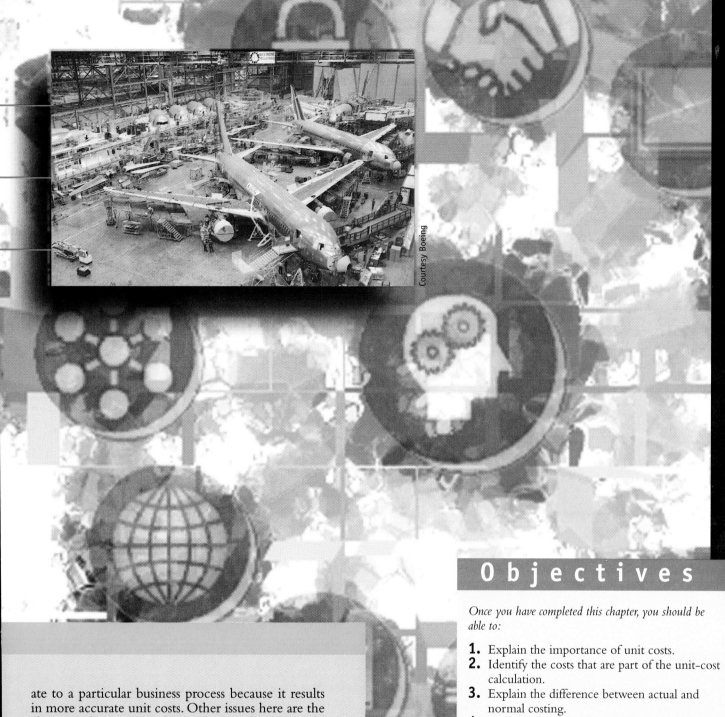

Courtesy Boeing

ate to a particular business process because it results in more accurate unit costs. Other issues here are the elements that go into the unit-cost calculation and the way unit-cost information is going to be used. Unit cost is not only a basis for managerial decision making; it also is a product of that decision making.

Major topics covered in this chapter include:
- The importance of unit costs to the management of manufacturing and service companies
- The elements that make up unit costs
- Decisions about how to measure costs: actual costing versus normal costing
- Determination of the most appropriate method for assigning unit costs
- Assignment of unit costs using job order and process costing

O b j e c t i v e s

Once you have completed this chapter, you should be able to:

1. Explain the importance of unit costs.
2. Identify the costs that are part of the unit-cost calculation.
3. Explain the difference between actual and normal costing.
4. Distinguish between job-order and process costing, and explain when each method is used.
5. Determine unit cost using job-order costing.
6. Describe cost flows in a process-costing system.
7. Determine unit cost using process costing.
8. Explain how job-order and process costing are used in the service sector.

THE ROLE OF UNIT COSTS

O b j e c t i v e   1
Explain the importance of
unit costs.

One of the most important pieces of information that management accountants develop for accounting reports and business decisions is the *unit cost*, **the cost of producing one unit of a specific product.** Managers use that cost to calculate the value of a company's inventories on its financial statements. Unit costs also play a key role in managerial decision making.

Placing a Value on Inventory

Exhibit 1 shows the flow of costs through the manufacturing process. In a manufacturing company, product costs are the costs of the direct materials, the direct labor, and the manufacturing overhead that go into producing a product. With each stage of the production process—as the product moves through the work in process inventories to the finished goods inventory—the value of the product goes up. In each state of the process, the company adds the value of more materials, more labor, and more overhead to the product.

Exhibit 1   Cost Flow in a Manufacturing Setting: A General Model

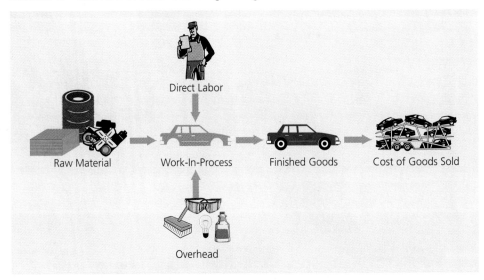

Accountants measure product costs and track the flow of those costs through the manufacturing process. They use that information to determine the unit cost of any product at any stage of production.

The process of determining unit cost is straightforward:

1. The costs incurred to date for direct materials, direct labor, and manufacturing overhead are measured and accumulated.
2. Those total costs are divided by the number of units produced.

The unit cost of a product, then, is the total cost of the product to date divided by the number of units:

Unit cost = total cost to date ÷ units

To value finished goods inventory at the end of a period or the cost of goods sold for the period, accountants have to identify the number of units available for sale at the end of that period or the number of units sold during that period, in addition to the unit cost. The value of ending inventory is the number of units available for sale at the end of the period multiplied by the unit cost:

Finished goods inventory = units available for sale × unit cost

The value of the cost of goods sold is the number of units sold during the period multiplied by the unit cost:

Cost of goods sold = units sold × unit cost

Managerial Decision Making

Unit costs play an essential role in establishing the value of a company's inventories. As Exhibit 2 shows, they also are a key element in the decisions managers make about products:

- How should we price the product?
- Should we continue to offer the product?
- What is the best way to allocate our limited production resources?
- On which products should marketing focus its efforts to maximize profits?

Exhibit 2   The Role of Unit Costs in Business Decisions and Business Performance

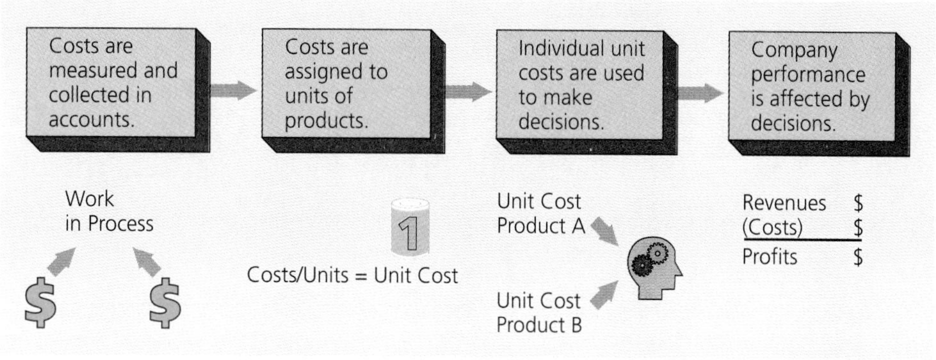

Product Pricing. Choosing the right price for its products is extremely important to the success of a company. A company that does not make an adequate profit on its products cannot survive over the long term. The pricing decision is based on three major considerations: product cost, the prices competitors charge for similar products, and market research on how customers will respond to different prices. Knowing how much it costs to make a product is very important when there is no competitive market for a product. In this case, the unit cost of the product may be the only information available to guide management in setting the price. The importance of unit cost to the pricing decision often depends on the company's marketing strategy for the product and where the product is in its life cycle.

   Marketing Strategy. Some companies choose to market a product on the basis of price. Other companies choose to focus their advertising on some other element of the product—its taste, its construction, its look, for example. **A** *differentiated prod-uct* **has some distinguishing characteristic or quality for which consumers are willing to pay a premium.** Still other companies adopt a combination strategy, advertising their product as the best product in its price range. That's the strategy that has given **Toyota Motor Corporation** a reputation for producing high-quality cars at low to moderate prices.

Remember that a company's need for accounting information depends on its marketing strategy. A company that uses a low-price strategy has a greater need for accurate unit-cost information than does a company that uses a differentiated strategy. Profit margins (price minus total cost) usually are lower on low-priced products. Lower margins mean that controlling costs is very important to ensuring profits. Accurate information about the amount of costs is required for careful cost control. A company that uses a differentiated strategy tends to have higher profit margins. For that company tight cost controls generally are less critical to the profitability of a product than are product quality and performance.

Product Life Cycle. Product life cycle also plays an important role in determining the need for accurate unit costs. Products tend to have finite lives characterized by growth, followed by stability, and then decline (Exhibit 3). Although the lengths of various products' life cycles may vary, a product's life cycle generally is characterized as follows:

(a) A company introduces a new product (growth stage).
(b) The company builds market share in anticipation of future profits (growth stage).
(c) The company focuses on holding the market share of the mature product (hold stage).
(d) The company maximizes the available return as the sales of the product fall (harvest stage).
(e) When profits are no longer adequate, the company eliminates the product (divest stage).

Exhibit 3   A Product Life Cycle

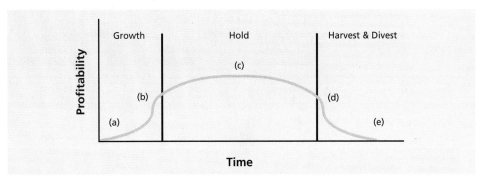

Market share **is that portion of sales a particular brand or company has of the total sales of all similar products.** For example, assume that the total sales of all brands of soft drinks is $25 billion per year. If the **Coca-Cola Company's** sales are $11 billion, the company has a 44% ($11/$25) market share.

In the growth stage (a) after a product has been introduced, the producer normally is interested in building market share. During this phase, the company often is willing to sacrifice profits to encourage new customers to buy the product. For example, when cellular phone companies give away phones, they are trying to encourage prospective customers to subscribe to their services. In the building phase (b) a company may not be concerned about maintaining tight cost control. It is willing to spend money on product improvements and marketing to build market share. As products mature (c), a company is less willing to spend money on further product and market development; instead, it concentrates on maintaining market share and profits. As the emphasis shifts to profits, cost control and accuracy of unit costs become more important because of greater emphasis on profitability. In the harvest stage (d), the company's focus is on earning as much profit as possible from the product until, finally, the product is eliminated (e).

Profit Margin. Unit costs also play a role in the decision to continue to offer a product. *Unit margin* **is the difference between the price per unit of a product and the unit cost.** If the unit margin of a product is too low to meet the company's profit goals for that product, the company may discontinue the product. (A company estimates its profit margin on a particular product by multiplying the unit margin times the number of units it expects to sell.) All companies operate with limited resources.

Allocating Resources. Unit costs help managers decide how to allocate limited production and marketing resources. When a company's production resources prevent the company from making enough different products to meet the demand for those products, managers must decide how much of each product to make. The question here is "What mix of products will provide the greatest profit for the company?" In the same way, when a company's marketing budget does not allow advertising to emphasize all of its products, managers have to decide which products to promote. Unit costs help managers make these kinds of decisions.

A word of caution: When managers base a decision on unit costs, they should remember that those costs can be inaccurate. The problem has to do with indirect costs, the manufacturing overhead costs that cannot be traced directly to a particular product but must be allocated (Exhibit 4). For instance, it is often difficult to determine how much of the cost of utilities (electricity, natural gas, etc.) are consumed by individual products. Decisions about how to allocate those costs can affect unit costs substantially. Managers need to be aware of the potential for cost inaccuracies in unit costs and how these inaccuracies can lead to poor decisions.

Exhibit 4 The Allocation of Costs

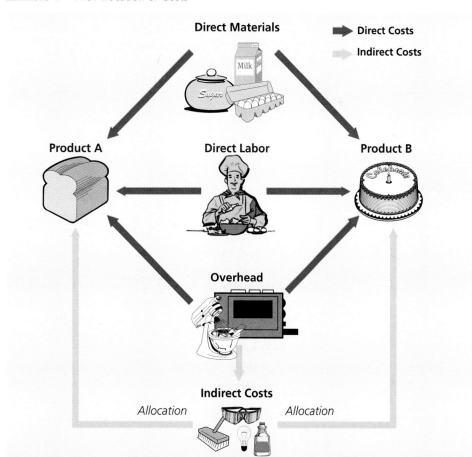

THE ELEMENTS OF UNIT COST

Objective 2
Identify the costs that are part of the unit-cost calculation.

The first step in calculating unit costs is determining the costs that should be included. Traditionally, direct materials, direct labor, and manufacturing overhead have been included in unit cost calculations. This is because generally accepted accounting principles (GAAP) require that the full costs of production be included in inventory costs in externally reported financial statements. Many companies use their financial accounting systems to provide information for management decisions. However, management accounting information does not have to conform to GAAP. Depending on how unit costs are used, they may or may not be based on all costs of production or may contain costs other than production costs.

For example, some companies compute the variable cost per unit of a product and ignore fixed costs in their unit cost calculations. Their reasoning: Because many fixed costs are indirect costs that are allocated to the units of a product arbitrarily, the unit costs can be distorted. A large amount of distortion can lead to poor decisions. We discuss these types of cost distortions in more detail in the following chapter.

In some cases, management may want to include non-manufacturing costs in calculating unit cost. Including only manufacturing costs ignores the costs of selling and distributing products. These costs often are large and may vary considerably among products and customers. If they do not include those costs in the unit cost of a product, managers may under- or overestimate the total cost required to provide the product to the customer. Problems with traditional methods of assigning unit costs have led to the development of activity-based costing and other new approaches to cost assignment.

In this chapter, we follow the usual convention of including the costs of direct materials, direct labor, and manufacturing overhead in unit costs. In later discussions of activity-based costing, however, we will include nonmanufacturing costs in unit cost computations. The costs that are part of the unit-cost calculation can have a significant effect on the accuracy and magnitude of the unit cost. Before they use unit costs to make marketing and production decisions, then, managers need to understand which costs are included in the unit cost computation.

MEASURING COSTS

Objective 3
Explain the difference between actual and normal costing.

Remember that total manufacturing costs include three components:

direct material costs + direct labor costs + manufacturing overhead costs

Two basic methods are used to measure those product costs: actual costing and normal costing. *Actual costing* **measures unit costs based on the actual costs of direct materials, direct labor, and overhead incurred in producing the units.** *Normal costing* **measures unit costs by adding the actual costs of direct materials and direct labor to an estimated overhead cost incurred in producing the units.** The difference between the two methods is whether actual or estimated overhead costs are included.

Actual Costing

When a company uses actual costing, it assigns the costs of direct materials, direct labor, and manufacturing overhead to the Work in Process Inventory account as those costs are incurred. Exhibit 5 shows a series of transactions for the Rogers Company, a valve manufacturer.

Exhibit 5   Rogers Company: Actual-Costing Transactions

Account	Cash	+ Other Assets	= Liabilities	+ Equity	+ Revenues	− Expenses
		Balance Sheet			**Income Statement**	
(a) Raw Materials Inventory		50,000				
Accounts Payable			50,000			
(b) Raw Materials Inventory		− 28,000				
Work in Process Inventory		28,000				
(c) Work in Process Inventory		15,000				
Wages Payable			15,000			
(d) Work in Process Inventory		17,000				
Accounts Payable			17,000			

Transaction (a) recognizes the purchase of raw materials for $50,000. Transaction (b) recognizes the use of $28,000 of raw materials during the period as part of the manufacturing process. Transaction (c) recognizes the direct labor costs incurred in the production process as wages are earned by factory employees. Transaction (d) recognizes manufacturing overhead costs such as equipment maintenance, utilities, supplies, and insurance. During the period, actual costs of $60,000 ($28,000 + $15,000 + $17,000) are transferred to Work in Process Inventory during the period. Although the amount of raw materials purchased totaled $50,000, only the portion of raw materials actually consumed in manufacturing during the period is transferred to the Work in Process Inventory account. The $22,000 ($50,000 − $28,000) of raw materials not consumed is available for use during the next period.

To determine the actual cost per unit, the company would divide the $60,000 of total actual cost by the number of units produced. If Rogers produced 100 units during the period, the unit cost would be $600 ($60,000 ÷ 100 units).

Measuring the costs of direct materials and direct labor usually is not difficult. Measuring manufacturing overhead, however, can be a problem. The company often does not know the actual cost of the overhead until after a product is produced or even sold. The total actual overhead cost is not known with certainty until the bills arrive. Because this cost can be critical to managerial decision making, many companies rely on estimates of overhead to measure product costs.

Normal Costing

As in actual costing, normal costing measures the actual costs of direct materials and direct labor incurred in producing a product. However, estimates of manufacturing overhead are assigned to units of product through the use of predetermined rates. Exhibit 6 shows the differences between actual and normal costing.

Exhibit 6   Actual Costing Versus Normal Costing

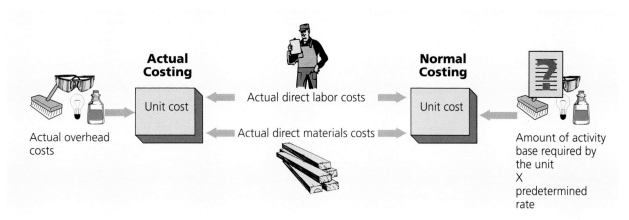

A *predetermined overhead rate* **is an estimate of the amount of overhead that management believes should be assigned to a unit of product.** To establish a predetermined rate, a company first must choose an activity base. An *activity base* **is a production activity (such as direct labor hours or machine hours) or a measure of the cost of production activity (direct labor cost, for example).** A company selects a particular activity base because its management believes that overhead costs are incurred in proportion to the amount of that activity base. At the beginning of the fiscal year, the company divides the total overhead it expects to incur during that year by the amount of the activity base expected for that period. Then, as products are manufactured during the period, the company multiplies the amount of the activity base used during the period by the predetermined overhead rate. The result is the estimated overhead cost for the products processed (Exhibit 7).

Exhibit 7   Assignment of Overhead Costs in a Normal Costing System

Summary of procedures:
Establishing the predetermined overhead rate

At the beginning of the fiscal year:
1. Estimate the total costs of manufacturing overhead for the period.
2. Choose a relevant activity or cost base and estimate the amount of that activity or cost for the year.
3. Calculate the predetermined overhead rate by dividing the estimate of total manufacturing overhead costs by the estimated amount of the activity or cost base:

**Predetermined overhead rate = estimated total overhead costs
÷ estimated total activity base**

Assigning overhead costs using the predetermined overhead rate

At the end of each accounting period:
1. Determine the actual amount of the activity base used during the period.
2. Multiply that amount by the predetermined overhead rate.

Estimated overhead costs = actual activity base × predetermined overhead rate

An example: Bloomington Carpets uses normal costing to measure its product costs. Currently, the company's controller is working on next year's production budget. He expects the company to produce 1 million rolls of carpet in the next fiscal year and to incur manufacturing overhead costs for the year of $25 million.

Assume that the management at Bloomington has decided to use direct labor hours as the activity base. If the company generally uses 5 direct labor hours to produce one roll of carpet, the activity base for that coming year is 5 million direct labor hours (5 direct labor hours × 1,000,000 rolls). The company's predetermined overhead rate for the coming year, then, is $5:

Predetermined overhead rate = estimated overhead costs ÷ estimated activity base
= $25,000,000 ÷ 5,000,000 direct labor hours
= $5

Over the coming year, for each direct labor hour *actually* worked, the company will add $5 to its cost of manufacturing the carpet.

Let's say that in January of the new fiscal year Bloomington uses 400,000 direct labor hours in the manufacturing process. At the end of the month, the company records $2 million (400,000 direct labor hours × $5) in manufacturing overhead costs in its Work in Process Inventory account. What about the actual overhead costs? As bills are received, those costs are accumulated in the company's Manufacturing Overhead account. Exhibit 8 demonstrates transactions in a normal costing system for Rogers Company.

Exhibit 8 Rogers Company: Normal Costing Transactions

Account	Cash	+ Other Assets	= Liabilities	+ Equity	+ Revenues	− Expenses
(a) Raw Materials Inventory		50,000				
Accounts Payable			50,000			
(b) Raw Materials Inventory		− 28,000				
Work in Process Inventory		28,000				
(c) Work in Process Inventory		15,000				
Wages Payable			15,000			
(d) Manufacturing Overhead		17,000				
Accounts Payable			17,000			
(e) Work in Process		18,000				
Manufacturing Overhead		− 18,000				

Many of the costs shown in Exhibit 8 are similar to those in Exhibit 5. The differences between the two exhibits relate to the treatment of overhead costs. In Exhibit 8, actual overhead costs of $17,000 are accumulated in the Manufacturing Overhead account (d). In transaction (e), the estimated cost of overhead ($18,000) is recorded in the Work in Process Inventory account. (If we assume that Rogers uses direct labor hours as its activity base, that company's predetermined overhead rate is $5 per direct labor hour, and that company actually uses 3,600 direct labor hours in this period.) Notice that in the same transaction, the company subtracts the estimated costs of overhead from its Manufacturing Overhead account. At the end of the period, Rogers will make whatever adjustment is necessary to bring the estimated costs of overhead in line with the actual costs of overhead.

Because normal costing uses estimates of overhead costs, the amount of overhead costs allocated to Work in Process Inventory often differs from the actual overhead incurred and recorded in Manufacturing Overhead. In Exhibit 8, the company *overapplied* its overhead costs. The amount of overhead costs applied to inventory ($18,000) was $1,000 more than the actual overhead costs ($17,000) incurred during the period. If the actual overhead costs had been more than the amount of overhead recorded in Work in Process Inventory, the company would have *underapplied* its overhead costs. At the end of the accounting period, the company adjusts for the variance between applied overhead and actual overhead by transferring the amount of over- or underapplied overhead to Cost of Goods Sold or proportionately to Cost of Goods Sold, Work in Process Inventory, and Finished Goods Inventory. Often companies investigate this variance to learn why it occurred and use that information to improve production efficiency. Sometimes, the information may be used to change the predetermined overhead rate and improve the accuracy of the allocation process. This happens, for example, when it is obvious that the predetermined rate has been badly estimated.

Suppose that actual manufacturing overhead for Rogers Company for 1997 was $3,650,000 and overhead applied to Work in Process Inventory using the predetermined rate was $3,400,000. The company has *underapplied* overhead in the amount of $250,000 (Exhibit 9).

Exhibit 9   Rogers Company: Adjusting for Underapplied Overhead

| | Balance Sheet | | | | Income Statement | |
Account	Cash	+ Other Assets	= Liabilities	+ Equity	+ Revenues	– Expenses
(a) Manufacturing Overhead		3,650,000				
Accounts Payable			3,650,000			
(b) Work in Process Inventory		3,400,000				
Manufacturing Overhead		– 3,400,000				
(c) Manufacturing Overhead		– 250,000				
Cost of Goods Sold						– 250,000

Because the company has not applied enough overhead, the Manufacturing Overhead account contains a positive balance of $250,000 at the end of 1997 (after transaction (b)). The adjustment (c) eliminates the balance in Manufacturing Overhead. It also corrects the balance in Cost of Goods Sold, *increasing* that balance for the year. (Remember that in the accounting equation Cost of Goods Sold normally has a negative balance because it is an expense that reduces net income.) When the amount of over- or underapplied overhead is significant, the difference should be allocated proportionately to Work in Process Inventory, Finished Goods Inventory, and Cost of Goods Sold.

SELF-STUDY PROBLEM 1

Russell Lumber Company uses an actual costing system which produced the transactions for March shown at the top of the next page.

The company's controller has been wondering what would be the effect on costs of using a normal costing system to assign overhead. She has determined that under the normal costing approach the predetermined overhead rate would be calculated based on machine hours. Russell Lumber Co. expects to use 50,000 machine hours during the year. Overhead is expected to be approximately $750,000 for the year. The company used 4,500 machine hours during March.

© PhotoDisc

Required

Compute the Work in Process Inventory using both actual and normal costing for the month of March. Explain why the numbers are different. Assuming that all of the products produced in March were sold in that month, what would be the amount of the adjustment to the Cost of Goods Sold account for the over- or underapplied overhead? Would Cost of Goods Sold be increased or decreased? Why?

The solution to Self-Study Problem 1 appears at the end of the chapter.

Self-Study Problem 1 (continued)

Account	Cash	+ Other Assets	= Liabilities	+ Equity	+ Revenues	− Expenses
		Balance Sheet			**Income Statement**	
(a) Raw Material Inventory		110,000				
Accounts Payable			110,000			
(b) Raw Materials Inventory		− 100,000				
Work in Process Inventory		100,000				
(c) Work in Process Inventory		40,000				
Wages Payable			40,000			
(d) Work in Process Inventory		60,000				
Accounts Payable			60,000			

Explanation of transactions:
(a) Raw lumber was purchased for $110,000.
(b) $100,000 in raw lumber was used in production.
(c) $40,000 in direct labor was incurred.
(d) $60,000 in overhead was incurred.

ASSIGNING UNIT COSTS

O b j e c t i v e 4
Distinguish between job-order and process costing, and explain when each method is used.

To develop unit costs, a company has to determine how to measure those costs and assign them to units of a product. The measurement decision involves choosing whether actual costs or estimated costs or some combination of the two will be recorded in the Work in Process account. Two methods have been used traditionally to assign unit costs: job-order costing and process costing. The overall goals of both methods are the same—to assign a unit cost to a product and to use that cost to determine the total cost and the selling price (Exhibit 10).

Exhibit 10   The Goals of Job-Order and Process Costing

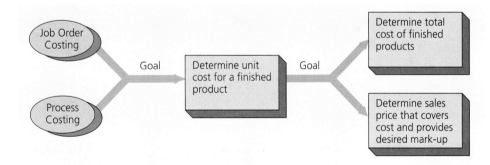

The two methods are fundamentally different. *Job-order costing* **assigns the costs associated with a particular job to the units produced in that job.** In contrast, *process costing* **totals the costs of all units produced in a given accounting period and divides by the total units produced to develop a unit cost.** Each method tends to be suited to a specific manufacturing situation.

Choosing a Costing Method

Job-order costing develops the unit cost of a *particular job*. Total production costs are tracked by the job and divided by the units produced in that job:

Unit cost for job A = production costs for job A ÷ units produced in job A

Job-order costing is effective, then, when a good or service is produced as an individual job.

Companies that build ships, manufacture airplanes, and repair automobiles would likely use job-order costing to assign unit costs to their products. Those products share certain characteristics:

- The units of a particular job are easy to identify.
- Much of the manufacturing cost or the cost of producing the service can be traced directly to a particular job.
- Individual goods or services have very different characteristics and costs.

In contrast, process costing assigns an average cost to all the products produced in a particular period:

Unit cost for period B = cost of production for period B ÷ units produced in period B

In a process costing environment, the products are very much alike, the processes used to manufacture those products flow from one into another, and the costs of producing the products cannot be traced easily to individual units.

Two examples: Suppose that **Boeing,** an aircraft manufacturer, builds two different types of planes—a jumbo jet and a small commuter plane—in the same plant. Obviously, the physical characteristics and the costs of producing the jumbo jet are very different from the characteristics and costs of producing a small plane. If the company assigns manufacturing costs by simply dividing its total costs for the period by the number of planes it has produced, it will assign too little cost to the jumbo jet and too much to the commuter plane. The company has to know the cost of producing each type of plane.

Think now about a petroleum processing plant, such as **Shell Oil,** where products are produced in a continuous flow and all units are very similar. The oil flows through a series of processes that transform it into gasoline and other petroleum products (Exhibit 11). Once produced and stored, it is impossible to distinguish one gallon of gasoline from another, much less to identify when that particular gallon was produced. A refinery cannot trace the cost of manufacturing gasoline to individual gallons. In this case, an average cost is sufficiently accurate because the physical characteristics and the costs of producing each unit of the product are very much the same.

Suppose that the cost of producing one airplane is the same as the cost of processing 25 million gallons of crude oil in a month. Exhibit 12 shows how each manufacturer would assign the costs of production.

Batch processing **combines elements of individual-job and continuous-flow processing.** When Bloomington Carpets, a carpet manufacturer, produces a batch of 100 rolls of high-grade carpet followed by a batch of 50 rolls of low-grade carpet on the same production line, it is using batch processing. When products are produced in batches, the decision to use job-order costing or process costing often depends on the answers to the following questions:

a. How much accuracy in the unit cost calculation does management require?
b. How accurate will process costing be compared to job-order costing?
c. How difficult and costly will it be to trace costs to individual batches using a job-order system?

If the actual costs and the activities that go into producing the different products are similar, process costing may produce a reasonably accurate unit cost. If the batches are run continuously, it may be difficult to trace costs to individual batches which means that it would be difficult to use job-order costing.

When products are processed in batches, the choice of a cost-assignment method involves weighing the need for accurate information against the cost of developing that information. The need for accuracy depends on the type of business and how

Exhibit 11   Continuous-Flow Processing: Petroleum Products

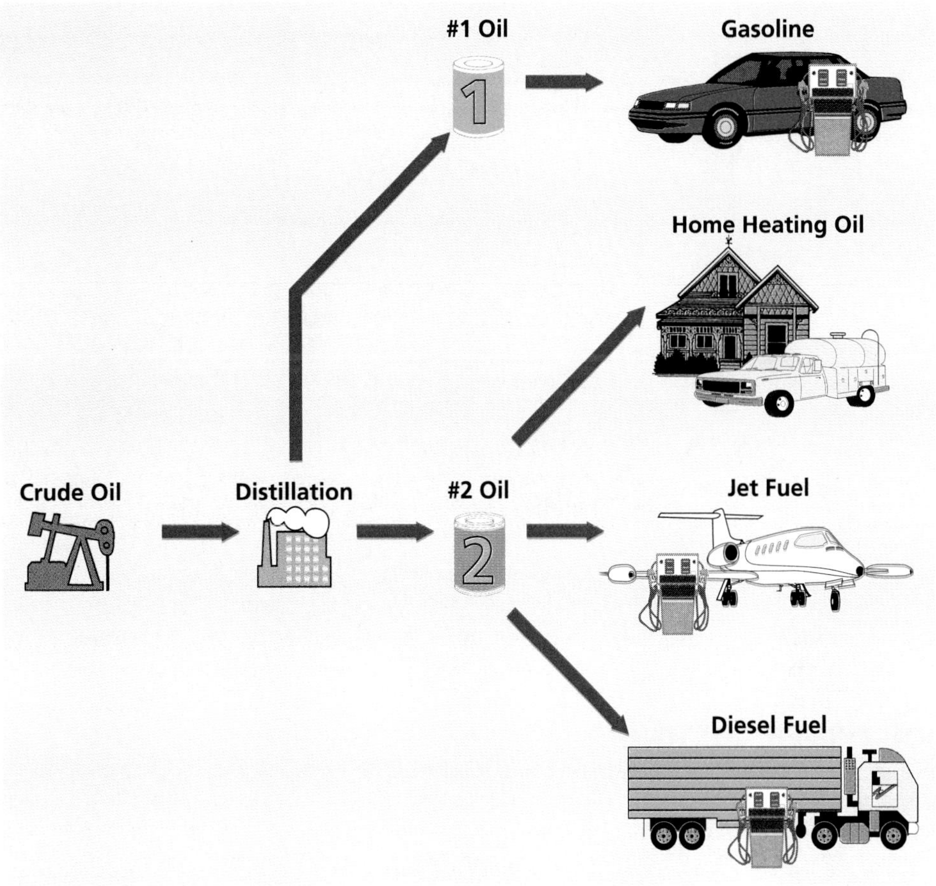

Exhibit 12   Job-Order Costing Versus Process Costing: The Production Process

Job-Order Costing	Process Costing
Airplane Manufacturing	Petroleum Processing
Total cost of job (one airplane): $18,500,000	*Total cost of month's production:* $18,500,000
	Gallons produced in month: 25,000,000
Cost per airplane: $18,500,000	*Cost per gallon:* $.74 ($18,500,000 ÷ 25,000,000 gallons)

the information is going to be used. The cost of developing accurate information is a function of the production process. Job–order costing generally is more accurate than process costing. However, a job–order system can be more costly and more difficult to implement in many manufacturing situations.

Exhibit 13 compares the two traditional methods for assigning costs to units of products: job–order costing and process costing. Job–order costing is more effective when jobs are manufactured separately rather than in continuous processes and when the units of each product vary in characteristics and costs. Process costing works best when production is continuous and when the units of each product are similar in characteristics and cost. Either method may be appropriate when products are made in batches, depending on the manufacturing context, the cost of collecting accounting data, and the need for accuracy.

Exhibit 13   Job-Order and Process Costing: Choosing a Cost-Assignment Method

	JOB-ORDER COSTING	**PROCESS COSTING**
Manufacturing Context	Products are manufactured in separate and distinct jobs. Both manufacturing costs and activities usually vary. Multiple jobs can run during a period.	Products are manufactured in a continuous process. Both manufacturing costs and activities are alike.
Computation of Unit Costs	Costs are traced to each job. The total cost of a job is divided by the number of units produced in the job to determine the unit cost of that job.	Costs are accumulated for all units produced during a period. To determine the unit cost of each product produced during the period, the total cost is divided by the number of units produced during the period.
Accuracy	Job-order costing tends to be more accurate because the costs of a particular job are traced to that job.	Process costing is usually less accurate because the unit cost is the average cost for all units produced during the period.

JOB-ORDER COSTING

Objective 5
Determine unit cost using job-order costing.

In a job-order costing system, a **job cost sheet** is used to identify each job and to accumulate the costs of manufacturing associated with that job. A job cost sheet can be either a piece of paper or a record in a computer file. Both forms allow space to record all the costs of direct materials, direct labor, and manufacturing overhead associated with a job. In effect the job cost sheet functions like a Work in Process Inventory account. If a company were to use only job-order costing, the total of all of its job cost sheets should equal the total of the Work in Process Inventory account. Exhibit 14 provides an example of a job cost sheet.

Exhibit 14   A Job Cost Sheet

Job Number	225P			Date	6-12-97		
Product	Designer lamps			By	Linda Smith		
Units	35			Ship	6-30-97		

Materials		**Direct Labor**				**Overhead**		
Requisition Number	Amount	Employee Number	Hours	Rate	Amount	Hours	Rate	Amount
X2134	$100.00	59	6	$9.35	$56.10	24	$26.50	$636.00
X2147	$420.00	107	18	$13.55	$243.90			
Total Materials	$520.00	Total Direct Labor			$300.00	Total Overhead		$636.00

In the job sheet illustrated, Job 225P was completed on June 12, 1997. Thirty-five units were produced. In this job, materials were issued twice—requisitions X2134 and X2147—in the amounts of $100.00 and $420.00. Thus, total material costs for the job were $520.00. Two employees worked on the job. Employee 59 worked 6 hours and was paid $9.35 an hour, and employee 107 worked 18 hours at a rate of

$13.55 per hour. Total direct labor cost for the job was $300.00 (6 × $9.35) + (18 × $13.55). The job sheet also shows the amount of overhead that has been applied to the job. In this example, the activity base is direct labor hours and the predetermined overhead rate is $26.50 per hour. Because 24 (6 + 18) labor hours were charged to job 225P, a total of $636.00 (24 × $26.50) of overhead was applied. The total cost of job 225P was $1,456, the sum of direct materials, direct labor, and overhead applied ($520.00 + $300.00 + $636.00). The cost per unit for the 35 units produced in this job was $41.60 ($1,456 ÷ 35 units). Once the job was completed, the costs of the 35 units were transferred to the Finished Goods Inventory account at $41.60 per unit. When the units are sold, the $41.60 unit cost will be used to determine the amount that appears on the income statement as cost of goods sold.

Materials are requisitioned for individual jobs using a **materials requisition** form like the one in Exhibit 15.

Exhibit 15   A Materials Requisition Form

Materials Requisition Number	X2134		Date	June 11, 1997
Job Number	225P			

Item Description	Quantity	Unit Cost	Total Cost
Metal sheets	100 lbs.	$1.00	$100.00
Issued by	*Murry Eel*		
Received by	*Electra Glowplug*		

According to that form, 100 pounds of metal sheets were used in job 225P. Each pound of material cost $1.00, the total cost to the job was $100. The document identifies the specific type and quantity of materials that have been drawn from the storeroom and the job to which the materials should be charged. The form is a means of controlling raw materials inventories because each requisition must be signed by the employee issuing and the employee receiving the materials. The form also is used as a source document for recording the actual materials used on a particular job.

SELF STUDY PROBLEM 2

Robotool Corporation is a machine shop that manufactures replacement parts for industrial machinery. Production at Robotool is characterized by small lot sizes and precision manufacturing. A recent production run of five gears, job 2B38, required the following activities and costs:

Raw materials requisitioned:

10 pounds of brass at $11.65 a pound

Labor:	Hours	Rate
Cutting and forming	3	$ 9.75
Lathe and milling	4	$11.50
Finishing	1	$10.00

© 91 Ed Wheeler/The Stock Market

Robotool applies overhead to jobs on the basis of direct labor hours at a predetermined rate of $25 an hour.

Required

Calculate the total cost of job 2B38 and the average cost per unit produced.

The solution to Self-Study Problem 2 appears at the end of the chapter.

PROCESS COSTING

Objective 6
Describe cost flows in a process-costing system.

Products that are produced in a process manufacturing environment usually pass through a series of steps or processes in production. In each step materials, labor, and overhead costs are added to the product. Processes usually are carried out in specific departments or process centers. Sometimes a department has more than one process center. Once the units of a product are completed, they are transferred as finished goods to a warehouse, where they wait for shipment to customers.

In a process manufacturing environment units of products generally are processed in a continuous flow through the production facility. Operations in that environment tend to share certain characteristics:

- Units of products are relatively homogeneous
- Units pass through a series of similar processes
- Costs are accumulated for a given period of time
- Each unit of product receives a similar amount of manufacturing costs
- The costs of manufacturing are averaged over the units produced for the period

The cost objective of process costing, like that of job-order costing, is to determine a unit cost for each type of finished product so that the total cost of finished products can be established. Costs are transferred to a Work in Process Inventory account at each process center. Beginning with the first process center, an average unit cost is computed for the units worked on in that process center during the accounting period. The average unit cost is multiplied by the number of units transferred to the next center to arrive at a total cost of units transferred. A similar calculation determines the cost of units transferred from the second process center to the third process center. That calculation is carried out for each successive process center. The last process center computes the average unit cost and total costs of units completed during the accounting period (Exhibit 16).

Exhibit 16   Tracing Costs in a Process Costing System

Department A	Department B	Department C	Finished Goods Inventory
Direct material costs + Direct labor costs + Overhead ___ Total costs of dept A ÷ units produced ___ = cost per unit × units transferred to dept B	►Total costs of units transferred from dept A + Direct material costs + Direct labor costs + Overhead ___ Total costs of dept B ÷ units produced ___ = cost per unit × units transferred to dept C	►Total costs of units transferred from dept B + Direct material costs + Direct labor costs + Overhead ___ Total costs of dept C ÷ units produced ___ = cost per unit × units transferred to finished goods inventory	►Units in ending finished goods inventory × cost per unit ___ = total cost of finished goods ending inventory Units sold × cost per unit ___ = cost of goods sold

An example: The Cow Hide Company manufactures baseballs. The Cow Hide production process involves three departments: Spinning, Covering and Sewing (Exhibit 17).

Exhibit 17   Cow Hide Company: Departments in the Manufacturing Process

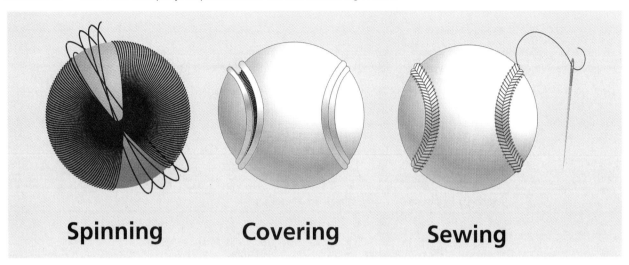

Spinning   **Covering**   **Sewing**

First, in the spinning department, twine is wound around a rubber core to produce the internal component of the balls. Next, workers in the covering department cut and glue the leather cover to each internal component. Finally, in the sewing department, workers sew the covers to finish the baseballs. Each department generates material, labor, and overhead costs that are added to the value of the product. Because the baseballs are almost identical, are processed continuously, go through the same processes, and incur very similar costs, Cow Hide uses process costing. The company traces the costs of the baseballs as they move from spinning to covering to sewing.

Equivalent Units. In process costing, manufacturing costs are accumulated by department and are applied to equivalent units of production. *Equivalent units* **are the number of units that would have been produced during a period if all of the department's efforts had resulted in completed units.** For example, two units that are each one-half complete would be treated as one complete unit for purposes of assigning costs. Equivalent units are computed separately for each process center. Cow Hide's covering department attaches two pieces of leather to the baseball cores. If at the end of the period that department has two baseballs, each with one piece of leather attached, the two balls would be treated as a single equivalent unit with respect to that department. The need to compute equivalent units arises because not all of a department's efforts result in fully completed units during a period.

Process costing is complicated by work in process at the end of an accounting period. Work in process for a particular department is made up of those units that are partially completed in that department. To compute a unit cost that reflects *all* of the work the department has done over a period, a company has to allocate costs to the equivalent units produced during the period. To accurately measure the output to which costs must be assigned requires a mathematical conversion of partially completed units to equivalent units of production. Exhibit 18 illustrates the relation between equivalent units and partially completed units.

Sequential and Parallel Process Systems. Process systems can be either sequential or parallel. In *sequential processing,* **units flow in sequence from one department to the next until they are completed.** Cow Hide processes baseballs sequentially: Basic materials are spun, covered, and sewn in sequential order (Exhibit 19).

Exhibit 18   Equivalent Units for Department B

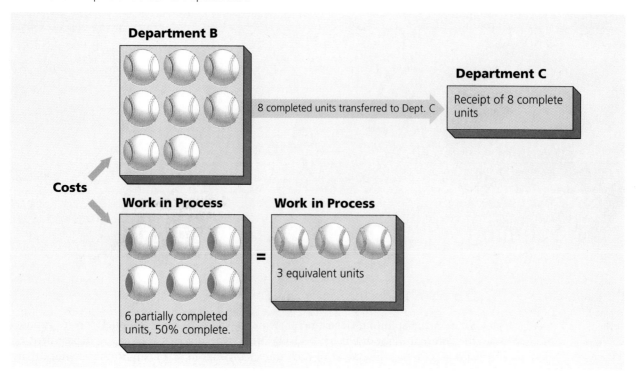

Exhibit 19   Cow Hide Company: Sequential Processing

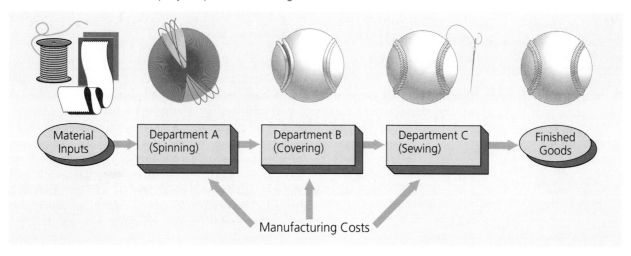

In *parallel processing* **the flow of products breaks off at some point so that different units go through different processing departments.** The petroleum industry uses parallel processing: Crude oil is refined to a certain point and then is processed further into different products. There are a number of parallel processing patterns. Exhibit 20 illustrates one of them.

Processing begins on all units in department J. After processing in department J, the units are processed separately. Some units move through department K and then department L. Once completed, those units become Product X. Other units are processed in department M, followed by department N. Those units become Product Y.

Refer to Exhibit 16. In a process-costing system, the flow of manufacturing costs follows the units of products as they move through production. Process costing maintains a separate Work in Process Inventory account for each department.

Exhibit 20 One Parallel Processing Pattern

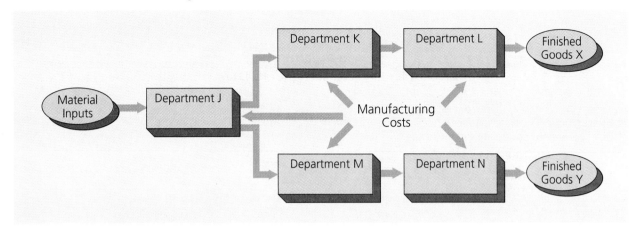

Manufacturing costs are accumulated in one department's account and are transferred to the next department's account as goods are transferred. In each department, additional materials, labor, and overhead may be added. After all processing is complete, the cost of the goods is transferred to the Finished Goods Inventory account. Once the units of product are sold, the costs associated with those units are transferred from the Finished Goods Inventory account to the Cost of Goods Sold account.

Companies track cost flows by *departmental production reports* **that describe the materials, labor, and overhead used by each department during a given accounting period.** The *initial department* **is the department that begins producing a product.** At Cow Hide the spinning department is the initial department. A *subsequent department* **is a department that continues production on a product.** Cow Hide's covering and sewing departments are subsequent departments. The cost flow follows the physical flow of the product as it moves from the initial department to subsequent departments. *Transferred-in costs* **are costs that have been transferred from an earlier department to a later department in the production process.** The manufacturing cost incurred in spinning one baseball is a transferred-in cost when that ball moves on to the covering department. To use process costing, the company must have a system for tracing production over a period, accumulating the costs incurred during the period, and applying those costs to the units produced in that period. The departmental production report summarizes all the activities that go on in the department's Work in Process Inventory account during a given period:

- The flow of units through a department
- The calculation of equivalent units
- The costs included in beginning inventory
- Any costs transferred in from a previous department
- The cost of materials, labor, and overhead incurred during the period
- The costs transferred to a subsequent department
- The costs assigned to the department's Work in Process Inventory account

Production reports function much like job cost sheets. We look at an example of one in the following section.

Using Process Costing to Determine Unit Cost. Exhibit 21 shows a departmental production report. In a production process, units can be partially completed at the end of the period. The computation of unit costs is complicated by the need to determine equivalent units of production for those partially completed units.

Exhibit 21 Departmental Production Report for Cow Hide Company

Cow Hide Company
October Production Report
Sewing Department

Account for Physical Flow of Units (Step 1)

Work in process, October 1	20,000
Units begun during October	120,000
Total units worked on in October	140,000
Units transferred out during October	110,000
Work in process October 31	30,000*

*   *materials 50% complete, conversion 40% complete*

Calculate the Equivalent Units of Production (Step 2)

	Materials	Conversion
	110,000	110,000
	15,000	12,000
October equivalent units	125,000	122,000

Account for the Department's Production Costs (Step 3)

	Materials	Conversion	Total
Work in process, October 1	$ 32,000	$ 42,000	
Costs transferred in from other departments in October	240,000	360,000	
Costs added during October in sewing department	65,000	90,000	
Total costs for October	$337,000	$492,000	$829,000

Calculate the Cost of Equivalent Units (Step 4)

Materials	$337,000 ÷ 125,000 equivalent units = $2.6960 per equivalent unit
Conversion	$492,000 ÷ 122,000 equivalent units = $4.0328 per equivalent unit
Total	= $6.7288 per equivalent unit

Assign Costs to Inventory (Step 5)

Costs assigned to units transferred out (110,000 units × $6.7288)			$740,166
Costs assigned to Work in Process Inventory:			
Materials	(30,000 units × 50% × $2.6960)	40,440	
Conversion	(30,000 units × 40% × $4.0328)	48,394	
Costs assigned to Work in Process Inventory			88,834
Total costs assigned to units in October			$829,000

Learning Note   The computations involved in process costing often are more complex than those described in this section. The method shown here is known as the weighted-average method. Some companies use a first-in first-out (FIFO) method to determine equivalent units—a process that is more complex than the weighted-average method (and the subject of a cost accounting course). The focus of this section is on concepts rather than computations.

O b j e c t i v e   7
Determine unit cost using process costing.

In order to compute the cost of the baseballs transferred from the covering department to the sewing department, it is first necessary to calculate the cost of partially completed baseballs transferred from the spinning department to the covering department. In other words, a unit cost must be calculated for the partially completed baseballs in each department prior to sewing in order to compute a final unit cost in the sewing department. For simplicity, only the computations for the final unit cost in the sewing department are shown. It is assumed that the computations for the spinning and the covering departments have already been completed.

Step 1: Account for the Physical Flow of Units. The first step in developing a production report is to account for the physical flow of units worked on during the month. The physical flow of units in Cow Hide's sewing department for October was as follows:

		Percentage Complete	
	Units	**Materials**	**Conversion**
Work in process, October 1	20,000		
Units started in production in October	120,000		
Total units in production in October	140,000		
Units completed and transferred out in October	110,000		
Work in process, October 31	30,000	50%	40%

At the beginning of the month, the sewing department had 20,000 unsewn baseballs. During October, another 120,000 baseballs were brought into sewing from the covering department. Of the 140,000 baseballs worked on during October in sewing, 110,000 were completed and transferred to the finished goods inventory, leaving 30,000 in the sewing department's ending inventory.

Step 2: Calculate the Equivalent Units of Production. In this step the company converts the physical units of production into equivalent units.

	Materials	**Conversion**
Units completed and transferred out in October (100% complete)	110,000	110,000
Work in process, October 31:		
30,000 units × 50% complete for materials	15,000	
30,000 units × 40% complete for conversion		12,000
Equivalent units of production for October	125,000	122,000

Conversion costs **are the direct labor and manufacturing overhead costs required to convert raw materials into finished goods.** Often, those costs are added together and are accounted for as a single cost in process-costing systems. Note that one physical unit that is complete in terms of all materials and conversion costs equals one equivalent unit. Therefore, at Cow Hide, the 110,000 physical units completed and transferred out of the sewing department equal 110,000 equivalent units.

Step 3: Account for the Department's Production Costs. In this step the company adds the costs of beginning work in process, the costs transferred into the sewing department during the month from the prior departments, and the costs added as a result of work performed in the sewing department:

	Materials	**Conversion**	**Total**
Work in process, October 1	$ 32,000	$ 42,000	
Costs transferred in from other departments in October	240,000	360,000	
Costs added during October in the sewing department	65,000	90,000	
Total costs for October	$337,000	$492,000	$829,000

As units of product flow from process to process, the costs associated with those units also must flow from department to department. As a result, *costs transferred in* appear on each department's production report after the units have passed the initial department. The sewing department receives units from the spinning department and the covering department. Production costs of those departments are transferred to the sewing department as units are transferred. Thus, as units flow through a process system, the costs associated with making those units continue to increase as they are transferred from one department to the next.

Step 4: Calculate the Cost of Equivalent Units. The fourth step in developing the production report is to divide total costs by equivalent units to obtain the cost per equivalent unit:

Materials	$337,000 ÷ 125,000 equivalent units =	$2.6960 per equivalent unit
Conversion	$492,000 ÷ 122,000 equivalent units =	$4.0328 per equivalent unit
Total		$6.7288 per equivalent unit

Step 5: Assign Costs to Inventory. In this step the company assigns production costs for the period to the units that are being transferred out of Cow Hide's sewing department's work in process inventory. They move into finished goods inventory, and the costs related to them are added to the company's Finished Goods Inventory account (and subtracted from that department's Work in Process Inventory account).

The costs transferred out equal the number of units transferred out multiplied by the total cost per equivalent unit. The costs assigned to the Work in Process Inventory account equal the number of equivalent units in work in process multiplied by the cost per unit:

Costs assigned to units transferred out		
(110,000 units × $6.7288)		$740,166*
Costs assigned to Work in Process Inventory:		
Materials (30,000 units × 50% × $2.6960)	40,440	
Conversion (30,000 units × 40% × $4.0328)	48,394	
Costs assigned to Work in Process Inventory		88,834
Total costs assigned to units in October		$829,000

* *A slight adjustment was made for rounding error.*

Notice that the total costs assigned to units in October equal the total costs to be accounted for in step 3.

Learning Note   Under process costing, a unit cost is determined for each department. That unit cost is used to calculate the cost of the units transferred to the next department or to finished goods inventory. Because the sewing department is the last department in processing baseballs, the costs computed in this department are used to compute the cost of the finished goods. During October, $740,166 was added to the Finished Goods Inventory account, represented by the 110,000 baseballs completed during October. Determining an overall unit cost of finished products in a process costing system involves calculating a series of unit costs as the product moves from department to department.

UNIT COSTS IN THE SERVICE SECTOR

Objective 8
Explain how job-order and process costing are used in the service sector.

Companies in the service sector also use unit costs to set prices and manage costs. Those companies can use job-order and process costing systems. For example, telephone companies, such as **MCI,** provide telephone services. MCI can use a process costing system to account for costs because the unit of product (one minute of telephone connect time) is like all of the other units, and each unit of product requires a similar amount of costs. The average cost of a minute of connect time gives MCI's

http://www.swcollege.
com/ingram.html

**Visit the home pages
of MCI, Sprint, and
AT&T.**

managers the information they need to decide how much they must charge for each minute of connect time to make a profit. On the other hand, MCI must set its price low enough to be competitive with other phone companies, such as **AT&T** and **Sprint.** If the unit cost of telephone connect time at MCI is too high for the company to earn a reasonable profit, MCI must look for ways to lower its costs. The telephone company cannot simply raise its price to earn higher profits without losing customers to its competitors.

Service organizations also can use job-order costing. For example, public accounting firms audit their clients' financial statements. The primary cost to those firms in providing this service is employee wages. Auditors track the time each individual spends on each task they perform in the audit. The times of all employees who work on the audit of a particular client are multiplied by a price per hour to assign costs to each audit.

SELF-STUDY PROBLEM 3

Fizz Pop produces one product (a soft drink) that flows through two departments, mixing and bottling.

Costs in Work In Process Inventory on March 1 included $4,000 of materials and $2,500 of conversion costs. Costs added during March included $50,000 of materials and $35,000 of conversion costs.

A production report for the mixing department for March showed the following information:

© 83 Doug Randel/The Stock Market

	Units	Percentage Complete	
		Materials	**Conversion**
Work in process, March 1	50,000		
Units started in production in March	600,000		
Total units in production in March	650,000		
Units completed and transferred out in March	570,000		
Work in process, March 31	80,000	100%	50%

Required

Compute the total and unit costs for March. Also compute the amount of cost transferred to the bottling department during March and the amount of Work In Process on March 31 for the mixing department.

The solution to Self-Study Problem 3 appears at the end of the chapter.

R E V I E W   *Summary of Important Concepts*

1. Unit costs have two primary functions.
    a. Accountants use unit costs to place a value on a company's inventories.
    b. Managers use unit costs as the basis of decisions about pricing products, continuing a product line, allocating limited resources, and establishing marketing strategies.

2. According to GAAP, unit costs must reflect the costs of direct materials, direct labor, and manufacturing overhead. Although some companies use that information as the basis of their managerial decision making, managers can choose to include nonmanufacturing costs or to exclude certain manufacturing costs in the unit-cost calculation when making decisions.

3. Most companies use one of two methods for measuring costs.
   a. Actual costing bases unit costs on the actual costs incurred for direct materials, direct labor, and manufacturing overhead.
   b. Normal costing uses the actual costs of direct materials and direct labor and an estimate of manufacturing overhead costs as the basis of units costs.
      (1) Estimated overhead costs are the product of the actual activity base multiplied by the predetermined overhead rate.
      (2) At the end of the accounting period, the company adjusts the Manufacturing Overhead account as necessary to make the estimated overhead equal the actual overhead.

4. Most companies use one of two methods—job-order or process costing—to assign costs to units of products.
   a. Each method is more effective in certain business situations.
   b. Key to the choice between job-order costing and process costing is the manufacturing context, the cost of collecting data, and the need for accuracy.

5. Job-order costing yields the unit cost of a particular job.
   a. It is most effective when a company produces very different products using very different processes and incurring very different costs, and when the costs of producing the product can be traced directly to the product.
   b. Companies that use job-order costing track job costs with job cost sheets.

6. Process costing yields an average cost for each unit produced during a particular period.
   a. It is most effective when a company's products are very much alike—both in physical characteristics and costs—and when a continuous flow of production makes it very difficult and costly to track the cost of individual units.
   b. As units of product move from one department to the next, the production costs of those products are transferred from department to department.
   c. Equivalent units are used to account for the costs of work in process.
   d. The departmental production report reflects the five steps in the calculation of an average unit cost. Those steps are repeated in each department until the units of products move into finished goods inventory.

7. Managers in the service sector are concerned with unit costs as well.

D E F I N E   *Terms and Concepts Defined in This Chapter*

activity base (80)	initial department (91)	sequential processing (89)
actual costing (78)	job-order costing (83)	subsequent department (91)
batch processing (84)	market share (76)	transferred-in costs (91)
conversion costs (93)	normal costing (78)	unit cost (74)
departmental production report (91)	parallel processing (90)	unit margin (77)
differentiated product (75)	predetermined overhead rate (80)	
equivalent units (89)	process costing (83)	

SOLUTIONS

SELF-STUDY PROBLEM 1

Under the actual costing system, the Work in Process Inventory account would contain the following costs: raw materials ($100,000), direct labor ($40,000), and actual overhead ($60,000) for a total of $200,000. Under the normal costing system, the account would contain: raw material ($100,000), direct labor ($40,000) and applied overhead ($67,500) for a total of $207,500. Thus, the difference between the two approaches would be $7,500.

Note: To assign overhead under the normal costing system, it is necessary to calculate the predetermined overhead rate. For Russell Lumber Co. the rate would be $750,000 expected annual overhead costs ÷ $50,000 expected annual machine hours = $15 per machine hour. Therefore, for March, the amount of overhead applied would be $15 × 4,500 actual machine hours for the month = $67,500.

The difference of $7,500 is the overapplied overhead. More overhead was assigned to the Work in Process Inventory account than was actually incurred. This means the Manufacturing Overhead account contains a positive balance of $7,500 and must be reduced to zero. The Cost of Goods Sold account is decreased by that amount also.

SELF-STUDY PROBLEM 2

The cost of Job 2B38 includes total direct materials, direct labor, and manufacturing overhead that has been applied as follows:

Direct materials (10 pounds × $11.65)		$116.50
Direct labor:		
Cutting and forming (3 × $9.75)	$29.25	
Lathe and mill (4 × $11.50)	46.00	
Finishing (1 × $10.00)	10.00	
Total labor		85.25
Overhead applied (8 labor hours × $25.00)		200.00
Total costs for Job 2B38		$401.75

The average cost per gear is $80.35 = $401.75 ÷ 5 gears produced.

SELF-STUDY PROBLEM 3

	Equivalent units:	
	Materials	**Conversion**
Units completed and transferred out in March	570,000	570,000
Work in process, March 31:		
80,000 units × 100% complete	80,000	
80,000 units × 50% complete		40,000
Equivalent units of production in March	650,000	610,000

Cost to account for:	**Materials**	**Conversion**	**Total**
Work in process, March 1	$ 4,000	$ 2,500	
Costs added during March in mixing department	50,000	35,000	
Total costs for March	$54,000	$37,500	$91,500

Cost per equivalent unit:
Materials $54,000 ÷ 650,000 equivalent units = $0.08308 per equivalent unit
Conversion $37,500 ÷ 610,000 equivalent units = $0.06148 per equivalent unit
Total $0.14456 per equivalent unit

Costs assigned to inventory:
Costs assigned to units transferred out 570,000 units × $0.14456 = $82,395*

Costs assigned to work in process inventory:
Materials   80,000 units × 100% × $0.08308 =   6,646
Conversion   80,000 units × 50% × $0.06148 =   2,459

Costs assigned to Work in Process Inventory   9,105

Total costs assigned to units in March ($82,395 + $9,105) $91,500

* *A slight adjustment was made for rounding error.*

EXERCISES

3-1. Write a short definition of each of the terms listed in the *Terms and Concepts Defined in This Chapter* section.

Obj. 1 **3-2.** Jeff Arnold recently graduated from a prestigious business school and joined the family business as a production manager. At his first management meeting with marketing, production, accounting and administrative personnel, he noticed that a lot of attention is focused on the unit cost of products. Explain why unit-cost information is so important to managers.

Obj. 1 **3-3.** Tip Top Manufacturing is in the process of enhancing its product costing system. Rick Pinkston, president of Tip Top, has asked the company's controller to explain why a product costing system is so essential and what purposes the costing system should serve. How should the controller respond?

Obj. 2 **3-4.** There are many expenses associated with a manufacturing process—for example, the costs of designing and building a manufacturing plant. Other expenses relate to specific products. Which of these types of expenses would be included typically in product cost?

Obj. 3 **3-5.** Rene Manzor plans to use a recent inheritance to buy a small factory that produces travel bags. Rene has done a great deal of reading about managing a business and realizes that she must establish a costing system to accumulate the costs of producing the bags. In her reading, she learned about two methods of accumulating product costs, actual and normal. Rene has no experience in accounting and is confused about the difference between the two methods. How would you explain the difference in cost accumulation between actual costing and normal costing?

Obj. 3 **3-6.** Hoy Heating and Air Company repairs heating and cooling equipment. Each time a service technician completes a job, a time sheet is turned in, and the job cost is computed. The company calculates the cost of each job by adding the cost of any materials used on the job, the labor cost of the service technician, and an overhead charge to cover administrative and support expenses. Hoy uses an estimated cost of support expenses in its calculation. Why do you think the company uses predetermined rates rather than actual costs in computing the costs of each service call?

Obj. 3 **3-7.** Roth Industries manufactures toy blocks for children. Maynard Industries manufactures computer-guided missiles for the military. Both companies use direct labor hours as the basis for applying overhead expenses to their respective products. Why would manufacturers of extremely different products—such as blocks and weapon systems—use the same basis for assigning overhead expenses to products? What factors should be considered in selecting an activity base for assigning overhead costs to products?

Obj. 3 **3-8.** Tom Brooks, production manager for Clarion Manufacturing was told that product overhead costs were too high, and that the amount of overhead which has been applied to inventory is less than the actual costs which have been incurred over the last few months. Tom responds that he doesn't understand what "applied" means when dealing with inventory costs. Explain to Tom what is meant by the statement overhead is *applied* to units of product? Must the actual amount of overhead costs incurred during a period always equal the amount of overhead that is applied to inventory?

Obj. 3 **3-9.** The income statement of Gardner and Associates, a manufacturer of kitchen utensils and accessories, has a line item called "Over or Under Applied Overhead." How would you explain this account to a user of the Gardner statements? If there is a significant balance in this account when financial statements are compiled, how might the under or over applied overhead account be adjusted?

Obj. 4 **3-10.** During a family get-together you announce that you are studying managerial accounting and fully understand product costing. Your brother says that he works for a company that assigns product costs using job-order costing. Your sister says that her company uses something called process costing to assign product costs. Uncle Nick asks you to explain the difference between job-order costing and process costing. What do you tell him?

Obj. 4 **3-11.** Which method, job-order costing or process costing, would be most appropriate for each of the following organizations? Briefly justify your answer.
a. A paint manufacturer
b. A glue manufacturer
c. An aircraft manufacturer
d. A home building company
e. An accounting firm
f. A hospital
g. A tire manufacturer
h. A manufacturer of specialty factory equipment
i. An interior decorator
j. A film studio
k. A brewery

Obj. 5 **3-12.** Snuffy Fitchen is the warehouse clerk for Big Chairs Limited. A production apprentice has asked Snuffy for a batch of raw materials, but he refuses to release the goods without the appropriate paperwork. What form is needed as supporting documentation for materials used in production? What are the essential parts of that form?

Obj. 5 **3-13.** Engineers at The Rose Company recently designed a new badminton racket for the company's sporting goods line. The technical drawings were sent to the production department, and the first lot of 1000 rackets has been manufactured. Management at Rose is anxious to see the cost sheet for this job. What information does the job cost sheet contain that would generate such management interest?

Obj. 6 **3-14.** Stan Meyer recently bought a shoe factory and plans to manufacture running shoes. As part of his business plan, Stan had to select a method of accumulating product costs. He understands that there are two different methods for accumulating product costs, job-order and process costing, but he wanted the less complicated method. Stan selected the process costing method. Why is cost accumulation under process costing less complicated than under job-order costing?

Obj. 6 **3-15.** Perfection Biscuit Company makes a variety of breads, rolls, buns, and snack cakes. Breads and rolls are manufactured in a sequential pattern, while some of the buns and all of the snack cakes are processed in a parallel pattern. Explain the difference in the movement of products through departments that are arranged in a sequential pattern versus a parallel pattern.

Obj. 6 **3-16.** During a tour of a local soft drink bottler, someone asked the tour guide: "What equivalent units of production are used to calculate unit costs in this department?" The guide understood the question, and responded "All production is accounted for on a per-barrel basis." What are equivalent units of production? Why would a soft drink bottler need to calculate equivalent units?

Obj. 6 **3-17.** Paula Locum is a department manager for the Dempsey Lumber Mill. She supervises the kiln drying operations and is directly responsible for ten employees and three large kiln dryers. Each month, Paula prepares a production report for the drying operation and submits her report to accounting. What are the key elements of a departmental production report?

Obj. 6 **3-18.** Carter Lumber Company processes timber into finished lumber. For 20 years, Carter has calculated the cost of lumber using job-order costing. Each production run was treated as a separate job. Carter recently changed accounting procedures and now calculates product costs using process costing. What methods could Carter use for calculating equivalent units?

Obj. 6 **3-19.** Pegasus Wire Harness Company produces an electrical-wire harness used in the automotive industry. Pegasus accounts for product costs using process costing. Managers of Pegasus focus on two components of product costs for planning and control purposes. What are the two elements that are assigned costs in process costing? Why are the two elements treated separately?

Obj. 7 **3-20.** Southern Brickyards processes clay and sand into bricks. Raw materials account for a small portion of the costs of the bricks Southern produces. Most of Southern's product costs are conversion costs. What are the two components of conversion costs?

PROBLEMS

PROBLEM 3-1   Job-Order Costing

Obj. 3

Harold Gordon operates a manufacturing company that uses a job-order costing system. The following activity was recorded in the Work in Process Inventory account for August:

Direct materials	$150,000
Direct labor	80,000
Manufacturing overhead applied	120,000
Completed production	(322,000)

Harold charges overhead to work in process on the basis of direct labor dollars. There were no jobs in process as of August 1. At the end of August, only one job was still in process (job 75). This job had incurred labor charges of $6,000 during the month.

Required

a. Compute the predetermined overhead rate that Gordon used in August.
b. Compute the amount of manufacturing overhead and direct materials costs that were incurred in job 75.

PROBLEM 3-2   Applying Overhead Under Job-Order Costing

Obj. 3

Tortolla Company is a manufacturing firm that uses a job-order costing system. The company uses machine hours to apply overhead to work in process. On January 1, Tortolla's management estimated that it would incur $700,000 in manufacturing overhead costs and 56,000 machine hours over the coming year.

Required

a. Compute the company's predetermined overhead rate for the year.
b. Assume that the company uses only 54,000 machine hours over the year and incurs the following manufacturing costs:

Maintenance	$ 56,000
Depreciation	206,000
Indirect materials	76,000
Utilities	164,000
Insurance	94,000
Indirect labor	64,000

Compute the amount of overhead that was applied to production and the amount of over- or underapplied overhead for the period.

PROBLEM 3-3 Applying Overhead Under Job-Order Costing

Obj. 3

TCC Inc. has prepared the following estimates for the current year.

Direct labor hours	80,000
Direct labor cost	$1,000,000
Machine hours	60,000
Manufacturing overhead	$600,000

Required

a. Compute the predetermined overhead rate based on (1) direct labor hours, (2) direct labor cost, and (3) machine hours.

b. Assume the following jobs were worked during the year:

Job	Labor Dollars	Labor Hours	Machine Hours
123	$204,000	18,000	9,500
124	132,000	8,500	4,800
125	86,000	5,100	5,200

Compute the amount of overhead that would have been applied to each of these jobs using the various overhead rates you computed in requirement (a).

c. Explain why the amount of overhead applied to each job varies with the activity base.

PROBLEM 3-4 Job-Order Versus Process Costing

Obj. 4

Clark Lights produces lightbulbs. The plant is new, and the process is highly automated. All production is completed in a single two-step department. First, a bulb casing is made and is passed to a second machine process where a filament is inserted. The company manufactures several different wattage bulbs, including 40, 75 and 100. Once the machinery is set up, the company will produce the same wattage bulb for up to four days before changing to another wattage bulb. The only difference in processing the different wattage bulbs is the size of the filament that is inserted in the second step. The cost difference of the different size filaments is insignificant. Clark produces approximately 5,000 bulbs of each wattage per month.

Required

a. Identify the costing procedure that would be most appropriate given the different style bulbs that are produced. Explain the reason for your answer.

b. Would your answer change if the cost of the materials was considered significantly different? Explain why or why not?

PROBLEM 3-5 Unit Costs Under Job-Order Costing

Obj. 5

The following information about job 272 is from the records of K-Say Manufacturing Company for October:

Work in Process Inventory, 9/30	$ 25,800
Material requisitions,	125,550
Payroll, 10/15	36,000
Overhead applied	99,400
Payroll, 10/31	35,400

Job 272 was completed on October 31, and a total of 12,886 units were produced.

Required

a. Calculate the per-unit cost of job 272.

b. Explain how K-Say's Work in Process Inventory account was affected by the completion of job 272.

PROBLEM 3-6 **Unit Costs Under Job-Order Costing**

Obj. 5

Basic Closet Company manufactures stand-alone cedar-lined wardrobe closets. Basic received an order for ten specially designed wardrobes to be delivered in eight weeks. The order was assigned job number 293. During production of the wardrobes, the following activities took place:

1. Requisitioned $2,500 of wood and $500 of hardware.
2. Time sheets revealed direct labor costs of $1,450 and indirect labor costs of $345.
3. Overhead was assigned using 130% of direct labor costs.
4. Completed units were shipped to the customer. The selling price was 140% of cost.

Required

a. Calculate the manufacturing cost of one wardrobe.
b. Calculate the selling price of each wardrobe.
c. Describe how Basic traces material, manufacturing overhead, and labor costs to job 293.

PROBLEM 3-7 **Job-Order Costing in a Service Environment**

Objs. 5,8

The law firm of Dewey, Louie, and Howe has six lawyers and ten support people. The firm uses a job-order costing system to accumulate costs by client. There are two departments, research and litigation. The firm uses a different predetermined overhead rate for each department. At the beginning of the year, the partners made the following estimates:

	Department	
	Research	**Litigation**
Planned attorney hours	2,500	11,600
Number of clients	1,000	230
Legal supplies	$ 12,000	$ 4,600
Direct attorney cost	$132,000	$696,000
Department overhead	$ 70,000	$406,000

The costs to clients are separated into three components: supplies, attorney costs, and overhead. Both departments base overhead on the number of attorney hours charged. Supplies are charged on a per-client basis. Clients are billed all costs plus 20%.

Case DR9312 was opened on January 3 and closed June 17. During that period, the following costs and time were recorded:

Attorney hours, research	55
Attorney hours, litigation	175
Attorney cost	$13,800

Required

a. Compute the rate each department should use to assign overhead costs.
b. Compute the amount per client that each department should use to allocate supply costs.
c. Using the rates computed in requirements a and b, compute the total cost of case DR9312, including overhead, supply charges, and attorney fees.
d. Calculate the billing for case DR9312.

PROBLEM 3-8 **Unit Costs Under Process Costing**

Obj. 7

Perfect Bread Company makes bread in its midwestern plant. The production process is described as follows:

> Flour, milk, yeast, and salt are combined and mixed in a large vat. The resulting dough is transferred by conveyor to a machine that shapes the dough into loaves and places the loaves into pans. The dough is allowed to rise for several hours. Then the pans move slowly through a long oven, where they bake for 45 minutes. When the baked bread

emerges from the oven, another machine removes the loaves from the pans. The bread cools for 10 minutes and then is fed through a slicing machine and wrapped.

Last week, Perfect produced 5,000 loaves of bread. The total cost of materials for the week, including ingredients and packaging, was $750. The costs of labor and overhead totaled $1,600. There were no beginning or ending inventories.

Required

a. Compute the unit cost of the 5,000 loaves produced during the week.
b. Perfect does not maintain work in process inventory. What implications does that fact have on the calculations the company must perform?
c. Suppose that Perfect uses the same machinery to produce rolls and buns but that processing those other products is significantly different in terms of cost. What implications would that have on the company's accounting procedures?

PROBLEM 3-9 Equivalent Units of Production

Obj. 7

Aladdin Company manufactures a product that passes through two processes. The following information was available for the first department for January.

1. All materials are added at the beginning of the process.
2. Beginning work in process consisted of 6,000 units, 33% complete with respect to conversion costs.
3. Ending work in process consisted of 4,400 units, 25% complete with respect to conversion costs.
4. 10,000 units started into production in January.

Required

a. Prepare a physical flow schedule for the department.
b. Calculate equivalent units for materials and conversion costs.

PROBLEM 3-10 Equivalent Units of Production

Obj. 7

Holbert Company produces a product that passes through two departments, mixing and heating. In the mixing department, all materials are added at the beginning of the process. All conversion costs are added uniformly during the process. The following information relates to activities in the mixing department for June:

Beginning work in process, June 1, 100,000 pounds, 60% complete as to conversion costs. Costs in beginning Work in Process Inventory were as follows:

Materials	$20,000
Labor	10,000
Overhead	30,000

Ending work in process, June 30, 50,000 pounds, 40% complete with respect to conversion costs.

Units completed and transferred out totaled 370,000 pounds. The following costs were added during the month:

Materials	$211,000
Labor	100,000
Overhead	269,500

Required

a. Prepare a physical flow schedule.
b. Prepare a schedule of equivalent units.
c. Compute the cost per equivalent unit.
d. Compute the cost of goods transferred out and the value of the ending Work in Process Inventory.

PROBLEM 3-11   Multiple-Choice Overview of the Chapter

1. Overapplied overhead would result if
   a.   the plant was operated at less than full capacity.
   b.   factory overhead costs incurred were less than estimated overhead costs.
   c.   factory overhead costs incurred were less than the overhead costs charged to production.
   d.   factory overhead costs incurred were greater than the overhead costs charged to production.

2. Scott Corporation uses labor hours as the basis for allocating manufacturing overhead costs to production. At the beginning of last year, Scott estimated total manufacturing costs at $300,000 and total labor hours at 75,000 hours. Actual results for the period were total manufacturing overhead costs of $290,000 and total labor hours of 75,000 hours. As a result of this outcome, Scott would have
   a.   applied more overhead to Work in Process Inventory than the actual amount of overhead costs for the year.
   b.   applied less overhead to Work in Process Inventory than the actual amount of overhead cost for the year.
   c.   applied an amount of overhead to Work in Process Inventory that was equal to the actual amount of overhead.
   d.   found it necessary to recalculate the predetermined rate.

3. Melrose Company uses a job-order costing system. The company recorded the following data for July:

| | July 1 | Added During July | |
Job number	Work in Process Inventory	Direct Materials	Direct Labor
475	$1,500	$ 500	$ 300
476	1,000	700	900
477	900	1,000	1,500
478	700	1,200	2,000

Melrose charges overhead to production on the basis of 80% of direct materials cost. Jobs 475, 477, and 478 were complete during July. Melrose's Work in Process Inventory balance on July 31 was:
   a. $7,280.
   b. $2,600.
   c. $3,160.
   d. $3,320.

4. Last year, the Rembrandt Company incurred $250,000 in actual manufacturing overhead costs. The company's Manufacturing Overhead account showed that overhead was overapplied in the amount of $12,000 for the year. If the predetermined overhead rate was $8 per direct labor hour, how many direct labor hours were worked during the year?
   a.   31,250.
   b.   30,250.
   c.   32,750.
   d.   29,750.

5. Birk Inc. uses a job-order costing system. The following information appeared in Birk's Work in Process Inventory account for April:

Balance, April 1	$ 4,000
Direct materials added	24,000
Direct labor added	16,800
Factory overhead applied	12,800
Transferred to finished goods	(48,000)

Birk applies overhead to production at a predetermined rate of 80% of direct labor costs. Work in process on April 30 includes direct labor costs of $2,000. The amount of direct materials in the ending work in process inventory for April was
a. $3,000.
b. $5,200.
c. $9,600.
d. $6,000.

6. During May, Roy Company produced 6,000 units of product X in job 344. The costs charged to job 344 were as follows:

Direct materials $10,000
Direct labor   20,000

At the beginning of the year, management estimated the following costs would be incurred to produce 120,000 units for the year:

Factory overhead $168,000
Selling expenses   84,000

Roy applies overhead to work in process on a per-unit basis. The cost to produce one unit of product X in job 344 was
a. $6.40.
b. $5.10.
c. $3.80.
d. $3.50.

7. Prism Company uses a process costing system. The company's work in process inventory on March 31 consisted of 20,000 units. Those units were 100% complete with respect to materials and 70% complete as to labor and overhead. If the cost per equivalent unit for March was $2.50 for materials and $4.75 for labor and overhead, the total cost on the March 31 in the company's Work in Process Inventory account was
a. $145,000.
b. $116,500.
c. $101,500.
d. $78,500.

8. In a process costing system, costs are accumulated by
a. department.
b. individual job.
c. both job and department.
d. neither job nor department.

9. Which of the following characteristics applies to process costing but does not apply to job-order costing?
a. the need for averaging.
b. the use of equivalent units of production.
c. separate, identifiable jobs.
d. the use of predetermined overhead rates.

10. A processing pattern in which, after a certain point, some units go through different processing departments than others is referred to as
a. sequential processing.
b. parallel processing.
c. operational processing.
d. throughput processing.

C A S E S

CASE 3-1 Unit Costing Policy

Objs. 1, 2

Knight Manufacturing produces three different products: A, B, and C. Knight applies overhead to the products on the basis of direct labor dollars. The company has collected the following information about its overhead and labor costs:

Manufacturing overhead:

Machine setup	$ 53,000
Depreciation	400,000
Receiving and handling	200,000
Factory operations	650,000
Packing and shipping	400,000
Total	$1,703,000

Total direct labor $225,000

Predetermined overhead rate 757% of direct labor dollars ($1,703,000 ÷ $225,000)

Knight can produce:
Product A—2 units per hour
Product B—3 units per hour
Product C—4 units per hour

The cost of direct materials and direct labor are charged to each product under a job-order costing system. The average cost per unit based on the first of several production runs is as follows:

	Product		
	A	**B**	**C**
Direct materials	$ 25.00	$ 35.00	$ 15.00
Direct labor*	10.00	6.67	5.00
Overhead applied	75.70	50.49	37.85
Total per unit cost	$110.70	$ 92.16	$ 57.85
Current selling price	$163.00	$125.00	$102.00

* *The average labor rate is $20 per labor hour.*

The company manufactures each product in different batch sizes. Product A is manufactured in lot sizes of 10,000 units per run, product B in lots of 5,000 units per run, and product C in lots of 1,000 units per run. The average shipment size is 2,000 units of product A, 500 units of product B and 100 units of product C. Over the past year, the company has sold 22,000 units of product A, 15,000 units of product B, and 32,000 units of product C.

In recent months, management at Knight has been puzzled by the company's sales and profit figures. The sales of product A have declined significantly since a competitor of that product reduced its selling price below Knight's current cost of manufacturing that product. In addition, Knight has increased its selling price of product C three times over the past year without losing any sales. Even though more product C is being sold, and it has the largest gross margin of the three products, overall profits have been falling.

Required

a. What problems do you see with the current unit-costing methods Knight is using?
b. What reasons can you suggest for the market reactions to the pricing of products A and C?
c. What changes would you suggest to management about its current costing policies?

CASE 3-2 Allocation of Overhead Costs

Objs. 1, 2, 5

Art's Custom Cabinetry manufactures and installs custom cabinetry built to customer specifications. The prices of cabinets depend on the quality of the lumber selected by the customers and the complexity of designs.

The company is owned and operated by Art Bruce. Five years ago, he started the company in his garage. Over the five years, Art has invested heavily in special equipment. The annual depreciation on that equipment is $1,200. He also has moved operations to a building he rents for $4,800 per year. During 1997, Art incurred the following costs: utilities, $1,500; repairs and maintenance $600; shop supplies $2,100; paint and varnish, $800; insurance and taxes $3,000. All of these costs are considered to be production costs and are assigned to jobs as overhead expense. These costs are expected to stay the same in 1998.

Art assigns job numbers by customer name. The only job still in process at the end of 1997 was Clara Cummins. That job had been charged with direct materials of $600, direct labor of $1,000 and overhead of $400, using an overhead allocation rate of 25% of direct costs (direct materials plus direct labor).

Art is the sole employee of the company. He works an average of 2,800 hours a year and is paid $20 an hour by the company. Art bids on all jobs in his spare time and feels his overhead rate has kept him from obtaining some of the jobs he has bid on.

A summary of activity for January is as follows:

Job	Direct Materials	Direct Labor Cost	Direct Labor Hours
Clara Cummins	$ 600	$ 800	40
John Ryan	1,200	1,000	50
Kyle Smith	750	700	35
Ken Woods	950	600	30

The Kyle Smith job was completed during January and billed at cost plus 10%. All other jobs are still in process at the end the month.

Required

a.   Comment on the overhead base used by Art's Custom Cabinetry. What changes would you recommend, if any, for the company?
b.   Select a base for 1998, and calculate the predetermined overhead rate that should be used in the coming year.
c.   Using your predetermined overhead rate (requirement b), calculate the total costs for each of the jobs Art worked on during January.
d.   Calculate the balance of the company's Work-in-Process Inventory account as of January 31, 1998. Which jobs are reflected in that balance?
e.   Calculate the cost of goods sold in January 1998.
f.   Calculate the unit margin that the company earned from jobs completed in January.

PROJECTS

PROJECT 3-1 Overhead Costs in a Service Environment

Obj. 2

On your next visit to a fast-food restaurant, make a list of items that would be considered overhead expenses. How much do you think each of those items add to the cost of each product. Would it be appropriate to include the cost of shake machines, deep fryers or soda fountains in the product cost of a hamburger? Write a short report of your observations and comment on the problems inherent in applying overhead expenses to products in this environment.

PROJECT 3-2   *Job-Order Versus Process Costing*

Obj. 4

Make a list of ten common items you use or buy frequently. Which costing method—job-order or process costing—would you consider most appropriate for each of these items? Is there a correlation between those items you use or buy frequently and the costing method most likely used by their manufacturers? Would the items that you buy very infrequently have a common costing method? Write a short report on the items you select and the costing method you think is more appropriate for each item. Briefly explain your reasons.

PROJECT 3-3   *Job-Order Versus Process Costing*

Obj. 4

http://www.swcollege.
com/ingram.html

**Search for catalogs on
the internet.**

Make a list of five products from a local store that probably are assigned costs using job-order costing and five items that most likely are assigned costs using process costing. In a short report describe the items and the assumptions you made in categorizing the products by costing system.

Cost Measurement

for

Management

Accounting and Management Decisions

Internal Control · Service Organizations · Cost Behavior · Unit Costs · **Cost Measurement** · Cost Allocation · Budgets · Performance Evaluation · Global Environment · Decentralized Organizations · Capital Budgeting

Overview

This chapter continues our examination of product costing with a discussion of two methods of costing: variable costing and absorption costing.

Variable costing classifies costs by the way in which they behave. Variable costs change with the level of production activity; fixed costs are not affected by production activity in the short run. The variable-costing income statement separates variable and fixed costs. It subtracts variable costs from revenues to obtain the contribution margin. Absorption costing classifies costs by their function, manufacturing or nonmanufacturing. That focus is reflected in the format of the traditional income statement.

The text describes how managers can use variable costing to understand the relationship among costs, volume, and profits and to make operating decisions.

Then it compares variable and absorption costing and explains why the two methods produce different cost and income amounts. In an examination of the implications of variable costing and absorption costing for managerial decision making, the text shows both the advantages and limitations of each method. The chapter ends with a discussion of measuring costs for decision making in service companies.

Major topics covered in this chapter:
- The contribution margin and the variable-costing income statement.
- Using cost-volume-profit analysis to make managerial decisions.
- A comparison of the unit product costs and the income

©Lawrence Migdale/PNI International

derived from the variable-costing and absorption-costing methods.
- The pros and cons of using variable costing or absorption costing to make managerial decisions.
- Measuring costs for decisions in service companies.

CONTRIBUTION MARGIN AND THE VARIABLE-COSTING INCOME STATEMENT

Objective 1
Explain what contribution margins and breakeven points are and how the contribution margin is reflected in a variable-costing income statement.

An organization has to assign costs to price its products and evaluate its performance. Managers have a choice. They can assign costs using either absorption or variable costing. *Absorption costing* **assigns costs by function, separating the costs of manufacturing products from the costs of selling, administration, and other nonmanufacturing activities.** Absorption costing is also called the *full-cost method.* That's because absorption costing assigns the full costs of manufacturing to product costs. It makes no distinction between variable and fixed manufacturing costs.

Variable costing **assigns costs by their behavior, separating them into variable and fixed components.** Using variable costing, just variable product costs go into the unit-cost calculation. Key to this costing method is the *contribution margin,* **the difference between sales revenue and variable costs over an accounting period.** (In fact, variable costing is sometimes called the *contribution-margin method.*) It is the contribution margin that covers a company's fixed costs and defines its profits.

Cost Behavior: A Review

Remember that there are two basic types of costs: variable costs and fixed costs. Variable costs vary in proportion to volume or activity. If production volume increases 50%, variable costs go up 50% too.

Exhibit 1   Variable Cost Behavior

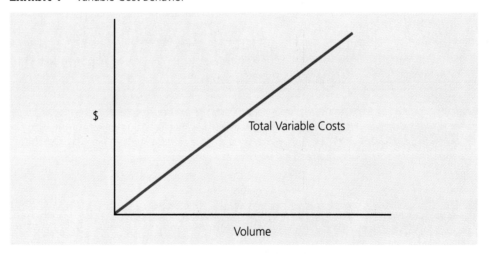

Exhibit 1 shows how total variable costs behave. The horizontal axis identifies the volume of activity—for example, the number of units produced. The vertical axis identifies the variable cost at any level of activity. As volume increases, cost increases in direct proportion. The costs of materials used in manufacturing products are variable costs.

Unlike variable costs, which increase proportionately with volume or activity, fixed costs remain constant over a wide range of activity. The rent on a factory building is a fixed cost: the rent stays the same regardless of how many units the factory produces. Exhibit 2 shows how total fixed costs behave. Notice that fixed costs do not change with volume. Cost behavior is important to decision making because it enables managers to forecast revenues and costs at different levels of production or service activity. Managers can then use these forecast revenues and costs to determine profits at different activity levels. This enables managers to decide on an activity level that will provide the greatest profit.

Exhibit 2 Fixed Cost Behavior

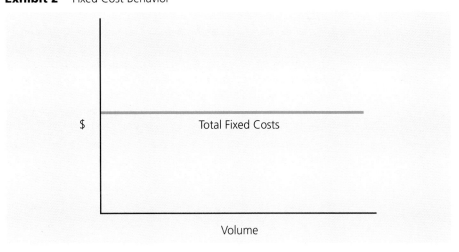

The Variable-Costing Income Statement

In the traditional income statement, the focus of cost data is on function: sales, the cost of goods sold, administration. The format does not distinguish between variable and fixed costs. In the administrative expenses entry, for example, both variable and fixed costs are reported as one amount. The traditional income statement tells investors and a company's suppliers what they need to know; it does not always give a company's management the information it needs to make planning and control decisions, however.

Managers need information in a format that can help them make decisions. **The** *variable-costing income statement* **is a managerial decision-making tool that measures net income by subtracting variable expenses from sales and then subtracting fixed expenses from the difference.** The difference between sales revenue and variable expenses for a period is the contribution margin. The contribution margin "contributes" to covering fixed expenses. What remains after fixed expenses have been covered is net income for the period. If the contribution margin is too small to cover all fixed expenses, the company reports a net loss. The order in which the contribution margin is applied is very important: first to cover fixed expenses, and then to provide profits.

Exhibit 3 shows a variable-costing income statement for Black & Blue Company, a small manufacturer of skateboards. Notice that the amounts are listed both in total and per unit. In their analysis of profitability, managers can look at both overall performance and the per-unit effect of variable expenses.

Exhibit 3 Black & Blue Company: A Variable-Costing Income Statement

	Total	Per Unit
Black & Blue Company		
Variable-Costing Income Statement		
For the Month Ended August 31, 1998		
Sales revenue (1,000 skateboards)	$20,000	$20
Less variable expenses	12,000	12
Contribution margin	$ 8,000	$ 8
Less fixed expenses	4,000	
Net income	$ 4,000	

Black & Blue generates a contribution margin of $8 per skateboard: Each skateboard the company sells contributes $8 toward covering fixed expenses. If the company sells enough skateboards to generate a $4,000 contribution margin, it can then cover all of its fixed expenses and break even for the month. **The** *breakeven point* **is that level of sales at which all variable and fixed expenses are covered, but no profit is generated.** Once sales reach the breakeven point, each additional unit sold contributes a profit equal to the contribution margin of that unit. As more units are sold, net income continues to go up by the contribution margin of each additional unit sold.

In addition to being expressed in total or on a per-unit basis, the contribution margin can be expressed as a percentage of sales as shown in Exhibit 4.

Exhibit 4   Black & Blue Company: Contribution Margin as a Percentage of Sales

	Total	Per Unit	Percentage
Sales (1,000 skateboards)	$20,000	$20	100%
Less variable expenses	12,000	12	60%
Contribution margin	$ 8,000	$ 8	40%
Less fixed expenses	4,000		
Net Income	$ 4,000		

The ratio (expressed as a percentage) of contribution margin to total sales is called the *contribution margin ratio* **or the profit volume ratio:**

Contribution margin ratio = contribution margin ÷ sales

When fixed costs stay the same, a company can use the contribution margin ratio to determine the effect on net income of a change in total sales. An example: Suppose that Black & Blue plans to increase its sales next month by $10,000. That means it plans to increase the total contribution margin by $4,000 ($10,000 increase in sales × 40% contribution margin ratio). If the company's fixed costs do not change, Black & Blue can expect its net income to go up by $4,000.

The contribution margin ratio can also help managers allocate limited resources. Products that have a higher contribution margin ratio are more profitable to a company, and so a company is more likely to focus its advertising and production resources on those products.

COST-VOLUME-PROFIT ANALYSIS

Objective 2
Understand the use of cost-volume-profit analysis in managerial decision making.

The variable-costing concept can be extended to help managers plan and make decisions about sales and profits. *Cost-volume-profit (CVP) analysis* **is the use of an understanding of the relationship among costs, volume, and profits to make managerial decisions.** A change in any one of those components affects the others. As Exhibit 5 shows, an understanding of the relationship among product prices, levels of activity, variable costs, and fixed costs can help managers develop marketing strategies, set pricing policies, and make resource decisions. Once costs have been separated into variable and fixed components, CVP analysis can be used to determine a company's breakeven point, to determine the sales volume necessary to earn a target profit, to measure the effect on net income of a change in expenses, and to determine the most profitable mix of products in a multiple-product environment. CVP analysis also helps managers evaluate sales options and a company's level of operating risk.

Exhibit 5   Cost-Volume-Profit Analysis and Managerial Decision Making

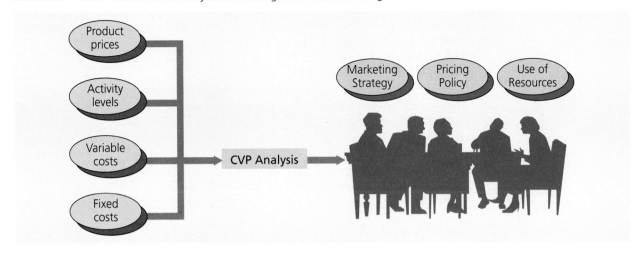

CVP analysis makes certain assumptions about costs and activities. If those assumptions are violated, the analysis can be flawed. One assumption, for example, is that fixed costs remain constant over the range of production. If fixed costs change, the analysis is not valid. A company can provide only a certain volume without adding workers or plant assets, which translates into higher fixed costs. If the existing machinery at Black & Blue is capable of producing just 60 skateboards a day, the company cannot produce 70 boards a day without additional equipment. That additional equipment would increase fixed maintenance expense, which is part of the fixed cost of production.

Fixed costs do change over time with inflation. That means that fixed costs usually are assumed to be fixed only for a given period. To be sure a CVP analysis is reliable, managers have to consult with one another about the possibility that fixed costs may change.

CVP analysis is complicated by mixed (semivariable) costs. Remember that mixed costs have both fixed and variable components. A salesperson's compensation, for example, is a mixed cost if it is made up of a (fixed) base salary plus a bonus that increases with sales. Exhibit 6 shows the behavior of a mixed cost. The distance between the origin (point zero) and point A on the vertical axis represents the fixed-cost component. The unit variable-cost component is the amount that variable costs increase with each additional unit produced.

Exhibit 6   Mixed-Cost Behavior

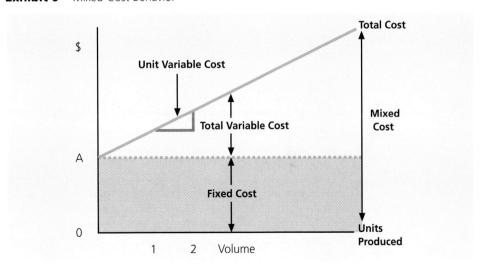

Whenever possible, mixed costs should be separated into their variable and fixed components. For example, some equipment is depreciated on the basis of units of production (say, $2 per unit produced). That is a variable expense. Other equipment is depreciated on a straight-line basis. That is a fixed expense. By keeping records of depreciation for individual pieces of equipment, a company can separate its depreciation expense into variable and fixed components.

Of course it's difficult to separate mixed costs because the costs are intermingled in the accounting records. For instance, a company may use a single account to record the costs of generating reports on a computer. The cost of reports that are produced weekly and sent to all departments in the company would be fixed. The cost of reports that are produced only at the request of a department would be variable. Although the company could separate the costs, it may choose not to if the additional accuracy does not justify the cost of keeping two accounts.

Learning Note Remember our discussion in an earlier chapter about costs and the need for accurate information. Generally the more accurate the accounting information, the more costly it is to produce.

CVP analysis also is complicated by the fact that the cost of materials for a unit of product may not remain constant. One factor here is the volume discounts that materials suppliers offer. As a company produces more units, it buys more materials, and as it buys more materials, volume discounts can lower the cost per unit of those materials. Another factor could be a shortage of materials in the market, which would push the price of those materials up. CVP analysis assumes that the cost of materials remains constant for each unit of a particular product. It is important, then, for managers using CVP analysis to talk with purchasing managers to be sure that variable costs per unit will not change over the period.

Breakeven-Point Analysis

Objective 3
Use CVP analysis to determine the breakeven point in sales and the sales volume necessary to earn a target profit.

Breakeven-point analysis is one of the most common uses of CVP analysis. **Breakeven-point analysis** is a technique used to find the volume of sales—in units or dollars—at which a company just covers its total costs. Two ways to calculate the breakeven point are the equation method and the unit-contribution method.

The Equation Method. The equation method builds on the relationship among sales, total costs, and profits. In its simplest form,

Sales − total costs = profits

The next step is to separate the variable and fixed components of total costs:

Sales − (variable costs + fixed costs) = profits

At the breakeven point, profits are zero. That means the equation can be rewritten this way:

Sales = variable costs + fixed costs

Remember that we're looking for the volume of sales at which a company covers its total costs. Fixed costs are a given: we assume that however many units a company sells, its fixed costs remain constant over the production run. Our focus is on two terms: sales and variable costs. For the sales term we can substitute the selling price per unit multiplied by the number of units sold; for the variable-costs term, we can substitute the variable cost per unit multiplied by the number of units sold:

Sales   = variable costs + fixed costs
Selling price per unit × units sold = (variable cost per unit × units sold) + fixed costs

How does it work? Black & Blue sells its skateboards for $20 apiece, each skateboard has variable costs of $12, and the company has fixed costs each month of $4,000 (see Exhibit 3). How many skateboards does the company have to sell each month to break even?

Breakeven sales   = variable costs + fixed costs
Selling price per unit × units sold = (variable cost per unit × units sold) + fixed costs
$20 × units sold   = ($12 × units sold) + $4,000
($20–$12) × units sold   = $4,000
$8 × units sold   = $4,000
Units sold   = 500

Black & Blue's breakeven point is 500 units a month. If it sells 500 skateboards a month, the company can cover its fixed costs.

The Unit-Contribution Method. The unit-contribution method also can be used to determine the number of units a company must sell to break even. The method is based on the idea that each unit sold contributes toward covering fixed expenses. To determine the number of units that must be sold to break even, then, we divide fixed costs by the contribution margin per unit:

Breakeven units = fixed costs ÷ unit contribution margin

According to Exhibit 3, Black & Blue generates an $8 contribution margin on each skateboard it sells. On that basis, the company has to sell 500 skateboards a month to break even:

Breakeven units = fixed costs ÷ unit contribution margin
                = $4,000 ÷ $8
                = 500 skateboards

The unit-contribution method also can be used to determine the breakeven point in sales dollars, the amount of sales in dollars at which a company covers its fixed costs:

Breakeven sales dollars = fixed costs ÷ contribution margin ratio

Black & Blue's contribution margin ratio is 40% (Exhibit 4). So the company must sell $10,000 in skateboards each month to break even:

Breakeven sales dollars = fixed costs ÷ contribution margin ratio
                        = $4,000 ÷ 40%
                        = $10,000

Target-Profit Analysis

CVP analysis also can be used to determine the sales (in units or dollars) necessary to earn a target profit. **A** *target profit* **is the profit that a company wants to make over a given period**.
    Suppose that Black & Blue wants to earn a profit of $2,000 a month. How many skateboards would it have to sell? One way to answer that question is to rework the breakeven-point equation, inserting target profit:

Target profit = (selling price per unit × units sold) −
                (variable cost per unit × units sold) − fixed costs
$2,000   = $20 × units sold − $12 × units sold − $4,000
$6,000   = $8 × units sold
Units sold = 750 skateboards

Black & Blue can earn its target profit by selling 750 skateboards a month.
    We can get the same answer using a variation of the unit-contribution method:

Units sold = (target profit + fixed costs) ÷ contribution margin
          = ($2,000 + $4,000) ÷ $8
          = $6,000 ÷ $8
          = 750 skateboards

Profit-Sensitivity Analysis

CVP analysis also answers questions about how profits would change if the selling price, the units sold, or costs change. An example: Right now Black & Blue is selling 750 skateboards for $20 apiece at a variable cost per skateboard of $12. Suppose that the company's management is thinking about lowering the selling price to $18, a change that should increase sales by 20%, and cutting the variable cost per unit to $11. Do the changes make sense in terms of the company's profits?

    To gauge the impact of the changes on profits, we can use the equation we used to determine the number of units the company would have to sell to earn its target profit. Here, though, we substitute profit for target profit:

Profit = (selling price per unit x units sold) −
       (variable cost per unit x units sold) − fixed costs
     = ($18 × 900)* − ($11 × 900) − $4,000
     = $16,200 − $9,900 − $4,000
     = $2,300
*** 900 units = 750 units × 1.20**

At the new selling price, the new sales volume, and the new variable cost per unit, Black & Blue's profit would go up $300 ($2,300 − $2,000).

Margin-of-Safety Analysis

A company's *margin of safety* **is the excess of sales over the breakeven point.** The margin of safety is the amount by which sales can fall before the company incurs a loss. It is a measure of the risk associated with the company's operations. To calculate the margin of safety in dollars, we use this formula:

Margin of safety dollars = sales dollars − breakeven sales dollars

Suppose that Black & Blue expects total sales for 1998 of $250,000 and that its breakeven point in sales dollars is $120,000. The company's margin of safety is $130,000 ($250,000 − $120,000). Even if sales fall $130,000, the company would still break even.

    Managers often state the margin of safety as a percentage or ratio. **The** *margin of safety ratio* **is the margin of safety dollars divided by total sales dollars:**

Margin of safety ratio = margin of safety dollars ÷ total sales dollars

Black & Blue's margin of safety ratio is 52% ($130,000 ÷ $250,000).

The margin of safety ratio answers the question "By what percentage can sales decrease and the company still break even?" A company with a low margin of safety ratio is operating closer to its margin of safety and so is at greater risk than is a company with a high margin of safety ratio.

For the margin of safety to be meaningful, it is important to know how and why sales vary. A $130,000 margin of safety may seem large in absolute dollars, but skateboard sales typically fall sharply during recessions. Black & Blue's managers should know how sales are likely to respond to different economic conditions. That means that the company's financial managers should consult with its marketing managers for estimates of future sales before concluding that the company's margin of safety is adequate. Second, Black & Blue's 52% margin of safety ratio is meaningful only if there's a *benchmark* against which to compare it. That benchmark could be a previous year's margin of safety ratio or an industry standard. By evaluating Black & Blue's ratio over time, management may be able to determine a trend. If the ratio is decreasing, the risk of not being able to break even is increasing. Management may need to take corrective action to avoid future losses.

SELF-STUDY PROBLEM 1

Calhoun Carpets is considering a new line of carpeting for boats. The carpet would cost $3.00 a yard to make and would sell for $10.00 a yard. Calhoun would have to build a new plant and buy new equipment—at an annual cost of $4.2 million—to produce the new line.

Required

1. How many yards of carpet would Calhoun have to sell annually to break even? What would the company's breakeven point in sales dollars be?
2. How many yards would the company have to sell to make a target profit of $700,000 on the line? What is the sales–dollars equivalent of that number of yards?
3. Calhoun's current margin of safety ratio is 25%. If the company sells the yards necessary to earn its target profit on the new line (see requirement 2), would its margin of safety ratio improve? Explain your answer.

The solution to Self-Study Problem 1 appears at the end of the chapter.

VARIABLE AND ABSORPTION COSTING: A COMPARISON

GAAP require that companies use absorption costing to develop their financial statements for external reporting. The Internal Revenue Service (IRS) requires the use of that method to determine federal tax liability. However, the choice of a method to use for internal purposes—to set the selling price of products and to evaluate a company's (and its managers') performance—is the company's. Some companies opt to use absorption costing for both external reporting and internal decision making. Other companies set up two accounting systems, using absorption costing for external reports and variable costing for internal reports.

The choice of an internal costing method affects both the unit product cost—a measure sometimes used to determine a product's selling price—and a company's net income—a performance measure.

Pricing Decisions: Unit Product Cost

A key measure in the pricing decision is the unit cost of the finished product—the unit product cost. That cost determines the value of finished goods inventory and, eventually, the cost of goods sold.

Remember that variable costing classifies costs by their behavior: variable or fixed. In calculating the unit product cost, variable costing uses only those costs that vary directly with production: the costs of direct materials, direct labor, and variable manufacturing overhead. Fixed manufacturing overhead costs are treated like period expenses. Like selling and administrative costs, those costs are expensed in the period in which they are incurred. The variable unit product cost never includes fixed costs.

Absorption costing, on the other hand, classifies costs by their function: manufacturing or nonmanufacturing. The unit product cost calculation using the absorption-costing method includes all the costs of manufacturing—variable and fixed. By definition, then, the variable unit product cost is always smaller than the absorption unit product cost. In the pages that follow, we look at the way each method determines unit product cost.

Objective 4
Calculate a unit product cost using variable costing.

The Variable-Costing Calculation. The variable unit product cost is a measurement that helps managers make decisions about cost-volume-profit relationships. For example, as you have just seen in the discussion of CVP analysis, the variable unit cost of a product is key to breakeven-point analysis, target-profit analysis, and profit-sensitivity analysis.

Exhibit 7 shows how variable costing is used to calculate unit costs.

Exhibit 7   Ply Wood Company: Calculating the Variable Product Cost per Unit

Number of units produced in the period	10,000
Variable costs per unit:	
Direct materials	$5
Direct labor	3
Variable manufacturing overhead	2
Variable administrative expenses	2
Fixed costs per period:	
Fixed manufacturing overhead	$50,000
Fixed administrative expenses	35,000
The variable unit product cost calculation:	
Direct materials costs per unit	$5
Direct labor costs per unit	3
Variable manufacturing overhead costs per unit	2
Total variable cost per unit	$10

Two things to remember: First, this unit cost is made up of variable costs only. Fixed costs are never part of the calculation. Second, the unit variable cost is a *product cost:* Only the costs of direct materials, direct labor, and manufacturing overhead are part of its calculation. Selling and administrative expenses—whether they are variable or fixed—are period expenses. Like fixed manufacturing overhead, they are recorded as expenses in the period in which they are incurred. The variable unit product cost times the number of units produced is recorded in Finished Goods Inventory and then charged to Cost of Goods Sold when the units are sold.

The Absorption-Costing Calculation. Absorption costing includes *all* production costs in the unit-cost calculations whether those costs are variable or fixed. So the

O b j e c t i v e   5
Calculate a unit product cost using absorption costing.

unit-cost calculation allocates fixed manufacturing overhead to each unit of product in addition to variable production costs. That means that the cost of each unit in finished goods inventory and the cost of goods sold has both variable and fixed components.

Exhibit 8 shows how costs are classified under variable and absorption costing.

Exhibit 8   Variable and Absorption Costing: Classifying Costs

Costs	Variable Costing	Absorption Costing
Direct materials	Product cost	Product cost
Direct labor	Product cost	Product cost
Variable manufacturing overhead	Product cost	Product cost
Fixed manufacturing overhead	Period expense	Product cost
Variable selling & administrative expenses	Period expense	Period expense
Fixed selling & administrative expenses	Period expense	Period expense

Notice that the only difference between the two methods is in the way each treats the costs of fixed manufacturing overhead.

Let's calculate a unit product cost using absorption costing from the information in Exhibit 7. The unit product cost for the period would be $15:

Direct materials costs per unit	$ 5
Direct labor costs per unit	3
Variable manufacturing overhead costs per unit	2
Fixed manufacturing overhead costs per unit*	5
Total cost per unit	$15

* $50,000 ÷ 10,000 units. See Exhibit 7.

Under the absorption-costing method, all production costs, both variable and fixed, are included in the unit product cost. The cost of one unit is carried in Finished Goods Inventory at $15 ($10 in variable costs and $5 in fixed costs). When the unit is sold, the company records $15 in the Cost of Goods Sold account.

Performance Evaluation: Net Income

O b j e c t i v e   6
Explain why net income differs under the variable- and absorption-costing methods.

Income using variable costing can differ from income using absorption costing. This difference is caused by changing finished goods inventory levels from period to period. Absorption-costing income is affected by changes in the ending inventory of finished goods. Variable-costing income is not affected by these changes. Note also that cost of goods sold using variable costing contains only the variable costs of manufacturing. This differs from cost of goods sold using absorption costing which contains both variable and fixed costs of manufacturing.

Exhibit 9 compares Ply Wood's income statements for January using the variable and absorption costing methods. Both statements are based on this information:

Direct materials costs per unit	$ 5
Direct labor costs per unit	$ 3
Variable manufacturing overhead costs per unit	$ 2
Fixed manufacturing overhead costs per unit ($50,000 ÷ 10,000 units)	$ 5
Unit selling price	$25
Units sold	8,000
Beginning finished goods inventory in units	0
Ending finished goods inventory in units	2,000
Administrative expenses	$35,000 fixed, $20,000 variable

Exhibit 9 Ply Wood Company: Income Statements for January

Absorption Costing

Sales (8,000 units × $25)	$200,000
Cost of goods sold (8,000 units × $15)	120,000
Gross margin	$ 80,000
Less administrative expenses ($35,000 fixed + $20,000 variable)	55,000
Net income	$ 25,000

Variable Costing

Sales (8,000 units × $25)	$200,000
Cost of goods sold (8,000 units × $10)	80,000
Gross margin	$120,000
Less administrative expenses ($35,000 fixed + $20,000 variable)	55,000
Less fixed manufacturing overhead costs	50,000
Net income	$ 15,000

Exhibit 9 shows a $10,000 ($25,000 − $15,000) difference in income between the two costing methods. That $10,000 difference is a function of the way the costs of fixed manufacturing overhead are treated. Using the absorption-costing method, the fixed overhead costs are carried as an asset in Finished Goods Inventory until the units are sold. Ply Wood produced 10,000 units (2,000 units in inventory + 8,000 units sold) in January; it sold just 8,000 units. The company assigned each of the 2,000 units in ending inventory $5 of fixed manufacturing overhead costs. That means $10,000 (2,000 × $5) of fixed manufacturing overhead costs remained in inventory until the units were sold.

Under the variable costing method, fixed manufacturing overhead is a period expense. The entire cost of fixed manufacturing overhead, $50,000, was deducted as an expense in the January period in which the costs were incurred. Again, using variable costing, all fixed overhead costs are recognized as expenses each period; no fixed overhead costs are recorded in inventory.

The differences in net income between the absorption- and variable-costing methods had to do with the level of finished goods. When the number of units in ending inventory *increases* from that of the *previous period*, net income reported under the absorption-costing method is *higher* than net income reported under the variable-costing method. When inventory *decreases*, however, net income reported under the absorption-costing method is *lower* than net income reported under the variable-costing method.

In January the number of units in Ply Wood's finished goods inventory increased over the previous month by 2,000 units. That increase translated into a higher net income using the absorption-costing method. Now let's look at what happens when the number of units in finished goods inventory falls from one period to the next. Exhibit 10 shows Ply Wood's income statements for February. Those statements are based on the following information:

Direct materials costs per unit	$ 5.00
Direct labor costs per unit	3.00
Variable manufacturing overhead costs per unit	2.00
Fixed manufacturing overhead costs per unit*	8.33
Total cost per unit	$18.33

* *$50,000 ÷ 6,000 units = $8.33.*

Unit selling price	$25
Units sold	8,000
Beginning finished inventory in units	2,000
Ending finished goods inventory in units	0

Exhibit 10   Ply Wood Company: Income Statements for February

Absorption Costing

Sales (8,000 units × $25)	$200,000
Cost of goods sold (6,000 units × $18.33) + (2,000 units × $15.00)	140,000
Gross margin	60,000
Less: administrative expenses ($35,000 fixed + $12,000 variable)	47,000
Net income	$ 13,000

Variable Costing

Sales (8,000 units × $25)	$200,000
Cost of goods sold (8,000 units × $10)	80,000
Gross margin	$120,000
Less administrative expenses ($35,000 fixed + $12,000 variable)	47,000
Less fixed manufacturing overhead costs	50,000
Net income	$ 23,000

The variable-costing net income was $10,000 ($23,000 − $13,000) higher than absorption-costing net income. In February, Ply Wood sold 8,000 units but produced just 6,000 units. The $10,000 difference in income for February ($13,000 versus $23,000) can be explained by the treatment of fixed manufacturing overhead cost. All 2,000 of the units in beginning inventory (from January) were sold in February, in addition to the 6,000 units produced in February. Because Ply Wood produced just 6,000 units in February, the $50,000 fixed manufacturing overhead costs for February were spread over 2,000 fewer units than in January. This means that under absorption costing, Ply Wood expensed the following fixed overhead:

January production:	2,000 units × $5.00 = $10,000
February production:	6,000 units × $8.33 = $50,000*
	$60,000

Rounded.

Under variable costing Ply Wood expensed the $50,000 in fixed overhead incurred in February. The difference between the $60,000 fixed overhead expenses under absorption costing and the $50,000 under variable costing explains the difference in the income figures between the two costing methods. Notice that the variable-costing net income was not affected by the change in the level of inventory. That is because variable costing treats fixed overhead costs as a period expense.

If manufacturing costs are constant (i.e., inventory levels do not change from the beginning to the end of a period) and production equals sales, variable costing and absorption costing produce the same net income. But production costs, inventory levels, and sales in a manufacturing company usually vary over time. That means that the methods should produce different income numbers from period to period. That difference can lead to important differences in managers' decisions, a subject considered in the next section.

SELF-STUDY PROBLEM 2

Kokomo Manufacturing Company produces a single product, model airplanes. Here is a list of selected cost and operating data for last year:

©Gary Hayes, 1991/PNI International

Beginning finished goods inventory in units	0
Units produced during the year	15,000
Units sold during the year	13,500
Ending finished goods inventory in units	1,500
Selling price per unit	$60
Manufacturing costs:	
Variable costs per unit:	
Direct materials	$20
Direct labor	12
Variable manufacturing overhead	8
Fixed manufacturing overhead	$60,000
Selling and administrative expenses:	
Variable costs per unit sold	$5
Fixed expenses	$50,000

Required

1. Assuming that Kokomo uses absorption costing, compute the inventory cost per unit, and prepare an income statement for the year using a *traditional format*.
2. Assuming that the company uses variable costing, compute the product cost per unit, and prepare an income statement for the year showing the *contribution margin*.
3. Explain the difference between the variable-costing and absorption-costing net income figures.
4. Assuming that Kokomo had finished goods in inventory at the beginning of the year, what would have happened to the company's net income if the number of units sold during the period had been greater than the number of units produced? Explain your answer.

The solution to Self-Study Problem 2 appears at the end of the chapter.

CHOOSING BETWEEN VARIABLE COSTING AND ABSORPTION COSTING

O b j e c t i v e   7
Explain how variable and absorption costing can be used in managerial decision making and the pros and cons of each method.

GAAP require that absorption costing be used to prepare external reports. But managers can choose between variable and absorption costing for internal reports. Which method is a better basis for managerial decision making? There is no simple answer to that question. The answer depends on the type of decision being made and the context in which it is made. This section discusses the pros and cons of each method.

Remember that the difference between absorption and variable costing is in the way the methods treat fixed overhead costs. GAAP require absorption costing because of the matching principle. Expenses should match the revenues with which they are associated. That means all product costs—including fixed costs—are assets until the units created by those costs are sold.

Arguments For and Against Variable Costing

Many accountants argue that variable costing is more accurate than absorption costing because it treats fixed overhead as a period expense. They insist that it is theoretically wrong to inventory fixed costs because most fixed costs are incurred whether or not any products are produced during a period. Another argument for variable costing is the usefulness of variable-cost information in certain types of analyses, like breakeven-point analysis and target-profit analysis. Variable costing clarifies the cost-volume-profit relationship.

Exhibit 11 shows the logic behind variable costing.[1] Sales revenue flows into a company much like water flows into a series of tanks. In the first tank, some of the revenue flow is drawn off to cover variable expenses. What remains—the contribution margin—fills a second tank, representing fixed costs. Any revenue greater than that needed to cover fixed costs spills over into a third tank, representing profit. In other words, profit is that revenue flow that remains after the flow that equals total costs has been drawn off.

Exhibit 11   Variable Costing: The Revenue Flow

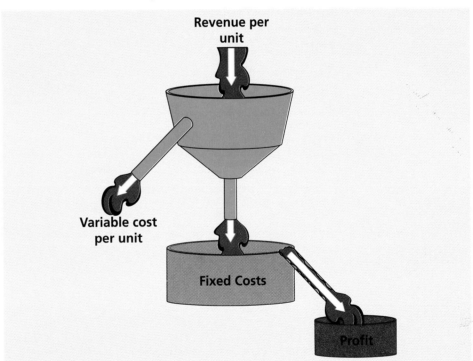

The picture shows that any sale that more than covers the variable costs of the units sold contributes to fixed costs and profit. If decision makers think of each sale independently from all other sales, any sale that covers its variable costs is good because it increases the company's contribution margin. But there are two difficulties with that

[1]   *This discussion and the figure are adapted from John K. Shank and Vijay Govindarajan,* Strategic Cost Analysis: The Evolution from Managerial to Strategic Accounting, *(Richard D. Irwin, © 1989) p. 27.*

logic. First, in the long run a company must cover its fixed costs and make a profit or it cannot survive. If an airline's average ticket price doesn't cover the fixed costs of buying airplanes, the company is not going to be able to replace its planes when they wear out. Second, often one sale is not independent of other sales. Airline customers who have flown on discount tickets that just cover variable costs are more likely to shop for low-priced tickets in the future. That makes it important for the airline to sell full-priced tickets. That also makes it difficult for the airline to cover its fixed expenses and make the profit it needs to stay in business.

To better understand the contribution fallacy, think about the discount fares that airlines offer to fill otherwise vacant seats. Airlines have high fixed costs: Planes are expensive to buy and maintain. The industry also has faced excess capacity (more seats than it can fill) for several decades. Airlines can increase the contribution margin of a flight by selling discounted tickets at any price greater than the variable cost of each additional passenger. Airlines, then, have an incentive to cut their fares and fill vacant seats. Many of them do just that, offering nonrefundable discounted tickets that must be purchased in advance. In some cases, the price of those tickets is below the absorption cost (all the variable and fixed costs) of offering passenger service.

Suppose that the costs of a particular flight are $40,000 plus $20 per passenger and that the flight can accommodate 200 passengers. If the regular ticket price for the flight is $420, the breakeven point is 100 passengers:

Breakeven sales	= total variable cost + fixed costs
Selling price per unit × units sold	= (variable cost per unit × units sold) + fixed costs
$420 × units sold	= ($20 × units sold) + $40,000
$400 × units sold	= $40,000
Units sold	= 100

Let's say that the airline usually sells 120 tickets for the flight. On average, then, the company earns $8,000 on this flight:

Average sales revenue ($420 × 120)	$50,400
Less average costs [($20 × 120) + $40,000]	42,400
Average profit	$ 8,000

Suppose that by offering discounted tickets at $200 each, the airline can sell an additional 50 tickets on this flight. The contribution margin for each of the discounted tickets would be $180 ($200 sales revenue − $20 variable cost). Therefore the company's profit would go up $9,000 ($180 contribution margin × 50 tickets).

But profit is not the only factor the airline's management should consider. Also important is the effect of discounted tickets on customers' buying habits. Over time, many customers have come to expect discounted tickets and buy them routinely, making it difficult for airlines to discontinue the discounted fares. In the long run, then, discounted fares have reduced profit for many airlines and probably have contributed to the failure of some of them. By not pricing tickets to recover the absorption cost of their operations and to make a reasonable profit, airlines have created a profitability problem for their entire industry.

Here's how it works. Suppose that the discounted fares lead to a change in customers' behavior. Now the airline can sell only 70 seats on average at the regular price. It also can sell 80 seats on average at the discounted price. Look at what happens:

Average sales revenue:
Full-priced tickets ($420 × 70 passengers)	$29,400	
Discounted tickets ($200 × 80 passengers)	16,000	
		$45,400

Less average cost:
Variable costs ($20 × 150 passengers)	$ 3,000	
Fixed costs	40,000	
		43,000
Average profit		$ 2,000

The company's average profit is only $2,000, $6,000 less than it was before the company began offering the discounted tickets.

Critics of variable costing argue that the method contributes to tactical (short-run) instead of strategic (long-run) thinking. They insist that managers who fail to see that sales are related to one another are not thinking about the long-term effects of pricing on their company. Those critics claim that the tactical thinking that variable costing encourages has been the downfall of some companies.

Learning Note | Many managers believe that variable-cost information is key to assessing the impact on profit of routine product-pricing decisions. Because fixed costs do not change in the short run with changes in volume or product mix, those managers feel that the best way to maximize profit is to maximize the contribution margin. In concept they are right, but as a practical matter that concept often does not work very well. In intensely competitive markets, variable costing is sometimes just an excuse to charge lower prices that over the long run fail to generate an acceptable return on investment.

Despite the contribution fallacy, variable costing and the contribution method can be helpful when managers understand how they should be used. For instance, it may be fine to price above variable cost but below absorption cost in selling a one-time order in a market in which a company normally does not do business. It can be very dangerous, however, to set prices this way in markets in which the company routinely does business. Variable costing also is useful in profit-sensitivity analysis (to determine the effect on profits as sales go up or down) and breakeven-point analysis (to measure operating risk). The key to its usefulness is remembering that variable costing can lead to decisions that seem good in the short run but create serious problems in the long run.

Arguments For and Against Absorption Costing

Because absorption costing is required by GAAP for external reporting, some companies also use it for internal decision making. Those companies do save money by investing in just one accounting system. However, cost-volume-profit decisions are more difficult using absorption costing. Ultimately, those companies are trading off the usefulness of information against its costs.

Supporters of absorption costing argue that it produces better strategic decisions in most areas. One area in which absorption costing can create problems, however, is in evaluating managers' performance.

The absorption-costing method gives managers an incentive to overproduce. Using absorption costing, managers can increase the net income figure by producing more units of product in a given period than are needed for sales and by keeping those units in finished goods inventory. Producing more units than needed spreads the fixed overhead costs over more units and reduces the cost per unit of finished product. Because the cost per unit is lower, less cost is expensed for units sold, and reported net income goes up.

An example: Steel Pot Company sells its small roasting pan for $20 a unit. The pan has variable costs of $10 a unit. The company's fixed costs are $10,000 a month. Steel Pot's breakeven point is 1,000 units a month:

Breakeven sales = total variable costs + fixed costs
$20 × units sold = ($10 × units sold) + $10,000
Units sold   = 1,000

Suppose that the company produces and sells 1,200 units in March. The fixed cost per unit would be $8.33 ($10,000 ÷ 1,200 units). The profit for the month would be $2,000:

Sales revenue ($20 × 1,200 units sold)		$24,000
Less total costs:		
Variable costs ($10 × 1,200 units sold)	$12,000	
Fixed costs	10,000	22,000
Net income		$ 2,000

Any evaluation of management's performance in March would be based on a $2,000 profit.

Now suppose that management had decided to produce 1,400 units in March, still expecting to sell 1,200 units. The fixed costs per unit would be $7.14 ($10,000 ÷ 1,400 units). The 200 units in inventory at the end of the month would have a value of $1,428 ($7.14 × 200). Look at what happens to the company's profit:

Sales revenue ($20 × 1,200 units sold)		$24,000
Less total costs:		
Variable costs ($10 × 1,200 units sold)	$12,000	
Fixed costs ($10,000 − $1,428)	8,572	20,572
Net income		$ 3,428

The company's profit is higher by the amount of fixed cost allocated to finished goods inventory, and management's performance seems much better. But the net income figure is an illusion, the result of more production, not more sales.

That net income is an illusion is one problem. That a company incurs real costs from inventory is another. It is expensive to carry inventory. A company has to pay for handling, storing, and insuring the finished goods. When those costs are added to the costs of management bonuses and other profit-linked compensation, overproduction can jeopardize the long-run profitability and even the survival of a company. A company has to be careful in using accounting information to evaluate managerial performance so that it is not creating incentives that could damage its welfare or that of its owners.

Ultimately, a company should exercise the same care in using absorption costing as it should in using variable costing. Neither method is without problems. Anytime accounting information is used carelessly, it can and often does lead to bad decisions.

MEASURING COSTS FOR DECISION MAKING IN SERVICE COMPANIES

Objective 8
Explain why costs are important for decision making in service companies.

Cost information is as important for service companies as it is for manufacturers. A bank, for example, has to know how much it costs to execute a particular transaction or provide a particular service in order to price that transaction or service. The cost of a car loan is more than the amount being borrowed. The loan application has to be printed and processed, the amount has to be updated each month, and a bad-debt assessment and the bank's target profit have to be included in the pricing.

The process of measuring costs in service organizations is often more complex than in manufacturing organizations. Two factors are at work here: First, services do not have the tangible, physical nature of products. It is much easier to trace the costs of materials and labor to a physical object than it is to trace costs to a particular service and the transactions that make up that service. Second, services often require many transactions that are carried out by a number of departments. The same employees may work on many different services. Again, this makes it difficult to determine the cost associated with a particular transaction and to trace the cost of that transaction to a particular service.

The following Case in Point demonstrates two important aspects of using costs to make decisions in service organizations: (1) the difficulty of tracing costs to services and (2) the way in which costing decisions can influence pricing, marketing, and operations.

SELF-STUDY PROBLEM 3

Sno–Blo Company manufactures several models of snowblowers. It markets the machines through its own franchise stores, which are scattered throughout the northern half of the country but are concentrated in the Northeast.

Sno–Blo has been approached by a large discount chain, Retail Warehouse Unlimited (RWU), Inc., with a one-time offer to buy 1,000 model X321 blowers. RWU has stores throughout the Midwest. The discounter is offering Sno–Blo a unit price of $80. At that price, it wants Sno–Blo to paint the machines a special color and sten-

©'92 Clark Mishler/The Stock Market

cil RWU's logo on them—processes that Sno-Blo's management expects would cost $10 per machine. Sno-Blo sells the model X321 for $200 a unit; RWU would sell the snowblower for considerably less.

Here is current cost and production information about the model-X321 snowblower:

Finished goods inventory on hand in units	2,000
Expected sales over the next 3 months in units	1,000
Production capacity over the next 3 months in units	1,000
Variable cost per unit	$50
Fixed cost per unit	$60

Required

Discuss the pros and cons of Sno-Blo's agreeing to the sale. If you were a manager at Sno-Blo, would you be for or against the sale? Explain your answer.

The solution to Self-Study Problem 3 appears at the end of the chapter.

In 1980, **First National Bank,** a bank, and **Home Federal Savings,** a savings and loan (S & L) association, were considering how to price a new service, a checking account that pays interest, called a NOW (negotiable order of withdrawal) account. In the past, the bank had offered checking accounts, but they did not pay interest. Based on cost estimates, the bank set a minimum balance of $2,200 for NOW accounts. The S&L set its minimum balance at $800. Why were the amounts so different?

In its estimates, the bank included all indirect costs of doing business. For example, it developed a charge for heating the building used by the customer service representatives who, in addition to their other duties, would handle customer's inquiries about their NOW accounts. Citing the difficulty of accurately estimating certain indirect costs, the S&L's management chose to ignore any indirect costs that it could not estimate easily. The result was that the bank's estimate of the NOW account costs was much higher than the S&L's.

The bank subsequently lost a great deal of its checking account business, but it continued to be very profitable. The S&L got many new accounts but was less profitable.

Which institution made the best pricing decision? It is difficult to say. The bank may have included costs that it should not have included. The S&L may have excluded too many costs. Arguably both benefited from their pricing decisions. But clearly the process of measuring costs to make decisions in service companies is not an easy one.

R E V I E W   *Summary of Important Concepts*

1. Companies can use two different methods to assign product cost.
    a. The variable-costing method classifies costs by behavior, breaking costs down into variable and fixed components.
    b. The absorption-costing method classifies costs by function, manufacturing and non-manufacturing.

2. Key to variable costing is contribution margin, the difference between sales and variable expenses over a period. Profit is the contribution margin less fixed expenses.

3. The variable-costing method helps managers understand the relationship among costs, volume, and profits, an understanding that is basic to breakeven-point analysis, target-profit analysis, profit-sensitivity analysis, and margin-of-safety analysis.

4. Both variable and absorption costing can be used to calculate unit product cost, an important element in a company's pricing decisions.
    a. Using variable costing, only those production costs that vary with volume are included in the unit product cost calculation.
    b. Using absorption costing, all product costs—fixed and variable—are part of the unit product cost calculation.
    c. The difference in the value of finished goods inventory between variable and absorption costing is a function of the way the methods treat fixed overhead costs.
        (1) Variable costing expenses all fixed costs in the period in which they are incurred.
        (2) Absorption costing holds fixed overhead costs in inventory until the products are sold.

5. The way in which the methods treat inventory also has an impact on the net income figure each produces—a factor in the evaluation of managerial performance.

6. Variable costing is a managerial tool.
    a. Its proponents insist that it is more accurate than absorption costing and that it is critical to managerial decisions about costs, volume, and profits.
    b. Its critics argue that it is a tactical decision-making tool, useful only for making short-run decisions.

7. Absorption costing must be used for financial reporting. Some companies also use absorption costing for internal decision making.
   a. Absorption costing can be more effective than variable costing for strategic decision making.
   b. One limitation of the method is that it can create an incentive for overproduction.

8. Service organizations, like manufacturing companies, rely on variable or absorption costing to make managerial decisions, particularly decisions about pricing.

D E F I N E *Terms and Concepts Defined in This Chapter*

Absorption costing   (112)
Breakeven point   (114)
Contribution margin   (112)
Contribution margin
  (or profit-volume) ratio   (114)

Cost-volume-profit (CVP) analysis
  (114)
Margin of safety   (118)
Margin of safety ratio   (118)

Target profit   (117)
Variable costing   (112)
Variable-costing income statement
  (113)

S O L U T I O N S

SELF-STUDY PROBLEM 1

1. Calhoun would have to sell 600,000 yards to break even:

   Unit contribution margin = $10 − $3
                            = $7 per yard
   Breakeven units   = $4,200,000 ÷ $7
                            = 600,000 yards

   The company's breakeven point in sales dollars would be $6 million (600,000 units sold × $10).

2. Calhoun would have to sell 700,000 yards of the carpet to earn a target profit of $700,000:

   ($700,000 + $4,200,000) ÷ $7 = 700,000 yards

   In sales dollars, sales of 700,000 yards equal $7 million (700,000 yards × $10).

3. Assuming that Calhoun reaches its target profit of $700,000, the margin of safety ratio on the new line is 14.29%:

   $7,000,000 − $6,000,000 = $1,000,000 margin of safety dollars
   $1,000,000 ÷ $7,000,000 = 0.1429
                           = 14.29%

   If Calhoun's margin of safety ratio is currently 25%, the new line would lower, not raise, the company's margin of safety ratio.

SELF-STUDY PROBLEM 2

1. Using absorption costing, both fixed and variable manufacturing costs are included in the unit product cost. The unit product cost is $44:

Direct materials costs per unit	$20
Direct labor costs per unit	12
Variable manufacturing overhead costs per unit	8
Fixed manufacturing overhead costs per unit	
($60,000 ÷ 15,000 units)	4
Total cost per unit	$44

The absorption-costing income statement looks like this:

Sales revenue (13,500 × $60)	$810,000
Less cost of goods sold (13,500 × $44)	594,000
Gross margin	$216,000
Less selling and administrative expenses*	117,500
Net Income	$ 98,500

*Variable selling and administrative	
expenses (13,500 units sold × $5)	$ 67,500
Fixed selling and administrative expenses	50,000
Total selling and administrative expenses	$117,500

2. Using variable costing, only variable product costs are included in the unit cost. The unit product cost is $40:

Direct materials	$20
Direct labor	12
Variable manufacturing overhead	8
Total cost per unit	$40

The income statement looks like this:

Sales revenue (13,500 × $60)		$810,000
Less variable expenses:		
Variable cost of goods sold (13,500 × $40)	$540,000	
Variable selling and administrative		
expenses (13,500 × $5)	67,500	
Total variable expenses		607,500
Contribution margin		$202,500
Less fixed expenses:		
Fixed manufacturing overhead	$ 60,000	
Fixed selling and administrative expenses	50,000	
Total fixed expenses		110,000
Net income		$ 92,500

3. Kokomo's absorption-costing net income ($98,500) is $6,000 more than the variable costing net income ($92,500). That difference equals the fixed overhead costs of the units that remained in finished goods inventory at the end of the year under the absorption-costing method:

   1,500 units in finished goods inventory × $4 fixed manufacturing overhead costs per unit = $6,000

4. If Kokomo had sold more units than it produced during the year, the absorption-costing net income would have been less than the variable-costing net income. Using absorption

costing, a company's selling more units than it has produced has the effect of releasing fixed overhead costs that were deferred in previous periods.

SELF-STUDY PROBLEM 3

One possibility is to use contribution-margin logic, to consider RWU's proposal a one-time special order that will not affect other sales. If the order promises a positive contribution margin, the order should be accepted. Sno-Blo would be justified in looking at the proposal as a special order and using the variable costing method. RWU is not a regular customer and generally does not do business in the same region of the country as most of Sno-Blo's franchisees. Furthermore, Sno-Blo has the ability to fill RWU's order and meet its regular demand:

Finished goods inventory on hand	2,000 blowers	
Productive capacity over next 3 months	3,000 blowers	
Total available over next 3 months		5,000 blowers
Regular demand over next 3 months	3,000 blowers	
Special order	1,000 blowers	
Total required over next 3 months		4,000 blowers
Excess of supply over demand		1,000 blowers

Would the order generate a positive contribution margin?

Sales revenues (1,000 blowers × $80)		$80,000
Less variable costs:		
Cost of manufacturing blowers (1,000 blowers × $50)	$50,000	
Cost of painting blowers (1,000 blowers × $10)	10,000	
Total variable cost		60,000
Contribution margin		$20,000

Because the contribution margin is positive, Sno-Blo should accept the order based on variable costing logic.

On the other hand, there are reasons that Sno-Blo might not want to use variable costing in making this decision. First, there would be some competitive overlap between RWU and Sno-Blo's franchisees, even if it is small. That presents both a moral and a marketing problem for Sno-Blo. RWU is a discount chain and probably would undersell Sno-Blo's franchisees in the areas where they do compete with each other. In effect, Sno-Blo would be undercutting its own franchisees' sales, an action that certainly would damage Sno-Blo's relationship with its franchisees. Even franchisees that would not be affected by the sale might be upset for fear that Sno-Blo would do the same thing in their areas. In the worst case: Some of Sno-Blo's franchisees might look to align themselves with other franchises. The end result: By selling RWU the machines, Sno-Blo will damage its marketing distribution channels.

While Sno-Blo would recover its variable costs on the RWU order, it would not recover its absorption cost ($120). If Sno-Blo accepts the order and RWU does well with the machines, the discounter may ask for the same terms again. At this point, if Sno-Blo refuses, RWU may turn to another snowblower manufacturer. Further, some of Sno-Blo's franchisees may ask for similar terms in order to compensate for lost sales. By lowering its price on the model X321 to accommodate RWU, Sno-Blo may weaken the market price for the model X321 blower.

In light of these strategic marketing factors, the RWU order does not look nearly as good as it does using contribution-margin logic. In this case, the risk to Sno-Blo of accepting RWU's proposal is too great. The company should turn the offer down.

EXERCISES

4-1. Write a short definition of each of the terms listed in *Terms and Concepts Defined in This Chapter* section.

Obj. 1

4-2. Jane Pratt is the president of Capital Products, Inc. Capital manufactures adjustable baseball caps embroidered with the logos of college teams. The company is planning to produce a special hat with the logo of a university that recently won the national football championship. The hats will be sold throughout the country over the next three months. After meeting with the managers of sales, production, and purchasing, Jane has determined that the special hat will have a positive contribution margin of $1.50. Capital currently is earning a profit for the year. What does the contribution margin represent? Why is it important to Jane?

Obj. 1

4-3. Taylor, Inc. produces a child's wall clock that chimes the tune "Three Blind Mice" every hour. The contribution margin for this clock is $8, and the breakeven point is 8,000 units. How much profit will Taylor make if it sells 11,000 clocks?

Obj. 1

4-4. Ampco Industries, Inc., produces audio and video circuit boards. Ampco sold 12,500 circuit boards last month, its breakeven point in sales units. Explain what the breakeven point is.

Obj. 2

4-5. Grabill Cabinet Company manufactures a single model of bathroom cabinet. The company's contribution margin ratio is 40%. Grabill is considering an advertising campaign that would cost $8,000 but is expected to increase sales by $21,000. Should Grabill buy the advertising? Explain your answer.

Obj. 2

4-6. Snow Manufacturing Company produces a snowshoe that is sold in many parts of the upper Midwest. The company's production manager has decided to change the materials used in the production process, a change that should produce a savings in direct materials costs of $12 per pair of snowshoes. The sales manager has decided to pass the savings on to the customer by reducing the selling price of the snowshoes $12 a pair. What effect will these changes have on Snow's breakeven point in units?

Obj. 2

4-7. Assume that a company that is operating above its breakeven point increases the selling price of its product without changing its fixed or variable costs. Also assume that the number of units sold stays the same. What effect would the change in selling price have on the company's margin of safety?

Objs. 2,3

4-8. Slinko, Inc. manufactures costume jewelry. The company's total sales last year were $2 million; its breakeven point was $1.2 million. What was Slinko's margin of safety? What does a margin of safety represent?

Objs. 1,4

4-9. The calculation of contribution margin is consistent with the variable method of inventory valuation since deduction of the variable cost of production from revenue will provide the contribution margin. Do you agree with the statement? Explain your answer.

Objs. 4,5

4-10. Hendee Productions Company does personal and commercial videotaping. Hendee accumulates the cost of each video production on a per-job basis using the variable-costing method. Pete Conrad, the owner of the company, recently noticed that selling and administrative expenses are not included in the costs of production. Pete is considering a switch to absorption costing. Would selling and administrative expenses be treated differently under absorption costing? Explain your answer.

Objs. 4,5 **4-11.** Sam Merchant was recently hired as a cost accountant by Dolls and Such Manufacturing. The controller has asked Sam to review the company's inventory records and to convert the carrying value of each item in inventory from an absorption-costing value to a variable-costing value. What differences does Sam have to consider in making his calculations?

Obj. 6 **4-12.** Over the past year, Darren, Inc. has seen its finished goods inventory go up significantly. Darren prepares financial statements for its stockholders using absorption costing. The company prepares another set of financial statements for its managers using variable costing. Which of the two statements is going to show a greater net income for the year? Why?

Obj. 6 **4-13.** Juanita Perez is the president of Allgood Manufacturing, Inc. Allgood manufactures electric power tools. The company uses the absorption-costing method. Over the past year, sales increased significantly at Allgood, reducing the company's inventories 60% from the beginning of the year. When she looked at the year's sales figures, Juanita was surprised that net income was lower than anticipated. What factors might have been at work here?

Obj. 6 **4-14.** Suppose that the number of units in a company's ending inventory equals the number of units in its beginning inventory and that its fixed costs have not changed from the previous year. Which costing method—variable or absorption costing—would yield a higher net income?

Obj. 7 **4-15.** Coyote Battery Company manufactures rechargeable nickel cadmium batteries. The company uses the variable-costing method to accumulate inventory costs. At the end of its fiscal year, Coyote has to prepare its financial statements and tax returns. Can Coyote use its inventory values for financial-reporting and tax purposes? Explain your answer.

Obj. 7 **4-16.** Jan and Fran Hook are hairdressers with over 40 years of experience between them. Recently they decided to combine their savings and buy a factory to produce men's hairpieces. Jan has assumed responsibility for administration, including the development of accounting procedures. Fran does not understand why the inventory value of a hairpiece should include plant and supervisory costs. How should Jan explain the process of placing a value on inventory to Fran?

Obj. 7 **4-17.** The controller of Dynaco, Inc., Rodney Jones, made this statement: "I prefer to use the absorption-costing method of inventory valuation because it requires less work than the variable-costing method." What do you think Rodney meant?

Objs. 5,6,7 **4-18.** Explain how absorption costing defers certain costs and how that deferral is in line with the matching principle. What costs are affected by the postponement?

Objs. 6,7 **4-19.** Randy Lightfoot is vice president of operations for MultiCo, Inc. He is responsible for the operations of the company's two manufacturing plants, one in Atlanta and one in St. Louis. Each plant has a manager who oversees the daily operations. During a recent review of operations for the year, prepared using absorption costing, Randy noted that the Atlanta plant reported net income and that the balance in finished goods inventory had grown significantly over the year. The St. Louis plant showed no net income, but its inventory fell over the year. According to MultiCo's policy, the Atlanta plant manager will receive a bonus this year based on the income generated at the plant; the St. Louis manager will not receive a bonus. Comment on Randy's observation. What conflicts are created when a company determines its managers' bonuses based on net income alone?

Objs. 6,7 **4-20.** Ruth Peevey is president of Tuffee Tools Company. Tuffee manufactures a wide variety of hand tools and sells them throughout the South. Ruth just completed a review of next year's budget and plans, which project an operating loss. Knowing that Tuffee's stockholders and the bank that is financing the company will not be happy with an operating loss, Ruth has asked the company's controller to recalculate next year's predetermined overhead rate to include 50% of all budgeted administrative costs. What problems does this create for the controller? Should the controller make the changes?

PROBLEMS

PROBLEM 4-1 **Contribution-Margin Income Statement**

Obj. 1

Double R Company's most recent income statement, prepared on a contribution-margin basis, is as follows:

	Total	Per Unit
Sales	$500,000	$25
Less variable costs	360,000	18
Contribution margin	$140,000	$ 7
Less fixed costs	110,000	
Net income	$ 30,000	

Required

Prepare a new income statement under each of the following independent conditions:

a. Sales volume increases 20%.
b. The selling price drops $4 per unit, and sales volume increases 30%.
c. The selling price increases $2, fixed costs increase $10,000, and sales volume decreases 5%.
d. The selling price increases 20%, variable costs increase $2 per unit, and fixed costs increase 20%.
e. Variable costs increase $2 per unit, and fixed costs decrease by $40,000.

PROBLEM 4-2 **Basic CVP Relationships and Analysis**

Objs. 1,2

Justin Company manufactures a product that sells for $25 a unit. Its variable costs are $13 per unit, and its fixed costs are $120,000 per year.

Required

a. What is the product's contribution margin ratio?
b. What is the breakeven point in sales dollars?
c. Assume that sales go up $50,000 next year. If fixed costs do not change, how does that increase affect net income (or net loss)?
d. Assume that Justin's operating results last year were as follows:

Sales revenue	$300,000
Less variable costs	156,000
Contribution margin	$144,000
Less fixed costs	120,000
Net income	$ 24,000

What was the company's margin of safety and margin of safety ratio?
e. If Justin spends $30,000 on advertising, sales should go up $60,000. If the increased sales do not change the company's contribution margin, should Justin buy the advertising?

PROBLEM 4-3 **Ethics and CVP Analysis**

Obj. 2

Nathan Dechter is the controller of Specialty Candies, Inc., a manufacturer of candies and confections. The company's executive planning committee has asked Nathan to prepare an analysis of two alternatives the committee is considering. The first alternative is labor-intensive. Nathan's analysis revealed the following:

Sales revenue (projected at 6,000,000 units)	$1,800,000
Less variable costs	1,000,000
Contribution margin	$ 800,000
Less fixed costs	600,000
Net income	$ 200,000

The second alternative would automate the factory, increasing fixed costs and reducing variable costs:

Sales revenue (projected at 6,000,000 units)	$1,800,000
Less variable costs	800,000
Contribution margin	$1,000,000
Less fixed costs	800,000
Net income	$ 200,000

Before sharing his analysis with the executive planning committee, Nathan thought about the probable outcome of the committee's decision making. He knows that if the committee decides to automate the plant, many of his friends in the production department will lose their jobs. Although both alternatives yield net income of $200,000 at the projected level of sales, Nathan is afraid that management will opt for automation. Nathan could recalculate depreciation using a method that would increase fixed costs in the short run, which would encourage management to reject the automation alternative.

Required

a. Is there an argument that Nathan could make to support the labor-intensive alternative without manipulating the financial data? (*Hint:* Calculate the breakeven point and margin of safety for each alternative.)

b. Do you think Nathan should alter the fixed costs of the automation alternative? Would that be ethical? Would the manipulation be justified if it helps a number of employees keep their jobs? Why or why not?

PROBLEM 4-4   Breakeven Point, Cost Structure, and Target Sales

Objs. 1,2,3

Plainfield Bakers, Inc., manufactures and sells a popular line of fat-free cookies under the name Aunt May's Cookies. The process Plainfield uses to manufacture the cookies is labor-intensive; it relies heavily on direct labor. Last year Plainfield sold 300,000 dozen cookies at $2.50 per dozen. Variable costs at this level of production totaled $1.50 per dozen, and fixed costs for the year totaled $150,000.

Required

a. Prepare a contribution-margin income statement for last year.

b. Calculate the company's contribution margin ratio and breakeven point in sales units for last year.

c. Calculate the company's margin of safety and margin of safety ratio for last year.

d. Plainfield's direct labor rate is going to go up $0.40 a dozen next year. Assuming that the selling price stays at $2.50 a dozen, calculate next year's contribution margin and breakeven point in sales units.

e. Plainfield's management is thinking about automating the production process, a change that would reduce variable costs by $0.60 a dozen but would raise fixed costs by $150,000 a year. If the company undertakes the automation project, how would its contribution margin and breakeven point in sales units be affected?

f. Assuming that Plainfield does go ahead with the automation project (see requirement e), how many dozen cookies would the company have to sell at $2.50 a dozen to earn the same income it earned last year?

PROBLEM 4-5 **Variable Costing and Breakeven-Point Analysis**

Objs. 1,2,3

Penquin Industries, Inc., manufactures a variety of plastic food containers and serving dishes. Here is the company's income statement for this year in a variable-costing format:

Sales revenue	$960,000
Less variable production costs	192,000
Less variable selling expenses	96,000
Contribution margin	$672,000
Less fixed manufacturing overhead	300,000
Less fixed selling expenses	139,000
Net income	$233,000

Penquin's management believes that it can increase prices by an average of 6% next year without affecting the number of products sold. Advertising costs are expected to go up next year by $9,000; administrative expenses, by $30,000. Production costs are not expected to change.

Required

a. Calculate Penquin's breakeven point in sales dollars for this year.
b. Use the estimates for next year to prepare a variable-costing income statement for that year.
c. Using the forecasted changes, calculate Penquin's breakeven point in sales dollars for next year.

PROBLEM 4-6 **Graphing the Cost-Volume-Profit Relationship**

Objs. 1,2,3

Below are two CVP graphs and cost information for two unrelated companies, each of which manufactures a single product.

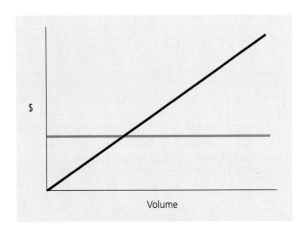

Company A
Fixed Costs = $400,000
Sales =$150 per unit
Contribution margin = $20 per unit

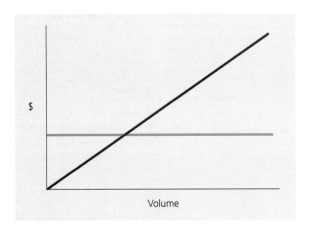

Company B
Fixed Costs = $400,000
Sales =$150 per unit
Contribution margin = $40 per unit

Required

a. Complete each graph by adding a total-cost line and the breakeven point, and by labeling each of the CVP graph lines.
b. Calculate the variable unit product cost for each company.
c. Calculate the breakeven point in sales units for each company.
d. Why are the companies' breakeven points different when both sell their products for the same price? How is that difference reflected in the CVP graphs in requirement a?

PROBLEM 4-7   Interpreting a CVP Graph

Objs. 2,3

The CVP graph below shows the relationships in one company among costs, volume, and profits:

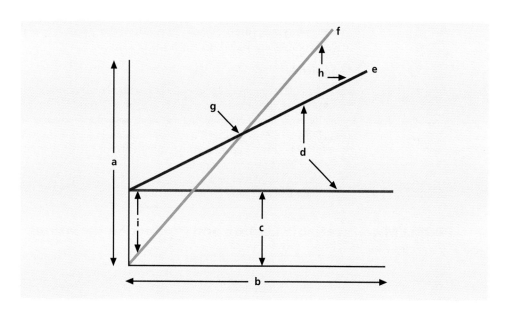

Required

a. Label each of the lettered elements on the graph.
b. List the lettered elements in the graph that would be affected by each of the following actions and the nature of the effect. Treat each case independently. Ignore the effect on element h.
   (1) The selling price per unit goes down from $50 to $45.
   (2) Variable costs per unit go up from $18 to $23.
   (3) Fixed costs fall $3,000.
   (4) Sales volume goes up 1,500 units.
   (5) The company sells a piece of production equipment, increasing labor hours and reducing fixed costs.
   (6) Both variable costs and the selling price go up 10%.
   (7) The company incurs advertising costs in the amount of $25,000 a year. Sales increase as a result.

PROBLEM 4-8   Absorption and Variable Costing

Objs. 4,5,6

Joan Tyler started a small manufacturing company, JT Enterprises, at the beginning of 1997. Joan has prepared the following income statement for the first quarter of operations.

JT Enterprises
Income Statement
For the Quarter Ended March 31, 1997

Sales revenue (25,000 units)		$1,200,000
Less variable costs:		
Variable cost of goods sold	$540,000	
Variable selling and administrative expenses	260,000	800,000
Contribution margin		$ 400,000
Less fixed costs:		
Fixed manufacturing overhead	$300,000	
Fixed selling and administrative expenses	150,000	450,000
Net loss		$ (50,000)

The variable cost of goods sold includes the costs of direct materials, direct labor, and variable manufacturing overhead. The company began the quarter with no inventory; it manufactured 30,000 units over the period. Variable selling and administrative expenses are based on units sold.

Required

a.   Calculate the unit product cost using absorption costing.
b.   Rework the income statement using absorption costing.
c.   Does the net loss figure change using absorption costing? If yes, explain why.
d.   During the second quarter of operations, JT again manufactured 30,000 units but sold 35,000 units. Prepare income statements for the second quarter using both the variable- and absorption-costing methods.
e.   Explain the difference in net income (or loss) in the second quarter between the two statements prepared in requirement d.

PROBLEM 4-9   **Variable Costing and Production Variations**

Objs. 1,4,5,6

Jerry Sanchez is president of Heatco, Inc., a manufacturer of a single product. He is comparing this year's income statement with last year's and is wondering why net income is different for the same level of sales. "Our costs have not changed at all, yet look at our income. What did we do right this year?" The statements, both prepared using absorption costing, look like this:

	This Year	Last Year
Sales revenue (40,000 units each year)	$800,000	$800,000
Less cost of goods sold	400,000	460,000
Gross margin	$400,000	$340,000
Less Selling and administrative expenses	300,000	300,000
Net income	$100,000	$ 40,000

Last year, the first year of operations, the company produced 40,000 units and sold them all. This year, the company increased production to maintain a margin of safety in its finished goods inventory. Fixed costs are applied to products on the basis of the number of units produced each year. Here is a summary of Heatco's production results, variable production costs, and fixed manufacturing overhead cost for both years:

	This Year	Last Year
Production in units	50,000	40,000
Production costs:		
Variable cost per unit	$4	$4
Fixed manufacturing overhead	$300,000	$300,000

Required

a. Calculate the unit product cost under variable costing and absorption costing.
b. Prepare an income statement for each year using variable costing.
c. Compare the net income figures in the variable-costing income statement (requirement b) and the absorption-costing income statement for each of the years. Explain any differences.
d. Why did Heatco earn more this year than last year using absorption costing, even though the company sold the same number of units?

PROBLEM 4-10
Objs. 4,5,6

Absorption and Variable Costing: Changes in Inventory

Proto, Inc. manufactures a single product. Here's a summary of the company's production results, sales, costs, and inventory levels last year:

Total production in units	96,600
Total sales in units	82,200
Fixed selling and administrative costs	$113,880
Selling price per unit	$12
Variable-costing net income	$11,880
Absorption-costing net income	$17,640

Required

a. Calculate the fixed manufacturing overhead cost per unit.
b. Calculate the total fixed manufacturing overhead costs.
c. Prepare an income statement using the absorption-costing method.

PROBLEM 4-11
Obj. 8

Variable and Absorption Costing in the Service Sector

PS Consultants specializes in computer systems design and programming. Most of the company's employees have a background in both computers and management. PS's average job takes three to four months to complete. The price PS quotes for consulting services is based on the expected number of consultant hours and an estimate of out-of-pocket expenses. When a job is finished, PS bases its charges on the actual number of hours and costs incurred on the job. The firm usually does not collect its fee until a consulting job is completed.

Currently PS records all of the firm's expenses in the periods in which they are incurred. Those expenses include the hourly wages of consultants and programmers as well as indirect costs—employee benefit packages, travel expenses, and other out-of-pocket expenses. Fixed overhead costs for administering the office, rent, advertising, depreciation on computer equipment, and software license fees also are expensed each period.

Leslie Rinauro is the firm's managing partner. She is concerned because the company's income fluctuates significantly from month to month. In the months when several jobs are billed, the firm shows respectable profits. In other months, the firm shows large losses, even though all of the consultants and programmers are busy. Leslie wants to use a costing method that will better reflect PS's income and smooth out the month-to-month profit fluctuations.

Required

a. How could PS better match the costs of its services with the income they generate?
b. How does the deferral of costs relate to PS's client services?
c. How do the concepts of variable and absorption costing affect PS?

PROBLEM 4-12

Multiple-Choice Overview of the Chapter

1. The breakeven point is that point where
    a. total sales revenue equals total variable and fixed expenses.

   b.   total contribution margin equals total fixed expenses.

   c.   both a and b are true.

   d.   neither a nor b is true.

2. Garth Company sells a single product that generates a positive contribution margin. If the selling price per unit and the variable cost per unit both increase 10% and fixed costs do not change, the

	Unit Contribution Margin	Contribution Margin Ratio	Breakeven in Units
a.	increases	increases	decreases
b.	no change	no change	no change
c.	no change	increases	no change
d.	increases	no change	decreases

3. Honeybee Company's contribution margin ratio is 60%; the company's breakeven point in sales is $150,000. If the company wants to earn net income of $60,000 over the period, its sales would have to be

   a. $200,000   c. $250,000

   b. $350,000   d. $210,000

4. Carlton Company sells its product for $40 per unit. The company's variable costs are $22 per unit; its fixed costs are $82,800 a year. Carlton's breakeven point is

   a. $184,000   c. $150,545

   b.   3,764 units   d.   2,070 units

5. The managers at Spice Company have made these estimates for the coming year:

Sales	$1,000,000
Breakeven sales	$ 700,000
Contribution margin	$ 600,000

   The company's budgeted margin of safety is

   a. $300,000   c. $500,000

   b. $400,000   d. $800,000

6. Last year Clarence Company sold 3,600 units at a price of $50 per unit. The company's variable cost per unit was $15; its fixed costs for the year were $40,530. If the company wants a margin of safety of $40,000 next year, all other factors remaining constant, it will have to sell

   a.   1,158 units   c.   2,300 units

   b.   1,958 units   d.   800 units

7. When production exceeds sales, absorption-costing net income generally

   a.   is less than variable-costing net income.

   b.   is more than variable-costing net income.

   c.   equals variable-costing net income.

   d.   is higher or lower than variable-costing net income because no generalization can be made.

8. Last year, Bone Company produced 10,000 units of product X and incurred the following costs:

Direct materials costs	$10,000
Direct labor costs	14,000
Variable manufacturing overhead costs	5,000
Variable selling and general expenses	3,000
Fixed manufacturing overhead costs	9,000
Fixed selling and general expenses	4,000
Total	$45,000

Under absorption costing, any unsold units of product X would be carried in the Finished Goods Inventory account at a unit cost of

a. $4.50   c. $3.80
b. $4.20   d. $2.90

9. Selling and administrative expenses are
    a. a product cost under variable costing.
    b. a product cost under absorption costing.
    c. part of fixed manufacturing overhead under variable costing.
    d. a period expense under both variable and absorption costing.

10. Last year Smith Company had net income of $125,000 using variable costing and $105,000 using absorption costing. The company's variable production costs were $20 per unit; its total fixed overhead was $176,000. The company produced 11,000 units. During the year, Smith's finished goods inventory
    a. increased by 1,000 units   c. decreased by 1,000 units
    b. increased by 1,250 units   d. decreased by 1,250 units

---

C A S E S

CASE 4-1   Variable and Absorption Costing

Objs., 1,2,6,7

Clyde Williams is the controller of Monroe and Sons, a manufacturer of bricks and patio blocks. Clyde and the other operating managers have just been dressed down by Pat Evans, Monroe's president, for the company's poor performance over the past year. Pat has pointed out that management changes would be made if things do not improve immediately.

After the meeting with Pat, several managers went to Clyde's office to talk about possible changes. Jim Salisbury, the company's sales manager, complained that Monroe's policy requiring full-cost bids was making it impossible to bid on jobs. Clyde suggested that the policy be changed, that bids be based on variable costing not full cost. He explained that variable costing would help the company set prices that would contribute to fixed costs, but not cover all expenses. Variable costing would let the sales staff bid aggressively for jobs during slow periods of production.

The suggestion was raised at the next administrative meeting. Pat questioned the wisdom of bidding any jobs below full cost. "If we don't cover all of our costs," she said, "we'll all be looking for new jobs because we won't be in business for long. Show me why you think this is a good idea."

That evening, Clyde collected the following information on 12 x 12 patio blocks, one of the products Monroe produces, and administrative costs:

Last-quarter production and sales in units	100,000
Selling price per unit	$0.90
Unit manufacturing costs:	
Direct materials	$0.22
Direct labor	0.14
Variable overhead	0.09
Fixed overhead	0.10
Total	$0.55

Selling and administrative costs per quarter:

Fixed	$30,000
Variable	5% of sales

The amount of overhead that was overapplied in the quarter was very small. Clyde took the information home with him to build a case for the variable-costing idea.

Required

a. Should Clyde rework last quarter's income statement in a contribution-margin format? Would that format support Clyde's position? Explain your answer.

b. Suppose that Clyde talks with the production and sales managers and learns that Monroe could have produced an additional 30,000 patio blocks last quarter and could have sold them for $0.54 apiece. Use absorption costing to calculate the gross margin on the sale of an additional 30,000 blocks. Calculate the contribution margin on the sale of the additional 30,000 blocks using variable costing. Discuss why those figures are different. Does this analysis support Clyde's position? Explain your answer.

c. Which of the figures calculated in requirement b would Clyde say best indicates the impact of selling an additional 30,000 blocks? Explain your answer.

d. Does Pat Evans have any basis for her contention that full costing is necessary to ensure a company's survival? Is it necessary to report inventory at full cost in the financial statements? When is variable costing useful, and how should Clyde use that information to make his point? Explain your answer.

CASE 4-2   **CVP Analysis: The Concepts**

Objs., 2,3,4,5

1. Carbon Industries, Inc., is considering buying new equipment to use in the manufacture of its product. The new machines would increase production capacity; they would also require annual fixed costs of $480,000. Carbon expects that variable costs would go down with more efficient use of materials and fewer direct labor hours. Those savings would be offset in part by higher variable manufacturing overhead costs related to machine maintenance. The net effect of the changes would be a 20% reduction overall in Carbon's variable manufacturing costs. Total sales are not expected to change in 1998. If the company does not buy the new machines, it expects the following costs next year:

Sales revenue	$8,000,000
Variable costs	70% of sales
Fixed costs	$1,600,000

   What impact would buying the new equipment have on Carbon's net income next year?

2. Atwater Enterprises sold 5,000 units of product A during July. It reported the following sales and cost information for the month:

Sales revenue	$400,000
Less variable costs	240,000
Less fixed costs	120,000
Net income	$ 40,000

   Suppose that Atwater increases the selling price of product A by 10%. How many units would it have to sell each month to continue generating a monthly income of $40,000?

3. Ample Company never advertises. The Kitch group, an advertising agency that has been trying to win Ample over, claims that an aggressive advertising campaign would increase Ample's sales by 22%. Here is a summary of Ample's sales and costs for the year just ended:

Units sold	150,000
Selling price per unit	$25
Variable manufacturing costs per unit	$15
Fixed costs:	
Manufacturing overhead	$800,000
Selling and administrative expenses	$700,000

Based on this information, how much could Ample pay for advertising and still earn a target profit of $200,000?

4. In planning its operations for next year, Petrie, Inc. estimated sales of $6,000,000 and the following costs:

| | Costs and Expenses | |
	Variable	Fixed
Direct materials	$1,600,000	
Direct labor	1,400,000	
Factory overhead	600,000	$ 900,000
Selling expenses	240,000	360,000
Administrative expenses	60,000	140,000
Total	$3,900,000	$1,400,000

What is Petrie's breakeven point in sales dollars? What is Petrie's margin of safety in sales dollars?

PROJECTS

PROJECT 4-1 A Comparison of Cost Structures
Objs. 1,2,3

Choose two different companies that sell the same basic product, but whose cost structures are obviously different (for example, a shop selling designers' clothes at a mall and a clothing store in a low-rent district of town, or a corner hardware store versus a discount outlet). Explain the differences in cost structure between the two companies. Do the companies treat variable costs differently? How does each company treat its fixed costs? How does cost structure affect a company's breakeven point in sales dollars?

PROJECT 4-2 Identifying CVP Concepts
Objs. 2,8

The basic principles of CVP analysis are everywhere, even at the movies. Although the script may not refer specifically to the relationship among costs, volume, and profit, that relationship is evident in what characters say and do. Write a short report on a movie you have seen in which the cost-volume-profit relationship is depicted. Describe the characters, the underlying situation, and how the cost-volume-profit relationships were used.

PROJECT 4-3 Relating Costs, Volume, and Profits to Individual Activities
Objs. 2,8

CVP analysis is more than a decision-making tool for managers. It is also a tool that individuals can use in the course of their daily activities. Identify three everyday situations in which CVP analysis came into play. Maybe an organization you belong to used CVP analysis to determine the number of raffle tickets it had to sell to cover the cost of the prizes. Describe the variable costs, the fixed costs, and the way CVP analysis helped the decision makers.

PROJECT 4-4 Variable and Absorption Costing
Objs. 6,7,8

Look through *The Wall Street Journal, Business Week,* or *Management Accounting* for articles that describe how a company costs its product or service. From the article, determine whether the company uses variable or absorption costing. Write a short paper on the article and describe why you think the company uses that costing method. What effect would the other method have on the company's costs?

Cost Allocation

and

Business Strategy

Accounting and Management Decisions

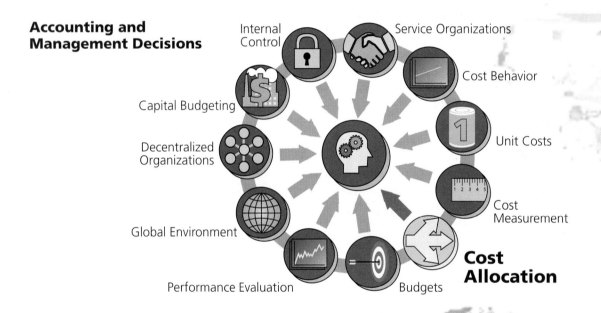

Internal Control

Service Organizations

Cost Behavior

Capital Budgeting

Unit Costs

Decentralized Organizations

Cost Measurement

Global Environment

Cost Allocation

Performance Evaluation

Budgets

Overview

The subject of this chapter is cost allocation, the process of assigning indirect costs to a product or service. Cost allocation is necessary because different products or services often share common resources. The work a plant supervisor does cannot be traced to a specific product, but it does add to the value of each product the plant manufactures. The work a nursing supervisor does cannot be traced to a specific patient, but it does add to the value of the service each patient receives. Manufacturing companies and hospitals cannot distribute the costs of supervision directly to a product or patient. Instead they allocate these costs. The accuracy of the allocation—and ultimately the usefulness of cost information in decision making—is a function of the allocation method an organization uses.

The traditional method of allocating overhead costs relies on a single activity base and a single predetermined overhead rate. The text examines the shortcomings of the traditional method and looks at new ways of estimating the unit cost of overhead. The product of activity-based cost systems is a unit cost that is far more reliable than the traditional unit cost. With more accurate cost information, managers are able to make better decisions.

As you study this chapter, think about cost allocation in terms of how costs behave in relation to the activities a company or department carries out? How does the design of a cost system affect both performance measures and managers' behavior? How do overhead costs affect not only manufacturing organizations but also service organizations?

Arnold Zann, 1983/PNI International

Major topics covered in this chapter:
- The limitations of the traditional method of allocating overhead costs
- Cost allocation in today's manufacturing environment
- How new methods of allocating costs help managers make better pricing and product design decisions
- How volume affects costs and the information managers use to make strategic decisions

Objectives

Once you have completed this chapter, you should be able to:

1. Explain the importance of overhead costs to manufacturing and service organizations.
2. Trace the development of manufacturing systems and the effect that development has had on overhead costs.
3. Explain the implications of overhead allocation for decisions about product mix and pricing and for performance measurement.
4. Identify the problems with traditional methods of allocating overhead costs.
5. Describe a hierarchy for classifying overhead costs.
6. Explain how activity-based costing works.
7. Explain how service organizations use cost information for decision making.

THE REASONS FOR COST ALLOCATION

Objective 1
Explain the importance of overhead costs to manufacturing and service organizations.

Managers rely on cost information to make important decisions about the resources for which they are responsible. When costs can be traced directly to a product or a service, managers typically are confident in the accuracy of those costs. But indirect costs—the costs of overhead—cannot be traced directly. Overhead costs have to be allocated to products or services in some logical way that can help managers make informed decisions. Managers cannot make an informed pricing decision, for example, if they do not have a good estimate of all product costs.

Recall that costs can be classified according to a number of criteria. One is the nature of the costs. *Direct costs*—the costs of direct materials and direct labor—are easy to trace to a specific product. Materials requisition forms document the type and amount of materials used in production, and time sheets record the hours workers spend on each job. On the other hand, *indirect costs*—the costs of materials handling, supervisors' salaries, and the depreciation of factory equipment, for example—usually cannot be traced to a particular product or product line. Instead, indirect costs are allocated to products.

The way in which overhead costs are allocated can affect unit product costs dramatically. Overhead costs also represent a major portion of a company's costs. It is not surprising, then, that managers are interested in finding allocation methods that accurately capture the behavior of overhead-generating activities.

VOLUME-BASED ALLOCATION: THE TRADITIONAL METHOD

Objective 2
Trace the development of manufacturing systems and the effect that development has had on overhead costs.

Most of the management accounting techniques for calculating the cost of goods and services and for evaluating managers' performance have been around a long time. In this section we briefly explore traditional techniques for allocating overhead costs and describe the changes that have taken place in manufacturing since those techniques first were used. In a later section, we examine today's business environment, an environment that has forced managers to find new ways to attach overhead costs to products and services.

Background

Many changes have taken place in manufacturing processes and in the information needs of managers since the early days of the industrial revolution in the United States.[1] Yet methods for allocating costs remain surprisingly similar to those used by early industrialists.

Before the industrial revolution, manufacturing was dominated by *cottage industries*. Skilled artisans worked in their homes on specialized tasks. Farmers concentrated on producing wool or cotton. Spinners produced yarn and usually were paid according to the pounds of yarn they delivered. Weavers produced cloth from yarn; they usually were paid by the yards of cloth they produced. Finally, tailors were paid a certain amount for each garment they sewed from the cloth the weavers supplied. To obtain a woolen shirt, for example, a merchant would have had to buy wool from a farmer, yarn from a spinner, cloth from a weaver, and the finished product from a tailor. The cost of each shirt was easy to calculate because each transaction was driven by market prices. The unit product cost was simply the sum of the various components purchased at market prices. Exhibit 1 shows how a merchant might have accumulated costs in preindustrial times.

---

[1] See H. Thomas Johnson and Robert S. Kaplan, Relevance Lost *(Boston: Harvard Business School Press)*, 1991.

Exhibit 1   A Preindustrial Cost Summary: 100 Woolen Shirts

Paid to Tom Farmer for wool	$ 200
Paid to Harriet Spinner to spin wool into yarn	800
Paid to Cynthia Weaver to weave yarn into fabric	600
Paid to Andy Taylor to sew shirts from fabric	500
Total costs	$2,100
Total shirts produced	100
Cost per shirt ($2,100 ÷ 100)	$ 21

The industrial revolution brought raw materials, equipment, spinners, weavers, and tailors together in one facility. Once factory owners hired craftspeople to work for them, they could not use external market prices to determine the cost of delivering a product. They needed a new source of information. Explosive changes in manufacturing practices, then, created new challenges for those who managed the operations of textile, steel, and transportation companies.

Many management accounting tools have been developed by engineers, not accountants, in response to changing production methods and competition. The difficulty is not with the direct costs of materials and labor. Those costs have been relatively easy to associate with a product or product family. For example, in many factories production workers electronically "log on" to a piece of equipment and identify the product on which they are working. In addition, through bar coding technology and electronic scanning devices similar to those found at checkout counters in a grocery store, direct material costs (and other material information) can be traced from a supplier to a final product. The problem is in allocating indirect costs, the overhead costs that are not directly related to products or processes. The problem has been made larger with the growing importance of those costs.

At one time, manufacturing overhead was a relatively small part of the total costs of manufacturing a product. Direct materials and direct labor costs dominated the costs of production. So a simple process for attaching overhead costs to inventory was developed. That process used **activity bases**—direct labor hours, direct labor dollars, or machine hours, for example—to apply overhead costs to products.

Today, cost structures have changed. Overhead has become the dominant cost in many manufacturing and service industries. Advances in technology have led to the dramatic growth of support functions, while the number of employees directly involved in assembly has dropped. Think what happens when automated equipment replaces skilled machinists. The machinists' wages, often a direct labor cost, are replaced with the wages of technical support engineers, an overhead cost.

Managers have to be able to attach overhead costs to products to understand the full cost (the absorption cost) of making a product. Unfortunately, traditional allocation bases often do not yield accurate product costs for individual products in a product line. The costs allocated to some products are too low, and those allocated to others are too high. Those misallocations can create problems for managers who have to make pricing and product mix decisions.

Predetermined Overhead Rates: A Review

Any cost-allocation method, by definition, relies on the use of estimates. When accountants prepare a company's financial statements, for example, they have to estimate the depreciation cost for plant assets. They also use estimates to prepare a company's internal reports. In fact, most of a company's planning activities are driven by a *sales forecast,* an estimate of sales volume. The sales forecast is the basis of the *production forecast,* an estimate of production volume. The production forecast is used to prepare the company's *budgets,* estimates of what the company is going to have to spend to meet production requirements.

Given expected levels of sales and production, a company generally can prepare a reasonable estimate of the costs of materials, labor, and overhead for the coming year. Budgets usually are stated in dollar amounts. But often those amounts have been converted from estimates of the machine hours and labor hours necessary to meet production targets.[2]

Recall our earlier discussion about the **predetermined overhead rate,** the rate a company uses to apply overhead costs to units of production. Why use a predetermined rate for overhead? Why not simply wait until actual overhead costs are known? The answer has to do with timing. A company that produces and delivers a product in March may not know its actual overhead costs until April, when the bills come in. However, management needs cost information well before March to negotiate prices with customers or to publish a price list. That means that overhead costs have to be estimated and because overhead costs are estimated, adjustments have to be made to certain accounts at the end of the period, when the actual costs of overhead are known. Remember that actual overhead costs rarely equal the costs applied to products using a predetermined overhead rate.

Let's look at an example. Suppose that Ryan Industries has forecast its sales for the coming year, and its managers have estimated the level of production necessary to support those sales. Based on those estimates, the company's accountants have budgeted total manufacturing overhead costs of $2 million for the coming year. Because overhead costs seem to vary in relation to the number of hours that production machinery is in operation, the decision is made to use machine hours as the basis for allocating overhead costs. Accountants often refer to the allocation base as a **cost driver.** Traditional volume-based cost drivers assume that manufacturing overhead costs vary in proportion to an allocation base. Examples of traditional allocation bases, or cost drivers, include direct labor hours, machine hours, and direct labor dollars. From sales forecasts, Ryan's production engineers expect to operate the machines 60,000 hours during the year. The predetermined overhead rate is $33.33:

Predetermined overhead rate = Estimated overhead costs ÷ estimated machine hours
$$= \$2,000,000 \div 60,000$$
$$= \$33.33$$

Throughout the year, then, overhead will be applied to the company's products at a rate of $33.33 per machine hour.

Now suppose that at the end of the year, the company actually has used 61,500 machine hours and has incurred overhead costs of $2,300,000. Throughout the year the company has applied $2,049,795 in overhead costs:

Applied overhead costs = actual machine hours × predetermined overhead rate
$$= 61,500 \times \$33.33$$
$$= \$2,049,795$$

That means that the company has underapplied $250,205 in overhead costs:

Actual overhead costs	$2,300,000
Less applied overhead costs	2,049,795
Underapplied overhead costs	$ 250,205

As described in an earlier chapter, a company must make adjustments when it under- or overapplies overhead costs. Remember that actual overhead costs are

---

[2]   *Industrial engineers often use time-and-motion studies to estimate the number of machine hours or labor hours needed to meet a given level of production. Accountants then convert those estimates into dollars.*

added to the Manufacturing Overhead account. The amount of applied overhead is subtracted from that account and added to the Work in Process Inventory account. Thus, it is the estimated overhead costs that are used to determine the value of work in process inventory, finished goods inventory, and the cost of goods sold. After applying overhead, the difference between actual and applied overhead is clear. When the Manufacturing Overhead account shows a positive balance, the company has underapplied its overhead costs. When the Manufacturing Overhead account shows a negative balance, the company has overapplied its overhead costs.

In the example here, the company's Manufacturing Overhead account shows a positive balance of $250,205 at the end of the year, the amount of underapplied overhead. To eliminate that balance, the company has to transfer a total of $250,205 in overhead costs to its Cost of Goods Sold account.

VOLUME-BASED ALLOCATION: TWO EXAMPLES

This section describes the operations of two companies.[3] Both manufacture ballpoint pens, but each has a very different marketing strategy. Click Pen Company produces just one pen; Wafer Pen Company produces six different pens.

Our focus here is on the way each of the companies uses the traditional method to allocate its overhead costs. As you read, though, think about two other important issues. First, as a company expands its product line, the manufacturing process usually becomes more complex. With each additional product, the costs of direct materials and direct labor generally go up. So do the costs of overhead. Additional materials have to be handled; additional products have to be inspected; additional inventory has to be carried.

Second, allocating overhead costs accurately is especially important in a company that produces multiple products. Two factors are at work here:

- Without accurate cost information, managers cannot make good decisions about the product mix. You cannot decide to eliminate product A if you cannot distinguish the costs of product A from those of products B and C.
- Also, as overhead costs go up—as they represent more of a company's costs—it becomes even more important to capture those costs and allocate them accurately.

We come back to these issues at the end of this section and later in the chapter. We discuss the shortcomings of the traditional cost-allocation method and the design of new methods to cope with the complexity of today's business environment.

Click Pen Company

Click Pen Company produces just one product, a high-quality, low-cost ballpoint pen. The company's founder adopted Henry Ford's philosophy, which she roughly paraphrases like this: "They can have any color ink they want, as long as it's black."

Click buys black ink cartridges in large volume. It manufactures blue plastic body tubes, black plastic caps, and black plastic tube plugs and assembles the components. The manufacturing process is shown in Exhibit 2. Raw materials—resin, dye, and ink cartridges—are received at a loading dock and moved by forklift to a storage area. Plastic resin and dye are loaded into an injection molding machine to produce the body tube, cap, and tube plug. Because just one type of component can be manufactured at a time, a machine setup is necessary between batches of body tubes, caps,

[3]   *The examples in this section were inspired by Robin Cooper and Robert S. Kaplan, 1988. "Measure Costs Right: Make the Right Decisions,"* Harvard Business Review, *September-October 1988, pp. 96-103.*

Exhibit 2   Click Pen Company: The Manufacturing Process

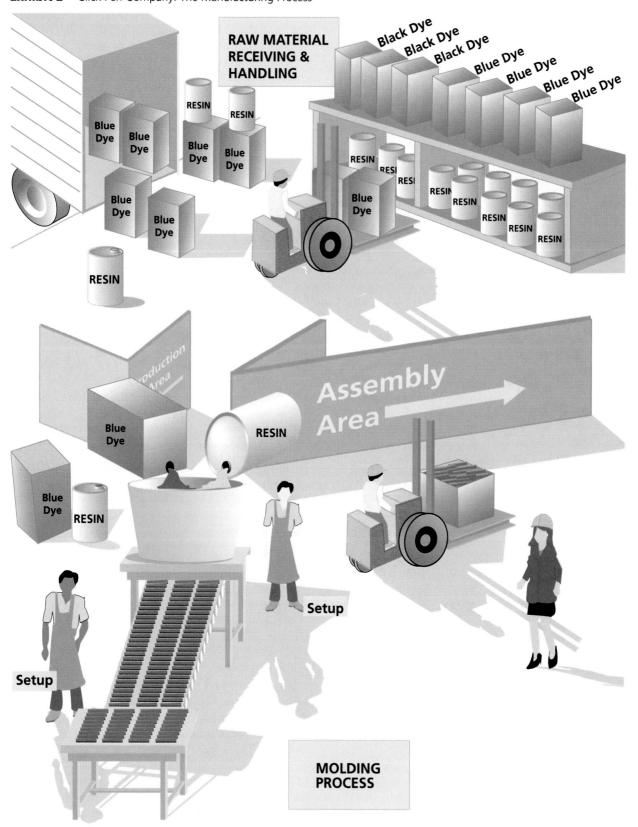

Exhibit 2, *continued*

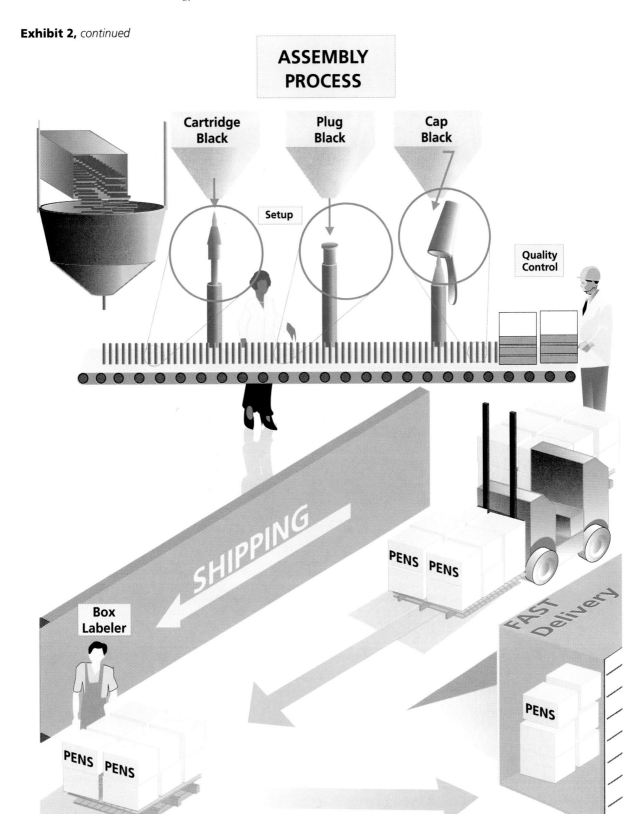

and tube plugs. A setup crew replaces the molds and changes the type and color of plastic resin to meet the engineering specifications for the next component being produced.

After the molding process, the components are taken to the assembly area and loaded into buckets that drop a steady flow of components into the assembly machine. That machine inserts an ink cartridge and end plug into each body tube and then attaches a cap. A quality control engineer monitors the process and periodically tests the pens to be sure that they conform to engineering standards. Once the pens are assembled, they are boxed and labeled and moved to a loading dock, where they are shipped to customers around the world.

Imagine the inside of Click's factory. Visualize the different kinds of activities that are going on. Start at the loading dock, where plastic resin, black dye (for the caps and tube plugs), blue dye (for the body tubes), and ink cartridges arrive by truck. Workers unload, count, inspect, and store the shipment. Next walk through a door into the production area. The plant supervisor, who has just finished talking with a machine operator, moves you out of the path of a forklift operator who is delivering raw materials to the injection-molding machine. You walk past the setup crew, who are busy preparing the injection molding machine for the next batch of components. Meanwhile, a forklift operator is moving a load of components from the molding area to the assembly area. Workers monitor the assembly process and ensure the raw material bins are loaded with the proper components. Every hour a quality control engineer draws a sample of pens to test. The pens are boxed, loaded on wooden pallets (low platforms used for shipping and storage), and labeled with the name and address of the customer. Finally, a forklift operator delivers the pallets to a loading dock for shipment.

Now think about the costs of the activities that make up Click's manufacturing process. It is easy to calculate the costs of direct materials and direct labor. But what about the costs of manufacturing overhead? Exhibit 3 shows a breakdown of the company's annual manufacturing overhead costs.

Exhibit 3   Click Pen Company: Annual Manufacturing Overhead Costs

Indirect labor costs		
Plant supervision (1 person)	$ 70,000	
Raw materials and component handling and transportation (2 people)	60,000	
Quality control inspections (1 person)	46,000	
Machine setups (3 people)	90,000	
Boxing, labeling, and shipping (1 person)	20,000	
Total indirect labor costs		$286,000
Other plant-related overhead costs		
Depreciation on forklifts, manufacturing equipment, and factory building	$100,000	
Electricity for plant operations	10,000	
Supplies and repairs	4,000	
Total other plant-related overhead costs		114,000
Total plant overhead costs		$400,000

Estimated machine hours per year (50 weeks per year × 40 hours per week) = 2,000
Estimated annual production volume
  (2,000 machine hours × 500 pens per hour) = 1,000,000 pens

Suppose that Click's marketing manager needs the unit product cost to make a pricing decision. The company uses machine hours as its activity base, and the estimated machine hours for the year is 2,000. The predetermined overhead rate is $200 per machine hour:

Predetermined overhead rate = estimated overhead costs ÷ estimated machine hours
= $400,000 ÷ 2,000
= $200 per machine hour

Click produces 500 pens per machine hour. The overhead cost per pen, then, is $.40 ($200 in overhead cost per machine hour ÷ 500 pens per hour). With the unit costs of direct materials and labor, the unit product cost schedule looks like this:

Direct materials (resin and dye cartridges) costs per unit	$.02
Direct labor costs per unit	.05
Manufacturing overhead costs per unit	.40
Total cost per unit	$.47

Suppose that Click sells the pens for $.60 a unit. The company's gross margin is $.13 per pen:

Selling price per unit	$.60
Less total cost per unit	.47
Gross margin per unit	$.13

Look again at the cost schedule. Click's overhead costs per unit make up 85% ($.40 ÷ $.47) of the company's total manufacturing costs per unit. Clearly if the company wants to increase its profits, a good place to begin is its overhead costs.

Wafer Pen Company

Click produces just one product, so it does not run the risk of misallocating overhead costs among several products. Most companies, however, produce more than one product. Click's competitor, Wafer Pen Company, produces a full product line. How does the added complexity of making several different products affect cost allocation?

Wafer Pen Company produces pens in six different colors: black, blue, red, green, silver, and gold. The body tube, plug, and cap match the color of the ink cartridge. Like Click, Wafer produces a total of 1 million pens a year. Exhibit 4 shows Wafer's annual production volume by product and in total.

Exhibit 4 Wafer Pen Company: Annual Production Volume

Product	Annual Production Volume
Black pens	500,000
Blue pens	250,000
Red pens	130,000
Green pens	60,000
Silver pens	50,000
Gold pens	10,000
Total	1,000,000

The layout of Wafer's factory is not very different from that of Click's factory (Exhibit 5). As you enter the facility on November 1, what do you see? On a loading dock, workers are counting boxes of black, blue, red, green, silver, and gold dye, verifying that the number received is both the number Wafer ordered and the number the supplier billed. Boxes of different-colored dyes are stacked in a corner, waiting to be sorted and stored. Materials handlers are busy arranging cartridge colors in the order of production. They remember a problem last month, when green cartridges were inserted into red body tubes. To prevent that kind of mistake, a quality control

Exhibit 5   Wafer Pen Company: The Manufacturing Process

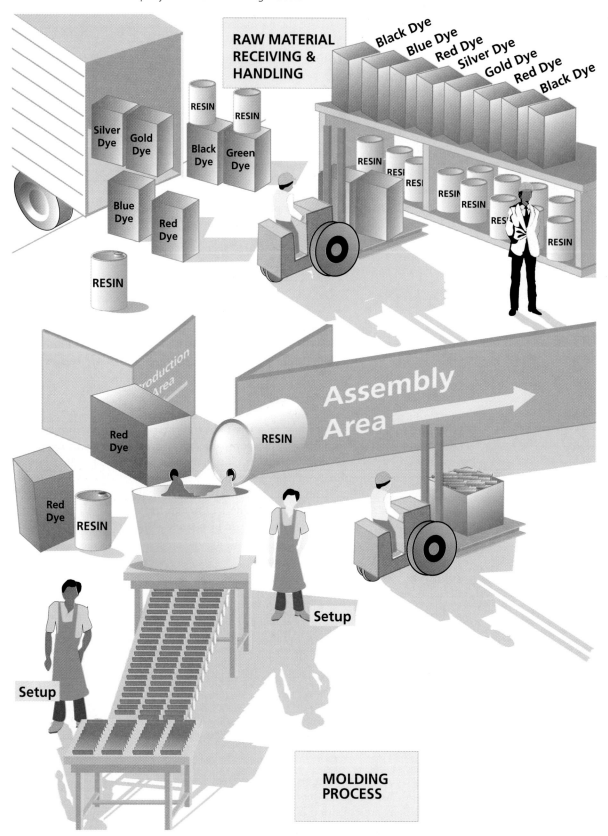

Exhibit 5, *continued*

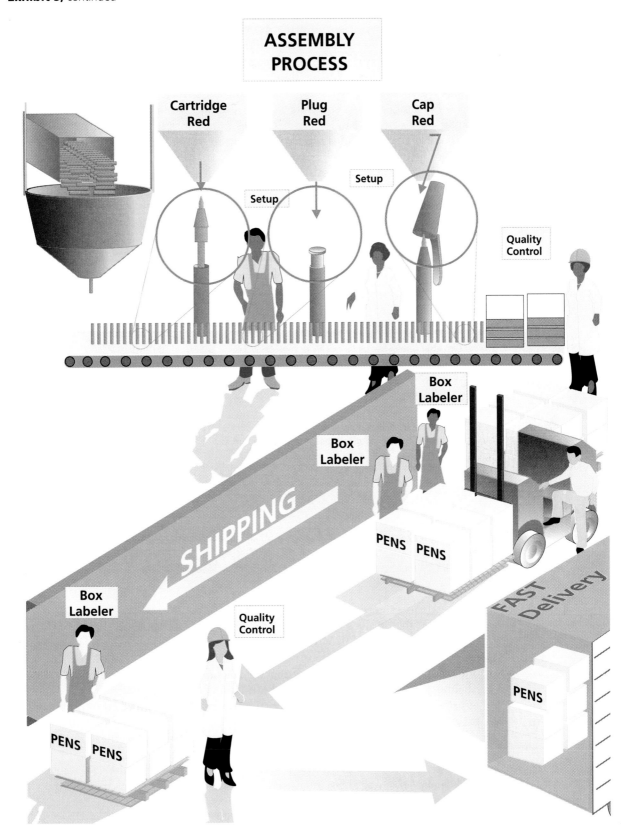

engineer is inspecting the parts that come off the injection-molding machine each time a different batch of pens is produced. Because Wafer manufactures six different pens, the company carries out many more inspections than Click does.

As you walk by the injection-molding machine, a setup crew is busy changing the dye color. Nearby a product manager is complaining about a shortage of gold cartridges, a hot item during the holiday season. The plant supervisor patiently explains that a strike at the supplier has slowed deliveries. More gold cartridges will arrive November 15. As you walk past the assembly machine, you notice much more activity than at the Click factory. You also notice that three people are working in the boxing, labeling, and shipping areas to keep the orders straight. In general, there seems to be a lot more activity in this factory than in the Click factory.

Because Wafer produces six different products, more materials have to be handled, more inspections have to be carried out, more machine setups are needed, and boxing, labeling, and shipping are more complicated. The more people needed to perform those tasks, the higher the company's overhead costs (Exhibit 6).

Exhibit 6   Wafer Pen Company: Annual Manufacturing Overhead Costs

Indirect labor costs		
Plant supervision (1 person)	$ 70,000	
Raw materials and component		
handling and transportation (3 people)	90,000	
Quality control inspections (2 people)	92,000	
Machine setups (4 people)	120,000	
Boxing, labeling, and		
shipping (3 people)	60,000	
Total indirect labor costs		$432,000
Other plant-related overhead costs		
Depreciation on forklifts, manufacturing		
equipment, and factory building	$100,000	
Electricity for plant operations	12,000	
Supplies and repairs	6,000	
Total other plant-related overhead costs		$118,000
Total plant overhead costs		$550,000

Estimated machine hours per year (50 weeks per year $\times$ 40 hours per week) = 2,000
Estimated annual production volume
   (2,000 machine hours $\times$ 500 pens per hour) = 1,000,000 pens

Notice that Wafer's total overhead costs are $150,000 more than Click's overhead costs (see Exhibit 3). Most of that difference has to do with higher costs of indirect labor. Wafer has one more person handling materials, one more person doing inspections, one more person setting up machines, and two more people boxing, labeling, and shipping. Even though both companies manufacture the same number of pens each year, clearly there is a lot more work and cost involved in producing six products than in producing just one.

How does Wafer's overhead cost affect its predetermined overhead rate? It is $75 higher than the rate Click uses ($275 per machine hour versus $200):

Predetermined overhead rate = estimated overhead costs ÷ estimated machine hours
                          = $550,000 ÷ 2,000
                          = $275 per machine hour

Exhibit 7 shows Wafer's unit overhead costs by product. Using the production figures from Exhibit 4, we have calculated the number of machine hours per product. That figure multiplied by the predetermined overhead rate equals the total cost

Exhibit 7   Wafer Pen Company: Unit Overhead Costs

| | A | × | B | = | C | D | C ÷ D |
| | **Machine Hours** | | **Cost per Hour** | | **Total Cost** | **Annual Production Volume (units)** | **Unit Cost** |
Product							
Black pens	1,000		$275		$275,000	500,000	$.55
Blue pens	500		275		137,500	250,000	.55
Red pens	260		275		71,500	130,000	.55
Green pens	120		275		33,000	60,000	.55
Silver pens	100		275		27,500	50,000	.55
Gold pens	20		275		5,500	10,000	.55
Totals	2,000				$550,000	1,000,000	

of overhead for each product. The unit overhead cost of each product is the total cost of overhead for that product divided by the units produced of that product. For example, to produce 500,000 black pens in a year, Wafer uses 1,000 machine hours (500,000 pens ÷ 500 pens produced per hour). Using the predetermined overhead rate, the company allocates total overhead costs of $275,000 (1,000 machine hours × $275 in overhead costs per machine hour) to the production of black pens. The per-unit cost of overhead for the black pens is $.55—the total cost of overhead for the black pens divided by the number of black pens produced.

Notice that each pen in Wafer's product line has the same unit overhead cost—$.55. That is because the traditional method for allocating costs is volume-based. Unfortunately, some overhead costs do not vary with the number of units or machine hours. Thus, volume-based allocations may distort unit costs.

If we assume direct materials and direct labor costs of $.07 (the same cost Click incurred), Wafer's unit product cost for each type of pen is $.62:

Direct materials (resin and dye cartridges) costs per unit	$.02
Direct labor costs per unit	.05
Manufacturing overhead costs per unit	.55
Total cost per unit	$.62

The average cost Wafer incurs to make a pen is $.62, $.15 more than Click's average cost of $.47.

Strategic Implications

O b j e c t i v e   3
Explain the implications of overhead allocation for decisions about product mix and pricing and for performance measurement.

Clearly the two companies we have been describing have very different overhead costs. Why? The answer, of course, is the number of different activities. Why do two companies that use the same basic manufacturing process to produce the same number of products each year have different numbers of activities? The answer is the complexity of their product lines.

Click manufactures just one pen. The company does not need as many materials handlers, quality control inspectors, setup crew members, or boxing, labeling, and shipping personnel as Wafer does. Click's strategy is to produce and sell a high-quality, low-cost pen in high volume without product diversity. Because of that strategy, Click can sell a black pen for less than it costs Wafer to manufacture a black pen.

Exhibit 8 lists the selling price, manufacturing cost, and profit (or loss) for each pen in Wafer's product line. Look at the entry for black pens.

Exhibit 8   Wafer Pen Company: Per-Unit Profit by Product

Product	Selling Price per Unit	Manufacturing Cost per Unit	Gross Margin per Unit
Black pens	$ .60	$.62	$(.02)
Blue pens	.65	.62	.03
Red pens	.75	.62	.13
Green pens	.75	.62	.13
Silver pens	2.00	.62	1.38
Gold pens	4.00	.62	3.38

Wafer has to meet its competitors' prices for black pens. The company loses $.02 with each black pen it sells. But look at Wafer's specialty products, the silver and gold pens. The marketing department is pleased with the full-line strategy because profits from the high-priced specialty items more than offset losses from the black pens.

How does a full-line strategy affect decision making at Wafer? For one thing, the company plans to add more low-volume, high-priced specialty colors to its product line. Also, Wafer pays its sales force higher commissions on specialty colors. It is not surprising, then, that the company's salespeople spend substantial selling time on the specialty colors and much less time on the traditional colors. Wafer has made the decision to settle for a low market share of black pens. All of those decisions are based on cost information. That information is based in large part on the method Wafer uses to allocate its manufacturing overhead costs. Does the traditional method of cost allocation give Wafer's managers the information they need to make good decisions about the company's marketing strategy? Is the information they are using to determine the company's product mix and to set its sales policies accurate? We answer these questions in the next section.

SELF-STUDY PROBLEM 1

Troy Company is a small manufacturer of high-quality home gardening tools. Each tool in Troy's line is the product of years of ergonomic research and development.

Troy's marketing manager is thinking about changing the selling price of certain products and has asked the company's accountant for a summary of production costs. Here is the information that was gathered from accounting and production records during the past six months:

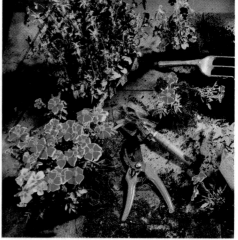

©Superstock

Depreciation on plant assets	$50,000
Energy for plant operations	$20,000
Indirect labor costs	$60,000
Manufacturing supplies	$12,000
Direct labor hours worked	10,000

Product A consumes $7 in direct materials and requires one-half hour of direct labor. Direct labor is paid at a rate of $10 per hour.

Required

1. Calculate the predetermined overhead rate Troy uses to allocate overhead to products.
2. Prepare a summary of the manufacturing costs for one unit of product A.

The solution to Self-Study Problem 1 appears at the end of the chapter.

THE PROBLEMS WITH VOLUME-BASED ALLOCATION

Objective 4
Identify the problems with traditional methods of allocating overhead costs.

The previous section described the manufacturing processes and costs of two manufacturers, Click and Wafer. Both companies base their marketing decisions on cost information. Is that information accurate? Does it make sense? For example, does each pen in Wafer's product line actually cost the same to manufacture?

Economies of Scale

If a company produces more than one type of product, some products are likely to be produced in higher volume than others. Managerial accountants call this phenomenon *volume diversity*. Any company that assembles components to produce a finished product could produce hundreds if not thousands of different products. Most manufacturers limit the number of different products they produce. They choose to make fewer types of products in higher volume. Why? Because of economies of scale. *Economies of scale* **are the savings a company realizes in unit costs by spreading fixed overhead costs over a larger number of units.** A company that is able to produce a product at a lower cost than its competitors has a distinct advantage in the market.

Look again at Exhibit 4. Wafer manufactures 500,000 black pens a year and just 10,000 gold pens. The company clearly can achieve economies of scale in producing the black pens that it cannot achieve in producing the gold pens. Machine setup is a good example. Let's assume that it costs Wafer $500 to set up the injection-molding machine. By running batches of 20,000 black pens, the company incurs a unit cost of $.025 ($500 ÷ 20,000 pens) per black pen. Even if Wafer was able to run all of the gold pens it produces in a year in a single batch, the unit cost of the machine setup for the gold pens would be $.05 ($500 ÷ 10,000 pens), twice that of the black pens.

One of the problems with the traditional method of allocating overhead costs is that it does not take economies of scale into account. The savings Wafer realizes from its higher-volume products are not reflected in the unit cost of overhead. Instead all of the company's products—high volume and low volume—are allocated the same overhead cost per unit.

The Allocation Base

A second problem with traditional cost allocation has to do with the allocation base, the activity base that is used to set the predetermined overhead rate. Think about manufacturing overhead in the Wafer plant. One example: When raw materials are received, workers unload, inspect, record, and store them. Those workers are paid wages, consume supplies, and use assets that depreciate. All of those costs are overhead costs. Another example: When a customer places an order for 100 green pens, the order has to be processed and the pens located, boxed, and shipped. The costs of those activities also are overhead costs.

Now think about the way Wafer allocates its overhead costs. The company uses machine hours as its activity base. How do machine hours relate to the costs of receiving materials or filling orders? Does the number of machine hours explain those costs? Does the use of machine hours produce those costs? No.

Critics of the traditional cost-allocation method argue that volume-based allocation distorts unit overhead costs. Remember that volume-based cost allocation systems assume that manufacturing overhead costs vary in proportion to an allocation base. Examples of traditional allocation bases include direct labor hours, machine hours, or direct labor dollars. If product A uses 10 machine hours and product B uses 5 machine hours, product A is allocated twice as much overhead as product B.

Are all overhead costs a function of machine hours? Do the costs of receiving and handling raw materials vary with the number of machine hours a product uses? No. Those costs have to do with the number of raw materials shipments the company processes or the size of those shipments.

Managers who want to cut overhead costs in their departments are given little guidance by a cost accounting system that assumes that all overhead costs are the product of machine hours or direct labor hours or direct labor dollars. Wafer's managers cannot reduce the number of machine hours and expect overhead costs in the receiving department to go down. Those costs simply are not affected by machine hours.

To understand the shortcomings of volume-based allocation, think back to the time in which the system was designed. Remember that overhead costs were a much smaller percentage of total costs. For internal decision making, then, overhead costs were not as important as they are today. Accounting systems were developed to help companies put a value on inventory in their financial statements.[4] External auditors were concerned that the value of total inventory on the balance sheet was correct. They did not care if the cost per unit of one product was overstated while the cost of another was understated.

COOPER'S HIERARCHY

Objective 5
Describe a hierarchy for classifying overhead costs.

Recognizing that overhead costs are not always related to volume, Robin Cooper, a management accounting professor, developed a hierarchy of overhead costs.[5] *Cooper's hierarchy* **is a framework that explains how overhead costs change with various activities.** The hierarchy organizes overhead costs into four categories—unit level, batch level, product level, and facility level—according to activity type (Exhibit 9).

Unit-Level Costs

Unit-level costs behave like variable costs. Remember that variable costs vary in total with the number of units produced but do not vary *per unit* with changes in volume. The costs of manufacturing supplies and utilities, for example, are a function of production volume. That means that traditional allocation bases—machine hours, direct labor hours, and direct labor dollars—are appropriate for allocating unit-level costs. An example: Suppose that the cost of electricity to run a machine is $2 an hour. If the machine produces 100 units in an hour, the cost per unit is $.02 ($2 ÷ 100 units). If the machine runs for 10 hours, the total cost of electricity is $20 ($2 × 10 hours), but the cost per unit is still $.02 [$20 ÷ (100 units per hour × 10 hours)].

Batch-Level Costs

The batch-level classification addresses one of the volume-related biases of the traditional cost-allocation method. That method, by using a single activity base to allocate

---

[4]   See *Thomas and Kaplan*, Relevance Lost.
[5]   Robin Cooper. "*Cost Classification in Unit-Based and Activity-Based Manufacturing Cost Systems,*" Journal of Cost Management, *Fall, 1990, pp. 4-14.*

Exhibit 9   Cooper's Hierarchy: Allocating Costs by Activity

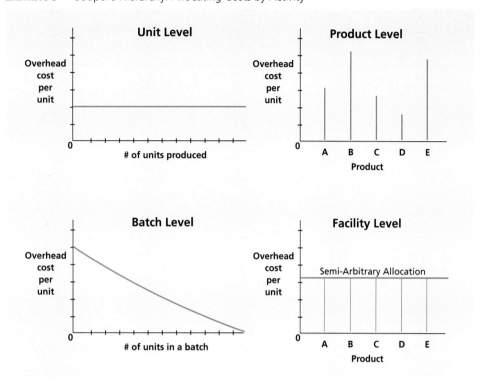

overhead costs, ignores economies of scale. It assumes that the cost of setting up a machine is the same per unit whether 10 units or 10,000 units are manufactured. In reality, certain types of activities—for example, raw materials handling and machine setups—are associated with each batch of production, whatever the number of units in a batch. To measure the overhead costs of a product accurately, batch-level costs must be allocated to specific production runs:

Batch-level cost per unit = total activity cost ÷ units in the batch

If a machine setup costs $200 and the company produces 10 units in the batch, the setup cost per unit is $20 ($200 ÷ 10 units). If the company produces 1,000 units in the batch, the setup cost per unit is just $.20 ($200 ÷ 1,000 units).

The batch-level cost per unit falls as the number of units in the batch goes up and rises as the number of units in the batch goes down. When the cost of an activity is fixed, the per-unit cost of the goods produced in a batch should relate to the number of units in the batch. The more units in a batch, the more units there are over which to spread the same cost. So the larger the batch, the lower the per-unit cost of the batch-level activity. The smaller the batch, the higher the per-unit cost.

Product-Level Costs

Product-level costs relate to a specific family of products. For example, suppose that a company that manufactures brake systems for automobiles and trucks tests 1 system out of 50 to be sure that the system complies with engineering specifications. Also, suppose that the test it uses on truck brake systems destroys the systems so that they cannot be sold. The specific costs of that test—the cost of the systems that cannot be sold—should be allocated to the truck brake system family of products. Another example is a design change. Usually a design change affects newer product lines. A new product is redesigned to make it easier to assemble or to use. The cost of an engineering design change should not be attached to well-established products that do not need modification. That cost should be associated with the product that does need modification. Otherwise a marketing manager might be misled into overpricing a mature product and underpricing a new one.

Facility-Level Costs

The costs at the facility level are a problem. Unfortunately, not all costs can be associated directly with a product. For example, the salary of a security guard does not relate directly to a specific unit, batch, or family of products. Therefore facility-level costs tend to be allocated arbitrarily.

Because the allocation is arbitrary, some companies choose not to allocate those costs at all. Their internal reports list the unit-level, batch-level, and product-level costs associated with each product and show facility-level costs as a lump sum.

SELF-STUDY PROBLEM 2

Highlands Machining Company produces bicycle gears from high-quality stainless steel. You are an assistant department manager helping develop a new cost-allocation system. Because you understand the weaknesses of the traditional volume-based method, you have been asked to classify some of the company's costs using Cooper's hierarchy. You have been given a list of four types of costs:

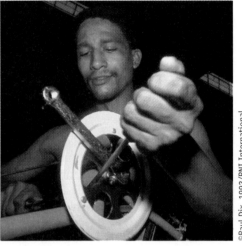

©Paul Dix, 1992/PNI International

- Lighting costs for the production areas
- Raw materials movement costs: the wages and supplies consumed in moving raw materials from inventory storage to a production area (Materials are moved each time a different production order begins.)
- The costs of cooling the metal-cutting equipment (Metal cutting equipment requires constant cooling during the production process. The costs include the costs of liquid coolant, pumps and hoses, and the energy to power the cooling system.)
- Research and development expenses incurred to develop a new product

Required

Classify each cost as a unit-level, batch-level, product-level, or facility-level cost, and explain your classifications.

The solution to Self Study Problem 2 appears at the end of the chapter.

ACTIVITY-BASED COSTING

Activity-based costing (ABC) **allocates overhead costs to a product based on the cost of the activities that are required to produce the product.** The allocation bases are cost drivers. These cost drivers should relate to the activities per-

O b j e c t i v e   6
Explain how activity-based
costing works.

http://www.swcollege.
com/ingram.html

Learn more about ABC.

formed while manufacturing a good or providing a service. Machine hours do not drive the costs of moving materials from a loading dock into storage or from storage to a production area. The number of movements does. So a company might choose the number of movements as a basis for attaching the costs of moving materials to products. Direct labor hours do not drive the costs of admitting patients to a hospital, but the number of admissions does.

In an ABC system, cost allocation usually involves two stages. In the first stage, costs (depreciation, salaries, and utilities, for example) are allocated to activity pools according to the type of activity carried out in each pool. *Activity pools* **are collections of costs that relate to an activity.** A pool for machine setups would include the costs of supplies, indirect labor, energy, and depreciation of equipment. A common method of allocating costs to a pool is in proportion to time or effort. Suppose that 60 percent of an engineer's time is spent on machine setups and 40 percent on quality control. The engineer's salary and benefits would be allocated in that proportion to a setup pool and a quality control pool.

In the second stage, costs are allocated from the activity pools to a cost object, such as a good or service. All of the costs in the setup pool, for example, would be divided by the number of setups to determine the cost per setup. Alternatively, if setups vary in complexity, the allocation base could be the estimated number of setup hours. In that case, output from the setup pool would be expressed in terms of a setup cost per hour.

Exhibit 10 shows Wafer Pen Company's total number of machine hours, batches, and special quality inspections by product. The totals are used in Exhibit 11 to calculate a cost per machine hour, batch, and quality inspection. Notice that in Exhibit 11, Wafer's overhead costs are classified into pools using Cooper's hierarchy. The total plant overhead costs have not changed (see Exhibit 6). The only difference is the classification.

Look, for example, at the costs of quality control inspections. The total cost of inspections—$92,000—has been divided between batch-level and product-level costs in proportion to the time Wafer's quality engineers estimate they spend on general quality control issues (90%) and special inspections of the silver and gold pens (10%).

Exhibit 10   Wafer Pen Company: Machine Hours, Batches, and Special Quality Inspections by Product

Product	Machine Hours	Batches	Special Quality Inspections
Black pens	1,000	12	0
Blue pens	500	12	0
Red pens	260	12	0
Green pens	120	12	0
Silver pens	100	12	1
Gold pens	20	12	1
Total	2,000	72	2

Notice that instead of using one predetermined overhead rate, Wafer is using four allocation bases: machine hours, batches, special quality control inspections, and overhead costs to date. Each of those bases is the denominator in an overhead rate calculation.

Exhibit 11   Wafer Pen Company: Overhead Cost per Unit of Activity by Activity Pool

Unit-Level Costs

Boxing, labeling, and shipping	$ 60,000	
Depreciation (forklifts, manufacturing equipment, factory building)	100,000	
Electricity (plant operations)	12,000	
Supplies and repairs	6,000	
Total unit-level costs		$178,000

Cost per machine hour:
$178,000 ÷ 2,000 machine hours = $89

Batch-Level Costs

Raw materials and component handling and transportation	$ 90,000	
Quality control inspections ($92,000 × .90)*	82,800	
Machine setups	120,000	
Total batch-level costs		292,800

Cost per batch: $292,800 ÷ 72 batches = $4,067

Product-Level Costs

Quality control inspections ($92,000 × .10)*		9,200

Cost per product: $9,200 ÷ 2 products requiring special inspections = $4,600

Total overhead costs to date		$480,000

Facility-Level Costs

Plant supervision		70,000

*Cost per overhead costs to date: $70,000 ÷ $480,000 total unit-, batch-, and product-level costs = $.1458***

Total plant overhead costs		$550,000

* The quality control inspectors spend 90% of their time on general inspections and 10% of their time on special inspections of the silver and gold pens.
**For every dollar of unit-, batch-, and product-level overhead cost applied to a pen, $ .1458 of facility-level costs also is applied.

In the second stage of activity-based costing, the costs are allocated to the products. In Exhibit 12 we have used the number of cost drivers from Exhibit 10 and the cost per activity from Exhibit 11 to calculate an activity-based cost for each product.

For example, the unit overhead cost in Exhibit 12 for the silver pens was calculated this way:

Unit-level costs:	100 hours × $89 per machine hour	$ 8,900
Batch-level costs:	12 batches × $4,067 per batch	48,804
Product-level costs:	1 product type × $4,600	4,600
Subtotal		$62,304
Facility-level costs:	$.1458 × $62,304 cost to date	9,084
Total overhead cost of the silver pen		$71,388

To calculate the overhead cost per unit, we divide $71,388 by 50,000 (Exhibit 4), the number of silver pens produced. The unit overhead cost is $1.43. The total cost per unit (including direct materials and labor cost of $.07 a unit) is $1.50.

Exhibit 12 Wafer Pen Company: Activity-Based Cost by Product

Overhead costs	Products						
	Black Pens	Blue Pens	Red Pens	Green Pens	Silver Pens	Gold Pens	Total
Unit	$ 89,000	$ 44,500	$23,140	$10,680	$ 8,900	$ 1,780	$178,000
Batch	48,804	48,804	48,804	48,804	48,804	48,804	292,824[1]
Product					4,600	4,600	9,200
Total overhead costs to date	$137,804	$ 93,304	$71,944	$59,484	$62,304	$55,184	$480,024[1]
Facility	20,092	13,604	10,489	8,673	9,084	8,046	69,988[1]
Total plant overhead costs	$157,896	$106,908	$82,433	$68,157	$71,388	$63,230	$550,012[1]
Production volume in units (Exhibit 4)	500,000	250,000	130,000	60,000	50,000	10,000	1,000,000
Manufacturing overhead costs per unit[2]	$.32	$.43	$.63	$1.14	$1.43	$6.32	
Direct materials costs per unit	.02	.02	.02	.02	.02	.02	
Direct labor costs per unit	.05	.05	.05	.05	.05	.05	
Total cost per unit	$.39	$.50	$.70	$1.21	$1.50	$6.39	
Selling price (Exhibit 8)	$.60	$.65	$.75	$.75	$2.00	$4.00	
Profit (loss) per unit	$.21	$.15	$.05	$(.46)	$.50	$(2.39)	

[1] *These totals differ slightly from those in Exhibit 11 because of rounding.*
[2] *Total plant overhead costs ÷ production volume.*

Exhibit 13 illustrates the design of Wafer's ABC system. Notice the elements in the first stage of allocation (costs are divided into activity pools) and the second stage of allocation (costs are allocated to the products). Notice, too, how the activity pools are classified according to Cooper's hierarchy.

Exhibit 13 Wafer Pen Company: The Conceptual Design of an ABC System

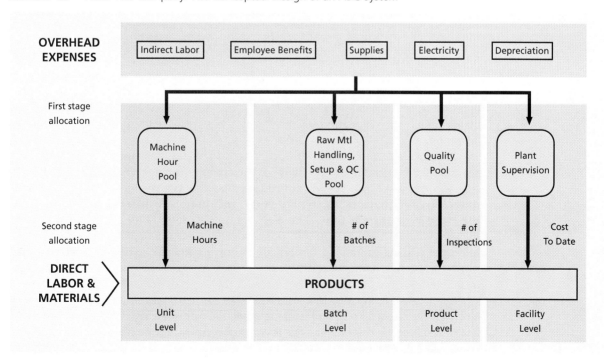

Exhibit 14 compares Wafer's unit product costs using traditional volume-based allocation with those using activity-based costing. The exhibit suggests that volume-based method overstated the unit costs of the black and blue pens and understated the unit costs of all the other pens.

Exhibit 14   Wafer Pen Company: Volume-Based Costs per Unit Versus Activity-Based Costs per Unit

Allocation Method	Black Pens	Blue Pens	Red Pens	Green Pens	Silver Pens	Gold Pens
Volume-based (Exhibit 8)	$.62	$.62	$.62	$ .62	$ .62	$ .62
ABC (Exhibit 12)	$.39	$.50	$.70	$1.21	$1.50	$6.39

Why do the two allocation methods yield different unit costs? More specifically, why does the ABC method yield different unit costs for the six pens? The unit-level costs listed in Exhibit 12 do not explain the differences in unit product costs among the six pens. Remember that each product is assigned overhead costs at a rate of $89 per machine hour. When the unit-level costs are divided by the number of units of each pen produced, the unit cost is $.178 whether Wafer makes a green pen ($10,680 ÷ 60,000 units = $.178) or a gold pen ($1,780 ÷ 10,000 = $.178).

The batch-level costs explain much of the difference in unit costs across Wafer's mix of products. Remember that batch-level costs address economies of scale. Here production volume does make a difference. Even though each product was allocated $48,804 for the costs of materials handling, quality control, and machine setups, some of the products were manufactured in much smaller quantities than others. The batch-level costs of the black pens, for example, are less than $.10 a unit ($48,804 ÷ 500,000 pens); the batch-level costs of the gold pens are $4.88 a unit ($48,804 ÷ 10,000 pens). By not recognizing economies of scale, (volume-based) allocation penalizes high-volume products and subsidizes low-volume products.

The product-level costs also help explain some of the variation in unit costs among the six pens. The ABC system tells managers that the silver and gold pens use quality control resources that the other pens do not. The costs of special inspections add to the unit costs of the metallic pens. What about the facility-level costs? Remember that those costs are assigned to products arbitrarily. Wafer assigned them proportionately to the total of unit-, batch-, and product-level costs to date. Because facility-level costs are allocated arbitrarily, they do not reflect a product's resource consumption as accurately as unit-, batch-, and product-level costs. That means that management may not find facility-level costs very helpful in making certain decisions.

What are the implications of our findings to Wafer's management? First, the silver and gold pens are not as profitable as the company's managers had thought. Product cross-subsidy is present. **Accountants use the term** *product cross-subsidy* **to describe a situation in which one product subsidizes (supports) the reported costs of another.** The high-volume black and blue pens are subsidizing the low-volume metallic pens. Although Wafer can sell the metallic pens for a higher price, the costs of producing those pens in low volume are extremely high. A long-run strategy of adding specialty pens to the company's product line could be disastrous.

Of course, a company's long-run strategies for marketing and production have to be based on more than manufacturing costs. A company may choose to offer a full line of products because retailers would rather order from one manufacturer than six. Also, a company may wish to establish its reputation as an expert, full-line producer.

A well-designed system for allocating costs to activities and products cannot answer all of management's questions. It can give the basic information managers need to chart the future course of their company.

C A S E

In Point

http://www.swcollege. com/ingram.html

Learn more about Siemens.

Siemens Electric Motor Works of Germany specialized in the production of electric motors used in industries ranging from pulp and paper to refrigeration. For many years the company emphasized high-volume standardized motors. However, for strategic reasons, the management of Siemens decided to begin producing special motors in small quantities. Those motors would require extra components and order-processing activities.

The traditional volume-based allocation system Siemens was using could not differentiate between the overhead costs of making a high-volume standard motor and the costs of making a low-volume special motor. In other words, the unit cost of producing one motor of a specific type was the same as producing the same motor in quantities of 20, 50, or 100. The company's ABC system painted a very different picture of overhead allocation. The special motors were much more expensive to produce. Not only were the costs of handling components and processing orders higher with each batch of special motors, each batch had fewer units over which to spread those costs. Using its ABC system, Siemen's management had more accurate information on which to base its pricing decisions. Though Siemens continued to produce the low-volume special motor, selling prices were based on a better understanding of production costs.

Source: The information here is based on R. Cooper, Siemens Electric Motor Works, *Case number 9-189-089 (Boston: Harvard Business School Press, 1993).*

COST ALLOCATION AND DECISION MAKING IN THE SERVICE SECTOR

Objective 7
Explain how service organizations use cost information for decision making.

Throughout this chapter, the term *cost object* has been used to refer to the product of a manufacturing process. ABC allows us to define cost objects very broadly. Services also can be cost objects. Services offered by organizations also may be classified as cost objects. The primary activities a service organization carries out are its *core activities;* its supporting activities are called *noncore activities.*

The core activity of a public school is education: teaching students such subjects as math, chemistry, biology, history, a foreign language, and English. To carry out that primary activity, schools rely on a host of noncore activities. For example, most school districts offer bus transportation to students. What are the costs of providing that supporting service? How do the people who manage school districts use that cost information?

Some school districts outsource their transportation services. For those districts the direct costs of transportation are defined in their contract with the bus company. For the districts that deliver their own transportation services, the direct costs of those services include the costs of buses, tires, fuel, drivers' wages and benefits, repairs, maintenance, and insurance. In both cases, there are the indirect costs of the administrators who set busing policy and develop the bus routes. A school district, then, could have several different activity pools that have to do with delivering transportation services.

How do school districts use activity-based costing in their decision making? For some, that information was a basis for the decision to outsource transportation services. By focusing on their core activity (education) and reducing noncore activities (such as busing), some districts have managed to reduce the costs of supporting activities and to apply the savings to core areas.

SELF-STUDY PROBLEM 3

Athena Company produces high-quality hand tools for woodworking. The company is conducting an ABC study. You are a manager at Athena, and you have been given the following information:

©Charles Gupton/Stock•Boston

Costs and Activity Rates by Overhead Category

	Unit Level	Batch Level	Product Level	Facility Level
Estimated cost	$50,000	$20,000	$10,000	$20,000
Estimated activity	500 machine hours	80 materials movements	25 engineering drawings	(applied as a percentage of unit-, batch-, and product-level costs)

You have been asked to calculate the overhead costs associated with products A and B. The units produced of and the resources consumed by products A and B are as follows:

Product	Units Produced	Machine Hours	Material Movements	Engineering Drawings
A	40	40	1	0
B	10	10	2	2

Required

1. Calculate the:
   a. cost per machine hour.
   b. cost per materials movement.
   c. cost per engineering drawing.
   d. predetermined overhead rate for facility-level costs.
2. Determine the total overhead costs and the unit overhead cost of products A and B.
3. Explain why the overhead costs of the two products are different.

The solution to Self-Study Problem 3 appears at the end of the chapter.

R E V I E W *Summary of Important Concepts*

1. The volume-based method of allocating costs to products was developed at a time when overhead costs were a relatively small portion of product costs.

    a.   The method uses a single activity base and a single predetermined overhead rate to allocate overhead costs to products.

    b.   Throughout a period, overhead is allocated to products by multiplying the actual amount of the activity base used (machine hours, for example) by the predetermined overhead rate.

2.   Today overhead costs make up the largest portion of a company's product costs.

3.   With the growing importance of overhead costs has come a need for greater accuracy in the allocation of those costs.

    a.   The traditional method ignores volume diversity; that is, it makes no allowance for economies of scale.

    b.   By limiting a company to a single activity base, the traditional method of cost allocation distorts costs.

4.   Cooper's hierarchy of costs is based on allocation by activity rather than volume.

    a.   Unit-level costs are like variable costs; they are constant per unit but change in total with the number of units produced.

    b.   Batch-level costs are like fixed costs; they vary per unit but are constant in total. These costs recognize economies of scale.

    c.   Product-level costs are incurred in manufacturing a product or product family.

    d.   Facility-level costs are not related to a particular unit or batch or family of products; they are necessary to sustain a company's overall operations.

5.   Activity-based costing allocates overhead costs on the basis of the activities that are necessary to produce a product.

    a.   In the first stage of the allocation process, a company assigns overhead costs to activity pools and chooses an activity base (a cost driver) for each pool.

    b.   In the second stage, activity pools are assigned to a cost object—a good or service.

6.   Activity-based costing gives managers of manufacturing and service companies the accurate cost information they need to make planning decisions.

DEFINE   *Terms and Concepts Defined in This Chapter*

Activity pool (165)   Cooper's hierarchy (162)   Product cross-subsidy (168)
Activity-based costing (ABC) (164)   Economies of scale (161)   Volume diversity (161)

SOLUTIONS

SELF-STUDY PROBLEM 1

1.   Troy's predetermined overhead rate is $14.20 per direct labor hour:

Predetermined overhead rate = estimated overhead costs ÷ estimated direct labor hours
= ($50,000 + $20,000 + $60,000 + $12,000) ÷ 10,000
= $142,000 ÷ 10,000
= $14.20 per direct labor hour

2. The unit cost of product A is $19.10:

Direct material costs per unit	$ 7.00
Direct labor costs per unit	5.00
Manufacturing overhead costs per unit	
($14.20 × 1/2 hour)	7.10
Total cost per unit	$19.10

SELF-STUDY PROBLEM 2

Lighting costs for the production areas are a facility-level cost. The lighting costs are not associated with any specific unit, batch, or family of products; they are related indirectly to all of the company's products.

Raw materials movement costs are a batch-level cost because raw materials are moved each time a new batch of products is placed into production.

The costs of cooling metal-cutting equipment are a unit-level cost. Those costs are a function of the number of hours the equipment is operating. When the equipment is idle, the cooling system also is idle.

The research and development expenses incurred to develop a product are a product-level cost. Those expenses can be associated with one product or product family. Although GAAP require that research and development costs be expensed in the period in which they are incurred, internal decision makers often treat those costs as overhead.

SELF-STUDY PROBLEM 3

1.
   a. The cost per machine hour is $100 ($50,000 ÷ 500 hours)
   b. The cost per material movement is $250 ($20,000 ÷ 80 moves)
   c. The cost per engineering drawing is $400 ($10,000 ÷ 25 drawings)
   d. The facility-level predetermined overhead rate is .25 [$20,000 ÷ (50,000 + $20,000 + $10,000)]

2.

	Product A	Product B
Machine hours:		
40 hours × $100 per hour	$4,000	
10 hours × $100 per hour		$1,000
Movements:		
1 movement × $250	250	
2 movements × 250		500
Engineering drawings:		
0 drawings × $400	-0-	
2 drawings × $400		800
Subtotal (cost to date)	$4,250	$2,300
Facility-level cost subtotal × $.25	1,063	575
Total overhead costs	$5,313	$2,875
Units produced	40	10
Overhead cost per unit	$133	$288

3. Economies of scale are evident in the lower cost per unit for product A, which is produced in a quantity four times that of product B. Also, product A was produced in one large batch versus two small batches of product B (one movement versus two). In addition, product A does not consume engineering services. Product A might be a mature product whose manufacturing process is stable and requires little attention.

EXERCISES

5-1. Write a short definition of each of the terms listed in the *Terms and Concepts Defined in This Chapter* section.

Obj. 1 **5-2.** In addition to the costs of direct materials and direct labor, what production costs are included in the value of manufactured products? Can those costs be traced directly to particular products? How do those costs become part of product costs?

Obj. 2 **5-3.** Last month, when his father, Nathan, retired, Norm Gregory became president of his family's manufacturing business. The company produces camping and mountain-climbing equipment that is sold in specialty shops throughout the country. At a retirement party, Nathan told his son, "I started this business 40 years ago producing a single model of tent. Now we make five models of tents and hundreds of other items! Our plant has been updated with the most modern equipment and manufacturing technologies." How do you think the company's expanded product line and technological advances have affected its allocation of manufacturing overhead?

Obj. 4 **5-4.** Quantro Enterprises has invested heavily in automated equipment over the past ten years. In that time Quantro has installed materials handling systems, automated flexible manufacturing cells, and machines geared for fast setup. All of those changes have allowed Quantro to reduce its labor costs by more than 35% while increasing production by 150%. Quantro has been applying overhead to products based on direct labor-hours. What impact do the changes in Quantro's manufacturing process have on its application of its overhead? What impact on overhead assignment is created by economies of scale? Explain your answers.

Obj. 5 **5-5.** Leslie Dunn is the controller of Demarco Company. Demarco produces six separate product lines in a single plant. Each line has a product manager who is accountable for the production costs of that line. Leslie is preparing for a meeting with the product managers to discuss the facility-level costs that will be allocated to each product line over the next year. She knows that the product managers are going to argue over those costs and the method of allocation to their product lines. Why would facility-level charges be a source of disagreement among the managers?

Objs. 4, 5 **5-6.** Denver Materials Company operates a recycling center that separates metals and then sells them to steel mills. The company uses large machinery to sort, move, and crush the metals. Denver's business throughout the year is uneven, in large part because the collection of recyclable materials varies greatly from month to month. In some months, the plant is slow. In others, supervisors have to authorize overtime to work the mountains of materials that the company receives. Management charges overhead costs to each job based on total machine hours for each batch processed. Explain how changes in volume and activity can distort the cost of each batch.

Obj. 6 **5-7.** Minor Medical Company is a manufacturer of blood pressure monitors, catheters, surgical instruments and other medical products. In each of the past five years, Minor has added approximately ten new products to its sales. Although its product line has become more diversified and its manufacturing processes more complex, Minor continues to apply overhead costs using a single activity base—direct labor hours. Explain why activity-based costing would benefit this company.

Objs. 4, 6 **5-8.** T-Bar Industries, Inc., manufactures radios and compact disk players. For years T-Bar's production process has been labor-intensive; its primary production cost has been the wages of many direct laborers who assemble components along its production lines. Management at T-Bar is considering an investment in new technology that would automate 80% of the production process. The new machinery and the computer systems to operate it cost hundreds of thousands of dollars. T-Bar historically has allocated manufacturing overhead on the basis of direct labor hours. What change in cost structure should T-Bar expect if the company decides to invest in the new technology? What problems would that change in cost structure create? Explain your answer.

Objs. 4, 6 **5-9.** Vera Hutchinson Company manufactures a wide variety of leather wallets, purses, and brief-cases. Each product has its own manufacturing process. Some of those processes are labor-intensive; others are highly automated. The company uses a single plantwide rate based on direct labor hours to allocate overhead costs to products. Would the company improve its allocation of overhead costs by increasing the number of overhead rates it uses? Explain your answer.

Obj. 6 **5-10.** Alice Glidden is the chief financial officer of Brown Ribbon Industries, Inc., a manufacturer of gift wraps, ribbons, and party supplies. A local Certified Management Accountant has suggested that Alice implement an ABC system. The accountant told Alice that activity-based costing would not "overload" high-volume products with overhead costs. What did the accountant mean?

Objs. 6, 7 **5-11.** Apply the concepts of activity-based costing to an airline flight in which each passenger is a "unit of product." Give examples of unit-, batch-, product-, and facility-level costs.

Objs. 1, 7 **5-12.** Jose Glass had a car accident last month and spent a night in the hospital. The bill came yesterday, and when he looked it over he noted that he had been charged $7 for a single dose of aspirin. Believing it was a clerical error, Jose called the hospital and was told that the charge was correct. The person he spoke to in the billing department said that the charge includes "overhead allocation." How would overhead allocation affect the cost of aspirin?

Objs. 4, 7 **5-13.** The law firm of Menard and Baker specializes in civil litigation. The overhead costs of operating the office are charged to clients as an administrative surcharge. The surcharge is based on attorneys' hours. The managing partner of the firm, Cynthia Menard, has noticed that clients who require extensive legal service often complain about the administrative surcharge. After reviewing costs and time sheets, Cynthia has determined that administrative costs usually are not a function of attorneys' hours, but of the time incurred by administrative personnel. How does volume affect the allocation of administrative costs? What changes should the firm consider? Why?

PROBLEMS

PROBLEM 5-1   Fill in the Blanks

Complete the following sentences with the appropriate term(s) from the chapter.

1. To calculate a single plantwide _____, a company does not have to separate indirect manufacturing costs into individual cost pools.

2. To calculate a burden rate, a company must estimate its indirect costs and a(n) _____.

3. _____ are the costs that sustain a company's general manufacturing facilities.

4. Activity-based costing more accurately traces the costs of production by shifting overhead costs from _____ goods or services to _____ goods or services.

5. _____ costs are incurred each time a batch of goods is processed.

6. Cost _____ is a problem when a company uses a single basis for allocating the costs of _____.

7. Using activity-based costing, overhead costs that vary in direct proportion to the number of units produced would be _____ costs.

8. Using activity-based costing, the costs of engineering a particular product line would be _____ costs.

9. The objective of activity-based costing is to associate as many costs as possible with specific _____.

10. The savings a company realizes by spreading fixed manufacturing overhead costs over a large number of products are called _____.

PROBLEM 5-2 The Ethics of Overhead Allocation

Objs. 2,3

Amanda Tubbs owns a small factory that produces buttons for the garment industry. Amanda wants to buy a new machine and has applied to a bank for financing. The loan officer has asked for operating statements for the past year. The company's net income has not been very good over that time, and inventory has grown substantially. Amanda is concerned that the bank is not going to be as optimistic as she is about future sales and the company's ability to reduce its inventory.

Yesterday, Amanda had this conversation with Willie Hancock, the company's controller:
Amanda: You know that I've applied for a bank loan and that the bank wants copies of our operating statements for the last twelve months.
Willie: I can have those ready for you in an hour.
Amanda: I'd like you to make some changes before you prepare those statements, Willie.
Willie: What sort of changes?
Amanda: I want you to increase our predetermined overhead rate by 25% and then recalculate the inventory figures and last year's income statement using the new rate. Also, move my salary and our office rent into the manufacturing overhead pool. I'll need those statements first thing in the morning.

Required

a. What effect would the change in predetermined overhead rate have on the company's inventory values?
b. What effect would the reclassification of Amanda's salary and the office rent have on the company's product costs?
c. Do you agree with the changes Amanda is asking for? What parts of the financial statements would reveal Amanda's changes to the loan officer?

PROBLEM 5-3 Multiple Cost Drivers: Calculating Predetermined Overhead Rates

Objs. 2,6

Randall Foundry uses four activity pools to assign costs to its products. Each pool has its own cost driver, the activity base used to calculate and apply overhead costs. Last year Randall prepared the following estimates of overhead costs and levels of activity for the first quarter of this year:

Activity Pool	Cost Driver	Estimated Overhead Costs	Estimated Level of Activity
Machine setups	Number of setups	$560,000	2,500 setups
Inspection	Number of inspections	$245,000	10,000 inspections
Receiving	Number of receipts	$ 21,300	1,200 receipts
Factory	Machine hours	$590,000	73,750 machine hours

The actual level of activity for each activity pool in the first quarter of operations this year was as follows:

Activity Pool	Actual Level of Activity
Machine setups	2,550 setups
Inspection	9,100 inspections
Receiving	1,750 receipts
Factory	71,000 machine hours

Required

a. Calculate the predetermined overhead rate for each activity pool.
b. Calculate the total overhead costs allocated to each activity center during the first quarter.
c. Randall is planning to run smaller batch sizes in an effort to reduce its inventories. The flow of raw materials will not be affected by that decision. What concerns should management address before it actually implements the plan?

PROBLEM 5-4 Multiple Overhead Pools: Assigning Overhead Costs to Products

Objs. 2,6

Randall Foundry (see Problem 5-3) traced the following levels of activity to the products it manufactured during the first quarter of this year:

		Actual Level of Activity			
Activity Pool	Total	Product A	Product B	Product C	Product D
Machine setups	2,550 setups	500	600	800	650
Inspection	9,100 inspections	3,165	2,155	780	3,000
Receiving	1,750 receipts	420	175	655	500
Factory	71,000 machine hours	19,250	14,300	21,500	15,950

Required

a. Using the predetermined overhead rates you calculated in Problem 5-3, determine the overhead costs charged to each product for the quarter. Show total overhead costs for each product and for each activity pool by product.
b. Reconcile the amount of overhead applied by product to the total overhead applied by activity pool in Problem 5-3.

PROBLEM 5-5 Overhead Allocation: The Effects of Volume

Objs. 3,6

Taylor Sweets, Inc., produces a popular brand of chocolate candies. The company's manufacturing process is labor-intensive: Chocolate, sugar, and other ingredients are measured by hand, blended in a large mixer, and then heated. Next, the mixture is spread by hand into molds. When the mixture is cool, the candies are removed from the molds, placed in paper cups, and then boxed. All of these steps are done by hand.

Tim Gabet, Taylor's President, is considering a modernization project that would significantly increase the amount of candy the company can produce. Under his plan, the measuring and mold-filling procedures would be automated, and a single machine would remove the candies from the molds, wrap them individually, and box them.

Tim is excited about the possibility of increasing production volume but realizes that automation can be very expensive. If automation would increase Taylor's overhead cost more than $.04 per unit, Tim knows he will have to reject the project. Taylor allocates overhead costs to production based on direct labor hours. Estimates of production volume and overhead costs under the current process and the automated process are as follows:

	Current Process	Automated Processes
Production volume in units	50,000	450,000
Total overhead costs	$15,000	$162,000

Required

a. Given Tim's target increase, should he go ahead with the automation project?
b. What is the minimum number of units (rounded to the nearest unit) that Taylor would have to produce at the expected level of overhead cost per unit to accept the project?

c. Suppose that Taylor allocates overhead on the basis of machine hours instead of direct labor hours. Would the project be accepted or rejected? Explain your answer.

PROBLEM 5-6 Product Costing: Different Activity Bases

Objs. 2,3,6

Mallory Chemical Corporation produces two products: A and B. The company's expected factory overhead costs for the coming year are as follows:

Overhead Category	Estimated Costs
Utilities	$ 300,000
Indirect materials	150,000
Indirect labor	50,000
Depreciation	100,000
Materials handling and storage	200,000
Repairs and maintenance	200,000
Supplies	180,000
Insurance	120,000
Other	50,000
Total	$1,350,000

Its expected levels of production activity are as follows:

	Product A	Product B
Machine hours	35,000	15,000
Direct labor hours	20,000	25,000
Number of units produced	10,000	5,000
Direct materials used, in pounds	75,000	125,000

All labor costs $10 per hour; materials cost $1.80 a pound for product A and $2.40 a pound for product B.

Required

a. Calculate the predetermined overhead rate based on direct labor hours and based on machine hours.
b. Calculate the unit cost of each product if overhead is applied on the basis of direct labor hours.
c. Calculate the unit cost of each product if overhead is applied on the basis of machine hours.
d. Compare the unit costs you have just calculated. Why does the choice of an activity base affect unit cost? What implications would the selection of an activity base for allocating overhead have on managerial decisions? What factors should management consider in choosing an activity base for assigning costs?

PROBLEM 5-7 Using Activity-Based Costing to Classify Cost Activities

Objs. 5,6

Dynamic Products, Inc., manufactures a wide variety of products in its plant in Macon, Georgia. Management has identified the following manufacturing and administrative activities:

1. Special equipment is used to add a protective finish to various products.

2. Purchase orders are issued to acquire raw materials.

3. Factory managers run training programs in quality control for new employees.

4. Machine setups are necessary for each batch of goods produced.

5. Janitors clean the offices and the plant floor each evening.

6. Warehouse personnel pull the stock needed for production and move the materials to the plant floor.

7. Receiving clerks inspect incoming materials and prepare receiving reports.

8. Quality control inspectors test each batch of goods before they are stored or shipped.

9. Payroll clerks process the factory workers' time cards and prepare weekly paychecks for distribution.

10. Engineers develop new-product specifications and redesign existing products as needed.

Required

a. Classify each of the activities listed as a unit-level, batch-level, product-level, or facility-level activity.
b. Identify a cost driver for each of the activities that could be used to apply costs to Dynamic's products.
c. For each activity, identify one or more traceable costs.

PROBLEM 5-8   Cost Allocation: Service Industry

Objs. 1,6,7

Franklin County Bank has a commercial loan department that makes loans to businesses that meet the bank's strict criteria. The department is staffed by eight loan officers. Each loan officer can grant loans up to a certain amount without the approval of the bank's lending committee. Loans that exceed that limit must be approved by the lending committee, which meets weekly.

The commercial loan department incurs significant costs administering and monitoring commercial loans. Among those costs are the wages of the credit analysts who review borrowers' financial statements; the wages of the administrative personnel who prepare loan packets; filing fees for security agreements; office rent; depreciation expense on office equipment, computers, and furniture; and fees for credit reports.

Anita Andrews, vice president of commercial loans, wants to allocate and collect administrative costs from borrowers in the form of a processing fee.

Required

a. What cost drivers could the bank use to allocate its overhead costs of processing commercial loans? What factors affect the choice of an activity base?
b. What estimates would be necessary to establish a processing fee if all costs are included?
c. How could activity-based costing be used to allocate overhead costs in the commercial loan department?

PROBLEM 5-9   Multiple-Choice Overview of the Chapter

1. Overhead allocation based on volume alone
   a. is a key element of activity-based costing.
   b. systematically overcosts high-volume products and undercosts low-volume products.
   c. systematically overcosts low-volume products and undercosts high-volume products.
   d. must be used to prepare external financial reports.

2. Using activity-based costing, overhead costs are accumulated in
   a. a single, companywide pool.
   b. departmental pools.
   c. pools created according to the number of cost drivers that can be identified.
   d. batches and allocated to products based on the costs of materials or labor.

3. Departmental overhead rates make more sense than plantwide overhead rates when
   a. the various departments in a plant carry out very different activities.
   b. all products require the same manufacturing effort in each department.
   c. most overhead costs are fixed.
   d. all departments in the plant are heavily automated.

4. Activity-based costing would be least effective when
   a. products differ substantially in volume and lot size.
   b. there is a close link between direct labor hours and overhead costs.
   c. managers use cost information to make pricing or other product decisions.
   d. the processes used to manufacture products differ substantially in terms of complexity.

5. All of the following are characteristic of activity-based costing except the
   a. use of cost drivers as a basis for allocating costs.
   b. accumulation of costs by activities.
   c. failure to recognize economies of scale.
   d. use of volume as a possible cost driver.

6. The allocation of overhead costs
   a. is used by service and manufacturing organizations to assign costs to products.
   b. is used only by manufacturing organizations.
   c. is used to assign the costs of direct materials and labor.
   d. must be based on sales or production volume.

7. The denominator used in calculating a predetermined overhead rate
   a. should have a causal relationship to the costs being assigned.
   b. is not affected by varying levels of volume.
   c. should change monthly to allow for fluctuations in volume.
   d. is determined once volume and actual costs are known.

8. The level of activity that is most likely to use volume for the allocation of overhead is the
   a. unit level.
   b. product level.
   c. batch level.
   d. facility level.

9. An example of a product-level cost is the cost
   a. of setting up machines for different products.
   b. incurred to operate a break room.
   c. of a factory's payroll.
   d. incurred to operate a product-testing center.

10. An example of a batch-level cost is the cost
    a. of setting up machines for different products.
    b. incurred to operate a break room.
    c. of a factory's payroll.
    d. incurred to operate a product-testing center.

CASES

CASE 5-1 Activity-Based Costing Versus Traditional Cost Allocation

Objs. 4,6

C. Berry Manufacturing Company produces two models of guitars. One is a standard acoustic guitar that sells for $600 and is constructed from medium-grade materials. The other model is a custom-made amplified guitar with pearl inlays and a body constructed from special woods. The custom guitar sells for $900. Both guitars require 10 hours of direct labor to produce, but the custom guitar is manufactured by more experienced workers who are paid at a higher rate.

Most of C. Berry's sales come from the standard guitar, but sales of the custom model have been growing. Here is the company's sales, production, and cost information for last year:

	Standard Guitar	Custom Guitar
Sales and production volume in units	900	100
Unit costs:		
Direct materials	$150	$375
Direct labor	180	240
Manufacturing overhead	135	135
Total unit costs	$465	$750

Manufacturing overhead costs:	
Building depreciation	$ 40,000
Maintenance	15,000
Purchasing	20,000
Inspection	12,000
Indirect materials	15,000
Supervision	30,000
Supplies	3,000
Total manufacturing overhead costs	$135,000

The company allocates overhead costs using the traditional method. Its activity base is direct labor hours. The predetermined overhead rate, based on 10,000 direct labor hours, is $13.50 ($135,000 ÷ 10,000 direct labor hours).

Nick Fessler, president of C. Berry, is concerned that the traditional cost-allocation system the company is using may not be generating accurate information and that the selling price of the custom guitar may not be covering its true cost.

Required

a. The cost-allocation system C. Berry has been using allocates 90% of overhead costs to the standard guitar because 90% of direct labor hours were spent on the standard model. How much overhead was allocated to each of the two models last year? Discuss why this might not be an accurate way to assign overhead costs to products.

b. How would the use of more than one cost pool improve C. Berry's cost allocation?

c. C. Berry's controller developed the following data:

Manufacturing Overhead Cost	Amount	Cost Driver	Standard Guitar	Custom Guitar
Building depreciation	$40,000	Square footage	3,000	1,000
Maintenance	15,000	Direct labor hours	9,000	1,000
Purchasing	20,000	Number of purchase orders	1,500	500
Inspection	12,000	Number of inspections	400	600
Indirect materials	15,000	Number of units	900	100
Supervision	30,000	Number of inspections	400	600
Supplies	3,000	Number of units	900	100

Use activity-based costing to allocate the costs of overhead per unit and in total to each model of guitar.

d. Calculate the cost of a custom guitar using activity-based costing. Why is the cost different from the cost calculated using the traditional allocation method? At the current selling price, is the company covering its true cost of production? Explain your answer.

CASE 5-2   Overhead Allocation: A Service Environment

Objs. 1,2,6,7

The East State Veterinary Clinic provides veterinary services for small domestic animals. Three certified veterinarians and four technical assistants work at the clinic. The clinic has three separate areas of operations: examination, surgeries, and laboratory tests. The technical assistants help with exams and surgery and perform the majority of laboratory tests.

The clinic allocates administrative and operating overhead to the three service areas using a single rate based on the veterinarians' direct labor-hours. Information about services and costs for the past fiscal quarter are as follows:

Area of Operations	Veterinarians' Direct Labor Hours	Number of Patients
Examinations	1,200	800
Surgeries	200	60
Laboratory tests	100	600
Total	1,500	

Overhead Item	Cost
Maintenance and supplies, exam rooms	$ 8,500
Depreciation, surgical equipment	6,000
Surgical supplies	2,000
Depreciation, laboratory equipment	2,000
Laboratory supplies	4,000
Total	$22,500

Required

a. Calculate the clinic's predetermined overhead rate based on the activity in the most recent quarter, and use that rate to allocate costs to each service area.
b. How does the use of a single activity base and rate disproportionately allocate costs among the three service areas? Explain your answer.
c. Calculate separate overhead rates for each of the three service areas using the veterinarian's direct labor hours incurred in each area as the activity base. Why do the rates differ for each service area? Calculate the overhead cost (rounded to the nearest dollar) that would have been allocated to each area using the three separate rates.

PROJECTS

PROJECT 5-1 Recognizing Overhead Costs

Objs. 1,3,5

Tour a business or manufacturing plant. During the tour make a note of the activities you see that incur overhead costs. In a short report, identify the company's product (good or service), and explain why the costs you noted during the tour are part of the company's product costs.

PROJECT 5-2 Overhead Application in Practice

Objs. 2,3,4,6

Ask a management accountant to come to a class and discuss the different methods of allocating overhead costs to production that he or she has used or observed. Ask how changes in manufacturing technologies have affected cost-allocation methods.

PROJECT 5-3 Effect of Volume on Cost

Objs. 2,3

Browse the Internet. Locate a Web site that describes a tangible or intangible product, or a news site that contains an article on a particular product. Prepare a report that outlines the content of the Web site and explains the effect volume, or market demand, has on the cost of the product.

Section 2

Control, Measurement, and Evaluation

The Role of Budgets in Decision Making

Accounting and Management Decisions

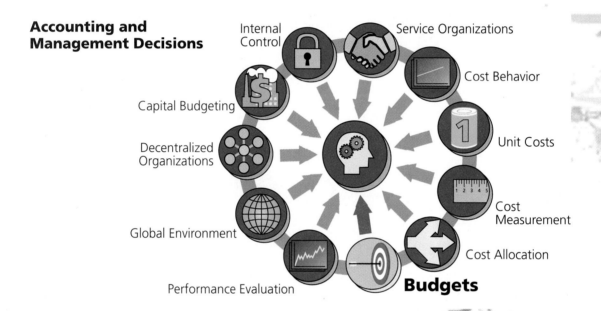

- Internal Control
- Service Organizations
- Cost Behavior
- Unit Costs
- Cost Measurement
- Cost Allocation
- **Budgets**
- Performance Evaluation
- Global Environment
- Decentralized Organizations
- Capital Budgeting

Overview

This chapter looks at the role of budgeting in decision making. Budgeting is an important tool in managing a company's financial performance. The discussion of budgeting includes the development of the master budget, which is a widely used concept in budgeting. Standard costs and quantities as an important part of budgeting are introduced. The current chapter presents the development of both operating and financial budgets and explains the concept of flexible budgets. Standard costs and flexible budgets are important because they help managers understand what costs should be, given different levels of sales and production. Finally, this chapter deals with how the company's budgeting culture, important considerations when budgeting, and the behavioral aspects of budgeting affect decision making.

Major topics covered in this chapter include:
- An overview of the master budget process.
- Development of a master budget.
- Basic analysis of budget data.
- Development of a sound budgeting culture in companies.
- How some companies construct effective budgets.
- Implications of budgets for management behavior.

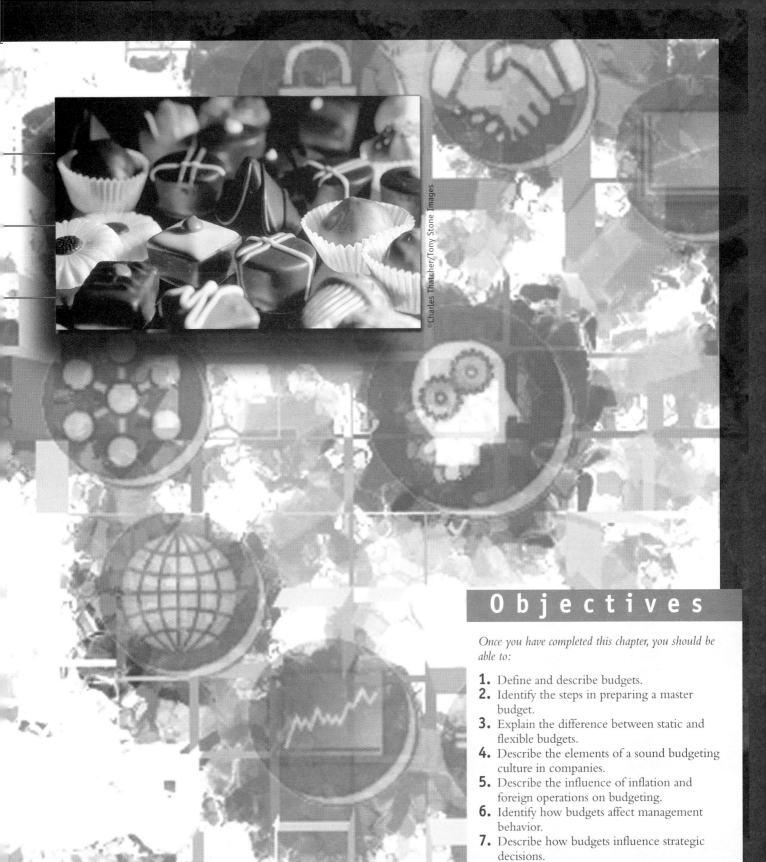

Charles Thatcher/Tony Stone Images

Objectives

Once you have completed this chapter, you should be able to:

1. Define and describe budgets.
2. Identify the steps in preparing a master budget.
3. Explain the difference between static and flexible budgets.
4. Describe the elements of a sound budgeting culture in companies.
5. Describe the influence of inflation and foreign operations on budgeting.
6. Identify how budgets affect management behavior.
7. Describe how budgets influence strategic decisions.
8. Explain the role of budgets in service organizations.

OVERVIEW OF THE MASTER BUDGET

Objective 1
Define and describe budgets.

A *budget* **is a detailed plan describing the use of financial and operating resources over a specific period.** A budget describes management's expectations for the company's future in terms of numbers and dollars. It contains specific details about management's financial goals and expectations for future resource requirements. It provides a means for managers to measure a company's progress toward specific financial goals. Consequently, managers in both manufacturing and service companies use budgets to monitor and control their operations. A budget is prepared for a specific period, typically a year for operating budgets. Some companies budget for longer periods.

A *master budget* **is a collection of related budgets covering sales, production, purchasing, labor, manufacturing overhead, administrative expenses, and financing activities.** Together, these individual budgets provide a strategic summary of a company's financial plans and goals. The master budget results in a set of pro forma financial statements. Pro forma means "before the fact." **Pro forma financial statements** identify expected, rather than actual, financial performance. Pro forma financial statements are prepared at the end of the budget process and include (1) a pro forma income statement giving the expected profit or loss for the budget period, (2) a pro forma balance sheet giving the anticipated levels of assets, liabilities, and equity at the end of the budget period, and (3) a pro forma cash flow statement (called a cash budget) giving the expected cash flows.

Exhibit 1   Components of a Master Budget

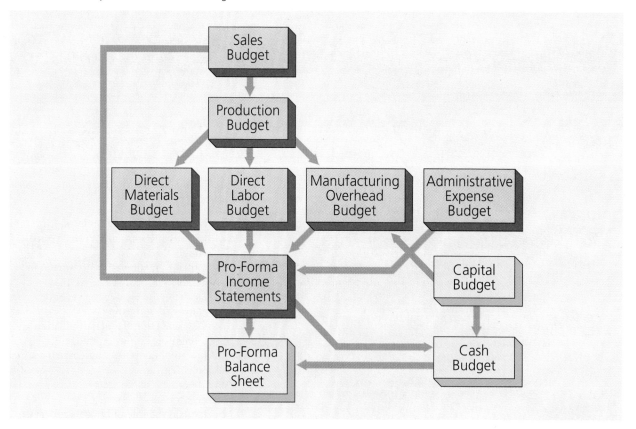

The master budget is a collection of several budgets, each of which provides financial details about part of a company's activities. Exhibit 1 illustrates the sequence in which the various budgets that form the master budget are prepared. These budgets can be separated into two subgroups, operating budgets and financial budgets.

Operating budgets **describe revenues, production costs, and general and administrative costs** and are shown with darker shading in Exhibit 1. *Financial budgets* **describe cash flows and financial position, including assets, liabilities, and owners' equity.** Financial budgets are developed after and rely on operating budgets and are shown with lighter shading in Exhibit 1. The financial requirements of a company's operations determine the expected amounts of assets and liabilities and the cash requirements.

DEVELOPING THE MASTER BUDGET

Objective 2
Identify the steps in preparing a master budget.

The components of the master budget referred to in Exhibit 1 are developed sequentially, beginning with the sales budget. Demand for a company's products is the driving force for production, and production creates production costs, such as the purchase of materials. This section examines each of the various master budget components.

Learning Note

This chapter does not cover **capital budgets,** which involve the acquisition of land, buildings, and equipment for plant expansion or replacement. Capital budgets are part of strategic planning and are covered in a later chapter.

A company normally develops a master budget for each month or quarter of the coming year. The Kirkland Company serves as an example of budget preparation in Exhibits 2 through 11. The company produces and sells gourmet chocolates that are marketed exclusively through fine-quality department stores. Kirkland prepares the following budgets on a quarterly basis:

1. A sales budget, including a schedule of expected cash collections.
2. A production budget.
3. A direct materials budget, including expected payments for raw materials.
4. A direct labor budget.
5. A manufacturing overhead budget.
6. A selling and administrative expense budget.
7. A cash budget.
8. A pro forma budgeted income statement.
9. A pro forma budgeted balance sheet.

Several calculations used in the development of the master budget for Kirkland require standard costs and quantities. *Standards* **identify the quantity and cost of inputs, such as materials and labor, expected for a single unit of product.**

Sales Budget

The *sales budget* **projects revenues from sales of a company's products or services.** It is prepared from a sales forecast, which is based on various factors such as past sales experience, pricing policies, unfilled orders, market research, general economic conditions, industry economic conditions, advertising and promotion plans, and competition. The sales budget is the starting point in preparing the master budget. Nearly all the other items in the master budget, including production requirements, purchases, and operating expenses, depend on the sales budget. Thus, it is important that the sales budget be as accurate as possible. Sales budget accuracy depends on an accurate sales forecast. Management sometimes sets unrealistic sales goals in the belief that these goals will inspire salespeople to sell more. Unrealistic sales forecasts, however, can lead to budgets that do not reflect the market for a company's products. Management accountants should work closely with sales and marketing personnel to ensure that the sales budget is realistic.

The sales budget is prepared by multiplying the expected sales in units by the unit sales price.

Expected sales dollars = expected sales (in units) × selling price (per unit)

If a company makes more than one product, this procedure is repeated for each product, and the dollar sales for all products are added together to calculate a total sales figure.

Generally, the sales budget is accompanied by a Schedule of Expected Cash Collections for the budgeted period. This schedule is needed for preparation of the cash budget. It is prepared along with the sales budget because the sales department generally controls the credit terms offered to customers. Expected cash collections for any given quarter are the sum of (1) expected cash sales during the quarter and (2) cash payments received for credit sales made in previous quarters. Exhibit 2 contains the sales budget and expected collection schedule for Kirkland.

Exhibit 2 A Sales Budget and Expected Cash Collections Schedule

Kirkland Company
Sales Budget
For the Year Ended December 31, 1998

| | Quarter | | | | |
	1	2	3	4	Year
Expected sales in units	1,000	3,000	4,000	2,000	10,000
Selling price per unit	$ 20	$ 20	$ 20	$ 20	$ 20
Total sales	$20,000	$60,000	$80,000	$40,000	$200,000

Schedule of Expected Cash Collections

	1	2	3	4	Year
Accounts receivable, 12/31/97*	$ 9,000				$ 9,000
First-quarter sales†	14,000	$ 6,000			20,000
Second-quarter sales		42,000	$18,000		60,000
Third-quarter sales			56,000	$24,000	80,000
Fourth-quarter sales‡				28,000	28,000
Total cash collections	$23,000	$48,000	$74,000	$52,000	$197,000

* *Assumed.*
† *Cash collections from sales are expected as follows: 70% in the quarter of sale, 30% in the following quarter. Note that the uncollected portion of sales at 12/31/97 was $9,000.*
‡ *The uncollected portion of fourth-quarter cash sales appears as Accounts Receivable on the year-end pro forma balance sheet.*

Production Budget

After the sales budget has been prepared, production requirements for the period can be calculated from existing inventories and expected sales, and a production budget can be prepared. **The** *production budget* **identifies the amount of a product that must be produced to meet a company's needs for sales and inventory.** In preparing the production budget, management must consider the amount of inventory needed for production requirements. Many companies prefer to keep some inventory of raw materials and finished goods on hand in case actual demand is greater than expected. Such inventories often are referred to as "just in case" inventories. In addition to producing enough units to meet sales demand, a company also must produce enough units to provide for the desired ending inventory levels. A portion of the production requirements will exist already in beginning finished goods inventory (last period's ending inventory).

Exhibit 3 shows a production budget for Kirkland. The production budget is developed by adding expected sales units to the desired ending inventory level and then subtracting the beginning inventory to arrive at the total number of units the company needs to produce.

Production budget = expected sales in units + desired ending inventory units − beginning inventory units

This process begins with the first quarter and moves sequentially to the fourth quarter. The ending inventory for each quarter becomes the beginning inventory for the following quarter. If a company manufactures more than one product, a production budget is developed for each product.

Recall that keeping inventory on hand is costly. Proper inventory planning is essential in order to avoid unnecessary inventory cost. The cost of keeping inventory should be compared with the possible loss of sales due to an inability to meet customer demand. Consequently, the amount of inventory kept on hand by a company will be determined by several factors, including (1) the ordering patterns of the company's customers, (2) the time required to produce and ship products, (3) the availability of raw materials, and (4) the reliability of suppliers of raw materials.

Exhibit 3   A Production Budget

Kirkland Company
Production Budget
For the Year Ended December 31, 1998

	Quarter				
	1	**2**	**3**	**4**	**Year**
Expected sales (from Exhibit 2)	1,000	3,000	4,000	2,000	10,000
Add desired ending inventory*†	600	800	400	**300**	**300**
Total needs	1,600	3,800	4,400	2,300	10,300
Less: Beginning inventory of finished goods‡	**200**	600	800	400	**200**
Units to produce	1,400	3,200	3,600	1,900	10,100

★   *Twenty percent of the following quarter sales (e.g., in the first quarter, 600 = 20% × 3,000 units that are expected to be sold in Quarter 2).*
†   *Note that Quarter 4 ending inventory is also the expected ending inventory for the year and is used when preparing the annual pro forma balance sheet.*
‡   *Beginning inventory is the assumed ending inventory from the prior quarter.*

Once a company's expected production requirements are known, resources used in production can be budgeted. The direct materials, direct labor, and manufacturing overhead budgets are based on the units forecast in the production budget.

Direct Materials Budget

The *direct materials budget* **identifies the amount of materials that will be required to support a company's total production needs.** The company will need enough materials to produce units for the period and to provide for the desired ending inventory levels of raw materials. Some raw materials will exist already in the form of beginning raw materials inventory. The remainder will be purchased from suppliers. For each successive period, the previous period's ending inventory becomes the beginning inventory for the period. If more than one material is required to manufacture a product, a separate schedule is developed for each material and the costs are combined to obtain a total cost of direct materials.

When this budget is constructed, generally a Schedule of Expected Cash Disbursements for materials also is prepared. This schedule is based on the credit terms the purchasing department anticipates receiving from its suppliers. The Schedule of Cash Disbursements is needed in preparing the cash budget. Exhibit 4 provides a direct materials budget for Kirkland. The number of units of product to be produced during each quarter is multiplied by the standard amount of raw materials needed to make a unit to determine the amount of raw materials required for production. The desired ending inventory of raw materials is added to this amount to obtain the total amount of raw materials needed. The beginning raw materials inventory is subtracted from the total amount needed to determine the amount the company needs to purchase.

Exhibit 4   A Direct Materials Budget

Kirkland Company
Direct Materials Budget
For the Year Ended December 31, 1998

	Quarter				
	1	2	3	4	Year
Units to be produced (from Exhibit 3)	1,400	3,200	3,600	1,900	10,100
Raw materials per unit (lbs.)	5	5	5	5	5
Production needs (lbs.)	7,000	16,000	18,000	9,500	50,500
Add desired ending inventory (lbs.)*	1,600	1,800	950	750	750
Total needs (lbs.)	8,600	17,800	18,950	10,250	51,250
Less: Beginning raw materials inventory (lbs.)†	700	1,600	1,800	950	700
Raw materials to be purchased	7,900	16,200	17,150	9,300	50,550
Cost of material purchases ($.60/lb.)	$4,740	$ 9,720	$10,290	$ 5,580	$30,330

* Ten percent of the following quarter production needs are desired as ending inventory each quarter (e.g., for Quarter 1, Quarter 2's production needs of 16,000 lbs. × 0.1 = 1,600 lbs.).
† Beginning inventory is the assumed ending inventory of the prior quarter.

Schedule of Expected Cash Disbursements

	1	2	3	4	Year
Accounts payable 12/31/97‡	$2,580				$2,580
First-quarter purchases§	2,370	$2,370			4,740
Second-quarter purchases		4,860	$4,860		9,720
Third-quarter purchases			5,145	$5,145	10,290
Fourth-quarter purchases¶				2,790	2,790
Total cash disbursements	$4,950	$7,230	$10,005	$7,935	$30,120

‡ Assumed.
§ Cash payments are expected to total 50% in quarter of purchase, and 50% in quarter following purchase.
¶ The unpaid portion of the fourth-quarter purchases appears in Accounts Payable on the year-end pro forma balance sheet.

Direct Labor Budget

Management also prepares the direct labor budget from the production budget. **The** *direct labor budget* **identifies the labor resources required to meet production needs.** Labor requirements can be predicted, and an organization can plan labor needs based on the direct labor budget. Failure to plan labor needs may result in labor shortages, unnecessary overtime, or unexpected layoffs. These results can affect employee morale and lead to high turnover. A direct labor budget also is necessary to project the total expected cost of direct labor.

Direct labor requirements are based on the number of units to be produced during a period, as determined in the production budget, multiplied by the number of direct labor hours required to produce one unit of product. The total direct labor hour requirements then are converted into expected direct labor costs. Though a company may face a wide range of labor costs due to different employees having different wage rates, an average rate often is used to compute direct labor costs. Some companies develop a separate schedule for each type of labor when rates vary across the types. A separate labor schedule must be developed for each product because different products consume different quantities of labor.

In some instances, organizations have contracts or employment policies that prevent them from laying off and rehiring workers. These commitments must be considered in calculating expected direct labor costs. Assume that Kirkland is able to adjust labor to its actual needs in Exhibit 5.

Exhibit 5 A Direct Labor Budget

Kirkland Company Direct Labor Budget For the Year Ended December 31, 1998					
	Quarter				
	1	**2**	**3**	**4**	**Year**
Units to be produced (from Exhibit 3)	1,400	3,200	3,600	1,900	10,100
Direct labor time per unit (hours)	0.8	0.8	0.8	0.8	0.8
Total hours of direct labor required	1,120	2,560	2,880	1,520	8,080
Direct labor cost per hour	$7.50	$7.50	$7.50	$7.50	$7.50
Total direct labor costs	$8,400	$19,200	$21,600	$11,400	$60,600

Kirkland's requirements for labor are least in Quarter 1, when only 1,400 units are expected to be produced. The requirements are greatest in Quarter 3, when 3,600 units are to be produced. Notice that the direct labor cost per hour remains constant at $7.50. If Kirkland had to use overtime to meet its labor requirements instead of hiring additional workers, this figure would increase because of the need to pay an overtime premium.

Manufacturing Overhead Budget

The *manufacturing overhead budget* **provides a schedule of all costs of production other than direct materials and direct labor.** Fixed and variable costs are separated for budgeting purposes. This separation permits actual and expected costs to be compared. From the manufacturing overhead budget, a predetermined overhead rate is developed by dividing the amount of expected overhead by the expected level of the activity base used to apply overhead.

Predetermined overhead rate = expected overhead ÷ expected activity base

Exhibit 6 illustrates the manufacturing overhead budget, by quarter, and the related expected cash disbursements, by quarter. Kirkland applies manufacturing overhead based on direct labor hours. From the total expected overhead cost and the number of labor hours expected, the company computes a variable rate of $2 per direct labor hour. Total fixed costs are budgeted at $6,060 per quarter, of which $1,500 represents noncash expense for depreciation. Further assume that all expenses will be paid in the quarter in which the expenses are incurred.

Variable manufacturing overhead costs can be determined by multiplying the variable overhead rate by the activity base (units produced, direct labor hours, machine hours, etc.).

Variable manufacturing overhead = variable overhead rate × activity base

For example, in Exhibit 6, variable overhead for the first quarter of 1998 is determined by multiplying the 1,120 budgeted direct labor hours by the variable overhead rate of $2.00 per direct labor hour to determine the budgeted variable overhead of $2,240.

Fixed manufacturing overhead remains constant over a wide range of activity levels and does not change based on production requirements. Fixed overhead is added to variable overhead to arrive at the total expected manufacturing overhead cost.

Exhibit 6   A Manufacturing Overhead Budget

Kirkland Company Manufacturing Overhead Budget For the Year Ended December 31, 1998					
	Quarter				
	1	2	3	4	Year
Budgeted direct labor hours (from Exhibit 5)	1,120	2,560	2,880	1,520	8,080
Variable overhead rate	$2	$2	$2	$2	$2
Budgeted variable overhead	$2,240	$ 5,120	$ 5,760	$3,040	$16,160
Budgeted fixed overhead	6,060	6,060	6,060	6,060	24,240
Total budgeted manufacturing overhead	8,300	11,180	11,820	9,100	40,400
Less: Noncash expenses	1,500	1,500	1,500	1,500	6,000
Cash disbursements for manufacturing overhead	$6,800	$ 9,680	$10,320	$7,600	$34,400

Selling and Administrative Expense Budget

The *selling and administrative expense budget* **contains a list of anticipated expenses for the period for activities other than manufacturing.** This budget generally is made up of many individual budgets prepared by managers with responsibilities for various functions. The number of items that compose this portion of the master budget can be quite large, depending on the size and complexity of an organization, and will include activities such as marketing, accounting and finance, and human resources.

The selling and administrative expense budget is based on the number of units expected to be sold, which is derived from the sales budget. Selling expenses, in particular, depend on the number of units sold, and many administrative functions also support the sales effort. The selling and administrative expense budget in Exhibit 7 for Kirkland identifies variable- and fixed-cost components. The exhibit assumes that variable selling and administrative expenses are expected to be $1.80 per unit sold. Fixed costs of advertising, insurance, executive salaries, and property taxes will be paid in the quarter in which they are incurred. Also, when preparing the selling and administrative expense budget, noncash expenses such as depreciation need to be identified for omission from the cash budget.

As shown in Exhibit 7, total variable expenses of $1,800 for Quarter 1 are determined by multiplying the 1,000 units to be sold by the $1.80 expected variable cost of sales for each unit. The $8,000 fixed selling and administrative expenses are added to the variable component to arrive at total budgeted selling and administrative expenses of $9,800. Noncash expenses for depreciation of $500 are then deducted to arrive at the cash expenditure for selling and administrative activity.

Note that the fixed expense varies from quarter to quarter even though it does not vary with the volume of production. This can result from factors such as changes in depreciation due to the addition and retirement of equipment during the year.

Exhibit 7   A Selling and Administrative Expense Budget

Kirkland Company
Selling and Administrative Expense Budget
For the Year Ended December 31, 1998

	Quarter				
	1	2	3	4	Year
Budgeted sales in units (from Exhibit 2)	1,000	3,000	4,000	2,000	10,000
Variable selling and administrative expenses per unit	$1.80	$1.80	$1.80	$1.80	$1.80
Budgeted variable expenses	1,800	5,400	7,200	3,600	18,000
Budgeted fixed selling and administrative expenses	8,000	8,190	11,775	9,815	37,780
Total budgeted selling and administrative expenses	9,800	13,590	18,975	13,415	55,780
Less: Noncash expenses	500	500	500	500	2,000
Cash expenditures for selling and administrative expenses	$9,300	$13,090	$18,475	$12,915	$53,780

SELF-STUDY PROBLEM 1

Bluffton Industries manufactures one product, a leather portfolio that sells for $20 per unit. This item is manufactured from a single raw material, tanned leather, that costs $2.00 a yard. It takes 1.5 yards of leather to produce a finished product. Each unit produced by Bluffton requires 0.25 hour of direct labor, which costs Bluffton $16 per hour. Variable overhead to produce a unit of product totals $3 per unit. Fixed overhead for the coming year, 1998, is expected to be:

© Jack Kurtz, 1994/PNI International

Depreciation	$25,000
Insurance	10,000
Property taxes	6,000
Supervision	35,000

Selling and administrative expenses for the coming year are expected to be $2 per unit sold plus the following fixed expenses:

Depreciation	$15,000
Sales salaries	30,000
Advertising	10,000
Office clerk	18,000
President's salary	60,000

At the beginning of 1998, Bluffton had 500 units of finished goods in inventory. The company wants to end the year with 2,500 units of finished goods in inventory. The company also requires 1,000 yards of raw material at year-end and began the year with 5,000 yards of material in inventory. A sales forecast indicates that 100,000 units will be sold during 1998.

Required

For 1998:

1. Prepare a sales budget.
2. Prepare a production budget.
3. Prepare a direct materials budget.
4. Prepare a direct labor budget.
5. Prepare a manufacturing overhead budget.
6. Prepare a selling and administrative expense budget.

The solution to Self-Study Problem 1 appears at the end of the chapter.

Pro Forma Budgeted Income Statement

The **pro forma budgeted income statement** is a projected income statement prepared from information developed in the budget process. The pro forma income statement is a key schedule in the master budget. It provides an estimate of an organization's profitability during a future period and often is the primary benchmark against which a company's performance during the period will be assessed. Exhibit 8 contains a pro forma income statement for Kirkland.

Exhibit 8   A Pro Forma Budgeted Income Statement

Kirkland Company
Pro Forma Budgeted Income Statement
For the Year Ended December 31, 1998

Sales (from Exhibit 2)	$200,000
Less: Cost of goods sold*	130,000
Gross margin	70,000
Less: Selling and administrative expenses (from Exhibit 7)	55,780
Net operating income	14,220
Less: Interest expense	1,400‡
Income before income taxes	12,820
Less: Income taxes (from tax return)	7,200‡
Net income	$ 5,620

*   *Based on the cost per unit as follows:*

Exhibit	Description	Quantity	Cost	Total
4	Direct materials	5 lbs.	$ .60/lb.	$ 3.00
5	Direct labor	0.8 hr.	$7.50/hr.	6.00
6	Manufacturing overhead	0.8 hr.	$5.00/hr.†	4.00
	Total			13.00
2	Units sold			× 10,000
	Budgeted cost of goods sold			$130,000

†   *$40,400 total budgeted manufacturing overhead ÷ 8,080 budgeted direct labor hours = $5.00 per hour.*
‡   *Assumed.*

Flexible Budget Approach

Exhibit 8 illustrates a pro forma income statement for a single level of activity developed using absorption costing. This statement is based on a *static budget* **because it identifies the income that would be earned at a predetermined level of sales activity.** Because the static budget reflects only one level of activity, it is unable to provide information about other levels of activity.

O b j e c t i v e   3
Explain the difference between static and flexible budgets.

Exhibit 9 illustrates a flexible pro forma income statement for Kirkland using the variable-costing approach. The *flexible budget* **enables a company to examine projected income over a *range* of sales levels.** Flexible budgets are best developed using the variable-costing format because this format separates the variable costs, which change with different levels of sales activity, from fixed costs, which remain constant over a wide range of sales and manufacturing activity.

Exhibit 9   A Pro Forma Flexible Budget Income Statement

Kirkland Company
Pro Forma Flexible Income Statement
Variable-Costing Format
For the Year Ended December 31, 1998

	Budget Formula (per unit)	Sales in units			
		9,000	10,000*	11,000	12,000
Sales	$20.00	$180,000	$200,000	$220,000	$240,000
Less variable expenses:					
Direct materials (from Exhibit 8)	3.00	27,000	30,000	33,000	36,000
Direct labor (from Exhibit 8)	6.00	54,000	60,000	66,000	72,000
Variable overhead[†]	1.60	14,400	16,000	17,600	19,200
Variable selling (from Exhibit 7)	1.80	16,200	18,000	19,800	21,600
Total variable expenses	12.40	111,600	124,000	136,400	148,800
Contribution margin	$ 7.60	68,400	76,000	83,600	91,200
Less fixed expenses:					
Manufacturing overhead (from Exhibit 6)		24,240	24,240	24,240	24,240
Selling and administrative (from Exhibit 7)		37,780	37,780	37,780	37,780
Taxes and interest[‡]		8,600	8,600	8,600	8,600
Total fixed expenses		70,620	70,620	70,620	70,620
Net income (loss)		$ (2,220)	$ 5,380[§]	$ 12,980	$ 20,580

* *Projected sales in the static budget.*
† *See Exhibits 5 and 6: $2 variable overhead rate per direct labor hour × 0.8 direct labor hour per unit = $1.60 variable overhead rate per unit.*
‡ *For simplicity, taxes and interest are the same at all levels.*
§ *The $240 difference between the variable-costing income of $5,380 and the absorption-costing income of $5,620 from Exhibit 8 can be explained as follows:*

  Increase in finished goods inventory
    (see Exhibit 3: 10,100 − 10,000 units)   *100 units*
  Fixed manufacturing costs deferred in ending inventory
    (fixed costs of $24,240 ÷ 10,100 units = $ 2.40 per unit) × $ 2.40 per unit
  Difference   *$240.00*

Cash Budget

The *cash budget* describes cash requirements for the budget period. The basic sources and uses of cash are shown in Exhibit 10.

Exhibit 10   A Cash Budget

Kirkland Company
Cash Budget
For the Year Ended December 31, 1998

	Quarter				
	1	**2**	**3**	**4**	**Year**
Cash balance, beginning	$ 4,250*	$ 4,000	$ 4,000	$ 4,050	$ 4,250*
Add receipts:					
Collections on account (from Exhibit 2)	23,000	48,000	74,000	52,000	197,000
Total cash available	27,250	52,000	78,000	56,050	201,250
Less disbursements:					
Direct materials (from Exhibit 4)	4,950	7,230	10,005	7,935	30,120
Direct labor (from Exhibit 5)	8,400	19,200	21,600	11,400	60,600
Manufacturing overhead (from Exhibit 6)	6,800	9,680	10,320	7,600	34,400
Selling and administrative (from Exhibit 7)	9,300	13,090	18,475	12,915	53,780
Income taxes (from Exhibit 8)*	1,800	1,800	1,800	1,800	7,200
Equipment purchases	3,000	2,000			5,000
Dividends	1,000	1,000	1,000	1,000	4,000
Total disbursements	35,250	54,000	63,200	42,650	195,100
Excess (deficiency) of cash	(8,000)	(2,000)	14,800	13,400	6,150
Financing:					
Borrowings	12,000	6,000			18,000
Repayments			(10,000)	(8,000)	(18,000)
Interest			(750)†	(650)‡	(1,400)
Total financing	12,000	6,000	(10,750)	(8,650)	(1,400)
Cash balance, ending	$ 4,000	$ 4,000	$ 4,050	$ 4,750	$ 4,750

★ *Assumed.*
† *Interest relates to $10,000 of the $12,000 borrowed in the first quarter: $10,000 × 0.1 × 3/4 = $750.*
‡ *Interest relates to $2,000 borrowed in the first quarter and $6,000 borrowed in the second quarter:*

$2,000 × 0.1 × one year = $200
$6,000 × 0.1 × 3/4 =   450

Total interest $650

The cash budget has four major sections:

1. cash receipts,
2. cash disbursements,
3. cash excess or deficiency, and
4. financing requirements.

The receipts section of the cash budget combines the beginning cash balance with expected cash receipts for the period. Generally, the major source of cash receipts is collections of accounts receivable and cash sales. Other cash receipts, such as interest from investments, also are included in this section.

The disbursements section of the cash budget contains all cash payments expected for the budget period. These payments include disbursements for raw materials, labor, manufacturing overhead, and administrative expenses as contained in these budgets. Other cash disbursements, such as income taxes, capital equipment purchases, and dividend payments, also are included.

The cash excess or deficiency section identifies the difference between cash receipts and cash disbursements. This section is important because it reveals the amount a company needs to borrow if a deficiency exists. If an excess exists, a company should plan for investment of its excess cash.

The financing section of the cash budget identifies amounts to be borrowed or repaid during the budget period. Also, it identifies interest to be paid on borrowings. This section of the cash budget allows an organization to work with lenders to ensure that cash is available when needed. Often, organizations have lines of credit available through banks to meet short-term needs. The financing section will assist managers in determining whether any special borrowing arrangements are necessary in addition to existing lines of credit.

Exhibit 10 provides a cash budget for Kirkland on a quarterly basis. The exhibit assumes that all borrowing takes place at the beginning of a quarter in which cash is needed and all repayments are made at the end of the quarter.

Additional information to complete the cash budget includes:

1. The company expects to pay $3,000 and $2,000 for equipment in the first and second quarters, respectively.
2. Dividends of $1,000 are planned for each quarter.
3. The company must maintain a minimum balance of $4,000 at the bank.
4. Interest is paid at the time of principal repayment.
5. No loans are outstanding at the beginning of the budget period.
6. The company must pay interest at an annual rate of 10% on any borrowed funds.

The cash budget is an important part of the master budget. Even if a company generates net income, it can experience serious difficulties if it does not have the cash it needs for day-to-day operations. For example, a company that cannot pay its accounts payable on a timely basis often loses discounts and may incur penalties for late payment. In extreme cases, suppliers may refuse additional credit to a company that does not pay on a timely basis. Consequently, planning for a company's cash needs is necessary for sound financial management.

Pro Forma Budgeted Balance Sheet

The **pro forma budgeted balance sheet** identifies the expected amount of assets, liabilities, and owners' equity at the end of the budget period. Exhibit 11 presents a comparative balance sheet showing actual beginning-of-year and pro forma end-of-year amounts for Kirkland.

The December 31, 1998, balance sheet figures are derived as follows. The ending cash balance (a) is projected in the cash budget, Exhibit 10. Accounts receivable (b) are projected as 30% of fourth-quarter sales from Exhibit 2 ($40,000 × 30%). Based on Exhibit 4, the ending raw materials inventory (c) was $420 (700 lbs. at $.60 per lb.) for 1997 and is projected to be $450 (750 lbs. at $.60 per lb) for 1998. Budgeted finished goods inventory (d) is projected from Exhibit 3 to be 300 units. Each unit is costed at $13 (see Exhibit 8) per unit (300 units × $13 = $3,900). Equipment purchases (e) will total $5,000 during the year as reflected on the cash budget (Exhibit 10). Accumulated depreciation is determined by the expected increase in total depreciation for the year. Depreciation charges (f) for the year are $6,000 (Exhibit 6) and $2,000 (Exhibit 7), for a total increase of $8,000 from the beginning of the year. Accounts payable (g) is forecast as one-half of the fourth-quarter raw materials purchases ($5,580) from Exhibit 4. Retained earnings is projected as shown below:

December 31, 1997 balance	$44,990
Add net income (from Exhibit 8)	5,620
	50,610
Less dividends paid (from Exhibit 10)	(4,000)
Balance at December 31, 1998	$46,610

Exhibit 11   A Pro Forma Budgeted Balance Sheet

Kirkland Company
Pro Forma Budgeted Balance Sheet
At December 31, 1997 and 1998

	1997 (Actual)	1998 (Pro forma)
Assets		
Current assets:		
Cash	$ 4,250	$ 4,750 (a)
Accounts receivable	9,000	12,000 (b)
Raw materials inventory	420	450 (c)
Finished goods inventory	2,600*	3,900 (d)
Total current assets	16,270	21,100
Plant and equipment:		
Land	8,000*	8,000*
Buildings and equipment	70,000*	75,000 (e)
Accumulated depreciation	(29,200)*	(37,200) (f)
Plant and equipment, net	48,800	45,800
Total assets	$65,070	$66,900
Liabilities and Stockholders' Equity		
Current liabilities:		
Accounts payable (raw materials)	$ 2,580	$ 2,790 (g)
Stockholders' equity:		
Common stock	17,500*	17,500*
Retained earnings	44,990*	46,610 (h)
Total stockholders' equity	62,490	64,110
Total liabilities and stockholders' equity	$65,070	$66,900

* *Assumed.*

A pro forma balance sheet provides information about expected assets and liabilities. This information can be useful for a variety of reasons. For example, management may want to determine if ending working capital (the difference between current assets and current liabilities) is sufficient for planned operations. Managers can use the pro forma statement to assess expected performance. Measures such as expected return on assets, expected return on equity, and expected debt to equity ratios involve balance sheet amounts.

DEVELOPING A SOUND BUDGETING CULTURE

O b j e c t i v e   4
Describe the elements of a sound budgeting culture in companies.

The budgeting methods adopted by a company will greatly influence how successful the budgeting process will be.

The culture of a business is the way people in the business think and behave. A sound budget culture relies on establishing a process that encourages participation by key employees in the development of budgets. Companies can undertake a variety of activities to develop such a culture. These activities include directing attention to the budget, educating participants in the budget process, ensuring availability of information necessary to develop the budget, evaluating actual versus budgeted results, and motivating management to be active in the budget process.

Some companies use **continuous** or **perpetual budgets,** which are updated each month or each quarter so that a full year of budgeted activity is always available. This approach is preferable to preparing and evaluating a budget only on an annual basis, because it requires managers to keep the budget and planning process always in their minds.

Preparation of the master budget requires the involvement of managers throughout an organization. Each department or manager who participates in the planning process should understand the goals of the budget and the methods used to develop it. Therefore, a company should educate managers about the goals and procedures of the budgeting process.

To create an accurate budget, a thorough understanding of an organization's cost structure is required. Managers must understand costs that affect their particular department or function. In addition, managers must understand the accounting methods a company uses in measuring costs and accumulating data in their area of responsibility. *Responsibility accounting* **assigns responsibility for the performance of a company's departments to department managers.** It requires that each manager's performance be evaluated on the basis of costs or revenues that are directly under the manager's control. Responsibility accounting reports are produced periodically for the purpose of evaluating a department manager's effectiveness in generating revenues or controlling costs.

Coordination is needed to bring the various components of the master budget together. In many organizations, a standing **budget committee** is responsible for the coordination of the master budget. This committee generally consists of the president, and vice presidents in charge of various departments, such as sales, production, administration, and finance. A role of the budget committee is to resolve disputes or misunderstandings among those involved in budget preparation.

Generally, the most successful budget processes are those that permit managers to participate in developing the budgets. *Participative budgeting* **is a process that allows individuals at various levels of a company to participate in determining the company's goals and the plans for achieving those goals.** It signals that senior managers value employee judgment and generally results in a greater degree of employee acceptance of the budget than if the budget is dictated by senior managers. Senior managers often are not in a position to know the details of day-to-day operations as well as employees involved in these operations. Therefore, participation by employees can result in more accurate and achievable budgets. Further, employees who are involved in the development of a budget are more likely to work toward achieving the budget goals. Participative budgeting will be discussed in detail later in this chapter along with other behavioral implications of budgeting.

CONSIDERATIONS IN IMPLEMENTING BUDGETS

Once an appropriate culture exists for budgeting, a formal budgeting process is necessary. This process is influenced by several factors. These include the scope of the budget, the existence of foreign operations, inflation, and the possible need to revise the budget because of changes that take place in the company's operations or costs.

Scope of the Budget

A company determines which activities to include in its budget. For example, some companies develop budgets for desired inventory levels, the levels at which inventory will be reordered, and the timing and size of inventory purchases. Some budgets may be prepared casually, whereas others require greater detail depending on the emphasis the company places on them.

Foreign Operations, Currency Fluctuation, and Inflation

Objective 5
Describe the influence of inflation and foreign operations on budgeting.

The marketplace in which companies trade is becoming more global. Many companies own foreign subsidiaries. Multinational companies face special budget problems because they operate in an international environment. Two of these problems are foreign currency exchange rates and inflation.

Foreign currency exchange rates refer to the relative values of the currencies of different countries. A U.S. company must translate the results of foreign operations into dollars. Consequently, its results are influenced by currency fluctuations, over which managers have no control. Foreign currency fluctuation presents a special risk when transactions, such as sales, are stated in a currency other than U.S. dollars. For example, suppose that the exchange rate on March 1 is 0.65 British pound sterling (£) for one U.S. dollar. U.S. Products Co., a U.S. company, agrees to sell furniture to England Imports, Ltd., a British company, for £65,000. The equivalent U.S. dollar value on March 1 is $100,000. Delivery and payment are to be made on April 1. If the value of the pound is £.70 for one U.S. dollar on the delivery date, the £65,000 that U.S. Products receives can be exchanged for only $92,857 (£65,000 ÷ £.70 per dollar). Consequently, U.S. Products Co. will have sustained a foreign currency exchange loss of $7,143 ($100,000 − $92,857). Such a loss is impossible to budget because the value of the dollar relative to the pound is not known until after the transaction is completed.

Inflation in some countries exceeds 100% annually. High inflation rates, called **hyperinflation,** create significant problems for budget preparation for multinational companies. Hyperinflation greatly reduces the ability of managers to compare budgets from period to period because it reduces the buying power of the foreign currency.

In addition to exchange rates and inflation, multinational companies must be sensitive to government laws and policies in the countries in which they operate when they set budgets. These laws and policies might affect labor costs, equipment purchases, cash management, or other budgeted items. For example, changes in tariffs and fees on imported raw materials will affect raw material costs.

Budget Revisions

Budgets forecast the future costs of inputs, such as raw materials and labor. These forecasts are not always accurate. Substantial differences between a company's actual costs and those assumed in developing the budget make the budget less useful. For example, a large increase in raw materials prices can cause the raw materials budget to be grossly understated in terms of actual raw materials costs. Evaluating personnel responsible for raw materials purchases against such a budget would be unrealistic and probably would be unfair. Consequently, companies may find it necessary to revise the original budget if there are unforeseen changes in costs.

Inaccurate forecasts raise two concerns. First, when is the forecast inaccurate enough to justify a change in the budget? If budgets are changed frequently because of minor differences in costs, they soon will lose meaning because managers will not view the budget as a goal to be achieved. Second, is the difference between the forecast and the actual cost due to a bad forecast or to the failure of the responsible managers to control costs? If managers are allowed to escape responsibility too easily, the budget again will lose its value. In deciding whether to permit a budget revision, senior management must weigh these concerns against the concern that the budget is inaccurate. Often, the decision will depend on the extent of the inaccuracy.

BEHAVIORAL CONCERNS IN BUDGETING

During the 1920s, a series of studies were conducted at the Hawthorne plant of the **Western Electric Company** to determine whether various elements of the physical environment in the plant affected employee efficiency and output. The experimenters

Objective 6
Identify how budgets affect
management behavior.

varied employee work environments and measured resulting employee performance. At first, the researchers believed that increasing the levels of light had a positive effect on productivity. They later discovered that productivity increased whenever the researchers measured employees' work, regardless of the change in the environment. The Hawthorne studies provide evidence that observing and measuring human behavior can alter that behavior. Budgets provide benchmarks for measuring performance. By observing and measuring performance, companies hope to improve the performance of their workers.

Changing Behavior

Changing the way the score is kept in a basketball game can change the strategy with which the game is played and the behavior of players. The 3-point rule offers evidence of such changes. An extra point for longer shots has resulted in more outside shooting. Consequently, the rule has changed the way many coaches and players view the game and prepare for it. This was the intent behind the 3-point rule. How we measure performance affects behavior.

Budgeting measures actual outcomes and compares these to expected outcomes. Budgets measure employee performance and are a means of keeping score of both the managers' and the company's performance. Well-designed budgets lead to desired changes in behavior and minimize any undesired behavior that results from the measurement process. For example, bank branch managers' performance often is measured against budgeted loan and deposit volume goals. These goals, when set properly, encourage branch mangers to solicit business from current and potential customers and result in greater loan and deposit growth. The bank benefits because its increased financial resources lead to higher profits.

Participation in the Budget Process

Different leadership styles on the part of top management can lead to different types of budgeting. Budgets can be described as either top-down or bottom-up, as shown in Exhibit 12. *Top-down budgets* **are budgets that are established by management and then provided to lower levels of an organization for compliance.** *Bottom-up budgets* **involve all levels of an organization working to achieve the organization's goals.** Top-down, nonparticipative budget setting is indicated by the one-way arrows in the left-hand figure in Exhibit 12.

For a bottom-up budget, the department managers usually submit proposed budgets and then negotiate with senior managers to create a master budget. This budget then is used to evaluate the departments' performance. There is two-way communication in bottom-up budgeting, as shown by the arrows in the right-hand portion of Exhibit 12. In bottom-up, participative budget setting, the chief executive officer might direct that the vice president of sales solicit information on budget goals for the coming year from the regional sales offices or departments. After reviewing the goals submitted by the regional sales offices and negotiating any desired changes with regional sales managers, the vice president of sales would present a consolidated sales budget for the company to the chief executive. If the chief executive accepts the proposed sales budget, no further action is required. If the chief executive does not accept the budget, the vice president of sales renegotiates the regional sales budgets with the regional sales offices until an acceptable budget is reached.

Resources are necessary to meet objectives, but resources usually are limited. In many companies, departments compete with one another for a greater share of available resources. Sound planning requires decisions about the allocation of limited resources. Middle and lower-level managers tend to accept these decisions about the allocations of limited resources more readily if they have an active role in planning and setting budget goals. Participative budgeting helps encourage the acceptance of

Exhibit 12   Nonparticipative and Participative Budgeting

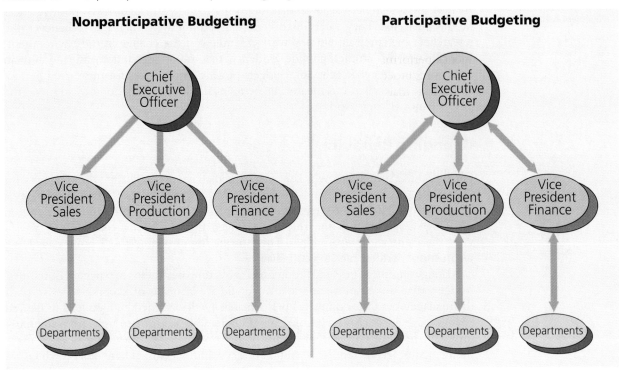

resource allocation decisions by creating a budget culture in which subordinates have a voice in these decisions.

Although it is a leader's responsibility to establish the overall mission, vision, and goals of a company, the leader affects the budgeting environment through his or her leadership style. Top managers can be responsive to new ideas and establish an environment of trust and openness by empowering managers at every level of the organization, or they can discourage involvement in the budgeting process. Usually it is better to develop an open and participative environment for the budgeting process because people make budgets work, and they usually will work harder to achieve goals that they had a role in setting.

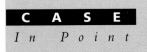

The **National Bank of Georgia** conducted an annual budgeting process that included loan and deposit goals for each of its branches. Top management established budget targets for the entire bank and for the branch division as a whole. Branch managers participated in this process by developing budgets for their branches and submitting these budgets to Branch Administration. Branch administrators reviewed the budgets and compared them to the targets set for the division. If the branch budgets were not as aggressive as the targets set by top management, branch administrators negotiated with individual branch managers in an attempt to get them to increase their budget targets so that the sum of the individual branches' goals was equal to the division's goal.

Slack in Budgets

When budgets are prepared, department managers have incentives to build slack into the budgets to make performance goals easier to achieve. Slack results in performance goals that are lower than what managers believe they can realistically achieve. This process of building slack into budgets is called **padding.** Budgets that have little or no slack are referred to as **tight budgets.** Research has shown that managers perform best when faced with moderately difficult but achievable goals. Not all factors that affect department performance are under the control of department managers. While managers have little control over external variables, such as the general economy, they should understand the effect those variables will have on their department's performance. Examples of external factors that should be considered in the budgeting process include economic forecasts related to a particular product, market conditions that affect a particular industry, and interest rates.

Because these external factors affect performance, even if managers run their departments well, department performance may not reflect their efforts. Budgetary slack reduces the risk that factors beyond the control of department managers will cause them to fail to meet their budget goals. On the other hand, if budgets contain too much slack, department managers can perform at a less than optimal level. Top or senior managers and department managers must work together to create budgets that will lead to satisfactory performance.

Budgets and Undesirable Behavior

Managers also should be aware that budget goals sometimes can cause subordinate managers to make decisions that are not in the best interest of the company as a whole. For example, suppose that a plant's maintenance costs are high relative to budget and the end of the budget year is approaching. Further assume that the plant manager expects to be promoted to supervisor of several plants if his particular plant's performance is superior to that of other plants. The plant manager may be tempted to defer needed maintenance in the hope of meeting the plant's budget targets and winning the promotion. The downside of such a decision, however, will be higher maintenance costs in the future because delaying necessary maintenance leads to abnormal wear of the plant's equipment.

Another example of budgets potentially leading to undesirable behavior was discussed in an earlier chapter. Absorption costing gives managers an incentive to overproduce inventory because fixed overhead costs are deferred in inventory, and so the department shows higher profits for the period. This excess inventory is costly for a company, although the costs are not fully captured in the current period's budget.

Managers need to be aware of the behavioral effects of budgeting and consider them in the budget process. With proper planning, managers can reduce behavior problems. For example, some slack can be included in the budget to reduce incentives for undesirable behavior. Companies can also attempt to detect behavior problems. As an example, a company can monitor unusual increases in inventories just prior to the end of budget periods to make sure a department is not producing unneeded inventory.

SELF-STUDY PROBLEM 2

Southeastern Bank owns a network of 60 branches. Each branch and branch manager is evaluated on the basis of performance relative to an annual budget. Growth in loans, deposits, and net income are the three principal measures on which managers are evaluated. The annual budget, for the fiscal year ending in December, is developed through a process of negotiation in a well-developed budget culture.

The process begins with senior managers providing general budget guidance to the branch managers. This guidance contains the branch's finan-

Photography by Alan Brown/Photonics

cial goals for the year. Each branch manager then develops a branch budget and submits this budget to senior management for approval. Branch managers know that they generally are expected to show positive growth in loans, deposits, and net income. However, since branch managers want to look as good as possible when their performance is compared against budget, they often try to pad their budgets by setting targets lower than what they actually believe they can achieve. Senior managers are aware of this tendency and frequently will not accept the budgets without an effort to get branch managers to accept higher targets.

Once the budgets are accepted, managers are provided with monthly reports that compare actual results to the budget targets. The results also are presented at quarterly meetings attended by branch and senior managers. If a branch manager is failing to meet budget targets, senior managers will ask the manager to explain why. At the end of the year, branch managers are given a performance appraisal. If the managers have met or exceeded their budgets, they are awarded a salary increase. If the managers have substantially exceeded their targets, they may receive a bonus in addition to a raise, unless the bank has had a bad year overall.

Occasionally, a manager who already has exceeded the loan growth goal for the year will wait until January to send in the paperwork on loans made in December. These loans then show up in the branch's January loan figures, rather than in the December figures. Deferring recognition of the loans enables the manager to get a head start on meeting next year's loan goals. Delays in recording a loan in the bank's accounting records do not affect the bank's cash flows. The bank loses no interest on the loans.

Required

Evaluate the strengths and weaknesses of this budget process from a behavioral standpoint. How well does the bank's budget process encourage managers to strive to meet its goals? What budgeting and ethical problems does the delay in recording loans present?

The solution to Self-Study Problem 2 appears at the end of the chapter.

STRATEGIC CONSIDERATIONS IN BUDGETING

Objective 7
Describe how budgets influence strategic decisions.

Budgets affect strategic marketing decisions. Recall that products have *life cycles* that consist of the following stages: (1) introduction of a new product, (2) building market share in preparation for future profits, (3) holding market share to ensure current profits on mature products, (4) maximizing available return while sales of a product are declining, and (5) eliminating the product when it is no longer sufficiently profitable.

Each stage has implications for the use and importance of budgets in marketing decisions. There is usually less reliance on budgets for decision-making purposes during the introduction and building stages because of uncertainty about financial performance. During these stages, little experience exists on which to base financial forecasts. Therefore, budgets tend to be less reliable during these stages and are used primarily as a short-term planning tool. Revisions to budgets are more likely to occur during the building stage because of changing information as the company gains experience with the product.

Managers of products in the introduction and building stages often have more input into the budget than managers of products in the holding and return-maximizing stages. Managers of products in the introduction and building stages operate in rapidly changing environments and have better knowledge of these changes than senior managers. In the holding and return-maximizing stages, sales tend to be more stable, and senior management can look to the company's prior experience with the product to set budget targets.

The frequency of contact between product managers and senior managers on strategic issues tends to be greater in the earlier stages of a product's life. Decisions about how to advertise the product, what markets to focus expenditures on, and how to respond to changing demand are more common in early stages than in the holding and harvesting stages. In contrast, there is more contact between product managers and senior managers on day-to-day operational issues during the later stages because of the need to manufacture the product at an economical cost.

During the earlier stages of product life, less importance is attached to meeting budget goals because these goals are not especially reliable and may need to be changed frequently. Holding product managers to tight budget targets during the building stage can result in poor decisions. For example, a manager concerned about making budget might prematurely discontinue a profitable product because it is less profitable than expected.

A company also must ensure that cash flows generated from products in the holding and profit-maximizing stages will be sufficient to support those products that are in the introduction and building stages. Meeting budget targets for products in the latter stages is important if a company is to generate the cash needed to produce and market new products. Therefore, budgets are important for strategic planning.

BUDGETING IN SERVICE COMPANIES

Objective 8
Explain the role of budgets in service organizations.

Service companies use budgets similarly to manufacturing companies. The preparation of budgets in service companies, however, can differ from budget preparation in manufacturing companies because service companies do not manufacture goods. Although service companies do not have to develop production and raw materials budgets, some aspects of budgeting can be more difficult in service organizations because it is often harder to trace costs to a particular service than to manufactured goods. In service companies, workers may be involved in the delivery of several different types of services during the same time period. In manufacturing companies, workers usually manufacture only one type of product at a time. When workers are involved with several different types of services at the same time, it is much more difficult to determine how much time (and therefore labor cost) is associated with providing one particular service. This makes it more difficult to develop budgets based on the expected amounts of services to be provided.

Consider checking account services, one of many services provided by banks. One of the costs bank management must budget for is the cost of the labor directly involved in providing checking accounts. This includes the work of tellers, new account personnel, and customer service personnel. These same personnel, however, help to provide many other types of services in addition to checking accounts, often at the same time they are dealing with checking accounts. For example, a teller may process a checking transaction, a loan payment, and a savings deposit for a given customer. How much of the cost of the teller's idle time should be assigned to each type of transaction? Although these cost allocation difficulties may be present in a manufacturing company to some extent, they are present to a greater extent in banks. The result is that banks are less able to accurately budget for the costs of providing for particular services than are manufacturing companies.

Although some aspects of service companies make budgeting more difficult than in manufacturing companies, other aspects potentially make budgeting easier and more useful. For example, some service companies, such as banks and automobile rental companies, operate many offices in different locations. The similarity of these separate offices provides a basis for analyzing budgets and evaluating performance that is not present in many manufacturing companies. The information for each unit can be compared with companywide averages. This makes determination of good and bad performers easier than with manufacturing companies.

SELF-STUDY PROBLEM 3

The 4 Square Corporation, a major manufacturer of carpet-related products, recently launched a new adhesive fastener that affixes carpet to flooring. The product had a development budget of $6 million. The company has a policy of budgeting future funding for all products, including products in the building stage of their life cycle, on the basis of recent actual versus budget sales performance. Senior management believes that all products should carry their weight and feels that this policy has served the company well. In creating the 1998 budget, 4 Square reduced the budget for the adhesive fastener because sales in 1997 were lower than projected in the marketing plan. The reduced budget did not permit extensive advertising efforts to continue. As a result, the adhesive fastener's sales did not increase at all during 1998, and the decision was made to discontinue the product. A problem occurred, however, when it was discovered that substantial additional costs were necessary to cancel contracts related to the product's development. Further, shortly after 4 Square abandoned the fastener, a competitor introduced a similar product that has been very successful.

© John Coletti/Stock•Boston

Required

Evaluate the policy of tying future funding for a product to the sales performance of that product during the previous year. What recommendations would you make to 4 Square to improve its policy?

The solution to Self-Study Problem 3 appears at the end of the chapter.

R E V I E W   *Summary of Important Concepts*

1. The master budget is a collection of related budgets.
   a. It is composed of many individual budgets.
   b. It leads to pro forma financial statements.
   c. It has both operational and financial aspects.

2. A master budget has the following components:
   a. The sales budget shows the quantity and price of goods expected to be sold during the coming period.
   b. The production budget shows the type and quantity of products expected to be produced.
   c. The direct materials budget reflects the amount of raw materials expected to be purchased and used in production.
   d. The direct labor budget indicates the expected labor requirements for production.
   e. The manufacturing overhead budget reflects anticipated overhead costs, both fixed and variable.

      f.   The selling and administrative expense budget shows anticipated cost, both fixed and variable.

      g. The cash budget shows expected cash receipts and disbursements.

      h. The pro forma income statement indicates the expected net income for the period.

      i.   The pro forma balance sheet indicates anticipated levels of assets, liabilities, and owners' equity.

3.   A sound budgeting culture has the following characteristics:
   a.   The culture encourages participation in budgeting at all levels of management.
   b.   Cross-functional coordination is required.
   c.   The budget provides motivational and performance measurement tools.
   d.   The budget defines responsibility for costs and activities.

4.   Some considerations in the budgeting process include the following:
   a.   Several budgeting methods are available, including static and flexible budgets.
   b.   International and foreign activities create special concerns, such as currency exchange rates and hyperinflation.

5.   A number of behavioral concerns should be taken into account in budgeting.
   a.   Leadership style greatly affects the budgeting process.
   b.   Budget negotiation and budget slack are important considerations in setting budget goals.
   c.   External forces related to economic conditions affect the budgeting process by imposing risk on subunit managers.
   d.   Subunit managers attempting to meet budget goals may make undesirable decisions.

7.   There are two important strategic considerations in budgeting:
   a.   Different product life cycle stages may have different implications for the use of budgets.
   b.   The implications of budgeting for product managers' decisions must be considered.

8.   Budgeting in service companies differs in some respects from budgeting in manufacturing companies.
   a.   Workers in service companies often perform more than one type of service at the same time, making budgeting the cost of individual services more difficult.
   b.   Service companies often operate many branches, providing a basis for analyzing budgets and evaluating performance that is not present in many manufacturing companies.

D E F I N E   *Terms and Concepts Used in This Chapter*

Bottom-up budget   (201)
Budget   (186)
Cash budget   (195)
Direct labor budget   (190)
Direct materials budget   (189)
Financial budget   (187)
Flexible budget   (195)

Manufacturing overhead budget (191)
Master budget   (186)
Operating budget   (187)
Participative budgeting   (199)
Production budget   (188)
Responsibility accounting   (199)

Sales budget   (187)
Selling and administrative expense budget   (192)
Standards   (187)
Static budget   (195)
Top-down budget   (201)

SOLUTIONS

SELF-STUDY PROBLEM 1

Sales Budget

Expected sales in units	100,000
Selling price per unit	$20
Total sales	$2,000,000

Production Budget

Units to be sold	100,000
Add: Desired ending inventory	2,500
Total needs	102,500
Less: Beginning inventory	500
Total units to produce	$102,000

Direct Materials Budget

Total units to be produced	102,000
Materials required per unit (yds.)	1.5
Total (yds.)	153,000
Add: Desired ending inventory	1,000
Total material needs	154,000
Less: Beginning inventory	5,000
Total materials to be purchased	149,000
Cost per yard	$2.00
Total material cost	$298,000

Direct Labor Budget

Units to produce	102,000
Labor hours per unit	0.25
Total labor hours required	25,500
Labor rate per hour	$16
Total labor cost	$408,000

Manufacturing Overhead Budget

Units to produce		102,000
Variable rate per unit		$3
Total variable overhead		$306,000
Fixed manufacturing overhead:		
Depreciation	$25,000	
Insurance	10,000	
Property taxes	6,000	
Supervision	35,000	
Total fixed overhead		76,000
Total manufacturing overhead		$382,000

continued

Selling and Administrative Expense Budget		
Units to be sold		100,000
Variable cost per unit		$2
Total variable selling expense		$200,000
Fixed selling and		
administrative expenses:		
Depreciation	$15,000	
Sales salaries	30,000	
Advertising	10,000	
Office clerk	18,000	
President's salary	60,000	
Total fixed expenses		133,000
Total selling and		
administrative expenses		$333,000

SELF-STUDY PROBLEM 2

The bank's budget process has several strengths. These include (1) making clear the major objectives for branch managers to focus on and therefore encouraging them to meet goals, (2) allowing branch managers to participate in setting budget goals, (3) encouraging branch managers to be aggressive in budget goals, (4) providing managers with periodic feedback, and (5) permitting some slack in the budget without allowing this slack to become too great. The negotiation process also permits the recognition in the budget of differences in opportunities of different branches. Two weaknesses are (1) the fact that high-performing managers may not receive a bonus if the bank had a bad year, and (2) distortions in the accounting system created by the late booking of loans in January. A question arises as to whether this constitutes unethical behavior. It may be argued that since the cash flows from the loans are not affected, the bank is no worse off. However, if many managers engage in this practice and the amount of loans made but not recognized at year-end is large, the bank's accounting records will be materially misstated. More likely, the underbooking of loans in December leads to an appearance of a higher loan volume in January than actually occurs and affects future budgets. The bank could institute a policy that all loans must be booked within a specified number of days after they are made.

SELF-STUDY PROBLEM 3

4 Square may be prematurely discontinuing new products by insisting that sales performance meet budgeted targets that were based on uncertain data. By doing so, 4 Square not only is losing the research and development costs sunk in these new products but also is forgoing the opportunity to make future profits. Such opportunities apparently exist, since a competitor marketed a product similar to 4 Square's adhesive fastener once 4 Square abandoned it. 4 Square could resolve this problem by implementing a policy in which new products are allowed a greater margin of error than more mature products in terms of meeting budgeted sales growth. The company could establish a range of likely sales performances based on differing market scenarios. Then, 4 Square could compare actual sales to what sales should be given the situation that actually prevails.

EXERCISES

6-1. Write a short definition of each of the terms listed in the *Terms and Concepts Defined in This Chapter* section.

Obj. 1

6-2. Paul Reynolds was recently hired as a salesman for The Rocky Company, which sells gardening tools and potting soil through retail outlets. Paul has been asked to attend a meeting next week to discuss the preparation of the master budget for the coming year. Paul has asked you to explain what is meant by a master budget so that he can prepare for the meeting. What would you tell Paul?

Obj. 2   **6-3.**   Susan Broyer is a marketing manager for Glow Industries, which produces lamps and lighting fixtures. Susan's department is preparing a sales budget for the company's lighting fixtures. She has issued a memo to her staff that says in part: "I expect an annual increase in sales next year of 12% across the board. Every line and product should reflect this sales increase." What budget(s) would be affected by the estimated increase in sales?

Obj. 2   **6-4.**   Den and Harry own a small ice cream shop in Kokomo, Indiana. They make their own ice cream, which is sold in gallons, quarts, pints, and over the counter in the form of cones. Den and Harry use a variety of information to forecast sales demand for ice cream in Kokomo each summer. Based on their forecasts, Den and Harry then prepare a sales budget for their shop. What is the difference between a sales forecast and a sales budget? Explain.

Obj. 2   **6-5.**   Markle Company is a *merchandising* firm that operates 26 stores. Marvle Industries is a *manufacturer* that operates a single plant. Both firms prepare detailed master budgets each year. How would the master budgets of the two firms differ?

Obj. 2   **6-6.**   Frank Sheffield is the vice president of finance for The Hercules Company. Recently, Hercules completed preparation of its master budget for the coming year. Frank has scheduled a meeting with the company's banker. What portions of the master budget, if any, do you believe Frank should review with the bank?

Obj. 2   **6-7.**   Vantage Incorporated is preparing a master budget for the coming quarter of operations. As part of the budget process, inventory policies are being reviewed at a senior management planning meeting. Which budgets would policies concerning the level of inventories affect? Why?

Obj. 4   **6-8.**   During a recent staff management meeting of Hoya Enterprises, a manufacturer of dog leashes, collars, and accessories, Rocky Findlayson, company controller, exclaimed, "We will never get a handle on our operating costs without responsibility accounting!" What is meant by the term *responsibility accounting*?

Objs. 4, 6   **6-9.**   Rick Nill is the president of The Toyco Company, which produces a wide variety of action combat toys for children. For the past few years, Rick has prepared an annual business plan at the beginning of the year, detailing his expectations for sales, production, income, and expenses. He does not share these plans with his senior managers, but rather is closely involved with each operating department, monitoring its activities and issuing directives that tell how to meet his objectives. How could Rick improve his planning and budgeting process? What benefits could Rick expect from your suggested changes?

Objs. 4, 6   **6-10.** A key concept underlying the budget process is that of responsibility accounting. The basic idea behind responsibility accounting is that each manager's performance should be judged by how well he or she manages those items that are directly under his or her control. Identify three possible limitations of responsibility accounting.

Obj. 6   **6-11.** Carla Eubanks is a production manager for Department 1 of Graham Packaging. Graham produces plastic bottles for detergents and cleaning supplies. Its management prepares detailed budgets at the beginning of each year covering all aspects of its business. Carla is preparing for an annual performance review with her supervisor and is certain that she will receive a positive review, since her department has achieved 20% greater production than the previous year. Is Carla correct in judging actual results based on past performance? Why or why not?

Obj. 6   **6-12.** Pat Houlihan is the chief executive officer of Alco Industries. Alco has business interests in many different communication fields, including publishing, television, radio, and cable. Pat has indicated that she expects 10 percent across-the-board cuts in operating cost in all of her company's segments in the coming year. Do you support such an approach? Why or why not?

Obj. 6   **6-13.**   Leroy Smith is the production manager of The Alum Company. In addition to his salary, Leroy receives bonus compensation based solely on his ability to meet the budgeted production of units. Comment on Leroy's bonus arrangement. What weaknesses might exist in this arrangement?

Obj. 6   **6-14.**   Discuss the implications associated with a budgetary approach in which budgetary data are imposed on managers from above. Contrast such an approach with one in which budgetary data are self-imposed in a participative manner.

Obj. 6   **6-15.**   Rona Abraham is the purchasing manager for Flextech Incorporated, a manufacturer of furniture and bedding. Rona knows that as part of her bonus compensation, she must meet the material purchasing budget that was established at the beginning of the year. In an effort to meet this budget, Rona has been purchasing lower-grade materials at reduced costs and is proud of her ability to spend less than the budgeted amounts on materials. What implications do Rona's actions have for Flextech as a whole?

Obj. 7   **6-16.**   Lester Arbuckle is owner of Sheetco, a manufacturer of snow shovels. Lester and his managers do no budgeting or planning for Sheetco. Sheetco management does not anticipate problems that arise, and as a result, the company has slow production, missed shipment deadlines, and lost sales. Discuss the reasons why Lester should wish to engage in budgeting and planning.

Obj. 8   **6-17.**   Service firms do not manufacture products; therefore budgeting is not important to service firms. Do you agree? Explain your answer.

PROBLEMS

PROBLEM 6-1   **Budgeted Cash Collections**

Obj. 2

Elm Company makes a product that has peak sales in September of each year. The company has prepared a sales budget for the third quarter of 1998, as shown below:

	July	August	September
Budgeted sales	$500,000	$600,000	$750,000

The company is in the process of preparing a cash budget for the third quarter and must determine the cash collections by month. Collections on sales are expected to be as follows:

70% in the month of sale
20% in the month following the month of sale
8% in the second month following the month of sale
2% uncollectible

The accounts receivable balance as of June 30 is $195,000, of which $45,000 represents uncollected May sales and $150,000 represents uncollected June sales.

Required

a.   What were the total sales for May and June?
b.   What are the expected cash collections for each month of the third quarter?

PROBLEM 6-2   **Production Budget, Inventory Considerations**

Obj. 2

The Stoner Company makes a popular Halloween mask. Peak sales are in October of each year. The company's partial sales budget, in units, for 1998 is as follows:

August	September	October	November
20,000	30,000	55,000	5,000

The company has an inventory policy in which the end-of-month inventory must equal 10% of the following month's sales. The inventory as of July 31 was 2,000 units.

Required

Prepare a production budget for the three months ended October 31, 1998. In your budget, show the number of units to be produced each month and for the quarter in total.

PROBLEM 6-3   Purchasing Budget, Inventory Considerations

Obj. 2

The Yucko Company produces vegetable candy bars called Veggy Bars. Each 6-ounce Veggy Bar contains 5 ounces of brussels sprouts, which Yucko purchases for $.05 an ounce. Budgeted production of vegetable candy bars for the first four months of 1998 is as follows:

	Units
January	100,000
February	120,000
March	110,000
April	100,000

Yucko has an inventory policy that ending inventory of brussels sprouts should be 10% of the following month's requirements.

Required

Prepare a purchasing budget for the first quarter of 1998 by month and for the quarter in total. Show the amount of materials required in unit and in dollar amounts.

PROBLEM 6-4   Direct Labor Budget

Obj. 2

Refer to the data in Problem 6-3. Each Veggy Bar requires 0.02 direct labor hour. The average labor rate is $10 per hour.

Required

Prepare a direct labor budget for the first quarter of 1998, showing the number of hours needed and the total labor cost required by month and for the quarter in total.

PROBLEM 6-5   Purchasing Budget, Quarterly Summarization

Obj. 2

A sales budget for the first six months of 1998 is given below for a product manufactured by Raven and Associates.

Month	**Budgeted Sales (Units)**
January	6,000
February	10,000
March	8,000
April	9,000
May	8,000
June	7,000

The inventory of finished goods on hand at the end of each month must equal 20 percent of the following month's budgeted sales. On January 1, 1998, there were 1,200 units of finished product on hand. There was no work in process inventory at January 1, 1998. Each unit produced requires 5 pounds of a product called Amco. Raven has the policy of maintaining enough Amco in stock to meet 10 percent of the following month's production needs. There was exactly 10 percent of January production needs in inventory as of January 1, 1998. The 1998 budgeted cost per pound of Amco is $3.10.

Required

Prepare a budget showing the amount of Amco to be purchased for each of the first three months of the year and for the quarter in total.

PROBLEM 6-6 Production Budget, Quarterly Summarization

Obj. 2

On April 30, Sterling Enterprises had an inventory of 38,000 units of finished goods, and it had accounts receivable totaling $85,000. Sales, in units, have been budgeted as follows for the next four months:

May	60,000
June	75,000
July	90,000
August	81,000

Sterling has a policy that 40% of the following month's sales should be maintained in ending inventory. Each unit sells for $2. All sales are on account. The budgeted cash collections anticipate that one-third of sales will be collected in the month of sale and the remainder in the following month.

Required

a. Prepare a production budget for the months of May, June, and July.
b. Prepare a schedule of budgeted cash collections for the months of May, June, and July.

PROBLEM 6-7 Direct Labor Budget, Quarterly Summarization

Obj. 2

Specialty Products Ltd. manufactures a collectible porcelain figurine. Labor at Specialty is provided under a union contract that requires that all workers be paid for a minimum 40-hour work week with a no-layoff policy. The guaranteed number of hours that Specialty must pay for each month is 1,600. The labor agreement also states that workers will provide overtime as needed, but will be paid time and a half for any overtime worked. Accordingly, an overtime premium must be budgeted for any labor required in excess of 1,600 hours per month. The amount of labor that is required for each unit is 0.05 hour, and the budgeted labor rate is $10 per hour. Budgeted production for the second quarter of 1998 is as follows:

	April	**May**	**June**
Production in units	26,000	46,000	29,000

Required

a. Calculate the number of labor hours that are required to meet production for each of the three months, and for the second quarter in total.
b. Calculate the total budgeted labor expense to be paid each month, and for the second quarter in total.

PROBLEM 6-8 Budgeting Behavioral Implications

Objs. 4, 6

An effective budget converts the goals and objectives of management into specific performance targets. The master budget serves as a blueprint that reflects management's plans for the budgeted period. Moreover, the master budget serves as a basis for control in that performance can be evaluated by comparing actual results to budgeted or planned results.

Given the importance of budgeting within a company, the creation of an effective budget is essential for the successful operation of the company. There are several methods of generating budget information that can be employed, all of which require extensive contact with people at various operating levels within the company. The way in which people see their involvement with the budget process is important to the successful use of the budget as a management tool.

Required

a. Discuss the behavioral implications associated with the budgeting process when the company employs:
   1. A budgetary approach in which budgets are imposed from the top down.
   2. A budgetary approach in which budgets are prepared in a participative manner.
b. Describe the difference in communication flows between these two different approaches to budgeting.

PROBLEM 6-9   **Budgeting Culture and Behavior**

Objs. 4, 6

Bob Haskins is the purchasing manager for Regal Products. Each year Regal Products develops a master budget. Bob is responsible for preparing a purchasing budget, which he bases on budgeted levels of production. Bob carefully plans purchasing costs and raw material inventory levels to meet production needs.

Each year, Yvonne Lang, president of Regal Products, conducts performance evaluations, and bonuses are paid to key employees, including Bob, based on meeting budgeted results. For the past two years, Bob has received a very small bonus and has been chided by Yvonne for poor planning. Specifically, Yvonne has pointed out that the purchasing department has not maintained adequate levels of raw material inventory and is always in a rush to obtain materials, resulting in increased shipping and handling charges. Further, Regal must often pay premium amounts for immediate shipment of materials. In her most recent evaluation, Yvonne stated to Bob, "The sales department and production department are doing an excellent job. They consistently exceed their budgets by 10 percent or more. I just don't understand why you can't meet your numbers. Perhaps it is time for some changes around here."

Required

a. Why might the purchasing department be experiencing problems with meeting its budget?
b. Is it appropriate to blame Bob for all of the purchasing problems?
c. If Yvonne does "make some changes," what changes would you suggest she consider?

PROBLEM 6-10   **Labor Requirement Planning, Service Provider**

Objs. 2, 8

Ceco Grass Care is a small lawn maintenance service that provides a variety of landscape services. A large part of Ceco's sales are generated through lawn maintenance. Jeff Roberts manages Ceco. Jeff has reviewed the job order log for the next 12 weeks (3 months ending July 26, 1998), and the log is full. Ceco recently acquired several commercial property accounts and has plenty of work planned. A summary of accounts shows that Ceco now has 11 commercial properties and 45 residential properties to maintain on a routine basis.

Each property is scheduled for maintenance every two weeks. The commercial accounts require 16 worker-hours to service, and the residential accounts require 4 worker-hours.

Ceco currently has a cutting crew of three, each of whom is paid $8.50 an hour.

Required

a. Prepare a direct labor budget for Ceco covering the next three months.
b. Does the budget raise any concerns for Ceco? Explain your answer.

PROBLEM 6-11   **Multiple-Choice Overview of the Chapter**

1. Which of the following represents the correct order in which the budget documents for a manufacturing company would be prepared?
   a. Sales budget, cash budget, direct materials budget, direct labor budget
   b. Production budget, sales budget, direct materials budget, direct labor budget
   c. Sales budget, cash budget, production budget, direct materials budget
   d. Production budget, direct labor budget, cash budget, pro forma financial statements

2. Which of the following is not included as one of the four major sections of the cash budget?
   a. The receipts section
   b. The financing section

   c. The selling and administrative expense section
   d. The cash excess or deficiency section

3. A major advantage of budgeting is that it
   a. eliminates major uncertainties associated with the business environment.
   b. ensures that management's objectives will be met.
   c. requires managers to give priority to the planning process.
   d. eliminates the need for stringent controls.

4. Which of the following is *not* correct with respect to the manufacturing overhead budget?
   a. Total budgeted cash expenses for manufacturing overhead are equal to total budgeted variable overhead plus total budgeted fixed overhead.
   b. Manufacturing overhead should be broken down by cost behavior.
   c. The manufacturing overhead budget should include all costs of production other than direct materials and direct labor.
   d. The budgeted variable cost of manufacturing overhead is dependent on the number of units to be produced, as shown in the production budget.

5. Budgeted production needs are computed by

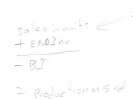

   a. adding budgeted sales to the desired ending inventory and deducting the beginning inventory.
   b. adding budgeted sales to beginning inventory and deducting the desired ending inventory.
   c. adding budgeted sales to the desired ending inventory.
   d. deducting beginning inventory from budgeted sales.

6. Which of the following represents a problem requiring special consideration when preparing budgets for multinational companies?
   a. The country in which the company is incorporated
   b. Foreign currency exchange rates
   c. Shipping and transportation of goods
   d. Most favored nation (MFN) trade status

7. Which of the following is *not* true with respect to a participative budgeting process?
   a. Participative budgeting requires less managerial involvement.
   b. Participative budgeting motivates managers by involving them in the budget process.
   c. Participative budgeting requires greater coordination between departments and disciplines.
   d. Participative budgeting relies on a bottom-up approach.

8. Which of the following statements is *not* correct?
   a. The strategic importance of budgets in decision making is affected by product life cycle stages.
   b. Operating budgets ordinarily are prepared for a year at a time and ignore monthly or quarterly amounts.
   c. Continuous, or perpetual, budgets cover a 12-month period and constantly add a new month or quarter on the end as the current month or quarter is completed.
   d. Continuous, or perpetual, budgets require managers to constantly think and plan a full 12 months ahead.

9. Identifying the costs that are to be controlled by a specific manager is
   a. an example of a top-down approach to budgeting.
   b. referred to as responsibility accounting.
   c. a way of ensuring that organizational policies are consistent.
   d. not necessary for the budgeting process.

10. Planning involves
   a. the development of future objectives and the preparation of budgets to achieve these objectives.

b. the steps taken to ensure that objectives set down by management are attained.
c. the steps taken to ensure that all parts of the organization function in a manner consistent with organizational policies.
d. comparing budgeted to actual results and investigating variations.

C A S E S

CASE 6-1 The Master Budget

Obj. 2

The Columbo Company manufactures a single model trench coat sold throughout the United States. Projected sales in units for the first five months of 1998 are as follows:

January	35,000
February	20,000
March	15,000
April	8,000
May	6,000

The following information relates to Columbo's production and inventory policies and balances:

1. Finished goods inventory is maintained at 80 percent of the following month's sales. Finished goods inventory at January 1, 1998, was 28,000 units.

2. Two materials are required for each trench coat manufactured, as follows:

Direct Materials	Yards per Unit	Cost per Yard
Polyester	5	$8
Lining material	3	2

Raw materials inventory is maintained at 10% of the following month's production needs. Inventory at January 1, 1998, was 51,000 yards of polyester and 30,600 yards of lining.

3. Direct labor used per unit is two hours. The average rate for labor is $9.50 per hour.

4. Overhead each month is estimated using a flexible budget format, with direct labor hours as the basis for variable costs. A summary of expected overhead costs is as follows:

	Fixed-Cost Component	Variable-Cost Component
Factory supplies		$1.00
Utilities		.75
Shop maintenance	$ 3,000	.50
Supervision	4,000	
Depreciation	60,000	
Taxes	5,000	
Other	10,000	2.00
Total	$82,000	$4.25

5. Selling, general, and administrative expenses are also calculated on a flexible budget basis based on the number of units sold. Cost estimates are as follows:

	Fixed-Cost Component	Variable-Cost Component
Salaries	$18,000	
Commissions		$3.00
Depreciation	22,000	
Shipping		.75
Other	10,000	1.50
Total	$50,000	$5.25

6. Each trench coat sells for $85.

7. All purchases are made in cash. All sales are on account. Collection of accounts receivable is planned as follows: 90% in the month of sale; 10% in the month following the month of sale. The accounts receivable balance at January 1, 1998, is $145,000, all of which is collectible. The cash balance at January 1, 1998, is $202,000.

Required

Prepare the following portions of the operating master budget, by month, for the first quarter of 1998:

a. Sales budget
b. Production budget
c. Direct materials budget
d. Direct labor budget
e. Overhead budget
f. Selling, general, and administrative expense budget
g. Cash budget

CASE 6-2   Budgeting in a Service Company

Objs. 7,8

Juanita Testor owns and operates a hair salon under the name Clips n' Curls. There are currently seven hair stylists, including Juanita. In addition to hair styling, Clips n' Curls sells nail care, facials, skin and hair care products, fashion jewelry, and tanning bed time.

A full-time receptionist is employed to arrange appointments and perform other clerical duties, such as counter sales and record keeping. The receptionist is paid $1,500 a month.

Juanita has eight styling bays, each equipped with a sink, cabinet, and vacuum system. Each stylist provides his or her own instruments. Each stylist, including Juanita, "rents" a bay at a cost of $400 per month. Charges for all client services are billed and collected by the receptionist, who accumulates totals for each stylist. Collections for services are paid to the stylists on a weekly basis after deducting bay rent and cost of supplies. Any supplies used by the stylists must be purchased through the shop, at Juanita's cost.

Nail care and facials are offered on a limited basis three days a week by a single individual, who receives 50% of collected billings as compensation. The tanning bed is owned by the shop. All income received from the bed goes to the shop. Variable shop costs are incurred based on the number of stylists. Based on a two-year study, Juanita has assembled the following information on monthly activity and costs to operate Clip n' Curl:

Average monthly billings per stylist	$4,000
Average product sales	600
Average gross margin on product sales	55%
Average gross nail and facial billings	$1,000
Average gross tanning bed billings	450
Fixed operating costs:	
Shop rent	500
Depreciation	400
Advertising	150
Other	100
Variable operating costs	
Maintenance, utilities, and other	1,400*

Note: Variable operating costs are incurred as follows: 50% by stylists, 30% by tanning and nails, 15% by product display, and 5% administrative.

Required

a. Assume that Juanita can hire an additional stylist who can generate the same average amount of business as the other stylists. Assume also that the additional stylist would have no impact on administrative expenses. What would be the change in average monthly shop income if Juanita hires the stylist to fill the remaining open bay? (*Hint:* Compare the change in revenues with the change in costs related to the incremental increase of one stylist.)

b. What is the average total monthly income of the shop given the number of stylists currently employed?

c. Juanita is considering a change in the bay rent agreement. Instead of charging a fixed amount per month, she is thinking of charging a stylist 12 percent of the stylist's billings. Would Juanita be better off with this new fee arrangement? Explain your answer.

PROJECTS

PROJECT 6-1   The Cash Budget

Objs. 1,2

Prepare a cash budget representing your own personal finances for the next six months.

PROJECT 6-2   The Master Budget

Objs. 1,2,4,5

Select a company or industry in which you have a personal interest. For each budget discussed in the chapter, describe the information this company or industry must consider in developing that particular budget. Prepare a short summary of your conclusions. For each budget, your summary should include the type of budget and the considerations that would be required in preparing it.

PROJECT 6-3   Personal Budgeting

Objs. 1,2,3

Speak with classmates who are planning to vacation over a class break. Find out if these students developed "budgets" for their trips. (The budget need not be formally written down.) What sort of things did the people consider in preparing a budget? What were the most prevalent items considered in vacation planning? Were any planned expenditures affected by volume? Did you note any incidence of "slack" in the planning process? Write a short report on these points as well as any other budgeting observations that you noted.

PROJECT 6-4   Budgeting Culture

Objs. 4,6

Budgets are used for planning and control purposes in almost every job. Interview 3 people with jobs to determine whether they are evaluated against budgets on their jobs. Write a short description of your findings. How many of these people are directly involved in the budget process? How many of these people have budgets forced on them without input? Are all of these people measured against the same kind of budget, or is a wide variety of budget types represented? Classify these budgets as operational or financial. Prepare a short report of your findings.

Evaluating Performance Within an Organization

7

Accounting and Management Decisions

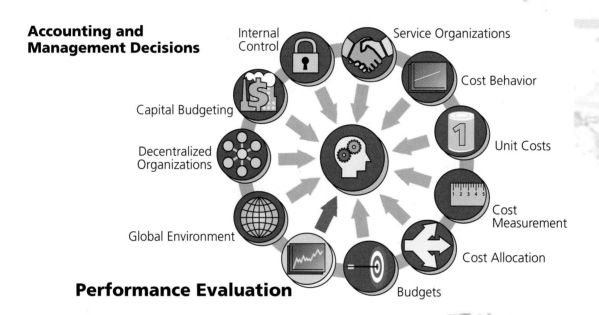

- Internal Control
- Service Organizations
- Cost Behavior
- Unit Costs
- Cost Measurement
- Cost Allocation
- Budgets
- Global Environment
- Decentralized Organizations
- Capital Budgeting

Performance Evaluation

Overview

Evaluating performance is a key responsibility of managers. This chapter considers a number of methods that managers of manufacturing and service organizations can use in determining how well their areas of responsibility are performing. Some of these methods are used to monitor production or service operations, while others are used by higher levels of management to evaluate the strategic direction of the company. Managers use these methods not only to evaluate overall performance, but also to isolate problems and identify solutions. This chapter is divided into two major sections as follows:

1. Performance evaluation using variance analysis to compare actual performance with predetermined standards

2. Other techniques for evaluating processes, including:
   a. Statistical process control methods to help managers classify problems resulting from unusual events, rather than normal or expected events
   b. Quality cost methods to understand the causes and cost of poor quality
   c. Methods for estimating the costs of variation in a process

Major topics covered in this chapter include:

- Interpretation of labor and materials variances for control and decision making.

© John Moss/Tony Stone Images

- Use of statistical process control charts in managing operations.
- Understanding of quality cost components and alternative views of quality measurement

Objectives

Once you have completed this chapter, you should be able to:

1. Calculate and evaluate cost variances for direct materials and direct labor.

2. Explain how managers may react when variance analysis is used to measure performance.

3. Explain how statistical process control provides useful information to managers of both production and administrative functions.

4. Identify four types of quality costs and explain how managers use these costs to improve performance.

5. Describe how variability can affect production costs.

6. Explain the application of performance evaluation methods in service organizations.

METALART: PERFORMANCE EVALUATION AND THE MANUFACTURING PROCESS

The examples in this chapter are based on the experience of MetalArt, a company that prints graphic designs on flat metal sheets. The sheets are processed by other companies to make containers for ground coffee sold in grocery stores. Exhibit 1 illustrates the manufacturing process at MetalArt. Four interrelated processes (coil shearing, coating, printing, and wrapping) are required to produce MetalArt's product line. The following section briefly explains the activities taking place within each process.

Coil Shearing

The manufacturing process begins with coils of steel and ends with printed metal sheets that will be cut and welded into coffee cans by MetalArt's customers. Large rolls of steel (weighing approximately 20,000 pounds and called *coils*) are loaded onto a spindle that permits the coil to rotate as it is unwound for processing. Next, the steel passes through a pinhole detector, an optical scanning device that identifies light passing through the steel sheet. This step ensures that the finished can will be airtight and provide a perfect seal.

As a coil unwinds, the steel is sheared (cut) into sheets approximately three feet square. The steel sheets are randomly tested for squareness and must fall within specification limits to be passed on to the next stage of production. Those sheets that meet the quality standards are stacked in preparation for coating.

Coating

Coating is the first step in the printing process. A coat of white paint is applied to the metal sheet to provide a base for colored ink to adhere to. Following the base coat application, the sheet advances into an oven for drying. Since 18 or more cans are cut from one sheet of steel, the base coat is applied in rectangular patterns with strips of bare steel separating the rectangles. This frame of bare metal, called the *weld margin,* (Exhibit 2) is very important. When the individual rectangles are cut from the sheet and welded to form the cylindrical can body, paint in the weld margin would cause major damage to the welding machine and disrupt the assembly process. Thus, a computer equipped with optical scanning devices monitors the coating of each sheet. A red flashing signal from the computer's control system lets the machine operator know when the coating process is beginning to produce weld margins that are too narrow. At the end of the coating step, the sheets are stacked and placed in a work in process area on the plant floor.

Printing

Printing is the next step in the process. The printing machines are capable of applying up to three colors to the sheets before they pass through a dryer that promotes rapid drying of the paint. The image that appears on the final product is printed using a process similar to silk screening. Three colors (such as red, blue, and yellow) are applied one after the other. Exhibit 2 illustrates a typical sheet of can bodies after coating and printing. At the end of the printing step, the sheets are stacked on platforms called *pallets* to await wrapping.

Wrapping and Shipping

Pallets of finished printed sheets are covered with plastic and bound with metal straps for shipping. Wrapping is a manual operation that requires two workers. After wrapping, pallets are loaded directly into trucks and delivered to customers. Finished goods inventory is not allowed to accumulate for more than a few hours.

Exhibit 1 The Manufacturing Process at MetalArt

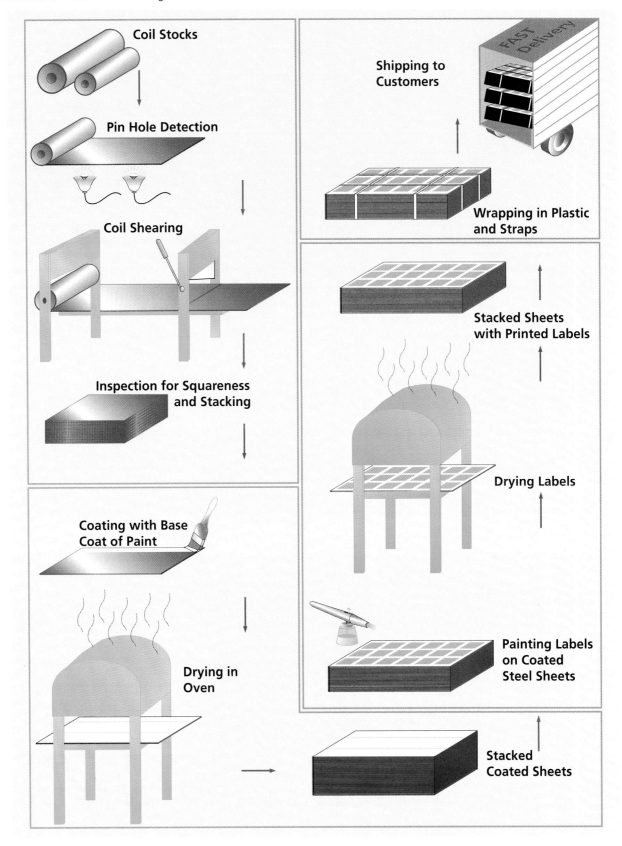

Exhibit 2   Sheet of Can Bodies

METALART: COST AND QUALITY MANAGEMENT

 This section documents the events occurring at MetalArt over a two-year period. The company found that its product quality was lower than that of its competitors. In addition, production costs were soaring out of control. MetalArt's managers discovered various cost management techniques to improve quality and reduce production costs.

We begin our discussion with the following events.

MetalArt—March 1995

Pat Allan, manager of the MetalArt plant, looked around the conference table in hopes that someone at the managers' meeting could explain why production costs had gone through the roof during the past few weeks. "I just don't understand. After all of our efforts to control costs, things have gotten worse. Corporate isn't going to be happy with our profitability figures."

Mary Smith, the production manager, replied, "Pat, remember the problems we had last week with bad raw materials? Everyone knows that rusty steel causes all kinds of headaches when we run it through the printing line. I suspect our profitability problems somehow are related to that. Also, I'm sure that some defective prints left the plant and that we'll hear about it from our customers. But we can't inspect everything; we don't have the resources."

"Mary, I don't think 'off-grade' material could have had *that* much impact on our bottom line," replied Lee Jones, the purchasing manager. "Anyway, by my estimates, I saved thousands of dollars by finding good steel prices."

Mary said, "Lee, we appreciate your efforts to control raw materials costs, but I scheduled a lot of overtime because our production line had to slow down to deal with off-grade raw material."

"I'm hearing two important issues," said Pat. "We have to find a way to measure the impact of material and labor cost overruns, and also to *prevent* production problems and their related costs before they get out of hand. It's clear to me that our disappointing financial results are linked to our operating problems. Let's get busy and put some controls in place that will help us improve operations and reduce costs. First, let's calculate cost variances for materials and labor. I'll evaluate those reports on a weekly basis to make sure we are staying on track."

"That's okay for you, Pat, but I need on-line, real-time tools to let me know when our process is out of control," said Mary. "I can't wait a week to find out that I need to look for a solution to a manufacturing problem. I think statistical process control methods would help us determine quickly when something has gone wrong."

"I agree," said Pat. "In addition, I think we should install a system for accounting for the costs of quality. I don't think we should rely on inspections to ensure that few defective units leave the plant. We can improve our processes so that they are reliable. In addition, we can illustrate to everyone from the shop floor worker to plant management how their actions affect our bottom line. We have good people, and I'm sure we can turn this plant around. Let's go to work!"

MetalArt—1997

Like other companies in the 1990s, MetalArt is constantly reviewing its operations, looking for ways to cut costs and improve quality. The employees have risen to the challenge and have managed to cut costs by 40% over the last two years while maintaining product quality. These improvements are due largely to employee suggestions and implementation efforts.

At each stage of production, the machine operator is assisted by software that signals when production quality slips out of control. With newer machines, data go directly from the machine to the computer. However, for older machines, the operator must enter the machine readings manually into the computer. The data are analyzed by a computerized statistical model that checks relevant variables to determine if production is within quality control limits. In addition, workers at all stages select samples from work in process, visually inspect printing quality, and reject products that do not meet very tight guidelines.

VARIANCE ANALYSIS FOR DIRECT MATERIALS AND DIRECT LABOR

Objective 1
Calculate and evaluate cost variances for direct materials and direct labor.

This section considers variance analysis as a tool for determining whether managers are using resources efficiently. We consider the environment in which the technique developed and its relevance to modern manufacturing companies. MetalArt is used to illustrate variance calculation and analysis.

MetalArt—April 1995

The first task undertaken by Pat Allan and the management team was to establish a standard cost reporting system that would allow *actual* material and labor costs to be compared with *standard* material and labor costs. *Standard costs* **represent the cost of the material and labor that should have been used to achieve actual production levels.** Accountants have used variance analysis for many years to evaluate how actual costs and quantities compare with predetermined standards.

In the later part of the nineteenth century and early part of the twentieth century, engineer-managers embraced a manufacturing philosophy known as scientific management. Frederick Taylor, who generally is regarded as the father of scientific management, believed that for every process, there was one best way of doing it. He identified standards for labor efficiency and material usage. Then he compared these standards with actual operating performance. Typically, *standards* **are based on engineering studies to determine the amount of a resource (such as labor hours or pounds of material) necessary to manufacture a product.** Thus, standards tell us how much of a resource we should use or how much we should pay for materials and labor, given the number of units actually produced. Today, managers use variance analysis, which evolved from scientific management, to evaluate performance and to help them identify solutions to production problems. In addition, managers of service organizations use variance analysis. For example, hospitals use it to monitor the amount of nursing labor and hospital supplies used in treating patients. Retail organizations often analyze sales performance by comparing actual costs at a certain sales level with standard (or expected) costs. Examples may include travel and entertainment expenses, sales commissions, and other administrative support costs.

Direct Materials and Direct Labor Variances

We will calculate and interpret cost variances for the direct materials and direct labor used by MetalArt. At the most basic level, a variance is simply the difference between an actual cost and a standard cost. Using the diagram in Exhibit 3, total *actual* costs are compared with total *standard* costs to determine a total variance. Whether direct labor or direct materials is analyzed, the format is the same.

Exhibit 3   Total Variance Diagram

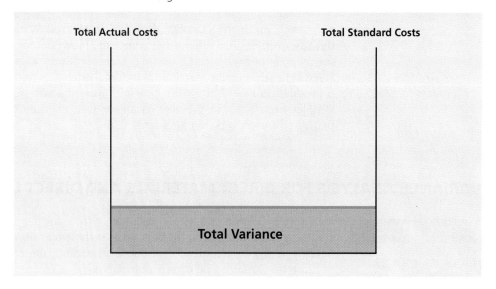

As shown in Exhibit 4, the total variance may be divided into two parts, a *price* component and a *quantity* component, by adding a middle prong to the total variance diagram. The reason for dividing a variance into its component parts is to determine whether a variance resulted from:

*   *costs* of resources consumed that differed from standards,
*   *physical amounts* of resources consumed that differed from standards, or
*   a combination of *both costs and physical amounts* that differed from standards.

Accountants typically use the terms material *price* and *quantity* and labor *rate* and *efficiency* to describe the price and quantity components of each variance.

Exhibit 4 Variances Divided into Price and Quantity Components

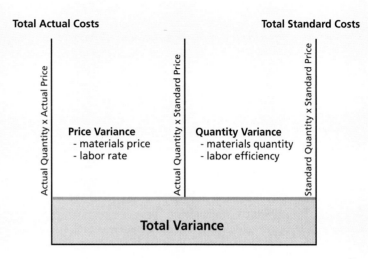

MetalArt's experience illustrates how to calculate and interpret variances. Under the direction of Pat Allan, a team consisting of an engineer, an accountant, a personnel manager, and a purchasing manager prepared the information in Exhibit 5. They wanted to understand how manufacturing costs went through the roof during the second week of March 1995, as discussed in the weekly managers' meeting.

Exhibit 5 Production Information for Calculating Materials and Labor Variances

Materials (Steel)		
Actual usage 500,000 pounds	× actual price per pound × $.25	= actual cost = $125,000
Standard usage 460,000 pounds	× standard price per pound × $.30	= expected cost = $138,000
Labor		
Actual usage 5,300 hours	× actual rate per hour × $29	= actual cost = $153,700
Standard usage 4,600 hours	× standard rate per hour × $24	= expected cost = $110,400

Materials (Steel). Production records indicate that the actual quantity of steel purchased and used in the second week of March 1995 was 500,000 pounds. However, according to engineering standards, only 460,000 pounds should have been used during this period to make 6,000,000 finished coffee cans. Engineers designed coffee containers to precise specifications for length, width, thickness, and weight. Therefore, by multiplying the actual number of coffee cans manufactured times the standard weight per can, MetalArt's accountants determined the amount of steel that *should* have been used in production. In addition to physical standards for steel consumption, MetalArt established raw materials cost standards to evaluate the effectiveness of the purchasing department. Recall that MetalArt's purchasing manager, Lee Jones, had found a "good deal" on steel coils and had paid only $.25 per pound, although the standard price was $.30 per pound.

Labor. MetalArt employs many factory workers, each of whom is scheduled to work 40 hours per week; however, some are willing to work overtime when necessary to achieve production targets. In our opening discussion, Mary Smith indicated that extra labor time was needed because the manufacturing process had to operate at slower speeds as a result of inferior raw materials. As shown in Exhibit 5, the total number of hours worked during the second week of March was 5,300, at an actual cost of $29 per hour. By contrast, only 4,600 hours should have been worked during the period, at a rate of $24 per hour, to achieve the actual production level. Engineers developed time standards for producing a printed image for a coffee container. By multiplying the number of containers actually produced by the standard time per container, MetalArt's accountants determined the number of labor hours that *should* have been worked. Standard labor rates also were provided by MetalArt's personnel department. Recall that overtime wages, which are higher, were paid, causing the actual average hourly wage ($29) to exceed the standard hourly wage ($24).

The differences between actual and standard costs and usage for both materials and labor have been identified. In addition to calculating the amount of a variance, accountants also classify variances as favorable or unfavorable. **A** *favorable variance* **results when the actual price (or quantity) is less than the standard price (or quantity) for materials or labor.** On the other hand, **an** *unfavorable variance* **results when the actual price (or quantity) exceeds the standard.** Because variances may be interrelated, you must be careful when interpreting favorable and unfavorable variances. The term *favorable* does not always imply that something good has happened.

Calculation and Interpretation of Materials and Labor Variances

Pat Allan called another managers' meeting in May 1995 to review the work of the standard cost team. This section summarizes the key elements of the meeting and outlines how to calculate materials and labor variances.

Total Materials Variance. The plant controller began the discussion after passing copies of the variance report to each member of the team. "Refer to Exhibit 4, where the left-hand side is defined as *actual* cost. We multiplied the actual quantity of steel purchased by the actual price per pound to determine the actual cost of our steel purchases. The right-hand side identifies the *standard* cost allowed for actual production. We multiplied the standard quantity of steel allowed for actual production by the standard price to determine the standard cost. Thus, the total materials variance represents the difference between actual cost and standard cost, calculated as shown here."

Total materials variance = (actual quantity × actual price) − (standard quantity × standard price)

| 500,000 x $.25 = $125,000 | **Total Materials Variance** | 460,000 x $.30 = $138,000 |

$13,000 Favorable

Pat examined the total materials variance and commented, "The plant's cost problems do not seem to be related to materials after all. A $13,000 favorable materials variance actually means that total material costs were *less* than the standards allowed."

However, Mary was quick to point out that a total variance does not tell the entire story. "Let's look beyond the total materials variance to the price and quantity elements and see what we find."

Materials Price Variance. "We divided the total variance for materials into price and quantity elements by adding a middle prong to the total variance diagram," explained the controller.

The middle prong shown in Exhibit 4 is defined as an actual quantity multiplied by a standard price. Thus, the price variance equation compares an *actual price* with a *standard price* to determine the *price variance per unit.*

MetalArt's controller continued, "We multiplied the number of pounds of purchased steel by the cost per pound (on the left side) and multiplied the actual number of pounds of purchased steel by the standard price (on the middle prong). The materials price variance is determined by subtracting the value found on the middle prong from that on the left side."

Materials price variance = (actual quantity × actual price) − (actual quantity × standard price)

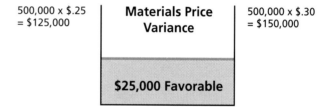

The purchasing manager, Lee Jones, smiled when the discussion turned to the materials price variance; he actually paid $.05 ($.30 − $.25) per pound less than standard rates for steel purchases. Since 500,000 pounds were purchased, the result was a favorable price variance of $25,000 (500,000 × $.05). Next, the discussion focused on the materials quantity variance.

Materials Quantity Variance. The plant controller continued, "As you know, we produced approximately 6,000,000 cans. Standards suggest that we should have used 460,000 pounds of steel. Thus, we multiplied the standard quantity of steel allowed for actual production by the standard cost per pound to arrive at the value found on the right side of the diagram. The materials quantity variance calculation compares the value on the middle prong with that on the right side."

Materials quantity variance = (actual quantity × standard price) − (standard quantity × standard price)

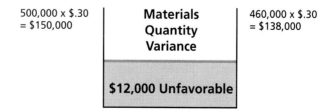

"Unfortunately, the materials quantity variance of $12,000 is unfavorable. The difference between the actual quantity of materials used (500,000 pounds) and the standard quantity allowed for actual production (460,000 pounds) represents excess consumption of 40,000 pounds of material at a standard cost of $.30 per pound," the controller explained. "Our calculations indicate that the total materials variance of $13,000 (favorable) can be divided into a $25,000 favorable price variance and a $12,000 unfavorable quantity variance ($25,000 favorable − $12,000 unfavorable = $13,000 favorable). As Mary suggested, off-grade materials affect the amount of steel required for production. The steel coils were blemished by small rust spots that did not affect the strength of the steel. Unfortunately, the blemishes were visible through the printed image, resulting in 40,000 pounds of scrap (500,000 actual pounds of steel − 460,000 standard pounds of steel)."

Jones leaned back in his chair. "So what's the problem? Even though we used $12,000 more materials than our standards allow, I saved $25,000 by finding good steel prices. The net effect is still positive."

Mary turned the page to the labor variance report. "Lee, look at the next report. Poor-quality materials affect our process in other ways. I think a clearer picture will emerge after we consider labor variances."

Learning Note

When the quantity of material purchased differs from the quantity actually used in production, the materials price variance is calculated using the actual quantity purchased, and the materials quantity variance is calculated using the actual quantity used in production. Thus, the purchasing agent is evaluated based on the amount purchased, whereas the production manager is evaluated based on the amount used. If more materials are purchased than are used, the difference is not a variance; it simply increases the value of the raw materials inventory.

Total Labor Variance. The controller continued, "The total labor variance is calculated in the same way as the total materials variance. Referring to Exhibit 4, the difference between actual labor costs and standard labor costs allowed for actual production (6,000,000 cans) is calculated as shown here."

Total labor variance = (actual hours × actual rate) − (standard hours × standard rate)

5,300 × $29 = $153,700	**Total Labor Variance**	4,600 × $24 = $110,400
	$43,300 Unfavorable	

"Look at how our labor costs were affected," said Mary.

"Wow, the $43,300 unfavorable labor variance wiped out my favorable materials variance. What caused the variance to be so large?" asked Lee.

Labor Rate Variance. The controller explained, "Lee, the labor variance is made up of two elements, the labor rate variance and the labor efficiency variance. Exhibit 5 identifies the actual and standard hourly labor rates as $29 and $24, respectively. We actually paid $5 per hour ($29 − $24) more than the standards allowed because we had to pay overtime. Since 5,300 hours actually were worked during the second week of March, an unfavorable labor rate variance of $26,500 (5,300 × $5) resulted. Many employees were asked to work overtime (at higher hourly wage rates) to achieve a production level of 460,000 pounds of printed steel. We computed the labor rate variance as shown here."

Labor rate variance = (actual hours × actual rate) − (actual hours × standard rate)

5,300 x $29
= $153,700

Labor Rate Variance

5,300 x $24
= $127,200

$26,500 Unfavorable

Labor Efficiency Variance. Mary said, "I not only paid higher hourly wages because of overtime, but also scheduled more hours trying to get materials to run properly. Our efficiency is really poor. Look at the labor efficiency report."

The controller explained, "We calculated the labor efficiency variance by subtracting the value found on the right side from the value on the middle prong."

Labor efficiency variance = (actual hours × standard rate) − (standard hours × standard rate)

5,300 x $24
= $127,200

Labor Efficiency Variance

4,600 x $24
= $110,400

$16,800 Unfavorable

"Only 4,600 hours were allowed by engineering standards to produce 6,000,000 cans. Our actual labor time was 5,300 hours. Thus, an excess of 700 hours (5,300 − 4,600) at a standard rate of $24 per hour caused an unfavorable labor efficiency variance of $16,800 (700 × $24). Our calculations indicate that the unfavorable labor variance of $43,300 is made up of an unfavorable rate variance of $26,500 and an unfavorable efficiency variance of $16,800 ($26,500 + $16,800 = $43,300)."

The team began to understand the financial impact of materials and labor variances. In addition, the relationship between purchasing and production decisions became apparent. Pat commented that perhaps management was to blame for the problem. In closing the meeting, Pat stated, "It appears that we are motivating managers to achieve local performance objectives without considering how their actions affect the organization as a whole."

"So, I'm not such a bad guy after all," quipped Lee.

"No, just a bit misdirected," teased Pat.

Learning Note
In a standard cost system, costs flow through the inventory accounts (Raw Materials Inventory, Work in Process Inventory, and Finished Goods Inventory) at standard values. Thus, the balance sheet reflects these standard costs. However, since actual costs of materials, labor, and overhead seldom equal standard costs, variances are created. At the end of an accounting cycle, these variances typically are closed out to the Cost of Goods Sold account on the income statement. Thus, the cost of goods sold calculation on the income statement reflects actual (rather than standard) costs.

LIMITATIONS OF TRADITIONAL VARIANCE ANALYSIS

The MetalArt example illustrates a potential problem associated with using price variances to motivate behavior. Because he was focusing only on meeting price standards, Lee Jones cut corners on quality. In addition, purchasing managers may be

O b j e c t i v e   2
Explain how managers may
react when variance analysis
is used to measure
performance.

encouraged to purchase inventory in quantities far greater than reasonable needs in order to receive volume purchase discounts. Unfortunately, costs saved on an initial purchase may be offset by inventory carrying charges, damage, and obsolescence.

In saving the company $25,000 in material costs, Lee Jones contributed to unfavorable variances totaling $55,300. Managers may add up the variances to determine whether a change (such as buying less expensive materials or using a different mix of labor) results in a favorable or an unfavorable net variance. In MetalArt's case, the unfavorable net variance may be calculated as follows:

Materials price variance		$25,000 favorable
Materials quantity variance	$12,000 unfavorable	
Labor rate variance	26,500 unfavorable	
Labor efficiency variance	16,800 unfavorable	55,300 unfavorable
Net variance		$30,300 unfavorable

While the MetalArt example suggests that poor raw material quality significantly contributes to the unfavorable labor efficiency variance, other factors also can hurt labor efficiency. For example, workers may simply make mistakes. In addition, poor training or problems with scheduling may affect workers' abilities to perform as desired.

The tendency in many organizations is to point the finger at plant managers when production-related variances occur. However, managers in marketing divisions can contribute to variances, as well. For example, when a manufacturing facility gears up for a certain level of production in response to a sales forecast made by the marketing manager, it often takes on additional labor and equipment. If actual sales do not meet expectations, the factory cannot immediately eliminate the unnecessary resources. The lag in the response time will result in some workers being temporarily idle, creating an unfavorable labor efficiency variance. Alternatively, if sales exceed the forecast, unexpected overtime costs will be incurred, thereby affecting the labor rate variance. Thus, proper planning is an important element of cost control.

Learning   Note   While variance analysis helps managers identify sources of inefficiency, some managers believe that the use of standards does not promote continuous improvement. For example, workers may focus merely on meeting the standards rather than finding better ways to manage existing processes.

In addition to materials and labor variances, some companies calculate variable and fixed overhead variances. Variable overhead variances are calculated in the same way as variances for labor and materials. In other words, variable overhead rate and efficiency variances may be calculated using the diagrams discussed earlier in this chapter. Many accountants, including the authors of this text, do not believe that overhead variances are especially useful; however, alternative methods for evaluating overhead are described in an earlier chapter. Also, recall that we have considered cost behavior with respect to volume; some costs change with activity levels, whereas others remain fixed. Fixed overhead can be analyzed in terms of two variances, budget and volume.

The fixed overhead budget variance is simply the difference between actual spending for fixed overhead and planned spending for fixed overhead. Alternatively, the fixed overhead volume variance is a measure of plant use. Managers who produce at higher levels have more units over which to spread fixed costs, making the fixed cost per unit smaller and creating more favorable variances. Thus, managers are encouraged to manufacture products in large quantities even if there is no market for them.

Many accountants argue that managers should focus instead on process improvements and product quality. The remainder of this chapter considers methods for evaluating processes and improving product quality. Both statistical process control charts and Taguchi's quality loss function were developed by statisticians and engineers for use in understanding factory operations. We also consider how accountants and managers can use engineering methods to improve administrative, as well as production, processes.

SELF-STUDY PROBLEM 1

Greasy Grimes is a chain of automotive repair shops owned by entrepreneur Terrel Grimes. Grimes established the company during the 1960s to compete with local garages and the service departments of new car dealerships. In addition to performing basic oil change and lubrication services, Greasy Grimes' mechanics do major and minor repairs on engine, transmission, and brake systems.

The company is unionized and has three labor classes, with the following wage rates:

© John Coletti/PNI International

	Hourly Rate
Apprentice mechanic	$25
Journeyman mechanic	$30
Master mechanic	$40

Each shop has a manager who prepares cost estimates for customers and assigns jobs to mechanics. Labor estimates are prepared using a book that identifies the number of standard labor hours required to perform various repairs.

Grimes is reviewing a monthly report that summarizes the transmission service activities of shop 222. The shop recently had a change in management, and Grimes is anxious to evaluate the new manager's ability to use labor effectively. Relevant data are presented below:

Shop 222
July
Transmission Services
Standard Labor Class: Apprentice

Actual Hours	Actual Rate	Standard Hours	Standard Rate
500	$30	800	$25

Required

Calculate the labor rate and labor efficiency variances for shop 222 during July and interpret your results.

The solution to Self-Study Problem 1 appears at the end of the chapter.

STATISTICAL PROCESS CONTROL[1]

Objective 3
Explain how statistical process control provides useful information to managers of both production and administrative functions.

As businesses seek to improve the quality of products and processes, methods for monitoring and evaluating performance have become increasingly important. One such tool that has become popular is the statistical process control (SPC) chart. Statistical process control charts can be applied to many different types of situations. When maintained continuously, they provide an early warning signal that a quality problem may exist. For example, control charts may be used to (a) identify errors or unpredictable processes and determine basic causes, (b) provide a warning of an unexpected change within a process, (c) evaluate service or product consistency over time, and (d) decrease process variability and associated inspection costs.

Control charts measure two types of variation, special cause and common cause. **A** *special cause variation* **has an identifiable source, such as faulty equipment or processes. Alternatively, a** *common cause variation* **is the result of randomness inherent in a process.** Statistical control results when special causes of variation have been eliminated. Once a process is in a state of statistical control, the process is considered stable and predictable. A process in a state of statistical control is not necessarily a good process; rather, it is a *predictable* process. Once a process is in control, managers can focus their attention on making improvements that reduce common cause variation.

Though companies use many different types of statistical process control charts, the charts have common elements. In general, a control chart is a graph that shows measurements for a characteristic of interest. The characteristic may be a quantitative variable such as weight, length, or thickness of material, or it may be a qualitative attribute such as whether or not a product is defective.

Statistical process control charts typically include (a) a center line, representing the expected value of a characteristic, (b) a line above and another below the expected value, indicating the limits within which a characteristic is considered to be in control, (c) a horizontal axis, indicating the time order of observations of the characteristic, and (d) a vertical axis, measuring the values of the observations. A control chart used to monitor the printing line at MetalArt serves as an example to illustrate the elements and uses of control charts.

As described at the beginning of this chapter, the printing line sprays paint onto steel sheets to produce a finished image. Paint is applied to the surface of metal sheets through sprayer nozzles. If the sprayer nozzles become clogged, printing quality is affected because the images do not receive the correct amount of paint. Thus, MetalArt maintains on-line control charts to monitor paint flow coming from the nozzles. Exhibit 6 is an example of a control chart used by MetalArt.

The vertical axis measures the flow volume per second through the sprayer nozzle. Values can range from zero, indicating no paint flow, to 120, indicating the maximum possible flow. The horizontal axis represents individual flow measurements taken throughout the day. Points on the chart represent flow values (y axis) for individual observations (x axis). A horizontal center line, or process average (expected value), is drawn through the center of the points. The process average (77.9) is the sum of the individual measurements divided by the total number of measurements $[(80 + 75 + 90 + 90 + 75 + 60 + 90 + 85 + 85 + 80 + 90 + 75 + 75 + 40) \div 14 = 77.9]$.

In addition to the center line, the MetalArt control chart has an upper and a lower control limit, placed at 109 and 47.2, respectively. The area between the upper

[1]   *The authors relied on the following articles in preparing the section on statistical process control:*
Albright, T. L., and H. P. Roth. 1993. *Controlling Quality on a Multidimensional Level,* Journal of Cost Management *(Spring): 29–37.*
Walter, R., M. Higgins, and H. Roth. 1990. *Applications of Control Charts,* The CPA Journal *(April): 90–93, 95.*
Duarte, J. 1991. *Statistical Process Control in Marketing and Finance,* CMA Magazine *(May): 20–23.*

Exhibit 6 Example of a Statistical Process Control Chart

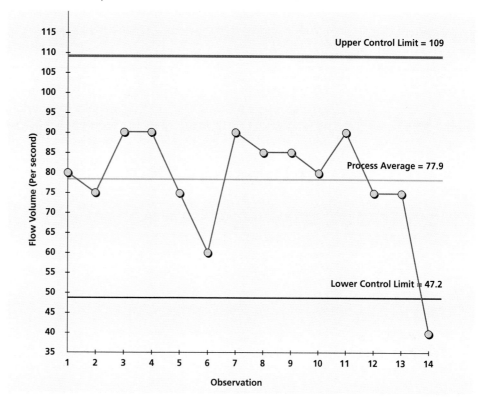

and lower control limits represents the band of normal variability for the printing process. **Control charts are designed to signal when a process is out of control.** At observation number 14, which exceeds the lower control limit, the sprayer process is no longer in statistical control. The chart informs the machine operator that an unusual situation has occurred so that the operator can take corrective action.

Thus, statistical process control charts are used to identify measurements of a characteristic that deviate from the process average and to discover changes in the measurement. If points on a control chart are randomly scattered around the center line and fall within the upper and lower control limits, the process is considered to be in statistical control. An out-of-control condition is indicated if points fall above or below the control limits. By analyzing conditions existing at the time an out-of-control signal occurs, a manager may discover the cause of the problem.

Control charts are appropriate for measuring and evaluating many different types of processes. Generally, they can be used in any repetitive situation in which a quantitative variable or qualitative attribute is measurable. However, statistical process control charts also can be used in other areas, including accounting, finance, and marketing. For example, MetalArt's accounting department prepares payroll checks and payments for inventory purchases. Internal auditors typically verify that proper internal control procedures, such as authorization of bills and approval to make payments, are used in preparing payroll checks and payments to suppliers. To do this, they can collect samples of paid invoices or canceled payroll checks and record the percentage of cases with proper authorization and approval on a control chart. An out-of-control signal would suggest that an unusually large percentage of cases did not conform to proper procedures. By investigating samples in which control limits are exceeded, auditors may trace the cause of errors. For example, a new employee may not be familiar with company policies. Employee training should keep this problem from occurring in the future. Thus, control charts may be used to identify and correct administrative problems, as well as problems within the manufacturing process.

Other examples of using control charts in an administrative capacity include monitoring (a) the number of invoices processed during each month, (b) the average age of accounts receivable, (c) the time required to prepare monthly financial statements, and (d) sales returns per salesperson. Thus, managers in many different areas can use statistical process control analysis to help them evaluate the quality of their activities.

When first implementing statistical process control methods, managers should use charts where they expect to find trouble. In addition, they should use charts in those areas where financial benefits from improving a process and reducing special causes of variability are most likely. Managers are more likely to support continued use of statistical process control methods if they are able to see positive, tangible financial results.

C A S E

In   Point

http://www.swcollege.com/ingram.html

Visit Polaroid's home page to learn more about the company.

Polaroid introduced the new Captiva camera in June 1993. The manufacturing process is monitored by a statistical process control system. Statistical process control charts are maintained in real time by the production organization and help Polaroid achieve a high level of quality. For example, the shutter subassembly line is part of a quality effort that attempts to minimize defects to one defect in three million units produced. A camera or shutter can be considered defective and rejected for any of 50 different reasons, ranging from shutters that stick to strobes that do not fire. Thus, Polaroid is using statistical process control to help ensure that its new camera meets or exceeds customer expectations.

Source: For more information, see A Picture of Quality, Quality (January 1995): 43–44, 46.

SELF-STUDY PROBLEM 2

Corporate managers at Greasy Grimes began collecting data from each service center to analyze material price and quantity variances. Some managers are concerned that too much is being paid for materials and too many materials are being used in conducting repairs.

Managers collected quantity data from the past 12 months to use as a comparison with the variance figures for July of the current year:

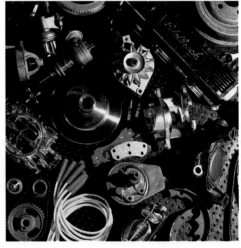

© Superstock

12-Month Material Quantity Variance Data

Jul.	$1,000 F	Jan.	$350 F
Aug.	1,000 U	Feb.	400 F
Sep.	500 F	Mar.	250 F
Oct.	750 F	Apr.	300 U
Nov.	800 U	May	250 U
Dec.	750 U	Jun.	150 F

July Material Price and Quantity Data

Actual price	$200
Actual quantity	25
Standard Price	$190
Standard Quantity	23

Required

1. Construct a statistical process control chart for material quantity variances. In calculating the process average, treat favorable variances as positive values and unfavorable variances as negative values.
   a. Calculate the process average for the 12 months listed above.
   b. Place the upper control limit at + $1,875.
   c. Place the lower control limit at − $1,825.
   d. Plot the materials quantity variances for the past 12 months.
2. Calculate the materials price and quantity variances for July of this year and add the quantity variance to your statistical process control chart.
3. Is the process in statistical control? Should managers investigate this July's materials quantity variance for special causes? Explain.

The solution to Self-Study Problem 2 appears at the end of the chapter.

QUALITY COST CONCEPTS[2]

Objective 4
Identify four types of quality costs and explain how managers use these costs to improve performance.

Quality costs **are costs incurred because poor quality can or does exist in a particular product, function, or business.**[3] Quality refers to conformance to design specifications. Thus, quality costs are costs incurred to ensure that quality standards are met or because quality standards are not met. These costs of conformance often are divided into three categories: prevention, appraisal, and failure.

Prevention costs are costs incurred to prevent the production of poor-quality units (in manufacturing organizations) or poor-quality services (in service organizations). MetalArt uses statistical process control to monitor production and to make necessary changes if a process slips out of control. Thus, the cost of implementing statistical process control techniques to prevent paint from being applied in the wrong place is an example of prevention costs.

Appraisal costs are costs incurred to identify poor-quality products (or services) before a customer receives the goods or services. The cost of inspections within the MetalArt plant is classified as an appraisal cost. A goal of world-class organizations is to design a production process that is in a state of control and exhibits little random variation. A good process that is in control produces high-quality products, making less inspection necessary. Therefore, a company usually benefits by investing in prevention, rather than appraisal, activities.

Failure costs are costs incurred because poor quality exists. Failure costs may be divided into two categories, internal failure costs and external failure costs. If a defective product or service is discovered before it is delivered to the customer, the cost is considered an internal failure cost. However, if a customer discovers a defective product or service, the cost is considered an external failure cost. For example, if paint is applied outside of the proper location during printing and subsequently damages welding equipment when a customer manufactures a can, MetalArt has incurred an external failure cost. Some failure costs are easy to quantify; however, customer ill will associated with discovering a defective product or service is difficult to measure. When W. Edwards Deming, a famous industrial statistician, said that the costs of poor quality are unknown and unknowable, he referred to the inability to determine the cost of unhappy customers.

Firms that measure quality costs wish to track the level of internal failure, external failure, appraisal, and prevention costs over time. Typically, a firm that embraces a quality program invests additional resources in prevention and appraisal activities to

---

[2] *This section draws heavily from the following article:*
Albright, T.L., and H. P. Roth. 1992. The Measurement of Quality Costs: An Alternative Paradigm, Accounting Horizons *(June): 15–27.*
[3] *The definitions in this section are based on Morse, Wayne J., Harold P. Roth, and Kay M. Poston,* Measuring, Planning, and Controlling Quality Costs *(Montvale, N.J.: National Association of Accountants, 1987).*

reduce failure costs. Over time, as processes become more reliable, failure costs decline. Of course, the objective is not merely to substitute one type of quality cost for another. Managers wish to see a decline in total quality costs as investments in improved processes produce results.

Exhibit 7 illustrates MetalArt's experience in managing quality costs. At first, failure costs were high. Then management implemented appraisal and prevention measures. Over time, the quality of production at MetalArt improved, and total quality costs began to decline. Finally, total quality costs reached a level far below their initial amounts.

Exhibit 7   Quality Cost Mix

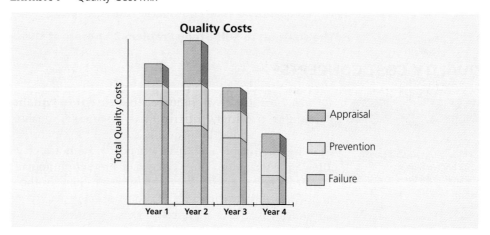

In attempting to use a quality cost system that classifies a product as defective or nondefective, several problems may be encountered. One of these problems is determining the amount of failure costs. Many failure costs, such as the costs of rework and warranty repairs, are available from accounting records, but others must be estimated. Costs such as lost customer goodwill, which occur because an organization produces poor-quality products, are not recorded by an accounting system. Thus, they often are referred to as hidden quality costs.

The traditional view of quality (defective versus nondefective) usually defines defective products as products with some characteristic that does not fall within the specification limits. By this definition, all units that fall within the specification limits are good, and all units outside the specification limits are defective. The problem with this view is all units within the specification limits are considered to be equally good, regardless of whether they fall near the target value or near the upper or lower specification limit.

C A S E

I n   P o i n t

Learn more about Xerox and the Malcolm Baldrige Award.

http://www.swcollege.com/ingram.html

Xerox received the Malcolm Baldrige Quality Award in 1989 for its manufacturing operations. A key element in its program was instituting a system of quality cost measures. The system helped managers determine the costs of activities such as inspecting products, making excessive engineering changes, doing rework, and repairing substandard equipment.*

In addition, Xerox implemented a quality cost system as a management tool within the sales and marketing division. This program saved an estimated $54 million in one year by increasing marketing efficiency. The company reported that no one was laid off and no drastic cost-cutting measures took place. Working smarter and changing poor processes contributed to the success of the quality cost program.

*Carr, Lawrence, 1992. Applying Cost of Quality to a Service Business, **Sloan Management Review** (Summer): 72.

Many quality experts believe that units that fall within specification limits are not all equally desirable. Even if a unit is within limits, higher costs may result as a unit's deviation from expected value increases. The Taguchi loss function, considered in the next section, attempts to measure these costs of variability.

TAGUCHI'S QUALITY LOSS FUNCTION

O b j e c t i v e   5
Describe how variability can affect production costs.

http://www.swcollege.
com/ingram.html

**Learn more about
Taguchi's quality loss
function.**

Genichi Taguchi is a Japanese engineer who recognized the relationship between variation and cost. He developed a model, termed the quality loss function (QLF), to explain in financial terms the engineering concept of variability. In theory, **the** *quality loss function* **measures the loss to society from a product that does not perform satisfactorily.** In the quality loss function model, costs increase dramatically as actual product characteristics deviate from a target (expected) value. The loss function is quadratic, which means that when the deviation from a target value doubles, the loss increases by four times.

Taguchi justifies the quality loss function on the basis of experience:

> This is a simple approximation, to be sure, not a law of nature. . . . But the tremendous value of QLF, apart from its bow to common sense, is that it translates the engineer's notion of deviation from targets into a *simple cost estimate* managers can use.[4] (Emphasis added.)

The quality loss function estimates the loss that results from producing products that vary from a target value, regardless of whether they fall inside or outside the specification limits. This differs from the traditional view of losses from poor quality, which is illustrated in Exhibit 8. The traditional view suggests that no failure costs or losses are incurred if actual product measurements fall within the specification limits. However, total loss in the form of scrap, rework, or warranty replacement occurs if the product's actual dimensions are outside the specification limits.

Exhibit 8   Traditional Cost Function

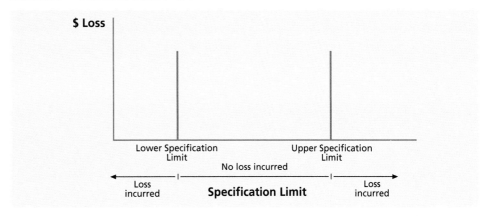

As an alternative to the traditional view, the quality loss function shown in Exhibit 9 shows a loss due to variability whenever a product deviates from a target value, even if the actual value falls within the specification limits. The loss is shown by the U-shaped curve that touches the horizontal axis at the target value. Thus, the quality loss function suggests that hidden quality costs exist any time a product varies

---

[4]   *Taguchi, Genichi, and Don Clausing, 1990. Robust Quality,* Harvard Business Review *(January–February): 68.*

from a target value. Once again, we use MetalArt to illustrate how a company may use the information from the quality loss function to make better decisions.

Exhibit 9   Taguchi Cost Function

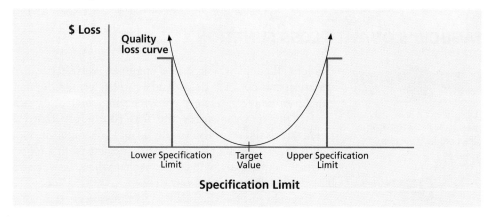

MetalArt—December 1996

Pat Allan, plant manager of MetalArt, called another managers' meeting to address the cost of variability and the intense competition from KolorKan. The team had made a great deal of progress since its original meeting to discuss production problems and related costs. MetalArt had installed a quality cost system and added extra inspectors to the process. However, the team knew that prevention costs in the form of statistical process control soon would allow them to shift resources away from inspections as processes improved.

Pat said, "As you know, KolorKan has made production changes to reduce variability in color density during the printing process.[5] Our market studies suggest that as color densities vary from target values, customers become dissatisfied."

"I could have told you that," interjected Mary. "Remember what happened when we shipped the load of containers with images that varied from dark pink to dark red?"

"I certainly do. We had to replace the cans, and I don't think we've been able to get any more orders from that customer," responded Pat.

"We have reason to believe that KolorKan's products follow a normal distribution with an average near the target value," said Pat, while wrestling to assemble an easel. Producing a flip chart containing the graphic shown in Exhibit 10, Pat continued, "However, a normal distribution means that some of their products actually fall outside the specification limits. Though these products did not conform to specifications, they were shipped to customers anyway because the plant did not strive for zero defects through inspections. Instead, the focus was on achieving output consistent with a target value."

After flipping the page to reveal a graph identical to that shown in Exhibit 11, Pat pointed out, "Alternatively, as indicated by the uniform distribution shown here, all of our products fell within specification limits."

"I'm glad to see that our investment in inspection costs is paying off," said Mary. "The inspectors are doing a great job. We didn't ship a single out-of-spec order."

"While it's true that inspections prevented some embarrassing deliveries, we still have much work to do to reduce our variability," responded Pat. "The uniform dis-

---

[5]   *The MetalArt example is based on Taguchi and Clausing's article describing the experience of Sony Corporation. Taguchi, Genichi, and Don Clausing. 1990. Robust Quality,* Harvard Business Review *(January-February): 65-75.*

Exhibit 10 Normal Distribution of KolorKan

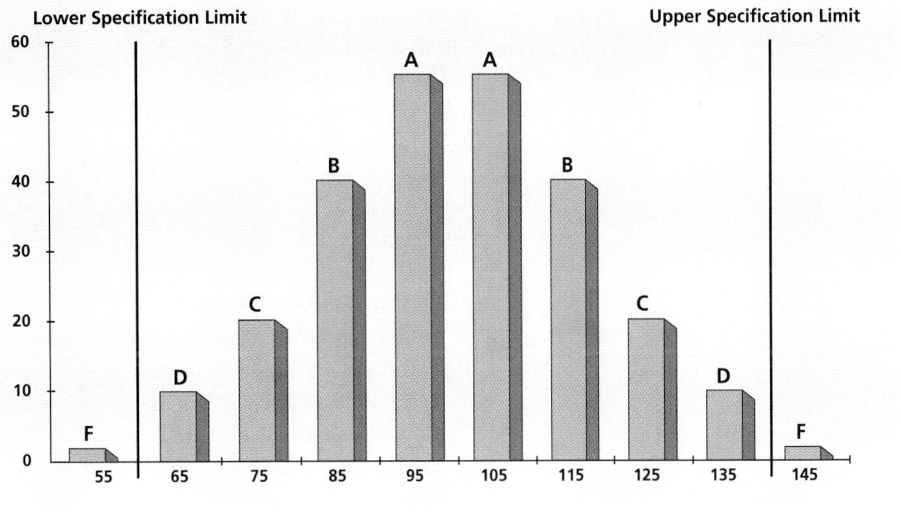

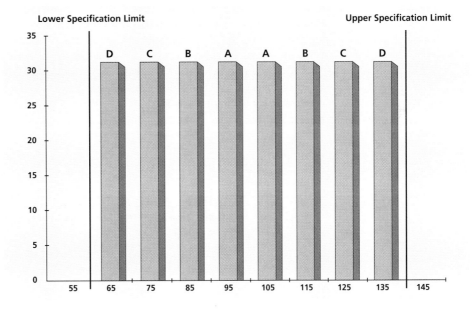

tribution shown here suggests that our process is equally likely to produce a product at the target value, the upper specification limit, or the lower specification limit."

"Pat, what are you driving at?" Mary asked. "Who cares about normal and uniform distributions? Our quality is good; we didn't ship any defective units."

Exhibit 11 Rectangular Distribution of MetalArt

Pat replied, "Assume that we want to assign letter grades to MetalArt and KolorKan; an A represents achieving target specifications, while an F represents exceeding specification limits. We may say that KolorKan produced many more As than we did, even if they did get an F now and then. Most of KolorKan's production was in the A and B range. We earned an equal number of As, Bs, Cs, and Ds. We also made some out-of-specification prints, but we didn't ship our Fs; they were inspected out of the process. KolorKan shipped everything it printed without bothering to inspect anything."

Pat continued to flip pages on the chart. "I think we may have discovered a hidden source of costs. If the Taguchi model is right, our quality costs are approximately *double* KolorKan's. I have made some estimates based on the cost of production and the way in which our customers respond to product variation. Let me summarize the Taguchi model in terms of how it affects us.

"First of all, let's review the elements of the model," said Pat, pointing to the easel containing the following equation and definitions:

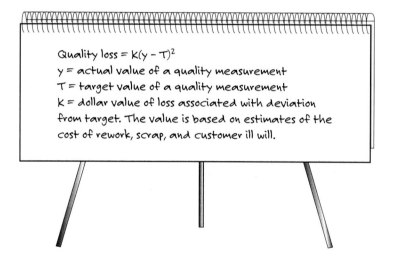

"In words, the loss function simply takes the difference between a target specification and an actual measurement ($y - T$) and squares the difference. Therefore, the larger the distance from the target value to the actual measurement, the greater the loss. Squaring the difference makes the cost increase dramatically!"

Lee responded, "So that means that as our products deviate more from a target value, our costs increase dramatically. The farther away they are, the greater the cost."

"Exactly. I've made some estimates of the cost of deviation; let's assume it's $5 and our target value for color density is 100. Assuming that our actual measure for color density is 95, our loss is $125." Pat turned the flip chart to reveal the following calculations:

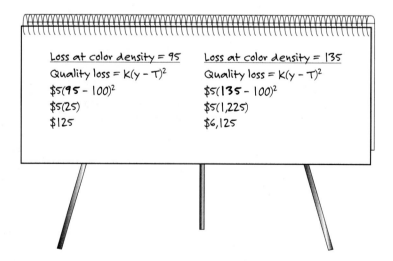

"By contrast," continued Pat, "if our actual measure for color density is 135, our loss is $6,125! The losses become large very quickly if we have many deliveries that are too far from the target specification."

Pat continued, "I have made some assumptions about KolorKan's process. If most of their production is close to the target value, as I have illustrated in Exhibit 12, their total quality costs approximate $359,000. On the other hand, our quality costs are approximately $651,000, because of variability in our process. We are equally likely to produce a unit at the upper specification limit, the lower specification limit, or the target."

Exhibit 12   Unit and Total Costs: The Taguchi Quality Loss Function

(From Exhibit 10)
KolorKan

Observed Value	Number of Units	Total Cost	Cost Per Unit
55	1	$ 10,125	10,125
65	9	55,125	6,125
75	20	62,500	3,125
85	40	45,000	1,125
95	54	6,750	125
105	54	6,750	125
115	40	45,000	1,125
125	20	62,500	3,125
135	9	55,125	6,125
145	1	10,125	10,125
Total	248	$359,000	

(From Exhibit 11)
MetalArt

Observed Value	Number of Units	Total Cost	Cost Per Unit
55	0	0	10,125
65	31	189,875	6,125
75	31	96,875	3,125
85	31	34,875	1,125
95	31	3,875	125
105	31	3,875	125
115	31	34,875	1,125
125	31	96,875	3,125
135	31	189,875	6,125
145	0	0	10,125
Total	248	$651,000	

Lee interjected, "Let me get this straight. Although we produced 248 units, the same number as KolorKan, our quality costs are approximately double theirs because our units are spread evenly between color densities of 65 and 135. On the other hand, KolorKan had most of their products clustered around the target value of 100."

After a few moments, Mary spoke. "I think I see the big picture. The manner in which we conduct our operations affects the income statement because costs and expenses reduce net income. Customer ill will also can affect net income through reduced sales. First, we used variance analysis, a tool that helps Pat and other upper-level managers compare actual performance with a standard. Statistical process control charts provide too much detail for the needs of upper management."

"That's right," responded Pat. "However, statistical process control tools help shop floor workers maintain control over their processes, thereby reducing operating costs."

"After we improve our processes and can maintain them in statistical control, we can work to reduce the common causes of variability. You have shown us that variability has a cost," Lee added. "All of our efforts are interrelated and ultimately affect profitability."

PERFORMANCE EVALUATION FOR SERVICE ORGANIZATIONS

Objective 6
Explain the application of performance evaluation methods in service organizations.

Service organizations such as CPA firms, law firms, hospitals, cable TV companies, and telecommunications companies face performance issues similar to those encountered by manufacturing organizations. Though these organizations do not manufacture a tangible product, managers can nonetheless evaluate the effectiveness of service delivery processes. For example, both CPA firms and hospitals often develop labor standards, or estimates of the time required to perform certain activities. A new staff accountant in a CPA firm is expected to prepare a client's payroll tax return in a certain (standard) amount of time. Additionally, hospitals often use critical paths to estimate the amount of services required for each type of medical procedure. Physicians whose use of services deviates significantly from a critical path may be asked to justify such deviations. Thus, as in manufacturing organizations, the efficiency of labor may be monitored. Service organizations often seek to improve customer satisfaction by making the experience pleasurable. For example, minimizing the time it takes to receive the service may result in satisfied customers. Therefore, managers often monitor customer satisfaction in order to improve the company's service quality.

Statistical process control charts originally were developed for use in manufacturing organizations. However, these charts commonly are used within service organizations to determine if a service process is "in control." For example, some hospitals maintain control charts to determine if the time from admission to the beginning of hydration (adding fluid) for a leukemia patient meets expectations. Another example would be plotting the variable cost of each appendectomy surgery to determine if certain physicians significantly exceed the average cost.

Many service organizations use quality cost systems that attempt to measure the cost of external failure. For example, many companies measure the amount of time a customer spends "on hold" before receiving assistance from a company representative. Additionally, many firms measure the number of customers who hang up while waiting to receive assistance. Costs or lost revenues associated with customers who "drop off" the line are seen as external failure costs. Thus, many processes in service organizations can be monitored in the same way as manufacturing processes.

SELF-STUDY PROBLEM 3

Terrel Grimes wishes to implement a quality cost program at each Greasy Grimes service center. His goal is to reduce total quality costs by 30% over the next five years, but he does not fully understand how quality costs are classified.

Required

Provide examples of each type of quality cost (internal failure, external failure, appraisal, and prevention) that Grimes may expect to incur at his service centers.

© Barbara Filet/Tony Stone Images

The solution to Self-Study Problem 3 appears at the end of the chapter.

Summary of Important Concepts

1. Companies may perform variance analysis of direct materials, direct labor, and overhead.
   a. A variance is defined as the difference between total actual costs and total standard costs allowed for actual production.
   b. Variances may be divided into a price (rate) component and a quantity (efficiency) component.
   c. Variances are defined as favorable if actual prices or quantities used are less than standard prices or quantities. However, because variances often are interrelated, *favorable* variances are not always good.

2. Statistical process control:
   a. Statistical process control charts separate special cause variation from random variation in manufacturing or administrative processes.
   b. Statistical process control charts have a center line (representing a process average) and upper and lower control limits.

3. Quality costs:
   a. Quality costs are classified as internal failure, external failure, appraisal, and prevention.
   b. External failure costs are the most expensive type of quality costs, though their amount can never be known with certainty. External failure costs include customer ill will as well as replacement and warranty costs.

4. Taguchi quality loss function:
   a. The Taguchi quality loss function is important because it associates costs with the engineering concept of variability.
   b. Customer dissatisfaction (and costs) occurs when product characteristics deviate from a target value, even if the characteristics are within specification limits.

5. Service organizations:
   a. Service organizations generally can establish standards for measuring the efficiency and effectiveness of their delivery process.
   b. Many processes in service organizations can be evaluated with statistical process control charts.
   c. Quality costs are not limited to companies that manufacture tangible products. Service organizations also incur quality costs in delivering services to customers.

Terms and Concepts Defined in This Chapter

Common cause variation (234)	Quality loss function (239)	Standards (226)
Favorable variance (228)	Special cause variation (234)	Unfavorable variance (228)
Quality costs (237)	Standard costs (225)	

S O L U T I O N S

SELF-STUDY PROBLEM 1

Labor rate variance	= (actual hours × actual rate) − (actual hours × standard rate)
	= (500 × $30) − (500 × $25)
	= 500 × ($30 − $25)
	= $2,500 unfavorable
Labor efficiency variance	= (standard rate × actual hours) − (standard rate × standard hours)
	= ($25 × 500) − ($25 × 800)
	= $25 × (500 − 800)
	= $7,500 favorable
Total variance	= $5,000 favorable ($7,500 favorable − $2,500 unfavorable)

The new manager appears to have changed the mix of labor for services. Typically, an apprentice mechanic, receiving the lowest wage rate, performs the transmission services. The new manager assigned higher-paid journeyman mechanics to these jobs and created an unfavorable labor rate variance. However, the experienced journeyman mechanics were more efficient in performing the service, as indicated by the favorable labor efficiency variance. In fact, the higher labor rate was more than offset by greater efficiencies. The shift in mix resulted in a net $5,000 favorable labor variance. The new manager has found a way to improve the efficiency of transmission service at Greasy Grimes.

SELF-STUDY PROBLEM 2

1. In summing the favorable and unfavorable variances for the 12 months, the average is calculated as follows:

$$(1,000 - 1,000 + 500 + 750 - 800 - 750 + 350 + 400 + 250 - 300 - 250 + 150) \div 12 = 25$$

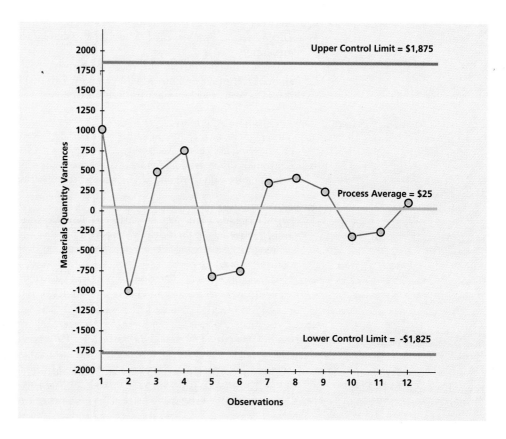

2. Price variance = (actual quantity × actual price) − (actual quantity × standard price)
    = (25 × $200) − (25 × $190)
    = 25 × ($200 − $190)
    = $250 U

    Quantity variance = (standard price × actual quantity) − (standard price × standard quantity)
    = ($190 × 25) − ($190 × 23)
    = $190 × (25 − 23)
    = $380 U

Refer to page 247 for the revised statistical process control chart.

3. The materials quantity variances are in a state of statistical control. Though the July variance deviates from the process average, it is within the control limits. The variation seems to be random and normal. Managers should not attempt to find a special cause for the variation during the month of July.

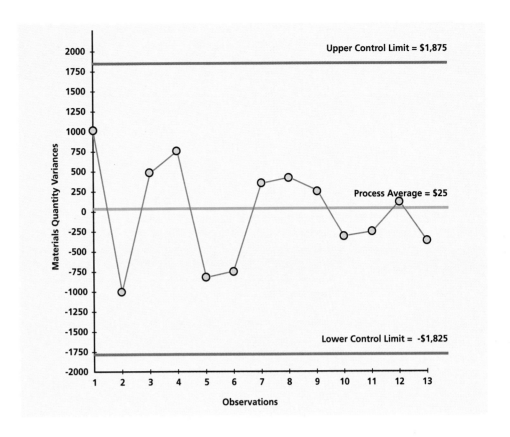

SELF-STUDY PROBLEM 3

Internal Failure. Costs resulting from repairs that have been performed incorrectly but are found before an automobile is returned to the customer are classified as internal failure. The costs of dealing with loose bolts or oil pan drain plugs that later could cause mechanical failure are examples.

External Failure. Costs resulting from repairs that were performed incorrectly and are discovered by the customer are classified as external failure costs. Examples include the cost of replacement parts, labor, customer ill will, and lost revenue (time spent reworking a repair is not available for other revenue-generating repairs). External failure costs also include the costs of lawsuits resulting from damages suffered by customers whose vehicles were damaged because of poor workmanship.

Appraisal. Appraisal costs generally relate to inspection costs. For example, the time spent by a mechanic on a test drive to ensure that repairs were made properly is an appraisal cost.

Prevention. Prevention costs can include training or technical workshops for mechanics. In addition, resources invested to identify reliable suppliers of high-quality parts are classified as prevention costs.

EXERCISES

7-1. Write a short definition of each of the terms listed in the *Terms and Concepts Defined in This Chapter* section.

Obj. 1

7-2. The Navaro Container Corporation produces various types of materials, such as bubble wrap and Styrofoam, that are used as packaging protection. Navaro utilizes a standard cost system for planning and control purposes. Navaro has recently invested in new machinery and technologies that are expected to improve production techniques, reduce scrap inherent in the production process, and improve product quality. In establishing production standards for the coming year, Navaro intends to rely on historical cost data, including average material usage and production times. Is past performance the best indicator for establishing standards for future production? Why or why not?

Obj. 1   **7-3.**   Managers are held accountable for variances that occur in the areas under their control. Variances may arise in a manufacturing environment, and in administrative functions, as well. In general, what is meant by the term *variance?*

Obj. 1   **7-4.**   The Doall Company is establishing production standards for the coming year. Matt Mellon, the production manager, argues that the standards need to be relaxed. "Last year's standards were based on ideal performance and did not reflect the practical realities of what could be achieved," he said. In establishing standards, what is the difference between practical and ideal standards?

Obj. 1   **7-5.**   The Adkins Manufacturing Company has called a planning meeting for the purpose of preparing operating budgets for the next quarter. "Before we begin," said Maria Sanchez, the president, "we need to establish standards for each of our products." "Why do we need to develop standards?" asked Paul Russel, production scheduler. "Can't we just establish an overall budget that everyone could work toward?" What is the difference between standards and a budget?

Obj. 1   **7-6.**   Keene, Incorporated separates material variances into price and quantity components for purposes of management control and analysis. Why are variances generally separated into price and quantity components? What effect, if any, can the price variance have on the quantity variance?

Obj. 1   **7-7.**   The cost records of the Prichter Company reveal that as the unfavorable material price variance increased, the unfavorable material usage variance decreased. What might this suggest?

Obj. 1   **7-8.**   The Fee Baggage Company utilizes a standard cost accounting system. Fee manufactures two styles of travel bags, one a soft-sided model and the other a hard-shell case. Labor rate variances are the responsibility of the human resources department, and labor efficiency variances are assigned to the production department for explanation. What impact, if any, would the labor rate variance have on labor efficiency variances?

Obj. 1   **7-9.**   Cadet Industries utilizes a standard cost system. When Cadet purchases raw materials, the materials are recorded at standard cost. Is this treatment by Cadet proper in a standard cost accounting system? Why or why not? What is the appropriate time to recognize material price and usage variances? Why?

Obj. 2   **7-10.**   In a manufacturing environment, who would most likely be responsible for the materials price variance? The labor efficiency variance?

Obj. 2   **7-11.**   In addition to material and labor variances, a company that utilizes standard cost accounting can compute fixed overhead variances. What are the two components of fixed overhead variance? What do the fixed overhead variances measure?

Obj. 2   **7-12.**   Tim Winker Manufactured Housing, Inc., produces prefabricated modular housing. The company manufactures four styles of homes and uses a standard cost accounting system. The company uses a single account for capturing material variances and another account for recording labor variances. During a review of the general ledger for the past operating period, Tim Winker, the president, noted that the material variances were favorable and the labor variances were unfavorable. In general, what do these variances indicate regarding production costs for the period? What further information would management find useful in analyzing production costs and variances for the period?

Obj. 2   **7-13.**   Pete Smith is the president of Home Products Manufacturing. During an executive planning meeting with senior managers, Pete made the following statement: "I am tired of all the finger pointing around here! Our costs are out of line, and we all know it! If each department does not take responsibility for its own mistakes and cost overruns, I will be forced to implement a standard cost accounting system to identify variances. If I have to take such drastic steps to identify who is responsible for cost overruns, then believe me, heads will roll once we pin down the problems!" Comment on Pete's planned use of standard cost accounting.

Objs. 1,2   **7-14.**   Techno-Global Products recently has implemented a standard cost accounting system. One of the products that Techno produces has a total standard cost for material, labor, and overhead of $1,328. The actual cost of material, labor, and overhead to produce these products was $1,363 per unit. In a standard cost system, what is the amount per unit that would be reflected in the Finished Goods Inventory account for these items? How would Techno treat the difference between the standard cost of production and the actual cost of production? On which financial statement, balance sheet or income statement, would these differences be recorded?

Obj. 3   **7-15.**   A machine operator cuts metal rods into 6-inch lengths, measures output periodically, and records the measurements on a statistical process control chart. Over an 8-hour shift, the operator notes that the measurements vary greatly but are always within the acceptable limits of plus or minus 0.005 inch. Are these variations most likely examples of common cause or special cause variations? Explain your answer.

Obj. 3   **7-16.**   Nathan Stuart is employed in the accounting department of a local manufacturer. During a recent management staff meeting, Nathan suggested that statistical control charts be established at key production steps to help increase quality and minimize defects. What is a statistical control chart? How is it used?

Obj. 3   **7-17.**   Penn Enterprises distributes office supplies through a mail order catalog that is sent to businesses. Penn distributes over 500,000 catalogs a year and ships an average of 150 orders a day. Penn maintains a central warehouse in South Carolina from which all orders are shipped. Over the past six months, many shipping errors have occurred because incorrect items were pulled from stock to fill customer orders. These errors have resulted in a high rate of customer returns and inventory out-of-stock conditions. How could Penn utilize statistical process control to help ensure that customer orders are filled properly?

Objs. 3,4   **7-18.**   Both statistical process control and the quality loss function are concerned with variability of production. If a company utilizes statistical process control, is the quality loss function still a useful tool, or are statistical process control and the quality loss function in essence so similar that to apply both concepts within an organization is redundant? Explain your answer.

Obj. 4   **7-19.**   Electro Industries wants to analyze the costs associated with quality conformance in its manufacture of electronic capacitors and transistors, which are sold primarily to manufacturers of cellular telephones. What four broad categories of conformance costs should Electro use? What are the differences between these cost groups?

Obj. 4   **7-20.**   Rayco Products manufactures audio speakers that are used in many applications. At the beginning of the current year, Rayco developed detailed operating budgets for all aspects of the company. Rayco now is considering purchasing new test equipment for the inspection department to use in checking the acoustical quality of speakers. This purchase was not considered during the preparation of operating budgets for the current year. If the equipment is acquired, depreciation will begin to be recognized immediately, using straight-line depreciation over an estimated useful life of five years; the result will be a monthly charge of $2,200. What effect would the equipment purchase have on quality costs and on meeting the company's current year budget?

PROBLEMS

PROBLEM 7-1   Material and Labor Standards and Variances, Three-way Analysis

Obj. 1

Multiflow Products manufactures a single product, for which the following standards have been developed:

	Standard Quantity or Hours	Standard Price or Rate	Standard Cost
Direct materials	5 feet	$3 per foot	$15
Direct labor	? hours	? per hour	?

During October, the company purchased 15,200 feet of direct materials at a cost of $47,880, all of which was used in the production of 3,000 units.

A total of 5,400 hours was spent on production during the month. The actual cost of direct labor was $61,560. The following labor variances have been computed:

Total labor variance	$1,185 Unfavorable
Labor rate variance	$ 540 Favorable

Required

a. For direct materials, compute (1) the actual cost paid for materials per foot, (2) the materials price variance, and (3) the materials usage variance.
b. For direct labor, compute (1) the standard labor rate per hour, (2) the standard hours allowed for the output of 3,000 units, and (3) the standard hours allowed per unit of product.
c. What is the value of direct materials and direct labor that has been applied to the Work in Process Inventory account during the month, in total and on a per unit basis?

PROBLEM 7-2 Material and Labor Variance, Shortcut Calculations
Obj. 1

Global Products has developed the following standards for one of its products:

Direct materials	25 pounds at $4 per pound
Direct labor	8 hours at $10 per hour

The following activity was recorded for the production of 12,000 units during the month of August:

Materials purchased	350,000 pounds at $4.12 a pound
Materials used	304,000 pounds
Direct labor	95,400 hours at $10.55 an hour

Required

Without completing the three-way variance model:

a. Compute the materials price variance.
b. Compute the material usage variance.
c. Compute the labor rate variance.
d. Compute the labor efficiency variance.

PROBLEM 7-3 Establishing Material and Labor Standards, Multiple
Obj. 1 **Departments**

TCC Industries produces specialty tires in a variety of sizes and tread designs for use on trailers and farm equipment. TCC is planning to implement a standard cost accounting system. Valerie Siewert, the controller, has accumulated the following information on the standard cost of a particular bias tractor tire.

Each tire requires 15 pounds of carbon black, the basic tire component, which is added in the mixing department. Other materials, such as zinc and sulfur, which are added in the molding department, are required in such small quantities that they are treated as indirect materials and included as part of overhead. Each tire requires 15 minutes of processing time to mold and cure. An additional 45 minutes of time is required to mix the ingredients in the mixing department.

The standard cost for carbon black is $3.50 a pound. The standard cost of direct labor in the mixing department is $10.00 per labor hour, while the standard cost of direct labor in the mold department is $11.00 an hour.

Required

a. Develop the standard cost of materials and labor for the tractor tire. The standard cost should identify the standard quantity, the standard rate, and the total standard cost per unit.

b. Identify the advantages of implementing a standard cost system.

c. Explain the role each of the following people would have in developing the standard costs:
   1. Purchasing manager
   2. Mixing department supervisor
   3. Mold department supervisor
   4. Cost accountant
   5. Product engineer

d. Assume that a batch of tires has been completed and the following actual amounts were used to produce the batch:
   1. Actual output: 4,500 tires
   2. Actual carbon black utilized: 68,000 pounds
   3. Carbon black purchased: 75,000 pounds at a cost of $258,000
   4. Direct labor in mixing department: 3,220 hours at a cost of $31,073
   5. Direct labor in mold department: 1,075 hours at a cost of $12,384

Compute the materials price variance and the material usage variance. Also, compute the labor rate variance and labor efficiency variance for each department.

PROBLEM 7-4 **Changes in Costs, Effects on Variances**
Objs. 1,2

Tempro, Inc., uses a standard cost accounting system. Variances for the year ended December 31, 1996, were as follows:

Material price variance	Unfavorable
Material usage variance	Favorable
Labor rate variance	Favorable
Labor efficiency variance	Unfavorable

Managers at Tempro are considering the following changes in operations for the year ending December 31, 1997.

1. An across-the-board pay increase of 5% will be given to all personnel.
2. The purchasing department will be allowed to purchase lower grades of materials.
3. Several key production workers will be transferred into managerial positions. These workers will be replaced either by new hires or by production personnel who will be transferred from another department.
4. Additional inspectors will be hired to ensure quality production. The cost of these inspectors will be considered administrative and general expense.

Required Assuming that product standards are not changed from the previous year, what impact, if any, would you expect each of the above changes to have on the company's variances? Consider each decision separately, and identify the variance that would be affected by the decision and whether the change would increase or decrease the prior year variance. Explain your answers.

PROBLEM 7-5 **Establishing Labor Standards**
Objs. 1,2

The Greenbriar Company is considering the addition of a new machine in its mold injection plant. Greenbriar already has five such machines that are operating three shifts a day. The company uses a standard cost accounting system. The number of pieces that currently are being produced on the existing machines is 300 per worker-hour. The vendor of the new equipment has stated that its studies indicate that the new machinery should be able to produce 400 pieces per worker-hour. Greenbriar engineers agree that under ideal conditions, the equipment should be able to generate 400 pieces an hour, and they support that rate as a labor standard. Production managers point out that the new machine is identical to the machines currently in use, and that the current production rate is only 300 pieces per worker-hour. Accordingly, production managers advocate the use of 300 as the labor rate standard. The accounting staff believes that the most appropriate standard labor rate would be 350 pieces per labor hour.

Required

a. What arguments are most likely to be offered by engineering, production, and accounting to support their respective proposed standard?
b. Which alternative do you support? Consider the motivational aspects of establishing a standard and explain the reasons for your choice.

PROBLEM 7-6   Performance Evaluation and Variance Analysis
Obj. 2

Timber Industries manufactures unfinished furniture, which it sells through retail outlets. Timber produces many different styles of bookcases, tables, chairs, desks, and dressers that customers finish themselves with stain or paint. Timber utilizes a standard cost system and performs variance analysis. The company recently increased production to meet anticipated demand from several new retail outlets that opened in new sales territories. To accommodate the expected increase in sales demand, the production department hired five new employees from a local community college program. These new employees were immediately assigned to various production processes, such as milling, lathe, and assembly.

To meet the anticipated production needs, the purchasing department had to seek additional sources of lumber. The company ordered large quantities of high-grade oak, maple, and pine. The purchasing department insisted on obtaining high-quality materials, since poor-quality materials result in excess scrap, rework, and defects during the manufacturing process. Some of the new suppliers delivered materials that were warped or had too many knots or blemishes. Instead of returning the materials, the purchasing department negotiated "quality" credits from the suppliers. The poorer-quality wood then was sorted, remilled by Timber, and used in places where lower-quality material was acceptable, such as drawer bottoms and sides.

Several of the new retail outlets did not reach the sales volume that was originally expected. The sales department insists that with time, the new stores will gain recognition, and their sales will increase. To deal with the increase in finished goods inventory, the sales department negotiated with a discount department chain to sell a limited line of Timber products in markets that did not compete directly with company-owned retail outlets.

Material and labor variances for Timber Industries were as follows:

Material price variance	Favorable
Material usage variance	Unfavorable
Direct labor rate variance	Favorable
Direct labor efficiency variance	Unfavorable

Required

a. Based on the facts stated, identify contributing factors for the variances noted.
b. Discuss how Timber Industries could use variance analysis to analyze the performance measures of the purchasing, production, and sales departments.

PROBLEM 7-7   Statistical Process Control Charting
Obj. 3

Power Source, Inc. produces electrical control harnesses used in the production of battery-powered carts and cars for children. These harnesses are sold to a toy manufacturer who requires close tolerances related to cable length. Power Source has implemented a statistical process control system to monitor harness production and performs statistical control charting related to cable length. Each harness cable is required to be 32 inches long. Based on previous observations, it is determined that 32 inches is the mean or expected value of the process average. Further, production is considered to be in control, and production is acceptable, if the cable harness is between 30.5 inches and 33.5 inches in length (plus or minus 1.5 inches). If the cable length is above or below these amounts, the process is considered to be out of control, and the operator must take corrective action to bring the process back to acceptable limits.

During a recent 4-hour morning shift, the operator on the cable assembly line performed a cable measurement every 20 minutes, and recorded the observation on a SPC control chart. The observed measurements were as follows:

	Measurement		Measurement
1	30.75 inches	7	33.50 inches
2	32.25 inches	8	31.95 inches
3	31.67 inches	9	32.00 inches
4	33.25 inches	10	31.08 inches
5	30.45 inches	11	30.99 inches
6	32.80 inches	12	32.15 inches

Required

a. Construct an SPC control chart. Identify the centerline value and the upper and lower control limit values. Record the observed measurements on the chart you have constructed.

b. Do any of the observed measurements indicate that an out-of-control condition exists? Which measurement(s)? What steps should be taken to remedy this situation?

PROBLEM 7-8 Quality Cost Analysis

Obj. 4

Management at Precision Manufacturing would like to analyze quality costs associated with the manufacturing process. In 1995, Precision implemented a statistical process control system. In 1996, further steps were taken in an effort to improve quality and focus on customer satisfaction. These included the addition of inspectors, expansion of statistical process control to additional processing steps, and further development of products through quality engineering. The benefits of the quality focus at Precision are apparent, as warranty costs and customer returns have declined since quality programs were implemented. However, total quality costs continue to be significant, and management is concerned that the quality focus has not reduced total costs, but has simply shifted costs from one area to another. Accordingly, management would like to analyze quality costs for the past two years. Precision had sales of $18,000,000 in both year 2 and year 1, and incurred the following costs related to quality control during those years:

	Year 2	Year 1
Inspection	$ 60,000	$ 30,000
Quality engineering	57,000	12,000
Quality training programs	26,000	40,000
Customer allowances	22,000	105,000
Scrap, net	24,000	8,000
Product testing	90,000	42,000
Rework	120,000	68,000
Statistical process control	50,000	35,000
Downtime due to defects	25,000	18,000
Warranty repairs	75,000	187,000
Field service	45,000	142,000
Testing supplies	15,000	16,000

Required

a. Categorize the above costs and compute the total costs of conformance for each year by category.

b. Evaluate the distribution of quality costs at Precision. Discuss the distribution of quality costs and any trends in cost distribution. What effect does the distribution of quality costs have on total quality at Precision? Explain your answer.

c. What future trends should Precision expect if the current focus of quality programs continues? Explain your answer.

PROBLEM 7-9 Quality Loss Function Analysis

Obj. 5

Gazette Paper Manufacturing produces newsprint paper for use in newspaper publishing. The thickness of the paper can vary slightly during the manufacturing process. If the paper is too thin, it will not hold up under the printing process and will tear, while paper that is too thick can result in printing press malfunction. As the paper is manufactured, it is rolled onto spools for shipping to newspaper publishers. Each spool is weighed after the manufacturing process is complete. The target value for a spool is exactly one ton (2,000 pounds). Management at Gazette has determined that each pound deviation from the target value will increase quality costs by $.50. The following production figures reflect production for the most recent month:

Spools of newsprint produced: 14

Spool Number	Total gross product weight (in pounds)
1	2,123.18
2	1,924.62
3	1,894.41
4	2,141.91
5	1,974.43
6	2,030.21
7	2,060.92
8	2,142.12
9	1,936.90
10	1,894.15
11	1,997.87
12	2,131.31
13	1,943.40
14	2,071.75

Required

a. Calculate the total quality loss cost for Gazette Printing Services, using the quality loss function.

b. What do your calculations suggest about the manufacturing process? What do your calculations suggest must be done by Gazette? Explain your answer.

PROBLEM 7-10 Variance Analysis, Service Environment

Objs. 1,6

Todd Judd separated from his wife, Stella, and filed for divorce. As part of the divorce, Todd realized that he would have to engage in a legal battle with Stella since the couple owned several parcels of property and had considerable investments, including a business Todd had acquired from his father. Todd spoke with several attorneys, explained his case, and asked each for an estimate of the cost to represent him in the proceedings. Perry Schmidt, a practicing attorney, provided Todd with the following estimate of costs if he were to represent Todd:

Item	Hours	Billing Rate	Total Cost
Attorney hours, planning and court time	150	$185 per hour	$27,750
Admin. and clerical support	60	75 per hour	4,500
Witness fees	n/a	n/a	1,500
Court costs	n/a	n/a	500
Total			$34,250

Todd hired Perry based on the above estimate. In the course of the trial several unforeseen issues arose, continuances were granted, and the proceedings dragged on for 18 months. At the end of the trial, Perry provided Todd with a bill totaling $42,840. The following billing detail was also provided:

Item	Hours	Total Cost
Attorney hours, planning and court time	187	$34,595
Admin. and clerical support	52	3,640
Witness fees	n/a	2,750
Deposition fees		1,255
Court costs	n/a	600
Total		$42,840

Perry offered the following explanations for the difference between the estimated and final billings.

1. Continuances and unforeseen issues resulted in the extra attorney hours.

2. Deposition fees were not anticipated in the original quote.

3. Although the number of filings was exactly as anticipated, Perry was not aware that the court had increased its filing fees resulting in an extra $100.

Required

a. Calculate the average rate per hour that Todd was billed for attorney time and clerical assistance.
b. Based on the original budget estimate, was the labor efficiency variance for attorney time favorable or unfavorable?
c. Would you describe the court filing fee variance related to volume? Explain your answer.
d. Calculate the labor rate, efficiency, and total variance associated with clerical support.

PROBLEM 7-11   Multiple-Choice Overview of this Chapter

1. A favorable material price variance coupled with an unfavorable material usage variance would most likely be the result of:
   a. labor efficiency problems.
   b. machine efficiency problems.
   c. the purchase and use of higher than standard quality materials.
   d. the purchase and use of lower than standard quality materials.

2. Standards preferably should be set so that:
   a. no allowance is made for machine breakdowns or other work interruptions.
   b. they are based on practical levels that can be achieved rather than on ideal levels.
   c. they reflect a level that can be achieved only by the most skilled and efficient employee working at peak effort 100 percent of the time.
   d. they can be used for motivational purposes rather than in forecasting cash flows and in planning inventory.

3. Inspection of products would be a(n):
   a. prevention cost.
   b. appraisal cost.
   c. internal failure cost.
   d. external failure cost.

4. Which of the following is NOT true with respect to statistical process control?
   a. It places the monitoring of quality at a workstation.
   b. It eliminates the need for a final inspection of goods.

    c.   It is considered a prevention cost.

    d.   It requires the charting of observed measurements.

Questions 5 through 8 are based on the following information.

    Jackson Industries employs a standard cost system in which direct materials inventory is carried at standard cost. Jackson has established the following standards for the costs of one unit of product.

	Standard Quantity	Standard Price or Rate
Direct materials	5 pounds	$ 3.60 per pound
Direct labor	1.25 hours	$12.00 per hour

During May, Jackson purchased 125,000 pounds of direct material at a total cost of $475,000. The total factory direct labor wages for May were $327,600. Jackson manufactured 22,000 units of product during May, using 108,000 pounds of direct material and 28,000 direct labor hours.

5. The price variance for the direct material acquired by Jackson Industries during May is:
    a. $21,600 favorable.
    b. $25,000 unfavorable.
    c. $28,000 favorable.
    d. $21,600 unfavorable.

6. The direct material quantity (usage) variance for May is:
    a. $7,200 unfavorable.
    b. $7,600 favorable.
    c. $5,850 unfavorable.
    d. $7,200 favorable.

7. The direct labor rate variance for May is:
    a. $8,400 favorable.
    b. $7,200 unfavorable.
    c. $8,400 unfavorable.
    d. $6,000 favorable.

8. The direct labor efficiency variance for May is:
    a. $5,850 favorable.
    b. $7,200 favorable.
    c. $6,000 unfavorable.
    d. $5,850 unfavorable.

9. For the month of January 1997, Crabapple's records disclosed the following data related to direct labor:

Actual direct labor costs $10,000
Labor rate variance $1,000 Favorable
Labor efficiency variance $(1,500) Unfavorable

For the month of January, actual direct labor hours totaled 2,000. What was Crabapple's standard direct labor rate per hour?
    a. $5.50
    b. $5.00
    c. $4.75
    d. $4.50

10. Quality costs:
    a.   relate only to the manufacturing process.
    b.   should focus on appraisal activities.
    c.   are minimized by having well-trained inspectors.
    d.   cut across departmental lines and are often not reported to management.

CASES

CASE 7-1 **Establishing Standards, Variance Analysis**

Objs. 1,2

Stellhorn Snacks produces high-quality potato chips. The manufacturing process is highly automated, yet requires labor to handle, inspect, and sort potatoes and chips. Stellhorn has accumulated product costs using process costing in the past and is considering adopting a standard cost accounting system.

At the beginning of the manufacturing process, potatoes are scrubbed and cleaned in an automatic washer. The potatoes then are placed automatically on a conveyor that feeds them into an automatic peeling machine. After the potatoes are peeled, they are inspected manually to remove blemishes and to cut out eyes. After inspection, they are placed on another conveyor that feeds them into an automatic slicing machine. The slicer feeds the chips into vats, which are loaded manually into deep fryers and monitored closely by production personnel. After cooking, the chips are drained and placed on another conveyor for final inspection and seasoning. At this point, unacceptable chips are sorted from good production, and the good chips are fed into an automatic bagger. The bagging process is highly automated, requiring one operator to load the empty bags for filling, and another person to remove the bags once they have been sealed and place them in cartons for final shipment.

Stellhorn expects to purchase potatoes of acceptable grade and quality for $.08 a pound. Based on historical records, Stellhorn has determined that it can produce 152 ounces of chips for every 10 pounds of potatoes placed into production. Each bag of chips produced contains 19 ounces of chips. Other direct materials include bags and boxes, which amount to $.14 per bag of chips. All other materials, such as oil and seasoning, are treated as indirect costs.

Stellhorn operates under a union contract and has 3 distinct classes, or categories, of employees. The established classes and the agreed-upon hourly rates for direct laborers are as follows:

Handlers	$ 8.00 an hour
Machine operators	$10.50 an hour
Inspectors	$12.00 an hour

For the coming year, Stellhorn expects to produce 6 million bags of chips. For this level of production, the company has determined that it will require 10,800 hours of handler time, 12,000 hours of machine operator time, and 14,800 hours of inspection.

Variable overhead is applied on the basis of direct labor hours and historically has averaged 110% of labor dollars. The budgeted fixed overhead for the coming year is $1,350,000, and also is applied based on direct labor hours.

Required

a. Discuss the benefits Stellhorn would realize by adopting a standard cost accounting system.

b. Using the following format, develop a standard cost sheet for material, labor, and overhead for each bag of potato chips.

Cost Category	Standard Quantity	Standard Cost or Rate	Total Standard Cost

For requirements c and d, assume that Stellhorn produced 6,200,000 bags of chips and incurred the following costs and levels of activity:

Materials: Potatoes 7,800,000 pounds of potatoes purchased and used, at a cost of $608,400.

Labor:

Handlers	12,480 hours, at an actual cost of $89,280
Machine operators	13,650 hours, at an actual cost of $130,200
Inspectors	15,475 hours, at an actual cost of $185,700

    c.   Calculate the material price and usage variances for potatoes.

    d.   Calculate the labor rate variance and labor efficiency variance for each labor category.

CASE 7-2   Establishing a Standard Cost Accounting System

Objs. 1,2

Tasha Smith is the president of Modern Machinery, Inc., which manufactures flexible manufacturing systems used in a wide variety of production processes. To remain competitive, Modern is continually improving product performance by increasing the sophistication of electronic controls, diversifying product offerings, and enhancing the quality of existing products. Many of Modern's customers dictate specific performance expectations and system designs. Modern employs a large engineering staff that coordinates system requirements with the designed components. Each manufactured system requires extensive design work and often results in over a hundred individual component drawings. Each drawing is developed in the engineering department and contains detailed manufacturing specifications. The use of computer-assisted design (CAD) allows Modern to provide system designs in an efficient manner, and has reduced design time. Since each system is manufactured to meet specific requirements, very few parts are interchangeable between systems.

Tasha is considering implementation of a standard cost accounting system. Her objective is to identify both rate and usage variances related to material and labor that are in excess of allowable standards. Tasha will require the engineering department to develop a standard cost sheet with each CAD design. The standard cost sheet will identify the amount of materials that should be used. For components already in use, the standard will assume the cost rates for materials that existed at the beginning of the year. For standards for new components, material costs will be taken from supplier catalogs. Standards for labor will be developed jointly by product and process engineers.

Tasha has determined that material price variances will be the responsibility of the purchasing department. Material usage and labor efficiency variances will be the responsibility of shop foremen in each of four manufacturing areas (Mill Shop, CNC Manufacturing, Electrical Shop, and Assembly). The labor rate variance will be the responsibility of the human resource department.

Required   Prepare a memo to Tasha Smith giving your advice concerning her plans. Specifically comment on the purpose of a standard cost system, the cost-benefit element of implementing such a system, and the inherent weaknesses in Tasha's proposed implementation plans.

PROJECTS

PROJECT 7-1   Identify Material Standards

Obj. 1

Identify ten common items in your home that have obvious material standards. For example, a deck of cards has 52 cards. Is the usefulness of these items impaired if the material standards are not met? Prepare a report listing the items and the expected standards.

PROJECT 7-2   Establish Material Standards

Obj. 1

Pick eight common household items for which material standards may not be immediately noticeable. Perform counts, weight tests, or other procedures to determine the standard quantity that should be allowed for a finished unit of output. For example, what is the "standard" quantity of M&M's® in a pack? What is the standard amount of materials in dinner plates? Do you note variances between items? Why do these variances exist? Write a report on your findings.

PROJECT 7-3   Identify Labor Standards

Obj. 1

Poll fellow students who have prepared a project, term paper, or assignment for a class. Determine the amount of time they each spent on the assignment. Can you develop the standard labor requirements for the assignment? What are some reasons the amount of time each person spent on the assignment differs?

PROJECT 7-4 **Statistical Process Control Observations**

Obj. 3

Identify a common daily procedure for which a target value can be determined. Identify the target value, establish upper and lower control limits, develop a control chart for this procedure, and then record 20 observations. For example, you might chart the dismissal times from your classes, with an upper limit defined as being held over five minutes and a lower limit defined as dismissal five minutes early. Or you might visit McDonald's or another fast-food restaurant and through observation establish the length of time to serve a customer. Chart actual observations.

PROJECT 7-5 **Identify Quality Cost Problems**

Obj. 4

Make a list of eight items you, or someone you know, have acquired for which there were quality problems. Describe each item and the problem, and explain how you believe the lack of quality might have been avoided. Identify the corrective steps you suggest as prevention costs, appraisal costs, internal failure costs, or external failure costs.

Management Accounting in a Global Business Environment

8

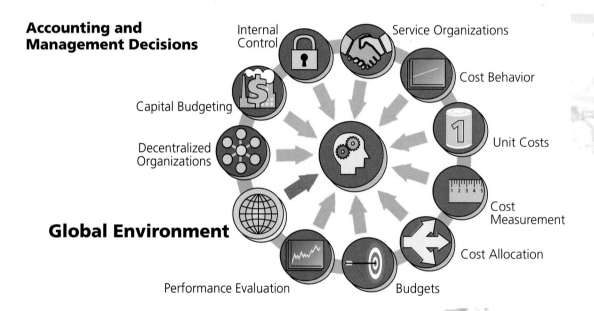

Accounting and Management Decisions

Internal Control — Service Organizations — Cost Behavior — Unit Costs — Cost Measurement — Cost Allocation — Budgets — Performance Evaluation — **Global Environment** — Decentralized Organizations — Capital Budgeting

Overview

The competitive global marketplace offers companies both challenges and opportunities as they seek to survive and prosper. A customer focus has become increasingly important because consumers demand high-quality products and services at competitive prices. Because of rapid technological advances, many companies are introducing products more frequently. This time-based competition means that companies must develop, manufacture, and deliver products and services to customers more quickly, and at lower cost, than their competitors. In an attempt to meet efficiently the demands of their customers, companies have embraced many new management and manufacturing philosophies. This chapter identifies and integrates several key developments that have become popular in the United States during the 1980s and 1990s. It is divided into three major sections as follows:

1. The new competitive environment, including total quality management (TQM)
2. Lean manufacturing systems, including just-in-time concepts
3. The theory of constraints

Major topics covered in this chapter include:
- Total quality management (TQM) techniques for empowering employees to deliver quality goods and services desired by customers
- Principles of just-in-time (JIT) systems to reduce inventory levels and manufacturing costs
- The theory of constraints (TOC) for managing bottleneck operations

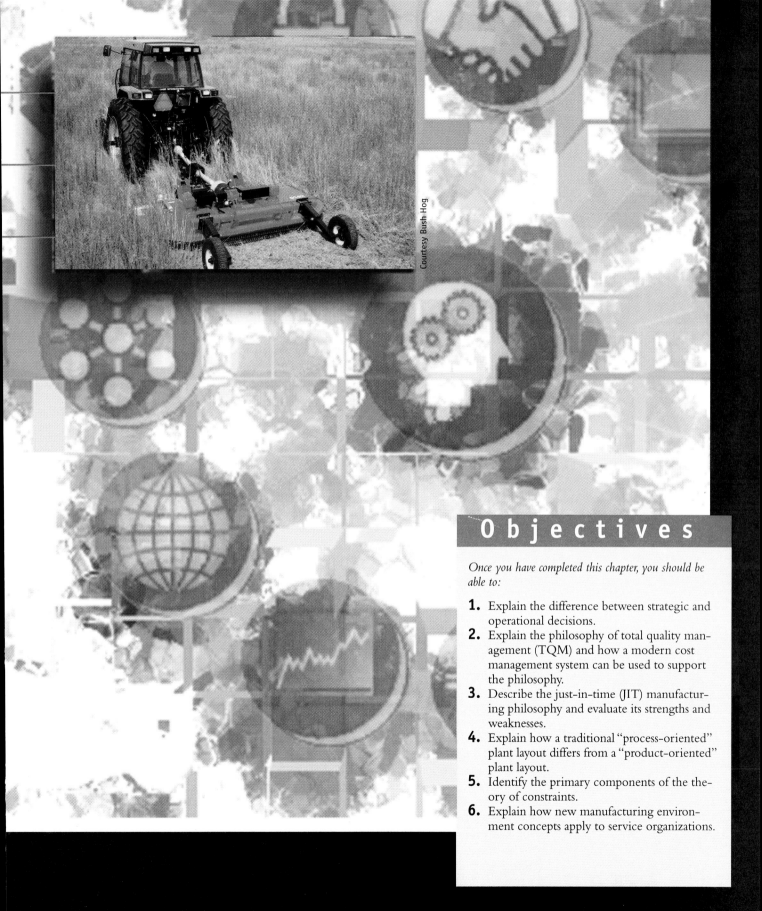

Courtesy Bush Hog

THE NEW COMPETITIVE ENVIRONMENT

Objective 1
Explain the difference between strategic and operational decisions.

The Japanese automobile industry generally is given credit for developing the concept of a lean enterprise.[1] The lean enterprise was born out of necessity. The Japanese automobile industry did not have a great deal of manufacturing equipment during the 1950s and 1960s. Thus, manufacturers were forced to produce automobiles in small quantities, using far less equipment than their competitors around the world. **Toyota** found ways to reduce setup time on metal presses from days to minutes. Small-batch production became economically possible as a result of efficient metal press setup times. Unfortunately, small-batch production created other problems that had to be resolved.

Because small-batch production results in lower inventory levels, extra components to replace a defective batch often were not available. Thus, lean production systems, while very efficient, demand strict attention to quality control. As a result, programs such as zero defects and total quality management (TQM) were developed to help minimize defects that could disrupt an entire production system. In summary, systems such as total quality management and just-in-time were developed in response to international competition. These concepts have been implemented by manufacturers around the world.

Examples in this chapter are based on the experiences of Tuff Cut, a company that manufactures rotary mowers used for industrial and agricultural purposes. Its rotary mowers are towed behind tractors to clear brush from rough, wide terrain. Tuff Cut has produced mowers in the United States for the past 40 years and has enjoyed consistent growth and loyal customers because of its high-quality product line. Customers include agricultural companies, individual landowners, and city, county, and state governments.

In recent years, some of Tuff Cut's market share has been eroded by competing products manufactured in the United States and abroad. Thus, managers at Tuff Cut are looking for ways to become more competitive in terms of price, quality, and delivery. As part of their effort, corporate officers are considering strategic changes in the way they manage their organization. **Strategic decisions** include decisions about the types of products a company should manufacture (such as commercial, agricultural, or residential) and how these products should be distributed (through wholesale distributors or company-owned retail outlets). In addition, questions concerning whether to enter new markets, such as China, Europe, Japan, and South America, are strategic issues. **Operational decisions** focus on day-to-day activities of the organization, but are linked directly to strategic objectives. For example, if receiving a product very soon after placing an order (lead time) is important to Japanese customers, improving machine setup times to reduce lead time is an operational activity that can be carried out at the factory floor level in support of strategic objectives.

Tuff Cut has embraced a "customer-focused" philosophy that places many operating decisions in the hands of teams of employees, rather than in the hands of management. To help reduce costs, improve competitiveness, and understand their position in the industry, Tuff Cut's managers evaluated the suppliers and manufacturing processes within the industry and used the information to assist in making strategic decisions. In addition, Tuff Cut made operational changes on the factory floor, such as maintaining very low inventory levels and strengthening relationships with suppliers. Finally, plant managers evaluated the flow of resources through their manufacturing facilities to identify bottlenecks and increase each plant's output. This chapter evaluates the changes implemented by Tuff Cut, and explores the manufacturing philosophies supporting these changes. First, let's begin with a description of the manufacturing process.

As shown in Exhibit 1, Tuff Cut's manufacturing process involves fabricating (cutting metal to desired specifications), welding, painting, and assembling steel sheets

---

[1]   Cooper, Robin. 1995. When Lean Enterprises Collide *(Boston: Harvard Business School Press).*

Exhibit 1 The Manufacturing Process at Tuff Cut

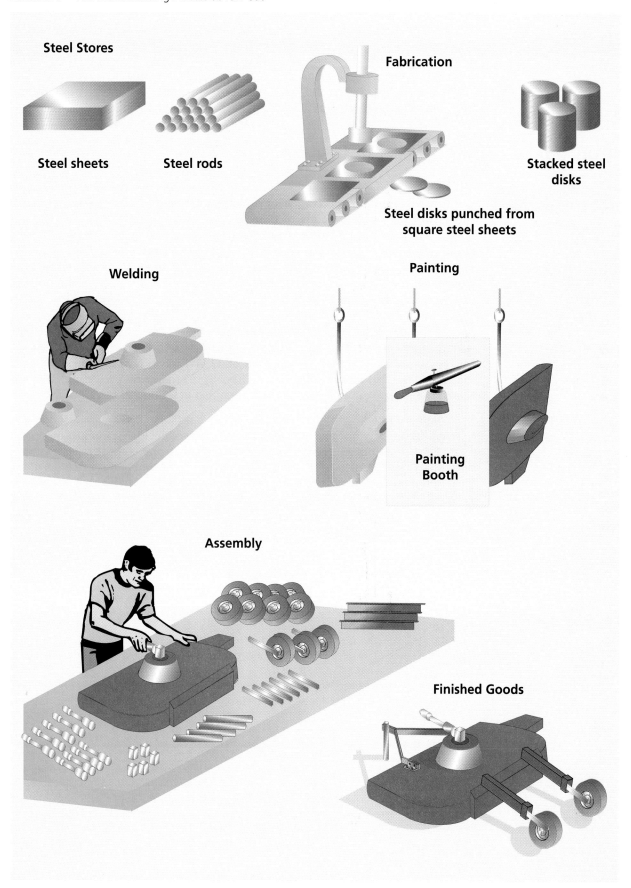

and components to conform to engineering specifications. Sheets of steel are removed by overhead crane from the steel stores area, located on the factory floor, and delivered to the fabrication area. In the fabrication area, steel is cut and pressed to the required shape. These cut shapes go to the welding area, where individual pieces of steel are welded together to make the mower body. Following the welding process, the mower body is painted and sent to the assembly area, where workers attach wheels, gear boxes, and various other components. Following assembly, finished units are transported to the loading dock for shipment to dealers.

TOTAL QUALITY MANAGEMENT AT TUFF CUT

Objective 2
Explain the philosophy of total quality management (TQM) and how a modern cost management system can be used to support the philosophy.

http://www.swcollege.
com/ingram.html

Learn more about TQM.

Total quality management (TQM) **is a management system that seeks continual improvement by asking everyone in an organization to understand, meet, and exceed the needs of customers.** A key question underlying all business activities should be, "Who are the customers, and what are their needs?" For example, total quality management as embraced by a university would include opening additional sections of classes to accommodate large student enrollments. Also, in response to long lines in university bookstores, managers may open additional cash registers to speed the checkout process at the beginning of each term.

Though total quality management is a continually evolving concept, the primary focus is on delivering value to a customer. As shown in Exhibit 2, every activity within an organization should contribute ultimately to the strategic objective of satisfying customers. Thus, the cascading set of TQM tasks shown in the exhibit links strategic objectives with operational activities. In the following paragraphs, Tuff Cut is used to illustrate examples of each task identified in Exhibit 2.

- *Identify the customers.* At first glance, we may be tempted to say that dealers and retail buyers are Tuff Cut's only customers. However, closer examination reveals additional customers internal, as well as external, to the company. For example, welders are customers of the fabrication process, and painters are customers of the welding process. Each operation produces output that is used by later processes.
- *Identify customer needs.* Having identified its customers, Tuff Cut prepared a list of customer needs. For example, *internal customers* demand rugged, high-quality raw materials consistent with engineering specifications. *External customers* require

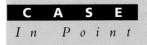

CASE
In Point

The **Wilson Sporting Goods** manufacturing plant located in Humbolt, Tennessee, produces golf balls. However, until the late 1980s the facility was considered to be one of the corporation's least effective plants. Recognizing that changes had to be made to achieve world-class competitiveness, plant leadership rewrote the mission statement to include the concepts of continuous process improvement, employee involvement, just-in-time manufacturing, total quality management, and low-cost manufacturing.

Wilson associates (employees) organized into teams and used TQM tools to aid them in identifying opportunities for improvement. For example, in training sessions, teams were instructed in the use of flowcharts and cause-and-effect diagrams. Associates were part of the team, and their opinions were valued and respected.

Over the last few years, the Wilson plant has reduced the standard cost per unit by 18%. In addition, Wilson's market share has grown from 2% to 18%, and the number of golf balls produced per employee has increased 104%. Wilson found that TQM principles empowered employees to achieve outstanding gains in customer satisfaction, quality, and productivity.

Source: For more information, see Wright, Pamela. 1993/1994. Team Wilson: S Shingo Award-Winning Approach to Golf Ball Manufacturing Excellence, National Productivity Review (Winter): 79–88.

dependable delivery times and sturdy products capable of withstanding the abuse associated with mowing rough terrain.

- *Identify product (or service) features.* For Tuff Cut customers, important *product* features include strong welds and sturdy gear boxes. Important *service* features include rapid delivery of spare parts and availability of repair services in the event of a mechanical breakdown.

- *Identify process (production or delivery) features.* Customers have identified rugged, high-quality products as essential. To meet this need, strong welds and sturdy components are required. Therefore, the next logical step is to design processes that result in strong welds and sturdy components. Tuff Cut evaluated various welding technologies, including robotic and manual, to ensure that these processes were consistent with the demands of the market.

Exhibit 2   Elements of TQM

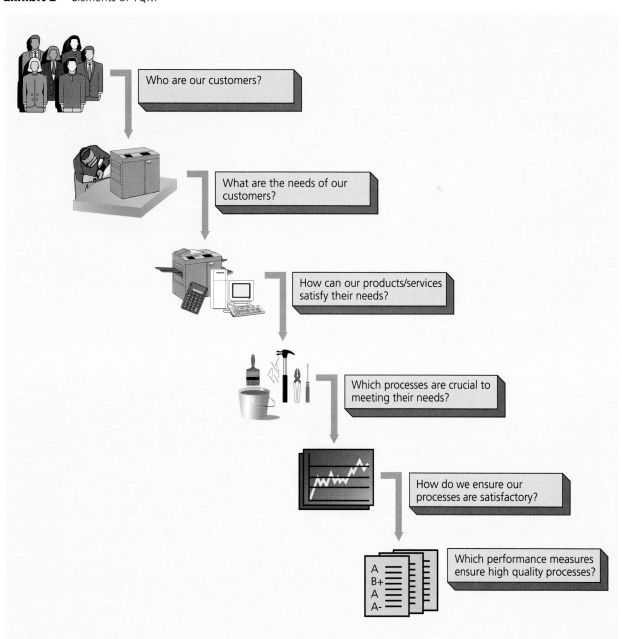

- *Establish controls.* Having identified key quality processes, management put controls in place to ensure that processes are performed at the appropriate quality level. Often, entire processes are redesigned to meet process requirements for quality.
- *Assess performance against goals from the perspective of both internal and external customers.* Tuff Cut must continuously improve production processes and service functions critical to ensuring that customers are satisfied. Managers assess performance on a number of quality criteria by comparing actual performance with predetermined targets (or benchmarks).

The remainder of this chapter explores two topics that are consistent with the objectives of total quality management. Just-in-time (JIT) inventory management and the theory of constraints have received much attention from business leaders in recent years. The operations of Tuff Cut are used to demonstrate these concepts. The purpose is to illustrate how real-world companies implement change in order to remain competitive in a dynamic environment.

SELF-STUDY PROBLEM 1

To illustrate the concepts in this chapter, all the self-study problems use the production process of Autobrake. Autobrake produces aftermarket (replacement) brake cylinders used by automobile repair companies. Autobrake purchases steel bar stock from wholesale distributors and manufactures and assembles components for brake cylinders at its plant. The purchasing manager seeks the lowest steel prices (consistent with strict quality standards) from a large number of vendors. Orders for raw materials must often be delivered very rapidly because of poor communication between the production floor and the purchasing department.

Photography by Joe Higgins

The company has been growing at a rapid pace because of its reputation for high-quality products. Thus, Autobrake is in the position of having more orders than it currently can process. As a result, it maintains a production backlog of approximately 12 weeks.

The manufacturing process consists of five steps. First, steel bar stock is placed into automatic turning equipment (lathes) (step 1). Clamps secure each end of the bar stock, which spins rapidly while a cutting tool cuts the external dimensions to meet engineering specifications. The process requires two turning operations, first stage and second stage. The operations are similar; however, second-stage turning further refines the shape of the component. Studies conducted by the industrial engineering department suggest that average processing times for first-stage and second-stage turning are 5 and 4 minutes per component, respectively. Both turning operations require machine setups between runs of different brake systems. These setups are lengthy and require highly skilled machine operators.

Following second-stage turning, a milling operation takes place (step 2). The component is held in place while a cutting tool removes metal according to specifications. Engineering studies have determined that the milling operation requires approximately 7 minutes for each component. The milling machines are old and subject to unexpected breakdowns. Because Autobrake does not maintain large amounts of work in process inventory, a machine failure often causes other machines to be idle from lack of input.

After milling, a component is ground to meet final specifications (step 3). The grinding operation requires approximately 3 minutes per component and is the last process before the cylinders are assembled.

Assembly of various components is a manual operation (step 4). The average assembly time per cylinder is 6 minutes. Following assembly, each cylinder is carefully packaged in an individual paperboard box that bears the name and logo of Autobrake (step 5). Autobrake gets its packaging materials from a company that buys rolls of paper stock from paper mills and produces custom-printed boxes. Management is considering automating the packaging line to reduce labor costs. Automated equipment would reduce the packaging time of 15 seconds to 8 seconds.

Autobrake contracts with trucking lines to transport its products to wholesalers, who then sell the brake cylinders to various retail stores. However, a major retailer of auto parts has contacted Autobrake to explore the possibilities of buying cylinders directly from the factory, without going through a wholesaler. In addition, the retailer wishes to buy cylinders in bulk containers, rather than in individual packages.

Required

1. Draw a simple flowchart showing the five-step process Autobrake uses. Include processing times.
2. Discuss how Autobrake might apply TQM principles to improve its competitiveness.

The solution to Self-Study Problem 1 appears at the end of the chapter.

PRINCIPLES OF JUST-IN-TIME MANUFACTURING

Objective 3
Describe the just-in-time (JIT) manufacturing philosophy and evaluate its strengths and weaknesses.

http://www.swcollege.com/inqam.html

Learn more about JIT.

Just-in-time manufacturing (JIT) has become popular in recent years. *Just-in-time manufacturing* **is a production system that pulls products through the manufacturing process on the basis of market demand.** Inventory levels are minimized (parts are delivered "just-in-time"), thereby improving asset turnover and reducing manufacturing costs. The concepts underlying just-in-time are not new; Japanese manufacturing companies have benefited from lean, integrated manufacturing systems for many years. A just-in-time manufacturing system typically has a number of related elements. For example, inventory is pulled through the system based on market demand. Companies using just-in-time have small inventories of raw materials and finished goods; therefore, high-quality raw materials are critical to success. Poor-quality raw materials can stop a production line. Because high-quality materials are extremely important, companies usually establish close business relationships with a small number of high-quality, certified suppliers. Engineers work to minimize machine changeover (setup) times to permit manufacturing products in small batches. Short manufacturing lead times result from small-batch production. Thus, just-in-time manufacturing is an important element of time-based competition. High-quality materials, rapid setup times, small-batch production, and minimal inventory levels are all important elements of just-in-time systems.

Just-in-time principles require inventory to be pulled through the plant based on market demand. For example, the last operation in a process acts as a trigger, signaling earlier (upstream) work centers to begin production. The pull system is in contrast to traditional "push" systems, which determine production levels from forecasted demand.

The push system is illustrated in Exhibit 3, panel A. Production is started in Department 1 based on market forecasts of customer demand. The goods produced are placed in inventory until they are needed. The alternative, the pull (or just-in-time) system, is illustrated in panel B of the exhibit. When a customer places an order, a signal is sent to the assembly department to begin production. The assembly department removes components from work in process and assembles them, and the product is delivered to the customer. When components are removed from work in process, a signal to process additional components is sent to the painting department.

Exhibit 3   Push System (A) of Production Compared to Pull System (B)

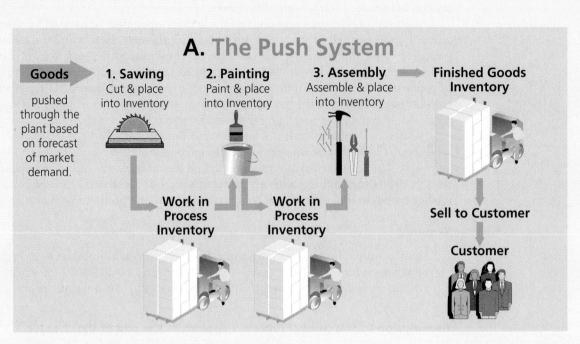

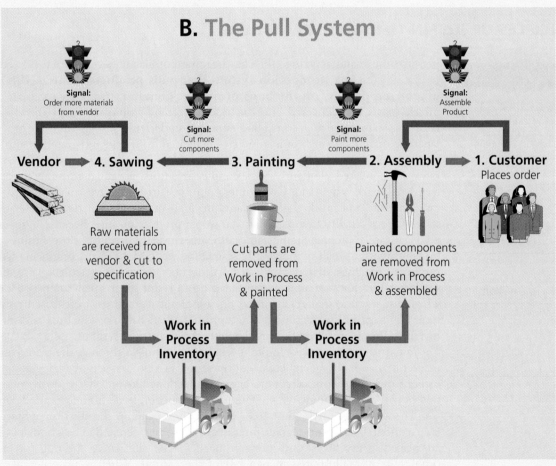

Thus, the painting department takes cut components from work in process, paints them, and places the painted components into work in process. By removing cut components from work in process, the painting department sends a signal to the sawing department to cut more materials. Therefore, the sawing department places an order for materials from an outside vendor. The materials are cut and put into work in process. In summary, a just-in-time system pulls products through the factory at the rate of customer demand. Information flows from right to left, as indicated by the blue arrows in Exhibit 3 (B). Materials flow from left to right, as shown by the red arrows in the exhibit. A key component of the pull system is low work in process inventory and rapid product movement.

To move products through a plant quickly, a company looks for ways to reduce machine setup (or changeover) times. By making setup times short enough, a company can produce units in small batches. Small-batch production results in low inventory levels because products move through the process in small quantities, rather than in large blocks. The company enjoys fast cycle times. Cycle time is considered in the following section.

Just-in-time principles require small amounts of all types of inventory, even raw materials inventory. Therefore, a good relationship with vendors is extremely important. Vendors must make many deliveries of small amounts of high-quality raw materials, rather than making weekly or monthly deliveries of large quantities. Because only small amounts are delivered at a time, quality must be high, or the production line will stop because of lack of raw material. To achieve the objectives of just-in-time, nonfinancial performance measures are used to evaluate critical factors such as lead time, cycle time, and throughput. The following section considers measures that are consistent with the philosophies of just-in-time and total quality management.

Nonfinancial Performance Measures

In today's manufacturing environment, employees often are asked to participate in cross-functional teams made up of individuals with various types of professional expertise. For example, teams may consist of accountants, industrial engineers, production managers, purchasing managers, and finance managers. Often, teams are responsible for improving processes, reducing manufacturing costs, and developing key nonfinancial performance indicators. Performance is no longer measured only in financial terms, such as net income or return on investment. Measurements such as *lead time, manufacturing cycle time, throughput,* and *bottleneck management* have been added to the list of performance criteria.

To illustrate these concepts, Exhibit 4 contains processing times for various work centers within the Tuff Cut plant. For example, the fabrication area has the capacity to produce 20 units per hour, while the welding, painting, and assembly areas are capable of processing 10, 30, and 25 units per hour, respectively. From these data, we can determine several key performance indicators for the Tuff Cut plant. The following sections consider the concepts of lead time, cycle time, and throughput rate.

Lead Time. *Manufacturing lead time* **is defined as the total time required to move a unit from raw materials inventory to finished goods inventory**. Lead time is the sum of two elements, processing time and waiting time. Exhibit 4 indicates that the processing time required to produce one rotary mower is:

	Processing Time (minutes)
Fabrication	3.0
Welding	6.0
Painting	2.0
Assembly	2.4
Total	13.4

Exhibit 4   Workcenter Processing Times Within the Tuff Cut Plant

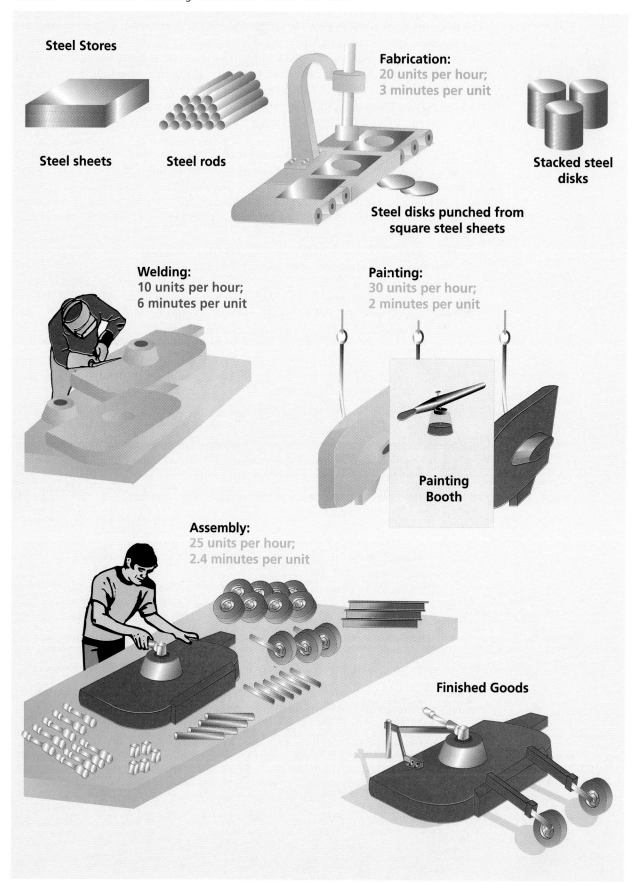

Steel Stores

Steel sheets

Steel rods

Fabrication:
20 units per hour;
3 minutes per unit

Stacked steel disks

Steel disks punched from square steel sheets

Welding:
10 units per hour;
6 minutes per unit

Painting:
30 units per hour;
2 minutes per unit

Painting Booth

Assembly:
25 units per hour;
2.4 minutes per unit

Finished Goods

Each rotary mower requires 13.4 minutes of total processing time from beginning (fabrication) to end (assembly). Processing time is the number of minutes in which value is added to raw materials. Does this mean that Tuff Cut can produce a unit from start to finish in 13.4 minutes? Probably not. Processing time is only one part of manufacturing lead time; the other part is the time a unit spends waiting to be processed. For example, assume that each work center has 6 hours of work in process inventory waiting to be processed. Six hours of work in process inventory represents the production of less than one shift. Most manufacturers have far more work-in-process inventory. Thus, 24 hours of wait time (6 hours before the fabrication area + 6 hours before the welding area + 6 hours before the painting area + 6 hours before the assembly area = 24 hours) are built into Tuff Cut's manufacturing process. Therefore, the lead time for completing one mower is calculated as follows:

Wait time (24 hours × 60 minutes)	1,440.0 minutes
Processing time	13.4 minutes
Manufacturing lead time	1,453.4 minutes

Wait time makes up the major portion of the lead time required to move a unit of product through the plant. Imagine a four-step class registration process at your university that requires a 6-hour wait at each step to accomplish a task requiring only a few minutes. You probably would say that the university registration process is inefficient. The same is true with a manufacturing process.

Why would Tuff Cut keep 6 hours of inventory at each work center? The answer involves process reliability. For example, without such inventory, if a work center becomes idle because of a mechanical breakdown, all later (downstream) work centers must stop processing because of lack of input. Therefore, inventory is viewed as insurance against unreliable equipment. Unfortunately, the insurance is not free. Just-in-time manufacturing practices require reducing the level of inventory to reduce carrying costs and to improve lead time.

So, why are lead time and work in process levels important? What is the downside of having high work in process levels and slow lead times? Maintaining high inventory levels is expensive because of the potential for damage or obsolescence as well as the cost of storage. Also, managers often are evaluated using return on assets[2] as a performance criterion. High inventory levels make the asset base larger and reduce a company's return. There are other considerations, as well. A company that has low levels of work in process inventory can move an order through the process in much less time than a company whose inventory levels require many hours of waiting time. Thus, fast-cycle companies may enjoy a strategic advantage in the marketplace by being able to deliver goods faster than their competition.

In addition to lead time, manufacturing **cycle time** often is used as a nonfinancial performance measure. The next section considers cycle time in connection with the Tuff Cut plant.

Cycle Time. Cycle time differs from lead time. The easiest way to visualize the concept of cycle time is to imagine standing at the final stage of a manufacturing process with a stop watch. Cycle time **is the number of minutes that pass between units leaving the final assembly area.** For Tuff Cut, which manufacturing center (fabrication, welding, painting, or assembly) drives cycle time? Exhibit 4 indicates that a finished Tuff Cut mower should roll off the assembly line every six minutes, provided there are no mechanical breakdowns or process interruptions. How do we

---

[2] Recall that return on assets = asset turnover × profit margin

$$= \frac{sales}{average\ assets} \times \frac{earnings}{sales}$$

know? **Cycle time is driven by the slowest process in the chain, the welding area.** Since the welders need six minutes to process a unit, it does not matter that the fabrication department can process one unit every three minutes, or that the painting department can process one unit every two minutes. The welders take the longest time to process a unit, and the system as a whole cannot move faster than the slowest process will permit. **Processes that produce at slow rates and restrict the flow of goods or services are termed** *bottlenecks*. Just as the small-diameter opening in a bottle restricts the flow of liquid, a production bottleneck restricts the output of a process.

The fabrication area can process units twice as fast as the welding area; however, processing at a rate faster than ten units per hour merely results in excess work in process inventory accumulating in front of the welding area. The painting and assembly areas also process faster than the welding area. Unfortunately, their production rates are held down by the welding area's inability to provide parts fast enough for them to achieve their potential. The production rate of the entire plant is determined by the slowest manufacturing center.

This section has evaluated lead time and cycle time as performance indicators. Another important measure of a manufacturing facility is the rate of throughput, which is discussed in the following section.

Throughput. *Throughput* **represents the number of units completed by a process in a given period of time.** Marketing managers are interested in both lead time and throughput. Lead time affects a salesperson's ability to deliver goods to customers quickly, and throughput affects the number of units available for sale. Throughput is related to cycle time. For example, to calculate the number of units Tuff Cut can produce in one eight-hour shift, divide the number of available hours by the cycle time. Thus, by dividing cycle time into available production time, the throughput for a process can be determined as follows:

```
8 hours per shift × 60 minutes per hour = 480 available minutes per shift
Cycle time                               = 6 minutes
Throughput          = 480 ÷ 6           = 80 units per eight-hour shift
```

Therefore, Tuff Cut has the ability to produce 80 units per eight-hour shift. During periods when demand for rotary mowers is high, managers must ensure that throughput is maximized to avoid lost sales. Exhibit 5 depicts a cycle time of six minutes between completed units leaving assembly. The number of completed units per shift illustrates the concept of throughput.

Product-Oriented Versus Process-Oriented Plant Layout

Objective 4
Explain how a traditional "process-oriented" plant layout differs from a "product-oriented" plant layout.

Some organizations have explored various approaches to plant organization in an attempt to improve operations and reduce manufacturing costs. Innovative plant layouts have been developed that can support minimal inventory levels, fast setup times, high-quality products, and responsive lead times. Traditionally, designs for manufacturing facilities were *process-oriented*. Each area of the plant was designed to carry out a certain type of process, and work in process inventory was transported between processes. For example, as illustrated in Exhibit 6, the steel storage area at Tuff Cut was located in the northwest corner of the plant. Materials were transported to the fabrication area in large batches by forklift. Following fabrication, the pieces were transported to the welding area to await processing. Following the welding operation, extensive handling and transportation was needed to move units to the painting process and back to final assembly. Clearly, Tuff Cut organized its factory by grouping similar processes together, an example of a process-oriented plant layout. *Process-oriented plant layouts* **typically are arranged according to machine function, with machines that perform similar functions placed together.**

Exhibit 5 The Relationship of Cycle Time to Throughput

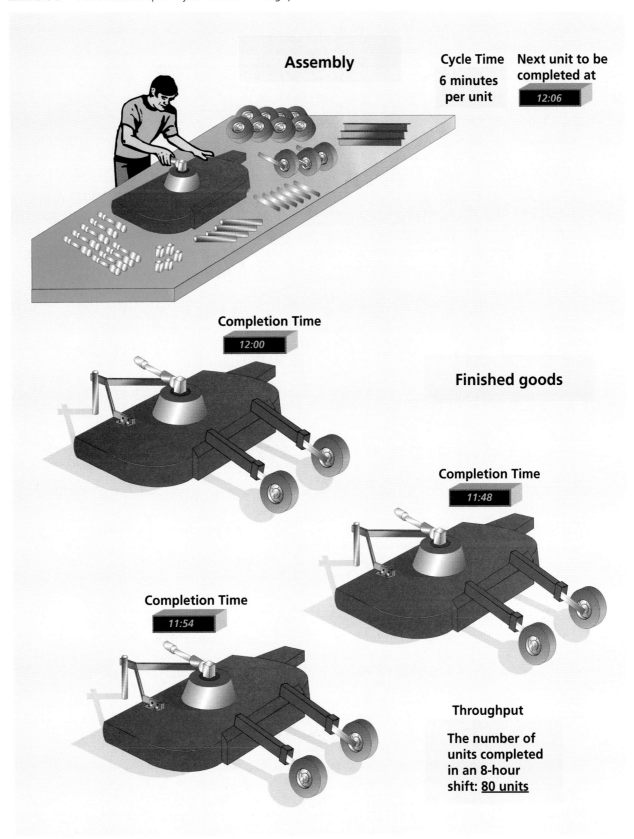

Exhibit 6   Traditional "Process-Oriented" Plant Layout

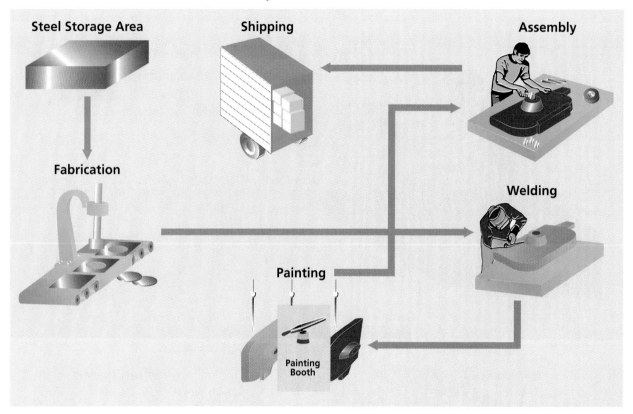

What are some of the cost considerations in a traditional process-oriented plant? First of all, to make efficient use of assets and the people who move parts from one workstation to another, a process-oriented plant typically produces in large batches. Therefore, work in process levels are high and lead times are long.

As an alternative, many companies are reorganizing their plants. As illustrated in Exhibit 7, a *product-oriented plant layout* **is based on manufacturing cells that meet the production requirements of products or product families (products that have similar characteristics).**

Because of rapid changes in product characteristics, manufacturing systems are developed to be flexible. Rather than buying a machine that serves only one function, such as drilling, cutting, or welding, companies are investing in flexible machinery that can perform a number of functions. Typically, flexible manufacturing systems are characterized by their ability to change rapidly from one type of process to another. For example, automatic tool changers may remove a drill bit that makes ½-inch-diameter holes and replace it with a drill bit that makes ¼-inch-diameter holes. In addition, many flexible systems contain automatic error detection in the form of statistical process control software. Finally, most flexible systems have the ability to increase or decrease the rate of output.[3]

A *manufacturing cell* **is a group of related machines, typically arranged in the shape of a U.** Raw materials enter one prong of the U, and finished goods exit from the other prong. Exhibit 7 illustrates how Tuff Cut might reorganize its plant floor to achieve a product-oriented layout. The industrial engineers designed work cells by placing equipment in two cells based on the manufacturing requirements of their product line. The painting process presented a few problems because the paint line cannot be divided. Thus, the design linked both cells to the painting area.

---

[3]   *For more information on flexible manufacturing systems, see Black, J. T. 1991.* The Design of the Factory with a Future *(New York: McGraw-Hill, Inc.).*

Exhibit 7   Cellular "Product-Oriented" Plant Layout

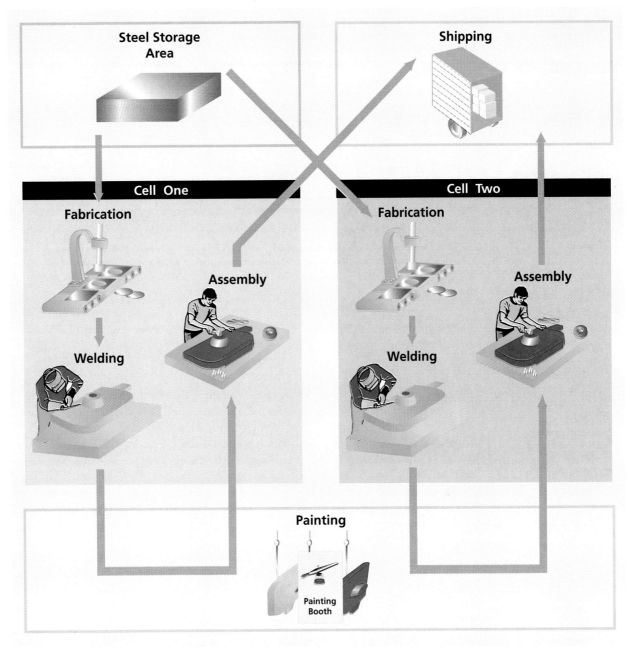

As indicated by the arrows in Exhibit 7, raw materials enter the cell and are processed, and completed products leave the cell. Because machines within the cell are close to one another, extensive handling and transportation of work-in-process inventory is not required. Work cells are arranged according to the needs of product families and are consistent with the concepts of just-in-time manufacturing. Because batch sizes are small, work in process levels are lower than those of process-oriented plants. Lead times also are much shorter because units do not sit for long periods of time waiting for processing. Plants that use a cellular design often have many cells, each dedicated to a product or product family.

Cellular manufacturing requires few arbitrary overhead allocations because costs associated with each cell tend to be direct. Thus, identifying the resources used by each product or product family usually is easier with a plant layout based on manu-facturing cells. In addition, since batch sizes are small, waste and scrap costs should be minimal. For example, if a machine operator makes an error in setting the width of a cut for a small batch, only a few units are affected.

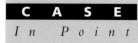

A manufacturer of commercial refrigerators, blast chillers, salad bars, and freezers explored cellular manufacturing as part of converting its operations to just-in-time. Three different types of equipment—a metal shear, a punch, and a brake press—were linked to form a cell. Metal shears cut steel sheets in much the same way that scissors cut paper. Punches cut holes in metal. A brake press bends flat sheets of metal into angular shapes. Thus, the company linked three different types of machines into a cell to manufacture a product.

Converting the plant to just-in-time required several major changes in addition to installing manufacturing cells. Machine setup times were reduced. In addition, union workers agreed to more flexibility in their job descriptions. The number of job classifications dropped from 33 to 11. Finally, a partnership arrangement was negotiated with the company's major supplier. Results included reduced labor costs, lower inventory levels, and faster customer response time. In addition, employees reported greater job satisfaction.

Source: For more information, see Howard, M., and R. Newman. 1993. From Job Shop to Just-in-Time—A Successful Conversion, **Production and Inventory Management Journal** *(Third Quarter): 70–74.*

Financial Benefits Resulting from Nonfinancial Performance Measures

Managers who make operational changes consistent with just-in-time management principles expect these changes to improve profitability. As discussed in this section, just-in-time principles help managers increase revenues as well as reduce operating costs. For example, companies maintain minimal levels of raw materials, work in process, and finished goods inventories when products are pulled through the factory at the rate demanded by customers. Reduced inventory levels result in lower carrying costs, which include costs of financing, obsolescence, and damage. Fast setup times contribute to short manufacturing lead times. Often, responsive factories gain a competitive advantage that translates into increased sales. This section considers the financial effects of reduced inventory levels, improved manufacturing lead times, and increased throughput.

Selected financial information for Tuff Cut is presented below. The company currently has sales of $93 million annually, while employing assets of $139.5 million. The controller estimates that variable manufacturing costs are 40% of sales. In addition, fixed manufacturing expenses and fixed administrative expenses are $28 million and $11 million, respectively. Thus, Tuff Cut's return on assets currently is 12%.

Annual Sales		$93,000,000
Variable manufacturing expenses, 40% of sales		
(0.40 × $93,000,000)	$37,200,000	
Fixed manufacturing costs	28,000,000	
Fixed general and administrative costs	11,000,000	76,200,000
Operating income		$16,800,000

Return on Assets before process changes:

Profit Margin	*Asset Turnover*	
(Operating income[4] ÷ sales)	× (sales ÷ assets[5])	= return on assets
($16,800,000 ÷ $93,000,000)	× ($93,000,000 ÷ $139,500,000)	= return on assets
0.18	× 0.67	= 0.12

[4] *Operating income is equivalent to earnings.*
[5] *The asset information given here is assumed to be equal to average costs.*

Let's consider how implementing just-in-time can improve Tuff Cut's return on assets. First, assume that demand for Tuff Cut's products exceeds supply and that improvements in throughput will result in a 10% increase in sales. Further, assume that reductions in raw materials, work in process, and finished goods inventories will result in a 1% decrease in assets. In addition, variable manufacturing costs will be reduced from 40% of sales to 38.5% of sales because inventory carrying costs and scrap rates will decrease. Product and process reengineering efforts often reduce fixed manufacturing costs. In this case, Tuff Cut's fixed manufacturing costs will decrease from $28 million to $27 million because of reductions in materials handling activities and the elimination of unnecessary manufacturing equipment. Finally, fixed administrative costs will be reduced from $11 million to $10 million because of changes in administrative support functions. For example, fixed administrative costs can be reduced by restructuring processes and reducing the amount of indirect labor and equipment. The following calculations summarize our assumptions:

Annual sales ($93,000,000 × 1.1)		$102,300,000
Variable manufacturing expenses,		
38.5% of sales (0.385 × $102,300,000)	$39,385,500	
Fixed manufacturing expense	27,000,000	
Fixed general and administrative expenses	10,000,000	76,385,500
Operating income		$25,914,500

Assets following a 1% decrease = $139,500,000 × .99 = $138,105,000

Return on Assets after process changes:

Profit Margin		*Asset Turnover*	
Operating income ÷ sales	×	sales ÷ assets	= return on assets
($25,914,500 ÷ $102,300,000)	×	($102,300,000 ÷ $138,105,000)	= return on assets
0.25	×	0.74	= 0.19

These calculations suggest that Tuff Cut's return on assets will improve from 12% to 19% as a result of implementing just-in-time principles. Our example illustrates the potential financial effects of changes in manufacturing strategy. Companies that have successfully implemented just-in-time see it as a strategy for long-run continuous improvement. Thus, just-in-time is not a "magic pill" that suddenly will improve a company's profitability. However, as our example illustrates, just-in-time includes sound operating principles that affect a company's revenues and costs.

Drawbacks to the Just-in-Time Manufacturing Philosophy

Just-in-time manufacturing is a system with many positive attributes; however, it has its disadvantages. In the economic recovery of the early 1990s, many companies reduced inventories to record low levels. Unfortunately, some companies experienced difficulties because of these low levels. Assume that you are the general manager of two plants, a manufacturing plant and an assembly plant. The manufacturing plant provides components to the assembly plant. Unexpectedly, the union at the manufacturing plant goes on strike. In the past, negotiations were lengthy and difficult, but at that time, the assembly plant had six months of components in inventory. Now, consistent with the just-in-time philosophy, the assembly plant has three days of inventory. How do you think just-in-time will affect your ability to bargain effectively? The union at the manufacturing plant has successfully closed two plants instead of one.

In a just-in-time environment, cost savings from reducing inventories can be off-set by increased delivery costs imposed by suppliers who are now making daily (or even hourly) deliveries. In addition, management must explain to workers why they are being asked to increase the number of batches and machine setups. Finally, in an economy experiencing rapid growth, managers may increase inventory to levels *inconsistent* with just-in-time because they fear that they will run out of inventory at a time when customers are ready to purchase goods.

On balance, just-in-time principles have helped many manufacturers improve operations and reduce waste. In addition, by reducing work in process inventory levels, bottlenecks become apparent. As we discussed earlier in this section, bottlenecks in a production process affect cycle time, and thus the number of units processed through the system (throughput). Understanding how to manage bottleneck resources is important for improving operating performance. The following section addresses the issue of managing bottlenecks.

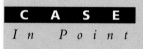

CASE *In Point*

Union workers went on strike at a **General Motors Corporation (GM)** assembly plant because of job security concerns. The strike immediately shut down nine other GM plants that depended on the assembly plant for parts. The strike was settled when GM agreed to cancel some layoffs and to add more workers and promised not to buy certain parts from outside suppliers.

Just-in-time practices have caused other headaches for the automaker. One plant once had to stop its production line because a delivery truck carrying parts broke down on the freeway.★ Though just-in-time offers many cost reduction possibilities, these examples confirm that just-in-time will not solve all manufacturing problems.

★ *Harper, Lucinda. Trucks Keep Inventories Rolling Past Warehouses to Production Lines.* **The Wall Street Journal,** *(February 7, 1994):A5.*

SELF-STUDY PROBLEM 2

Refer to the information presented in Self-Study Problem 1.

Required

1. Calculate the following for the manufacturing process at Auto-brake:
   a. Cycle time
   b. Total processing time
   c. Throughput per hour
2. Why would you expect lead time to be different from the total processing time calculated in part (b) above?
3. Assume that management at Auto-brake is considering redesigning the plant layout from a process-oriented layout to a product-oriented layout by establishing work cells. Discuss the benefits of a product-oriented plant layout.

The solution to Self-Study Problem 2 appears at the end of the chapter.

THE THEORY OF CONSTRAINTS

Objective 5
Identify the primary components of the theory of constraints.

As indicated in the previous section, the welding area of the Tuff Cut factory was found to be a bottleneck. In this area, steel sheets are assembled to form the mower housing. As part of the strategic objective of reducing lead time and increasing throughput, management began reducing the level of work in process inventory. In doing so, they observed some troubling outcomes. Certain machines were forced to become idle, which resulted in a *decrease,* rather than an increase, in throughput.

While touring the plant in search of answers to the decline in productivity, managers noticed several things that suggested the presence of a bottleneck. First, in the welding area, managers observed large stacks of work in process inventory sitting in front of the welding machines waiting to be processed. Though work in process inventories in most areas of the plant contained the output from only a few hours of production, the work in process inventory in the welding area contained the output from several days of production. Second, after observing the welding operation over a number of days, managers noticed that the welders never were idle, except during scheduled breaks. In contrast, they noticed that the downstream painting process often was forced to shut down temporarily because workers had no materials to paint. From observing the manufacturing process, management reasoned that the welding area must be a production bottleneck, or constraint.

Bottleneck processes exist in almost every manufacturing plant. They result when the processing speed of a machine or production area is less than that of other machines or production areas in the plant. Bottlenecks never can be eliminated entirely, because as the processing capability of one machine or production area is increased, *a different* machine or production area often becomes a bottleneck. Thus, in the spirit of continuous process improvement, managers continually adjust processes to improve throughput and reduce operating costs.

Steps to Improve Performance

This section explores various steps management can take to improve throughput consistent with the theory of constraints.[6] **The** theory of constraints (TOC) **states that by identifying a constraint, such as a bottleneck, that exists in the processing of a good or service and taking corrective steps, the process will be improved.** The five steps recommended for process improvement are as follows:

- Step 1: Attack a bottleneck by **identifying** the system's constraints.
- Step 2: Decide how to make the **best use** of the constraint.
- Step 3: **Subordinate** all other decisions to those made in step 2.
- Step 4: **Improve the performance** of the constraint.
- Step 5: If a constraint has been broken (the old bottleneck is gone) but a different bottleneck has been created, **go back to step 1 and start over.**

Implementation of the Theory of Constraints

Let's assume that managers at Tuff Cut have correctly identified the welding area as a bottleneck. Thus, the second step involves deciding how to make the best use of

---

[6] *The principles of the theory of constraints were developed and discussed in Goldratt, Eliyahu M. and Jeff Cox. 1992.* The Goal *(Great Barrington: North River Press).*

the welding area. For example, because a minute of lost time on a bottleneck results in a minute of lost production for the entire plant, the bottleneck resource must never be allowed to remain idle during lunchtime and breaks. If automated equipment is used, workers simply make certain the raw material supply bins are filled with parts before they leave the work area for a break. Alternatively, workers may be encouraged to have flexible break times and lunchtimes to ensure that the bottleneck is not idle.

Another way to reduce the effect of the bottleneck is to inspect materials before they are processed at the bottleneck. For example, if scrap rates are a problem in the manufacturing process, inspection centers can be located before the bottleneck. Thus, the bottleneck does not waste valuable processing time on parts that will be unusable.

Step 3 suggests that all other decisions should be subordinated to those made in step 2. In other words, the entire plant should be scheduled and managed by considering the bottleneck. For example, components that require processing on a bottleneck resource should receive highest priority at nonbottleneck work centers. Thus, all work centers should schedule production orders to ensure that the bottleneck resource is never idle.

The fourth step requires managers to improve the performance of the bottleneck. What are some strategies Tuff Cut can use to improve performance on the bottleneck in the welding area? They can minimize downtime on the bottleneck by making machine setups less time-consuming. One method of reducing setup time is to convert on-line setup time to off-line setup time. Production machinery often has removable parts, such as saw blades, grippers, and drill bits, called machine tools. Complex tool changes can be made more quickly if two or more sets of tools are used. While a machine is actively producing with one set of tools, a machinist prepares the settings of a second set of tools at a workbench. Changeovers become rapid because one set of tools is simply replaced by a second set that already has been prepared. Thus, productive time is gained by reducing downtime associated with setup activities.

Extra capacity can be created for the bottleneck resource in several ways. Purchasing additional machinery can reduce the effects of a bottleneck by providing more processing capability. If management decides that capital for additional equipment is not available, some components could be purchased from external sources, thereby increasing the output of the entire plant. Additionally, more workers can be hired. At Tuff Cut, management acquired a new machine to operate along with existing equipment. The new machine provided the capacity needed to increase throughput, while decreasing inventory. Let's assume that the new equipment was more efficient and increased the number of units processed from 10 per hour to 25 per hour. How will the investment affect throughput?

Exhibit 8 illustrates the relationships among Tuff Cut's processing centers after adding the new equipment. What is the cycle time for a unit of product under the new arrangement? Just as before, the bottleneck controls the rate of product flow through the plant. Do we have the same bottleneck as before?

Exhibit 9 indicates that with the capacity of the welding department increased to 25 units per hour, the fabrication department, with a productive capacity of 20 units per hour, now becomes the process bottleneck. Thus, cycle time has changed from one completed unit every 6 minutes (10 units per hour = 6 minutes per unit) to one completed unit every 3 minutes (20 units per hour = 3 minutes per unit). The theoretical throughput per 8-hour shift is calculated by dividing the number of minutes in an 8-hour shift (60 minutes × 8 hours = 480 minutes) by the cycle time between units rolling out of the assembly area. As the following calculations illustrate, improving the process capability of the bottleneck resource dramatically increases the throughput rate from 80 units per shift to 160 units per shift.

Exhibit 8   Revised Workcenter Processing Times Within the Tuff Cut Plant

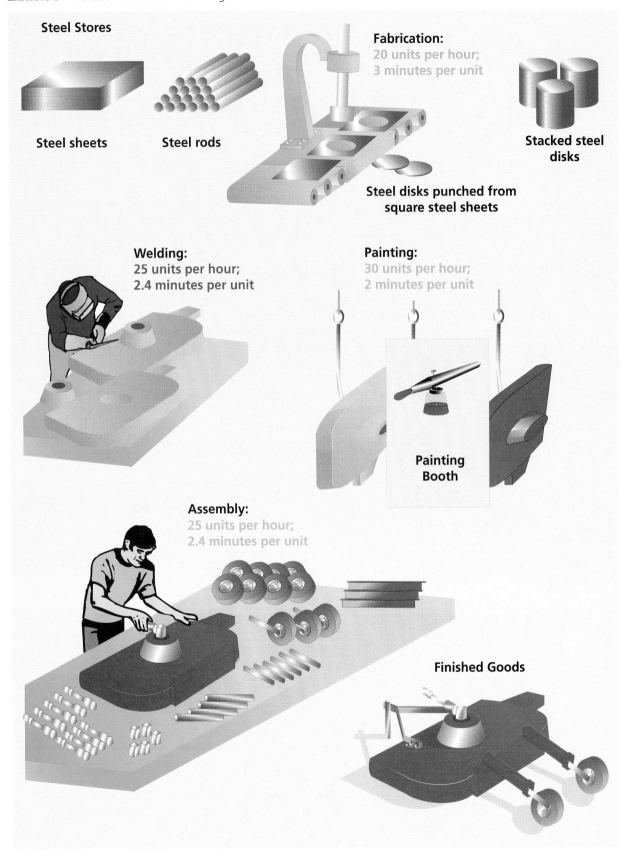

Steel Stores

Steel sheets

Steel rods

Fabrication:
20 units per hour;
3 minutes per unit

Stacked steel disks

Steel disks punched from square steel sheets

Welding:
25 units per hour;
2.4 minutes per unit

Painting:
30 units per hour;
2 minutes per unit

Painting Booth

Assembly:
25 units per hour;
2.4 minutes per unit

Finished Goods

Exhibit 9   Throughput Comparison, Old System versus New System

	Before new CNC welder	**After new CNC welder**
Bottleneck	Welding area	Fabrication area
Cycle time	6 minutes per unit	3 minutes per unit
Throughput		
per 8-hour shift	480 ÷ 6 = 80	480 ÷ 3 = 160

Exhibit 10, panel A represents the four processes of Tuff Cut and work in process levels between each process. Under the old system, large amounts of inventory piled up in front of the welding area because it was the bottleneck, or slowest work center in the plant. The work in process areas before the painting and assembly processes were empty because these processes were faster than the welding process. Thus, painting and assembly workers had idle time between completing a unit and receiving another one from the welding area.

The new system is presented in Exhibit 10, panel B. Now, the fabricating department is the bottleneck, or slowest work center in the plant. What is the difference in work in process levels between panel A and panel B? In panel B, since all processes are faster than the first one in the sequence, no work in process inventory accumulates between work centers. In other words, the welding, painting, and assembly work centers can complete a unit of product before the fabricating department places another unit into work in process.

In the spirit of continuous process improvement, the fifth step requires management to start over with step 1. As indicated by Exhibit 9, the improvements have shifted the bottleneck operation from the welding area to the fabrication area. Therefore, managers must look for ways to reduce the new constraint, the fabrication area.

If managers increase the processing capacity of nonbottleneck resources, will throughput increase? What if the managers of Tuff Cut learn of robots that can double the speed of the *assembly* process? Thinking every modern manufacturing plant needs advanced technology to survive, they redesign the assembly process and install robots. Press conferences are held in the community to advertise how the company has modernized the plant and how modernization will carry the company forward into the twenty-first century. The plant managers eagerly await the productivity reports in the month following the installation. What result do you predict? Assume the same information presented in Exhibit 8 except that the assembly department now produces at 50 units per hour. Where is the bottleneck? What is the cycle time? What is the throughput for an eight-hour shift? Of course, the fabrication area remains the bottleneck, the cycle time continues to be the processing rate of the slowest production area, and the throughput does not increase at all. What has happened? Managers invested in faster machines in an area that already had excess capacity. In other words, the bottleneck (the fabrication area) already restricted the rate at which the assembly area could produce. Adding speed to a nonbottleneck resource does nothing for throughput. However, it increases costs and investment, thus reducing operating income and return on assets.

Just-in-Time and Theory of Constraints Similarities and Differences

This chapter used the operations of Tuff Cut to illustrate the concepts of just-in-time inventory management and the theory of constraints. Just-in-time emphasizes external relationships in an attempt to improve operations and profitability. An example includes developing stronger relationships with fewer suppliers. Also, just-in-time emphasizes fast-cycle, low-inventory manufacturing practices. Performance measures consistent with just-in-time include lead time, setup time, and work in process inventory levels.

Exhibit 10   Bottleneck Identification

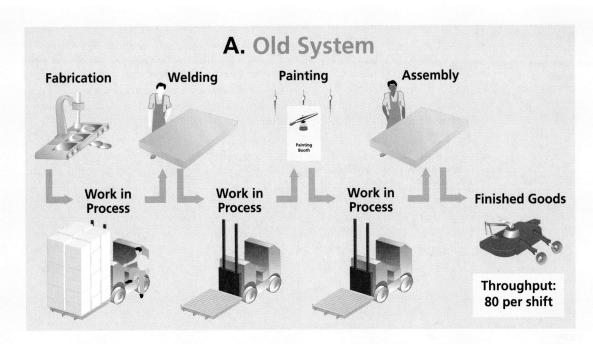

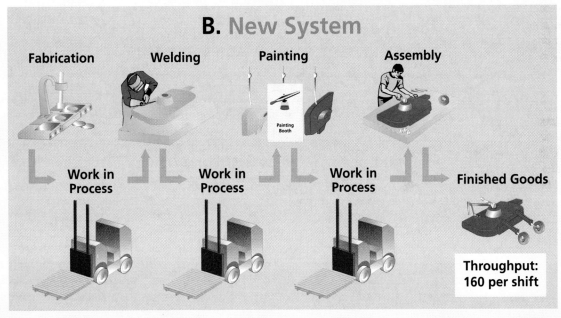

The theory of constraints also emphasizes the external environment by considering market demand when determining production levels. Both just-in-time and the theory of constraints have the objective of reducing work-in-process inventory levels; however, the theory of constraints emphasizes placing small amounts of inventory in front of constraints to ensure that they are never idle. Both just-in-time and the theory of constraints emphasize the importance of reducing lead times. Thus, just-in-time and the theory of constraints embrace the concepts of total quality management with respect to satisfying customer needs.

Though the approaches discussed in this chapter have different characteristics, a pattern emerges. To compete in the global economy, companies are learning that identifying and serving customer needs is crucial. In addition, inventory management and cost control are major elements of most companies' competitive strategies.

SERVICE ORGANIZATIONS IN A GLOBAL BUSINESS ENVIRONMENT

Objective 6
Explain how new manufacturing environment concepts apply to service organizations.

The concepts illustrated in this chapter also are directly applicable to companies that deliver services, rather than tangible products, to their customers. For example, an insurance company specializing in automobile coverage can apply TQM principles in its quest to meet the needs of policyholders. Assume that Fender Bender Insurance Company knows that customers want their insurance claims processed quickly in the event of an automobile accident. Fender Bender may analyze activities in its claims processing department to discover ways to reduce lead time.

Assume that a study conducted by Fender Bender showed that the average policyholder waits three weeks (15 working days) after submitting a claim before receiving a check. Further studies showed that it takes four hours to process an average claim. Thus, value-added time represents a very small portion of total lead time. Why does a claim remain in work in process so long? Perhaps a bottleneck exists.

For Fender Bender, the number of claims processed is equivalent to throughput for a manufacturing company. Thus, to improve throughput, bottleneck activities must be identified and improved. The check preparation function is an example of a bottleneck within Fender Bender. After cost estimates are received from three separate repair facilities and an insurance adjuster gives final approval, the final step is check preparation. Fender Bender's checks are computer-generated; however, an office employee must enter the amount and the payee into the computer. Fender Bender discovered that the employee responsible for entering check data sometimes waited three or four days between processing batches of checks. Rather than preparing checks several times per day, the employee allowed claim forms to accumulate for processing in one large batch. Thus, work in process levels and lead time increased, resulting in slower claims service and dissatisfied policyholders.

The check processing activity is only one potential bottleneck, but it illustrates the concepts of a customer-focused total quality management philosophy, bottlenecks, throughput, and lead time within a *service* organization. Understanding administrative processes permits managers in various service industries to deliver value to their customers. Other examples of customer-oriented services include one-day mortgage loan approval offered by certain mortgage lenders, fast checkout procedures offered by major hotel chains, and rapid car rental and drop-off services provided by leading car rental agencies.

SELF-STUDY PROBLEM 3

Autobrake wishes to identify bottlenecks in the production process.

Required

1. How would you identify potential bottlenecks by observing a manufacturing process?
2. If the bottleneck in Autobrake's process is idle for one hour, what is the effect on plant throughput?
3. How would an hour of lost time on a nonbottleneck machine affect throughput?
4. Identify some ways to ensure that production time on the bottleneck process is not wasted.

© Mark Bolster/International Stock

The solution to Self-Study Problem 3 appears at the end of the chapter.

REVIEW *Summary of Important Concepts*

1. Total quality management includes the following activities:
   a. Identify customers.
   b. Identify customer needs.
   c. Identify product (good or service) features.
   d. Identify process (production or delivery) features.
   e. Establish controls and conduct operations.
   f. Assess performance against goals from both internal and external customer perspectives.

2. Just-in-time (JIT) has the following key elements:
   a. High-quality input and output are required.
   b. Inventory levels are reduced.
   c. Cycle times become shorter.
   d. Suppliers become partners, rather than adversaries.
   e. Machine changeover (setup) times must be short.
   f. Production batch sizes are small.
   g. Inventory is pulled through a plant based on market demand.

3. The theory of constraints has the following key steps:
   a. Identify the process constraint (the bottleneck).
   b. Decide how to make the most efficient use of the constraint.
   c. Subordinate all other decisions to those identified as making efficient use of the constraint.
   d. Improve the processing capability of the constraint.

4. The concepts of total quality management, just-in-time, and the theory of constraints can be applied to service organizations.
   a. All organizations use processes to deliver their goods or services to customers.
   b. TQM principles apply to service organizations as well as to manufacturing companies.
   c. Processes within service organizations can contain bottlenecks that affect lead time and throughput.

DEFINE *Terms and Concepts Defined in This Chapter*

Bottleneck   (272)
Cycle time   (271)
Just-in-time manufacturing   (267)
Manufacturing cell   (274)

Manufacturing lead time   (269)
Process-oriented plant layout   (272)
Product-oriented plant layout   (274)
Theory of constraints (TOC)   (279)

Throughput   (272)
Total quality management (TQM)   (264)

SOLUTIONS

SELF-STUDY PROBLEM 1

1.

Step 1

| First-stage turning (5 minutes) |
| Second-stage turning (4 minutes) |

Step 2

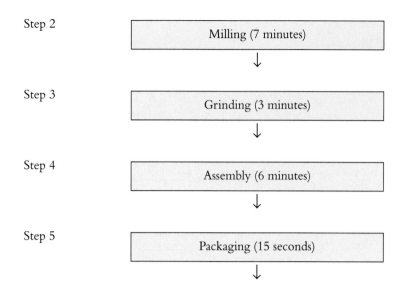

Milling (7 minutes)

↓

Step 3

Grinding (3 minutes)

↓

Step 4

Assembly (6 minutes)

↓

Step 5

Packaging (15 seconds)

↓

Within the plant, raw material goes through five operations: turning (first and second stage), milling, grinding, assembly, and packaging. Following packaging, cylinders are shipped to wholesalers, who sell and ship to retailers.

2. Using TQM principles, there are several clues for improvement in the process description. For example, Autobrake orders raw materials from many vendors, using the lowest cost as a criteria. In addition, communication between the plant floor and the purchasing department often is very poor. Perhaps Autobrake could reduce the costs of acquiring raw materials by working closely with a few selected vendors. Understanding suppliers' cost drivers may also help Autobrake reduce acquisition costs. For example, production needs could be forecast well in advance and provided to vendors, who then might pass along savings resulting from better communication between the two companies. Delivery costs often can be reduced by careful planning.

    The process description also suggests that setup times between batches of different products are very lengthy. Since the process appears to be capacity-constrained (Autobrake has a backlog of orders), an hour used to set up equipment cannot be used to make brake cylinders. Therefore, if a faster method of performing machine setups can be developed, nonproductive setup time can be converted into productive manufacturing time.

    The scenario at the close of the problem suggests that Autobrake has the opportunity to sell directly to a large retailer and to eliminate packaging costs. Packaging includes raw materials (in the form of paperboard boxes) and also labor and overhead costs associated with handling.

    Thus, by identifying key process features and establishing controls to ensure that Autobrake meets or exceeds demands placed on these processes, Autobrake's quality may be improved and costs may be reduced. The end result is a satisfied customer who receives a quality product at a competitive price.

SELF-STUDY PROBLEM 2

1. a. Cycle time is defined as the number of minutes between completed products. The production process consists of the following steps and associated manufacturing times:

First-stage turning	5 minutes	
Second-stage turning	4 minutes	
Milling	**7 minutes**	**(Milling is the bottleneck.)**
Grinding	3 minutes	
Assembly	6 minutes	
Packaging	¼ minute (15 seconds)	

To determine the cycle time, identify the slowest process because it determines the rate of flow through the plant. In the Autobrake facility, the milling department requires 7 minutes to process a component; thus, we would expect to see a component available for shipment every 7 minutes.

b. Total processing time is determined by adding the time required to process a unit at each step in the process, as follows: $5 + 4 + 7 + 3 + 6 + \frac{1}{4} = 25\frac{1}{4}$ minutes.

c. Plant throughput per hour (assuming no breakdowns) is calculated by dividing 60 minutes by the cycle time (60 minutes per hour $\div$ 7 minutes = 8.6) Thus, the plant would produce approximately 9 cylinders per hour.

2. Total processing time should be shorter than lead time. Lead time is the sum of two variables, processing time and waiting time. The lead time required to move a unit of product from the raw materials inventory to the finished goods storage area is the sum of all processing and waiting times. Waiting and moving time are considered non–value-added activities. Alternatively, processing time is value-added time, in which materials are converted from their original form.

3. Traditionally, plants were organized according to the machine functions, and products were transported through the plant to carry out various manufacturing steps. These process-oriented plants consume many resources in moving and handling materials. Alternatively, work cells typically are U-shaped and consist of machines dedicated to a product or product family. Machines are arranged according to product requirements. Work in process inventory levels usually are small, and lead times usually are short. In addition, materials moving and handling is reduced greatly as a result of locating machines close together. From a cost management perspective, production costs are associated more easily with products and product families because many costs can be traced directly to cells and then to products manufactured within the cells.

SELF-STUDY PROBLEM 3

1. Since bottlenecks produce at a slower rate than other machines in the plant, stacks of work in process inventory usually are piled up in front of the bottleneck to await processing. Other clues include a machine or work center that constantly is active. In other words, bottleneck resources do not have slack time because they are attempting to catch up with faster processes that continue to add work to their "to do" list.

2. An hour of lost time on a bottleneck resource translates into an hour of lost production for the entire plant. In Self-Study Problem 2, the throughput rate of the plant was found to be approximately 9 units per hour. Therefore, an hour of lost time on the bottleneck resource results in a loss of 9 units.

3. An hour of lost time on a nonbottleneck resource may have no impact on throughput. Since the rate of flow through the plant is determined by the processing speed of the bottleneck, other machines have faster processing speeds and can "make up for lost time."

4. Inspection points can be placed in front of the bottleneck, so that valuable time is not spent processing defective units. Also, workers can be asked to cooperate with respect to lunch and break periods, to permit constant operation of the bottleneck resource. Setup times can be reduced by either devising ways to perform setups faster or developing part or all of the setup "off-line" while the machine is engaged in production. This technique is referred to as converting on-line setup time to off-line setup time.

EXERCISES

8-1. Write a short definition of each of the terms listed in the *Terms and Concepts Defined in This Chapter* section.

Obj. 1   **8-2.**   NCCB produces pool tables and billiard supplies. The company is considering changes in the billiard ball production process that would reduce operating costs but would not affect any physical aspects of the product. It also is considering an expansion of operations whereby it would begin manufacturing pinball machines, a product it has not produced in the past. Which of these plans represents an operating decision? Which represents a strategic decision? What is the difference between operating and strategic decision making?

Obj. 2   **8-3.**   The Madrid Manufacturing Company produces roller skates designed for use in indoor skating rinks. Over the past five years, Madrid has seen sales decline significantly. The company has not added any new products or changed manufacturing processes in the past 20 years. Some changes have been made in materials, but the basic product has not changed. The company produces standard roller skates with four polyurethane wheels and leather uppers. How could elements of TQM assist Madrid in improving performance and meeting customer needs?

Obj. 2   **8-4.**   Maxwell Tree Service provides tree feeding, trimming, and removal services. Tim Maxwell, the owner of the tree service, has noted that many repeated activities are performed. For example, to remove a tree, workers cut the tree into pieces and load it onto a truck, using tractors, cranes, and heavy equipment. The wood is brought to a dump location, where it is unloaded and cut into smaller pieces. How could Tim simplify operations and eliminate activities by using TQM philosophies? Explain your answer.

Obj. 2   **8-5.**   Quick Drain Plumbing has six full-time plumbers who perform residential and commercial plumbing services. Based on a review of service records over the last several months, it was noted that, on average, plumbers must return to the shop to obtain parts or equipment on one out of every three service calls. How could TQM philosophies improve the performance of the plumbers? Explain your answer.

Obj. 3   **8-6.**   Nina Patel is the production manager at Donahue Enterprises. Nina is implementing a new pull system in the manufacturing process in an effort to reduce inventory. How does a pull system work? How does such a system differ from traditional push systems?

Obj. 3   **8-7.**   Many manufacturing companies experience inventory losses. These losses often result from excess inventory that must be handled, stored, and accounted for, and that in the process risks being damaged, lost, or becoming obsolete. Explain a key cause of excess inventory in an organization.

Obj. 3   **8-8.**   Sara Collins is the purchasing manager for Southwest Manufacturing. Sara has been able to obtain low-cost raw materials through competitive bidding and volume discounts. Southwest is planning to implement a just-in-time manufacturing system. What changes should Sara expect in the purchasing area with the implementation of this system?

Obj. 3   **8-9.**   Implementation of a just-in-time manufacturing system results in no buildup of inventory at any stage of the production process. It is easy to see how this concept would affect the amount of inventory on the plant floor, but how would just-in-time affect the amount of raw materials inventory?

Obj. 3   **8-10.** Dexter Pharmaceuticals manufactures a variety of over-the-counter pain relievers. Each employee in the production area of Dexter has been trained on a single piece of equipment, which they operate during eight-hour shifts. How would implementation of a JIT philosophy at Dexter affect the workforce?

Obj. 3   **8-11.** In a JIT environment, who is responsible for maintaining quality control of raw materials and work in process? Explain your answer.

Obj. 3   **8-12.** Mitchell Gabriel is the plant manager for the Carry-All Company. Carry-All produces a soft shell book bag/attaché that is popular with students and young business professionals. During production, the bag passes through a number of steps, such as cutting, sewing, assembly, and finishing. Mitchell wants to increase the number of products being packaged for shipment each day. What advice would you give Mitchell to help increase production output?

Obj. 3   **8-13.** Leeza Vicaro is a divisional manager for Liddon Industries. Leeza is responsible for the production at three of Liddon's plants. Production at plant 1 provides components to plant 2, which in turn provides components to plant 3. In the second and third plants, component parts from the previous plant are added to raw materials during the production process. Leeza is considering the implementation of JIT manufacturing at all three plants. What are some drawbacks of adopting the JIT system that Leeza should consider?

Objs. 2,3 **8-14.** Tom Mast is a lathe operator for a company that manufactures precision metal products. The lathe is the first step in the manufacturing process. Jobs begin at the lathe based on customer orders that call for specific numbers of pieces to be shipped. When an order is started, Tom generates the number of pieces ordered, plus a 10% cushion. According to Tom, "This over-run is necessary to allow for errors and scrap in subsequent manufacturing steps." Since production begins based on customer demand, is the company using a JIT system? How could principles of TQM and JIT help the company?

Objs. 2,3 **8-15.** Brayton Manufacturing has been utilizing JIT concepts in its single manufacturing plant for the past year. One of the key elements in Brayton's production process is the ability of any worker to completely stop the entire production line if he or she detects quality problems. Why is it essential for employees to have such control in a TQM production environment? Explain your answer.

Obj. 4   **8-16.** Excalibur Products manufactures many different styles and types of sink faucets. Many different products flow through processes organized by departments. Management estimates that before the average faucet is completed, the component parts are moved, stored, and handled by at least 18 different individuals as the parts move from one department to the next. How could Excalibur improve its production process by improving plant layout?

Obj. 4   **8-17.** Alverez Manufacturing produces five different types of battery-operated hand tools. There are four production departments at Alverez, each of which performs similar functions on the various products. A great amount of time is spent in each department changing tools and setting up machinery to work on the different products. How could a product-oriented plant layout assist Alverez in reducing cost and improving production? Explain your answer.

Obj. 4   **8-18.** Traditionally, companies have designed their plant floors so that similar machines are grouped together. Such a functional layout results in all drill presses in one place, all lathes in one place, and so forth. How does the traditional plant layout add cost to the manufacturing environment? How would this layout change with the implementation of a product-oriented manufacturing system? Explain your answer.

Objs. 3,4 **8-19.** A large manufacturing company rearranged its plant layout and organized its products into individual flow lines. The company determined that this change reduced the distance one product traveled in the plant from 2 miles to 150 feet. This change also increased throughput by 33%. What is throughput, and why would a change in plant layout have such a dramatic effect on it? Explain your answer.

Objs. 2,5 **8-20.** Why is a commitment to continuous improvement necessary for the successful implementation of a total quality production process? Is the commitment to continuous improvement isolated to the manufacturing process? Explain your answer.

PROBLEMS

PROBLEM 8-1   JIT: Supplier Relationships

Obj. 3

Sung Yu Chen is a purchasing manager for Hilbert Construction, a builder of custom homes. Hilbert is implementing JIT philosophies and has informed Sung Yu that new purchasing procedures need to be developed. For the past 10 years, to obtain the lowest possible cost on building materials, Hilbert has requested quotes from many different suppliers.

Building materials usually are stored in the company's stock yard, where employees select the materials needed for the day, load the materials, and take them to the job site. Materials received in the stock yard are inspected by the shop foreman. Sometimes the inspection occurs days after receipt. After inspection, poor-quality materials are separated and returned to the supplier.

Under the new plan, the stock yard would be eliminated, and suppliers would deliver materials directly to job sites. The delivery of materials must be made as construction progresses, with no buildup or excess inventory held at any site.

Required

a. What changes in supplier relationships will result from the implementation of JIT philosophies?
b. How will the implementation of JIT affect internal and external communications?
c. Under the new plan, how would the inspection process change?

PROBLEM 8-2   Measuring Cycle Time and Throughput

Obj. 3

Wabash Products, Inc., manufactures a dust-free computer enclosure that is designed to be used on plant floors and in other harsh environments. The steps required to manufacture the all-steel enclosure and the amount of time each step takes on a per unit basis are as follows:

Department	Processing Time per Unit
Forming	6 minutes
Milling	12 minutes
Grinding	10 minutes
Assembly	35 minutes
Finishing	22 minutes

Required

a. Calculate the minimum cycle time for a completed enclosure.
b. Assume that the company has a total of 385 minutes per day available in each department. Calculate the total daily throughput of completed enclosures.
c. Assume that the company currently is incurring total manufacturing lead time of 124 minutes per enclosure. Calculate the total process time and total wait time for an enclosure. What does the wait time reveal about the manufacturing process?
d. Which of the departments represents a manufacturing bottleneck? If all departments are operating at maximum output, what effect does the bottleneck have on inventory levels and unit output? Explain your answer.

PROBLEM 8-3   JIT, Ethical Considerations

Objs. 2, 3

McMahon Food Services is a provider of vending machine meals, snacks, and sandwiches. The company operates under a JIT philosophy. Each morning, food is received at the company's commissary, where meals are prepared and packaged. Company route drivers load trucks and deliver the food to vending machines throughout a large metropolitan area.

On a daily basis, the company relies on suppliers providing fresh food materials that are free of contamination, mold, and foreign objects. The only materials that McMahon stockpiles are cases of soda, which are purchased on a weekly basis and are stored in the company's warehouse.

Management at McMahon has received a notice from a food supplier indicating that a delivery of coffee may have been contaminated with a nontoxic cleaning solution used in the supplier's packaging machine. The notice indicated that the cleaning solution posed no risk to health, but would cause a significant foul taste in the coffee.

Managers at McMahon do not wish to recall the coffee from vending machines. They believe that the cost of retrieving the coffee is not warranted, since there is no foreseeable health risk involved. In support of this position, they also note that federal law allows food to contain small traces of foreign substances, provided there is no risk to consumers.

Required

a. What does the coffee contamination suggest about supplier responsibilities and a company's selection of supply sources under a TQM system?

b. In measuring the quality of the product, what ethical considerations should McMahon consider?

c. Comment on the measurement of quality in this situation. Who measures the quality and what implications do those measurements have for McMahon?

PROBLEM 8-4   Plant Layout and Work in Process

Objs. 3,4

Brown and Pickens manufacture a variety of battery-operated hand tools, including a cordless screwdriver, drill, and hand saw. The company produces these items in a plant organized in a process-oriented layout in two separate buildings. Batteries are outsourced to a dependable, high-quality supplier who makes deliveries to Brown and Pickens on a daily basis.

The main components of the tools are a motor, gears, and a casing. The company winds motors in one area of the plant, using coil-winding machines. The casings are manufactured in another area of the plant, using an injection molding machine. The gears are milled in the machine shop, using computer-controlled milling machines. All of the component parts are moved to the assembly area, where they are combined to form a finished product. Setup time on these machines is significant. To change any of these machines from one product to another takes over an hour.

The manufactured motors are moved to the assembly area by forklift every other day. The casings are produced in large batches and stored in a warehouse adjacent to the assembly area. The gears are manufactured in a separate building, across the street, and are held in that building until needed by assembly. The assembly area maintains just enough gears to meet production needs for a single day. Gears are delivered to the assembly department in small batches as needed to keep production flowing.

Required

a. How would having a manufacturing cell for each of the products differ from the current plant layout? What changes would this create in the product flow? How would work in process inventory be affected?

b. How could changes in the plant layout improve material handling and storage practices at Brown and Pickens? What effect would a change in plant layout have on the value of work in process? Explain your answer.

c. The gears are delivered in small batches just as needed by production. Would you consider this proper use of JIT? Why or why not?

PROBLEM 8-5   Push vs. Pull Inventory Systems

Objs. 2,3,4

Lamar Manufacturing produces radio alarm clocks. The company offers three clock models with various features. Each clock is assembled in a single plant that is laid out in a functional format. Each worker has been highly trained to perform a particular function in the manufacturing process.

In department 1, circuit boards are combined with electrical components and attached to a "base." When a batch is completed, the base units are forwarded to department 3, where they are shelved in work in process bins until needed.

In department 2, speakers are attached to the radio cabinet, and buttons and knobs are attached. Each batch of cabinets is then forwarded to department 3, where the units are also stored until needed in production.

Department 3 is the finishing department. In this area, the radio cabinets are attached to the base unit and the clock is packaged. The work in process area of department 3 is always full. If a completed batch from an earlier department is found to be defective, department 3 workers will automatically stop work on that particular model and work on another while the error is corrected.

Completed units are stored in the company's finished goods warehouse. On average, clocks are stored in the warehouse for 45 days before shipment.

Required

a.   Is the company operating a push or a pull system of inventory management? Explain your answer.
b.   What changes would be necessary to adapt the plant layout to a product-oriented facility? What benefits would the company realize from such changes?
c.   Assume that the company implements total quality management by arranging the plant into a product-oriented facility and is successful in reducing work in process and finished goods inventories. What further actions should the company take to achieve total quality?

PROBLEM 8-6   Performance Evaluation, Constraints

Obj. 5

The Corsair Window Company manufacturers custom-insulated windows and screens for residential and commercial uses. Each window is manufactured to specific building measurements. Corsair utilizes a JIT approach to manufacturing, and plans each production run so that it can be shipped as soon as it is completed. Shipping dates are very important to Corsair, as most sales contracts contain a monetary penalty for late delivery.

All windows pass through a finishing station. At this station, hardware is installed, screens are attached, and an inspection is performed to ensure that the windows meet specifications. The company has only one finishing station in its plant. Managers have long talked about adding a second station, but the amount of processing time at this station is so small in relation to other steps in the production process that they have determined that a second station is not warranted. On average, a window is in the finishing station for 15 minutes, which is the least amount of time a window spends in any single process.

Recently, a large shipment of windows was not delivered on time, and the company incurred a significant penalty. After review of the manufacturing logs for these windows, it was determined that the shipment was late because all 48 windows in the order were delivered to the finishing station on the afternoon the windows were to be shipped. In addition, several of the windows had to be returned to other stations in the plant for minor rework and adjustments.

Required

a.   How does the finishing station impose a constraint on production?
b.   How does the finishing station constraint affect the utilization of other work stations and the amount of work in process in the other areas of production?
c.   Should the inspection process be placed ahead of the finishing station? Where should the inspection process occur? Explain your answer.

PROBLEM 8-7   Continuous Improvements, Behavioral Implications

Objs. 2, 5

Franklin Berm & Company is a manufacturer of sporting goods. The company employs over 700 workers, who are organized under a labor union contract. Management at Franklin plans to implement total quality management and reorganize the company's operations into a product-oriented layout. The company's plans include the restructuring of production so that teams of 15 employees will work on specific product lines. The company wants to eliminate several layers of factory supervisors and place responsibility for production quality on the team leaders.

The company's plan will result in fewer job classifications by reducing the number of employee job descriptions and pay rates. The new job classifications will require broader employee knowledge and ability. In order for an employee to receive a raise under the plan, the employee will be required to learn additional skills and advance to a new job level. Compensation also will be tied to the quality of employee output.

Union leaders have reviewed the plan and are concerned that the restructuring is an attempt to eliminate jobs and limit employee pay. They argue that the plan will discriminate against slow learners and will require workers to dilute their technical skills by spreading their time among more activities. They are concerned that quality will not improve without new machinery and equipment, and that failure to achieve improved quality will be blamed on the workers.

Required

a. Why might labor constrain the successful implementation of quality-oriented programs?
b. What ethical obligations does management have toward workers implementing quality programs?
c. What role do employees have in implementing quality programs and continuous improvement?

PROBLEM 8-8   **TQM in a Service Environment**

Objs. 2,6

Olympic Insurance provides home and auto coverage to policyholders in six states. Olympic has agents in many cities, but has a central office in Atlanta, Georgia. This office issues policies and settles all claims.

If policyholders wish to file a claim, they contact their local agent. The agent gathers information, prepares a report on the damage, and submits the claim to the home office for processing. Managers at Olympic have determined that it takes three weeks from the filing of the agent's report to the issuance of a check. Many customers have complained about the three-week delay, and Olympic would like to speed up the processing time.

Managers have determined that the delay in issuing checks occurs in the accounting department. The average claim is held in the accounting department for more than one week before it is processed and a check prepared. Accounting personnel insist that weekly check runs are adequate to settle claims in a timely manner. The main reason for delays, they say, is incomplete files submitted by the claims processors that must be sent back to the processors for further work.

Required

a. How could Olympic utilize total quality management techniques to improve claims processing?
b. What does the information related to the accounting department suggest about processing time and product quality?

PROBLEM 8-9   **Multiple-Choice Overview of the Chapter**

1. A key concept of the JIT inventory system is to:
   a. utilize work in process as a cushion for production when material deliveries are late, or a department is unable to operate.
   b. purchase raw materials from many suppliers.
   c. keep large stocks of raw materials in order to maintain a high rate of productivity.
   d. keep inventories to minimum levels, or eliminate them entirely, through careful planning.

2. The flow of goods through a JIT system is based on:
   a. a department completing a batch of units as quickly as possible so that the units can be pushed to the next department.
   b. processing goods in large batches rather than less economical small batches.
   c. maintaining a stockpile of raw materials in anticipation of errors in production.
   d. meeting customer demand by pulling inventory through production, with no buildup of inventory at any point in the production process.

3. A successful JIT system is based upon which of the following concepts?
   a. A large number of suppliers ensures frequent deliveries of small lots.
   b. Suppliers offering the lowest prices should always be accepted.
   c. Long-term contracts with suppliers should be avoided.
   d. Suppliers make frequent deliveries, thus avoiding the buildup of material inventories on hand.

4. The plant layout under the JIT concept emphasizes:
   a. a functional approach, in which machines performing the same function are grouped together.
   b. a product approach, in which all machines needed in the production of a particular product are grouped together.

    c.   a facilities approach, in which all machines of a similar nature are located in one plant building.

    d.   a contractual approach, in which the processing of certain subassemblies is performed by a small number of independent machine shops under contract to the manufacturing company.

5. The term *throughput* means:
   a. the length of time required to turn materials into products.
   b. the total volume of production through a facility during a period.
   c. the time involved to prepare a machine for the production of a different item.
   d. production of goods without the accumulation of raw materials or work in process inventories.

6. A cluster of two or more related machines at a single workstation is referred to as:
   a. a manufacturing cell.
   b. an activity center.
   c. a functional layout.
   d. a bottleneck.

7. Which of the following statements regarding total quality management is *not* correct?
   a. Inspection of finished goods is performed by quality control inspectors.
   b. Total quality demands that suppliers provide prompt delivery of goods that are free of defects.
   c. Defective components can halt the entire manufacturing process.
   d. The inspection function for incoming goods is shifted from the company to its suppliers.

8. Cycle time refers to:
   a. the total amount of time to move a unit from raw materials inventory to finished goods.
   b. the number of units completed by a process in a given period of time.
   c. the number of minutes that pass between units completed.
   d. the amount of time needed to prepare a machine for its next operation.

9. Under a total quality management system:
   a. understanding customer needs is critical.
   b. once a popular product has been perfected, a company can be assured that customers will continue to buy it.
   c. the primary focus is on accumulating quality accounting information.
   d. always having a lot of inventory available is critical.

10. Under JIT, the plant floor:
   a. is laid out in a functional format, with similar types of machines grouped together.
   b. is laid out in a product-oriented flow.
   c. is laid out in a single line through which all products must pass.
   d. is usually cluttered with excessive work in process.

C A S E S

CASE 8-1   Just-In-Time Objectives

Obj. 3

Apex Technologies produces automotive filters that are used by original equipment manufacturers of automobiles and light trucks. The company also markets a line of replacement filters that are sold through retail distribution.

Apex operates a single plant that manufactures over 100 different filters. The first manufacturing department is metal fabrication. This department stamps out casings and housings that are needed by other departments later in the production process. The metal fabrication department has implemented a JIT system with respect to raw material purchases. No other departments at Apex have yet implemented a JIT system.

Juan Spanoza is the production manager of the metal fabrication department. Although work in process inventories have declined significantly since the implementation of JIT, Juan is frustrated at the amount of time that he now spends coordinating with suppliers and with other departments in order to meet production demands. With no buildup of inventory in his department, Juan must now tend to problems immediately, since failure to do so could halt the department's production.

Other managers at Apex have observed Juan's problems and are reluctant to implement JIT in their areas. The plant manager, Chris O'Connor, has scheduled a meeting to discuss further JIT implementation plans for the plant with department supervisors.

Required

a. What are the objectives of a JIT system that Chris should communicate to the department supervisors?
b. What are some actions that Apex could take to ease the transition to a JIT system?
c. In order to successfully implement the JIT system, what arrangements must the company make with vendors? How will these arrangements be formalized?

CASE 8-2 Reducing Process Time

Objs. 3, 5

Many companies have made shortening the cycle times of various processes their primary goal. Most of these companies have reviewed costs and eliminated as much product cost as feasible. Now the focus is on speed. The commitment to speed affects every phase of a company's business. Administration, sales, engineering, and production are all expected to complete tasks faster and more efficiently than ever before. Improved computer technologies have allowed companies to organize, synthesize, and analyze information, giving firms that can operate faster a competitive advantage. For a company to operate faster, every process it undertakes must be performed faster, but quality also must be improved.

Required

a. Explain how faster processes can be applied in areas such as engineering and administration. How can reduced process times in these areas help a company be more competitive?
b. Explain why improved quality is essential to a company that is able to work faster and reduce process times.
c. Teamwork is essential to any successful efforts to reduce process time and speed up processes. Do you agree? Why or why not?
d. What are potential problems that may arise from the increased speed of processes?

PROJECTS

PROJECT 8-1 Total Quality Management

Objs. 2, 6

Find a company in your area that has adopted JIT or other elements of total quality management. Discuss the benefits the company expects to receive with a representative of the company. Ask the representative to identify problems that came up during the implementation of quality programs. Identify the departments and personnel who were involved in the implementation. Ask the representative to address your class, or prepare a report from your discussions and present it to the class yourself.

PROJECT 8-2 Total Quality Management

Objs. 2, 6

Anti-lock brakes have made cars safer since they were introduced to the market in the late 1980s. Find a product that has changed its style or character and has become better or less expensive. Write a report that details the changes in the product and explain how its quality has increased.

PROJECT 8-3 Just-in-Time Manufacturing

Objs. 3,6

Select a company in an industry with which you are familiar or about which you can find substantial information. Write a narrative outlining a plan for successful implementation of JIT. Address changes that were needed in the areas of production, plant layout, and supplier relationships, and the potential behavioral impacts. Present a report of your plan to your class.

Controlling Decisions in Decentralized Organizations

9

Accounting and Management Decisions

Internal Control

Service Organizations

Cost Behavior

Capital Budgeting

Unit Costs

Decentralized Organizations

Cost Measurement

Global Environment

Cost Allocation

Performance Evaluation

Budgets

Overview

As organizations grow in size and scope, top-level managers cannot continue to make all of the necessary decisions. Thus, they must rely on help from lower-level managers. A company is highly centralized when all major decisions are made by a few owners or top-level managers. On the other hand, a company is decentralized when lower-level managers are responsible for many of a company's major decisions.

The value of a company depends on managers making decisions that are consistent with owners' interests. Stockholders must depend on top managers, and top managers must depend on lower-level managers, to make good decisions. The issue that we consider in this chapter is how incentives can be created to ensure that managers at all levels make proper decisions. Performance measurement systems are designed to encourage managers to make decisions that are consistent with owners' goals.

This chapter considers the organizational structure of decentralized companies. Then it describes various methods used to evaluate managerial performance within these organizations. In addition, problems associated with intracompany transactions are considered. When one division buys goods or services from another division within the same company, there must be policies for determining the appropriate price at which the purchase (or transfer) takes place. The price charged by the selling division and paid by the buying division is termed the transfer price. The transfer price affects the income of both divisions. Unfortunately, managers have incentives to make decisions that enhance their division's profitability, without regard to overall company prof-

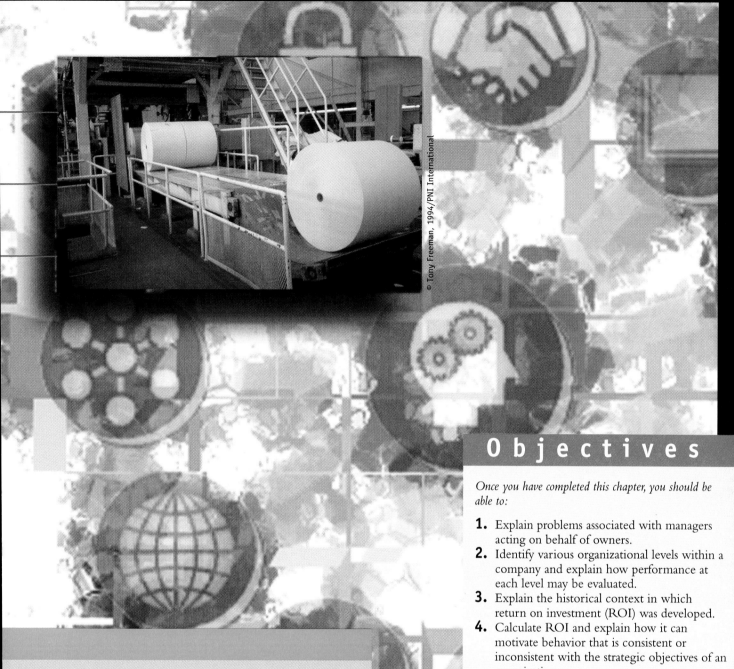

© Tony Freeman, 1994/PNI International

itability. This chapter considers the merits and problems of transfer pricing in multidivisional companies.

Major topics covered in this chapter include:
- How and why companies are decentralized
- Performance measurement using return on investment (ROI) and the balanced scorecard
- Transfer pricing

Objectives

Once you have completed this chapter, you should be able to:

1. Explain problems associated with managers acting on behalf of owners.
2. Identify various organizational levels within a company and explain how performance at each level may be evaluated.
3. Explain the historical context in which return on investment (ROI) was developed.
4. Calculate ROI and explain how it can motivate behavior that is consistent or inconsistent with the strategic objectives of an organization.
5. Discuss the four elements of the balanced scorecard approach to evaluating performance.
6. Explain how a manager who acts in the best interests of a division may harm the company as a whole.
7. Discuss various transfer pricing methods that have been developed to influence managerial behavior.
8. Explain how the performance of managers can be evaluated in decentralized service organizations.

THE AMERICAN PAPER COMPANY

This chapter uses American Paper Company to illustrate the concepts of responsibility centers, performance evaluation, and transfer pricing. American Paper is organized into two divisions, Pulp and Paper. Each division is responsible for producing and selling its products. Though most of the output from the Pulp Division is sold to external customers worldwide, some of it is sold to the Paper Division to be used as raw material.

As shown in Exhibit 1, pulp manufacturing begins with timber in the form of logs or wood chips. If raw materials are received in the form of logs, the first step in the process is debarking. A rotating debarking drum tumbles the logs to remove the bark. After the debarking, chippers cut the logs into one-inch cubes.

The second step in the process is "digesting." Wood chips are cooked to break down the gluelike material bonding the wood fibers. Chemicals used in the digestor are reclaimed and used in future pulp production. Following the digesting process, brown fibers, which are used in manufacturing so-called natural-colored coffee filters and paper towels, are washed and screened. A bleaching process may be used to convert natural-colored brown pulp into white pulp, which is used to manufacture products such as writing and printing paper. As a final step, the pulp mixture is dried, cut into sheets, and packaged for shipment.

The Paper Division of American Paper manufactures large rolls of paper. These rolls are sold to companies that convert the paper into writing, printing, and computer paper. As shown in Exhibit 2, the paper manufacturing process begins with the mixing of pulp with water and chemicals in the first stage of a paper machine. The mixture is spread out on a porous wire mesh; the actual formation of paper begins in this step. The wire mesh travels through a press that forces the pulp mixture against the wire to remove water from the mixture and make the paper the desired thickness. The material then proceeds to a drying section, where it travels across numerous cylindrical dryers that are heated with steam. In the final section of the paper machine, long sections of paper are rolled up into "parent rolls" and removed from the machine. The parent rolls are processed further by American Paper's customers to make various types of printing paper.

A paper plant requires a large amount of expensive production equipment—a new pulp mill can cost $750 million. In addition to the initial investment in equipment, these mills consume resources in the form of pulp, water, and chemicals. Some mills purchase electricity to power their operations, while others use heat produced by the chemical recovery process to generate electric power. The capital and organizational structures of a company, as well as its operating costs, are directly related to decisions managers face in a decentralized environment. The remainder of this chapter considers the related topics of responsibility accounting, performance measurement, and transfer pricing.

THEORETICAL FRAMEWORK FOR BEHAVIOR WITHIN ORGANIZATIONS

Objective 1
Explain problems associated with managers acting on behalf of owners.

This text emphasizes how managers use accounting information to make marketing and operations decisions. In most large companies, professional managers make these decisions, thereby acting as agents for the owners (shareholders). *Agents* **are hired by owners and are expected to manage the company in a way consistent with the owners' interests.** Thus, a major consideration when designing a performance evaluation system is to build incentives for managers to act according to the owners' wishes.

Economic theory assumes that the objective of a company is to maximize stockholder wealth. However, theory does not assume that managers will always behave in a way consistent with this objective. Thus, compensation packages often are constructed to give the managers incentives to maximize company value. For example,

Exhibit 1 The Pulp Manufacturing Process

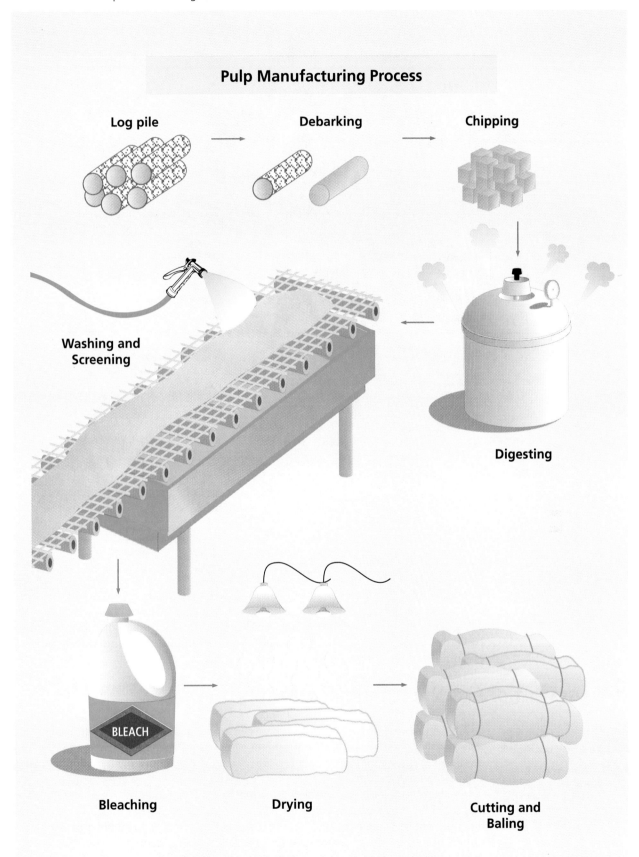

Exhibit 2   The Paper Manufacturing Process

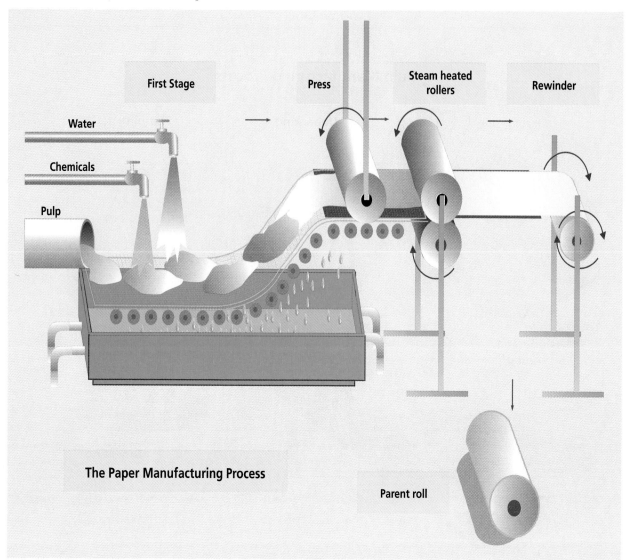

The Paper Manufacturing Process

compensation arrangements often include bonuses when certain income targets are met. In a decentralized organization, divisional managers have authority to make many types of decisions, but are held accountable for the results of their decisions. Next, this chapter addresses various types of responsibility areas within decentralized organizations, and how managers of these areas may be evaluated.

MANAGEMENT OF DECENTRALIZED ORGANIZATIONS

O b j e c t i v e   2
Identify various organizational levels within a company and explain how performance at each level may be evaluated.

Exhibit 3 presents the organization chart of American Paper. Each division manager reports to a corporate-level vice president. Operations managers, who report to the division managers, are responsible for supervising the activities of the manufacturing and marketing functions.

Managers typically are evaluated on the basis of variables over which they have control. Thus, managers at different levels within an organization are evaluated by different criteria. For example, some managers can control costs, but not revenues. Other managers may be responsible for controlling costs, earning revenues, and making decisions about acquiring additional plant assets. Thus, divisions within an organization often are categorized according to the types of responsibilities placed on managers. For example, the organizational structure of American Paper consists of four levels or types of responsibility centers:

- Cost centers
- Revenue centers
- Profit centers
- Investment centers

Exhibit 3   American Paper Company—Organizational Chart

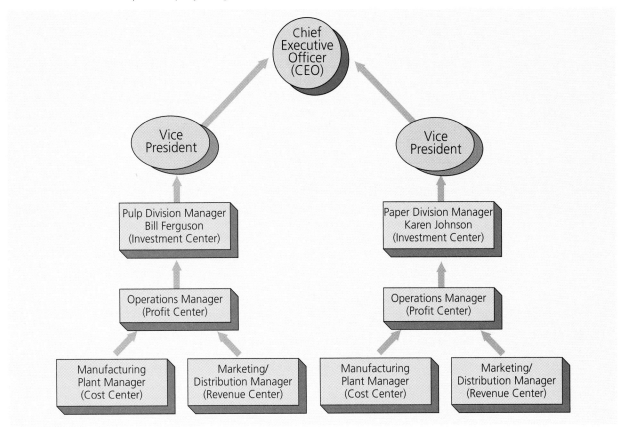

A *cost center* **is a division of an organization that consumes resources while performing its responsibilities, yet has no direct involvement in generating sales or acquiring property.** Thus, managers of cost centers are evaluated on their ability to control costs. For example, manufacturing plant managers can influence materials, labor, and overhead costs, but they cannot set selling prices for products, manage marketing campaigns, or acquire equipment without approval from divisional or corporate-level management. Thus, to evaluate the performance of a manufacturing plant manager on profitability would not be consistent with the objective of evaluating managers on activities over which they have control. Additionally, cost center managers often are evaluated on their ability to meet quality standards and delivery schedules. The two manufacturing plants identified in Exhibit 3 are examples of cost centers.

A *revenue center* **is a division of an organization that has responsibility for generating sales.** Thus, managers of revenue centers often are responsible for meeting sales quotas and managing distribution channels. However, these managers do not control most of the costs that affect net income. Therefore, revenue center managers should be evaluated using sales, rather than income, as a performance criterion. In addition, revenue center managers may be responsible for managing inventory and may be evaluated using inventory measures. The Marketing and Distribution functions shown in Exhibit 3 are examples of revenue centers.

A *profit center* **is a division of an organization that is responsible for both generating sales and controlling costs and expenses.** Profit center managers typically have the responsibility for setting prices for products, determining product mix, and monitoring production activities. Thus, profit center managers are responsible for costs, sales volume, and profitability. As shown in Exhibit 3, American Paper has two operations managers whose departments function as profit centers. Since profitability is determined by the difference between sales revenue and costs, operations managers who are evaluated on profitability must have control over both variables.

An *investment center* **is a level within an organization that has the strategic responsibility for generating profits and managing assets.** In the American Paper example, division managers are considered investment center managers. Typically, performance measures such as return on assets (ROA) or a similar measure, return on investment (ROI), are used to evaluate investment center managers because they have control over (a) costs, (b) revenues, and (c) assets. Investment center managers are evaluated using these measures because profit, or operating income, tells only part of the story about their effectiveness as managers. Typically, measures such as ROI or ROA are appropriate only if managers can determine the level of assets used by their area of responsibility. In this example, division managers can acquire and dispose of equipment. Thus, it is appropriate to evaluate division managers using ROA or ROI as a performance criterion. In addition, investment center managers are responsible for the strategic direction of the company. Thus, they are responsible for improving market share and successfully introducing new products.

Exhibit 4 summarizes responsibility centers often found within decentralized organizations and gives examples of relevant performance measures.

Exhibit 4 Performance Measures by Type of Responsibility Center

Performance Measures	
Cost centers	Manufacturing cost (materials, labor, overhead) Quality (defect rate) Percentage of on-time deliveries
Revenue centers	Sales volume in units Inventory turnover Sales revenue
Profit centers	Manufacturing costs Distribution costs Sales volume Profitability
Investment centers	ROI Market share Successful new product introductions

Benefits of Decentralization

A decentralized organization permits local managers, such as bank branch managers who are located far from corporate offices, to make certain decisions without approval from a central administrator. Localized decision making has many benefits for an organization. For example, local managers should be in touch with the economy and business conditions in their geographical areas; therefore, they often are in a better position to make informed judgments than their supervisors, who may be located hundreds of miles away.

The decentralized structure offers other benefits, as well. Lower and middle managers are given the opportunity to develop and exercise their skills in preparation for greater responsibilities. Thus, a decentralized structure provides a training ground for future top-level managers. In addition, lower and middle managers' job satisfaction should be enhanced because they are allowed to have control over their areas of responsibility and should experience pride of ownership.

C A S E

In   Point

http://www.swcollege. com/ingram.html

Learn more about PeopleSoft, Inc.

Decentralization can work well for companies that establish international branch offices. Often, branch managers are responsible for the success of their newly established branches. **PeopleSoft, Inc.,** provides an example of how one decentralized software company successfully established international branch offices by helping local managers develop business plans and then permitting them to implement their plans.

PeopleSoft, Inc., is a decentralized software maker with annual sales of $113 million. The company began its international expansion by setting up offices to assist existing clients that had foreign operations. When establishing a new business in a foreign country, PeopleSoft begins by identifying local managers and working with these managers to establish a business plan. After a short time, each new unit is basically left to develop its own accounting, sales, training, and support functions. Corporate-level reviews of individual operations take place on a quarterly basis. The company believes that this "hands off" policy allows local managers to customize their services and respond more quickly to changes in the local business environment.

Source: For more information see Toll, Eric E. 1995. Hands Off, **World Trade** *(Vol. 8, Issue 4): 66–70.*

SELF-STUDY PROBLEM 1

Assume that you are the plant manager for a medium-sized company that manufactures a variety of types of telephones. The phones are produced by assembling an array of components, including electronic circuit boards that are purchased from another division within the company. Every Friday morning, your corporate headquarters faxes you a production schedule indicating the type and amount of products to be produced during the following week. Thus, a major aspect of your job is meeting production schedules as efficiently as possible. Selling prices are set by senior-level management.

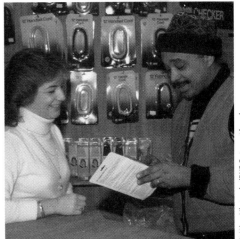

The following income statement and supporting schedule reflect sales, product costs, and expenses for your plant during the last twelve months. As you prepare for your annual performance evaluation, you recall a conversation from last year in which upper management set a net income target for products manufactured in your plant. However, you believe that certain costs on the income statement are beyond your control. Also, you wonder why net income is used to evaluate your performance at the plant level.

Required

1. In preparation for your meeting, identify the costs over which you have control.
2. Should your plant be evaluated as a cost center, revenue center, profit center, or investment center? Explain.

Income Statement

Sales	$100,000,000	
Cost of goods sold	75,000,000	
Gross margin		$25,000,000
Selling and administrative expenses:		
Depreciation on corporate aircraft	1,000,000	
Sales commissions and other sales expenses	10,000,000	
Other direct plant-related expenses	13,000,000	
Total expenses		24,000,000
Net income		$ 1,000,000

Cost of Goods Sold Schedule

Beginning finished goods inventory	$ 5,000,000
Cost of goods manufactured	77,000,000*
Total	82,000,000
Ending finished goods inventory	(7,000,000)
Cost of goods sold	$75,000,000

* *Cost of goods manufactured includes materials, labor, and overhead costs. Overhead includes allocated corporate-level costs, such as quality assurance and computer time used for production scheduling.*

The solution to Self-Study Problem 1 appears at the end of the chapter.

PERFORMANCE EVALUATION USING ROI

Objective 3
Explain the historical context in which return on investment (ROI) was developed.

http://www.swcollege.com/ingram.html

Find out about the DuPont Company today.

Recall that return on assets (ROA) is a ratio used to understand financial performance. This chapter considers a similar measure, return on investment (ROI), commonly used by internal managers to evaluate performance. The measures are used for different purposes. In this section, ROI is calculated and divided into its two components. In addition, the strengths of using ROI as a performance indicator to motivate managers are evaluated, and some criticisms of using ROI as the sole measurement of performance are considered.

Johnson and Kaplan[1] trace the roots of return on investment (ROI) to the **Du Pont Powder Company.** Three cousins purchased the assets of **E.I. du Pont de Nemours and Company** in exchange for corporate bonds and created the Du Pont Powder Company in 1903. The bond interest rate was based on the earnings of the old company. The new owners had to use the company's resources wisely in order to generate sufficient earnings to pay the bond interest and produce a profit. The cousins developed ROI for the purpose of assessing the performance of various departments and for making resource allocation decisions. They could not afford to invest assets in projects that earned less than the interest rate they were paying on the bonds issued to acquire their assets.

Of what benefit is ROI? Why don't managers simply compare the net incomes from their various operations to determine which is the most and least profitable? Net income tells only part of the story; other factors also must be considered. For example, assume that you are a senior manager in a corporation that has two divisions. Both division managers report directly to you. During the past year, both managers reported $500,000 in net income. Do you evaluate them equally? How would

---

[1] Johnson, H. Thomas, and Robert S. Kaplan. 1991. Relevance Lost *(Boston: Harvard Business School Press).*

your answer change if you assume that one division employed assets of $2,500,000, while the other division employed assets of $5,000,000? A different picture now emerges; the smaller division (in terms of assets employed) produced the same net income as the larger division. This suggests that the smaller division is managed more efficiently than the larger division.

Recall that ROA can be divided into two components, profit margin and asset turnover. Profit margin is determined by dividing net income (adjusted for interest expense) by operating revenues (sales). Asset turnover is computed by dividing operating revenues (sales) by average total assets. From an external perspective, such analysis provides useful information about a company as a whole. For example, we can determine whether a company uses a high margin, low turnover strategy, in which the profit on each sale is high and the amount of sales compared to assets is low (as is the case with a phone company like **Southwestern Bell**), or a low margin, high turnover strategy, in which the profit on each sale is low and the amount of sales compared to assets is high (as is the case with a discount store like **Wal-Mart**). *Return on Investment (ROI)* **is calculated by dividing operating income by operating assets.** Like ROA, **ROI** can be divided into two components, *margin* and *turnover.* As illustrated in Exhibit 5, *margin* **for ROI is operating income expressed as a percentage of sales.** For example, a 6% margin suggests that 6 cents of operating income are earned for every dollar of sales. *Turnover* **for ROI is sales divided by average operating assets employed.** A turnover value of 1.07 indicates that $1.07 of sales were generated for each dollar of operating assets used. Thus, as shown in Exhibit 5, ROI for the Pulp Division is margin times turnover ($0.064 = 0.06 \times 1.07$).

Objective 4
Calculate ROI and explain how it can motivate behavior that is consistent or inconsistent with the strategic objectives of an organization.

Managers typically use *operating income* as the numerator of the margin calculation and *average operating assets* as the denominator of the turnover calculation. Operating income, rather than net income, is used because operating income is not affected by nonoperating revenues and expenses (such as interest and taxes). **Recall that** *operating income* **is Sales − (cost of goods sold + other operating expenses).** *Operating assets* **are those assets controlled by the division; they include investments in cash, accounts receivable, inventory, and plant assets used in production.** Excluded from operating assets are assets such as land held for investment or long-term investments in marketable equity securities. While ROI and ROA are similar in their approach to measuring margin and turnover, ROI uses assets, revenues, and expenses that are more directly related to the daily operations of an investment center.

In the following paragraphs, information about American Paper Company is used to illustrate the calculation of margin, turnover, and ROI. In addition, the types of decisions managers make to improve ROI for their areas of responsibility are considered. From the organization chart, note that the managers of the Pulp and Paper Divisions are Bill Ferguson and Karen Johnson, respectively. These division managers compete with each other; their salary levels, bonuses, and opportunities for promotion are related to their performance. Exhibit 5 presents information that permits us to evaluate the performance of each division using ROI.

Discussion of Results

The Pulp Division has a higher *ROI* than the Paper Division. An ROI of 0.064 means that for every dollar of assets, the Pulp Division earns almost six and a half cents. In contrast, the Paper Division earns only five and a half cents from every dollar of assets. How could Karen Johnson, manager of the Paper Division (who is embarrassed by her performance relative to the Pulp Division), improve her division's margin, turnover, and ROI?

Margin. To improve an investment center's margin, a manager must increase the size of operating income relative to sales. In other words, Johnson needs to earn more operating income from each dollar of sales. Since operating income is determined

Exhibit 5   ROI Data and Calculations for the Pulp and Paper Divisions

	Pulp	Paper
Average operating assets	$750,000,000	$200,000,000
Sales	$800,000,000	$275,000,000
Cost of goods sold	$640,000,000	$206,000,000
Operating expenses	$112,000,000	$ 58,000,000
Operating income	$ 48,000,000	$ 11,000,000

Pulp Division

Margin	×	turnover	=	ROI
$\dfrac{\text{Operating income}}{\text{Sales}}$	×	$\dfrac{\text{sales}}{\text{average operating assets}}$	=	ROI
$\dfrac{\$48,000,000}{\$800,000,000}$	×	$\dfrac{\$800,000,000}{\$750,000,000}$	=	ROI
0.06	×	1.07	=	0.064

Paper Division

Margin	×	turnover	=	ROI
$\dfrac{\text{Operating income}}{\text{Sales}}$	×	$\dfrac{\text{sales}}{\text{average operating assets}}$	=	ROI
$\dfrac{\$11,000,000}{\$275,000,000}$	×	$\dfrac{\$275,000,000}{\$200,000,000}$	=	ROI
0.04	×	1.38	=	0.055

by subtracting cost of goods sold and operating expenses from sales, managers usually focus on cost control to improve the *margin* element of ROI. Of course, another alternative is to raise selling prices. However, managers typically are reluctant to raise prices because of competitive pressures. Margin may be expressed as follows:

$$\text{Margin} = \frac{\text{operating income}}{\text{sales}} = \frac{\text{sales} - (\text{cost of goods sold} + \text{operating expenses})}{\text{sales}}$$

Let's assume that Johnson decides to reduce costs in the next period to improve the division's margin. She predicts that she can achieve a cost savings of $2,750,000 by reducing production overhead costs (which become part of cost of goods sold) by $2,000,000 and reducing operating expenses by $750,000. Specifically, Johnson plans to change administrative procedures to eliminate costs associated with activities such as purchasing and payroll. She understands that if non-value-added work can be eliminated, the associated costs also will disappear. Most of the savings will be realized by reducing the size of support departments and eliminating unnecessary job classifications.

In addition, Johnson plans to realize savings from redesigning the product mix and manufacturing process. For example, analysts within the plant currently are examining the product mix to eliminate product types (termed "grades") that are manufactured in small batches, or that require special handling or expensive finishing operations. Exhibit 6 provides examples of the product and volume diversity within Johnson's plant. The process of changing the paper machine from the production of one grade to another results in scrap, and so Johnson expects to reduce the plant's scrap rate by making fewer grade changes. The number of grade changes can be reduced by eliminating products that are manufactured in small quantities. This should result in significant scrap reductions and cost savings. Eliminating some of the product line will not affect the plant's overall output. The remaining grades will simply be produced in larger quantities, which Johnson is confident will be sold. Additionally, she plans to redirect the quality control engineers' efforts to pulp inspection. If only top-quality raw materials are allowed into production, scrap rates and related costs should further decline.

Exhibit 6 Product and Volume Diversity within the Paper Plant

Before Product Mix Changes

Production Volume in Tons	.015	.0175	.02	.025	.0275	.03	**Total**
	100 Tons	80 Tons	90 Tons	30 Tons	10 Tons	5 Tons	315 Tons

After Product Mix Changes

Production Volume in Tons	.015	.0175	.02				**Total**
	120 Tons	100 Tons	95 Tons				315 Tons

As illustrated in Exhibit 5, the Paper Division's cost of goods sold and operating expenses are $206,000,000 and $58,000,000, respectively. Let's evaluate the Paper Division's margin under the proposed cost-cutting program as follows:

$$\text{Margin} = \frac{\text{operating income}}{\text{sales}} = \frac{\text{sales} - (\text{cost of goods sold} + \text{operating expenses})}{\text{sales}}$$

$$0.05 = \frac{\$13,750,000}{\$275,000,000} = \frac{\$275,000,000 - (\$206,000,000 - \$2,000,000 + \$58,000,000 - \$750,000)}{\$275,000,000}$$

$$= 0.05$$

This calculation indicates that the Paper Division's margin should improve from 0.04 to 0.05 after establishing the cost-cutting program. Therefore, if Johnson's predictions are correct, the cost-cutting program will improve the division's ROI from 0.055 to 0.069, as follows:

	Margin	×	**turnover**	=	**ROI**
Paper Division ROI before cost-cutting program	0.04	×	1.38	=	0.055
Paper Division ROI after cost-cutting program	0.05	×	1.38	=	0.069

In addition to cost-cutting strategies, managers also can improve ROI by effectively managing assets under their control. The next section addresses turnover decisions.

Turnover. Sales are divided by operating assets to calculate turnover. Because larger turnover values are preferred to smaller values, managers are motivated to keep asset levels low while maintaining or increasing sales levels. Let's use the information from Exhibit 5 to illustrate the concept of turnover and to consider the types of decisions managers may make in an attempt to improve turnover within their area of responsibility.

Assume that Johnson has identified assets in the form of inventory, accounts receivable, and equipment totaling $25,000,000 that can be eliminated. For example, she plans to aggressively pursue collections of accounts receivable. She plans to permanently reduce the level of accounts receivable and submit excess cash to the corporate offices. In addition, by reducing the level of raw materials, finished goods, and supplies inventory, Johnson can reduce the asset base of her plant. She may do this by employing just-in-time inventory techniques. Modifying the product line and manufacturing process may make certain types of equipment unnecessary. Thus, further decreases in the asset base will be possible. How would these reductions affect the Paper Division's turnover ratio? After removing $25,000,000 from the asset base, turnover is calculated as follows:

$$\text{Turnover} = \frac{\text{sales}}{\text{operating assets}} = \frac{\$275,000,000}{\$200,000,000 - \$25,000,000} = 1.57$$

This calculation indicates that eliminating $25,000,000 from the asset base improves turnover from 1.38 (before reducing the asset level) to 1.57 (after reducing the asset level).

How does improving the turnover ratio affect the Paper Division's ROI? First, let's look at the improvement in ROI attributable only to improved turnover. Then we calculate the predicted ROI if both margin and turnover ratio are improved.

$$\text{Margin} \times \text{Turnover} = \text{ROI}$$

Paper Division ROI—improved turnover only $0.04 \times 1.57 = 0.063$

If Johnson improved only turnover, without undertaking a cost-cutting campaign, her division's ROI would improve from 0.055 to 0.063.

However, by improving both margin and turnover, Johnson can report an ROI of 0.078, as follows:

$$\text{Margin} \times \text{Turnover} = \text{ROI}$$

Paper Division ROI—improved margin and turnover $0.05 \times 1.57 = 0.079$

This analysis shows that Johnson can improve ROI *in the short run* by increasing margin, turnover, or both margin and turnover simultaneously. In a competitive environment, managers make decisions to improve the measures that are used to evaluate their performance. Unfortunately, a focus on short-term performance may have disastrous long-term consequences.

Criticisms of Using ROI to Evaluate Performance

Earlier, this chapter discussed managers' roles as agents and the objective of selecting performance measures that align the interests of agents with those of owners. How can using ROI as a performance indicator achieve this objective? What does it communicate to managers? Using ROI instructs managers to earn the greatest net income possible, while minimizing assets employed. Thus, managers are motivated to increase the numerator and to reduce the denominator of the ROI calculation. The discussion of margin identified strategies to increase the income component (numerator) of the ROI calculation, while the discussion of turnover considered methods to reduce the average operating asset level (denominator) of the ROI calculation.

Some accountants argue that focusing on ROI promotes short-sighted decision making that can harm a company in the long run. The following discussion gives examples of decisions that improve ROI in the short run but may have negative long-term effects. The first set of examples involves decisions affecting the margin component of ROI. Since managers are encouraged to reduce operating costs and administrative expenses, they may be encouraged to sacrifice "investments" necessary for future growth. Such investments include research and development (R&D) expenses.

Generally accepted accounting principles (GAAP) require companies to expense R&D in the period incurred, even though most companies view R&D as an investment to benefit future periods. By cutting R&D expenses, managers may realize an immediate improvement in operating income. However, the long-term consequences of a reduced R&D budget may include less competitive products, which are likely to lead to lost market share and lower profitability.

Managers also may capture short-term savings by reducing maintenance expenditures for manufacturing equipment. Typically, maintenance costs, such as lubricants, spare parts, and salaries of maintenance crews, are treated as overhead cost items. Therefore, trimming maintenance costs may improve a division's operating income in the short run. However, a reduced maintenance program may result in very large equipment repair or replacement costs in the future.

Finally, since using ROI encourages reduced asset levels, some managers may be reluctant to make the investments in plant assets necessary to ensure superior quality and reliable product delivery. Therefore, while ROI has many positive attributes as a performance measure, if used improperly, it may encourage managers to make short-term decisions that negatively affect long-term performance.

Exhibit 7 summarizes some of the criticisms of using ROI as the only measure of performance.

How do managers design performance measurement systems that encourage behavior consistent with the long-term objectives of an organization? The next section considers an evaluation method that permits performance criteria to be linked to a company's strategy. Both financial and nonfinancial performance criteria are used in the approach termed the balanced scorecard.

THE BALANCED SCORECARD APPROACH

Objective 5
Discuss the four elements of the balanced scorecard approach to evaluating performance.

http://www.swcollege.com/ingram.html

Learn more about the balanced scorecard.

People use information continuously to evaluate their environment and to help them make appropriate decisions. For example, if you drove a car to class today, you probably monitored your speed, checked the rear-view and side-view mirrors to evaluate the position of other vehicles relative to yours, glanced at the gasoline gauge, and so forth. However, while the rear-view mirror is certainly an important piece of safety equipment, driving your car using only the rear-view mirror would produce disastrous results. People must view and react to many different types of performance measures at the same time.

Some accountants have argued that ignoring important nonfinancial performance measures while focusing exclusively on financial measures can spell disaster for organizations. Therefore, managers need a short list of key indicators that signal current as well as future performance. A "balanced scorecard"[2] approach has been used by some companies to bring together many different aspects of their corporate *strategy* in one report. **The** *balanced scorecard* **has key performance criteria in four categories: financial, customer satisfaction, innovation and learning, and internal business.** Thus, operating performance measures are developed that are consistent with an organization's strategic goals. In addition, the balanced score-

[2]   *For more information see Kaplan, R., and K. Norton. 1992. The Balanced Scorecard—Measures that Drive Performance. Harvard Business Review (January–February): 71–79.*
Kaplan, R., and K. Norton. 1993. Putting the Balanced Scorecard to Work. Harvard Business Review (September–October): 134–147.

Exhibit 7   Criticisms of Using ROI as the Only Measure of Performance

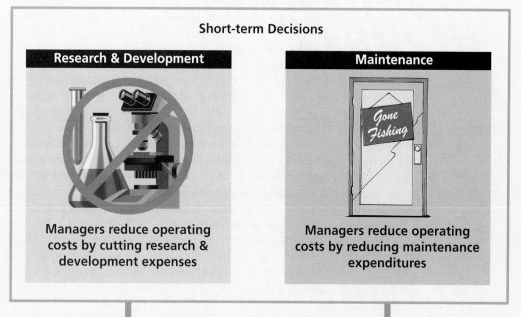

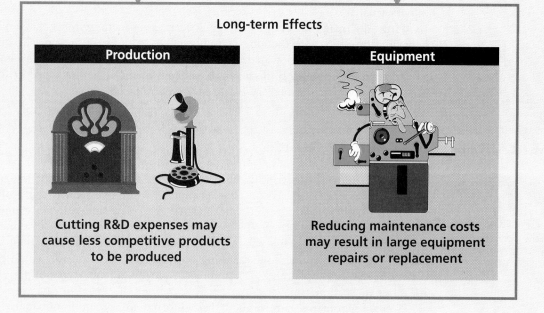

card prevents managers from improving only one aspect of performance while simultaneously allowing other important aspects of performance to decline.

The balanced scorecard approach to performance evaluation is based on linking a company's strategic goals with specific, concrete measures designed to motivate behavior consistent with factors that will help the organization achieve success in the long run. The approach views a financial measure, such as ROI, as an important indicator, but not the only measure at which managers must excel. Thus, the approach represents a broader, more balanced view of an organization's success in achieving its long-term strategic goals.

Financial performance measures motivate managers to consider how the company looks in the eyes of the shareholders. Typically, managers are evaluated using criteria such as profitability, ROI, market share, and cash flow. Thus, managers are encouraged to make decisions that increase revenues, contain costs, or both.

In line with the objectives of total quality management (TQM), the balanced scorecard contains a category of indicators that encourage managers to consider how their company looks in the eyes of customers. Customer satisfaction performance measures may include the percentage of on-time deliveries and customer response time for service or other assistance. When customer satisfaction is included as a key performance indicator, managers are encouraged to make decisions consistent with customers' needs.

The innovation and learning category asks how managers can continue to improve processes and products and to create value. Examples of measures are the rate of new product introduction and the percentage of sales from new products. The long-term focus of the innovation and learning performance measures links directly to a continuous-improvement philosophy. Thus, managers are encouraged to invest resources in ways that will result in new, innovative products for the long run.

Managers who are evaluated by internal business criteria ask themselves, "At what must we excel?" Once again, the link to customer satisfaction is made explicit. Managers are encouraged to improve processes internally to ensure customer satisfaction. Internal business indicators include measures that promote manufacturing excellence, such as cycle time, scrap rate, and lead time from placing an order until delivery. Managers are encouraged to improve internal processes that add value for customers. Once again, the balanced scorecard emphasizes long-term investments and continuous improvement, rather than short-term savings from cost reductions.

Exhibit 8 illustrates the relationships among the various components of the balanced scorecard, using the Paper Division of American Paper Company as an example.

Exhibit 8 Performance Measures Using the Balanced Scorecard Approach for the Paper Division of American Paper Company

Perspective	Actual	Desired
Financial		
ROI	0.055	0.08
Customer		
On-time deliveries	80%	85%
Response time to inquiries	2 days	3 hours
Innovation and Learning		
Percentage of sales from new products	8%	25%
Internal Business		
Cycle time	6 weeks	5 weeks
Scrap rate	5%	2%
Manufacturing lead time	10 hours	8 hours

Using American Paper Company as an example, how would Johnson's decision to restructure the division and reduce costs affect other important factors identified by a balanced scorecard approach? Certainly reducing the scrap rate (and presumably improving the quality of products delivered to customers) would be viewed favorably from the customer perspective. Additionally, reducing the number of different products would result in faster cycle and delivery times. However, her strategy to pursue collections of accounts receivable aggressively may have an adverse effect on customer relations (though in the short run cash flow would be improved).[3] Finally,

---

[3] *Customers who wish to purchase all of their paper from one supplier may be disappointed to learn that Johnson no longer produces a full line of products. These customers may take all of their business elsewhere.*

using ROI as a measure does not encourage Johnson to invest resources in seeking opportunities to develop new products. In a mature industry such as pulp and paper, innovation may result in long-term financial rewards.

This section has considered how to evaluate performance in decentralized organizations and how to motivate behavior to achieve long-term success. The next section examines how transfer pricing policies can affect decisions made by divisional managers. Often, financially based performance measures encourage managers to optimize divisional earnings, yet harm the overall organization. Thus, transfer pricing and performance measurement issues are of key importance to managers in decentralized organizations.

SELF-STUDY PROBLEM 2

Refer to the financial information presented in Self-Study Problem 1. In addition to the financial statement data, your records indicate that the division employed operating assets valued at $20,000,000.

Required

1. Calculate the division's operating profit margin and describe various ways a manager may improve his or her performance with respect to operating profit margin.
2. Calculate the division's turnover and describe various ways a manager may improve his or her performance with respect to turnover.
3. Calculate the division's ROI.
4. What are some of the criticisms of using ROI as the sole performance measure?
5. Identify other measures that may promote organizational success in the long run.

The solution to Self-Study Problem 2 appears at the end of the chapter.

TRANSFER PRICING

Objective 6
Explain how a manager who acts in the best interests of a division may harm the company as a whole.

Transfer pricing **involves setting appropriate selling prices for goods or services when both buyer and seller are within the same company.** Thus, transfer pricing decisions typically arise within multidivisional organizations. In a decentralized business, managers are free to make many decisions locally. Some of the decisions managers make relate to the acquisition of materials, labor, and overhead to be used in production. When a corporation has many divisions, situations often occur in which one division buys products from another division. Because internal transfer prices affect revenues (for the selling division) and costs (for the buying division), transfer pricing policies affect a division's ROI. Thus, divisional managers are very interested in the price at which goods are transferred internally.

The classical transfer pricing problem involves setting a transfer pricing policy that encourages managers to act in the best interests of the overall organization. Naturally, when *divisional* managers are evaluated by a measure such as ROI, they take actions that produce the highest possible *divisional* ROI. To maximize ROI, what options are available to a manager? Since ROI boils down to operating income ÷ operating assets, the manager has an incentive to increase income or reduce assets (or some combination of the two). For purposes of our discussion, let's focus on the management of operating income. If you are Bill Ferguson, manager of the Pulp Division, you wish to receive the highest possible price for pulp sold to the Paper Division. On the other hand, if you are Karen Johnson, manager of the Paper Division, you maximize ROI by paying the lowest possible price for raw materials (assuming quality is not affected adversely). As a result of divisional competition and performance evaluations exclusively based on ROI, the following scenario is unfolding within American Paper Company.

The Scenario

Karen Johnson, manager of the Paper Division, was unhappy with her division's performance in comparison to that of the Pulp Division (refer to Exhibit 5). Her division purchased all of its raw materials from the Pulp Division at a transfer price of $400 per ton. However, Karen wondered if she could outsource (buy pulp from an outside supplier) at a cost below that quoted by her sister division. Since the divisions were decentralized and had a *market-based* transfer pricing policy, she was free to purchase raw materials from any source. **A** *market-based transfer pricing policy* **requires buyers and sellers to transfer goods based on externally verifiable market prices.** Thus, bids from outside vendors often are used to establish a market price to serve as a basis for transferring goods.

Karen knew that market prices for pulp had been falling because of worldwide oversupply. Thus, she requested a bid from Southland Pulp Company to determine if the transfer price charged by her sister division was competitive. This morning, a bid of $350 per ton arrived by fax from Southland. The bid specified that to qualify for the reduced price of $350 per ton, the Paper Division must purchase one-half of its annual demand from Southland. Karen quickly made a few computations to determine the potential impact on her division's ROI.

She understood that her division's cost of goods sold ($206,000,000, as shown in Exhibit 5) represented pulp costs as well as other manufacturing costs incurred by her division to convert pulp into paper. She estimated that one-half of the cost of goods sold value, $103,000,000 ($206,000,000 ÷ 2 = $103,000,000), represented pulp costs. The remaining portion of the cost of goods sold value represented labor, electricity, water, chemicals, and overhead costs for depreciation and supervision. Thus, "If our annual pulp cost is $103,000,000 at an average of $400 per ton, we must have used 257,500 ($103,000,000 ÷ $400) tons last year," Karen reasoned. "Southland wants one-half of our volume, or 128,750 tons."

"Wow," Karen said under her breath. "Bill isn't going to like losing the sale of almost 130,000 tons, especially in this slow market."

Karen continued to work with the bid. "Let's see, what's the bottom-line savings if I agree to this deal? Okay, at a savings of $50 per ton ($400 from Bill versus $350 from Southland), that works out to be a total savings of $6,437,500 ($50 per ton × 128,750 tons to be purchased). What does that do for my ROI?" Karen said to herself as she continued to enter values into her calculator.

"Our operating income was $11,000,000, to which we can add an expected savings of $6,437,500. That results in an estimated operating income of $17,437,500. Now, if I divide by operating assets of $200,000,000, I have a predicted ROI of 0.087."

Karen reclined at her desk. The prospects for outsourcing one-half of her pulp requirements looked promising. Assuming that her sales and other expenses remained at a constant level, she could improve the division's ROI from 0.055 to 0.087, a whopping 60 percent improvement [0.60 = (0.087 − 0.055) ÷ .055]! Karen did not look forward to announcing her intentions to Bill Ferguson, manager of the Pulp Division.

Bill had been in a bad mood recently because of soft market conditions and a union contract that required a forty-hour work week for each of his three shifts.

Because of sluggish demand, each shift required only thirty hours per week in production time. The remaining ten hours were spent maintaining equipment and making general repairs. Therefore, Bill was watching sales volume fall, while most of the division's manufacturing costs continued unchanged. Karen was certain that her decision to outsource one-half of the Paper Division's pulp requirements would send shock waves throughout the corporation.

Karen was correct. Her company subscribed to a "hands-off" policy with regard to letting divisional managers make their own decisions. However, Karen contacted Deborah Truth, a vice president at the corporate office, and revealed her intention of acquiring one-half of her pulp requirements from an external supplier. Karen's phone rang, and Deborah was on the other end of the line, requesting a meeting with both divisional managers as soon as possible to discuss their transfer pricing problem.

A few days later, Karen made her way from the airport to the corporate offices. Because her flight had arrived before Bill's, she had a few minutes to review her notes before the meeting. Deborah was the next to enter the conference room, and finally Bill arrived. Following greetings and casual chatter, Deborah began the meeting by referring to the analysis Karen had faxed after receiving the bid from Southland.

"You must admit," Karen began, "a $50 savings per ton can have a dramatic effect on my division's profitability. That represents a 13% price reduction. Do you realize how difficult it would be to reduce operating costs by that amount and still maintain the same level of quality?"

Bill could hardly contain himself any longer. "Karen, let's talk about quality. The first time you ship a load of unbleached paper that contains strands of chlorinated fibers, there will be trouble." Bill was referring to "twilight pulp" that is temporarily produced between production runs of bleached and unbleached pulp. This "twilight" mixture is produced until the system cleans out all the chlorine from the pulp mill. Bill's mill has stringent quality control measures to prevent the shipment of mixed, or twilight, pulp.

Karen understood Bill's point. Customers who are environmentally sensitive will not tolerate bleached fibers mixed with environmentally friendly "unbleached" fibers. She certainly had no complaints about the quality she was receiving from Bill.

"And what about reliable delivery?" Bill continued. "In a continuous-process manufacturing environment, such as pulp and paper, you know very well what happens if production interruptions occur. You can't just turn your paper machines on and off like a saw. Remember the studies that show how scrap costs are associated with paper machine downtime? If you start messing around with your process and making late shipments yourself, you'll soon see that 13% cost savings evaporate into thin air."

Karen knew that Bill was right. A paper process is complex. Any production interruption introduces instabilities into the process, with undesirable consequences. However, Karen also knew that Bill was suggesting that Southland's quality was poor and their delivery times were unreliable. Admittedly, Karen had never had a problem with quality or on-time delivery from Bill's division.

Bill was on a roll, and he continued his assault against Southland. "Furthermore, I'll bet Southland will give you one contract at that price and later will raise their bid. I think they are bidding below market price so that they can get their foot in the door."

Objective 7
Discuss various transfer pricing methods that have been developed to influence managerial behavior.

Deborah considered all that had taken place. She knew why Bill was fighting to keep Karen's business. Since Bill had idle capacity (the division could produce more pulp than the market currently required), his production costs per unit were increasing. "Let's try to remember we are all on the same team here," Deborah began. "Bill has made some good points regarding quality, delivery reliability, and cost. We need to work together to make sure that American Paper Company doesn't suffer as a result of decisions that improve divisional performance." Deborah walked to the board at the head of the conference table and wrote the following outline:

Transfer Pricing Methods
A. Market-based
B. Cost-based
   Variable cost
   Fully absorbed
C. Negotiated

"What do you two remember from your college accounting course about different ways to set up transfer pricing policies?" Deborah asked.

"Not much," admitted Bill. "I memorized some formulas, but beyond that . . ."

"Then, let's reason through these methods and consider the pros and cons of each. Maybe we can find a mutually agreeable solution to our transfer pricing problems," continued Deborah.

"Market-based. That's our existing policy," volunteered Karen. "The market determines the value at which transfers take place. As a buyer, I'm in favor of a market-based approach because it keeps guys like Bill honest."

Karen continued, "I operate a division that sells paper to the outside market at competitive prices. If my costs are too high, I can't compete. Therefore, using a market-based policy throughout the company seems to be a control that forces our internal divisions to be competitive with those outside our company. I'll buy from Bill if he meets the external price. I'd like to keep the business within the company."

Bill walked to the board and scribbled the following numbers:

Variable cost per ton	$110
Fixed cost per ton	250
Total cost per ton	$360

"Karen," he said, "I recently completed a major capital expansion at my plant. As a result, I estimate that next year my cost structure will look like this. As you can see, if I sell at $350 a ton, I won't even cover my costs. My variable costs include items such as timber, chemicals, water, and electricity; however, the majority of my costs are fixed. These fixed costs include depreciation on my plant equipment and most labor costs. Unfortunately, those costs will be incurred whether the machines are making pulp or not."

Karen looked at the figures. She now understood why Bill was fighting so hard to convince her to reject the Southland bid. If Bill's production volume declined further, the cost of each ton would become larger because his fixed costs would be spread over fewer tons. To cover his higher unit costs, he would have to raise prices. However, raising prices would cause further declines in volume, which in turn would raise his unit costs—definitely not a happy scenario.

Deborah interjected, "Bill, you have moved the discussion to the topic of cost-based transfer pricing policies. Leave your numbers on the board. Some accountants advocate using a cost-based approach," she added. "However, two distinct versions of cost definition emerge, variable and fully absorbed. Variable-cost transfer prices include only variable manufacturing costs, while fully absorbed transfer prices include both variable and fixed manufacturing costs."

Karen spoke quickly, "As a buyer, I'd be in favor of a cost-based approach if cost is defined as variable cost."

Bill retorted, "Sure you would. Your profits would look great because you would leave me holding the bag for all the fixed costs of your raw materials production. I could not pass those along to you. How could you expect me to show a profit under those circumstances?"

Deborah intervened. "Most companies do not use a variable-cost transfer policy for that reason. The buyer's profitability is overstated, and the seller's profitability is understated."

Bill added, "What about using a full cost approach, one that includes both variable and fixed costs? Admittedly, I would not earn a profit, but at least I could recover my costs. Since sales to Karen represent only a portion of my total sales volume, a breakeven situation would not hurt my division's profitability too badly."

Karen squirmed in her seat. "Bill, remember our discussion about market-based policies. I really don't want to have my profitability affected by your decisions. If your costs increase, a full-cost transfer price permits you simply to pass them along to me. I find that unacceptable."

Deborah interjected, "Perhaps there is room for compromise. The third method for determining transfer prices is through negotiation. Perhaps we can put aside our divisional interests momentarily and look at the problem from the corporate point of view." Deborah returned to the board and wrote the following equation:

$$\text{Transfer price} = \text{variable cost} + \text{opportunity cost}$$

"Bill, is this the equation you memorized for your accounting class?" asked Deborah.

"I think so. Somehow it looks familiar," responded Bill.

"Karen, what is the most you would be willing to pay per ton?" Deborah asked.

"I can't see why I should pay more than Southland's bid of $350, all other things being equal," responded Karen.

Deborah wrote $350 on the board with the word Ceiling beside it. Next, she turned to Bill. "What is the lowest price you would be willing to accept?"

"Deborah, I've already told you. I need $400 per ton to cover my costs and make a decent profit," responded Bill.

"Let's step back a moment. What is American Paper Company's cost to make a ton of pulp?" asked Deborah.

"Look at the board. It's $360 per ton," responded Bill.

"But, what is our direct out-of-pocket cost?" continued Deborah.

"Are you talking about my variable cost of $110 per ton?" asked Bill.

"Exactly," said Deborah. "You have already told us that your fixed costs are incurred whether you make pulp or not. Thus, let's use your variable cost as a floor, below which you would never consider selling the product." Deborah completed the board, which now looked like this:

$$\text{Transfer price} = \text{variable cost} + \text{opportunity cost}$$

Ceiling	$350
Floor	$110

Deborah began the discussion. "Bill, if you could sell every ton you could produce at $400, would you be willing to negotiate with Karen for a lower price?"

"Of course not. Why should I? If I can sell everything I can make at $400 per ton, why should I take less?"

"Let's put your answer into our formula," responded Deborah. "In other words, your 'opportunity cost' of taking a ton off the market and selling it to Karen is the difference between the selling price of $400 and your variable costs of $110, as follows:"

```
Selling price                                    $400
Variable cost                                     110
Contribution margin (opportunity cost)           $290
```

"If we add your variable cost to the opportunity cost, our transfer price formula gives us a value of $400, or the original selling price."

```
Transfer price  =  variable cost +  opportunity cost
$400            =  110           +  290
```

"That makes sense," replied Bill. "Since I can sell all I can make at $400 per ton, the formula says that if Karen wants some of my tons, she will have to pay $400 for them. Otherwise, I'll sell them to other customers."

"Exactly," responded Deborah.

"But, Bill, aren't you forgetting something?" interjected Karen. "You have excess capacity—you can't sell everything you make. Thus, you are not forgoing profits by selling me a ton of product because you cannot sell that product to someone else. Your opportunity cost is *zero* when you have excess capacity. According to Deborah's model, if your opportunity cost is zero, the transfer price should be $110, your variable cost. When you have idle capacity, the opportunity cost becomes zero because external sales are not forgone."

Karen walked to the board and plugged new numbers into the equation as follows:

```
Transfer price  =  variable cost +  opportunity cost
$110            =  110           +  0
```

"Karen, you seem to be suggesting that I sell to you at variable cost. We already dismissed that plan when we discussed cost-based transfer policies."

Deborah once again broke into the conversation. "What do these calculations suggest? From a companywide viewpoint, what can we learn from our model?"

Bill spoke first. "Since I have excess capacity, the model says that the company is better off if I sell to Karen at a price that at least covers my variable costs. Since my fixed costs are incurred whether I produce or not, they are not relevant to the decision. From the company's perspective, the variable cost to produce pulp is $110; if we purchase it from Southland, the variable cost to the company is $350. Thus, the company would lose $240 per ton."

Karen responded, "So that's what the floor and ceiling represent. The floor represents the minimum acceptable transfer price to the seller, and the ceiling represents the maximum acceptable transfer price to the buyer."

"Exactly," said Deborah.

Bill spoke after a few moments of thought. "Deborah, you've certainly given us a lot to think about. But somehow, I can't help but believe that the problem is not with the transfer pricing policy, but rather with our performance evaluation policies.

Everything is tied to divisional profitability and ROI. Who knows how many times decisions are made that may affect corporate profitability in the long run, but in the short run make managers look good on paper."

Deborah agreed. "That sounds like a problem for another day. Think about what we discussed and let me know what you decide. I appreciate the time you took from your busy schedules to meet with me today. Have a safe flight home."

As Karen and Bill left the room, they both knew that corporate management would not permit them to optimize divisional performance at the expense of the overall organization. American Paper was decentralized; however, corporate management had sent a strong signal regarding the outsourcing decision. Both Karen and Bill knew that the transfers would take place internally; however, they had a great deal of work still to do to negotiate a transfer price acceptable to both of them.

Transfer Pricing Summary

Given the preceding exchanges, how can we summarize the key issues with regard to transfer pricing? The exclusive use of financially based performance measures such as ROI and profitability may encourage managers to make decisions that benefit their divisions, but at the same time harm the overall organization. The use of market-based transfer prices helps managers assess their efficiency with respect to external companies producing similar products. Market-based transfer pricing policies rely on external market prices for identical (or comparable) goods or services to establish transfer prices. Cost-based transfer prices are easy to calculate and apply; however, their use can cause problems because inefficiencies may be passed along to subsequent departments. *Cost-based transfer pricing policies* **use either full cost or variable cost as a basis for determining a transfer price.** *Negotiated transfer pricing policies* **permit managers to consider factors such as cost and external market prices when negotiating a mutually acceptable transfer price between two business units.**

Capacity issues should affect decisions concerning appropriate transfer prices. If a division has excess capacity, a transfer price between the variable cost of the selling division and the outside market price may be negotiated. Theoretically, if a company has excess capacity, it would be worse off if it purchased goods from an external supplier at a purchase price that exceeded the internal variable cost. Exhibit 9 summarizes the key points of each of the major transfer pricing methods.

Learning Note   When divisions sell goods exclusively to other divisions within a company, market-based and negotiated transfer pricing policies generally are not used. If a division does not sell to external customers, the division should be evaluated as a cost center, rather than as a profit center, and transfers should take place at standard costs. The division managers' performance would be based on their ability to control costs when compared to standards.

MANAGEMENT OF DECENTRALIZED SERVICE ORGANIZATIONS

Objective 8
Explain how the performance of managers can be evaluated in decentralized service organizations.

In this chapter, a manufacturing company was used to demonstrate issues facing decentralized organizations. However, managers of service organizations face many of the same issues. For example, banks often have branch offices in various locations. Rather than referring all loan applications to a centralized loan committee, branch managers are given authority to make certain types of lending decisions. Thus, a decentralized structure often permits faster processing of loan applications. In addition, local managers may better understand the risks associated with granting loans if they are familiar with the local economy.

Exhibit 9   Transfer Pricing Methods

Cost-based
   Strengths: Cost-based transfer pricing methods are easy to apply because standard (or actual) product costs generally are available from the accounting system.
   Weaknesses: Cost-based transfer pricing methods do not encourage and reward efficiency. Often, costs are transferred from one department to the next without concern for the price at which the final product will sell.

Market-based
   Strengths: Market-based transfer pricing methods force departmental managers to be as cost-efficient as the best competitor.
   Weaknesses: Market-based transfer pricing methods require time and effort because external bids must be acquired and evaluated.

Negotiated
   Strengths: Negotiated transfer pricing methods encourage dialogue among division managers. Such conversations may promote transfers internally when they are in the best interest of the overall company.
   Weaknesses: Negotiated transfer pricing methods take management time and can result in stronger negotiators acquiring better deals. Thus, performance may be affected by negotiating skills, rather than by a manager's ability to control costs.

Decentralized service organizations can be made up of cost centers, profit centers, revenue centers, and investment centers. For example, branch banks often are evaluated as profit centers. The performance of bank branch managers is evaluated using a number of criteria. For instance, they are responsible for generating profits by charging more interest on money loaned to their customers than they pay to depositors. In addition, they are responsible for increasing the amounts of deposits and loans at their branch. Thus, two common performance measures within the banking industry are (1) yield (a measure of loan profitability) and (2) loan growth (the rate by which a manager increases the dollar value of loans outstanding). Analogies in manufacturing organizations include ROI and sales growth. While this example illustrates financial measures of performance, service organizations also may use a balanced scorecard approach to evaluate performance. In addition to performance evaluation issues, managers in service industries face other challenges often associated with manufacturing companies.

In a manufacturing organization, transfers between divisions occur when one division buys goods from another division. Transfer pricing is a major issue in banking also. For example, to meet legal requirements aimed at protecting depositors and other interested parties, banks must maintain a certain ratio of loans to deposits. A loan-to-deposit ratio of 65 percent means that a bank has loaned 65 cents for every dollar it holds in deposits. Assume that an aggressive branch manager has exceeded the maximum loan-to-deposit ratio, while another branch manager (within the same banking corporation) has not. Corporate management would transfer funds from the branch with excess funds to the branch exceeding the limit. The funds transfer would involve "interest charges" to the borrowing bank and "interest revenues" to the lending bank. The interest rate selected for the transfer is similar to the transfer price in a manufacturing organization. Many options exist for determining the interest charge, or transfer price. For example, the interest charge could be based on the corporation's average cost of funds, or perhaps on the highest rate paid on deposits. Thus, like manufacturing organizations, banks transfer goods and services among divisions and must determine an acceptable price for the transaction.

This chapter has shown that manufacturing and service organizations may use a decentralized organizational structure. The banking example illustrates the way service organizations face many of the same challenges as manufacturing organizations face. Managers of service organizations must find ways to be responsive to a changing environment, evaluate performance using a variety of indicators, and determine the cost of resources transferred among divisions.

Learning Note	Both service and manufacturing companies make special pricing decisions to attract customers that would otherwise buy goods or services from competitors. When negotiating special pricing arrangements, a manager must understand which costs are relevant and which costs are not relevant. Costs that change between alternatives typically are considered relevant to special pricing decisions. For example, pricing that covers variable costs of materials, labor, overhead, and special handling expenses will benefit the company in the short run. However, many academics warn against the long-term consequences of continuously basing prices on variable rather than full (variable + fixed) costs. Though special sales may appear profitable in the short term, all costs of production must be recovered in the long term if the company is to survive.

SELF-STUDY PROBLEM 3

Refer to the financial data presented in Self-Study Problem 1. The financial statements represent the operations of your division during the past 12 months. Assume that you are a divisional manager who purchases raw materials from other divisions within the company. Your company has a market-based transfer pricing policy. Thus, managers commonly seek transfer prices consistent with bids submitted by outside companies.

Before entering into price negotiations to purchase raw materials from the manager of Division B, you wish to understand Division B's cost structure and other factors that may affect the negotiations. Respond to the following questions.

1. You estimate that 25% of the materials used by your division was purchased from Division B. Assuming that your division's total cost of materials was $40,000,000, what was the cost of materials purchased from Division B?
2. If the selling division (Division B) typically earns a 20% gross margin [(Sales − cost of goods sold) ÷ sales], what was Division B's cost of goods sold?
3. You recall from past meetings that Division B is very capital-intensive (they use expensive equipment, whose costs are fixed in the short run). Their variable costs are 30 percent of total manufacturing costs, while fixed costs make up the remaining 70 percent.

   Using the transfer pricing equation, Transfer price = variable cost + opportunity cost, calculate the minimum acceptable transfer price (from the seller's perspective). Assume that Division B is operating at full capacity.
4. Should the manager of Division B consider negotiating a lower transfer price if the division is not operating at capacity? Explain.

The solution to Self-Study Problem 3 appears at the end of the chapter.

© Matthew Borkoski, 1994/PNI International

REVIEW *Summary of Important Concepts*

1. A responsibility center is defined as any business unit or segment over which managers have control and managerial authority.
   a. Cost center managers are evaluated on their ability to control costs.
   b. Revenue center managers are responsible for generating sales, or revenues.
   c. Profit center managers are responsible for both costs and revenues.
   d. Investment center managers are held accountable for costs, revenues, profits, and efficient asset use.

2. Managerial performance is often evaluated using ROI.
   a. Return on investment (ROI) is made up of two elements, margin and turnover.
   b. Margin is defined as operating income $\div$ sales.
   c. Turnover is defined as sales $\div$ operating assets.
   d. The use of ROI for performance evaluation encourages managers to maximize operating income while at the same time minimizing the level of assets employed.

3. Performance evaluation using the balanced scorecard includes four sets of measures:
   a. Financial: How do we look to shareholders?
   b. Customer satisfaction: How do customers see us?
   c. Innovation and learning: How may we continue to improve and create value?
   d. Internal business: At what must we excel?

4. A number of transfer pricing issues can arise in organizations.
   a. Transfer pricing issues typically occur in decentralized organizations.
   b. Financially based evaluation programs often encourage managers to act in the best interests of their own division, rather than the best interests of the company as a whole.
   c. Typically, three methods are used for determining transfer prices among business units:
      (1) Cost-based transfer pricing policies use either full cost or variable cost as a basis for determining transfer prices.
      (2) Market-based transfer pricing policies rely on external market prices for identical (or comparable) goods or services to establish transfer prices.
      (3) Negotiated transfer pricing policies permit managers to consider factors such as cost and external market prices when negotiating a mutually acceptable transfer price between two business units.

5. Many of the same issues arise in service organizations.
   a. Service organizations often are decentralized and face many of the same challenges as manufacturing companies.
   b. Managers of decentralized service organizations must develop financial (and nonfinancial) measures with which to evaluate performance.
   c. Transfer pricing policies are important to decentralized service organizations because services are transferred among divisions.

DEFINE *Terms and Concepts Defined in This Chapter*

agents (300)
balanced scorecard (311)
cost center (303)
cost-based transfer pricing policy (320)
investment center (304)

margin (307)
market-based transfer pricing policy (315)
negotiated transfer pricing policy (320)
operating assets (307)

operating income (307)
profit center (304)
return on investment (ROI) (307)
revenue center (303)
transfer pricing (314)
turnover (307)

SOLUTIONS

SELF-STUDY PROBLEM 1

1. A plant manager typically is responsible for controlling materials, labor, and overhead costs within the plant. These costs are included in the cost of goods manufactured as shown on the cost of goods sold schedule. Some of the overhead costs appear to be allocated from the corporate level and are not directly controllable by you, such as the cost of corporate computer time used for production scheduling. The income statement also includes corporate cost allocations over which a plant manager has no control, such as depreciation on corporate aircraft (used by the senior-level executives). Finally, as plant manager, you have no control over sales commissions and expenses.

2. The scenario presented suggests that the plant manager determines neither product mix nor selling prices. Thus, to evaluate the plant manager on his or her ability to generate income is not consistent with the principles of performance evaluation. This manager should be evaluated on his or her ability to manage costs, meet production schedules, and achieve quality specifications. Thus, the plant in our example should be evaluated as a cost center, rather than a profit center.

   Senior-level managers may evaluate a plant's ability to contribute to corporate income. An analysis based on income is appropriate at higher levels because higher-level managers make product mix and pricing decisions. However, the plant manager in our example is not responsible for decisions such as these.

SELF-STUDY PROBLEM 2

1. Margin = operating income ÷ sales
   = $1,000,000 ÷ $100,000,000
   = 0.01

   Managers may consider ways to reduce direct materials, direct labor, manufacturing overhead, and other general or administrative costs. Such actions would increase operating income, assuming no changes in sales volume.

   Another approach involves raising prices to generate more operating income per sales dollar. Managers must be careful when raising prices because both sales volume and operating income could decline, resulting in a lower profit margin.

2. Turnover = sales ÷ operating assets
   = $100,000,000 ÷ $20,000,000
   = 5

   Turnover motivates managers to create lean organizations by producing greater sales volume while simultaneously employing fewer operating assets. Thus, turnover can be improved by
   a. Increasing sales while maintaining the same level of operating assets,
   b. Reducing operating assets while maintaining the same level of sales, or
   c. Increasing sales and reducing the level of operating assets.

   Strategies to reduce assets may include (a) collecting on accounts receivable and submitting excess cash to corporate management, (b) reducing inventory levels, and (c) eliminating unnecessary equipment that creates excess capacity.

3. Margin × turnover = ROI
   0.01   × 5   = 0.05

4. Focusing exclusively on financial measures of performance may encourage managers to sacrifice long-term success for short-term gains. For example, managers may cut back on research and development expenditures, quality programs, and preventive maintenance in order to improve short-term performance.

5. The balanced scorecard identifies four classes of performance measures: financial, customer, innovation and learning, and internal business. Financial measures may include ROI or market share. Customer measures may include percentage of on-time deliveries or external failure rate (percentage of products delivered that are defective). Innovation and learning measures may include such things as the number of technological innovations. Internal business measures may include such things as scrap rates.

SELF-STUDY PROBLEM 3

1. $40,000,000 cost of materials $\times$ 0.25 = $10,000,000.

2. First, let's establish the relationship among sales, cost of goods sold, and margin as follows:

Sales − cost of goods sold = gross margin
Gross margin = 0.20 $\times$ $10,000,000 = $2,000,000

Selling price	$10,000,000	100%
(less) Gross margin	(2,000,000)	20%*
Cost of goods sold	$ 8,000,000	80%

$$^* \quad \frac{\$10,000,000 - \$8,000,000}{\$10,000,000} = 20\%$$

Therefore, it cost Division B $8,000,000 to produce the goods it sold to your division.

3.
Variable cost 0.3 $\times$ $8,000,000	=	$2,400,000
Fixed cost 0.7 $\times$ $8,000,000	=	$5,600,000
Total cost		$8,000,000

Opportunity cost	=	sales	−	variable cost
$7,600,000	=	$10,000,000	−	$2,400,000

Transfer price	=	variable cost	+	opportunity cost
$10,000,000	=	$2,400,000	+	$7,600,000

Thus, the manager of Division B would have no incentive to reduce the selling price from $10,000,000 because all units could be sold to external buyers at a price of $10,000,000. Therefore, negotiations could be difficult.

4. Theoretically, the manager of Division B should be willing to make price concessions if the division has idle capacity. The transfer pricing formula suggests that if excess capacity exists, managers may consider prices that are sufficient to cover the variable costs of production as follows:

Transfer price = variable cost + opportunity cost
$2,400,000 = $2,400,000 + 0

When a division has idle capacity, the opportunity cost becomes zero because external sales are not forgone.

EXERCISES

9-1. Write a short definition of each of the terms listed in the *Terms and Concepts Defined in This Chapter* section.

Obj. 1 **9-2.** Heather Stone is a production manager for Bohemia Company. Her father, Alex, is a shareholder of the company but does not work for Bohemia. Which of the Stones would be considered an agent for Bohemia? What role does an agent play in an organization?

Obj. 2 **9-3.** Tenco Company manufactures high-quality playground equipment. There are several plants within Tenco. Plant A produces plastic slides and swings that are used in manufacturing at Plant B. What type of responsibility center is Plant A? Explain your answer.

Obj. 2 **9-4.** Assume that the performance of the plant manager at Tenco's Plant A, discussed in Exercise 3, is being evaluated by the vice president of operations at Tenco's headquarters. What performance objectives are most likely to be used to evaluate the manager's performance?

Obj. 2 **9-5.** The T. H. Hucksley Corporation is a multidivisional company with locations in several countries. The Electronics Division of Hucksley has three plants, including one in Austin, Texas. The Austin plant employs over 600 workers and maintains marketing and engineering personnel that support the production process. The plant has no administrative staff and must rely on divisional headquarters for administrative support. The managers of the plant independently establish production schedules and market its product. The profitability of the plant is reported to divisional headquarters, where it is combined with that of other plant operations to determine total divisional income. What sort of responsibility center is the Austin plant? Explain your answer.

Obj. 2 **9-6.** Granite Industries is a multidivisional corporation in which each division operates autonomously. Division A is considered an investment center of Granite. Given this, would you expect the divisional manager of Division A to be able to make decisions regarding the acquisition of new machinery and equipment necessary to conduct divisional business? Explain your answer.

Obj. 2 **9-7.** Logistics, Inc., is a decentralized company with branch operations in 15 of the largest metropolitan areas of the United States. Each division is operated as a separate profit center, and there is a corporate vice president in charge at each location. The company has a decentralized decision-making philosophy by which the vice president at each location is empowered to make the necessary decisions to operate the profit center. What benefits would be realized from the decentralized decision-making philosophy at Logistics? What sort of localized decisions would the profit center managers be expected to make?

Obj. 2 **9-8.** Leslie Greenwood is a plant manager for Ambrose Manufacturing. Leslie's plant is operated and evaluated as a profit center. Leslie has reviewed the plant's sales and costs for the last 12 months in preparation for her annual review. She has noticed that while margins and the cost of goods manufactured have improved over the last year, overall profitability has declined as a result of increased corporate cost allocations. The corporate controller has told Leslie that the cost allocations relate mainly to insurance, interest, and data processing costs, which have increased significantly over the prior year levels. What arguments should Leslie be prepared to make when her performance is evaluated?

Obj. 3 **9-9.** Assume that two different companies, Company A and Company B, have earned net income of $10 million and $1 million, respectively, over the same fiscal period. Would it be fair to say that Company A earned a higher ROI than Company B?

Obj. 4 **9-10.** Roseanne Creole is a divisional manager for The Southland Group of Companies. Roseanne's compensation includes a bonus arrangement that is based on her division's ROI and turnover. In the last month of the year, her division acquired new machinery with a cost of $12 million. The addition of this machinery significantly increased the division's year-end asset value. Roseanne is concerned that the large increase in assets will result in an unfavorable ROI and turnover rate, and that she will miss out on her bonus. What would you tell Roseanne to ease her concerns with respect to the calculation of the performance figures?

Obj. 4 **9-11.** The manager of Zelta Corporation's southeast region, Art McCormick, must improve the investment center's margin in order to achieve the performance goals established for his segment of the company. A 5% increase in sales price would achieve the desired margin. After meeting with the sales and marketing staff, however, Art is sure that an increase in sales price would result in a loss of sales and that target income would not be achieved, even though margins would increase. If sales prices cannot be increased, how can Art attain the desired margins?

Obj. 4 **9-12.** Davidson Manufacturing produces two models of barbecue grills. One of the models, the "King Cooker Deluxe," is produced from a higher grade of material and is manufactured in smaller batches than the standard "King Cooker" model. The cost of producing the deluxe model is higher than the cost of producing the standard model, yet the deluxe model provides a greater sales margin than the standard unit. Because of production constraints, management at Davidson is planning to discontinue the deluxe model. Assuming that the increase in the number of standard units sold will equal the number of discontinued deluxe models that would have been sold, what effect will the change in the product mix have on Davidson's ROI?

Obj. 4 **9-13.** Elmer Woods is a plant manager for the Lima Corporation, a producer of paints and solvents. Elmer's performance evaluation, and his bonus compensation, is based in part on his plant's turnover ratio. Elmer wants to increase the turnover ratio in order to maximize his bonus. What are the two elements of turnover, and how would they need to change in order to increase Elmer's turnover ratio?

Objs. 4,5 **9-14.** The board of directors at the Mays Company calculates the company president's performance based strictly on the turnover ratio. The denominator for the calculation is cash, accounts receivables, inventory, and fixed assets. The company has been engaged in a plant revitalization project over the past two years and has added or upgraded many of the fixed assets. How will these changes in fixed assets affect the president's performance evaluation, assuming sales do not increase? Do you agree with the method the board uses to evaluate the president? Why or why not?

Obj. 6 **9-15.** Lana Martinez is a divisional manager with Power Source, Inc. Over the last several years, Lana has trimmed equipment maintenance costs in an effort to improve her division's operating income and improve financial performance measures. What effect, if any, will such a move have on the long-term profitability of the division?

Obj. 6 **9-16.** The Choice Products Company operates three plants in the United States. Each plant manufactures different products, but they depend on each other for subcomponent assemblies needed in the final assembly of their respective products. Each plant manager wants to establish a transfer price to the other divisions that will maximize the manager's own plant's return on investment. Why may these transfer pricing policies not be in the best interest of the company as a whole?

Obj. 6 **9-17.** Compton Enterprises sells inner tubes and rubber products. Several inner tube lines are imported to the company's California warehouse from Korea. These tubes then are transferred to other divisions at cost. Kelly Hardaway, manager of the Tennessee plant, has argued that the tubes should be transferred at the import cost, rather than the California division's "marked up" cost. The California warehouse insists that the markup is necessary to cover its own operating costs related to processing, storage, and handling. How would you resolve this dispute between divisions?

Obj. 7 **9-18.** Tandem Manufacturing transfers a product between two plants. The product has variable costs of $65 per unit, and fixed overhead costs per unit of $25. This product can be purchased from an outside source with acceptable levels of quality and quantity at $83 per unit. Assuming that Tandem has excess production capacity for this product, what would be the acceptable ceiling and floor transfer pricing amounts for the product?

Obj. 7 **9-19.** The Frame Division of Reliable Computers manufactures storage housings for personal and midsize computers, which it sells externally to computer manufacturers. The division is operating at full capacity. One of the most popular size housings has variable costs of $34 and is sold to outside customers at $52 per unit. These housings also are needed by the Component Division of Reliable, which produces a line of small business computers. The Frame Division can sell all of its production to outside customers at $52 or can transfer a significant amount of its production to the Component Division. At what cost should the Frame Division transfer production? Why?

Obj. 7 **9-20.** For establishing transfer prices between divisions of a company, what alternative is there to using current market prices or a cost-based formula? What are the strengths and weaknesses of such an approach?

PROBLEMS

PROBLEM 9-1 Recognizing Responsibility Centers

Obj. 2

The following are independent situations.

1. LonnMark Inc. operates a satellite plant that produces components for many of the company's products. The plant is operated by a plant manager, who coordinates scheduling and material acquisition with the company's home office. The plant manager also is directly responsible for a labor force consisting of 350 employees. This manager controls overhead, but may not add any equipment without home office approval.

2. A nationally known soft drink company acquires a coal mining company. The decision to acquire the mining operation is strategic and is based on anticipated growth in the industry. The mining operation is run by a local management group independent of soft drink management.

3. Black and Runyan, Inc., of Chicago, owns a grain elevator and storage facility in rural Iowa. The grain facility is run by Dave Bailey. Dave and 22 other grain facility operators report to the senior vice president of operations, located in Chicago. Dave has day-to-day control in running the Iowa facility and routinely buys and sells grain.

4. Sandra Falls is the California senior account representative for a national copier manufacturer. Sandra has overall responsibility for the 12 showrooms located in the state. Each showroom employs approximately 6 sales representatives. Sandra's representatives sell copiers, but maintenance on the copiers is provided by certified subcontractors who are coordinated through the national headquarters.

Required Categorize each of the above underlined organizations as either a cost center, profit center, revenue center, or investment center. Briefly justify your answers.

PROBLEM 9-2 Calculating Return on Investment, Turnover, and Margin

Obj. 4

The following information for the past two years relates to a division of Axle Company:

	1997	1998
Sales	$30,000,000	$40,000,000
Net operating income	2,500,000	3,000,000
Average operating assets	56,000,000	56,000,000

Required

a. Compute the return on investment for both years.
b. Compute the margin and turnover ratio for each year.
c. Explain why the return on investment increased from 1997 to 1998 despite a lower margin in 1998.

PROBLEM 9-3   Margin, Turnover, ROI

Obj. 4

	Company 1	Company 2	Company 3	Company 4
Sales revenue	$12,000	$20,000	$158,000	?
Expenses	8,000	?	136,000	?
Net income	4,000	8,000	?	?
Average assets	24,000	25,000	65,000	100,000
Margin	?	40%	?	7%
Turnover	?	0.8	?	2
ROI	?	?	?	?

Required   Calculate the missing information for each of the four companies above. Treat each company independently.

PROBLEM 9-4   Enhancing Return on Investments: Ethical Considerations

Obj. 4

Connor Consumer Products has three operating divisions, which are appropriately treated as investment centers. Each of the investment centers is run by a divisional manager. The managers are evaluated on the basis of ROI performance. Those managers with the best ROI figures are most likely to be promoted to higher-level corporate positions. Maurice Dubois is one of the divisional managers for Connor. He is an ambitious person who desperately wants a promotion to headquarters. The investment center for which Maurice is responsible manufactures a line of patio furniture. This investment center has two plants, which employ over 500 workers. Operating results for each of the plants and for the division in total for the most recent year are as follows:

	Total	Plant A	Plant B
Revenues	180,000	120,000	60,000
Expenses	150,000	100,000	50,000
Net income	30,000	20,000	10,000
Average operating assets	160,000	100,000	60,000

Sales, marketing, and production managers who work for Maurice have proposed adding production capabilities for the manufacture of picnic table umbrellas. They have compiled figures that show that the estimated cost of the assets needed to produce an umbrella line is $1.2 million. They further estimate that the umbrella line would increase net income by $120,000 a year. After careful consideration, Maurice rejected the idea and added, "This is no time to add to our production facilities. In fact, I've been thinking of closing Plant B and moving its production to Plant A."

Required

a. What is the most likely reason why Maurice turned down the proposal to produce umbrellas? Provide computations to support your reasoning.
b. Would the company as a whole be better off by producing the umbrellas? Explain your answer.
c. Why do you believe Maurice has suggested closing Plant B? How does ROI as a performance measure adversely affect the company in total?

PROBLEM 9-5   Balanced Scorecard Approach to Performance Evaluation

Obj. 5

Carol Rolfson is a divisional manager for Klinger Products. Carol operates a division that manufactures clocks and timepieces that are distributed through retail stores. Over the past year, Carol's division recorded the highest net income in the division's history. Internal records indicate that customer returns have declined significantly as a result of the division's improved quality. Many of the improvements were generated as a result of a vigorous program of enhanced technology in which most of the division's equipment was replaced or updated over the last 18 months.

Carol has noticed a change in morale as a result of the plant improvements. Employees have become more interested in their work and have suggested additional improvements to the production process. One of the suggestions led to a new product that has shown strong sales potential. The improved processes have also resulted in lower scrap rates and more timely shipments.

As a divisional manager, Carol is eligible for an annual bonus under Klinger's executive compensation plan. She has been notified, however, that her bonus for the year will be significantly less than in prior years. The executive compensation plan calculates a manager's effectiveness based solely on return on investment. The president of Klinger pointed out to Carol that while her division's income has improved, the addition of all the new equipment overshadowed the higher earnings.

Required

a. What weaknesses do you see in Klinger's executive bonus plan?
b. How does the company's current compensation plan differ from a balanced scorecard approach to bonus compensation?
c. If the company utilized a balance scorecard approach, what do you believe would be the impact on Carol's bonus compensation? Explain your answer.

PROBLEM 9-6   Performance Evaluations

Objs. 2,5

The Promotion and Advertising Department at Jefferson Corporation coordinates point of purchase promotions for its distributors. Employees of this department are graphic art or marketing majors who develop campaign materials and conduct market research. The department does not collect any revenue for these services. The department manager is evaluated based on the department's ability to operate within its budget. For the last several years, the manager has had to curtail many promotional programs a month before year-end in order to stay within budget.

Sales personnel, marketing representatives, and customers frequently complain when these services are terminated. Dan Beck, the department manager, told a colleague, "I hate taking all this heat every year. But I just can't afford to blow the budget." He also noted that "soon the new budget will be out, and I can give everyone what they want!"

Required

a. What type of responsibility center is the Promotion and Advertising Department?
b. How is the department currently being evaluated? What are the important elements on which the department should be evaluated?
c. What appear to be the reasons for the department's budget problems? What implications does this have for the company?

PROBLEM 9-7   Transfer Pricing, Idle Capacity

Objs. 6,7

At its Video Division, Kessler Enterprises manufactures color computer monitors. These can be sold internally to the EDD division of Kessler or externally to independent customers. Sales and costs of the most popular monitor are as follows:

Per unit selling price	$135.00
Per unit variable cost	102.00
Per unit fixed costs*	28.00
Full production capacity	10,000 units per month
Current level of production	8,000 units per month

* Based on full production capacity

The Video Division of Kessler plans to sell a maximum of 96,000 of these monitors to outside customers in the coming year. The EDD division of Kessler plans to buy 20,000 identical monitors from an outside supplier at a price of $135. The manager of the Video Division has offered to supply these 20,000 monitors to the EDD Division at a price of $130.

Required

a. What is the minimum transfer price for the monitor that the Video Division should be willing to accept on an internal transfer? What is the maximum price the EDD division should be willing to pay for these monitors on an internal transfer?

b. Suppose the managers of the EDD Division learn of the idle capacity at the Video Division, and make an offer of $120 for these monitors. Would you expect the Video Division to accept? What would be the effect on net income for the Video Division of accepting this offer?

c. What would be the effect on net income for Kessler as a whole if the transfer price of $120 were accepted?

PROBLEM 9-8 Transfer Pricing, Full Capacity

Objs. 6,7

The USA Company's Box Division produces cardboard boxes used for packaging microwavable fast foods. The Consumer Products Division produces a variety of fast food entrees that are packaged in boxes. In the past the Consumer Products Division has purchased its boxes from the Box Division for $0.15 each. The Box Division currently is producing at capacity and sells 6,000,000 of these boxes each year at a price of $0.15. The Consumer Products Division has offered to buy 500,000 boxes per year from the Box Division at an internal transfer price of $0.13 per box. The Box Division's cost to produce each box consists of $0.09 of variable costs and $0.04 of fixed costs.

Required

a. What is the minimum transfer price that would be acceptable to the Box Division without hurting the company as a whole?

b. Assume that by selling the boxes internally, the Box Division would avoid $0.03 of variable costs. Should the internal transfer be accepted at $0.13 per box?

c. Assume that the Box Division accepts a price of $0.13 for the internal transfer of 500,000 boxes. How much better off (or worse off) would the company as a whole be than if it sold the boxes externally at a price of $0.15?

PROBLEM 9-9 Transfer Pricing in a Service Environment

Objs. 6,8

Waldo and Company, LLP, is a partnership that provides public accounting services. Waldo has three offices in Louisiana, which are located in New Orleans, Baton Rouge, and Lafayette. Each of the offices employs approximately 30 professional accountants who are recruited and hired by and work solely for the office to which they are assigned. The offices are run independently, and there is a managing partner in charge of each office. Bonuses are paid to each managing partner based on criteria that include the number of staff hours worked and total billings for the respective office.

The Lafayette office was recently hired by a large petroleum company to conduct an audit. This engagement will require more accounting personnel than are currently available in the Lafayette office. Nancy Bloom, managing partner of the Lafayette office, has asked the other offices to "lend" her some professional staff to assist on this engagement. The other offices want to help, but are concerned that "lending" their personnel will reduce the number of staff hours worked in their own offices, thereby reducing their billings and resulting bonuses.

Required Why does this situation reflect a transfer pricing problem for the firm? How should the firm handle the interoffice transfer of personnel from a pricing standpoint? If there are professional staff available in the New Orleans and Baton Rouge offices who are not servicing clients, would the interoffice transfer price be affected?

PROBLEM 9-10 Multiple-Choice Overview of the Chapter

1. Which of the following responsibility centers would appropriately be evaluated in terms of the margin and turnover together?
   a. cost center
   b. profit center

    c.   investment center
    d.   revenue center

2.   Which of the following is true regarding return on investment?
    a.   An increase in sales would affect the margin but not the turnover.
    b.   Return on investment is applied only to profit centers.
    c.   An increase in assets will decrease the return on investment when sales remain constant.
    d.   Plant and equipment are the only assets used to calculate the return on investment.

3.   A company establishing transfer prices for products between divisions should:
    a.   transfer products at prices that would be paid by outside customers.
    b.   utilize transfer prices that will result in the highest income to the transferring division.
    c.   allow negotiated prices that result in the greatest benefit to the corporation as a whole.
    d.   require the transferee division to accept price quotes without negotiation.

4.   A principal expectation for agents is that:
    a.   agents will operate the company in a way consistent with the owners' interests.
    b.   agents may not act on behalf of owners in important business matters.
    c.   agents must always operate a company in order to maximize shareholder wealth.
    d.   agents' compensation should not include incentives, as this can create conflicts of interest.

5.   A decentralized organization:
    a.   permits managers to make decisions based on local economic situations.
    b.   allows middle managers to develop skills in preparation for greater responsibilities.
    c.   is characterized by multiple divisions or operating segments.
    d.   all of the above.

6.   The return on investment performance evaluation tool:
    a.   is calculated by dividing operating assets by net income.
    b.   is calculated by dividing sales revenue by operating assets.
    c.   is calculated by dividing operating income by operating assets.
    d.   is not meaningful since it is subject to manipulation by division managers.

7.   The turnover ratio:
    a.   is considered to improve when the ratio decreases.
    b.   demonstrates the effectiveness of asset management.
    c.   encourages managers to increase the asset base.
    d.   cannot increase unless the company's margin also increases.

8.   The balanced scorecard approach to performance evaluation includes:
    a.   financial performance measures.
    b.   customer satisfaction measures.
    c.   internal business criteria.
    d.   all of the above.

9.   The transfer pricing policy that requires managers to transfer goods based on external price conditions is referred to as:
    a.   negotiated transfer pricing.
    b.   a market-based transfer policy.
    c.   a cost-plus transfer policy.
    d.   none of the above.

10. When a division is operating at less than full capacity,
    a.   the company as a whole would be better off utilizing a market-based transfer pricing policy.
    b.   internal transfers generally should be made at a price that equals the variable cost of production.
    c.   the turnover ratio will increase.
    d.   fixed costs are being fully recovered.

```
C A S E S
```

CASE 9-1 Segment Reporting and Analysis

Obj. 4

The following is Play Safe's financial statement for the year ending December 31, 1998 in total and by division:

	Total	Division A	Division B
Assets:			
Cash	$ 40,000	$ 10,000	$ 30,000
Accounts receivable	85,000	37,000	48,000
Inventory	188,000	72,000	116,000
Fixed assets	1,750,000	900,000	850,000
Total	$2,063,000	$1,019,000	$1,044,000
Liabilities:			
Accounts payable	$ 65,000	$ 28,000	$ 37,000
Bank debt	1,500,000	800,000	700,000
Total	$1,565,000	$ 828,000	$ 737,000
Stockholders' equity	498,000		
Total liabilities and equity	$2,063,000		
Revenues	$1,600,000	$ 600,000	$1,000,000
Expenses	1,300,000	400,000	900,000
Net income	$ 300,000	$ 200,000	$ 100,000

Required

a. If the stockholders own shares of the company in total, and not in the individual divisions, how can the divisional managers' performance be evaluated in terms of building stockholder wealth?

b. From a ROI perspective, which of the two divisions has shown better performance? (Assume that ending assets reflect average operating assets for the year.)

c. Assume that management at Play Safe is considering a capital investment that is expected to provide a return of 8%. As an alternative, it can invest the amount in either of the two divisions, returning that division's ROI. Which investment should management make? Explain your answer.

CASE 9-2 Transfer Pricing

Objs. 6, 7

Cameo Products has two divisions: Office Products and Furniture. Divisional managers are encouraged to maximize income and ROI at their respective divisions. Managers are free to decide whether goods will be transferred internally and to determine the prices at which transfers will occur.

The Furniture Division would like to purchase a particular chair manufactured in the Office Products Division and sell it with a computer desk the division recently has designed. The Furniture Division can purchase a similar chair from an outside supplier for $45. The Office Products Division currently is producing this chair at full capacity and sells it to outside customers at $45. The manager of the Furniture Division is hoping to receive a price concession if the chair is bought internally. The full cost to produce the chair is $40 ($32 represents variable costs). If the chair is sold internally, $3 of variable selling expenses can be avoided.

The managers of the two divisions met to discuss the possible transaction. After some discussion and negotiation, it was decided that the Furniture Division would purchase the chair at the current outside selling price for the next six months. At the end of six months, negotiations can be reopened by either party if desired.

Required

a. Based on current information, what is the highest price that the Furniture Division should be willing to pay for the chair? What is the lowest price that the Office Products Division should be willing to accept?

b. Assume that the outside sales price of the chair increases to $47. How would this affect the internal transfer price of the chair?

c. Assume that because of soft market conditions, demand for the chair has decreased significantly, creating excess idle capacity within the Office Products Division. How would this change affect the internal transfer price of the chair?

d. Why is it in the best interest of the company as a whole to allow the division managers to negotiate internal transfer prices instead of using a fixed, nonnegotiable formula for establishing transfer prices?

PROJECTS

PROJECT 9-1 Transfer Pricing

Obj. 7

Identify a company that manufactures component products that are required in at least one of its other operating plants. Identify the type of products manufactured and the different methods that may be used in establishing transfer prices between the locations. Write a short paper on your findings.

PROJECT 9-2 Transfer Pricing

Objs. 7,8

Identify a company in your area that produces parts or services for other divisions. Invite a manager from a division to address your class on transfer pricing policies at the company. Ask the person what method is used to establish transfer pricing policies. Inquire whether all production costs are recovered in the transfer price. Is there another market for the parts or services that are transferred? How does the existence (or lack thereof) of outside markets affect transfer pricing policies at this company?

PROJECT 9-3 Return on Investment

Obj. 4

Review the published financial statements of a publicly held company that provides segment information for its various divisions. Calculate the return on investment for each of the company's segments. Write a short report on your findings.

Decisions About Capital Investments

10

Accounting and Management Decisions

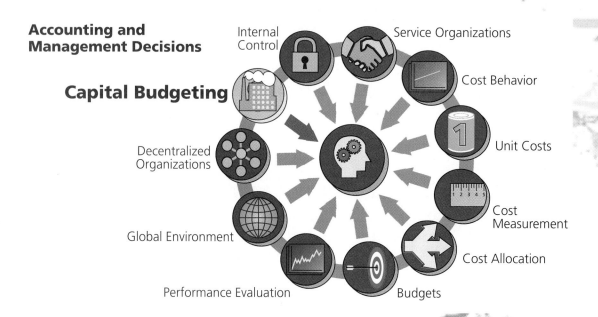

Internal Control

Service Organizations

Capital Budgeting

Cost Behavior

Decentralized Organizations

Unit Costs

Global Environment

Cost Measurement

Cost Allocation

Performance Evaluation

Budgets

Overview

Acquiring long-term assets often requires a large outlay of funds. The success or failure of these investment decisions can be of great importance to a company. Capital investment decisions may put significant financial resources at risk for long periods of time. With changes in the business environment, such as total quality management, the importance and risk of capital investments are increasing. This chapter discusses factors that affect the risk of capital investments.

Two types of quantitative tools are available to capital investment decision makers: discounting and nondiscounting. Discounting techniques often are preferred because they consider the time value of money. Thus, many companies use discounted cash flow methods, such as net present value (NPV), as the principal tools for making capital investment decisions. This chapter describes several common discounting and nondiscounting techniques and discusses the danger of relying too heavily on these tools. For example, traditional discounting techniques often fail to consider the costs of *not* investing in new technology. Not considering these costs can be harmful in the new business environment, where international competition requires companies to deliver high-quality products. Distinguishing between operational and strategic investments is important because the techniques that are useful for making operational capital investment decisions may be of limited use for strategic decisions.

Managers often must decide whether to continue to fund capital investments once they are begun. In some instances, because of the way managers are being evaluated, they have incentives to

© Charles Thatcher/Tony Stone Images

continue to fund unsuccessful investments. It is important to identify these situations so that they can be avoided. Thus, companies should evaluate carefully the success of their investments before committing additional resources.

Major topics covered in this chapter include:
- Factors that affect capital investment decisions.
- Traditional approaches to capital investment decisions.
- The effect of the new manufacturing environment on capital investment decisions.
- Making capital investment decisions in the new manufacturing environment.
- Identifying and ending unsuccessful investments.

Objectives

Once you have completed this chapter, you should be able to:

1. Identify factors that affect capital investment decisions and explain why these decisions are important to companies.

2. Calculate net present value, internal rate of return, payback, and accounting rate of return.

3. Explain how service life and residual value, the income tax effects of depreciation, and risk affect capital investment decisions.

4. Describe the effect of the new manufacturing environment on capital investment decisions.

5. Identify factors that are important for strategic decisions.

6. Explain how evaluation systems can produce incentives to continue to fund unsuccessful investments and how companies can reduce the funding of such investments.

7. Describe the factors affecting capital investment decisions in service organizations.

FACTORS AFFECTING DECISIONS

Objective 1
Identify factors that affect capital investment decisions and explain why these decisions are important to companies.

When a company makes a decision to invest in long-term assets such as plant and equipment, it is making a *capital investment decision.* These decisions often involve large outlays of cash for long periods. **The process of making these decisions is known as** *capital budgeting.*

Capital investment decisions can be classified in various ways. One such way is to view these decisions as either operational or strategic. *Operational capital investment decisions* **are those that affect only a part of a company's operations, have easily predictable lives, and represent relatively small capital outlays for a business.** *Strategic capital investment decisions* **affect all or a considerable part of a company's operations, have uncertain lives, and require large investments.** The risks associated with strategic capital investment decisions are different from and considerably greater than those associated with operational capital investment decisions.

Capital investments affect a company's revenues, expenses, and cash flows as well as its assets. For example, Exhibit 1 illustrates that the purchase of new equipment, such as a computer, results in:

- A payment of cash for the equipment
- A payment of wages for employees
- Additional interest on money borrowed to finance the purchase
- Additional depreciation expense
- Additional revenues from the sale of goods or services

Exhibit 1   Financial Effects of Capital Investment Decisions

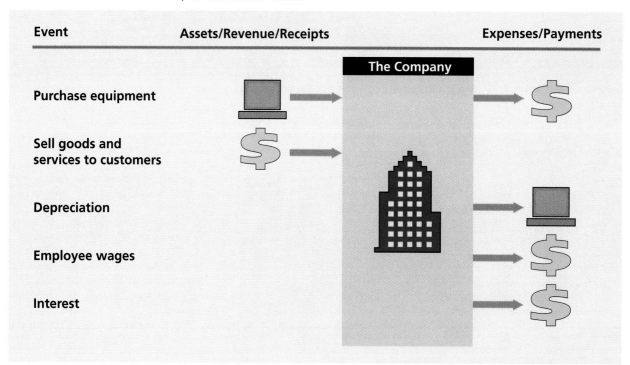

Risk

Exhibit 2 depicts several factors that affect the risk associated with capital investment decisions. The outcomes of most investment decisions are uncertain. In addition to the effect of a decision on expected cash flows, risk is an important factor in determining the value of an investment.

Exhibit 2 Factors Affecting the Risk of Capital Investments

FACTORS THAT *INCREASE* RISK	FACTORS THAT *DECREASE* RISK
1. Large investment size relative to the company's total investment (assets). 2. Long-term recovery of the cost of the investment. 3. Management inexperience with similar investments. 4. Difficulty in reversing the investment decision. 5. High uncertainty about whether the asset will perform as expected.	1. Large potential for recovery of investment through resale of the investment asset. 2. Recovery of the investment in a short time period. 3. Management experience with similar investments.

A company is at greater risk financially if an investment fails when the investment is large relative to the company's financial size. For instance, a company that invests all of its investment funds in one large project is accepting greater risk than a similar company that invests its funds in five different projects. In addition, the longer it takes to recover the cost of an investment, the greater the risk of the investment because the opportunity for the investment to fail is greater. When the expected performance of the asset is uncertain, prior experience with similar investments can help reduce risk.

Companies typically invest large amounts of money in capital investments. Usually, a company cannot recover the amount it has invested if a project is unsuccessful. For example, consider the construction of a new bank branch. The bank must acquire land and have a building designed, constructed, and landscaped. Specialized construction is necessary, such as installation of a vault. A sign with the bank's logo must be erected, and drive-in windows must be installed. If the branch is unprofitable, other banks may be unwilling to purchase it for an amount close to its original cost. A nonbank purchaser would not need or pay for the specialized assets. As a result, banks are careful in making decisions about construction of branches so that they can avoid losses from unsuccessful investments.

Another factor that increases the risk associated with capital investments is uncertainty about performance, such as that associated with new technology. In general, the newer the technology, the greater the uncertainty about its performance. In addition, there is the risk that competitors will develop newer technology that will make a company's existing technology out of date and result in the loss of business. Often, it takes time to make new technology work correctly.

C A S E

In Point

http://www.swcollege.com/ingram.html

Visit Intel's home page to learn more about the company.

Intel experienced a problem with the accuracy of calculations made by its Pentium® processor, which **IBM** and other companies installed in their personal computers. New versions of the processor corrected this problem. However, the problem was an embarrassment to the company and required the costly replacement of many processors.

Generally, the greater the amount of the original investment that can be recaptured through the sale of the assets, the lower the risk. In the case of a branch bank, it is unlikely that a significant portion of the initial cost could be recovered unless the branch were sold to another bank. Likewise, the greater the value of the asset at the end of its service to a company, the smaller the portion of the investment that must be recovered in cash flows during its service to the company. For example, suppose computers purchased by a software development company can be sold at the end of their service lives for 50% of their cost. In this case, only half of the investment in the computers will have to be recovered during their operation at the software company. The rest will be recovered by their sale.

Finally, the more experience management has with a particular type of investment, the less likely the company is to develop problems. For example, if a company's usual business is making corrugated cardboard boxes for packaging, purchase of equipment to improve the efficiency of the business is less risky than purchase of equipment to enter a new line of business, such as making specialty gift boxes. The new line will require management to gain experience with a new manufacturing process and new markets.

Controlling Capital Investments

Large capital investment decisions often involve company politics. Different divisions of companies compete for investment funds. Capital investment projects usually must meet a minimum rate of return requirement before a company will commit funds. Often managers have a strong interest in having their projects funded. Thus, they are likely to make favorable assumptions about the projects. However, since some of these projects actually will deliver lower rates of return than were estimated, key decision makers in companies tend to be very careful when they evaluate projects. They try to determine if assumptions are realistic.

Capital investment decisions often involve cash outflows over more than one period. Therefore, these projects must be monitored over time. Monitoring helps ensure that projects are developing satisfactorily and that continued investment is justified. Companies often use a milestone approach to monitoring. *Milestones*, **which are major decision points,** are established at the beginning of a capital investment project. At each milestone, the project is reevaluated and a continue or discontinue decision is made. These decisions may be difficult because investments often do not produce positive returns for some time after an initial investment is made. The absence of positive returns during the developmental stage of projects increases investment risk. (Recall that the longer it takes to recover the cost of the investment, the higher the investment risk.)

Consider the decision by **General Electric** to produce a new model of refrigerator. This new model requires additional plant space, equipment, and tools. Considerable cost will be incurred before production can begin. If the model is unsuccessful, much of this cost will not be recovered. However, General Electric may be better off accepting its losses rather than continuing to invest in the product in an effort to make it successful. *Sunk costs* **are costs associated with decisions that have already been made.** For example, the cost of designing and making specific tools that are useful only in producing the new model of refrigerator are sunk costs. Sunk costs are not relevant for future decisions because future decisions cannot alter these costs.

Monitoring the progress of investment projects can be difficult, as can evaluation of the managers responsible for the projects. To develop forecasts about the amount and timing of returns on these projects, assumptions are necessary. It is frequently difficult to forecast the amount of time it will take to develop and market a new product. For example, Food and Drug Administration approval is required for new pharmaceutical products. In developing a new pharmaceutical product, there is often a long approval process during which the product is tested. In the meantime, the life span of the patent on the product is passing. This means that the pharmaceutical company will have fewer years in which it can market the product exclusively before its patent expires and generic brands begin to erode its sales. If delays occur, they may not be the fault of project managers. It is difficult to assess performance accurately because of uncertainty about what the performance should be.

TRADITIONAL APPROACHES

Objective 2
Calculate net present value, internal rate of return, payback, and accounting rate of return.

As discussed in the previous section, capital investments often involve long-term cash outlays. Consequently, the time value of money is an important consideration in making capital investment decisions. There are several tools that can assist managers in deciding whether or not to make a capital investment and in choosing between competing projects. Traditional tools can be divided into discounting and nondiscounting methods. *Discounting methods* **are those that rely on the time value of money.** *Nondiscounting methods* **ignore the time value of money.** Each method has advantages and disadvantages. Nondiscounting methods are less reliable than discounting methods, though some companies use them because they are easier to use.

An important point to remember about the application of these methods to capital investment decisions is that they can be misleading when used improperly. This section describes how these methods are used in making capital investment decisions. Subsequent sections will discuss some of their shortcomings, especially in the new manufacturing environment. Also, it is important to keep in mind that these methods require long-term revenue and cost estimates, which often are uncertain. The most difficult task in using these methods is developing reasonable forecasts of revenues and costs.

Net Present Value

Recall that an important attribute of money is that it can be invested to earn interest. A dollar today is not worth the same as a dollar a year from now. **The translation of future dollars into current dollars is known as** *discounting*. **The** *net present value (NPV)* **of an investment is the difference between the present value of expected future cash inflows from the investment and the present value of expected cash outflows invested.**

The net present value compares the present value of expected cash inflows and cash outflows associated with a project as shown in the following equation:

$$NPV = \Sigma[C \div (1 + R)^t] - I$$
where I = amount invested at the beginning of the project
   C = net cash inflow expected in period t
   R = required rate of return
   t = time period
   Σ = summation for all periods

Thus, the net present value of an investment is the difference between the present value of expected future cash flows and the amount invested. Exhibit 3 illustrates an example. Assume that Stockdale Company has an opportunity to invest $60,000 in new equipment. Management expects the company to receive cash inflows of approximately $25,000 per year from the investment. The equipment is expected to have a useful life of three years. In considering the investment, Stockdale's managers determine that the company has $30,000 available in an investment account that earns 8% interest per year. It would have to borrow the remaining $30,000 at 12% per year. Should Stockdale invest in the equipment?

To answer this question, consider the rate of return Stockdale will require. If the company uses the $30,000 from its investments, it will forgo the 8% interest on the invested funds for the coming year, or $2,400 (0.08 × $30,000). The $2,400 of lost interest is an opportunity cost that should be considered in the decision. (*Opportunity costs* **are the costs associated with not taking a particular course of action.**) Also, the cost to borrow $30,000 is $3,600 (0.12 × $30,000) for the next year. Thus, to break even, Stockdale will need to recover the $60,000 invested and earn an additional $6,000 ($2,400 + $3,600) per year. Any amount earned over

Exhibit 3   An Illustration of Net Present Value

		Time		
Present		**Year 1**	**Year 2**	**Year 3**
Expected future cash flows		$25,000	$25,000	$25,000
Discounted to present value at 10%				

$22,727 \leftarrow \$25,000 \div 1.10^1$
$20,661 \leftarrow \$25,000 \div 1.10^2$
$\underline{18,783} \leftarrow \$25,000 \div 1.10^3$
$62,171$

Less:
 Amount invested $\underline{60,000}$

Net present value $\underline{\underline{\$\ 2,171}}$

$6,000 will increase company value and make the investment desirable. The $6,000 represents Stockdale's *cost of capital,* **which is the cost of funds that can be used to finance a project.** The rate of return necessary to earn $6,000 is considered Stockdale's *required rate of return.* **This rate sometimes is referred to as a** *hurdle rate* **because it is the rate that must be earned before an investment is made.** It is also known as the **discount rate** because it is the rate used to discount (reduce) future cash flows to their present value. In this case, Stockdale requires a 10% rate of return ($6,000 ÷ $60,000 = 10%).

Using the discount rate of 10%, we can compute the present value of the cash flow expected from the investment at the end of each of the three years.

$$PV = \frac{\$25,000}{(1.10)^1} + \frac{\$25,000}{(1.10)^2} + \frac{\$25,000}{(1.10)^3}$$
$$= \$22,727 + \$20,661 + \$18,783$$
$$= \$62,171$$

Alternatively, we can use the interest factor for an annuity from Table 2 (inside front cover) for three periods at 10%: $25,000 × 2.48685 = $62,171. Recall that an annuity results when the same amount is received each period over the life of an investment. The net present value, then, is the difference between the present value of the expected net cash inflows and the amount invested.

Year	Cash Flow	Present Value
1–3	$25,000*	$62,171
0	(60,000)+	(60,000)
Net present value		$ 2,171

* *Net cash inflows.*
+ *Amount invested at the beginning.*

A positive net psresent value indicates that the initial investment has been recovered and a return greater than the initial investment and cost of capital has been received. Thus, if the net present value is greater than zero, the investment is acceptable. If the net present value is less than zero, the investment should be rejected because it will earn less than the required rate of return.

To use net present value analysis, an organization must identify an appropriate discount rate. Usually, the discount rate is the average cost of all sources of financing available to a company, such as bank loans and returns to stockholders. Generally, managers should select those projects that promise the highest net present value.

SELF-STUDY PROBLEM 1

The management of Joyful Car, Inc., is considering replacing the company's current semiautomated car washing equipment with a fully automated system that would eliminate all labor except that required to clean car interiors. Though the new system will reduce labor costs, it represents a substantial capital investment for the small company. Management has developed the following data regarding the investment:

Cost of the new system	$100,000
Sales value of the old system	40,000
Sales value of the new system at the end of its five-year life	0
Required rate of return	10%
Net decrease in annual operating costs	15,000

Assume that Joyful has the cash to pay for the new equipment, and ignore any tax effects.

Required

Evaluate the investment using the NPV method. Assess the factors that increase or reduce the risk associated with the capital investment decision in this case. Explain whether you consider the investment to be an operational or a strategic decision for the company, and why. (*Hint:* The net decrease in annual operating costs can be treated as a net cash inflow.)

The solution to Self-Study Problem 1 appears at the end of the chapter.

Internal Rate of Return

Another discounting method is the internal rate of return. **The** *internal rate of return (IRR)* **is the interest rate that results in the present value of cash outflows being equal to the present value of cash inflows from an investment.** In other words, it is the interest rate that results in a net present value of zero. The following equation can be used to determine a project's IRR:

$$PV = \Sigma[C \div (1 + R)^t]$$

where PV = present value of the project
        C = cash inflow to be received in period t
        R = required rate of return
        t = time period
        Σ = summation for all periods

Let's consider the Stockdale Company's investment decision using the internal rate of return method. Recall that an investment of $60,000 is estimated to return $25,000 each year for three years. The cost to Stockdale of the $60,000 it will invest is $6,000, or 10%, which is the hurdle rate.

Using the internal rate of return method, the investment would be accepted if its internal rate of return is greater than 10%. The internal rate of return is the interest rate that equates $25,000 each year for three years with $60,000 today. The IRR would be calculated as follows:

$$PV = \Sigma[C \div (1 + R)^t]$$
$$\$60,000 = \frac{\$25,000}{(1 + R)^1} + \frac{\$25,000}{(1 + R)^2} + \frac{\$25,000}{(1 + R)^3}$$

We can find R by trial and error, or we can approximate the value using Table 2 from the front of the book. Table 2 provides an interest factor that associates the present value of an annuity with expected future cash flows:

$$PV = C \times IF$$
where PV = present value
C = expected cash flow each period
IF = interest factor
Therefore, $PV = C \times IF$
$\$60,000 = \$25,000 \times IF$
$\$60,000 \div \$25,000 = IF$
$2.4 = IF$

Look at the third row of Table 2. Note that an interest factor of 2.4 is the approximate value in the 12% column.

Thus, the internal rate of return is 12%. Because the internal rate of return is greater than the required rate of return of 10%, the investment should be accepted. The internal rate of return is higher than the cost of capital; thus, accepting the investment would add value to the company.

The internal rate of return for a multiyear project where the net cash inflows are not the same each year is the interest rate that will make the present value of the cash flows equal to the initial cash investment. Consider a project with an initial investment of $15,403 that is estimated to return cash flows of $4,000, $4,000, $5,000, and $8,000 for years 1 through 4 of the project, respectively. Again, the interest rate that will make the cash flows from operations equal to the initial cash outlay can be found by trial and error. Exhibit 4 calculates the present value of cash flows from operations using a discount rate of 10% and the interest factor from Table 1 (inside front cover). (Table 2 cannot be used because the expected net cash inflows are not the same amount each year.)

Exhibit 4   Present Value Calculation

Year	Expected Cash Flow		Interest Factor for 10% from Table 1		Present Value
1	$4,000	×	0.90909	=	$ 3,636
2	4,000	×	0.82645	=	3,306
3	5,000	×	0.75131	=	3,757
4	8,000	×	0.68301	=	5,464
					$16,163

The present value of the project is $16,163. This amount is greater than the initial investment of $15,403; therefore, 10% is *not* the IRR. A different interest rate must be tried. Should a higher or a lower rate be used? **The higher the interest rate, the lower the present value.** Since $16,163 is greater than $15,403, a higher interest rate must be used so that a lower present value is obtained. The present value using a rate of 12% is shown in Exhibit 5.

At 12% the present value of future cash flows from operations is exactly equal to the initial investment.

Exhibit 5 Present Value Calculation

Year	Expected Cash Flow		Interest Factor for 12% from Table 1		Present Value
1	$4,000	×	0.89286	=	$ 3,571
2	4,000	×	0.79719	=	3,189
3	5,000	×	0.71178	=	3,559
4	8,000	×	0.63552	=	5,084
					$15,403

Since the interest rate that makes the cash flow from operations equal the initial investment is 12%, this is the IRR for the investment. A trial-and-error procedure must be used to determine the IRR when the cash flows from operations are not the same each year. Computer programs such as Excel® and Lotus® contain functions that simplify the calculation. Even these programs begin with an estimated rate of return and use trial and error to find the internal rate of return.

Although the internal rate of return is easily understood by managers, a major disadvantage is that it does not differentiate between two projects that have identical rates of return but that differ in some other important way. For example, consider a $100 investment and a $100,000 investment, both of which have a 15% rate of return. Using the IRR method, both investments would be equally desirable, since they have identical returns. However, these investments are not equal because of the substantial difference in the cash outlays required.

Another disadvantage of the IRR method is that it assumes cash flows from operations can be reinvested at the internal rate of return. For example, if a project is expected to have an IRR of 20%, it is assumed that each time a cash flow from operations is received, the company will be able to reinvest the cash and earn 20% over the remaining life of the investment. This assumption is not always true and is a weakness of the IRR method. If the reinvested cash flow earns only a 15% return, the overall return on the investment will be less than 20%.

Payback Period

An approach to capital investment decision making that does not involve discounting is based on the payback period. **The** *payback period* **is the time required to recover an original investment from expected future cash flows.** For example, if the original investment is $100,000 and the estimated cash inflows are $50,000 per year, then the payback period is two years ($100,000 ÷ $50,000 per year). When the future cash flows for each period are expected to be equal, the payback period can be computed as follows:

Payback period = original investment ÷ periodic cash inflow

If the periodic cash inflows are not the same, the payback period is computed by adding each cash inflow until the sum equals the invested amount. Management decides on a time period in which the invested amount is to be recovered. A project that does not pay back its original investment within this period is rejected. There are shortcomings to such an approach, however. Consider the following cash flows for two projects, each requiring an initial investment of $100,000.

	Investment A	Investment B
Year 1	$20,000	$90,000
Year 2	80,000	10,000
Year 3	5,000	10,000

Both investments have payback periods of two years ($20,000 + $80,000 = $100,000, and $90,000 + $10,000 = $100,000). Thus, if a manager uses the payback period method, both would be equally desirable. In reality, however, B should be preferred over A. Project B returns $90,000 in the first year, compared to $20,000 for project A. The extra $70,000 can be invested in other projects during year 2. In addition, project B continues to return greater cash flows after year 2. Accordingly, the payback method ignores total profitability and the time value of money.

Many companies use the payback period as one of several criteria when making investment decisions. In addition, managers may use the payback method to choose among projects of similar value or attributes.

Accounting Rate of Return

The accounting rate of return is another commonly used decision-making method that does not require discounting. The *accounting rate of return (ARR)* **is the average accounting income a project generates per period divided by the amount of the investment in the project.** ARR differs from discounting methods in that it uses income rather than cash flows to measure return. ARR is computed as

Accounting rate of return = average income ÷ investment

The average income of a project is obtained by adding the net income for each period of the project and dividing by the number of periods over which the project will produce income. To illustrate the computation of accounting rate of return, assume that an investment requires an initial outlay of $100,000. The life of the investment is five years, and it is expected to produce net income as follows:

Year	Net Income
1	$10,000
2	10,000
3	20,000
4	15,000
5	25,000
Total	$80,000

The average net income is $16,000 ($80,000 ÷ 5), and the accounting rate of return is 16% ($16,000 ÷ $100,000).

Unlike the payback method, the accounting rate of return considers a project's profitability. Like the payback method, the accounting rate of return ignores the time value of money. Failure to consider the discounted time value of money may lead a manager to select a project that does not maximize company value. However, sometimes future cash flows are not easy to determine. Many investments involve combinations of resources such as plant assets, working capital, and labor, making cash flow from a project difficult to estimate. ARR, therefore, may be used instead of cash flows to get some idea of the return on investment.

Other Considerations

Objective 3
Explain how service life and residual value, the income tax effects of depreciation, and risk affect capital investment decisions.

In addition to the considerations discussed in the prior section, there are other considerations that affect the use of discounting models. Three of these considerations are: (1) the service lives and residual values of investments, (2) the effects of income taxes on investment cash flows, and (3) the risk associated with capital investment decisions.

The trade-in or *residual value* **of an investment refers to its market value at the end of its useful life or service life to a company.** *Service life* **refers to the period during which an investment is expected to be used.** A residual value must be estimated in order to make net present value and internal rate of return calculations. Failing to include the residual value understates the cash flows from an investment and could lead to rejection of an acceptable investment. Residual values can be difficult to estimate for an investment in equipment that has an uncertain life.

Sometimes managers overestimate the service lives of assets such as computers because they fail to consider the rate of change of technology. When new technology becomes available (for example, the Pentium® processor), management must decide whether to continue to operate with old assets or to purchase new assets sooner than expected.

Recall that depreciation is a noncash expense. However, depreciation reduces a corporation's taxable income because it is a tax-deductible expense. This reduction in taxes is cash that the company will not have to pay out. Therefore, although depreciation itself does not affect cash flows, its effect on taxes does. As a result, it is important to include the income tax benefits of depreciation when calculating the net present value or internal rate of return of capital investment projects. The following example illustrates how service life, residual values, and depreciation can affect investment decisions.

The Merchants' Bank is considering an investment in a new computer system to replace the old computer that is used to process deposits, loans, and other customer transactions. The bank uses the net present value method in its analysis of investment decisions.

The new system, including workstations, a network, and software, will cost $450,000 and will have an estimated useful life of five years. The expected residual value at the end of five years is $50,000. Straight-line depreciation is used for accounting and tax purposes. The old computer system, which has been depreciated to its residual value, can be sold for $20,000. The bank's income tax rate is 35%, and its required rate of return is 10%. Bank managers believe that the bank can save $100,000 each year if the new system is purchased. Should the bank invest in the new computer system?

Exhibit 6 provides an analysis of the investment to answer this question. The analysis involves a series of steps. In step 1, the amount to be invested ($430,000) is determined. In step 2, the amount of depreciation ($80,000 per year) and the effect of depreciation on taxes (savings of $28,000 per year) are calculated. In step 3, the expected cash flows associated with the investment each year are identified. Step 4 involves calculating the present value of the expected cash flows ($516,267). Finally, in step 5, the net present value of the investment ($86,267) is determined.

Because the net present value of $86,267 is greater than zero, the bank should invest in the new computer. In this analysis, the effect of tax savings is important. It adds $106,142 to the present value of the investment (step 4). Without these savings, the present value would be $410,125 ($516,267 − $106,142), and the investment would be unacceptable. Thus, it is important to consider all of the financial consequences of an investment in making a capital budgeting decision.

When managers are unsure about the accuracy of assumptions used in making investment decisions, they often test the sensitivity of their decisions to these assump-

Exhibit 6 Net Present Value Analysis of Computer Purchase

Step 1: Amount of Investment

Cost of new computer	$450,000
Less: Sale price of old computer	20,000
Amount to be invested	$430,000

Step 2: Tax Savings per Year

Cost of computer	$450,000
Less: Residual value	50,000
Amount to depreciate	$400,000
Expected life	÷ 5
Depreciation per year	$ 80,000
Income tax rate	× 0.35
Tax savings per year	$ 28,000

Step 3: Expected Future Cash Flows

Year	Cost Savings	Tax Savings	Residual Value
1	$100,000	$28,000	
2	100,000	28,000	
3	100,000	28,000	
4	100,000	28,000	
5	100,000	28,000	$50,000

Step 4: Computation of Present Value of Expected Future Cash Flows

Present value of annuity of $100,000 per year for 5 years at 10%:	
$100,000 × 3.79079 (interest factor from Table 2) =	$379,079
Present value of annuity of $28,000 per year for 5 years at 10%:	
$28,000 × 3.79079 =	106,142
Present value of single amount of $50,000 at the end of 5 years at 10%:	
$50,000 × 0.62092 (interest factor from Table 1) =	31,046
Total present value of expected future cash flows	$516,267

Step 5: Computation of Net Present Value of Investment

Total present value	$516,267
Amount to be invested	430,000
Net present value	$ 86,267

tions. For example, suppose the managers of the Merchants' Bank are unsure about the cost savings they expect from investing in the new computer system. They believe that the savings are most likely to be $100,000 per year, but that they could be as low as $75,000 per year. What effect would the lower level of savings have on the decision? The present value of an annuity of $75,000 per year for 5 years at 10% is $284,309 ($75,000 × 3.79079). Therefore, the total present value of expected cash flows (step 4) would be $421,497 ($284,309 + $106,142 + $31,046), and the net present value (step 5) would be −$8,503 ($421,497 − $430,000). At the lower cost savings, the project would be rejected. The managers now must decide whether they believe the lower cost savings are likely to occur or whether they are confident that the higher savings are likely. Net present value analysis, like other decision tools, does not make decisions for managers. It provides them with information to help them with their decisions.

THE NEW MANUFACTURING ENVIRONMENT

The new manufacturing environment has changed the way capital investment decisions are viewed. Before the new manufacturing environment, many companies relied heavily on methods such as net present value to justify capital investments. Traditional capital investment analysis focused mainly on the immediate direct benefits, such as labor savings, reduced waste, lower inventories, and improved capacity. Less tangible benefits such as improved quality often were not considered. In the 1980s, foreign companies that produced high-quality products began to compete with U.S. companies. This competition increased the pressure on U.S. companies to improve the quality of their products, which, in turn, increased the need to consider quality improvements when making capital investments.

Increased automation is a major feature of many production processes in the new manufacturing environment. Automation has become a priority for many companies as they replace older equipment. Much U.S. equipment is old compared to that in many other industrialized nations. Much of the older U.S. equipment is not computer-controlled, in contrast to that used in countries like Japan.

Automation and Modern Manufacturing

The objective of automation often is not only to increase capacity but also to produce high-quality goods in a consistent, rapid, and economical manner. Used effectively, automation can improve a company's ability to deliver high-quality products, to create value for customers. The new manufacturing environment requires a fresh look at the ways capital investment decisions are made. The costs of quality and efficiency are important to many capital investment decisions. These costs are especially relevant when companies automate their production processes.

Frequently, automation is part of a plan to redesign the value chain. Redesigning the value chain can involve many activities, from changing a company's production process to eliminating activities such as inventory storage, material handling, and excessive rework.

In the new manufacturing environment, capital investments involving automation can be classified into four categories, as illustrated in Exhibit 7 on the next page.

1. *Stand-alone tools,* such as robots used to weld steel, are commonly controlled by computers. Stand-alone tools are the most common form of automation. They can improve quality, speed, or capacity. The amount invested is relatively small compared to that needed for other types of automation. Also, the payback period is relatively short.
2. *Cells of machines* consist of multiple pieces of isolated equipment grouped closely together. An example of a cell is a computer-controlled machine for materials handling grouped with computer-controlled molding equipment to manufacture automobile body parts. These machines have a short setup time and can be quickly changed from the manufacture of one part to another. The amount of the investment often is much higher and the payback period much longer than for stand-alone tools.
3. *Linked islands* consist of cells of machines connected through computerized information networks. Islands give a company the ability to respond rapidly to developing markets by creating new, custom-designed products. Investments are large, and payback periods are long. Also, if one component of an island fails, the entire island is likely to fail.
4. *Computer-integrated manufacturing* links an entire manufacturing process through an extensive information network. For example, **Monsanto Plastics Division** manufactures plastics for use in automobiles, computers, and other products. In its old manufacturing process, changing from one type of plastic to another took hours. The division installed a computer-integrated manufacturing system that permits much faster changeover times, improved quality, and less waste.

Automated production can give a company a powerful competitive advantage in the global marketplace because it allows improved product innovation and quality, shorter delivery time, efficient production scheduling, and lower cost. Computer-integrated manufacturing can involve what are sometimes referred to as "greenfield

Exhibit 7   Categories of Automation

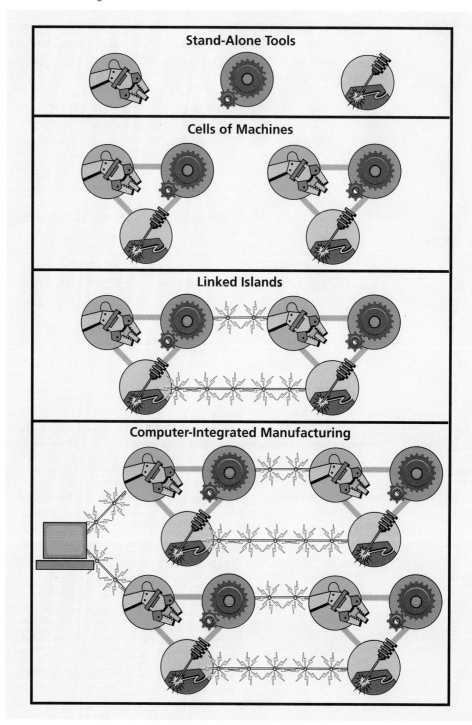

factories" because virtually the entire factory is redesigned. This type of capital investment has been referred to as a "you bet your company" decision because of the high level of risk involved. Failure of the strategy often means failure of the company.

These capital investment categories in the new manufacturing environment involve different levels of decisions, ranging from lower-level, operational decisions for stand-alone tools to very costly strategic decisions for computer-integrated manufacturing. The new manufacturing environment has changed the way many companies make capital investment decisions:

- Investments are becoming more significant. Automation can be large in scope and affect an entire company.
- Equipment is more complex and expensive than the equipment that was the focus of traditional investment decisions.
- The cash flows required to justify capital investments are received over a longer period of time.

In short, capital investment decisions have become longer-term and riskier. The next section examines how managers make capital investment decisions in this new strategic environment.

MAKING SOUND STRATEGIC DECISIONS

Objective 5
Identify factors that are important for strategic decisions.

Managers making capital investment decisions in the new manufacturing environment do not rely solely on traditional methods, such as net present value. This section highlights problems in making capital investment decisions and provides guidance on how these decisions should be made in the new manufacturing environment to avoid such problems. These problems have led some companies to underestimate the value of strategic investments that would improve their ability to compete in the new manufacturing environment. In some cases these investments are necessary for the survival of companies in intensely competitive markets.

Problems in Making Decisions

What are these problems? First, residual values often are critical to investment decisions. Estimating residual values can require managers to forecast technological, economic, operational, strategic, and market developments over several years. Residual values are especially difficult to estimate because they come at the end of the investment's expected service life. For example, a company may have difficulty estimating the residual value of a computer system in five years because the value depends on new systems introduced by manufacturers during the five-year period. Managers sometimes ignore the residual value of an asset because of uncertainty about its value. However, because strategic decisions usually involve high residual values, the failure to include estimates of residual values in discounting models biases decisions against strategic investments.

Second, because strategic investments in the new manufacturing environment often are long-term, the discount rate has a major effect on capital investment decisions. Many companies use discount rates that are higher than their current cost of capital. Setting discount rates too high biases decisions against strategic investments by decreasing the present value of the future cash flows.

Third, managers often fail to include the opportunity costs associated with not making a strategic investment. In the new manufacturing environment, these opportunity costs usually consist of the loss of future potential sales as a result of inferior quality, slower and less reliable delivery, and the inability to respond rapidly to customer demands for new products. These typical customer concerns in the new manufacturing environment often require strategic investments. Unfortunately, difficulty in estimating these opportunity costs often leads managers to omit them from their discounting models. Yet, consideration of the opportunity costs of not investing can be critical, not only to a single investment decision but also to the future of a company or a division.

As an example of a case in which opportunity costs are important, consider the following Case in Point, the World Transmission Project at the **Allison Transmission Division of General Motors.**

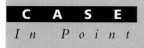

Allison Transmission is a world leader in making transmissions for heavy trucks. Allison has long been a very successful division of General Motors Corporation, with a reputation for consistently generating good cash flows.

During the 1980s, existing technology for making heavy transmissions was becoming obsolete. Further, foreign competitors threatened to build state-of-the-art facilities to manufacture a new generation of transmissions if Allison chose not to take this step. At the same time, General Motors was experiencing a financial downturn that made Allison's positive cash flows important to the company.

The facility that Allison needed if it was to continue to dominate the truck transmission market required an investment of over $500 million in robotics and built-in quality controls such as cameras that detected incorrectly assembled parts. Production scheduling and operations would be governed by a computer system that would integrate virtually all aspects of manufacturing.

Allison drew up plans for the new plant, called the World Transmission (WT) Project. It would take years to build the facility, to develop a new generation of transmissions, to train the workforce that would operate the new equipment, and to establish the products in the marketplace. Consequently, it would be some time before the new facility would begin to show positive cash flows. This presented a dilemma for General Motors. If Allison did not go forward with the WT Project, one of several foreign competitors probably would build a similar plant, and Allison would lose its edge in the market. If Allison built the plant, it would no longer produce positive cash flows for some time to come.

GM used traditional discounting methods to justify capital investments by its many divisions. The long term of the WT Project placed it at a disadvantage compared to short-term projects with high payoffs. As a result, the decision was delayed for a few years. Finally, GM authorized Allison to go forward with the WT Project. The ultimate success or failure of the project is still unknown.

Avoiding Problems

How should managers avoid the pitfalls associated with making capital investments in the new manufacturing environment? First, in applying traditional techniques for making capital investments, managers need to be careful in estimating residual values and discount rates. Second, managers need to include the opportunity costs of not investing in their strategic decisions. Third, managers should recognize the uncertainty of cash flows in many strategic investment situations.

Moving Baseline Concept

Traditional capital investment techniques compare the expected results of new investments with the company's current operating results. This comparison assumes that the company's current operating results will continue indefinitely and will not be hurt by the decision not to make an investment. If this assumption is wrong, the company will experience an opportunity cost by not investing in assets that will allow it to maintain its market share.

One method that addresses this issue is the *moving baseline concept*. Instead of assuming that current operating cash flows will continue indefinitely, **this concept assumes that if the investment is not made the cash flows will decrease because of the competition's superior quality.** For example, assume that the Sandy States Insurance Company is considering an automated customer service system that will lower costs and improve customer service. The lower costs will result in an improvement in existing net cash inflows of 30% each year. The system will cost $450,000, and additional cash outflows of $300,000 will be required each year to operate and service the system. The system will be in service for at least seven years.

Between year 1 and year 4, the project will generate increasing cash inflows in the form of reductions in operating costs. Cash inflows equal cash outflows after two and one half years. The project will generate net cash inflows of $450,000 per year by year 7, when all accounts will have been moved to the new system.

If Sandy States does not switch to the new system, it will begin to lose some business each year as a result of customer dissatisfaction. These losses are expected to reach $300,000 by year 7 as the old system becomes increasingly obsolete, leading to greater and greater customer dissatisfaction. Including the losses due to customer dissatisfaction in the analysis is what is meant by the moving baseline approach. Management has two choices: to assume that the current cash flows will continue or to assume that cash flows will decrease if the investment is not made.

Exhibit 8 compares the cash flows with the moving baseline (line a) to those without the moving baseline (line b). The moving baseline approach (line a) includes the quality benefits from investing in the new system, both in terms of reaching the break-even point sooner (c versus d) and in terms of total cash flows over the seven-year period. Including the cash inflows that are preserved by the quality benefits of the new system in the investment decision could make the difference between Sandy States investing and not investing.

Exhibit 8   Comparison of Cash Flows With and Without Moving Baseline

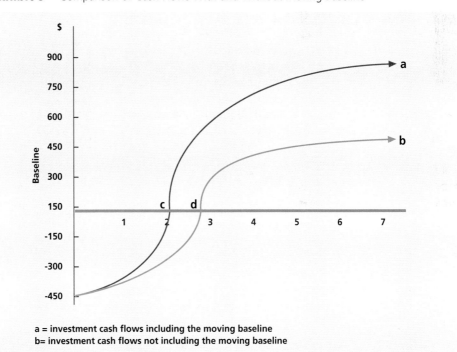

a = investment cash flows including the moving baseline
b= investment cash flows not including the moving baseline

Uncertain and Hidden Costs

Strategic investments often involve uncertain costs that are difficult to measure but that are extremely important to the decision. An example is a decision by a company to develop a new product line for unfamiliar markets. For example, **Pennzoil** made the mistake of underestimating warranty costs when it decided to invest in quick-change oil facilities. The failure of employees to remove and properly reinsert plugs in oil pans led to engine failures and unexpectedly high warranty costs. The company's lack of experience in the automobile maintenance business resulted in its failure to include adequate warranty costs in its investment decision.

The problems associated with strategic capital investments are not limited to manufacturing companies. Service companies can face similar decisions that have far-reaching consequences. Furthermore, marketing assumptions often are critical to the success of a strategic capital investment project, regardless of whether a company is a manufacturing or service business. Self-Study Problem 2 provides examples of two banks that made strategic capital investment decisions. In both cases, subjective marketing considerations were instrumental in the banks' decisions to fund the project. In analyzing this problem, keep the following points in mind:

- Capital investment decisions sometimes are made for reasons other than just return on investment. For example, management may believe that being in a particular market improves the company's image. Image may be important to a company's marketing strategy. If return on investment is much lower than expected, however, any marketing advantage may be more than offset by the cost of the investment.
- Where uncertainty about future cash flows is high because of uncertainty about revenues and costs, managers should consider a range of possible outcomes resulting from the capital investment.
- In situations where cash flows are uncertain, managers should be careful that their assumptions regarding factors that could affect future cash flows are realistic.

SELF-STUDY PROBLEM 2

In the middle 1970s, the **National Bank of Georgia (NBG)** seized an opportunity to establish a branch in a major office complex that was being built in downtown Atlanta. The facility represented a new concept in urban office space for the city. It was to contain its own shops, restaurants, and branch banks. Workers in the office space could work, shop, eat, and bank without ever leaving the complex. Some were touting this approach as the wave of the future. The complex attracted a great deal of attention, and branch banks

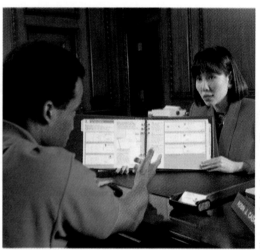

Photography by Alan Brown/Photonics

located in it were expected to be high-profile signals of the banks' presence in the downtown Atlanta market. At the time, NBG was the fifth largest bank in the city but was considered smaller than the leading banks, a position it had long held. NBG's management was trying to make a major push to become larger and more visible and to establish an image as a major player in the city's market. Although the lease expenses and costs of improvements would be very high, the new office complex seemed to afford the type of opportunity the bank wanted.

At about the same time NBG was considering its branching decision, **Home Federal Savings** of Rome, Georgia, was considering a strategic branching decision of its own. Rome was a small city of approximately 40,000 people. Home Federal was a small, independent S&L that was totally oriented toward making home loans and accepting savings deposits from individuals. It had long had a conservative banking philosophy. Despite its retail orientation, it operated from only one downtown location, unlike most of its competitors, which long ago had embraced branch banking. Home Federal's management, however, had come to the conclusion that the city's growth was headed in a westerly direction and that it had to establish a branch on that side of town or lose customers who considered the drive into town too inconvenient. Home Federal had the opportunity to acquire and remodel a vacant facility that had been used as a fast food restaurant at a cost that, although significant, was considerably lower than the cost of building a new branch. The facility was in a highly visible location. Home Federal's logo would be seen by thousands of motorists driving by each week.

Both banks elected to make the capital investments in branching. NBG's investment failed. The branch was closed within two years because the new office concept failed to generate enough customers. Leasing of office space in the complex was slower than expected, and far fewer customers than expected used the shops and restaurants. Conversely, Home Federal's branch was a great success. The branch was profitable within months after opening and continued to show good growth and profitability thereafter.

Required

What factors could account for the difference between these two strategic investment decisions? Why are marketing assumptions often critical to the success or failure of strategic capital investment decision?

The solution to Self-Study Problem 2 appears at the end of the chapter.

RESPONDING TO BAD CAPITAL INVESTMENT DECISIONS

O b j e c t i v e   6
Explain how evaluation systems can produce incentives to continue to fund unsuccessful investments and how companies can reduce the funding of such investments.

Capital investment projects sometimes are funded in stages. Decisions are made at each stage about whether to continue to fund a project. Once it becomes apparent that the project has failed, these decisions pose serious difficulties because a decision to continue can be very costly. This problem occurs in a bank when a loan officer continues to lend money to a failing customer to delay recognizing a loss. Managers should know that there is a tendency to continue funding failed projects and be able to recognize the causes of this tendency.

Costs of a project that cannot be recovered are sunk costs. Decision makers should ignore these costs when deciding whether to invest additional money in a project. Unfortunately, they often fall into a sunk cost trap, as shown in Exhibit 9.

When decision makers become aware that an investment is failing (a), they reexamine the investment (b) and weigh the benefits of terminating the investment (c) against the benefits of continuing (d). If the estimated costs of terminating the project are greater than the benefits, decision makers should withdraw from the project and accept the losses associated with withdrawal (e). However, if their commitment to the project is high (f), decision makers may continue to fund it (g) even though it is failing (h).

For example, suppose that a bank loaned money to a remanufacturer of automobile parts to buy raw materials for inventory production. Because of bad management practices, the remanufacturer used these funds to make inventory it could not sell. The remanufacturer then asked the bank for more money to buy raw materials to manufacture more inventory. The bank, fearing that the remanufacturer would fail if it did not loan the funds, made the second loan. The remanufacturer repeated its first mistake and ultimately failed. The bank lost considerably more money than it would have lost if it had recognized its first mistake and not loaned the additional funds. The bank focused on the sunk cost of the first loan and loaned additional money instead of cutting its losses.

In this cycle, information about a project's performance causes a reexamination of the project. If managers are committed to a project, they often fund the project until additional information is received.

Why do they do this? The reasons can be divided into four categories:

- *Project determinants:* These are objective features of a project. For instance, large sunk costs that cannot be recovered if the project is discontinued or the fact that

Exhibit 9   The Escalation Cycle

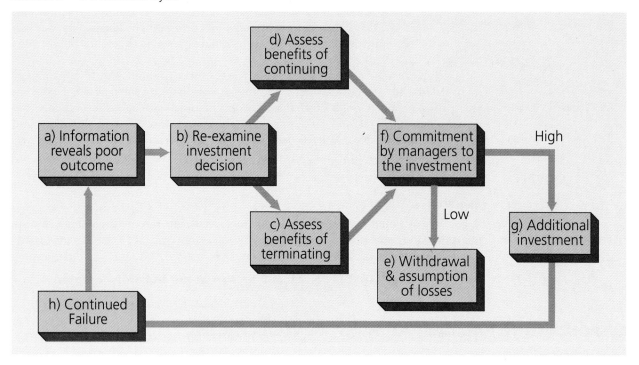

Adapted from Barry M. Staw and Jerry Ross, "Behavior in Escalation Situations: Antecedents, Prototypes, and Solutions," **Research in Organizational Behavior,** *1987, pp. 39–78.*

there are no competing projects that provide higher returns are both features that may contribute to the decision to continue.

- *Psychological determinants:* These are forces that can introduce error into managers' estimates of the gains and losses. Such forces influence the decision to continue or discontinue a project and can lead to greater investment. Examples: (1) Managers may have made the earlier decision to invest in the project and may feel a strong desire to continue investing because of their earlier decision. (2) Decision makers may believe withdrawing from the project will mean a loss of money already sunk instead of viewing the withdrawal as saving money not yet spent.

- *Social determinants:* These are pressures within the organizational environment. The need to save face, the desire to beat a competitor, the support of others for a project, and attitudes such as "never quit no matter what" encourage increased investment.

- *Structural determinants:* These are features of the organization itself. For example, the absence of appropriate project controls and a desperate need for a company to show progress can lead to continuing a project.

To avoid these problems, a company periodically may replace some members of the project management team with new members to bring fresh insights and to prevent too much personal identification with the project. Also, initial investment decisions can be separated from later investment decisions by requiring rejustification of a project with every funding decision. Companies can reduce the threat of failure for decision makers by acknowledging that well-managed projects are sometimes unsuccessful. For example, many banks encourage aggressive lending by loan officers. Loan officers who never generate loan losses are not sufficiently aggressive.

Identifying the opportunity costs associated with continuing to invest in failing projects may help managers make termination decisions. Also, it may be helpful to identify the potential costs of terminating a project before initial funding of the project, so that these costs will be more obvious from the beginning. Some risk of failure is associated with any project, and some failures must be expected. Managers should learn to evaluate and accept some failures.

CAPITAL INVESTMENT DECISIONS IN SERVICE COMPANIES

Objective 7
Describe the factors affecting capital investment decisions in service organizations.

Like manufacturing companies, service companies must make capital investment decisions. A service company must invest in those fixed assets that are necessary if it is to provide a service to its customers. This may mean investment in long-term construction projects such as railroad tracks, telephone lines, and even telecommunication satellites.

When making capital investment decisions, managers in service companies must take the same factors into consideration as managers in manufacturing companies. In addition, service companies such as railroads, telecommunication companies, and power companies often are government-regulated. Regulators frequently set the rates that service companies can charge their customers. They become concerned if they believe that the customers are being charged too much or are not being given good service. Regulators monitor regulated service companies' capital investments to determine whether they will lead to requests for higher rates and how they will affect customer service.

Remember that investment capital usually is scarce, so managers must put it to the best possible use. Managers in regulated service companies sometimes must choose between capital investments that will provide better service to different sets of customers. In such cases, regulators may exert pressure on the company to limit capital investment of one type in order to be sure that enough capital is invested in other services. This may be true even if the investment that the regulators limit has the potential to provide greater cash flows.

C A S E
I n   P o i n t

http://www.swcollege. com/ingram.html

Learn more about Matav.

The Hungarian telecommunications company, Matav, is responsible for providing basic telephone service to thousands of residences. Many of these residences do not yet have basic service. At the same time, Matav would like to expand its commercial services to businesses which provide the company with higher returns on investment. Matav does not have enough investment capital to provide both types of service to the extent it would like. The Hungarian government is forcing Matav to increase residential service each year. Therefore, the company must limit its investment in commercial equipment.

SELF-STUDY PROBLEM 3

Refer to the Case in Point involving General Motors' decision to fund the Allison Transmission "World Transmission Project." GM originally expected to spend approximately $500 million on the WT Project. After the project had been underway for several years, it became obvious that cost overruns would result in the project's costing in excess of $600 million. By the time the overruns became known, GM already had spent over $250 million on the project. Further, Allison experienced some production problems with the new transmissions. The division's cash flows were negative.

© Linc Cornell/Stock Boston

Required

Assume you are part of GM management. What factors would you consider in deciding whether to invest the additional $100 million to complete the WT Project? Discuss the factors in terms of the four categories of reasons for continuing to fund unsuccessful investments. What alternative(s) to abandoning the project might GM consider?

The solution to Self-Study Problem 3 appears at the end of the chapter.

R E V I E W *Summary of Important Concepts*

1. Capital investment decisions are important decisions about acquiring long-term assets.
    a. Operational decisions are those decisions that affect the day-to-day operations of the company and the short-run outcomes of those operations.
    b. Strategic decisions are those decisions that affect the major directions the company is taking and the long-run outcome of those directions.

2. Capital investment decisions often involve large outlays of cash for long periods of time.
    a. Several factors affect the risk associated with capital investments.
    b. Capital investment decisions can be difficult to reverse without large losses.
    c. Capital investment decisions often are political because different divisions compete for funds.

3. Traditional approaches to justifying capital investments are of two types, discounting and nondiscounting.
    a. Discounting methods take into account the time value of money.
        1. The net present value method compares the net present value of expected cash inflows and outflows associated with the investment.
        2. The internal rate of return method involves determining the interest rate that results in the present values of cash inflows and outflows being equal.
    b. Nondiscounting methods do not consider the time value of money.
        1. The payback period method involves determining the amount of time required to recover the initial investment.
        2. The accounting rate of return method uses the average accounting income a project generates per period divided by the amount of the investment.

4. Several additional factors should enter into capital investment decisions.
    a. The service life is the period during which an investment is expected to be used.
    b. Residual value is the market value of an investment at the end of its useful life.
    c. The income tax effects of depreciation on cash flows must be considered, because although depreciation is a noncash expense, it is tax-deductible.
    d. When there is uncertainty about future cash flows, managers should test the sensitivity of their decision to their assumptions.

5. The new manufacturing environment has changed capital investment decision making for many companies.
    a. Capital investment decisions have become more strategic.
    b. The costs of capital investments are increasing, and the payback periods are becoming longer.

6. Making sound strategic capital investment decisions requires managers to avoid several pitfalls.
    a. Managers should carefully consider salvage values and use appropriate discount rates.
    b. Managers should consider in their decisions the opportunity cost of not making a capital investment.

7. Managers often are reluctant to terminate a failing project.
   a. Reasons for this reluctance can be divided into project, psychological, social, and structural determinants.
   b. Managers can reduce this reluctance by being aware of the problem and taking steps to prevent it.

D E F I N E *Terms and Concepts Defined in This Chapter*

accounting rate of return (ARR) (346)
capital budgeting (338)
capital investment decision (338)
cost of capital (342)
discounting (341)
discounting methods (341)
hurdle rate (342)

internal rate of return (IRR) (343)
milestones (340)
moving baseline concept (352)
net present value (NPV) (341)
nondiscounting methods (341)
operational capital investment decision (338)
opportunity costs (341)

payback period (345)
required rate of return (342)
residual value (347)
service life (347)
strategic capital investment decision (338)
sunk costs (340)

S O L U T I O N S

SELF-STUDY PROBLEM 1

Evaluation using net present value method

YEAR Cash Flow	0 Present Value	1	2	3	4	5
Purchase of new system	$(100,000)					
Net decrease in operating costs	56,862*	15,000	15,000	15,000	15,000	15,000
Sales value of old equipment	40,000					
Net present value	$ (3,138)					

* $15,000 × 3.79079 from Table 2.

In this case, the net present value analysis indicates that the new investment should be rejected because the net present value is negative.

Joyful Car is already in the car washing business, so this is an investment in a business in which management has experience. This tends to reduce the risk. On the other hand, this would seem to be a large investment for a small company, increasing the risk. It is likely that part of the $100,000 total investment cost is installation cost for the new system, which probably would not be recaptured if the system had to be sold before the end of its useful life. This also increases the risk. Overall, this would appear to be a strategic investment for Joyful Car. Even though a car washing system may not seem like a major investment for many companies, it is for Joyful Car.

SELF-STUDY PROBLEM 2

The difference in the outcomes of the two branching decisions can be explained by the fact that Home Federal appears to have been much more careful to reduce its risk than NBG. Home Federal kept its costs down by buying a building at a reduced cost and renovating it.

Home Federal also appears to have a better understanding of its market. While NBG was inexperienced in dealing with the marketing environment of its new branch, Home Federal's management had observed the population movement in the area of its new branch for some time and was confident that the trade would support the branch.

Capital investment decisions often depend greatly on marketing assumptions. NBG's branch was inside a large office complex and not visible from the street. People driving by might not be aware of its existence. NBG gambled on a new concept in self-contained office space and hoped that the stores and restaurants would bring in enough outside clientele to support the branch. This did not happen—at least, not in time to save the branch. In contrast, Home Federal's branch was in a visible location seen by many potential customers. NBG took a significant risk and lost, partly encouraged by the hope that being in a prestige location would enhance its image. Home Federal took the safe road and was successful.

SELF-STUDY PROBLEM 3

GM should reconsider the costs and benefits of the WT Project. Among the factors to be reconsidered probably would be (1) the future stream of cash inflows and outflows based on revised marketing and production forecasts, (2) the likelihood of resolving the production difficulties with the new transmissions, and (3) any costs associated with abandoning the project, such as contract cancellation costs.

The WT Project falls into the category of computer-integrated manufacturing in terms of the level of automation. Virtually the entire manufacturing operation was controlled by computers.

It is difficult to determine at this point whether the WT Project is an escalation situation. After several years and over $500 million invested in the WT Project, it is unlikely that GM would abandon the project for several reasons. Some of these, categorized in terms of Staw and Ross's four determinants of escalation, are:

Project determinant: There is the possibility that the setback in the WT Project is only temporary and that it still might succeed in the long run.

Psychological determinant: There is a very large sunk cost in the WT Project that GM management would be reluctant to write off.

Social determinant: GM might naturally be reluctant to admit to a high-profile mistake such as the failure of a project like the WT Project.

Structural determinant: GM is in a battle with foreign competitors in many of its markets. Maintaining its position as the leading manufacturer of high-quality transmissions for heavy equipment could be important to GM's image.

GM did continue to fund the WT Project. However, it attempted to sell Allison Transmission to other corporations in the hope of eliminating the negative cash flows associated with the WT Project.

EXERCISES

10-1. Write a short definition of each of the terms listed in the *Terms and Concepts Defined in This Chapter* section.

Obj. 1　　**10-2.** Managers at Precision Products are considering a change in the method used to apply paint to the company's products. The new method represents the newest technology. Instead of traditional "wet" painting, it uses electromagnetics to make powdered paint adhere to product surfaces. Precision's major competitors already have adopted the new paint method. The new method would require replacement of the paint booths currently being used, resulting in a $250,000 capital expenditure. Nearly all of Precision's products require painting. The new paint method is expected to improve the paint quality, reduce the product rejects, and enhance customer satisfaction. Is the decision to change painting methods an operational or strategic capital investment decision? Explain your answer.

Obj. 1　　**10-3.** A local manufacturing company is planning to purchase a new computer software system that will affect the entire company. The new system will allow the receptionist to log all incoming calls and messages on the company's electronic mail system so that users will have immediate notice of incoming calls. The cost of the new system will be $20,000, and it is estimated that the investment will have a useful service life of five years. Would this investment be considered operational or strategic? Explain your answer.

Obj. 1   **10-4.**   Tim and Tom are brothers who split a large inheritance. Tim used all of his money to buy a company that manufactures a single product used in high-tech industries. Tom used his money to lease two small retail stores in a nearby mall, one that sells candles and another that sells yogurt. He also purchased inventory and equipment to start the businesses. Assuming that neither of the brothers has any experience in his new endeavor, which of the brothers has the greater investment risk, and why?

Obj. 1   **10-5.**   Caltron Enterprises operates a multimillion-dollar plant and is considering an expansion of its facilities to support a new product line. Should the cost of the company's existing plant and equipment affect the expansion decision? Explain your answer.

Obj. 2   **10-6.**   Assume that a friend has asked to borrow $100 from you. You agree, as long as your friend pays you 6% annual interest to provide for the time value of money. Your friend wants to know what is meant by "time value of money." How would you explain this concept?

Obj. 2   **10-7.**   Erin Brady won a $500 prize in a raffle. The winning ticket states, "Prizes are payable in six months from contest date, or may be discounted at 10% for immediate payment." Erin has asked you what is meant by the term "discounted." What would you tell her?

Obj. 2   **10-8.**   Douglas Wright has calculated the net present value of a proposed project investment and has obtained a negative amount. Assuming that Douglas calculated the net present value properly, what does the negative amount indicate about this investment?

Obj. 2   **10-9.**   Julie Russo attended a company meeting to discuss a potential investment in new machinery. The company uses the payback method to analyze potential investments. After reviewing the figure, Julie commented, "These figures are not reliable. They have not been discounted." Do you agree with Julie? Why or why not?

Obj. 2   **10-10.**   Bill Rubble, president of Melinco Company, reviewed a proposal for a project investment that was submitted by the vice president of production. Bill attached a note to the proposal that said, "Please recalculate this proposal—adjust the rate of return by 2% to compensate for the higher risk involved." Should the vice president increase or decrease the rate of return when recalculating the proposal?

Obj. 2   **10-11.**   Samuel Sanchez is a project manager for Johnson Industries. Samuel wants to analyze a potential investment. He seeks a method that considers the project's profitability but is not affected by the time value of money. What method would you suggest Samuel utilize?

Obj. 2   **10-12.**   Capital budgeting models such as NPV, internal rate of return, payback, and accounting rate of return make managing easier, because future projects can be approved immediately if target values are obtained. Do you agree or disagree? Why?

Obj. 3   **10-13.**   Paul Bruce, controller of Chief Industries, performs investment analysis for all of the company's capital projects. Paul has complained that investment analysis is difficult because there are so many estimates that must be made. What are some of the variables that typically must be estimated in a capital budgeting decision?

Obj. 3   **10-14.**   Assume that the internal rate of return on a particular capital investment project has been calculated and is exactly equal to the target rate a company has established for such projects. If tax rates are expected to increase in the future, would the investment become more or less desirable from an internal rate of return standpoint?

Obj. 4   **10-15.**   Tanguchi Equipment Company manufactures cabs and chassis for fire trucks, ambulances, and other emergency vehicles. Parts manufactured by Tanguchi require precision and quality. The company employs a highly trained workforce that produces most parts by hand and has maintained a moderate level of production quality. How would quality affect capital decisions at Tanguchi?

Obj. 4 **10-16.** The Newhart Company is planning a major capital investment program to automate its production processes, which are currently labor-intensive. What impact on its cost structure should the company expect from its factory automation program?

Obj. 5 **10-17.** Everyday Plastics Corporation wants to invest in new machinery that would allow the company to be more responsive to changes in customer demand. The company has an excellent credit rating and can borrow funds at the prevailing prime interest rate. To be on the "safe" side, however, the company has analyzed the potential investment using a discount rate 3% above the prevailing prime interest rate. Why would the company want to increase the discount rate to be on the safe side, and what is the likely effect of using a rate higher than the available borrowing rate on the company's analysis of the investment decision?

Objs. 3,5 **10-18.** Chambers Industries manufactures copper tubing used in many mechanical applications. The company believes that it must invest in a new facility if it is to remain competitive with foreign manufacturers. A preliminary analysis of the proposed investment indicates that property, plant, and equipment costing more than $50 million would be needed to bring the facility into operation. The residual value of the investment would be $1.5 million at the end of 15 years. Failure to commit to the new investment would cause the company to realize an estimated $250,000 a year in lost income. What are the relevant costs that Chambers should include in its capital investment decision, and why?

Obj. 5 **10-19.** In an effort to convince the president of Utah Instruments to expand the company's product lines, Lynnette Peters, vice president of marketing, inflated potential future sales figures on a proposed product. Lynnette believed that without the inflated marketing estimates, the new product would not be pursued. If the new product is undertaken, extensive capital investment will be required. How could improper or poor estimates of market conditions adversely affect a capital investment decision?

Obj. 6 **10-20.** Allen Hardaway is president of Fly High Shoes. Allen recently approved the purchase of several acres of land near the company factory to build a retail shoe outlet. Allen's plan to sell shoes directly to the public at the factory store was met with immediate disapproval by several of Fly High's largest customers, who have threatened to take their business to a competitor if the factory outlet is opened. "Never mind them," said Allen. "This project is a great idea. Besides, we already bought the land and paid an architect for store plans. We can't stop now!" Do you think Allen is throwing good money after bad if he pursues the factory outlet investment? What advice would you give Allen?

PROBLEMS

PROBLEM 10-1 **Operational and Strategic Decisions**

Obj. 1

Classify each of the following capital investment decisions as either operational or strategic. Briefly justify your answers.

1. A bank decides to build a new branch in the same town where it has 15 other branches. The new branch will cost $200,000, and will have an estimated service life of 25 years with a $150,000 residual value.

2. A bank decides to add automatic teller machines (ATMs) in the lobby of each of its 15 branches. The bank has never offered ATMs to customers in the past. The machines will have an estimated service life of 15 years with no residual value.

3. A company automates an entire production process that had not previously been automated. The automation includes computer-controlled equipment linked together in work cells. The machines will improve quality and increase the number of products offered, and they are expected to head off entry into the market by a major competitor. The machines will have an estimated useful life of nine years with a residual value of $350,000.

4. A company updates several pieces of factory equipment with new models. The new models have increased safety features and can operate faster than the older models. The new machines also have new features that will allow workers to perform tasks that the old machines could not perform. The estimated service life of the new machines is 10 years, and they will have a residual value of $75,000.

PROBLEM 10-2 Basic Net Present Value Analysis

Obj. 2

Community Drycleaning would like to purchase a new machine for cleaning large quilts and comforters. The current cleaning operation on quilts and comforters is done by hand. The new machine would cost $12,500. The estimated service life is 12 years, at which time it is estimated that the machine could be sold for $500.

The company estimates that it would cost $700 per year to operate the machine. The current cost of manual cleaning is $3,000 per year. In addition to reducing costs, the new machine would increase the drycleaner's ability to clean quilts and comforters by 600 per year. The company realizes a contribution margin of $1.50 per quilt or comforter. A 10% rate of return is required on all investments. Community expects its tax rate to be 30%.

Required

a. What are the annual net cash inflows that would be realized from the new machine?
b. Compute the net present value of the investment (round to the nearest dollar).

PROBLEM 10-3 Present Value Calculations

Obj. 2

Terry Partee received severance pay from an employer and invested the money in stock. On January 1, 1996, Terry bought 200 shares of Cinco, Inc., for $12,000. In each of the following three years, he received dividends of $420 cash, which he did not reinvest, but rather, used to pay monthly bills. On December 31, 1998, he sold the stock for $15,000. Terry would like to earn at least 12% on his investment, and a local stockbroker who wants Terry's business has promised that he can invest the proceeds from Terry's stock sale and earn 12% annual interest. Terry is not sure if he earned 12% return on the Cinco stock and would like some help with the necessary computations.

Required Determine whether Terry earned the required 12% annual interest on his investment for the last three years. Is the broker's guaranteed 12% return better than the return he realized on the Cinco investment? (Round calculations to the nearest dollar.)

PROBLEM 10-4 Accounting Rate of Return and Payback

Obj. 2

Brad Koester has an opportunity to invest in a bicycle franchise shop under a nationally recognized brand name. Brad has assembled the following information and estimates relating to this opportunity:

1. Rent on a operating facility would total $3,000 per month.

2. Estimated sales income would total $800,000 per year, and the variable cost of goods sold would be 70% of sales revenue.

3. Costs to operate the shop would include $87,000 per year for salaries and benefits, $4,000 per year for insurance, $15,000 per year for utilities, and $10,000 per year for office expenses.

4. Display racks, repair equipment and other fixed assets would cost $270,000 and have an estimated service life of 15 years, with no salvage value at the end of service life. Brad would use the straight-line depreciation method.

5. Brad must pay a commission of 5% of sales to the bicycle supplier.

If Brad does not invest in the bicycle shop, he could invest his funds in long-term bonds that would pay 12% annual interest.

Required

a. Determine the net annual income that Brad would realize from the franchise, ignoring income taxes. (Use the contribution approach format income statement.)

b. Compute the accounting rate of return that would be obtained by the franchise. Based on the accounting rate of return, would Brad be better off financially by investing the franchise or the long-term securities?

c. Compute the payback period on the franchise. If Brad wants a payback period of five years or less, should he invest in the franchise? (Ignore income taxes.)

PROBLEM 10-5 **Internal Rate of Return**

Obj. 2

The Wild Side Bowling Alley is planning to invest in pinball machines and pool tables for use by its patrons. The equipment will cost $3,896 to acquire and will have an estimated service life of seven years with no residual value. Based on estimates by the owner, the tables and games will generate approximately $800 a year of cash inflow after all expenses have been met.

Required

a. Compute the internal rate of return promised by the table and games.

b. Assume that the owner will not invest in the equipment unless it has a 12% internal rate of return. Compute the amount of annual cash inflows that would be required on the initial investment to obtain this rate of return.

PROBLEM 10-6 **Payback, Rate of Return**

Obj. 2

A piece of labor-saving equipment is available to the Armtech Company that could be used to reduce costs at one of its plants. Relevant data related to this particular equipment are as follows:

Purchase price of equipment	$432,000
Net annual cash savings provided by the new equipment	$ 90,000
Estimated service life of equipment	12 years
Required rate of return	14%

Required

a. Compute the payback period for the new equipment. If the company requires a payback period of four years or less, would you recommend purchase of the equipment? Explain your answer.

b. Compute the internal rate of return on the equipment. Use straight-line depreciation based on the equipment's estimated service life. Would you recommend that the equipment be purchased? Explain your answer.

PROBLEM 10-7 **Net Present Value and Automation Decision**

Objs. 2,4

Tony Setimi, president of Solidex Machinery, is considering the purchase of an automated stamping machine. In reviewing the figures prepared by the production department, Tony has noted that the machine would cost $500,000 plus another $80,000 for controls and programming. In addition, the production department estimates that the machine would cost $3,000 a month to maintain. Further, the production department estimates that repairs totaling $45,000 would be required at the end of seven years.

Tony gave the figures to Becky Roberts, the controller, and asked her to analyze the situation and be prepared to offer her opinion in the morning. Becky determined that the new machine would replace six workers and save $108,000 a year in labor costs. She also determined that $6,500 a year in scrap costs could be avoided and that the current equipment being replaced could be sold for $12,000. She then calculated depreciation on the new machine, assuming it would last 12 years and have a residual value of $20,000. She noted that the company's current cost of capital is 11%.

Required

a. Compute the net annual cost savings that would be realized from the new machine. (Ignore income taxes.)

b. Using the data from requirement a and information from the problem, compute the new machine's net present value. (Ignore income taxes.)

c. Assume that there are intangible benefits such as reduced setup time, improved quality, and greater flexibility of production. What annual dollar value would the company have to assign to these intangible factors in order to make the new machine an acceptable investment?

PROBLEM 10-8
Objs. 2,5

Capital Investment Decision, Changing Environment, Moving Baseline

Rita Sanchez, the president of your company, has asked for your help in a capital investment decision. The company has an opportunity to invest in a new piece of equipment that will cost $400,000. This equipment represents the latest technology and will be able to perform certain tasks that were previously labor-intensive. Rita is concerned that the investment is too costly compared to the cost of the laborers who are currently performing the tasks. She is aware, however, that a major competitor is investing in similar equipment, and she is worried that failure to invest may result in lost sales. Rita has asked that you draft a memo explaining how the investment should be analyzed and how the new technology might be justified.

Required Draft a memo to Rita explaining the use of net present value as a tool for making capital investment decisions and explain why the moving baseline approach is necessary in such a decision. In your memo, be sure to explain both the strengths and the potential weaknesses of capital investment analysis.

PROBLEM 10-9
Objs. 2,3,5

Impact of Errors on Decision Making

Westco, Inc., is considering a capital investment project. Explain how each of the following situations would affect the capital investment decision Westco is considering. Explain whether each situation would make the project more or less likely to be accepted. Consider each situation independently:

1. The net present value of the proposed investment is zero.

2. The estimated service life used to evaluate the investment was 10 years, when in reality the actual service life is 12 years. The investment was analyzed using the accounting rate of return model.

3. The company desires a 12% return on the investment but inadvertently used a 14% factor in its analysis. The company utilizes the net present value method of investment analysis.

4. In its original internal rate of return analysis of the investment Westco failed to consider the income tax effects of depreciation on the investment. The net present value model was used in the analysis.

5. The residual value of the project under consideration was estimated at $30,000, when in reality the actual residual value of the project is $20,000. The company utilized the net present value method of investment analysis.

PROBLEM 10-10

Multiple-Choice Overview of the Chapter

1. In which of the following situations would it be appropriate to accept a project under the net present value method?
   I. Net present value is positive.
   II. Net present value is zero.
   III. Net present value is negative.

a.   Only I.
b.   Only II.
c.   Both I and II.
d.   Both II and III.

2. An investment for which the net present value is $300 would result in which of the following conclusions?
    a.   The net present value is too small, and so the project should be rejected.
    b.   The investment project promises more than the required rate of return.
    c.   The net present value method is not suitable for evaluating this project.
    d.   The investment project should be accepted only if the net present value is zero.

3. Which of the following statements regarding investments in automated equipment is not correct?
    a.   The cost of automating a process is usually minor compared to other alternatives.
    b.   The total cost to automate a process consists of outlays for machinery and equipment.
    c.   The benefits of automation are often tangible, direct, and easy to quantify.
    d.   A decision to automate usually results from a commitment to quality and customer satisfaction.

4. When a company considers an investment in automated equipment, it should:
    a.   focus primarily on ways to reduce direct labor cost.
    b.   select only automation projects with positive net present values.
    c.   consider both the tangible and intangible benefits of automation.
    d.   automate the entire process rather than take a piecemeal approach to automation.

5. The Wilson Company purchased a machine with an estimated useful life of seven years. The machine will generate cash inflows of $8,000 each year over the next seven years. If the machine has no salvage value at the end of seven years and the company's discount rate is 10%, what is the purchase price of the machine if the net present value of the investment is $12,000? (Round to the nearest dollar.)
    a. $38,947
    b. $26,947
    c. $12,000
    d. $50,947

6. Elizabeth Rankin invested $60,000 to start a business at the beginning of 1996. She withdrew $10,000 at the end of each year for the next five years. At the end of the fifth year, Elizabeth sold the business for $100,000 cash. At a 12% discount rate, what is the net present value of Elizabeth's business investment. (Round to the nearest dollar.)
    a. $60,000
    b. $36,048
    c. $56,743
    d. $32,791

7. Anthony operates a part-time auto repair service. He estimates that a new diagnostic computer system will result in increased cash inflows of $1,200 in Year 1, $2,300 in Year 2, and $3,500 in Year 3. If Anthony's cost of capital is 10%, then the most he would be willing to pay for the new computer system would be (rounded to the nearest dollar):
    a. $4,599.
    b. $5,502.
    c. $5,621.
    d. $5,107.

8. The moving baseline concept is based on the assumption that:
    a.   currect cash flows can continue indefinitely into the future.
    b.   customer dissatisfaction can be avoided with increased quality.
    c.   a competitor will adversely affect a company's cash flows if an investment is not made.
    d.   investment in new equipment is an opportunity cost.

9. A manager who fails to terminate a failing capital investment project:
   a. is probably unaware that the investment is failing.
   b. may do so because sunk costs are not being ignored.
   c. may be reacting to pressures within the organizational environment.
   d. all of the above.

10. Which of the following items must be estimated when a capital investment decision is made?
    a. Service life of investment
    b. Residual value of investment
    c. Both a and b
    d. Neither a nor b

C A S E S

CASE 10-1
Obj. 2
Capital Investment Decision, Discounting and Nondiscounting Methods of Analysis

Leroy Mandel is investigating the possibility of starting a hardware business. Leroy would sell home products, supplies, and maintenance materials. He has determined that the initial cost of the store would be $400,000 to acquire a suitable lease, obtain store fixtures, and fund working capital requirements. To obtain the needed funds, Leroy intends to sell $300,000 of stock and borrow $100,000 from a bank. The stock would pay annual dividends of 8% and the bank loan will carry interest of 16%.

Leroy also has estimated that the store will generate an annual cash inflow of $50,000. For purposes of analysis, Leroy expects to operate the business for 20 years and then retire. Leroy does not want to invest unless he can fully recover his investment within nine years. There will be no residual value at the end of the 20 years, as the lease will expire, the inventory will be sold through normal operations, and store fixtures will be scrapped.

Required

a. Compute Leroy's cost of capital.
b. Calculate the payback period.
c. Assuming that depreciation is $10,000 per year, compute the accounting rate of return. (Ignore income taxes.)
d. Compute the net present value of the investment.
e. Compute the internal rate of return of the investment.
f. If you were Leroy, would you invest in the store? Why or why not?

CASE 10-2
Objs. 2,5
Investment Analysis, NPV, Payback, Uncertainty

The Perfect Chef Company is constantly developing and marketing new cooking accessories. Based on past experience in forecasting cash flows for a new product, Perfect Chef has been able to predict cash flows within 10 percent of actual results. The longer the estimated life of a particular product, the greater the uncertainty surrounding future cash flows. The company currently is evaluating a project that is expected to have a five-year service life.

Accordingly, in performing net present value analysis of new product offerings, the company computes three different net present value figures: most likely, optimistic, and pessimistic. On a five-year project, the pessimistic computation assumes that the cash flows are overstated by 10% in the first three years of the project and by 50% in the last two years. The optimistic computation assumes that the estimates are understated by 10% in the first three years and 50% during the last two years. The most likely computations use the estimates without adjustment.

Perfect Chef is developing a new pressure cooker. To produce the pressure cooker, $625,000 must be invested in special equipment. The following are estimated net annual cash inflows that have been developed to analyze the potential product:

Year	Projected Net Annual Cash Inflows
1	$200,000
2	250,000
3	200,000
4	150,000
5	100,000

The company's cost of capital is 8%.

Required

a. Prepare a schedule of cash flows for five years based on the three methods described above.
b. Compute the net present value for each of the three methods.
c. Compute the payback period for each of the three methods.
d. Based on your calculations in requirements b and c, would you advise Perfect Chef to produce the cooker? Explain your answer.
e. Explain why Perfect Chef might not want to invest in a product that has a payback period greater than three years.

PROJECTS

PROJECT 10-1
Obj. 2

Rate of Return on Stocks

Select 10 publicly traded stocks for which prices are quoted in *The Wall Street Journal*. Obtain a recent copy of *The Wall Street Journal* and a copy from the prior year. Compare the current closing price to that of a year ago. Based on changes in the stock price, calculate the rate of return for each of the stocks. Don't forget to include any dividends that have been paid over the past year in your analysis. Rank your selections from highest return to lowest, and prepare a summary of your findings.

PROJECT 10-2
Objs. 4,7

The New Business Environment

Review a trade or industry publication of your choice. These publications frequently describe new technologies that are available within the industry. Write a short narrative explaining the nature of the new technology and its potential impact on both product cost and customer expectations. Present your findings to the class.

PROJECT 10-3
Objs. 1,2,4,7

Factors Affecting Capital Investment Decisions

Interview a manager who has been involved in capital investment decisions for a company in your area. Determine what methods the manager has used in making an investment decision. Classify the investment decision as operational or strategic. Determine whether the manager used numerical calculations such as NPV and IRR in the analysis, and identify other concerns such as competition and customer expectations that may have affected the decision. Write a summary of your interview and present it to your class.

Section 3

Expanded Topics

Internal

Control

Accounting and Management Decisions

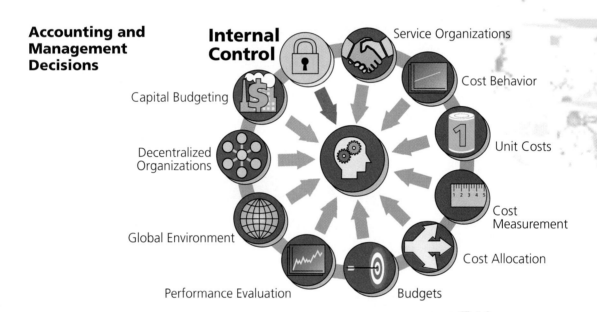

Internal Control

Service Organizations

Capital Budgeting

Cost Behavior

Decentralized Organizations

Unit Costs

Cost Measurement

Global Environment

Cost Allocation

Performance Evaluation

Budgets

Overview

Previous chapters consider the importance of accounting as an information system that is useful in making management decisions. Managers use accounting information in planning for future operations and in evaluating progress toward meeting organizational goals. To be useful for any of these purposes, accounting information must be reliable. If a division reports sales of $2 million for the current month or total assets of $20 million at the end of the month, those amounts must be accurate or management decisions are likely to be flawed. This chapter examines the role of accounting in ensuring the reliability of information and protecting a company's resources. This role generally is known as the internal control function of accounting. It is a major management accounting activity in most organizations.

A variety of problems can cause inaccurate information. Errors in recording transactions can lead to incorrect account balances. For example, recording revenues before goods are sold will overstate income for a period. Also, theft of assets or intentional misstatement of account balances can produce errors in accounting numbers. For instance, inventory balances will be overstated if employees routinely steal materials or merchandise for personal use or sale. Internal control systems are designed to prevent theft or misuse of a company's assets and to ensure the reliability of information. Also, they are designed to detect these problems if they exist.

This chapter examines the purpose of internal control systems and how these systems function to protect a company's assets and ensure the reliability of accounting and other information. It considers

© Kenneth Jarecke 1986/The Stock Market

the structure of internal control systems and the types of problems these systems are designed to solve.

Major topics covered in this chapter include:
- The purpose and objectives of internal control systems.
- Human behavior problems that create a need for internal controls.
- The structure of internal control systems.
- The function of internal auditing.

Objectives

Once you have completed this chapter, you should be able to:

1. Define internal control and identify its objectives.
2. Explain human behavior problems that create a need for internal control systems.
3. Identify the components of an internal control system.
4. Explain why a company's organizational environment is important for meeting internal control objectives.
5. Explain why risk assessment is an important component of an internal control system.
6. Identify primary types of control procedures and the types of activities to which they are applied.
7. Explain why communications are important in internal control systems.
8. Describe ways in which companies monitor their internal control systems and explain why monitoring is important.
9. Describe the purpose and functions of an internal auditing department.

INTERNAL CONTROL OBJECTIVES

Objective 1
Define internal control and identify its objectives.

Internal control **refers to the methods a company uses to protect its assets and promote their efficient use, to ensure accurate and reliable information, and to encourage adherence to laws and regulations.**[1] Internal control can be very valuable to a company. It can prevent losses due to theft and misuse of resources. It can promote quality decisions by ensuring that the information managers use is reliable. It can evaluate whether management policies and plans are being carried out throughout a company. It can help prevent legal action against a company because of violation of trade, product, or labor laws. Therefore, internal control systems are integral to the operations of most companies. In fact, all corporations that report to the **Securities and Exchange Commission** are required to maintain a system of internal control that is evaluated as part of the annual external audit. Failure to maintain an effective internal control system casts serious doubt on the reliability of the accounting information reported externally to investors and used internally by managers.

A company designs its internal control procedures to accomplish several objectives:

- To encourage effective and efficient operations to promote profitability and protection of assets
- To ensure the reliability of accounting information to avoid misstated and misleading reports
- To ensure that a company does not violate laws and regulations of the jurisdiction where it does business

The first and second of these objectives are closely related. Accounting information is not accurate unless it reflects a company's economic activities and resources. Exhibit 1 illustrates this relationship. The first panel of the exhibit assumes that a company receives $10,000 from customers. The cash is placed in a cash register. Sales invoices indicate that $10,000 was received, and this amount is recorded in the company's accounts. If the amount of cash and the amount recorded are the same, the resulting accounting information matches economic reality.

Exhibit 1 The Relationship Between Accounting Information and Economic Activities

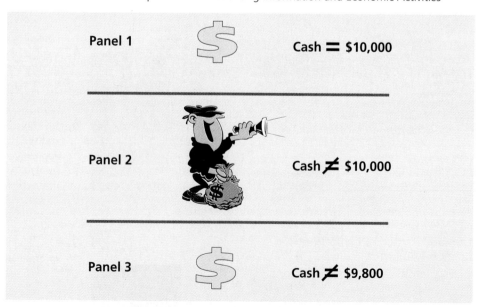

---

[1] *Adapted from Committee on Auditing Procedure,* Internal Control *(American Institute of Certified Public Accountants, 1949).*

Suppose, however, as in the second panel, that an employee steals some of the money from the cash register. Sales invoices indicate that $10,000 was received, and this amount is recorded in the company's accounts. Though sales of $10,000 were made, the company's Cash account balance does not match the actual amount of cash the company has. Thus, the accounting records are misstated.

As a third alternative, shown in panel three, $10,000 of cash may be received from customers and placed in the cash register. However, sales invoices indicate that only $9,800 of cash sales were made, and this amount is recorded in the company's accounts. Again, the accounting records are misstated. Therefore, it is important that a company both protect its assets and properly record its transactions in order for accounting information to be accurate.

The third objective of internal control, to ensure that a company does not violate laws and regulations of the jurisdiction where it does business, is also important for a company's economic performance and the validity of its accounting information. If a company violates laws and regulations, it can be subject to litigation, fines, and other penalties. In such cases, accounting information may not fully reflect the expected future performance of a company unless the economic effects of legal problems are considered.

C A S E

In Point

http://www.swcollege.com/ingram.html

Learn more about the Valdez oil spill.

Corporations can face major litigation and fines for violating laws and regulations. One of the most notable cases is that of **Exxon Corporation,** which paid approximately $1 billion to settle claims related to the Valdez oil spill in Alaska. Fines are not uncommon in the oil industry. **Chevron** paid $8 million in fines for actions involving drilling off the coast of California. Fines are common for other types of companies, as well. **Bristol-Myers Squibb,** a pharmaceutical company, was fined $3.5 million for illegally polluting waters near its plant in East Syracuse, New York. **Metropolitan Life Insurance Company** faced fines of $20 million for its sales practices in Florida and other states. Before its bankruptcy, **Eastern Airlines** was fined $3.5 million for falsifying airplane maintenance records. All of these cases involved negligence and improper behavior that led to violations of laws and regulations.

INTERNAL CONTROL AND HUMAN BEHAVIOR

Objective 2
Explain human behavior problems that create a need for internal control systems.

Internal control systems are based on the theory that workers do not always behave in ways that are in the best interests of their company or its owners. The ways in which the interests of employees and their employer differ increase with the size and complexity of a company. Consider a small company, Hammer's Hardware. Helen and Harry Hammer own and manage the store. One of them is in the store at all times, and they keep their own accounting records. The economic interests of the Hammers and their company are the same. Their livelihood depends on the success of their store. Therefore, they have incentives to make sure the company is run efficiently and effectively. In contrast, consider a large corporation like Lowe's. Lowe's operates a chain of hardware, lumber, and household supplies stores. The company employs thousands of people. The success of the company depends on these employees doing their jobs efficiently and effectively to meet the needs of customers. If employees fail to serve customers promptly and courteously, if they steal cash or inventory or permit them to be stolen, or if they do not maintain a clean and safe work environment, the company is not likely to be successful. Internal control systems are used to increase the likelihood that employees will do what is best for the company. These systems are designed to deal with both intentional and unintentional behavior.

The design of many internal controls considers three related human behavior problems, as illustrated in Exhibit 2. Problems involving intentional behavior may result when employees or managers perceive a need such as more money, more power, or more leisure time than is provided currently by their job. Though employees often perceive such needs, most do not try to satisfy them through unethical behavior. The decision to behave unethically depends, in part, on opportunity. An employee who has access to cash or other assets (or control over transactions that can provide this access) often has an opportunity. In addition to perceived need and opportunity, the ability to rationalize one's actions is an important factor in unethical behavior. Employees rationalize their actions, convincing themselves their behavior is justified because of such beliefs as:

- They are being underpaid by their employer.
- Everybody else is behaving the same way.
- They will pay back the amount taken the first chance they get.
- Their supervisors do not care what they do.
- Nobody is really being hurt.

Exhibit 2   Human Behavior Problems Underlying Internal Control Systems

Problem 1
A perceived need exists on the part of an employee or manager, such as a need for more money.

Problem 2
A perceived opportunity exists to meet the need, such as access to company cash.

Problem 3
An ability exists on the part of the employee or manager to rationalize improper or unethical behavior.

Internal control systems are designed to deal with these human behavior problems. These systems identify the types of problems that could exist and try to prevent those problems. Perceived needs can be reduced by encouraging employees to discuss their problems with supervisors, to understand the importance of their jobs, and to take pride in their work. The controls try to reduce opportunity by making it difficult for individuals to steal or manipulate transactions without being detected. Also, they can reduce employees' ability to rationalize their behavior by making clear what is expected and the consequences of improper behavior.

Unintentional behavior problems arise primarily because people make mistakes. Numbers are recorded incorrectly, a customer is given the wrong amount of change, or goods are shipped to the wrong place. Internal control systems are designed to reduce these problems also by detecting errors or making them more difficult to commit.

Most companies develop policies and procedures for employees to follow to help them avoid mistakes. Policies describe proper employee behavior in various situations. For example, a company's policy may be to accept returned merchandise from customers in an efficient and prompt manner. Procedures describe the steps employees should take in dealing with various problems and situations. For example, a customer returning merchandise should be referred to a particular employee, who is responsible for receiving the merchandise and authorizing a refund.

An important role of internal control is ensuring that employees understand company policies and procedures and follow them properly. Providing written policies and procedures to employees and training them in the use of these policies and procedures is an important internal control activity. Monitoring employee behavior to determine that policies and procedures are being followed also is an important internal control activity. Such activities protect a company, its employees, and its owners.

To illustrate the importance of policies and procedures, consider the question of safety in a manufacturing plant. Manufacturing usually involves the use of equipment, tools, chemicals, and other devices that are potentially dangerous. Employee safety is important because it increases efficiency and employee morale, reduces health care and litigation costs, and protects workers. Therefore, companies often have policies designed to encourage safe behavior and limit opportunities for accidents. Physical barriers may limit access to dangerous locations. Protective clothing, such as hard hats, may be required in certain locations. Other safety devices, such as earplugs, may be required to prevent injury to employees.

Internal controls ensure that policies and procedures to protect workers are in place. Workers then are observed to make sure they follow these policies and procedures. Supervisors and other employees are responsible for controlling behavior by enforcing these policies and procedures. Companies also identify and track accidents in an effort to avoid future problems and to discover whether policies and procedures are working properly.

Most internal control activities affect the financial condition of a company, and therefore accounting information, directly or indirectly. For example, employee safety has an important indirect relationship with accounting information. If a company disregards the safety of its employees, there are likely to be accidents, and the company may incur accident-related costs, some of which may be significant. These costs include health benefits to injured employees, higher insurance costs, and litigation costs. Fines and penalties also may be imposed by governmental agencies. These costs reduce a company's profits and, in extreme cases, can endanger its existence. A major purpose of accounting is to inform owners and other external parties of management decisions and the realized and potential outcomes of these decisions. Risks associated with management disregard for safety are relevant for external decision makers because of the financial damage that may be done to the company.

SELF-STUDY PROBLEM 1

Internal controls are important in many organizations. College instructors employ internal controls in classroom situations to encourage learning, to prevent improper evaluation of learning, and to prevent unauthorized access to information.

© 1995 Tom Stewart/The Stock Market

Required

1. Identify the kinds of intentional human behavior problems (need, opportunity, and rationalization) that arise in a classroom setting that require the use of internal controls.

2. Identify examples of internal controls often used to address these problems.

The solution to Self-Study Problem 1 appears at the end of the chapter.

THE STRUCTURE OF AN INTERNAL CONTROL SYSTEM

Objective 3
Identify the components of an internal control system.

An internal control system has five major components:[2]

1. The organizational environment in which the system exists

2. The risks that affect the ability of a company to meet its objectives

3. The activities a company uses to control its risks

4. The methods, records, and reports a company uses to communicate with employees and external decision makers

5. The procedures a company uses to monitor its internal control system to make sure it is functioning properly

Organizational Environment

Objective 4
Explain why a company's organizational environment is important for meeting internal control objectives.

The top managers and board of directors of a company determine its organizational environment. Their behavior affects the behavior of other managers and employees. If top managers behave ethically and responsibly, other employees are likely to follow their lead. If top managers are concerned about the reliability of information and other control issues, they are likely to ensure that there is a strong internal control system within their company.

The integrity and ethical values of managers are primary determinants of the strength of a company's internal controls. Managers who believe in a strong control system will develop such a system and communicate their expectations throughout the company. These expectations often include statements about company and personal values and ethical conduct. Many companies have established codes of conduct to reinforce this commitment. Professionals in all disciplines have a duty to maintain skills and attitudes that are consistent with their responsibilities and to exercise these skills ethically and competently. Exhibit 3 contains the code of ethics developed by the Institute of Management Accountants for the management accounting profession. This code is typical of those of other professions and those of companies that expect similar behavior from their employees. Although it is not a guarantee of ethical behavior, a code of conduct communicates to a company's employees expectations about what the company considers to be proper behavior.

The organizational environment affects employees' incentives to engage in activities that are inconsistent with long-run company value. In addition to formulating a code of conduct, top managers communicate expectations about ethical and legal conduct to employees by the way they monitor, evaluate, and reward employees. Consider the case of Hardley Scruples, a sales representative with a major manufacturing company. His sales target for the first quarter of 1998 was $2.5 million, 10%

---

[2]   *The outline and general content of this section are adapted from The Committee of Sponsoring Organizations of the Treadway Commission,* Internal Control—Integrated Framework, *1992.*

Exhibit 3 Ethical Conduct for Management Accountants

STANDARDS

Management accountants have an obligation to the organizations they serve, their profession, the public, and themselves to maintain the highest standards of ethical conduct. In recognition of this obligation, the Institute of Management Accountants has promulgated the following standards of ethical conduct for management accountants. Adherence to these standards is integral to achieving their *Objectives of Management Accounting*. Management accountants shall not commit acts contrary to these standards nor shall they condone the commission of such acts by others within their organizations.

COMPETENCE

Management accountants have a responsibility to:
- Maintain an appropriate level of professional competence by ongoing development of their knowledge and skills.
- Perform their professional duties in accordance with relevant laws, regulations, and technical standards.
- Prepare complete and clear reports and recommendations after appropriate analysis of relevant and reliable information.

CONFIDENTIALITY

Management accountants have a responsibility to:
- Refrain from disclosing confidential information acquired in the course of their work except when authorized, unless legally obligated to do so.
- Inform subordinates as appropriate regarding the confidentiality of information acquired in the course of their work, and monitor their activities to assure the maintenance of that confidentiality.
- Refrain from using or appearing to use confidential information acquired in the course of their work for unethical or illegal advantage either personally or through third parties.

INTEGRITY

Management accountants have a responsibility to:
- Avoid actual or apparent conflicts of interest and advise all appropriate parties of any potential conflict.
- Refrain from engaging in any activity that would prejudice their ability to carry out their duties ethically.
- Refuse any gift, favor, or hospitality that would influence or would appear to influence their actions.
- Refrain from either actively or passively subverting the attainment of the organization's legitimate and ethical objectives.
- Recognize and communicate professional limitations or other constraints that would preclude responsible judgment or successful performance of an activity.
- Communicate unfavorable as well as favorable information and professional judgments or opinions.
- Refrain from engaging in or supporting any activity that would discredit the profession.

OBJECTIVITY

Management accountants have a responsibility to:
- Communicate information fairly and objectively.
- Disclose fully all relevant information that could reasonably be expected to influence an intended user's understanding of the reports, comments, and recommendations presented.

RESOLUTION OF ETHICAL CONFLICT

In applying the standards of ethical conduct, management accountants may encounter problems in identifying unethical behavior or in resolving an ethical conflict. When faced with significant ethical issues, management accountants should follow the established policies of the organization bearing on the resolution of such conflict. If these policies do not resolve the ethical conflict, management accountants should consider the following course of action:
- Discuss such problems with the immediate superior except when it appears that the superior is involved, in which case the problem should be presented initially to the next higher managerial level. If satisfactory resolution cannot be achieved when the problem is initially presented, submit the issues to the next higher managerial level.

  If the immediate superior is the chief executive officer, or equivalent, the acceptable reviewing authority may be a group such as the audit committee, executive committee, board of directors, board of trustees, or owners. Contact with levels above the immediate superior should be initiated only with the superior's knowledge, assuming the superior is not involved.
- Clarify relevant concepts by confidential discussion with an objective advisor to obtain an understanding of possible courses of action.
- If the ethical conflict still exists after exhausting all levels of internal review, the management accountant may have no other recourse on significant matters than to resign from the organization and to submit an informative memorandum to an appropriate representative of the organization.

Except where legally prescribed, communication of such problems to authorities or individuals not employed or engaged by the organization is not considered appropriate.

Source: Statements on Management Accounting: Standards of Ethical Conduct for Management Accountants, Statement No. 1C 1983. **Copyright by Institute of Management Accountants. Reprinted with permission.**

higher than in the previous year. Hardley receives a 20% bonus if he meets his target. The company is known to replace representatives who often fall short of their targets. Hardley usually has trouble meeting his target in the first and second quarters, but he has less difficulty in the third and fourth quarters, when demand is stronger. To meet his first- and second-quarter targets, Hardley sometimes delays reporting fourth-quarter sales until the first quarter of the next year. Also, he sometimes reports third-quarter sales as though they were made during the second quarter. In addition, he encourages customers to delay orders at the end of the fourth quarter and to order late in the second quarter rather than waiting until the third quarter. Some of this encouragement is in the form of kickbacks to purchasing agents of customer companies, who receive under-the-table payments for their cooperation. As a result, Hardley almost always meets his target and receives his bonus. He has gained the reputation of being one of the top sales reps in his company and several times has been voted "salesperson of the year." His supervisors pay little attention to the way Hardley operates, not wanting to mess with a good thing. Indeed, they encourage other reps to follow Hardley's lead. Because of his success, Hardley's sales targets increase each year, giving him more incentive to use creative sales techniques.

Hardley Scruples provides an example of how an internal control problem can result from an organizational environment. Environmental problems include:

- An extreme emphasis on short-term results
- A reward system that emphasizes current financial performance
- Ineffective monitoring of employee activities
- Lack of concern by top management about employee behavior

When employees are pressured to perform and receive little supervision or guidance concerning acceptable behavior, they are encouraged to bend rules and operate unethically, and sometimes illegally. The problem stems from the top of the organization. The organization creates a perceived need that the employee is attempting to meet. Problems are created by the organizational environment when management is unconcerned about internal control issues, does not provide policies to communicate expected behavior to employees, and does not monitor behavior to determine that expectations are being met. The organization creates the perceived opportunity for an employee to meet the perceived need and provides a basis for rationalizing this behavior.

The costs of these problems can be high. In the case of Hardley Scruples, the company's sales information is misstated each quarter. Thus, its financial projections are distorted. If Hardley's sales targets continue to increase, he will have a harder time meeting them. He will pay out greater amounts of his bonuses to purchasing agents and will have to move larger and larger sales amounts from one period to another. If Hardley's sales tactics become known by top managers, other employees, competitors, and customers, his company is likely to suffer along with him. Customers may react to the treatment they have received and turn to new suppliers. Litigation is likely from companies whose employees took payoffs and from other companies that lost sales because of these illegal practices. Company management will have little defense because of their failure to supervise their employees.

A strong organizational environment can help protect a company against improper behavior. A primary characteristic of a strong environment is concern by top management about ethical behavior. A clear set of rules and effective communication with employees are critical. Lines of authority should establish who makes decisions and how the decisions will be monitored and evaluated. Concern with personnel and performance evaluation policies also is important. In a strong environment, policies are created to control hiring, training, supervising, evaluating, and compensating employees. These policies help to ensure that employees are competent and understand their responsibilities. Involving employees in setting performance goals and compensation arrangements can avoid extreme pressure and the perception of a "succeed at all costs" attitude.

A strong organizational environment could limit the damage caused by Hardley Scruples. Company policies should identify clearly how and when sales should be reported. These policies should state that illegal behavior, such as paying kickbacks, is unacceptable. Top managers should make employees aware that the policies will be enforced and let them know the penalties for failure to adhere to the policies. Employee behavior should then be monitored carefully to ensure that the policies are being followed. In addition, top managers should work with employees, such as Hardley, to create compensation arrangements that consider product demand in different periods and that emphasize long-term relationships with customers and long-term profits, rather than placing an extreme emphasis on short-term sales. These policies would reduce the incentive and opportunity for employees to engage in unethical or illegal behavior.

Risk Assessment

Objective 5
Explain why risk assessment is an important component of an internal control system.

All companies face risks. Risks are associated with events that threaten a company's ability to meet its objectives. Risk assessment involves identifying potential risks and ways to manage those risks. Risks result from external and internal factors. Technological change, product innovation, changes in competition, and changes in laws and regulations are examples of external risks. Internal risks often involve how managers and employees respond to changing conditions. For example, these risks are realized when managers fail to follow company policies or shirk their responsibilities to the company. Any time a company is going through major changes, such as developing new product lines or acquiring a new plant, it is particularly susceptible to risk. Employees are learning new skills, production and information systems are being modified, and new policies are being implemented.

Managing risks is a major task in most companies, as illustrated in Exhibit 4. Risk management requires a clear understanding of the risks faced throughout a company. These risks should be analyzed to determine the likelihood that an event will occur and the potential effects of the event if it does occur. Once those risks that

Exhibit 4   Issues Considered in Effective Risk Management

What risks does a company face?
Example: The company depends on computer systems for accounting, customer orders, production, and other purposes.

What is the likelihood an event will occur that creates a risk of loss?
Example: What is the likelihood of the computer system being damaged or destroyed?

What are the potential losses if an event occurs?
Example: If systems are destroyed, managers and employees will not have needed information for making decisions.

What can be done to prevent the events from occurring?
Example: On a regular basis, prepare backup data that can be used on a replacement system.

are significant have been identified, action can be taken to reduce them. To illustrate, most companies use computerized information systems to record, store, analyze, and report important operating information. These systems pose major risks to a company. Physical damage to hardware or failure of hardware or software can render a system useless. Data may be destroyed or falsified. Also, data can be accessed by unauthorized users. The result can be large losses stemming from this damage, misinformation, theft, or sabotage. Information system risks are particularly important to the reliability of accounting and other information used by decision makers. System failure or manipulation can lead to major losses because information is unavailable or misstated. Using passwords, controlling physical access to hardware and software, maintaining copies of important data, maintaining backup systems, and proper supervision and training of computer operators are ways in which a company can reduce information system risks.

Behavior such as that of Hardley Scruples is another source of risk to a company. A company should recognize this type of risk and try to prevent or detect improper behavior. Hardley's behavior could be prevented or detected by comparing the dates sales were reported against the dates goods were shipped, by identifying patterns in the timing of large sales, and by identifying patterns in sales to particular customers.

A thorough examination of risks and ways of preventing the risks from becoming problems for a company is a major task of an internal control system. The system should identify and document areas of risk, and it should identify procedures that managers and employees should use to protect the company against those risks.

SELF-STUDY PROBLEM 2

Margie Qualms is in charge of purchasing for a chain of ladies' apparel stores. She orders merchandise from manufacturers, submits purchase orders to the company's accounting department for payment, and receives merchandise for the company. She then allots the shipments to individual stores. The company provides her with an expense account to travel to fashion shows and to meet with designers and manufacturers. She submits requests to the accounting department for reimbursement and receives checks for her expenses.

© Tim Brown/Tony Stone Images

Required

Identify risks that Margie's company faces because of her responsibilities and describe internal control procedures that the company could use to protect itself from these risks.

The solution to Self-Study Problem 2 appears at the end of the chapter.

OTHER ASPECTS OF INTERNAL CONTROL STRUCTURE

In addition to the operational environment and risk assessment, internal control structure includes internal control activities, communications, and monitoring.

Internal Control Activities

O b j e c t i v e   6
Identify primary types of control procedures and the types of activities to which they are applied.

Internal control activities include policies and procedures that a company uses to address significant risks.[3] These activities may be designed to prevent an event from occurring, to discover an event if it does occur, or to correct a problem once it is discovered. For example, the use of passwords to access a computer system is a control activity designed to prevent unauthorized access. A system can be programmed to print a log of the users who accessed a system and the time of their access. This log can be reviewed to determine if unauthorized users accessed the system. Identifying how unauthorized users gained access and checking the files that they accessed allows problems of unauthorized access to be corrected.

Typical types of control procedures include:

1. Reviewing reports that describe actual and expected (or budgeted) amounts to identify unexpected results that may suggest control problems, such as excessively large amounts of sales at the end of a fiscal period

2. Checking the accuracy of recorded transactions to determine if they correspond to documents, such as sales or purchase invoices, and making sure that transactions were properly authorized (for example, payments were approved by appropriate managers)

3. Securing cash, inventories, and equipment to prevent theft, and comparing physical counts with recorded amounts

4. Comparing financial with other data, such as production or shipping data, to determine if they are in agreement (for example, the number of units shipped to a customer agrees with the amount billed and recorded revenue)

5. Segregating duties so that the people who authorize transactions are different from those who record the transactions and physically handle cash and other assets

As mentioned earlier, many control activities involve policies and procedures. Policies provide guidelines for proper behavior: what should be done in various circumstances. For example, a policy might require that a sales clerk check a customer's credit record before accepting a check for a purchase. Procedures describe the specific actions to be taken to implement a policy. For example, a credit check procedure might require a clerk to examine a computer file or listing of customers who have issued bad checks. The clerk might initial the check to indicate that the file had been examined and the check was approved. If the check was not approved, the procedure might require the clerk to call a store manager or direct the customer to the appropriate employee.

Many internal control procedures focus on those company activities that are particularly susceptible to theft or mismanagement. High-risk activities are those involving:

http://www.swcollege.com/ingram.html

Learn more about internal controls.

- Cash
- Accounts and loans receivable
- Inventory and purchasing
- Payroll and other expenses

---

[3]   *Some of the examples and ideas contained in this section were adapted from a videotape: National Association of Certified Fraud Examiners,* The Corporate Con: Internal Fraud and the Auditor, *1992.*

Cash. Cash is particularly risky because it is readily available to many employees, such as sales clerks. Also, it is easily concealed, and its source is hard to trace. For example, a clerk can easily remove cash from a cash register. Another method of taking cash involves issuing fictitious sales refunds to customers. Sales clerks often have the authority to receive returned merchandise from customers and issue refunds. A clerk can forge return slips and pocket the cash.

Internal controls for cash include using locked cash registers to secure cash. Sequentially numbered sales slips ensure that all sales are recorded. Cash registers often issue sales slips automatically whenever sales are entered. Bar coding of merchandise removes the need to enter merchandise codes or prices, thus reducing the chance of error. The total of the sales slips can be verified against the contents of the cash drawer at the end of each shift to ensure that the cash balance is correct. Each clerk has a separate cash drawer, so responsibility for cash is easily determined. Both the sales clerk and a supervisor are responsible for verifying the cash. Sales returns must be authorized by a supervisor, and returned merchandise is logged with a return slip so that it can be returned to stock or returned to the manufacturer if it is defective.

At higher levels in a company, the responsibility for depositing cash should be separated from the responsibility for accounting for cash receipts or selling goods. Exhibit 5 illustrates a typical segregation of duties involving cash. The receipt of cash is separated from accounting for the cash. Documentation such as sales and deposit slips and bank statements provides independent evidence of the amount of cash received and deposited. Because sales slips are numbered sequentially, accounting personnel can verify that all sales are reported. Accordingly, neither the sales clerk nor the supervisor can easily take cash from the company. Altered or missing documents are a clear sign of potential problems that should be examined by those responsible for the internal control system.

Exhibit 5   Segregation of Duties Involving Handling and Accounting for Cash

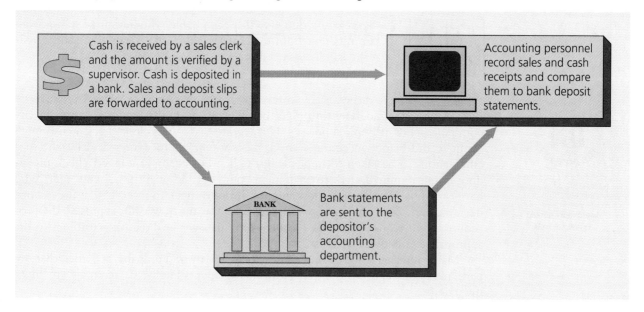

Accounts and Loans Receivable. Accounts receivable often are a major internal control problem, especially for companies with large amounts of receivables and many sales representatives who submit orders from numerous customers. A typical problem involves lapping. For example, assume that Minnie Morals is a cash receipts clerk for Electro Supply Company. She receives payments from customers and records the payments to the customers' accounts. She receives a payment from

L. Plugg for merchandise purchased on account. However, instead of recording the payment to Plugg's account and depositing the cash, she pockets the cash (or forges an endorsement on the check and deposits it in her personal account). Later, Minnie receives a payment from E. Wire. Instead of recording the payment to Wire's account, she records it to Plugg's account. Thus, she conceals her theft of Plugg's payment by lapping his account with that of Wire.

Internal controls for receivables include independent verification of account balances with customers. Customers are mailed a statement giving the customer's accounts receivable balance. Customers verify the balance and return the statement to the company. Any discrepancies between recorded amounts and amounts reported by customers should be examined. Trends in account balances also can be examined. For example, an unexpected increase in the ratio of accounts receivable to sales would indicate that customers are not paying their accounts as quickly as expected.

Requiring employees to take vacations is another important internal control procedure. For scams such as Minnie's to work, the employee has to perform the same duties without interruption so that he or she can continue to lap customer accounts. If someone else receives customer payments, a lag will occur between when payments are made and when they are recorded. For example, if L. Plugg pays his account in May, he does not expect to receive a statement at the end of May indicating that he still owes money to Electro Supply Company. Minnie has to make sure that a payment is recorded to Plugg's account before statements are mailed. If she is on vacation, she will be unable to ensure that this payment is recorded. Many cases of theft and embezzlement have involved "loyal" employees who never took vacations.

Receivables are a special problem for banks and other financial institutions that lend money to customers. Top managers or loan officers in these institutions can authorize loans to customers in exchange for kickbacks from the customers. For example, suppose Stella Spendthrift needs $10,000 for her business but is having difficulty getting a loan because of her prior credit history. Freddie Freelender, an officer at First Fraud Bank, agrees to provide the loan. Instead of a $10,000 loan, however, Freddie authorizes a $15,000 loan to Stella. Stella then pays the extra $5,000 to Freddie, or they share the amount. Later, Freddie might write off the loan or some portion of it as a bad debt. Some savings and loan failures of the 1980s can be traced to loans to high-risk customers who paid kickbacks to officers of the institutions. When these customers were unable to repay the loans, some of the institutions became insolvent. Problems also can result when officers authorize loans, often at favorable rates, to businesses in which they have a major ownership interest or when loan officers receive expensive gifts from favored clients.

Internal controls are critical in banks. Loans should require the approval of a loan committee that acts independently of those who accept loan applications. Careful monitoring of customers to identify who is receiving loans and whether loans are being repaid can reveal loan problems. Banks and other companies also can observe the lifestyles of their officers and employees. Companies should be suspicious when employees are able to spend much more than they earn.

Inventory and Purchasing. Inventory can be stolen by customers or taken by employees for personal use. Many companies tag their merchandise so that an alarm will sound if the merchandise is removed from the store without being purchased. Expensive merchandise may be kept in locked cabinets or in special areas where customers can be watched carefully. Manufacturing materials and extra merchandise can be locked in storage facilities until needed. Employees must sign forms showing the type and amount of materials or merchandise removed from these facilities. Unauthorized personnel are not permitted access. Materials or merchandise can be tagged or bar coded so that individual items can be tracked from the time they are received until they are transferred to other departments or to customers.

Misstating inventory is one type of fraud committed by top managers. Such fraud often is hard to detect because these managers can manipulate reported accounting numbers and supporting documents. These cases often involve millions of dollars and, once detected, severely damage a company's finances and reputation. Stockholders of **Comptronix Corporation,** a computer software developer, won a $10 million settlement from the company because of overstated earnings. The company's top managers inflated the company's earnings by reporting fictitious sales. To balance the company's accounts, they overstated inventories and other assets. Inventories are a popular target for manipulation by unscrupulous managers because the amounts often are large and misstatements can be concealed. Typically, the managers report inventories that do not exist, resulting in overstated assets, understated expenses, and overstated net income.

To prevent overstatement, a company should periodically count the inventory and compare the actual amounts with accounting records. A thorough count would have revealed the Comptronix fraud. In addition, an analysis of accounting numbers can reveal major problems. For example, although Comptronix overstated its earnings, it could not create the cash that would normally accompany them. Thus, its reported earnings were much higher than its reported operating cash flows over the several years during which the fraud was committed. Exhibit 6 shows the relationship between Comptronix's net income and operating cash flows during the period of the fraud. Net income was consistently higher than operating cash flow during this period. In its cash flow statement, the company reported large increases in inventories to justify the difference between earnings and cash flows. This large difference could have alerted company directors and lower-level managers of a potential problem. Again, the fraud could have been detected by a careful count of inventory.

Exhibit 6   A Comparison of Net Income and Cash Flow for Comptronix Corporation.

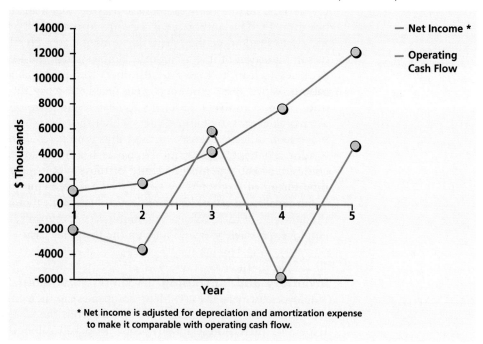

* Net income is adjusted for depreciation and amortization expense
to make it comparable with operating cash flow.

Internal controls also are needed to deal with purchasing problems. Purchasing department employees have been caught embezzling from a company by writing fictitious purchase invoices. The invoices indicate that purchases were made and payments are owed to suppliers. The invoices are submitted for payment through regular channels. The employee then has the checks sent to his or her home address or a post office box and deposits them to a personal account. The employee adds the amount of each purchase to the company's inventory account as though an actual purchase had been made.

This kind of problem can be prevented or detected by segregating custody of assets (such as receipt of inventory) from the authorization and recording of purchase transactions. Payments should be made only after independent documentation, showing that goods were ordered and that the ordered goods were received, arrives from two separate departments. Unexpected changes in the amount of cost of goods sold and ending inventory also can suggest a potential problem. The addresses of suppliers can be checked against those of employees and against telephone directories to ensure that the suppliers are legitimate. A physical count of inventory also can detect discrepancies between actual inventory amounts and accounting records.

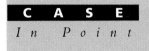

An employee of an insurance company was responsible for settling customer claims for auto accidents. The employee investigated claims, determined the company's responsibility, and authorized payment to a repair shop. With a friend, the employee created an auto repair company. The company owned no repair facilities. Instead, it hired other companies to do the work. These companies billed the employee's fictitious company for the actual work. The fictitious company inflated the bills so that the charges were much higher than the actual charges. The employee then submitted the inflated bills to the insurance company. The company paid the amounts charged by the fictitious company, which then paid the real charges. The employee and his friend kept the difference. The scam was uncovered when the insurance company discovered that the fictitious company was owned by the employee. The insurance company might have become suspicious if it had examined the frequency of payments to the fictitious company.

Payroll and Other Expenses. Payroll and other expenses also are susceptible to manipulation. Payroll personnel can create fictitious employees, write checks to these employees, and deposit the checks in personal accounts or have them sent to relatives or friends. Employees who have been terminated can be left on payroll records. Checks to these former employees then can be diverted to a current employee's account. Employees can claim overtime in excess of amounts worked. Various steps can be taken to prevent or detect these problems. Companies can use time clocks to verify hours worked. Careful comparison of employee lists and changes in employees with documentation from departments where employees work can identify payments to fictitious or former employees.

Other expense accounts also are subject to manipulation. For example, employees can submit requests for travel expenses that are overstated. Employees who control advertising, legal, and other budgets can submit fictitious bills for payment and then have the payments diverted to their personal accounts. A review of trends in account balances can reveal unexpected increases in expenses. For example, an unexpected increase in advertising expenses for a particular branch or region might suggest that the expenses should be examined to make sure they are legitimate. A check of addresses can detect if payments are being sent to employees rather than actual companies. Correspondence with other companies can reveal whether submitted bills are based on actual services performed and whether the amounts are correct. Limits can be placed on the amounts an employee can authorize.

The number and types of internal control procedures can be extensive in large organizations. The examples provided in this chapter illustrate some of these procedures. The procedures used in a particular company depend on the risks faced by that company.

Communication of Internal Control Policies and Problems

Objective 7
Explain why communications are important in internal control systems.

Internal control policies and procedures must be communicated to those who use or rely on them. Employees should understand that these are important activities. Also, they should be trained to use the policies and procedures properly. Communication also means that information must be reported on a timely basis to those who use it. If the file of customers who have issued bad checks is not updated often, the control activity of examining the file before accepting customer checks will be ineffective.

Employees should understand how to communicate problems or concerns. They should know to whom they report and the types of information that should be reported. Also, they should understand the consequences of reporting or failing to report. For example, an employee who sees a supervisor stealing materials from the factory floor should know to whom the information should be reported and should be protected from any harm as a result of this action.

Communication is especially important for accounting activities. The reliability of accounting information depends on the proper use of procedures to ensure timely and accurate recording of transactions and other information. Activities associated with the communication of accounting information involve making sure that all transactions:

* Have been identified and recorded, so that data are complete
* Are measured properly, so that reported amounts are accurate
* Are recorded in the proper period, so that amounts for each period are correct
* Are summarized and reported properly, so that financial statements and other reports are reliable and are received by the appropriate decision makers on a timely basis

Much of the effectiveness of an internal control system depends on timely and accurate communications. Internal control requires good data about expected and actual results and prompt feedback if problems are identified. To illustrate, consider a company that transports hazardous waste materials to disposal sites. The company operates trucks that pick up waste and take it to other locations, often across state lines. If a state changes its regulations concerning the shipping of hazardous waste—for example, which roads may be used or authorities to be informed about shipments—the company may face stiff penalties and delays if drivers are not told of the changes promptly. Further, if violations occur and the drivers do not report them to the company promptly, other drivers may face similar problems.

Effective communication can reduce the likelihood that employees will engage in unethical behavior. Many employees are unaware that their employer has the ability to detect theft or other improper behavior. For example, sales clerks have been caught stealing when they were not aware that they were being videotaped. Surprise audits of cash in a sales clerk's cash register drawer can identify discrepancies. These are valuable control procedures for detecting improper behavior. They also are valuable for preventing improper behavior. Making employees aware that these types of controls exist reduces the opportunity employees perceive to engage in improper behavior.

Monitoring

Objective 8
Describe ways in which companies monitor their internal control systems and explain why monitoring is important.

Internal control systems must be monitored. Organizations change, and the effectiveness of internal controls changes. Controls have to be modified from time to time because of new risks. Also, a control system is not effective if it is not being used. If control procedures are not being implemented, opportunities increase for risks to go undetected or unprevented. Many large organizations have separate internal auditing departments that are responsible for monitoring internal control systems to make sure that they are being implemented and that they are meeting their objectives. The next section of this chapter examines internal auditing.

Some monitoring of internal controls is continuous. For example,

- Managers compare operating activities with reports of those activities on an ongoing basis. If reports differ from actual activities (for example, if reported sales differ from number of units shipped), internal controls are not functioning properly.
- Customers and suppliers also provide monitoring on an ongoing basis. If the amounts that they are paid or charged differ from their records of sales or purchases, they are likely to notify a company of problems with financial records and therefore with internal controls.
- Supervisors are responsible for monitoring employees' activities to make sure that they are following appropriate procedures.
- Employees can be trained to spot internal control problems and can be given periodic updates about control system changes.

Other monitoring activities are periodic. Often these activities involve planned investigation and evaluation of internal control systems. In many companies, these activities are performed by internal auditors.

INTERNAL AUDITING

Objective 9
Describe the purpose and functions of an internal auditing department.

http://www.swcollege.com/ingram.html

Learn more about internal auditing.

Internal auditing **is an independent evaluation function in an organization designed to assess various activities of the organization to help the organization meet its objectives.** An internal audit department often is responsible for independent evaluation of a company's internal control systems. Internal auditors are responsible for evaluating the operations of other departments to determine whether internal controls are working properly. In addition, internal auditors perform activities that are part of an internal control system, such as taking physical counts of cash or inventory and assessing whether management policies are being carried out. Also, internal auditors analyze and evaluate the efficiency and effectiveness of other departments in a company and advise the company's top managers about how the company is functioning. Internal control, efficiency, or effectiveness problems are passed on to top managers for action.

Because of their responsibilities, it is important that internal auditors be independent of other divisions or managers in a company. They must be objective in their evaluations and not subject to pressure that might bias their findings. Often internal auditors report directly to a company's board of directors. A company's board of directors and top management should be careful to separate the internal audit function from other functions so that internal audit findings cannot be suppressed.

An internal audit department should include employees with a wide range of knowledge and skills so that they can understand a company's operations. Disciplines represented in this department often include accounting, finance, information systems, production, and law.

The work of internal auditors involves a series of steps, as illustrated in Exhibit 7. An internal audit begins with a carefully planned evaluation of all major aspects of a company's operations. Each department and activity of the company should be evaluated periodically, including an examination of department operations and data. Internal auditors should regularly visit each of the company's stores, branches, and production facilities. The auditors examine the procedures used for handling and accounting for cash, receivables, payroll, purchasing, inventory, fixed assets, and other items as appropriate to the facility. The auditors may examine the overall security of the facility and the ability of that security to protect the facility's assets, employees, and information systems. Findings should be documented and reported to appropriate managers or directors.

Exhibit 7   Activities in an Internal Audit

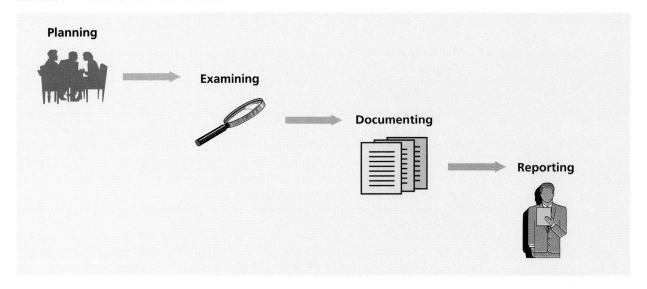

Internal auditors document the internal control procedures used in a facility, whether the procedures are being followed properly, and any discrepancies between company policy and the observed procedures. For example, company policy may call for purchase orders to be written and approved at the time an order is placed with a supplier, even if the order is by phone. A discrepancy would occur if auditors observed purchase orders being prepared after goods were received. Internal auditors observe operations to determine what activities are taking place. They observe documents and transactions, and they interview managers and employees to obtain information about actual operations and the use of internal control procedures.

Once problems are identified, the auditors prepare a report of their findings and make recommendations for eliminating any problems. The report is submitted to appropriate company officials. In later audits or follow-ups, the auditors evaluate whether recommended changes have been made.

Internal auditors also examine the performance of various departments or divisions of a company. These evaluations often are referred to as *operational audits.* Operational audits focus on opportunities for improving effectiveness and efficiency and for changing division activities to improve performance. They consider changes in policies and procedures that can save money or improve the quality of goods and services provided to customers.

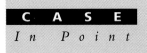

A performance review of a publisher revealed that company employees routinely used Express Mail for most correspondence with authors. The use of Express Mail normally results in mail being received in one or two days rather than the three or four days when first-class mail is used. However, responses from authors usually were not received for two or more weeks. Consequently, internal auditors questioned whether the faster delivery was necessary. They discovered that employees used Express Mail because it was readily available and they did not have to consider other options. By restricting the use of Express Mail to high-priority correspondence that required immediate response, the company was able to save $40,000 a year.

To perform an operational audit, internal auditors must become familiar with the activities of the division they are auditing. After reviewing the division's purpose, functions, and operating activities, the auditors survey its operations to identify important activities that might be sources of problems or areas for improvement. The auditors then plan a series of activities to evaluate the division's performance and to collect data about that performance. These activities include interviews; evaluating documents, reports, computer files, and systems; and observing procedures used in the division. After collecting enough data to reach conclusions, the auditors prepare a report of their findings and recommendations. These reports usually are confidential and are shared only with the appropriate company and division managers.

Internal auditing, like other aspects of a company's internal control system, is designed to improve the ability of a company's managers and employees to meet the overall goals of the organization. Good management requires reliable information and efforts by managers and employees to implement company policies and protect the interests of company owners.

SELF-STUDY PROBLEM 3

Isoflex Company is a manufacturer of exercise equipment. Raw materials are accepted by the receiving department and stored in a warehouse. Factory workers take materials from the warehouse as needed for work in process based on a production schedule developed from sales forecasts. The production process involves five departments: assembly, painting, finishing, testing, and packaging. Completed goods are shipped to retailers.

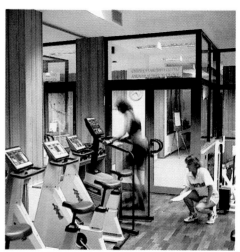

©1995 Robert Essel/The Stock Market

Required

Describe internal control objectives that Isoflex should consider in designing an internal control system for its manufacturing process. What kinds of monitoring procedures should the company use to make sure its internal control system is functioning properly?

The solution to Self-Study Problem 3 appears at the end of the chapter.

R E V I E W   *Summary of Important Concepts*

1. Internal control refers to the methods a company uses to protect its assets and promote their efficient use, ensure accurate and reliable information, and encourage adherence to laws and regulations.

2. Internal control systems are necessary because of intentional and unintentional human behavior problems.

3. An internal control system has five components: the organizational environment, the risks inherent in the environment, internal control policies and procedures to control those risks, communication, and monitoring.

4. The organizational environment depends on the attitudes and actions of top managers with respect to ethical behavior and the importance of internal control systems.

5. Risks that jeopardize the ability of a company to meet its objectives should be identified as a basis for designing control procedures.

6. Internal control policies and procedures are designed to prevent, detect, and correct problems in a company's operations.

7. The effectiveness of an internal control system depends on communication with employees and ensuring that reliable and timely information is provided to decision makers.

8. Internal control systems must be monitored to ensure that they are functioning properly.

9. Internal auditing is an independent evaluation function in an organization that is designed to help the organization meet its objectives, including monitoring its internal control system.

DEFINE *Terms and Concepts Defined in This Chapter*

internal auditing   (387)   internal control   (372)   operational audits   (388)

SOLUTIONS

SELF-STUDY PROBLEM 1

1. Needs generally are associated with a student's desire for a grade in a course. Students need credit for the course, need to maintain or increase their grade point average, and need confirmation of their personal worth. Faculty also have needs: need for control of the educational environment, need to be perceived as good teachers, or need to perceive importance in their teaching activities. Opportunity arises when students perceive that they can cheat to secure a grade that they have not earned. Faculty have the opportunity to perform at a lower level than their responsibilities as teachers demand. Students can rationalize cheating by arguing that exams are unfair, that they are too busy to prepare adequately, that other students cheat, that faculty don't really care if students cheat, or that grades are more important than learning. Faculty can rationalize poor performance by arguing that they are underpaid; that teaching is not important in their evaluation, promotion, or raises; that students don't care about learning; or that they are too busy to prepare adequately.

2. Frequently used internal controls to protect against cheating include monitoring students during exams, requiring student identification during exams, securing exam materials so that students do not have access, and securing grades from unauthorized access. Frequently used controls to protect against poor instructor performance include student evaluations; evaluations by other faculty members, who review teaching materials or evaluate teaching activities; coordination or supervision of teaching materials and exams; and evaluation of teaching as part of salary and promotion reviews. To protect students and faculty from misunderstanding classroom requirements, faculty usually prepare syllabi describing objectives, grading, and assignments.

SELF-STUDY PROBLEM 2

Margie's company faces the risk that Margie may use her position for personal gain at the company's expense. Because she is responsible for both ordering and receiving goods, she controls both the merchandise and authorization for the merchandise. She can submit fictitious orders that are not subject to independent authorization or verification. She can submit vouchers for payments to fictitious companies and have the payments sent to her or to a friend. Also, she can steal merchandise from the company because she has control over the merchandise when it is received. There is no independent verification of the merchandise received, so the company does not know if all merchandise is transferred to stores for sale.

Margie's travel account also provides opportunity for personal gain. She can submit for reimbursement expenses that she did not incur or submit amounts that are larger than her actual expenses. Her travels also give her an opportunity to arrange deals with suppliers. She may use her expense account to provide kickbacks to suppliers, or she may arrange for suppliers to overcharge for orders. She may negotiate personal payments or gifts from suppliers in exchange for placing orders for their goods.

Internal control procedures that the company could use include separating the purchasing and receiving functions, so that Margie authorizes purchases but does not have access to merchandise. Receipt of merchandise should be independently verified and the merchandise shipped to stores based on company policies covering how much is shipped to each store. The receiving stores should submit documentation of the goods received so that the amounts can be compared with the amounts submitted for payment by suppliers. Large or unusual amounts could be verified with the supplier. The company can obtain price lists from suppliers or independent verification of their prices to compare with the amounts it is paying. Also, it can monitor the amount of purchases from various suppliers to determine if excessive orders are being placed with certain suppliers or if the pattern of orders changes over time. The company should also require Margie to submit receipts for her travel expenses so that the expenses can be verified.

SELF-STUDY PROBLEM 3

Primary internal control objectives for manufacturing include ensuring that production is limited to those items that are needed and authorized and safeguarding inventories, equipment, and production facilities. Reliable and timely sales forecast information is important in order to ensure proper scheduling of goods demanded by customers. Accurate measurement of materials, labor, and overhead costs is important to ensure the reliability of the Raw Materials Inventory, Work in Process Inventory, Finished Goods Inventory, and Cost of Goods Sold accounts.

Protection of assets involves proper authorization for obtaining materials and for transfer between departments. Materials and work in process (the number of units and types of materials) should be tracked throughout the production process to prevent theft. Scrap and defective products should be accounted for. Units can be tagged or bar coded to make tracking easier, and signed authorizations can be used to ensure proper transfer of goods throughout the manufacturing process. Responsibility for physical access to assets (storage and manufacturing departments) should be separated from the information functions (accounting and production systems) and from the authorization function (planning and scheduling). Security for the manufacturing process can be obtained by controlling access to the facility and requiring employee identification.

Monitoring of internal controls involves continuous supervision of the manufacturing process to ensure that controls are being implemented and are working properly. Documents should be checked for proper signatures. Records of transfers, scrap, and defective units should be checked to ensure that all materials are accounted for. Account balances should be checked to ensure that relationships among materials, work in process, finished goods, and cost of goods sold are reasonable. Periodic internal audits of the manufacturing process should examine the process by observing procedures and documents that are part of the internal control system.

EXERCISES

11-1. Write a short definition of each of the terms listed in the *Terms and Concepts Defined in This Chapter* section.

Obj. 1   **11-2.** How does the existence of federal laws such as the Family Leave Act and the Americans with Disabilities Act affect a company's system of internal control?

Obj. 1   **11-3.**   What is meant by a company's system of internal control policies and procedures?

Obj. 1   **11-4.**   Stan Duvall is the controller of Midland Enterprises. Stan stated, "Midland has strong internal controls. The ledger must always balance, and this ensures that all transactions are properly transferred to our general ledger." What do you think of this comment?

Obj. 2   **11-5.**   Senior management at The Stylex Corporation realizes that the company has a very weak system of internal control. It has come to management's attention that an employee with the responsibility for handling transactions involving large amounts of cash is experiencing financial difficulties as the result of a costly personal divorce. What steps should management take with respect to this individual?

Obj. 2   **11-6.**   What role do employee training and written policies and procedures have in a properly designed system of internal controls?

Obj. 4   **11-7.**   Terry Curtis is the president of Bunker Enterprises. Employees of Bunker notice that Terry routinely uses the company truck for personal reasons, and it is widely known that Terry's expense reports often contain many personal expenses. How does Terry's behavior affect the company's system of internal control?

Obj. 4   **11-8.**   Edwin Holeyfield is a management accountant for a nationally known company. Does the code of ethical conduct developed by the Institute of Management Accountants explain how Edwin should act in specific ethical situations? Explain your answer.

Obj. 4   **11-9.**   Rita Gall is a management accountant for Drexel Enterprises. Rita has decided to leave Drexel and has secured an interview with a major competitor of Drexel. In an effort to make a good impression on the prospective employer, Rita shared specific cost information about Drexel's main product with the interviewer. Did Rita act appropriately? Explain your answer.

Obj. 4   **11-10.**   Elsa Wagoner is a management accountant who prepares product cost reports for Medley Industries. Her good friend Mark Camino is a production superintendent for one of Medley's product lines. The production figures for the past month revealed a substantial increase in the cost of production on Mark's line. In an effort to help him look better, Elsa shifted some of the costs from Mark's line to another production line before completing the monthly product costing reports. The shift in costs were never detected. Did Elsa act appropriately? Explain your answer.

Obj. 5   **11-11.**   The data processing system at Integrated Technologies allows any computer user to access software program files. A report is written at the end of the day that lists all users and the programs that were accessed. What internal control weakness exists in these procedures, and how may they be strengthened?

Obj. 5   **11-12.**   Mary Czentnar is the president of Olympic Foods. At a recent management meeting, Mary instructed her managers to prepare a detailed internal and external risk assessment for their respective departments as the beginning of a companywide evaluation of internal control. Why is risk assessment necessary to establish effective internal controls?

Obj. 6   **11-13.**   Anthony Keaton is a sales clerk at a large department store. Over the past few months, Anthony has been involved in a scheme in which he prepares sales return forms and takes money from the cash register in the amount of the fictitious sales return. What are some control procedures that would be effective in detecting this sort of scheme?

Objs. 4,5   **11-14.**   General Machine and Lathe Company is a metal processing firm that grinds, welds, and shapes metal parts. In the machining process the company uses solvents and coolants that by law must be properly disposed of through a licensed treatment center. However, the company dumps these chemicals in a ditch along the back of its property. What risks does the company face by improperly dumping these chemicals?

Obj. 6   **11-15.**   Goshen Products has a written policy that states in part: "All employees are strictly prohibited from accepting any gratuities, gifts, donations, or any other remuneration from vendors, suppliers, or salespeople for which the fair market value of such gift, gratuity, or donation exceeds $5." How does such a policy strengthen the company's system of internal control?

Obj. 4 **11-16.** Assume that the president of Goshen Products, described in Exercise 11-15, routinely accepts invitations from the company's bankers, lawyers, and accountants to play golf, attend sporting events, and eat dinner at no cost. What effect do these actions have on the organizational environment at the company?

Obj. 6 **11-17.** Like Nature sells vitamins and nutritional products to health food stores throughout the country. All sales are made on account, with terms that require payment 45 days after shipment. The company sends an invoice with each shipment and expects its customers to remit payment from these invoices. Statements are never sent to customers. If the company sent statements to its customers on a periodic basis, would this strengthen control over accounts receivable? Explain your answer.

Obj. 6 **11-18.** Poppy's Wallcoverings is a manufacturer of wallpaper products. The company maintains a central warehouse inventory consisting of thousands of rolls of wallpapers and borders. The company does not perform a periodic count of its inventory, but rather controls its stock by analyzing sales and inventory records. How could the periodic inventory counts strengthen the company's internal controls?

Obj. 7 **11-19.** Todd Adelstein is a staff accountant at Huber Industries. Todd is responsible for preparing monthly remittances of state payroll taxes which have been withheld from employee checks. The state recently changed its rules concerning the timing of tax remittances, and has increased the penalty for failing to file returns within the prescribed time limits. While his supervisor was aware of the rule changes, Todd was not, so Todd filed the September taxes based on the old guidelines. How would stronger communications at Huber have helped strengthened controls and possibly prevented this situation from occurring?

Obj. 8 **11-20.** At a drive thru window of a fast food chain you notice a sign that reads "If the amount you pay is not the same as your sales receipt, your meal is free." Would you consider this policy as a method of monitoring internal controls at the restaurant? Explain your answer.

Obj. 9 **11-21.** The internal audit department at Iso Industries works directly for the company controller. The controller assigns the auditors' work, most often having the auditors check the work of the accounting department. After the auditors have completed their work, they prepare written reports that are delivered directly to the controller. What weaknesses do you see in this arrangement?

PROBLEMS

PROBLEM 11-1 Missing Terminology

Complete each of the following sentences with the proper terminology.

1. The methods a company uses to protect assets and ensure reliable information are referred to as _____.

2. Properly designed internal control procedures protect a company's assets and ensure _____ of accounting information.

3. The behavior of top management of a company directly affects the company's _____.

4. The set of rules established by the Institute of Management Accountants that governs the behavior of management accountants is known as _____.

5. To resolve an ethical conflict, a person should first discuss the problem with his or her _____.

6. The identification of internal and external conditions that jeopardize the ability of a company to meet its objectives is known as _____.

7. Securing inventory to prevent the possibility of theft is an example of a(n) _____.

8. Separating the physical control of assets from the record-keeping process is an example of _____.

9. Receiving payment from one customer and applying it to another's account is known as _____.

10. Effective control over inventory requires that periodic _____ be compared to _____.

PROBLEM 11-2   Internal Control and Cash

Objs. 2,6

Jack Rashad is the controller for a small manufacturing company. Jack is responsible for ensuring that the company's bills are paid in a timely manner. His immediate supervisor, the president, is most concerned with maintaining a perfect credit record for the company and expects all bills to be paid as soon as possible. Before a check is written, Jack is given a memo with the signature of the appropriate department head indicating that the goods or services were received and instructing that the payment be made. All department heads have the authority to acquire the goods and services needed to operate their departments. No document other than the department head's memo is needed to make a disbursement.

When Jack receives a memo from a department head, he writes a check, signs it, and then mails the check. At the end of the month, Jack receives the bank statement and reconciles the company's checking account, looking for any unusual items such as a check endorsed over to a department head by the payee.

Required

a. What internal control weaknesses exist with respect to cash procedures?
b. What changes could be implemented to enhance internal controls over cash?

PROBLEM 11-3   Payroll Expenses and Collusion

Objs. 2,6

Sunbury Products employs over 600 workers in its manufacturing plant. Payroll is processed by the company's personnel department and distributed to employees by the department supervisors on a biweekly basis. On the advice of a management consultant, the supervisor of the personnel department decided to conduct a payroll distribution for one pay period using senior managers rather than department supervisors to distribute checks.

Each employee was required to show a photo identification in order to collect his or her paycheck from the manager. As a result of this pay distribution, a scheme was uncovered in which two "ghost" employees had been added to the payroll system in one department. After further investigation, it was discovered that the department manager and a payroll processing clerk had colluded to operate the scheme. Two extra checks were prepared each pay period. One of these was kept by the payroll clerk, and the other was taken by the department manager. The checks then were cashed at a bank.

Required

a. How could this scheme have been detected earlier under a proper system of internal control?
b. Would a review of payroll journals have prevented this scheme if the department manager was solely responsible for reviewing the journals?
c. What is collusion, and how did it affect this situation?

PROBLEM 11-4   Communication and Internal Control Weaknesses

Objs. 6,7

The First State Bank operates seven branch locations throughout the county. There are over 35 bank tellers who work for First State. When bank tellers are hired, they are provided with a week of teller training, which includes instruction on bank operating procedures, computer terminal operations, and bank policies for processing transactions. During the training period, the new tellers are never informed that teller drawers are subject to independent counts and verification on a periodic basis by the bank's internal audit staff.

Kelly O'Donnell was hired as a teller for one of the bank's drive-up windows at a branch office and received the one week of training. After Kelly had worked at the branch for six months, an audit of Kelly's cash drawer by the internal audit staff found the drawer short $2,500. It was subsequently learned that Kelly had been fired by a previous employer for misappropriating company assets.

Required

a. How would communication of the internal audit procedures during the teller training period reduce the risk of thefts such as this?
b. What role did the lack of internal control over personnel hiring policies play in the bank's loss?

PROBLEM 11-5   Internal Audit Functions

Obj. 9

Quick Flow, Inc., is a manufacturer of fuel pumps and hoses. The company's stock is traded nationally. Quick Flow has an internal audit staff made up of over 40 employees. Most of the internal audit employees are accountants, but there are also computer experts and an engineer on the staff. The director of internal audit reports directly to the audit committee of the company's board of directors. Each year the director presents an audit plan to the audit committee, detailing the financial and operational audits that will be conducted during the coming year. The director also reviews the results of the prior year's audits with the audit committee, along with recommendations for operational improvements.

Required

a. Why would the internal audit staff include computer experts and an engineer?
b. Why does the director of internal audit report to a committee of the board of directors?
c. Why is it appropriate for the director to outline the planned audit procedures to the audit committee before they are conducted?

PROBLEM 11-6   Internal Control and Human Behavior

Objs. 2,4,5

The USA Pie Company produces pies, cakes, and snacks. The company, which produces over 10,000 cakes, pies, and snacks each month, uses a manual production and accounting information system.

The owner of the company, Ralph Lloyd, expects the controller, Anita Nichols, to prepare monthly financial statements within three business days after the end of each month. In order to close the books and generate financial statements, Anita must summarize production information, ensure that all shipments have been invoiced, accrue all liabilities, and perform other necessary calculations for the month end. With a staff of only three assistants, Anita finds the imposed deadline of three business days difficult to meet. There is no time to double-check work, review information for unexpected results, or confirm recorded transactions against supporting documentation.

After the financial statements have been prepared and submitted to Lloyd, Anita often finds errors that must be corrected. These are often the result of human error, such as mathematical inaccuracies or failure to cross-check totals. Lloyd becomes upset when the statements must be changed and has demanded that the original statements presented to him be accurate. Lloyd has threatened to fire Anita if the financial statements are not accurate and timely.

Required

a. How does the imposed three-day deadline affect the company's internal control structure?
b. If the company implemented a computerized production and accounting system, what impact would this have on the company's organizational environment and need for risk assessment?
c. What implications for human behavior does the three-day deadline have?

PROBLEM 11-7   **Inventory Control Weaknesses**

Objs. 6,9

The Jefferson Manufacturing Company produces chemical products for use by plastics manufacturers. The plant operates two shifts a day, five days a week. Raw materials are received at the back of the plant and may be signed for by any employee who is available at the time. The materials then are stored near the first department that uses them and are used in production as needed.

The first department foreman sends a memo to the controller on a weekly basis, stating that materials have been received and indicating the number of units that were produced. The controller calculates material usage based on standard quantities of production and records both the receipt of materials and the usage of materials on a weekly basis.

At the end of each quarter, a physical count of raw materials is conducted by first department personnel. The results of their counts are sent to the controller, who adjusts inventory accounts to reflect the actual amount of materials on hand. Adjustments to the Raw Material Inventory account are common and can be rather large.

Required

a.   What weaknesses are there in the inventory control procedures at Jefferson?
b.   What improvements would you recommend to strengthen inventory control?
c.   Assume that Jefferson has an internal audit department. What role could this department play in strengthening internal control over raw materials?

PROBLEM 11-8   **Monitoring Control Systems**

Obj. 8

Jerry Itt is a trustee for a municipal township. The trustee is an elected official who is responsible for administering programs that assist the needy. Jerry works full time at a local bank and performs the trustee duties on a part time basis. As trustee, he employs a staff of clerks and case workers that meet with clients. Tom Peterson is the supervisor in charge of all case workers. The case workers accumulate information from clients and process payments to service providers that assist clients with the cost of shelter, utilities and medical expenses. Client expenses are paid directly to the services provider.

Jerry is concerned that case workers may be tempted to make improper expenditure of funds and has established the following procedures and controls related to the administration of client assistance:

1.   Any new service providers must be approved by Tom before they can receive payment.
2.   All payments must be processed by Carol Shelton, the adminstrative clerk.
3.   Jerry will sign all checks.
4.   Jerry will reconcile the bank statement each month.

Required

a.   Assume a case worker prepares a check for a fictitious service provider that is payable to a close relative. What controls would minimize the risk of this occurrence? What controls are in place to detect this theft?
b.   If Tom Peterson works in collusion with a case worker to make unauthorized payments to a third party, are there controls in place that would prevent or detect this activity? Explain your answer.
c.   Assume that Jerry allows the clerk to use a signature stamp to sign checks after they have been prepared. Which controls become critical to ensuring that funds are not stolen?

PROBLEM 11-9   **Multiple Choice Overview of the Chapter**

1.   Management accountants are best described as:
   a.   employees who audit company transactions for purposes of reporting to shareholders.
   b.   employees of an organization who may work in finance, accounting, or internal audit.
   c.   independent contractors unrelated to the corporation.
   d.   required by SEC regulations.

2. Communication of a company's ethical issues to authorities outside the organization
   a. is a violation of ethical standards unless it is required by law.
   b. is appropriate if management refuses to take action to correct the issue.
   c. is appropriate if the issue involves the highest level of management.
   d. may be appropriate, depending on management's actions.

3. When faced with an ethical dilemma, a manager should first:
   a. confront the parties involved.
   b. identify the potential person or persons affected by the dilemma.
   c. identify the ethical issues involved.
   d. resign from the organization.

4. The primary purpose of an effective system of internal control is to:
   a. ensure that no unauthorized transactions occur.
   b. safeguard a company's assets.
   c. provide management with a tool to assess risk.
   d. provide management with a tool to manage risk.

5. A reward system that emphasizes current financial performance:
   a. is an effective method of reducing control risk.
   b. is an example of an environmental control problem.
   c. is ineffective for motivating managers.
   d. does not encourage employees to engage in activities inconsistent with long-run goals.

6. Which of the following would not be considered an element of internal control?
   a. A computerized accounting system.
   b. An internal audit staff.
   c. Well-trained, competent personnel.
   d. None of the above; they are all elements of internal control.

7. Proper internal control over cash would include which of the following?
   a. The person who keeps the cash box also records all cash transactions.
   b. The person who records cash receipts opens the incoming mail.
   c. Cash receipts and cash disbursements are performed by the same individual.
   d. The person who writes and signs checks does not reconcile the bank account.

8. Which of the following would reflect a good internal control procedure?
   a. All employees must take a full week of vacation at least once a year.
   b. The inventory storeroom clerk performs a count of all inventory on hand at least once a year.
   c. The accounts receivable billing clerk opens all incoming mail.
   d. None of the above.

9. Effective risk management:
   a. requires a strong internal control structure.
   b. requires proper segregation of duties.
   c. requires risk assessment, evaluation, and prevention.
   d. is effective only when human behavior is properly controlled.

10. The internal audit function:
    a. is independent of other divisions of the company.
    b. may include employees other than accountants.
    c. evaluates efficiency and effectiveness by performing operational audits.
    d. all of the above.

C A S E S

CASE **11-1**   **Ethical Conflict**
Obj. 4

Able Axle Company, a nonunion company that employs approximately 300 factory workers, produces axles that are sold to a major auto and truck manufacturer. Faced with pressures from its customers, company management has begun to stress cost reduction at all levels. Factory supervisors are pressured constantly to achieve greater output and reduce labor cost. Skilled workers are required to operate the production machinery. Many of the factory workers have been with Able for over 15 years and make a significant hourly wage. Plant supervisors claim that it is difficult to cut labor costs when the average hourly worker makes over $20 an hour.

One of the company's department supervisors has demanded that employees continue to work *after* they have clocked out, in order to increase productivity without adding cost. When employees argued that they should not work without pay, the supervisor responded that (1) if the employees were able to get the job done during their normal shift, they wouldn't need to work late, (2) administrative employees often work extra hours when needed without receiving extra pay, (3) the employees should welcome the opportunity to do a little something extra for their company, and (4) the extra work is only temporary in order to make the department look good to management.

Required

a.   Were the supervisor's actions ethical? What would be the managerial accounting impact of work without pay?
b.   What would you suggest the workers do if the supervisor continues to demand work without pay?
c.   Assume that management agrees with the supervisor's position. Do the factory employees have any recourse? Explain your answer.

CASE **11-2**   **Accounts Receivable Lapping**
Objs. 2,4,6

Roberta Dunn was an accounts receivable clerk for Speedco Products. Each day, Roberta received a large batch of unopened payments from a courier, who picked up the mail from the company's post office box. Roberta developed a sophisticated lapping scheme whereby she diverted some of the collected funds to a bank account she had opened in the company's name from which funds could be withdrawn on Roberta's signature. Roberta kept careful records, holding on to customer payments and then using cash receipts from other customers to pay these payments a few days later. Soon, the total misappropriation grew to a sizable amount, with customer payments being recorded nearly three weeks after the initial payment was received.

Eventually, Roberta was discovered. Management was surprised that such an old and faithful employee, who was never sick and never took a vacation, would pull such a scheme. Upon being caught, Roberta turned over unprocessed customer payment notices in excess of $85,000. Management immediately called for an investigation, and the following facts were discovered:

1.   Roberta worked for the controller.
2.   Roberta prepared the bank deposit each day.
3.   Roberta gave the customer payment notices to the EDP processing clerk for posting each day. The EDP clerk posted the amounts to customer accounts.
4.   Roberta took the deposits to the bank each day.
5.   Roberta gave the stamped bank copy of the deposit ticket to the controller each day.
6.   The controller compared the deposit ticket to a list of customer payments processed by the EDP clerk. No discrepancies between the total deposit and the amounts processed were ever noted.
7.   Customers were not sent statements; rather, their following month's billing would reveal any unpaid amounts.
8.   Customer inquiries concerning account balances and billing statements were directed to Roberta.

Required

a.   Identify problems in Speedco's system that allowed the misappropriations by Roberta.
b.   What changes would you recommend to ensure that these problems do not recur?

PROJECTS

PROJECT 11-1   Ethics
Obj. 4

Working in a group of three or four students from your class, prepare a role play demonstrating an ethical dilemma for a fictitious company. Present your role play to the class. Identify the ethical conflict and then show through role play how you would resolve the conflict.

PROJECT 11-2   Internal Control And Losses
Objs. 2,6

Find an article in a national business publication that identifes a situation in which poor internal control procedures resulted in the loss of assets to a company. Write a short narrative on the article, explaining the internal controls that apparently were lacking and the result of the control failure. Explain what controls could have been implemented to reduce the possibility of the loss.

PROJECT 11-3   Internal Control Procedures
Obj. 6

Write a short narrative discussing a job you have had or currently have. What are some of the internal control procedures that you experienced in your employment? What assets or resources was management protecting by these control procedures? Were the procedures effective?

A Closer Look
at Service
Companies

12

Accounting and Management Decisions

Internal Control

Capital Budgeting

Decentralized Organizations

Global Environment

Performance Evaluation

Budgets

Service Organizations

Cost Behavior

Unit Costs

Cost Measurement

Cost Allocation

Overview

This chapter considers managerial accounting issues that are particularly important to service companies. Although manufacturing companies are vital to the U.S. economy, 75% of employees work for service companies.[1] Service companies include CPA, law, consulting, and architectural firms; hospitals; schools; banks; airline companies; and day-care facilities. In addition, companies such as McDonald's are considered part of the service sector even though they sell a tangible product.

Service companies use processes to create the services their customers purchase. Although most service companies do not deliver tangible products, managers of service companies must understand the cost of providing various services to their customers. Those managers must develop appropriate performance measures to help them improve the effectiveness and efficiency of their processes.

Although service companies are similar to manufacturing companies in many ways, they may have unique problems. Because services often are tailored to a client's specific needs, the cost of providing these services often depends on the specific needs. As a result, the cost of providing a particular service varies by client. In most manufacturing settings, the cost of producing a product does not depend on the characteristics of the customer who purchases the product. Additionally, service companies must manage their output volume carefully because a large proportion of their cost tends to be fixed.

This chapter considers cost management systems used by service organizations. It identifies methods used to allocate indirect support department costs to revenue-producing departments in order to understand the total cost of providing services. In addition, the chapter identifies strategies service organizations

© Kurt Coste/Fertility Institute of New Orleans/Tony Stone Images

use to improve their processes. To illustrate these methods and strategies, this chapter uses the experiences of Stonebrook Medical Center, a medical services company.

Major topics covered in this chapter include:
- Allocation of support department costs to revenue-producing departments
- Cost management systems used to attach costs to services
- Measuring and improving process performance within service organizations

1   Martinson, Otto. 1994. Cost Accounting in the Service Industry, A Critical Assessment. *Montvale, NJ: Institute of Management Accountants.*

Objectives

Once you have completed this chapter, you should be able to:

1. Explain how costs are classified within service organizations.
2. Allocate support department costs to revenue-producing departments.
3. Calculate costs of providing various services to customers and discuss how service costs may be used to make better decisions.
4. Describe various strategies used by service organizations to improve quality and reduce costs.

BACKGROUND AND ENVIRONMENT OF STONEBROOK MEDICAL CENTER

A major insurer asked us to bid on performing all of its open-heart surgeries in the south-east United States. We prepared a bid by pulling cost information from our old cost system on all open-heart surgery patients we had treated. We did not get the contract, and we had *no idea* whether to be disappointed or relieved. From talks with third-party payers and major employers, we believed that we would be bidding for portions of business, like open-heart surgeries, on a regular basis. We realized that we needed a much better under-standing of our costs if we were to be able to compete effectively.
—Jay Williams, Administrative Leader, Stonebrook Medical Center

Stonebrook Medical Center is a for-profit medical facility that offers a wide range of health-care services, including extended outpatient surgery, labor and delivery, psy-chiatry, and heart surgery. In addition, Stonebrook has initiated a number of pro-grams to promote knowledge and wellness in the community. These programs include health and fitness courses, a cancer program, and a diabetes program.

The health-care industry currently is receiving more and more attention by the media, government, and public as a result of increasing health-care costs. In order to survive, providers must cope with constantly changing conditions. They must deliver high quality health-care services in a time of intense competition.

The market for health-care services includes both patients and insurance compa-nies. Thus, medical facilities are expected to deliver high quality health-care services, while controlling health-care costs. Stonebrook and many other medical facilities are taking steps to improve their cost reporting systems. In addition, hospitals are redesigning health-care delivery processes to reduce costs and improve quality.

Jay Williams, an administrative leader at Stonebrook Medical Center, selected a group of individuals with diverse professional backgrounds to serve on a committee to improve the clinical and financial outcomes at Stonebrook. The team consisted of Beth Rogers, the cost accounting manager; Linda Reynolds, a specialty nurse; and Tim Harris, a clinical case manager. Linda and Tim were asked to join the team because they have clinical and managerial experience. Beth and Jay brought account-ing and business systems knowledge to the group.

Jay and his team had to find ways to improve the health-care delivery processes within the hospital. In addition, because of pressure from insurance companies, they had to reduce costs and at the same time improve the quality of care delivered to patients at Stonebrook. The health-care environment is changing rapidly because of managed-care systems. Employers often contract with insurance companies to pro-vide health-care coverage for their employees at a fixed annual rate per employee. The insurance companies then contract with health-care providers, such as Stone-brook, to provide care at predetermined rates. Thus, hospitals that offer lower costs while providing quality care are more successful in securing contracts with managed-care systems. As a result, hospital cost systems have become increasingly important to managers as they attempt to understand the cost of providing services such as open heart surgery and cancer treatment.

As indicated by Jay's quote at the beginning of this section, Stonebrook is facing a rapidly changing environment. The existing cost management system is inadequate for the decisions that managers must make. Of growing concern is the unexplained variation in physicians' practice patterns. As administrators attempt to control costs and modify physicians' behavior, accurate information on resource use by physicians would prove very useful. It is difficult to improve processes without accurate cost data.

An analysis of the effectiveness of care also would permit decisions about the types of clinical procedures Stonebrook and member physicians performed. Evaluat-ing the effectiveness of a medical procedure involves clinical understanding. Thus, to be adequate for decision making in tomorrow's health-care environment, an infor-mation system must include the ability to gather and distribute information about the results of clinical procedures.

Other decisions that administrators face include cost versus value of care. For example, new medical technologies are developing continually. The decision to make investments in new technology is a complex process that compares existing clinical results with those promised by the new technology. Often, cost information can be a key factor in decisions about purchasing new technology.

Cost management systems for hospital use are evolving. Until recently, many hospitals used a facilitywide cost-to-charge ratio to estimate the cost of a medical procedure. This ratio is similar in principle to manufacturers using a facilitywide predetermined overhead rate to apply overhead to products. Thus, total annual facilitywide costs were divided by total annual facilitywide charges (billings) to determine a facilitywide cost-to-charge ratio. To estimate the cost of a procedure, the charge (amount billed) was multiplied by the facilitywide cost-to-charge ratio. For example, assume the following costs and charges for Stonebrook:

Cost and Revenue Data for 12 Months Ending December 31, 1996

Revenue Center	Total Costs	Total Charges
Radiology	$ 7,000,000	$ 7,000,000
Psychiatric care	5,000,000	6,000,000
Intensive care	9,000,000	9,200,000
Chemotherapy	5,000,000	7,000,000
Coronary care	7,200,000	7,400,000
Nursing/surgical	8,000,000	9,000,000
Emergency room	6,300,000	6,800,000
Operating room	26,000,000	46,000,000
Labor and delivery	9,000,000	11,200,000
Laboratory	5,000,000	15,000,000
Diabetes center	500,000	400,000
Total	$88,000,000	$125,000,000

The facilitywide cost-to-charge ratio is calculated as follows:

$$\frac{\text{Total costs}}{\text{Total charges}} = \frac{\$88,000,000}{\$125,000,000} = 0.704$$

If Stonebrook charged $5,000 for an appendectomy procedure, the estimated cost would be $3,520 ($5,000 × 0.704). Also, if charges for an open-heart surgery were $30,000, the estimated costs would be $21,120 ($30,000 × 0.704). The system was adequate for determining the average cost of all procedures; however, it was not useful in helping managers determine the cost of a specific procedure. Unfortunately, many hospitals continue to use the cost-to-charge ratio to estimate costs. However, better cost management systems are becoming a necessity for survival as hospitals submit bids to insurance companies to acquire managed-care contracts.

MODERN COST MANAGEMENT SYSTEMS FOR SERVICE ORGANIZATIONS

Objective 1
Explain how costs are classified within service organizations.

Jay and Beth sat at a table and sketched the structure of a cost system that would accurately trace costs to revenue-producing departments. Their sketch is reproduced in Exhibit 1. The system had to be one that could be understood easily because cost management systems for health-care decisions must be accessible by everyone in the organization. They began by classifying departments as either support departments or revenue-producing departments.

Revenue-producing departments at Stonebrook included the operating room, psychiatric care, radiology, the diabetes center, and coronary care. Each revenue-producing department incurred direct costs, such as supplies and salaries. Departments

Exhibit 1   Conceptual Design of the Stonebrook Medical Center Cost Accounting System

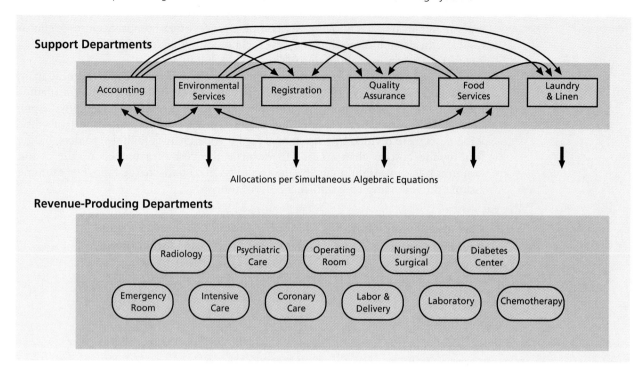

such as accounting, environmental services (janitorial and maintenance), registration, and quality assurance supported the revenue-producing departments. Jay and Beth reasoned that the total cost of providing operating room services should include direct operating room costs plus part of the support department costs. Thus, allocations were necessary to transfer support department costs to revenue-producing departments.

In addition to providing services to revenue-producing departments, support departments often provide services to other support departments. For example, the environmental services department cleans the accounting department offices. Likewise, the accounting department provides payroll functions for the environmental services department. **A** *reciprocal service arrangement* **exists when support departments exchange services.** Health-care cost systems commonly use either a step-down or a simultaneous algebraic equation method to allocate costs among support departments. Simultaneous equations for real organizations are too complex to be solved manually. However, the following simple example illustrates key principles found in complex computer-based cost systems.

Step-down and Simultaneous Algebraic Equation Methods for Allocating Reciprocal Support Costs

O b j e c t i v e   2
Allocate support department costs to revenue-producing departments.

For illustration purposes, assume that Stonebrook has only *two* support departments, accounting and environmental services. In addition, assume that Stonebrook has only two revenue-producing departments, operating room and psychiatric care. A study conducted by the accounting department revealed that its efforts were distributed among the other three departments as follows: environmental services, 5%; operating room, 45%; and psychiatric care, 50%. A manager of the environmental services department estimated that the department's efforts and resources were consumed as follows: accounting, 10%; operating room, 60%; and psychiatric care, 30%. Exhibit 2 illustrates the relationships among the support departments and revenue-producing departments. Direct costs (before allocations have been performed) for each department are shown in Exhibit 3.

Exhibit 2   Reciprocal Service Relationships (Chart of %)

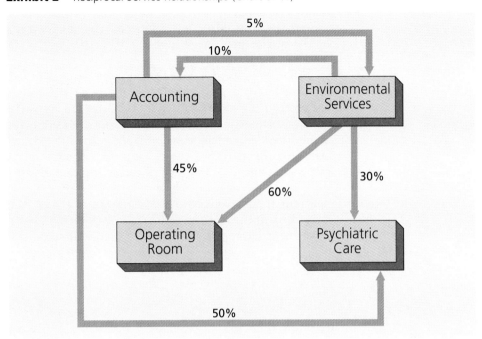

Exhibit 3   Departmental Direct Costs Prior to Allocation

Accounting	$ 100,000
Environmental services	300,000
Operating room	1,600,000
Psychiatric care	1,000,000
Total	$3,000,000

This section considers two methods for allocating service department costs to revenue-producing departments: step-down and simultaneous algebraic equations. Allocations of service department costs using the step-down method recognize reciprocal relationships to only a limited extent because cost allocations flow in only one direction. Once costs are transferred out of a department, they do not flow back into it. Typically, departments that provide the most resources to other departments are allocated first. Using Stonebrook as an example, the step-down method first allocates the costs of environmental services to accounting, operating room, and psychiatric services. Next, the accounting department's costs (beginning costs and those transferred from environmental services) are allocated to the operating room and psychiatric care departments. Exhibit 4 illustrates the cost flows using the step-down method.

Exhibit 4   Graph of Cost Flows Using Step-down Method

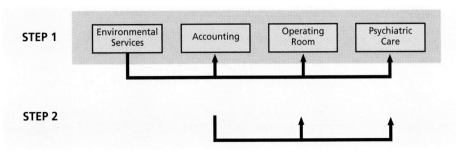

As indicated earlier, environmental services department costs were allocated as follows: accounting, 10%; operating room, 60%; and psychiatric care, 30%. Thus, to allocate the costs of the environmental services department, $300,000 is multiplied by the service percentages ($300,000 \times 0.10 = 30,000$; $300,000 \times 0.60 = 180,000$; $300,000 \times 0.30 = 90,000$).

After the costs of environmental services are allocated, the next step is to allocate the accounting department's costs. Although the accounting department provides resources to environmental services, the step-down method does not permit costs to be allocated into a department whose costs already have been allocated. Thus, the accounting department costs are allocated to the operating room and psychiatric care. From Exhibit 2 we know that the operating room and psychiatric care departments consume 45% and 50% of the accounting department's services, respectively. As a result, the allocation base is 95% (45% + 50%) rather than 100%. Thus, the operating room receives $61,579 ($130,000 \times 0.45 \div 0.95$), and the psychiatric services department receives $68,421 ($130,000 \times 0.50 \div 0.95$) from the accounting department. Exhibit 5 summarizes the allocation process for the step-down method.

Exhibit 5   Cost Allocation from Service to Revenue-Producing Departments, Step-down Method

	Environmental Services	Accounting	Operating Room	Psychiatric Care	Total
Beginning	$300,000	$100,000	$1,600,000	$1,000,000	$3,000,000
Environmental services distribution	(300,000)	30,000	180,000	90,000	
Accounting distribution		(130,000)	61,579	68,421	
Ending	$ 0	$ 0	$1,841,679	$1,158,421	$3,000,000

The step-down method was commonly used in health-care organizations before sophisticated computer packages became generally available. This method recognizes reciprocal transfers among service departments to only a limited degree because costs flow in only one direction. The primary advantage of the step-down method is the ease of calculation. Also, because simultaneous equations or matrix algebra is not required, users of information easily understand how costs are allocated. However, the team at Stonebrook decided to use a computerized system to perform allocations based on simultaneous algebraic equations. Before the system could crunch the numbers, mathematical models of departmental relationships had to be constructed. The group asked Jay to develop these mathematical relationships.

Jay began to define the relationships among departments in mathematical terms. For example, the cost of providing environmental services equals $300,000 plus 5% of the costs incurred by the accounting department. The cost of providing accounting services equals the direct costs of $100,000 plus 10% of the cost incurred by environmental services. These relationships may be expressed mathematically as follows:

Environmental services = $300,000 + (0.05 × accounting)
Accounting   = $100,000 + (0.10 × environmental services)

Because of reciprocal service arrangements, the cost of the environmental services department is affected by the cost of the accounting department, and the cost of the accounting department is affected by the cost of the environmental services department. Thus, simultaneous equations are used to arrive at a solution. First, solve the equation for the environmental services department as follows:

Step 1. *Define the mathematical relationship.*

Environmental services = $300,000 + (0.05 × accounting)

Step 2. *Substitute the mathematical definition of accounting.*

Environmental services = $300,000 + 0.05 ($100,000 + 0.10 × environmental services)

Step 3. *Distribute 0.05 across both terms in parentheses.*

Environmental services = $300,000 + $5,000 + (0.005 × environmental services)

Step 4. *Subtract 0.005 × environmental services from each side of the equation.*

Environmental services − (0.005 × environmental services) = $300,000 + $5,000

Step 5. *Combine terms.*

0.995 × environmental services = $305,000

Step 6. *Divide each side of the equation by 0.995.*

Environmental services = $306,533

Therefore, the cost of operating the environmental services department is $306,533 after considering costs allocated from the accounting department. Next, solve the accounting equation by substituting $306,533 for the environmental services term in the equation.

Step 1. *Define the mathematical relationship.*

Accounting = $100,000 + (0.10 × environmental services)

Step 2. *Substitute the value from Step 6 above into the accounting equation.*

Accounting = $100,000 + (0.10 × $306,533)

Step 3. *Multiply terms within parentheses.*

Accounting = $100,000 + $30,653

Step 4. *Combine terms.*

Accounting = $130,653

The simultaneous equations produce values for environmental services and accounting that are allocated among each of the four departments according to the percentages identified in Exhibit 2. This method commonly is used by hospitals to allocate the costs of service departments to other service departments and finally to revenue-producing departments. Though a computer routine performs the complex algebraic calculations, managers should understand the underlying concepts.

Having determined service department costs, Jay prepared the allocation schedule shown in Exhibit 6. He prepared a column for each department and placed the direct costs from Exhibit 3 into the columns to represent beginning balances before allocations. He noted the total cost of $3,000,000. Jay began by allocating the accounting department's costs. The algebraic solution stated that $130,653 was incurred by the accounting department. Thus, Jay subtracted $130,653 from the accounting department to distribute among environmental services, operating room, and psychiatric care using the percentages from Exhibit 2 ($130,653 × 0.05 = $6,533; $130,653 × 0.45 = $58,794; $130,653 × 0.50 = $65,326). Next he subtracted $306,533 from the environmental services column to distribute among accounting, operating room, and psychiatric services using the percentages identified in Exhibit 2 ($306,533 × 0.10 = $30,653; $306,533 × 0.60 = $183,920; $306,533 × 0.30 = $91,960). As shown in Exhibit 6, after the service department costs are distributed, both the accounting and the environmental services columns contain zero balances, while the revenue-producing departments, operating room and psychiatric care, contain all the costs from the service departments. Notice also that the total costs before and after allocation equal $3,000,000.

Exhibit 6   Cost Allocation from Service to Revenue-Producing Departments

	Accounting	Environmental Services	Operating Room	Psychiatric Care	Total
Beginning	$100,000	$300,000	$1,600,000	$1,000,000	$3,000,000
Accounting distribution	(130,653)	6,533	58,794	65,326	
Environmental services distribution	30,653	(306,533)	183,920	91,960	
Ending	$ 0	$ 0	$1,842,714	$1,157,286	$3,000,000

Managers use cost reports containing allocations to make various kinds of decisions. An objective of support department cost allocation is to understand the revenue-producing departments' total cost of providing services. To make pricing decisions, managers must understand how total resource consumption rates vary across revenue-producing departments. For example, in a hospital, the operating room and the psychiatric department consume support department resources differently because each has its unique function. Thus, the cost system must trace support department costs to revenue-producing departments accurately to allow managers to understand the cost of providing different types of services. When reciprocal service arrangements occur among service departments, cost allocation among these departments is necessary to determine each service department's total cost.

To improve processes and reduce costs, managers must understand cost drivers, the activities that cause costs. Choosing appropriate cost drivers, or allocation bases, helps managers understand the sources of costs and where to look for clues as to how to reduce costs. For example, managers may look at the allocated cost of lab services and consider whether the value of the services received equals the cost. If costs are thought to be excessive, consumption patterns may change, or a manager may decide to purchase these services from an independent laboratory. Finally, accurate allocations are necessary to reduce cross-subsidy among services provided. The cost-to-charge ratio averages many types of costs across various services. As a result, some services are reported at a cost greater than the actual, while other services are reported at a cost less than the actual. This is known as *cross-subsidy*. Eliminating cross-subsidy is important because managers using costs based on averages may make poor pricing decisions.

SELF-STUDY PROBLEM 1

The Liberty School is a private institution offering preschool and kindergarten classes. All teachers are experts in the field of early childhood education. To support the primary function of classroom instruction, Liberty maintains a personnel department and an administrative department. The manager of the administrative department estimates that her department provides services to other departments as follows:

Personnel	15%
Preschool instruction	50%
Kindergarten instruction	35%
	100%

The manager of the personnel department estimates that his department provides services to other departments as follows:

Administrative	30%
Preschool instruction	45%
Kindergarten instruction	25%
	100%

The departmental direct costs are as follows:

Administrative	$100,000
Personnel	75,000
Preschool instruction	300,000
Kindergarten instruction	500,000
Total	$975,000

Required

1. Discuss the circumstances that create reciprocal relationships among service departments.
2. Draw a chart of the relationships among the four departments.
3. Allocate the service department costs to revenue-producing departments using the step-down method.
4. Set up the equations to mathematically explain the cost of providing administrative and personnel services.
5. Determine the costs of maintaining the administrative and personnel departments using simultaneous algebraic equations.
6. Allocate the costs from the administrative and personnel departments to the preschool and kindergarten departments.

The solution to Self-Study Problem 1 appears at the end of the chapter.

Cost Management Systems for Service Companies

Managers of service organizations, like their counterparts in manufacturing, need to understand the cost of providing goods or services to their customers. They must

Objective 3
Calculate costs of providing various services to customers and discuss how service costs may be used to make better decisions.

understand how costs change with activity levels if they are to determine appropriate prices for their services. Additionally, managers may use cost accounting information to help them identify expensive, inefficient processes that are candidates for improvement. Finally, having accurate cost information may permit managers to compare the cost of their services with those of competitors. The cost structure of most service organizations presents interesting challenges for managers. This section illustrates the design and use of a cost system in a service environment.

A Health-Care Cost Report for an Appendectomy Procedure. A cost system for attaching costs to services may use a two-stage process. In the first stage, support department costs are allocated to revenue-producing departments. In the second stage, costs are attached to a specific product, service, or customer.

Jay and Beth continued to work on their drawing of a new cost system for Stonebrook. Their final objective was to design a cost system that would attach costs to each patient based on resources consumed while treating the patient. Thus far, their model allocated costs among support departments and to revenue-producing departments. These support-related costs were added to the direct costs of the revenue-producing department, as illustrated in Exhibit 6. Their next step was to ensure that costs from revenue-producing departments were allocated to the patient, based on the resources consumed. Exhibit 7 illustrates the model designed by Jay and Beth.

Exhibit 7 extends the model shown in Exhibit 1 by adding allocations from revenue-producing departments to patients. As in manufacturing cost systems, a variety of allocation bases are used to attach costs to patient procedures. For example, from discussions with the clinical members of their team, Jay and Beth knew that some costs are incurred as a function of hours, whereas others are incurred at a daily rate. Finally, other costs should be applied to procedures using the actual cost, such as supplies.

Exhibit 7   Design of the Cost Allocation System.

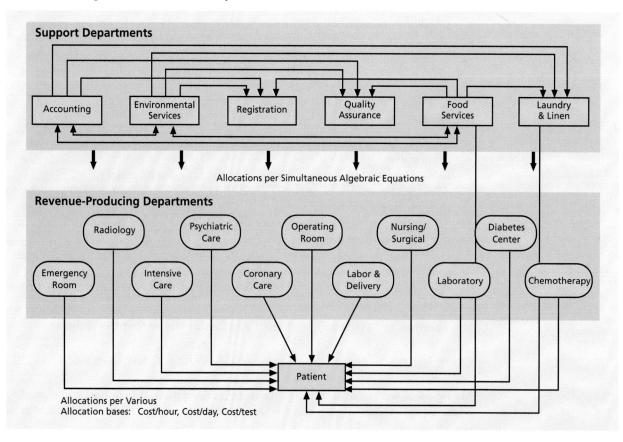

Jay and Beth pulled data on a patient who recently received care at Stonebrook. Their cost analysis is shown in Exhibit 8. The patient was admitted to the emergency room for an appendectomy procedure. Jay and Beth identified departments and the description of services provided. Linda Reynolds, the specialty nurse, said that patients could receive various levels of nursing attention. Thus, when designing the system, Jay and Beth allocated nursing costs to patients based on a daily rate at various acuity levels. **Acuity levels** identify the amount of care required; higher acuity levels indicate sicker patients. The patient in their report required one day at acuity level 1 and two days at acuity level 2.

Exhibit 8   Appendectomy Cost Report

Department Description	Product Description	Cost	Quantity	Total Cost
Nursing—surgical	Acuity level 1—daily rate	$313.00	1	$ 313.00
	Acuity level 2—daily rate	369.00	2	738.00
Operating room (OR)	Major surgery—1 hour	449.00	1	449.00
Operating room supplies	Sutures	24.00	5	120.00
	Basic surgical pack	23.00	1	23.00
	Additional OR supplies	251.50	1	251.50
Food services	Daily hospital service	42.00	3	126.00
Laundry/linen	Daily hospital service	15.00	3	45.00
Emergency room (ER)	ER visit level II—intensive	222.00	1	222.00
				$2,287.50

Jay and Beth used an hourly charge to allocate costs from the operating room. As shown in Exhibit 8, the patient spent one hour in the operating room. In the cost model, operating room supplies and central stores supplies are assigned to the patient using the items' actual costs. For example, 5 sutures costing $24 each were required for the appendectomy procedure.

Food services and laundry/linen costs were attached to the patient using a daily rate because costs of meals and laundry service typically do not vary significantly by the type of patient or procedure. Finally, emergency room costs of $222 were associated with the patient.

By way of comparison, Jay calculated the cost of the appendectomy procedure using the cost-to-charge ratio and compared the result with that found using his new cost system. Pulling data on the appendectomy patient, he found that the charge was $8,100. Thus, using the facilitywide cost-to-charge ratio of 0.704, Jay calculated the cost as follows $8,100 × 0.704 = $5,702. The cost-to-charge ratio had greatly overestimated the cost of this patient's appendectomy procedure. How could Stonebrook possibly use information based on the cost-to-charge ratio to submit bids? No wonder it had been unsuccessful in winning bids for procedures. Using this case as an example, Stonebrook would have overestimated its costs by $3,414 ($5,702 − $2,288). Jay then had a frightening thought. If Stonebrook overestimated its costs (and bids), the worst that would happen was that another hospital would win the contract. What if the cost-to-charge ratio caused Stonebrook to underestimate its costs, thereby winning long-term contracts for procedures whose actual costs exceeded contract revenue!

Clinical Decisions Using Cost Information. The cost system designed by Jay and Beth as shown in Exhibit 7 is far superior to systems that estimate costs using a facilitywide cost-to-charge ratio. Like managers of manufacturing companies, managers of health-care facilities can use cost reports to understand the way in which clinical procedures consume resources. Opportunities for both cost control and quality improvement may be identified by careful analysis. For example, physicians can make decisions about the cost/benefit relationship of laboratory tests. They may reduce the number of unnecessary lab tests performed by specifying only required tests, rather than ordering an entire list of tests. Physicians may order lab tests every other day, rather than daily, if this is consistent with proper clinical practice. Where appropriate, physicians also may consider early discharge. In addition, carefully selecting the level of care may have a positive impact on costs. In the appendectomy example, the patient received two days of care at acuity level 2 and one day at acuity level 1. The physician can evaluate whether the additional clinical attention at acuity level 2 ($369 per day) rather than acuity level 1 ($313 per day) is necessary. Thus, better cost systems assist managers in making various types of operational decisions.

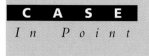

A sample of service organizations revealed that 55% of the companies surveyed were planning to make changes in their cost accounting systems. The companies in the sample represented the accounting, legal, architectural, engineering, communications, banking, financial, health-care, software, marketing, public utilities, research and development, and transportation industries. Though managers indicated a variety of reasons for making changes, continuous improvement was the dominant theme. Managers indicated that they need to make decisions that will help improve quality, increase the number of services delivered, and reduce non-value-added activities. The cost management system is an important tool to help them with improvement efforts.

Martinson, Otto. 1994. **Cost Accounting in the Service Industry, A Critical Assessment.** *Montvale, NJ: Institute of Management Accountants.*

The next section considers various ways service organizations may evaluate processes to reduce waste. While many factors are important to the delivery of health-care services, the cost system may highlight areas for improvement. However, many decisions and clinical assessments must be made by those who have medical, rather than financial, knowledge. Once again, a team approach to cost management is an effective management tool.

SELF-STUDY PROBLEM 2

Paradise Air is a small airline company located in the Florida Keys. The company provides transportation services to various Caribbean islands. Because Paradise Air competes directly with major carriers, controlling costs and setting appropriate fares are vital to the company's survival. Thus, management is preparing an analysis to assist it in understanding the cost of providing various services to customers. Five categories of costs have been identified:

1. Ticketing
2. Fuel, wages, maintenance, and operating expenses

3. First-class on-board services
4. Coach-class on-board services
5. Baggage handling

Managers at Paradise predicted the following costs and activity levels for the next month:

Ticketing	$10,000
Passengers	1,500 coach-class
	500 first-class
Fuel, wages, maintenance, operating expenses	$1.50 per passenger mile*
Baggage handling	$9,000
Number of baggage transfers	3,000
First-class in-flight service	$25,000
Coach-class in-flight service	$15,000

* *Assume that management at Paradise had conducted a long-term study and determined the cost to be $1.50 per passenger mile. Therefore, to determine the fuel, wages, maintenance, and operating expenses cost of each ticket, $1.50 was multiplied by the number of miles traveled.*

Ticketing costs are assigned using a cost per passenger basis. Fuel, wages, maintenance, and other operating expenses are assigned using cost per mile as a basis. Baggage handling costs are assigned using the number of times baggage is transferred. Finally, costs of in-flight services, including food, beverages, and other amenities, were estimated for each class of service.

Required

1. Describe the "product" delivered by Paradise Air.
2. Calculate the cost of providing first-class service to a passenger who requires two baggage transfers and travels 200 miles.

The solution to Self-Study Problem 2 appears at the end of the chapter.

PERFORMANCE MEASUREMENT AND COST MANAGEMENT STRATEGIES IN THE SERVICE ENVIRONMENT

O b j e c t i v e 4
Describe various strategies used by service organizations to improve quality and reduce costs.

Jay and the team understood that developing a new management information system was only part of the plan to improve quality and reduce cost at Stonebrook. He and Beth had relied heavily on various clinical experts when designing the new cost system. Once again, a team orientation would be required to make the organizational changes that were necessary if Stonebrook was to become competitive in a managed-care environment.

In reaction to changes in the reimbursement policies of health-care payers, many health-care providers are making strategic changes in the way they deliver services. Though this chapter uses a health-care organization as an example, the same principles apply to other service (and manufacturing) organizations. Three strategies for improving the health-care delivery process are illustrated.

The team had gathered to consider the next step in restructuring the clinical-care delivery system at Stonebrook. *Operations restructuring* **involves a complete evaluation of the relationships among multiple processes and is conducted to improve the quality and efficiency of services provided to customers.** After months of design and implementation effort by Jay and Beth, the new cost system was in place. Armed with better cost information, the team considered the next step in the restructuring process. While the cost system was under development, the clinical team members, Linda and Tim, had pursued another aspect of the restructuring effort.

Linda began, "As you know, the purpose of our restructuring effort is to improve efficiency and reduce the costs of our clinical delivery process. The result should be increased customer satisfaction and improved patient outcomes."

"We used the blood specimen procurement system as a trial process," continued Tim. "It was a very complex system, consisting of over 100 steps and requiring ten employees. Everyone from the patients to the clinicians was dissatisfied with it."

"We studied the process and made recommendations for changes," Linda went on. "The new system is far less inconvenient for patients because the number of steps has been drastically reduced. Clinical staff members also appreciate the efficiency."

"The new process is less costly, too," added Beth.

"That's right. Beth helped clinicians see their processes from a financial perspective. She was a great help as clinicians struggled to let go of old ways of providing care," Tim said.

"Operations restructuring is the first strategy for becoming more competitive," said Linda. "Our new blood procurement system is an example. We think two other strategies are crucial to successfully changing the way we deliver care. The first is 'outcomes data dissemination,' and the second is 'critical path utilization.' Outcomes data dissemination involves communicating financial and clinical data to physicians and others who make clinical and resource decisions at Stonebrook."

Tim added, "Critical path utilization standardizes treatment routines for various medical procedures."

Outcomes Data Dissemination

The Stonebrook team decided that a key component of successfully improving clinical and financial outcomes involved communicating and acting on relevant data. *Outcomes data dissemination* **is the practice of sharing process and outcomes information with those who make resource decisions.** As with manufacturing processes, the people involved in the delivery of services must understand key process variables. Thus, Linda and Tim collected cost and outcomes data to help physicians improve their practice patterns so that they resulted in better outcomes and lower costs. An example of Linda and Tim's data is shown in Exhibit 9, which summarizes the cost per case for six physicians (A through F).

Exhibit 9   Outcomes Data Dissemination: Cost per Case

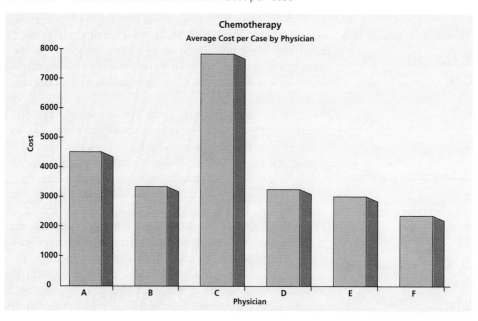

Linda pointed out that Physician C appears to have a high cost per case relative to other physicians in the group. In addition, Exhibit 10 suggests that Physician C's patients remain in the hospital longer than the patients of other physicians. At first, the team thought that Physician C's patients were sicker than those of other physicians. However, Exhibit 11 identifies AWAS (average weighted admission severity) scores for each physician. An AWAS score is a measure of patients' clinical conditions at the time of admission to the hospital; higher scores indicate sicker patients. Physician C's average patient AWAS score is lower than those of almost all of the other physicians in the group. Thus, upon admission to the hospital, Physician C's chemotherapy patients are not as sick as other chemotherapy patients in the sample, but they stay longer and have a higher average cost per case.

Exhibit 10   Outcomes Data Dissemination: LOS Data

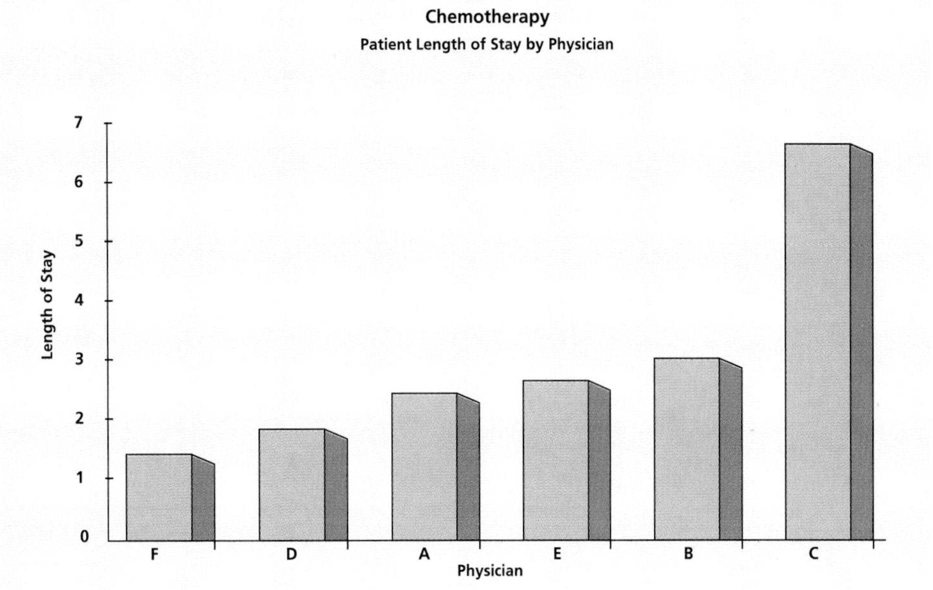

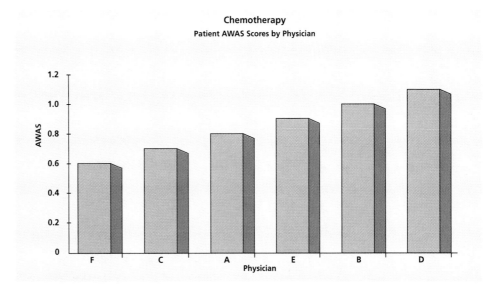

Exhibit 11   Outcomes Data Dissemination: AWAS

"Physician C contacted us for assistance," noted Tim. "He was interested in reducing his cost per case in order to be attractive to a managed-care company."

"We looked at his practice patterns. Using the new cost system, we made clinical recommendations for reducing waste. We also estimated the resulting cost savings," continued Linda. "For example, Physician C typically asks for a full list of lab work on all admissions. We recommended ordering lab work only for specific tests."

"In addition, most of the electrocardiograms and chest x-rays could be eliminated or completed on an outpatient basis. Full labwork would be completed only on selective groups as needed," said Tim.

Jay and his team borrowed numerous techniques traditionally used by manufacturing organizations. For example, they viewed each service as a process. To determine whether these processes were in a state of statistical control, the team used SPC (statistical process control) charts. One such process, called hydration, involves administering fluids to chemotherapy patients prior to treatment. As shown in Exhibit 12, the elapsed time from admission to the beginning of hydration for chemotherapy patients is plotted to determine if the process is in a state of statistical control. The average time from admission to the beginning of hydration is 89 minutes. However, significant variation in time exists among patients. As indicated by the point above the upper control limit, the chemotherapy administration process is not in a state of statistical control. Using their clinical expertise, Tim and Linda evaluated the process to discover underlying causes of variability and to made recommendations for improvement. They understood that reducing waiting time is important for patient satisfaction and continuous process improvement.

Exhibit 12   Statistical Process Control Chart for Hydration Data

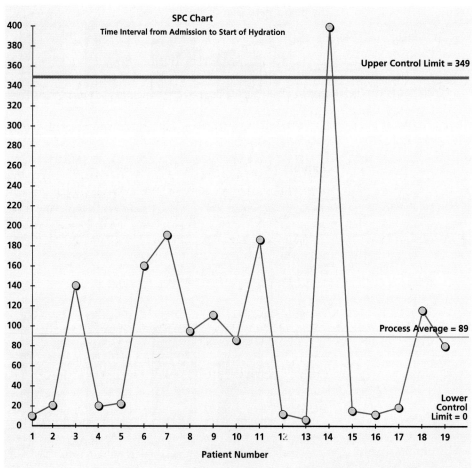

Critical Path Utilization

Before further improvements could be made in delivering clinical care to patients, the team found it necessary to develop standard treatment protocols. Thus, they developed critical paths for various clinical procedures. **A** *critical path* **outlines the steps needed to complete a process.** In the case of a health-care organization, this could be the sequence of tests, treatments, and medication provided to patients. The quantity and type of all procedures, tests, and lab work needed by patients were specified by the critical path. Cost data were evaluated to choose procedures that presented opportunities for cost and quality improvement.

This text has illustrated manufacturing processes that use concepts similar to a critical path. For example, as described in an earlier chapter, TuffCut products were manufactured according to a "critical path" consisting of cutting, welding, painting, and assembly. Exhibit 13 illustrates a critical path for chemotherapy treatment.

Exhibit 13   Critical Path Chemotherapy Treatment

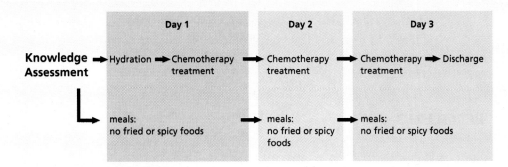

"The use of critical paths helps standardize and improve the delivery of care," said Linda. "Critical paths help everyone—patients, family, nurses, and physicians—understand the order and sequencing of care. Communication and understanding are improved."

"At the same time, adopting the best clinical practices for procedures improves the average quality of care," added Jay.

"We have evidence that suggests that costs decline, as well," added Beth.

Jay said, "We should be very pleased with our progress. Having redesigned the cost system and restructured many of the clinical delivery systems, we are preparing to meet the challenges of providing health care into the next century. I'm certain that next time we are asked to submit a bid for services, we'll have the information to make an informed analysis. We have better clinical delivery systems than most of our competitors, and we understand our costs. Let's keep up the momentum."

Summary

Stonebrook illustrates a service organization that is taking steps to restructure its operations. Its goal is to improve efficiency and quality, while reducing costs. The team approach used by Stonebrook to restructure operations is appropriate for many types of service organizations. For example, airline companies attempting to restructure services could benefit from the advice of pilots, flight crews, mechanics, and accountants.

Stonebrook illustrates various approaches for analyzing and improving systems. For example, the team used SPC charts, commonly found in manufacturing companies, to statistically analyze delivery processes. Additionally, financial information, including cost per case, was provided to physicians who used the information to help them manage costs while treating patients. A high-quality cost management system is an integral part of a service company's efforts to restructure its processes.

Teams at Stonebrook developed standard clinical processes, termed critical paths. The critical path served many different functions. For example, patients and relatives are informed of the sequencing of treatments prior to admission. In addition, critical paths helped reduce communication problems among physicians and nurses. Finally, critical paths could be used to develop standard costs for various medical procedures.

C A S E

In Point

ON THE INTERNET

http://www.swcollege.com/ingram.html

Find out about employment projections.

As consumers purchase services such as dining, health care, travel, and auto repairs, the service sector continues to play a major role in the U.S. economy. In addition, though companies may spend less on capital equipment, such as computers, they continue to invest in consulting services and outside computer specialists to remain competitive. Therefore, even if the manufacturing sector slips into a recession, many experts believe the economy can continue to grow if the service sector remains healthy. The Bureau of Labor Statistics estimates that the service sector grew by 300,000 new jobs in 1995. Approximately one-third of these jobs were in data processing services.

Bleakley, F. Feb. 16, 1996. U.S. Economy Can Thank Service Sector: These Jobs Fuel '90s Growth as Manufacturing Idles. **The Wall Street Journal, p. A2.**

SELF-STUDY PROBLEM 3

Refer to Self-Study Problem 2 for an introduction to Paradise Air.

Required

1. Discuss various strategies Paradise Air can use to improve quality and reduce the cost of performing maintenance services on aircraft. Use the techniques discussed in connection with Stonebrook to direct your answer.
2. Identify appropriate team members to analyze costs and recommend improvements in maintenance service.

©1996 PhotoDisc, Inc.

The solution to Self-Study Problem 3 appears at the end of the chapter.

R E V I E W *Summary of Important Concepts*

1. Service organizations deliver intangible products (or services) to their customers.
   a. Though their products are intangible, service organizations have processes for delivering their services.
   b. Service companies may use tools developed by manufacturing companies to help them evaluate and improve processes.

2. Support department costs must be allocated to revenue-producing departments for a full understanding of the cost of delivering services.

    a. Reciprocal service arrangements exist among support departments when support departments provide (and consume) services of other support departments.

    b. The step-down and simultaneous algebraic equation methods are commonly used to allocate service department costs to revenue-producing departments.

3. Service companies need high-quality cost management systems to understand the cost of providing services to their customers.

4. Like manufacturing companies, service companies monitor their operations and seek ways to improve their processes to promote efficiency and improve quality.

    a. Operations restructuring involves evaluating the relationships among multiple processes.

    b. Outcomes data dissemination is used to communicate important financial and operating information to decision makers.

    c. Critical paths are used to standardize the processes for cost reduction and quality enhancement.

D E F I N E   *Terms and Concepts Defined in This Chapter*

critical path (417)
operations restructuring (413)

outcomes data dissemination (414)

reciprocal service arrangement (404)

S O L U T I O N S

SELF-STUDY PROBLEM 1

1. Reciprocal service arrangements occur when support departments provide services to other support departments, as well as to revenue-producing departments. To recognize properly the cost of maintaining a support department, all costs must be recognized, including those provided by other support departments.

2.

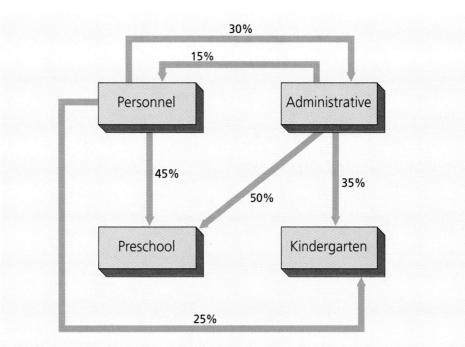

3.

	Administrative	Personnel	Preschool Instruction	Kindergarten Instruction	Total
Beginning	$100,000	$75,000	$300,000	$500,000	$975,000
Administrative	(100,000)	15,000*	50,000	35,000	
Personnel		(90,000)	57,857†	32,143	
Ending	$ 0	$ 0	$407,857	$567,143	$975,000

* $100,000 × 0.15 = $15,000
† ($90,000 × 0.45) ÷ (0.45 + 0.25) = $57,857

4. Personnel = $75,000 + (0.15 × administrative)
Administrative = $100,000 + (0.30 × personnel)

5. Step 1. Personnel = $75,000 + (0.15 × administrative)
Step 2. Personnel = $75,000 + [0.15 × ($100,000 + (0.30 × personnel))]
Step 3. Personnel = $75,000 + $15,000 + (0.045 × personnel)
Step 4. Personnel = 0.045 × personnel = $75,000 + $15,000
Step 5. 0.955 × personnel = $90,000
Step 6. Personnel = $94,241

Step 1. Administrative = $100,000 + (0.30 × personnel)
Step 2. Administrative = $100,000 + (0.30 × $94,241)
Step 3. Administrative = $100,000 + $28,272
Step 4. Administrative = $128,272

6.

	Administrative	Personnel	Preschool Instruction	Kindergarten Instruction	Total
Beginning	$100,000	$75,000	$300,000	$500,000	$975,000
Administrative	(128,272)	19,241	64,136	4,895	
Personnel	28,272	(94,241)	42,408	23,561	
Ending	$ 0	$ 0	$406,544	$568,456	$975,000

SELF-STUDY PROBLEM 2

1. The product delivered by Paradise Air is airline transportation. In addition to safe and timely travel, the company must provide dependable baggage handling and high-quality in-flight cabin service.

2.
Ticketing cost: $10,000 ÷ 2,000 passengers	$ 5
Fuel, wages, maintenance, operating expenses:	
$1.50 × 200 miles	300
Baggage handling: $9,000 ÷ 3,000 transfers = $3 per transfer;	
$3 × 2 transfers	6
First-class cabin service: $25,000 ÷ 500 first-class passengers	50
Total cost	$361

SELF-STUDY PROBLEM 3

1. Maintenance is one of the many processes required to provide airline services to customers. Using the Stonebrook techniques of outcomes data dissemination and critical path utilization, one may consider the following:

Outcomes data dissemination—Information regarding costs for routine maintenance may be distributed to the aircraft mechanics.
Critical path utilization—The team may develop a critical path for performing maintenance services. As with a critical path in a hospital, aircraft maintenance may be specified according to the number of hours of operation and other variables. Various tests and preventive maintenance may be routinely performed according to a schedule.

2. Teams consisting of mechanics, cost accountants, and managers should be formed to analyze processes. Presumably, mechanics have the necessary technical skills to recommend improvement in maintenance processes. Managers may add insights about forecast passenger demand and FAA regulations. Accountants may assist with analyzing and interpreting financial information.

EXERCISES

12-1. Write a short definition of each of the terms listed in the *Terms and Concepts Defined in This Chapter* section.

Obj. 1 **12-2.** Big Al's Car Care provides auto repairs such as tune-ups, brake work, and engine overhauls on all models of cars. Over 60% of the revenue generated by Big Al's is from the sale of parts. Would you consider Big Al's a service organization? Explain your answer.

Obj. 1 **12-3.** Nickles Consulting Services is a nonprofit organization that provides free legal assistance to clients who meet certain income criteria. The company's funding is obtained by means of fund-raising activities conducted by the board of directors. The directors are not compensated for their time, but Nickles does reimburse them for any out-of-pocket expenses that they incur in conducting company activities. Would the board of directors be classified as a cost center? Why or why not?

Obj. 2 **12-4.** Estella Rodriquez is a staff accountant for Baylor Software. Baylor has two separate departments, programming and consultation. The programming department provides services for small manufacturing companies that are not large enough to employ their own programmers. The consultation department designs special software that is marketed under the Baylor logo. The president of Baylor has asked Estella to prepare an allocation of the company's in-house computer costs, dividing the costs of operating the company's large mainframe computer between the two departments. What is meant by cost allocation, and how can cost allocation be used by managers?

Obj. 2 **12-5.** What information must be known or estimated in order to allocate support department costs to revenue-producing departments?

Obj. 2 **12-6.** After allocating the maintenance department's support costs to revenue-producing departments using the step-down method, Stewart Cohen, controller of Saint Anthony's Hospital, discovered that human resource support costs should be included in maintenance department costs. How should Stewart handle the additional costs in the allocation process?

Obj. 2 **12-7.** Trans Comm Airline flies domestic routes among several large regional airports. What information would management need in order to allocate the costs of services such as baggage handling, ticketing, and customer service among revenue-producing departments?

Obj. 2 **12-8.** Would you consider the step-down method of cost allocation to be more accurate than the simultaneous algebraic equation method of allocating service costs? Why or why not? What are the limitations or weaknesses of the step-down method?

Obj. 2 **12-9.** The accounting department at Brown Manufacturing provides support for both the manufacturing department and the maintenance department. A total of 80% of the accounting department effort is provided to manufacturing, with the remainder provided to maintenance. The maintenance department provides 90% of its efforts to the manufacturing department and the remainder to accounting. Express the cost of accounting services provided to the manufacturing department in the form of an algebraic equation reflecting the reciprocal service arrangement with the maintenance department.

Obj. 3   **12-10.**   Digital Communications provides local and long-distance telephone service to nearly 2 million households. Explain why it is important for Digital to have accurate cost information regarding the services it provides.

Obj. 3   **12-11.**   Service industries do not deliver a product to their customers; therefore, product costing concerns are limited to manufacturing organizations. Do you agree or disagree? Explain your answer.

Obj. 4   **12-12.**   Southern Technical College is an accredited university that grants two- and four-year degrees. The registration process at Southern requires students to stand in long lines to obtain forms for the courses they desire, then take the forms to a service window where they are processed. Could operations restructuring assist Southern in improving the quality or efficiency of the service provided to customers? Explain your answer.

Obj. 4   **12-13.**   A-1 Appliance Repair provides in-home service for major brands of household appliances. The company has six trucks staffed by service technicians, which it dispatches based on phone orders. Mark Maddox, owner of A-1, has noted a wide range of charges from his different technicians for similar repair work. He is worried that certain technicians may be performing excess repairs, or that others may be failing to identify problems that should be considered. How could A-1 use data dissemination to improve its service process?

PROBLEMS

PROBLEM 12-1   Incomplete Terminology

Complete each of the following sentences with the appropriate missing terminology.

1. Two methods that are commonly used to allocate service department costs to revenue-producing departments are _____ and _____.

2. In order for managers of service organizations to make informed decisions regarding process improvements, it is necessary to have available _____.

3. Service department costs often are not directly traceable to specific products and must be _____.

4. The act of reengineering a process in order to better provide service to customers is known as _____.

5. An outline of the sequence of processes involved in providing a service is known as the _____.

6. A department that provides support or assistance to other departments but does not engage in revenue-producing activities is known as a(n) _____.

7. A measure of activity that is used to charge service department costs to revenue-producing departments is commonly referred to as a(n) _____.

PROBLEM 12-2   Service Departments in a Manufacturing Environment
Obj. 2

The Omega Manufacturing Company has two production divisions, industrial products and consumer electronics, and three service departments, administration, personnel, and maintenance. Budgeted costs for each service department are as follows:

Administration	$600,000
Personnel	280,000
Maintenance	320,000

Management has decided that administration and personnel service costs should be directly allocated based on the number of employees in each revenue-producing department, and maintenance should be directly allocated based on the dollar amount of assets employed in each revenue-producing department. The number of employees and dollar value of assets employed by each revenue-producing department are as follows:

	Number of Employees	Dollar Value of Assets Employed
Industrial products	225	$4,000,000
Consumer electronics	275	6,000,000

Required

a. Calculate the amount of service costs that should be allocated based on number of employees.
b. Determine the allocation percentages based on both number of employees and dollar value of assets employed.
c. Calculate the amount of service costs that would be allocated to industrial products and consumer electronics.

PROBLEM 12-3 Service Department Cost Allocation

Obj. 2

First State Bank has two revenue-producing departments, demand deposits and loans. The bank also has three service areas, administration, personnel, and accounting. The direct costs per month and the interdepartmental service relationships are reflected below. The bank allocates costs in the following order:

1. Administration
2. Personnel
3. Accounting

	Direct	Percent of Service Used By				
Department	Costs	Administration	Personnel	Accounting	Deposits	Loans
Administration	$40,000		10	10	30	50
Personnel	60,000	10		20	40	30
Accounting	60,000	10	10		40	40
Demand deposits	50,000					
Loans	80,000					

Required

a. Compute the total cost for each revenue-producing department using the step-down method.
b. Define the algebraic equations reflecting the reciprocal service cost functions for the personnel, administration, and accounting departments.

PROBLEM 12-4 Service Department Cost Allocation

Obj. 2

Med Alert is a 24-hour walk-in medical service provider that has two revenue-producing departments, laboratory and patient care. It also has two service departments, administration and custodial services. Service costs for the most recent year of operation were as follows:

Service costs:	
Administration	$ 340,000
Custodial services	100,000
Laboratory	250,000
Patient care	739,000
Total costs	$1,429,000

Med Alert utilizes two different allocation bases, labor hours worked and service space occupied, in assigning service department costs. Information on these allocation bases for the most recent year was as follows:

Labor hours worked:
Administration	12,000
Custodial services	6,000
Laboratory	18,000
Patient care	30,000

Service space occupied (square feet):
Administration	10,000
Custodial services	0
Laboratory	5,000
Patient care	45,000

Administration costs are allocated to revenue-producing departments based on labor hours. Custodial services costs are allocated based on service space occupied.

Required

a. Assume that Med Alert currently allocates costs to the revenue-producing departments individually and without regard to any reciprocal service arrangements. Determine the service costs that would be allocated to the revenue-producing departments using this approach.

b. Compute the cost of the revenue-producing departments using the step-down method to allocate service costs. Allocate administration costs first.

c. Which method of allocation provides a more accurate indication of service cost in the revenue-producing departments?

PROBLEM 12-5   Budgeted Versus Actual Allocation Costs

Obj. 2

Dempsey Manufacturing operates a cafeteria for the benefit of all employees. The cost of operating the cafeteria is allocated to the operating departments on the basis of number of employees in the respective departments. Budgeted and actual data for operating the cafeteria during the previous month are shown below:

	Budgeted	**Actual**
Cafeteria services	$60 per employee	$72 per employee

The budgeted and actual number of employees in each operating department during the previous month were as follows:

	Departments			
	Receiving	**Assembly**	**Machining**	**Administration**
Budgeted number of employees	12	240	175	44
Actual number of employees	11	243	173	43

Required

a. For purposes of allocating cafeteria service costs, should budgeted or actual cost be used? Explain your answer.

b. Determine the amount of cafeteria service costs that should be allocated to each of the four operating departments.

c. How should cafeteria service costs be treated when evaluating the costs of each of the four operating departments for purposes of comparing actual to planned performance?

d. How should cafeteria service costs be treated by receiving and administration if these service department costs are also allocated to assembly and machining?

PROBLEM 12-6   Service Cost Allocation, Step-down Method
Obj. 2

The Eldarodo Manufacturing Company has three service departments and two operating departments. Selected data for each of the five departments are presented below:

| | Service Departments & Operating Departments | | | | | |
	A	B	C	1	2	Total
Department costs	$86,000	$72,000	$40,000	$260,000	$504,000	$962,000
Number of employees	72	58	145	300	600	1,175
Square feet occupied	2,500	10,000	8,000	26,000	30,000	76,500
Machine hours				12,000	25,000	37,000

The company allocates service department costs by the step-down method in the following order, utilizing the following allocation bases:

Department A	Number of employees
Department B	Square feet occupied
Department C	Machine hours

Required

a. Using the step-down method, make the necessary allocation of service department costs.
b. Compute the total cost of operating departments 1 and 2 after all service costs have been allocated.

PROBLEM 12-7   Service Activities
Obj. 3

Public Airlines provides low cost commuter flight service between 10 cities in the northwest United States. During a recent stop in Seattle, the plane for Flight 107 had 4,000 pounds of passenger baggage and 2,000 pounds of commercial freight unloaded. Similar amounts of baggage and freight then were loaded onto the plane in preparation for the next leg of its flight. During this stop over, airline custodial personnel boarded the plane to clean the lavatories, seat pockets and floors. The airline catering crew performed an inventory of drinks and restocked the refreshments. The catering crew loaded in-flight meals into the plane's galley. Laundry personnel exchanged soiled pillows, blankets and first class linens with clean supplies. While all this activity was occurring, ground crew mechanics were busy inspecting and refueling the plane. Ticket agents issued seat assignments, and flight attendants checked passengers onto the aircraft.

Required

a. Why must management at Public understand all of the activities that occur on a plane during layover? What impact do these activities have on the cost of the flight?
b. How will the cost of these activities be recovered by Public? What can Public do in order to reduce some of the cost associated with providing these activities?
c. Airlines such as Public desire to minimize the amount of time it takes to prepare an aircraft for service. Why do you believe it is important for an airline to decrease a plane's "turnaround" time?

PROBLEM 12-8   Costing and Pricing Service Activities
Obj. 3

Ace Auto Repair Shop provides service repairs for most domestic car models. Ace charges customers based on the time and materials that are used for service repairs. At the beginning of each year, the shop calculates a standard labor rate that is based on estimated costs plus a per hour markup. The markup is based on the competitive environment that management must assess each year. For the coming year, management believes that a $5 per labor hour markup would be acceptable based on current market conditions. Any parts that are used during service repairs are billed to the customer at cost plus 15%. The 15% markup is expected to cover the cost of ordering parts, providing a parts manager, and other carrying costs. Estimated operating costs for the coming year are as follows:

Mechanic wages	$320,000
Employee benefits	36,000
Supervision	40,000
Supplies	2,400
Utilities	42,000
Property taxes	9,200
Depreciation	88,400
Environmental	12,000
Total	$550,000

Management estimates that there will be 25,000 mechanic hours charged during the coming year.

Required

a. Calculate the billing rate that should be used during the coming year.
b. Assume a customer service job results in the following: Labor time = 4 hours; Parts (at cost) = $200. Calculate the total cost for this particular service job.

PROBLEM 12-9 Service Provider, Ethical Dilemma

Obj. 4

Ted Macintosh is a computer programmer for Warsaw Products. The computer programming department at Warsaw provides service support to every other department within the company, including other service departments such as accounting and human resources. The gossip at Warsaw is that upper management is considering the elimination of the programming department and outsourcing of programming requirements to a third-party consulting firm. According to the rumors that Ted has heard, the main reason for this possible change is the high cost of maintaining an in-house programming staff.

In response to these rumors, Ted has begun making unauthorized changes to many programs in an effort to "hide" certain programming costs and to make special use programs too difficult for third parties to understand. Ted hopes that his actions will keep the programming staff from being eliminated.

Required

a. Many services that are provided within an organization can be obtained from outside sources. What are some of the main concerns management should consider before outsourcing a particular service?
b. If the programming staff at Warsaw is eliminated, would the allocation of service costs to other departments be eliminated as well? Explain your answer.
c. What are some arguments for and against Ted's actions? What is the ethical dilemma raised here?

PROBLEM 12-10 Cost and Quality Control

Obj. 4

Medic Delivery provides transportation services between doctors' offices and a hospital laboratory. The company owns three small cars and a minivan. Each morning the company runs specific routes to the offices of various physicians and collects lab specimens that then are delivered to the hospital for testing. Upon reaching the laboratory, the driver collects the previous days examination results, if any, and delivers the results back to the physician offices in the afternoon. Every route covers over 100 miles each morning and afternoon. The drivers take the company vehicles home at night and begin their respective routes directly from home.

When a driver picks up either a lab specimen or test result, he or she records the pickup in a log book. Physicians are charged a fixed fee for each lab specimen or exam result that is handled by Medic personnel. If a physician has no specimens to be transported, or lab results to be delivered, there is no charge for the day.

Required

a. What data do the managers at Medic need to properly operate and control the business? How would this information improve quality or reduce operating costs?

b. How could the route drivers assist in improving the company's service and profitability?

PROBLEM 12-11   Multiple-Choice Overview of the Chapter

1. Service department costs must be allocated to revenue-producing departments in order to:
    a. determine the proper value of services provided.
    b. assist in determining the profitability of services provided.
    c. provide managers with information to assist in planning and control.
    d. do all of the above.

2. The use of statistical process control in a service industry:
    a. is not possible, since services do not result in the fixed, measurable activities on which statistical process control is based.
    b. is impractical, since the outcome of services cannot be measured on a control chart.
    c. can be an effective management tool.
    d. will not reveal common cause exceptions.

3. Which of the following reflects a similarity between manufacturing and service companies in the use of accounting information?
    a. Both manufacturing companies and service companies use accounting information to value inventories.
    b. Both manufacturing companies and service companies can utilize just-in-time theories to control inventory purchases.
    c. Both manufacturing companies and service companies utilize processes that require accounting information to analyze and control.
    d. There are no similarities between manufacturing and service companies.

4. The allocation of service department costs to revenue-producing departments is necessary:
    a. only in service organizations.
    b. to accurately reflect the total cost of providing a particular product or service.
    c. unless reciprocal service relationships exist.
    d. only in manufacturing organizations.

5. The basic difference between a service department and an operating department is that:
    a. operating departments can have no reciprocal relationships with other departments.
    b. service departments have no identifiable customers.
    c. operating departments generate revenues, whereas service departments do not.
    d. service departments are not essential to the organization's product or service.

6. Which of the following would not be considered a service organization?
    a. a mortuary
    b. an airline company
    c. an advertising agency
    d. all of the above are service organizations

7. In order for services to be delivered in a more efficient and cost-effective manner:
    a. service managers must receive information regarding process outcomes.
    b. interrelated services must be evaluated in order to improve quality.
    c. the critical service path must be identified by service providers.
    d. all of the above must be true.

C A S E S

CASE 12-1 Cost Allocation, Step-down Method

Obj. 2

Applegate Mortgage Company provides mortgage servicing for financial institutions. As a mortgage servicer, Applegate collects mortgage payments from homeowners on behalf of banks and other mortgage lenders. Applegate collects the payments, and then transfers any cash collected to the appropriate bank or lender with a report of which customers have made payments. The bank, or lender, pays Applegate 1/2 of 1% of all funds collected as a fee for performing this service. The department that generates these revenues is called the mortgage service center.

Applegate also coordinates escrow accounting, collecting funds from mortgagees that are used to pay real estate owners' taxes and insurance. Twice a year, Applegate sends a report to each homeowner explaining the amount of escrow funds that have been collected and disbursed. Each time Applegate processes an escrow analysis, it charges the lending bank a flat rate of $2.50. This revenue is generated by the escrow analysis department.

Applegate maintains two departments that support mortgage servicing and escrow analysis: financial administration and computer services. The financial administration department provides accounting and auditing services for the two departments. Computer services provides the necessary computer hardware and programming for each department. The computer services department also supports the financial administration department.

It is estimated that computer services dedicates approximately 70% of its efforts to support mortgage servicing, 20% to support escrow analysis, and 10% to support financial administration. The financial administration department has determined that approximately 80% of its efforts are in support of mortgage servicing, with the remaining 20% supporting escrow analysis.

The direct costs to operate each department for the most recent year, prior to any cost allocation, were as follows:

Mortgage servicing	$376,000
Escrow analysis	284,000
Financial administration	235,000
Computer services	315,000

Costs are allocated in the following order: 1) computer service; 2) financial administration

Required

a. Calculate the total cost of mortgage servicing and escrow analysis based on the step-down method of allocation.
b. Calculate the cost of mortgage servicing and escrow analysis using simultaneous algebraic equations.

CASE 12-2 Service Cost Allocation, Multiple Departments and Bases

Obj. 2

The Majestic Manufacturing Company has three service departments: maintenance, cafeteria, and material handling. The company also has two operating departments: fabrication and assembly. The service departments provide services to each other as well as to the operating departments. The bases for service department cost allocation are as follows:

Department	Allocation Base
Maintenance	Square footage occupied
Cafeteria	Number of employees
Material handling	Direct labor hours

Service costs are assigned using the step-down method in the following department order:

1. Maintenance
2. Cafeteria
3. Material handling

The following costs were incurred during the most recent quarter of operations:

Maintenance	$130,000
Cafeteria	74,000
Material handling	42,000

The following operating data relate to the most recent quarter of operations:

Department	Number of Employees	Square Footage of Space Occupied	Direct Labor Hours
Maintenance	6	3,000	
Cafeteria	9	4,000	
Material handling	30	1,000	
Fabrication	190	8,000	300,000
Assembly	250	13,000	500,000

In addition to the above, the fabrication department incurred $1,240,000 of manufacturing overhead, and the assembly department incurred $1,536,000 of manufacturing overhead during the most recent quarter.

Required

a. Determine the amounts that should be used as a basis for allocating service costs to each of the operating departments, assuming the step-down method is used.
b. Prepare a cost allocation schedule for the most recent quarter using the step-down method.
c. Determine the total indirect cost of operating the fabrication and assembly departments for the most recent quarter.

PROJECTS

PROJECT 12-1 Service Department Identification

Objs. 1,2

Choose an industry with which you are somewhat familiar and list seven or eight major support or service departments associated with this industry. What service does each of these departments provide? Is there a reciprocal relationship between these departments? Write a brief narrative of the industry and present your findings to your class.

PROJECT 12-2 Service Cost Identification

Objs. 1,2,3

Interview managers who work for different companies in your area. Identify the different service departments that exist within their respective businesses. Determine whether the company allocates the costs associated with these service areas to other operating departments within the business. If so, identify the method that is used in the allocation process. If no allocation of service costs is performed, what ramifications might failure to recognize service cost allocations have on this business? Write an account of your interviews and present your findings to your class.

PROJECT 12-3 Service Industry Concerns

Objs. 3,4

Review articles published in a periodical such as *The Wall Street Journal* or *Business Week* that discuss a particular cost concern of a service industry. Write a brief discussion of the article, explaining the particular cost concern and how this concern affects other operating areas of the industry or company discussed in the article.

The

Japanese

Perspective

**Accounting and
Management Decisions**

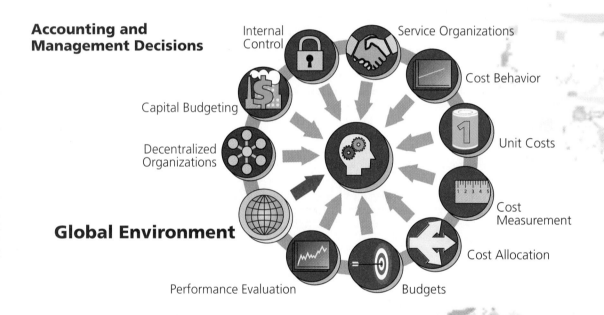

Internal Control

Service Organizations

Cost Behavior

Capital Budgeting

Unit Costs

Decentralized Organizations

Cost Measurement

Global Environment

Cost Allocation

Performance Evaluation

Budgets

Overview

This chapter[1] considers survival strategies used by lean manufacturing companies that compete using a confrontation strategy. Lean manufacturing companies are characterized by the delivery of high-quality products that are produced efficiently. Mass producers in the Western Hemisphere traditionally have tried to avoid competition and gain a sustainable competitive advantage by either positioning themselves as a low-cost producer or differentiating their products. The low-cost strategy discourages competition because the most efficient producer can simply reduce prices and make less efficient competitors unprofitable. Alternatively, by differentiating its products in some manner, a company can create a barrier to entry into its markets because competitors cannot duplicate a critical aspect of the product. Unfortunately, many companies cannot avoid com-

petition because they can neither establish themselves as the low-cost producer nor differentiate their product from others in the market.

The concepts introduced in this chapter are based on a confrontation strategy, rather than a strategy of avoiding competition through cost leadership or product differentiation. The techniques described are used by various Japanese manufacturing companies that compete head to head using similar manufacturing technology. Since no single company enjoys a sustainable competitive advantage, companies continually compete along three dimensions, cost (or price), quality, and functionality. Companies strive to reduce costs while simultaneously improving the quality and functionality of their products.

This chapter considers target costing, value engineering, and interorganizational cost management

© Kessler Photography

systems to help in managing the costs of products under development. In addition, the chapter addresses product costing, Kaizen costing, and operational control techniques used by Japanese manufacturers to manage production costs of existing products. Finally, the chapter describes the use of profit centers and pseudo-profit centers to motivate employees.

Major topics covered in this chapter include:
- Confrontation strategy and the survival triplet
- Japanese cost management techniques for managing future costs
- Japanese cost management techniques for managing existing costs

[1] *This chapter is based on the work of Robin Cooper. For more information about Japanese cost management techniques and the survival triplet, see Cooper, Robin. 1996.* When Lean Enterprises Collide. *Boston, MA: Harvard Business School Press.*

Objectives

Once you have completed this chapter, you should be able to:

1. Contrast the confrontation strategy with the strategy of developing a sustainable competitive advantage through product differentiation or cost leadership.
2. Identify and describe the elements of the survival triplet for lean enterprises.
3. Discuss various cost management techniques used by Japanese manufacturing companies to control future costs and improve competitiveness.
4. Explain what Kaizen is.
5. Understand how techniques used by Japanese companies can be applied to service organizations.

CONFRONTATION STRATEGY AND THE SURVIVAL TRIPLET

Objective 1
Contrast the confrontation strategy with the strategy of developing a sustainable competitive advantage through product differentiation or cost leadership.

KnitCo is an athletic apparel manufacturer specializing in high-quality sports uniforms for high school athletics. Patented innovations in fabric design that reduce wear and tear have permitted KnitCo to dominate its market for many years. However, as companies worldwide have worked to expand market share, KnitCo is facing increasing competition in its primary market. Management is considering developing new products for other markets to replace lost sales in the primary product line. For example, KnitCo currently is developing a warm-up suit to be marketed in sporting goods stores to customers of all ages. The new product extends the product line and also diversifies the type of customer KnitCo serves.

The manufacturing process for athletic apparel traditionally has been labor-intensive. However, KnitCo uses technology as a strategy to reduce costs and provide consistently high-quality products. As shown in Exhibit 1, the first step in the manufacturing process involves spinning yarn from cotton and synthetic fibers that are purchased from suppliers. Next, the yarn is woven into fabric and dyed, using a process that ensures colorfast materials. Because athletic apparel is subjected to strains beyond those faced by ordinary fabrics, high-quality materials, dyes, and construction are very important. Next, the fabric is cut using computer-controlled laser equipment and sewn to produce athletic uniforms for a variety of sports.

Exhibit 1 KnitCo: The Production Process

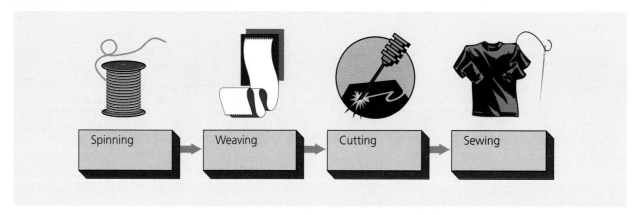

As a result of increased competition, KnitCo's management began to look for ideas to improve their position. They decided to participate in an executive exchange program with a number of Japanese companies to learn more about Japanese cost management techniques. Three managers, representing accounting, marketing, and operations, who participated in this program have returned and are explaining their insights into the techniques they saw in Japan. Ann Rogers is the controller, Jan Barrett is the marketing vice president, and John Case is the vice president of operations. Also present are Bob Miller from production, Carolyn Sykes from accounting, and Bruce Caruthers from marketing.

These six individuals had assembled to discuss what the group had learned in Japan. Ann began the discussion. "We toured companies that manufacture many different types of products, from automobiles and optics to soy sauce and sake. Though their products and processes varied widely, we observed many common themes. The companies use target costing, value engineering, and interorganizational cost management systems to help them manage the costs of new products under development."

John added, "We also learned about ways to continuously improve manufacturing processes and control the costs of existing products."

"Japanese companies are doing some interesting things with performance measurement," commented Jan. "They are dividing the organization into small centers and making these centers responsible for profits. They call them micro profit centers."

Bruce asked, "Did you visit textile companies that are using these techniques? I'm not convinced that our process or market is comparable to that of a soy sauce producer or automobile manufacturer."

"No, we didn't visit textile producers; however, a broad range of companies successfully applies many of the concepts we would like to discuss today. We think some of these techniques are relevant to KnitCo," replied Jan.

John followed up on Jan's comment. "We've all heard about companies that raced to implement the 'latest and greatest' manufacturing technology, only to discover that the new systems were inferior to their old ones. Someone inevitably misunderstood a critical aspect of a new technique. Let's ask ourselves hard questions and try to understand how these techniques apply to KnitCo."

Jan said, "Before we address specific cost management techniques, let's discuss our competitive environment. We need to understand the factors that drive competition in our industry before we can develop strategies to compete successfully. For example, how would KnitCo compete and survive if three or four major garment producers entered the high school athletic uniform market?"

Bruce responded, "I don't see a problem. We have established our reputation as a high-quality manufacturer; our logo is recognized internationally. Athletes would not accept 'Brand X' sportswear."

"So, you are saying we have a strategy of differentiation. Our brand name implies quality, and everyone knows that quality teams wear quality uniforms," Ann commented.

"Yes, that's right," responded Bruce. "But there is more to our product than brand recognition. Our investment in research and development also helps differentiate our products."

Jan continued, "Do you think we can sustain our competitive advantage indefinitely?"

Bruce admitted, "Recently, we have seen competitors developing similar products and spending large sums on advertising. I suppose we may someday compete head to head as their products gain brand recognition. Under those circumstances, we need to produce even better products at a lower cost."

Jan interjected, "Exactly! You are describing the confrontation strategy we studied in Japan. **A** *confrontation strategy* **is a management approach that creates numerous temporary competitive advantages when a sustainable competitive advantage is not possible.** Rather than avoiding competition by differentiating our brand and expecting customer loyalty, we may need to confront our competitors on three dimensions."

The Survival Triplet

O b j e c t i v e   2
Identify and describe the elements of the survival triplet for lean enterprises.

Jan walked to a blackboard in the conference room and sketched the diagram shown as Exhibit 2.

"This three-pronged diagram represents crucial success factors for firms using a confrontation strategy. **Three elements, cost/price, quality, and functionality, are known as the** *survival triplet*. A company's position with respect to each of the three factors may be plotted on the graph."

Jan pointed to her graph. "Bruce, you said we must produce a better product at a lower cost than our competition." She made a mark on the cost dimension of her chart as shown in Exhibit 3.

Exhibit 2   The Survival Triplet

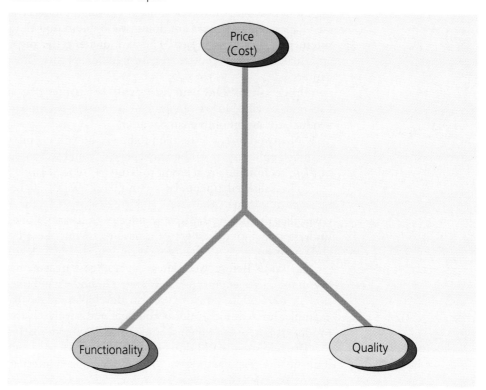

"Let's say point A represents the lowest cost for which we can produce our product. You used the term 'better product.' Let's define 'better' in terms of quality and functionality."

Bruce responded, "The quality aspect of our apparel includes durability, comfort, and possibly rapid delivery times."

Exhibit 3   The Survival Triplet: Point A

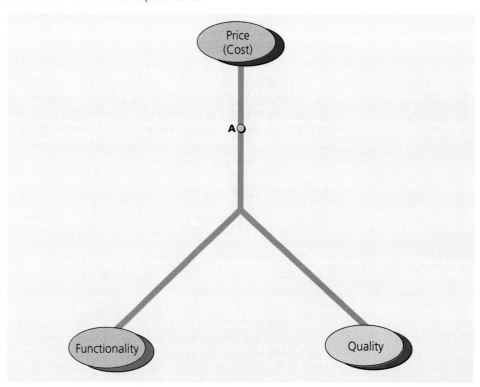

"The functionality component measures a product's characteristics on many dimensions," added John. "For example, the water-resistant fabric used in our uniforms represents a functional improvement over fabrics that do not repel water. We also pioneered a hollow-core synthetic fiber that dramatically increases the insulating properties of our fabric."

"Remember," said Carolyn, "we also developed new spinning, weaving, and dyeing processes because these new fibers had characteristics very different from those of our traditional materials."

Jan asked, "Who do you suppose defines the minimum acceptable values for quality and functionality?"

"Our customers, I presume," responded Bruce. "In our case, they compare the cost, quality, and functionality of various brands of athletic wear. We have been successful in our market because customers perceive our quality to be far superior to that of our competitors."

Jan added to her graph (Exhibit 4). "Let's identify minimum acceptable quality and functionality values as defined by our customers and connect all three points."

Exhibit 4 The Survival Triplet: Minimum Acceptable Values

Carolyn added, "It seems to me that our customers define not only minimum acceptable levels of quality and functionality, but also the maximum acceptable price. Though we may develop exotic fabric technology, there are limits to the price a customer will pay for athletic wear."

In response to Carolyn's comment, Jan added a mark at the upper range of the cost/price axis of her graph. In addition, she placed marks on the quality and functionality axes, representing maximum values of each element, and colored in the area between the minimum and maximum values for each dimension. Jan's chart illustrating the survival zone is shown in Exhibit 5.

Jan continued, "Carolyn, you are right. As a manufacturer, we determine the maximum quality and functionality possible at a given cost, while the customer determines the minimum acceptable quality and functionality at a given price."

Exhibit 5   The Survival Zone

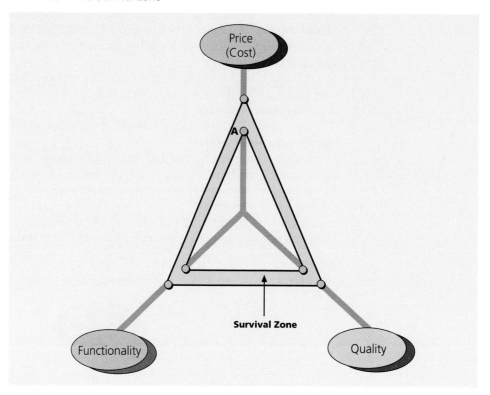

John said, "In Japan, we learned that companies there use a confrontation strategy based on these three dimensions. Because few companies can develop a sustainable competitive advantage, companies constantly seek to improve along these dimensions: cost, quality, and functionality. We can think of the shaded area of Jan's graph as a *survival zone*. For example, if a company's product is outside the acceptable zone defined by price, quality, or functionality, customers will not purchase it. A confrontation strategy involves improving one or more dimensions of the survival triplet."

Ann interjected, "Carolyn touched on this concept a moment ago when she said that price limits exist for athletic apparel, regardless of quality or functionality. By using exotic fabric technology, a company may place itself outside the survival zone with respect to the price variable."

Carolyn thought for a moment, then added, "Our graph suggests that a company may gain a temporary advantage if it can improve one dimension. For example, we may reduce the price component while maintaining the same level of quality and functionality."

"Or, we may maintain the selling price while delivering higher quality or functionality, or both," added Bob.

Jan was quick to respond. "That's right! Let's illustrate how the survival triplet would look if we developed an innovation, such as a better fabric dye, that significantly improved quality while functionality and cost remained unchanged." Jan sketched the new survival triplet. It appears as shown in Exhibit 6.

Bob observed, "Since we have redefined the survival zone by improving quality, presumably all our competitors now fall outside the survival zone. We should enjoy a temporary advantage until competitors catch up with our innovations."

Jan responded, "That's right, Bob. **The name of the game in a confrontation strategy is to continually improve one or more dimensions of the survival triplet.** In doing so, we redefine the survival zone and gain a temporary advantage in the market."

Exhibit 6   The Survival Triplet: Added Innovation

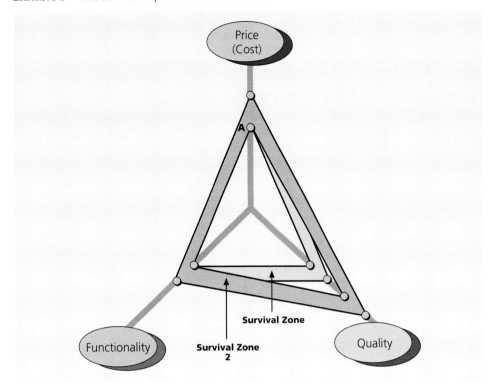

John summarized, "The survival triplet helps us understand the motivation behind the Japanese cost management techniques we are going to discuss. The first technique, target costing, is used to control the cost of future products. Let's take a break; we'll discuss target costing when we return."

SELF-STUDY PROBLEM 1

The survival triplet illustrates key relationships for surviving in a confrontation strategy.

Required

1. Draw the three-pronged diagram of the survival triplet and label the prongs.
2. Add a survival zone to your diagram by indicating high and low values for each prong. For each point, discuss whether a customer or a company defines the value.
3. Assume that a company decided to compete by increasing the functionality of its products while keeping quality and price constant.

    a. Give an example of how a company may increase the functionality of a product.

b. Add the new survival zone to your graph. Discuss the competitive implications.

The solution to Self-Study Problem 1 appears at the end of the chapter.

TECHNIQUES TO CONTROL FUTURE COSTS

Objective 3
Discuss various cost management techniques used by Japanese manufacturing companies to control future costs and improve competitiveness.

After everyone had returned, John began the discussion. "In Japan, we learned techniques to help manage the costs of a new product from conceptualization to production. In particular, we learned how to maintain control over costs during the design stage so that we can deliver a product whose cost is acceptable to our customers."

Target Costing

John continued, "Let's begin with the marketing aspect. Jan, when we develop a new product, how do we set prices? In other words, what factors do we consider in determining a selling price?"

Jan responded, "We are sensitive to many factors, such as the cost of manufacturing, delivery requirements, customer service demands, and special customer needs. Also, we speculate on our competitors' costs and pricing policies before we submit bids to high school athletic departments. Competitive bids actually determine the market prices of our products. However, we use manufacturing cost as a starting point in preparing our bids."

"So, we begin by estimating manufacturing cost and adding a markup to calculate our bids," replied John.

"That's right," said Jan. "After a new product has been developed and manufactured, our customers tell us whether they are willing to pay the prices we have established. If they abandon our product in favor of lower-priced athletic wear, we may be forced to reduce our prices accordingly."

John followed up, "Let me rephrase Jan's explanation of our pricing policy for new products. First, we design and manufacture a product that we think will be attractive to our customers. Next, we analyze all manufacturing costs and add a markup. Finally, our customers tell us whether they like the product and whether they will accept our price."

"In Japan, we learned about another way to introduce new products," Ann added. "The technique is called target costing. *Target costing* **is used to determine the cost at which a new product must be manufactured to achieve desired profitability.** After companies develop a basic idea for a new product, they ask their customers to help them identify important product features that should be added, and also to identify features that can be eliminated. They ask potential customers to estimate a price range for such a product. From this price range, companies set a target selling price.

"Next, managers determine a target profit margin consistent with the long-term goals of the company," Ann continued. "The target profit margin, which is a target percentage times the selling price, is subtracted from the target selling price to determine an allowable target cost."

Learning Note

A company may establish a target margin after evaluating future product mix and desired profitability. Computer simulations sometimes are used to help managers predict earnings under various competitive scenarios. Corporate earnings expectations and historical information also are factors in determining a target margin.

Jan wrote the following equation on the board:

Target selling price − target profit margin = allowable target cost

Carolyn noted, "The process is very interesting, but target costing seems backward. You start with an estimated selling price and work backwards to determine a manufacturing cost. Jan told us we use the manufacturing cost to help determine our selling price."

Bruce considered Carolyn's comment and added, "Carolyn, we have three variables to consider: selling price, manufacturing cost, and profit margin. We can't control the selling price, especially in a highly competitive market. The manufacturing cost of most products is determined by decisions made in the design stage, before the product is actually produced. Therefore, if the selling price is below our expectations, while at the same time we cannot make significant cost reductions in the product, what is the inevitable outcome?"

Jan interjected, "Our profit margins must decline."

Carolyn responded, "Oh, I see. If we understand the future selling price of a product, we can set targets for product costs in the development stage to ensure an appropriate level of profitability."

Jan added, "That's right. As you may know, KnitCo is planning to introduce a new line of warm-up suits marketed through sporting goods stores to the general public. While the market for athletic uniforms is limited, warm-up suits have much broader demand. Our new line should fit the needs of various customer groups, from the serious athlete to the 'athlete in spirit.' As casual wear, the garment makes a statement about the wearer.

"We visited a Japanese auto maker that uses the term 'mindsets' to classify their customers' preferences for products," Jan continued. "Because customers often select a car to project an image, many automobile producers manufacture a mix of cars, including sport, economy, and luxury models, to meet diverse customer 'mindsets.' For example, I know some middle-aged guys who drive sports cars to project a youthful image."

"Why is everybody looking at me?" Bob asked, pretending to ignore Jan's innuendo.

"At any rate, we think a broad market exists among customers of all ages who think of themselves as athletic and wish to project that image. The suit will be functional as athletic apparel and comfortable as casual attire," said Jan.

Bruce added, "Our marketing department could conduct customer surveys to help us understand the characteristics that add value from the customer's perspective. The information would be helpful in designing new products and estimating the eventual selling prices. Next, we could conduct an analysis to determine the profit margin necessary to achieve long-term profitability."

John moved to the board. "Determining the desired profit margin for a new product is a fairly complex process that involves forecasting sales volumes and profitability under various assumptions. Companies often use computer simulation models to help with these forecasts. They first plot the profitability of existing products across a multiyear time span. Doing so helps managers understand a company's future profitability without including the new product in their mix. Next, desired profit margins for the new product are entered into the model to estimate a company's overall future profitability if the new product is introduced. Finally, management's long-term profit goals are compared with predicted profitability to help determine a target profit margin for the new product."

Jan added, "After the study to determine a target selling price and target profit margin is completed, the calculation of an allowable target cost is very straightforward. We simply subtract the required margin from the estimated selling price. Thus, the target cost system will help us do a better job of managing costs."

Bob interrupted, "Jan, we already manage costs; we constantly try to reduce our production costs."

"But, do you set strict targets for cost reduction?" Jan asked.

"No, we are always mindful of cost and try to make reductions as we can," responded Bob.

"Target costing demands that specific cost objectives be achieved. But there is a much larger issue here. By using target costing, we may identify opportunities for cost reduction in the *design* phase, before production begins. In other words, we manage future costs in the design phase, where most costs are determined," added John. "In the design phase we make decisions about materials and equipment to be used in the manufacturing process. Often, new production equipment or tools must be purchased as a result of decisions made while designing a new product. For these reasons, significant cost reductions are not likely once a manufacturing process has been designed and production has begun."

Bruce asked, "How do Japanese companies decide whether introducing a new product is appropriate?"

"Good question," responded John. "Japanese firms that use target costing typically identify a broad mix of products that achieves their desired level of market coverage. Typically, new products are introduced after conducting a thorough consumer analysis. The companies we visited indicated that target costing helps them impose the necessary discipline to set limits on the number of products a company offers."

Ann added, "Target costing is a strategic planning tool that helps companies manage their product mix and control future costs. A major element of the target costing process is value engineering. We learned that value engineering is used to help achieve target costs by designing costs out of the manufacturing process."

Value Engineering

John continued, "*Value engineering* **is an engineering approach in which cost reduction techniques are applied during a product's design phase by a multidisciplinary team. Representatives from design engineering, manufacturing, and purchasing work together to find ways to trim costs from a product before the manufacturing stage.** Suppliers also are invited to join the discussions because they too may have insights for cost reduction."

Ann added, "We learned that the objective of value engineering is not simply to minimize cost, but to achieve a specified level of cost. The target costing process begins by determining an *allowable* target cost that becomes the *final* target cost after a number of development phases."

John added, "Value engineering requires teams to make trade-off decisions about functionality and cost, two of the three elements of the survival triplet. The process often requires many attempts to find ways to trim costs from the proposed product and manufacturing process."

Ann continued, "We saw that new product development typically requires four different phases as follows: phase 1, conceptual design; phase 2, product development; phase 3, prototype development; and phase 4, production."

Conceptual Design. "At the conceptual design phase, teams try to identify new forms of functionality that have not existed previously," Ann stated. "Even in the earliest stages of product development, teams ask whether a new product can be manufactured at a profit."

John added, "Consumer mindsets help teams identify a preliminary conceptual design for a new product. As we have already discussed, consumers help determine the expected selling price range for a product meeting certain functionality characteristics. After subtracting our target margin, we arrive at the allowable target cost. Next, an estimate of the cost to produce the new product is prepared and compared with the allowable cost from the target costing study."

"That's right," said Ann. "The cost estimate is based on our current costs of the various components required to make the new product. For example, we may add the cost of fabric, zippers, and elastic to arrive at the current cost."

"What happens if the cost estimate exceeds the allowable target cost?" asked Bruce.

"Good question. Value engineering is used to eliminate the difference between allowable target cost and estimated cost," responded Jan.

"We learned that the estimated cost typically exceeds the allowable cost," said Ann. "Therefore, a cross-functional team, whose members represent product design, engineering, production engineering, manufacturing, and parts supply, meets to determine the allowable cost of each *product function*. We toured an automobile facility whose product functions included transmission, engine, and air conditioning. The object of value engineering in the conceptual design phase is to make the sum of the costs of all the major functions equal the total allowable cost as determined from the target costing exercise."

"Just as automobile manufacturers identify costs by function (transmission, air conditioning, sound system), we can classify the costs of our warm-up suit by function," said John.

"I understand the automobile example, but what is an example of a function found in a warm-up suit?" asked Carolyn.

"I have been thinking about this question since I left Japan, and I think I have some answers," responded Jan. "A major function of the warm-up suit is to help regulate body temperature. Various fibers and weaves may be used to accomplish this task."

Bruce added, "Another function is the method of closure. For example, the jacket requires a closure system, such as a zipper, buttons, snaps, or Velcro."

"Exactly!" responded Jan. "Choices made at the conceptualization stage affect the cost of manufacturing the product. Within each function, there are numerous ways to design a product. Here, the systems are analyzed for cost and functionality trade-offs. For example, should we offer warm-up suits with external pockets and hoods in addition to the basic suit? However, if our estimated cost exceeds the allowable target cost, we have to go back and rethink various functions. For example, we might offer top-of-the-line warm-up suits that offer breathable water-repellent material at higher prices. Another strategy would be to use less costly materials that do not provide water resistance."

"Our objective in the conceptual design stage is to define a product whose estimated costs are close to our allowable target cost," Ann summarized. "However, further opportunities for cost reduction occur in later stages of value engineering. We have a basic understanding of how the conceptualization phase applies to us; now let's consider the product development phase."

Product Development. Jan continued, "The product development phase results in the second iteration of the allowable cost, termed the draft target cost. Upon completing the conceptualization stage, our design engineers would prepare a detailed order sheet identifying all components to be used in assembling the warm-up suit—fibers, yarn, fabric, elastic, lining material, and zippers."

Ann interjected, "At this point, decisions are made concerning which components will be purchased from outside suppliers and which ones will be manufactured internally. For example, we would outsource zippers and possibly synthetic yarn, while we would continue to spin cotton yarn internally."

"During the product development stage, we must involve our suppliers. If we slightly alter the specifications on certain components, suppliers may be able to provide greater cost savings," added John.

"When do engineers actually produce drawings of the new product?" asked Carolyn.

"Representatives at the automobile company said that engineers produced drawings following receipt of the detailed order sheet," John answered. "Then, cross-functional teams use value engineering to reduce the component cost for each *product function*. For example, at the auto facility, individual functions such as air conditioning and transmission systems were examined to discover opportunities to reduce parts costs."

"Value engineering," Ann added, "also involves tearing down competitors' products to understand the materials and parts used, and how the components function. In addition, companies try to gain insights into the manner in which products are manufactured or assembled. The teardown stage attempts to discover ways to reduce direct manufacturing costs as well as investments in equipment required in the production process."

Prototype Development. Jan continued, "The third iteration of value engineering results in the final target cost. After the conceptualization and product development phases, a prototype of each product is produced. For example, we would produce prototypes of various warm-up styles—hooded, zippered, Velcro, water-resistant, etc. During this stage, we would discover any problems encountered in the assembly process."

John added, "Changes in the manufacturing process can be made during this stage, and these changes can be factored into the estimated cost of the product. Once again, before production is initiated, the cost is compared with the allowable cost as originally defined."

Production. "While production facilities are expected to achieve target costs, few efforts are directed at cost reduction during the production phase of a product. Because life cycles for many products are very short, companies rarely make major changes in production systems because of the disruptive nature of changes. Of course, minor changes are made in the spirit of continuous process improvement. Major changes are reserved until the next model is introduced," recalled John.

"During the production phase, the final target cost determined during the prototype development phase is compared with actual costs," Jan added. "The final target cost is used as a benchmark against which actual costs are compared."

Carolyn asked, "As an accountant, I find the concept of continually comparing actual costs with benchmarks, or standards, very reasonable. However, in your explanation of target costing, I heard very little about the accountant's role. How are we involved in the process?"

Ann responded, "Carolyn, that's a good question. As you have heard, the design and cost control efforts are the responsibility of various engineering groups. In Japan, employees typically rotate among various job responsibilities within a company. Thus, engineers receive on-the-job training in accounting and develop strong cost management skills. The target costing system forces engineers to manage costs while developing new products and new manufacturing systems. Therefore, the primary role of accountants is to help set the final target cost and to serve as watchdogs to ensure that actual manufacturing costs do not exceed targets."[2]

Decision Makers Affected

Target costing and value engineering are processes that affect many different functions within an organization. Thus, decisions are made by groups representing marketing, product design, production, and accounting. Because target costing begins by identifying customer needs, marketing professionals must identify key product characteristics that consumers value. These characteristics are communicated to engineers, who develop products and manufacturing systems that permit efficient

---

[2]   *Cooper, Robin. 1994.* Cost Management in a Confrontation Strategy: Lessons from Japan—Instructor's Guide. *Boston: Harvard Business School.*

production. Accountants design systems that capture the costs of design, manufacturing, and delivery. Thus, the process is a joint effort that spans multiple disciplines.

Cost, quality, and functionality trade-offs are made to achieve the target cost. However, an organization often is incapable of successfully controlling costs by working exclusively within its organizational boundaries. To effectively compete using a confrontation strategy, costs must be managed across the entire supply chain. Thus when developing new products, companies often work in conjunction with suppliers. The next technique to control the future cost of products is interorganizational cost management.

Interorganizational Cost Management Systems

Ann began, "We noticed a common theme across the various industries we visited. Lean enterprises using a confrontation strategy have done a good job managing the elements of the survival triplet within their organizational boundaries. However, most have taken cost management one step farther. **They are forming** *interorganizational cost management systems,* **which are alliances across organizational boundaries for sharing cost information to develop an efficient supply chain."**

John added, "We learned that firms shared research and development information with suppliers. They also have employee exchange programs that help suppliers and customers understand each other's processes and products. Employees of suppliers can see firsthand how their products affect their customer's production process and final product."

"The communication network is helpful because all suppliers in the supply chain understand the demands of the final customer in terms of price, quality, and functionality," added Jan. "All too often suppliers define their customer as the company that purchases their product. However, many unseen customers are affected by each supplier in the chain."

Bruce added, "That's right, if we purchase defective zippers from our supplier, the defect affects KnitCo and our customer, the wholesaler. It also affects the retail store, and finally the athlete who purchases the warm-up suit."

"By understanding the demands of the final customer, companies in the supply chain can work together to promote efficiency and cost reduction. For example, each supplier in the chain should understand the quality, functionality, and price demands of the final customer. In doing so, companies may discover opportunities to modify specifications that result in cost savings," added Ann.

"Many companies maintain interorganizational cost management systems," Jan volunteered.

Bob objected, "Are you suggesting that we share proprietary information about our products and processes with our vendors? That sounds very risky. Many of our vendors also supply raw materials to our competitors."

"We face an interesting dilemma," Jan replied. "If we do not share information and participate in an efficient supplier chain, we may lose opportunities to improve quality and to reduce costs. However, by sharing information with the industry, we may lose our ability to differentiate our product."

Who Benefits from Target Costing and Value Engineering?

"John, at the beginning of our meeting, you challenged us to ask hard questions about whether a technique applies to us. Are there certain company or industry characteristics that make target costing more or less applicable?" asked Bob.

"That's a fair question," responded John. "From our observations, we believe that companies that have products with short life cycles benefit from target costing because new products constantly replace older models."

"For example, high-tech companies may benefit," added Bob.

"That's right," John replied. "I think the garment industry also can benefit because styles constantly are changing. Our product life cycle isn't short because our products wear out, it is short because customers want a fresh look each season. On the other hand, companies in mature industries producing standardized products or commodities, such as paper and steel, rarely make significant changes in their product designs. If new products are rarely introduced, target costing is not practical."

SELF-STUDY PROBLEM 2

Lightning Communications, Inc., manufactures cables used for fiber-optic data transmission. Lightning purchases optical fiber from outside suppliers. These fibers are used to produce insulated bundles of communication cable that are installed by businesses throughout the world.

Lightning traditionally has developed new products based on market research. Selling prices were determined by adding a profit margin to the manufacturing cost. Selling prices were adjusted when necessary to meet competitive market prices for similar products. Recently, corporate management has identified cost containment and product quality improvement as objectives. Target costing has been recommended when new products are proposed.

Required

1. How does target costing differ from Lightning's existing approach to new-product development?
2. Why might Lightning use multidisciplinary teams to implement value engineering?
3. Discuss how Lightning can use interorganizational cost management to help improve quality and reduce costs.

The solution to Self-Study Problem 2 appears at the end of the chapter.

TECHNIQUES TO CONTROL CURRENT COSTS

Objective 4
Explain what Kaizen is.

"Our discussions so far have focused on techniques to manage the costs of new products prior to the manufacturing stage. While we were in Japan, we also explored how lean enterprises manage costs during the production phase," John stated.

"While the focus of target costing is to design away manufacturing inefficiencies and costs, many companies continue to look for ways to improve manufacturing processes. **Continuous improvements resulting in greater levels of quality and lower costs are termed** *Kaizen*," added Ann. "Obviously, the shape of the survival zone will change over time, as product and manufacturing innovations are developed. The target costing system helps ensure that a product is profitable at introduction. However, because of innovations developed by competitors, a product may become unprofitable."

http://www.swcollege.
com/ingram.html

**Learn more about
Kaizen.**

"How do lean enterprises respond when competitors move the survival zone?" asked Bruce. "Presumably companies constantly are developing new products, but what about products that are in the production phase?"

John responded, "Because quality and functionality dimensions have been largely established before the production stage, few significant changes along these dimensions of the survival triplet are possible. Thus, the cost dimension typically is the element of the survival triplet that is managed after a product is in the production phase."

"The focus of Kaizen costing is continuous process improvement and cost reduction. Not all companies use Kaizen costing because many of them have eliminated most significant inefficiencies through the target costing and value engineering processes," added Jan. "Also, major changes during the production phase often are not beneficial because product life cycles are short. Process interruptions may cost more in lost production time and retraining than would be saved by making changes. We observed that Kaizen cost systems were more prevalent among companies that have products with long life cycles."

"How do Japanese firms motivate teams to achieve targets set as part of Kaizen?" asked Carolyn.

"Employee teams are rewarded for their cost reduction efforts," answered Jan. "For example, we saw picture boards illustrating processes before and after improvement initiatives. Team members are given credit for innovative improvement ideas."

"Ann, we have heard about ways Japanese companies manage costs when introducing new products," said Carolyn. "I would like to know how their cost accounting systems differ from those with which we are familiar."

Ann responded, "The product costing systems we saw in Japan were very similar to those found in Western firms. Few companies had introduced an activity-based costing (ABC) system. This is not altogether surprising, given the purpose of ABC systems. For example, ABC systems often are used to understand how resources are consumed by activities, and which products demand activities. If a company has used target costing and value engineering to develop products, the target costing process already has given companies insights into the manner in which products consume resources."

John added to Ann's explanation, "We observed that many companies assigned production costs to product lines, rather than to individual products. Since product lines often have dedicated areas within the factory, cost assignment at the product line level is straightforward. Also, most decisions are made at the product line level, rather than the individual product level. Thus, the importance of understanding the cost of individual products is diminished."

Bruce interjected, "Earlier you mentioned that operational control systems were used to help ensure that costs do not differ from standards."

"That's right," answered Ann. "As we discussed, the accountant's role in target costing is to ensure that actual costs do not significantly exceed the final target cost. Here, a very traditional form of variance analysis is used to compare actual costs with standards developed by the target cost system."

John moved the conversation toward the topic of designing organizations to motivate behavior. "Japanese cost management practices also encompass changes in the way a company views its organizational structure," he said. "We observed how some Japanese companies are restructuring to create incentives for increasing profits. You may recall that the performance of cost center managers is based on their ability to manage costs, and the performance of profit center managers is based on their ability to both generate revenues and control costs. In these companies, business segments that traditionally had been organized and evaluated as cost centers have been restructured to become profit centers or *pseudo-profit centers.*"

Carolyn asked, "How do companies decide whether to use profit centers or pseudo-profit centers?"

"Good question," responded John. "Cost centers that can sell their products to outside customers become profit centers. Their goods are transferred to other divisions at current market prices. Alternatively, cost centers that cannot sell their products externally are established as **pseudo** (or false) **profit centers.** Their goods are transferred to buying divisions at cost plus a markup.

"At KnitCo we could organize the spinning, weaving, cutting, and sewing departments as profit centers," remarked Ann.

"I'm not convinced that these departments are true profit centers," replied John. "We sell only finished goods to external customers."

"However, our intermediate outputs such as yarn and fabric could be valued using external market prices for identical or similar goods," Ann responded.

Bruce asked, "Why are such measures necessary? Why isn't providing incentives to control costs sufficient?"

"When divisional or departmental managers are held responsible for profits, they focus on both revenues and costs," responded Jan. "In other words, companies have created incentives for managers to increase production levels if they can sell their products to other buyers. Using a cost center concept, managers are responsible only for controlling costs of production."

"In addition to using increased volume as a strategy to improve profitability, some companies reward profit centers for higher-quality products," John added. "For example, a profit center's products may be classified according to various levels of quality. Higher levels of quality command higher prices."

"We also learned of downsides associated with using small profit centers to motivate improvements," recalled Ann. "Sometimes economies of scale are lost because communication and coordination across numerous small profit centers is difficult. As in companies that use negotiated transfer pricing policies, sometimes conflicts arise among competing profit centers within an organization."

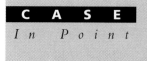

CASE
In Point

The internal audit department at **The Boeing Company** benefits from top management support that encourages employee participation. Auditors develop performance objectives and design personal strategies to achieve their objectives. The role of managers at Boeing involves removing constraints that limit an auditor's effectiveness, promoting career advancement, publicly recognizing auditor performance, and ensuring that stated improvement targets are met. The Kaizen program at Boeing directly affects the quality of internal audits provided to management. Thus Kaizen, or continuous improvement, principles apply equally to service and manufacturing.

Source: Didis, Stephen K. 1990. Kaizen. **Internal Auditor** *(August) 66–69.*

SERVICE ORGANIZATIONS

Objective 5
Understand how techniques used by Japanese companies can be applied to service organizations.

The techniques discussed in this chapter originate in the manufacturing industry. We easily can envision engineers designing a product and then using value engineering to achieve a target cost. For example, trade-off decisions, such as substituting a less expensive plastic lens for a glass lens in a compact camera, commonly are made in manufacturing environments. How do these techniques apply to service organizations, which often do not deliver a tangible product to their customers?

Consider a bank manager who is analyzing a proposal to offer on-line cash management services to customers. To offer the new service, software that permits transaction data downloading and other cash management activities must be developed and distributed to customers. In addition, various processes within the bank will be affected by customers having on-line access to account information. The manager must understand whether customers will value the new services and determine an acceptable monthly fee. Using target costing methodology, the manager would subtract the bank's required profit margin from the estimated monthly fee to determine a target cost for developing and delivering the on-line services. Using value engineering, processes and activities would be analyzed to discover and eliminate inefficiencies and waste. Though on-line cash management services are not tangible products, target costing and value engineering are useful tools for helping the bank manager deliver a service that will be profitable and valued by customers.

SELF-STUDY PROBLEM 3

Sweet Imagination Candy Company produces chocolate-covered peanut clusters in a three-step process. In the first step, peanuts are shelled, sorted, and roasted. In the second step, chocolate is melted in vats and the roasted peanuts are added to the mixture. Next, the clusters are poured onto a conveyor belt and allowed to cool. In the third step, the peanut clusters are packaged in plastic bags and prepared for shipment.

©Jim Pickerell

Currently, each process is evaluated by management as a cost center; however, the managers are considering reorganizing the cost centers into profit centers.

Required

1. Why would management consider converting the cost centers into profit centers?
2. Since revenues would become an important factor in performance evaluation, how might profit center managers increase reported profits?
3. What factors will determine whether management organizes the departments as profit centers or pseudo-profit centers?

The solution to Self-Study Problem 3 appears at the end of the chapter.

R E V I E W   *Summary of Important Concepts*

1. A confrontation strategy is used by companies that cannot maintain a sustainable competitive advantage through product differentiation or cost leadership.

2. The survival triplet is used to explain three variables on which companies employing a confrontation strategy compete.

3. The three variables of the survival triplet are cost (or price), quality, and functionality.

4. Target costing is used to help control costs of future products and to manage the product mix.

5. Value engineering is used by multidisciplinary teams to help remove costs from a new product before the product is manufactured.

6. Interorganizational cost management systems encourage teams to work with suppliers and customers so that additional cost savings may be realized.

7. Kaizen costing is used to continually reduce costs and improve quality during a product's production phase.

8. Japanese product costing systems typically trace costs to a product line, rather than to an individual product.

9. Operational control often consists of comparing actual costs with standards developed during the target costing process.

10. Cost centers can be organized as profit centers or pseudo-profit centers to encourage teams to consider ways to improve revenues and reduce costs.

D E F I N E   *Terms and Concepts Defined in This Chapter*

Confrontation strategy   (433)   Kaizen   (444)   Target costing   (438)
Interorganizational cost management   Survival triplet   (433)   Value engineering   (440)
   systems   (443)

S O L U T I O N S

SELF-STUDY PROBLEM 1

1.

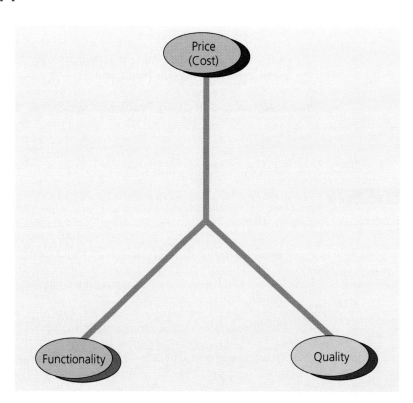

2.

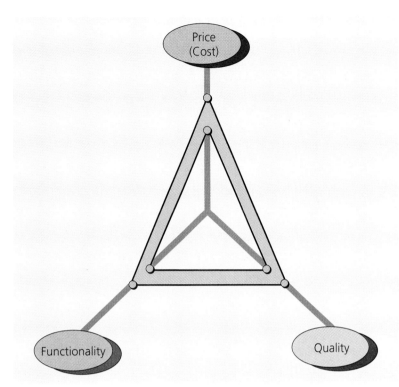

The outer boundaries of the functionality and quality elements are defined by the producer, and the inner boundaries of these dimensions are defined by the customer. The outer boundary of the cost (price) element is defined by the customer because it indicates the maximum price he or she is willing to pay. The inner boundary of the cost (price) element is determined by the producer. It illustrates the minimum possible cost to produce a product meeting customer specifications for quality and functionality.

3. a. A company may increase the functionality of a product by improving the product's ability to meet customer needs. For example, color capability can be added to black-and-white ink-jet printers. Camera systems may be upgraded to include various features, including auto-focus, red-eye reduction, time lapse capability, or water-resistant camera bodies.

    b.

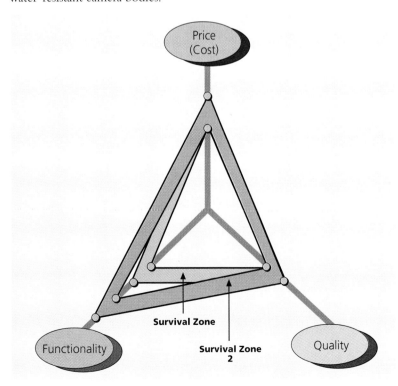

By increasing the functionality dimension of the survival triplet, a company may enjoy a temporary advantage in the marketplace until competitors respond with innovations of their own. This advantage occurs because the innovating company has shifted (increased) the minimum acceptable functionality demanded by a customer. Other companies that were located safely within the old survival zone find themselves suddenly outside the zone. Competitors must introduce innovations to alter the shape of the survival zone so that they once again are placed within it.

SELF-STUDY PROBLEM 2

1. Lightning may continue to use its market research program to help identify ideas for new products. However, a target costing program differs from the current policy of adding a markup to manufacturing costs to determine a selling price. For example, under target costing, market research may indicate important characteristics and possible selling prices for new products. This market-derived selling price is the basis for determining a target cost. A profit margin is subtracted from the expected selling price to arrive at a target cost.

2. Many firms use value engineering to develop manufacturing processes that ensure that target costs for products or services can be met. A multidisciplinary approach is used because many different functional areas are affected by new-product development. For example, those responsible for product design, raw materials purchasing, and manufacturing system design can contribute ideas that help deliver a new product that meets expectations for target cost.

3. Lightning may expect suppliers to help reduce costs and to improve the quality of the optical fiber used in Lightning's products. Suppliers may make recommendations for changes in product specifications that result in lower costs without sacrificing quality. Employee exchange programs also improve understanding and communication between Lightning and its suppliers. Improved communication may result in all members of the supply chain gaining a better appreciation of how their product and processes affect the final customer.

SELF-STUDY PROBLEM 3

1. Cost reductions are only one aspect of improving a company's profitability. When they are responsible for profitability, managers must consider ways not only to reduce costs, but also to increase revenues.

2. Managers may increase revenues by increasing production volume (assuming demand exists). Alternatively, some companies classify their intermediate products and pay higher prices for higher-quality goods. Thus, managers may be encouraged to improve the quality of their products to generate higher unit sales prices.

3. Typically, if the intermediate product cannot (or will not) be sold to external buyers, pseudo-profit centers are created. However, if market prices exist for intermediate products, and managers may sell intermediate products externally, profit centers are created.

EXERCISES

13-1. Write a short definition of each of the terms listed in the *Terms and Concepts Defined in This Chapter* section.

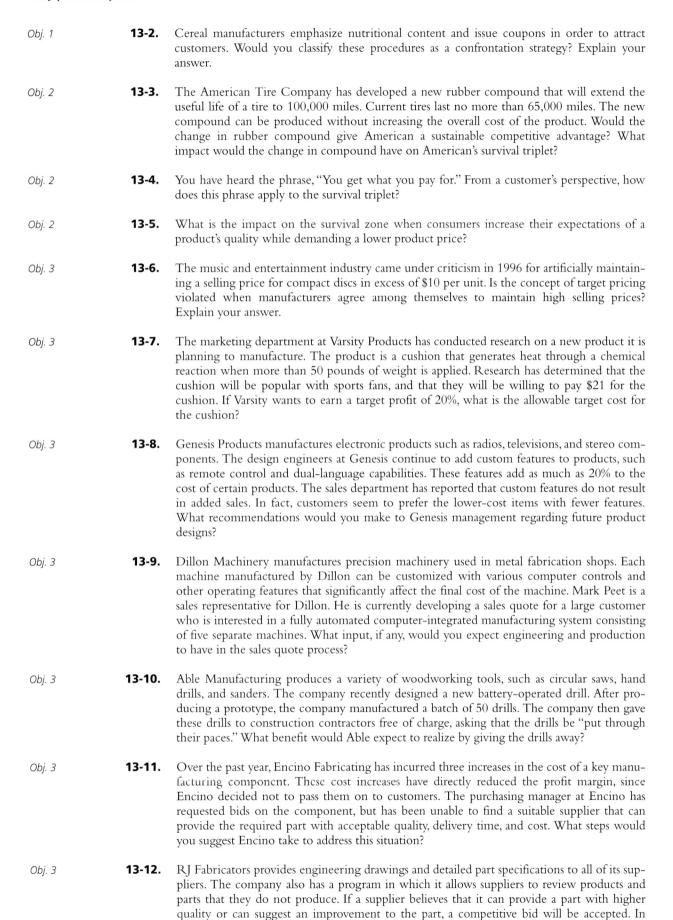

Obj. 1 **13-2.** Cereal manufacturers emphasize nutritional content and issue coupons in order to attract customers. Would you classify these procedures as a confrontation strategy? Explain your answer.

Obj. 2 **13-3.** The American Tire Company has developed a new rubber compound that will extend the useful life of a tire to 100,000 miles. Current tires last no more than 65,000 miles. The new compound can be produced without increasing the overall cost of the product. Would the change in rubber compound give American a sustainable competitive advantage? What impact would the change in compound have on American's survival triplet?

Obj. 2 **13-4.** You have heard the phrase, "You get what you pay for." From a customer's perspective, how does this phrase apply to the survival triplet?

Obj. 2 **13-5.** What is the impact on the survival zone when consumers increase their expectations of a product's quality while demanding a lower product price?

Obj. 3 **13-6.** The music and entertainment industry came under criticism in 1996 for artificially maintaining a selling price for compact discs in excess of $10 per unit. Is the concept of target pricing violated when manufacturers agree among themselves to maintain high selling prices? Explain your answer.

Obj. 3 **13-7.** The marketing department at Varsity Products has conducted research on a new product it is planning to manufacture. The product is a cushion that generates heat through a chemical reaction when more than 50 pounds of weight is applied. Research has determined that the cushion will be popular with sports fans, and that they will be willing to pay $21 for the cushion. If Varsity wants to earn a target profit of 20%, what is the allowable target cost for the cushion?

Obj. 3 **13-8.** Genesis Products manufactures electronic products such as radios, televisions, and stereo components. The design engineers at Genesis continue to add custom features to products, such as remote control and dual-language capabilities. These features add as much as 20% to the cost of certain products. The sales department has reported that custom features do not result in added sales. In fact, customers seem to prefer the lower-cost items with fewer features. What recommendations would you make to Genesis management regarding future product designs?

Obj. 3 **13-9.** Dillon Machinery manufactures precision machinery used in metal fabrication shops. Each machine manufactured by Dillon can be customized with various computer controls and other operating features that significantly affect the final cost of the machine. Mark Peet is a sales representative for Dillon. He is currently developing a sales quote for a large customer who is interested in a fully automated computer-integrated manufacturing system consisting of five separate machines. What input, if any, would you expect engineering and production to have in the sales quote process?

Obj. 3 **13-10.** Able Manufacturing produces a variety of woodworking tools, such as circular saws, hand drills, and sanders. The company recently designed a new battery-operated drill. After producing a prototype, the company manufactured a batch of 50 drills. The company then gave these drills to construction contractors free of charge, asking that the drills be "put through their paces." What benefit would Able expect to realize by giving the drills away?

Obj. 3 **13-11.** Over the past year, Encino Fabricating has incurred three increases in the cost of a key manufacturing component. These cost increases have directly reduced the profit margin, since Encino decided not to pass them on to customers. The purchasing manager at Encino has requested bids on the component, but has been unable to find a suitable supplier that can provide the required part with acceptable quality, delivery time, and cost. What steps would you suggest Encino take to address this situation?

Obj. 3 **13-12.** RJ Fabricators provides engineering drawings and detailed part specifications to all of its suppliers. The company also has a program in which it allows suppliers to review products and parts that they do not produce. If a supplier believes that it can provide a part with higher quality or can suggest an improvement to the part, a competitive bid will be accepted. In order to participate in this program, suppliers must sign a nondisclosure agreement. What benefit would RJ realize from such a program? Why do you think suppliers must sign a nondisclosure agreement?

Obj. 4 **13-13.** Trentco Electronics utilizes a working relationship with suppliers that requires suppliers not only to provide key subcomponents of its products, but also to install the parts in the end product right in Trentco's factory. The president of Trentco is pleased with this working relationship and points out that as a result of this arrangement, the suppliers are footing the bill for much of the capital investment that is required to support subassembly production. What other benefits do you think Trentco would realize from this arrangement with suppliers?

Objs. 1, 3, 4 **13-14.** The Garden Mark Company produces lawn mowers, rototillers, and edgers. Each year the company spends thousands of dollars purchasing competitors' equipment and putting it through vigorous tests. What benefit would you expect Garden Mark to realize from this activity?

PROBLEMS

PROBLEM 13-1   **Confrontation Strategy**

Objs. 1, 2

Blackstone Construction Company was founded by Lewis Blackstone shortly after his graduation from high school. During high school, Lewis enrolled in every construction trade course available, excelled in his studies, and decided that he would pursue a career constructing new homes. Using funds that he had saved from summer construction jobs, Lewis purchased two lots in a newly formed subdivision. After hiring a small work crew, he built a three-bedroom, two-bath home on one of the lots. He hoped to sell it quickly, turn a profit, and build an even larger home on the other lot. Lewis believed that the quality of his home would ensure its quick sale. Unfortunately, after it had been on the market for nine months, the home still had not sold.

Lewis determined that the reason his home had not sold was that in the same subdivision there were more than 15 other homes of similar size and with similar features that had lower selling prices. He further determined that most of the other homes for sale contained prefabricated versions of many components, such as roof joists and fixtures, that Lewis's crew had manufactured by hand. Accordingly, Lewis determined that his home had taken more time, materials, and hence had cost more. Lewis is beginning to plan the construction of the second home, and wants to ensure that this second home is sold faster than the first.

Required

a.   Explain how Lewis could use a confrontation strategy.
b.   What are some factors Lewis should consider in developing a confrontation strategy?

PROBLEM 13-2   **Product Differentiation**

Objs. 1, 2

Taylor Equipment Company manufactures factory equipment that is used in metal fabricating. The machines sold by Taylor include presses, lathes, and welders. Historically, machines of this nature have been a major cause of factory accidents. Accordingly, Taylor designs its machinery with electro-photostatic eyes and beams that automatically shut down a machine if any foreign object, including hands or arms, gets too close to the machine and obstructs the safety beams. The insurance industry has placed its "stamp of approval" on Taylor's machines, and many insurance companies have offered discounts on workers' compensation insurance policies if a manufacturer replaces old equipment with Taylor's new technology.

Required

a.   How does Taylor utilize a strategy of product differentiation?
b.   Assume that Taylor's safety features add significant cost to each machine. What is the impact of these costs from the customer's perspective?

PROBLEM **13-3** **Survival Triplet Analysis**

Obj. 2

Cole Enterprises manufactures two products, whose three-prong survival triplets are shown below.

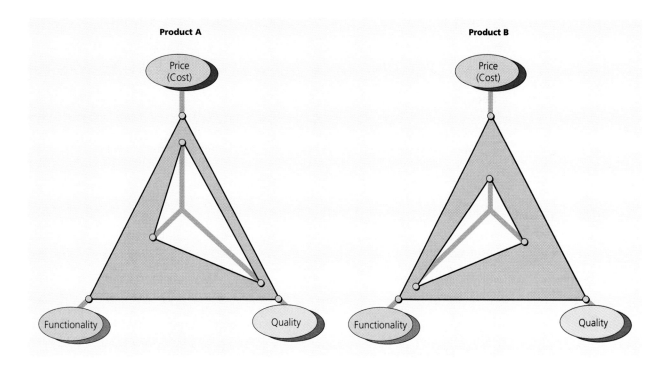

Product A   Product B

Price (Cost)   Price (Cost)

Functionality   Quality   Functionality   Quality

Required

a. Which of the two products would most likely be rejected by customers if the sales price were increased to compensate for additional costs? Explain your answer.

b. Which of the two products would most likely have an increase in sales if Cole added features and benefits to the product and passed the cost of the additional features on to customers in the form of a higher selling price? Explain your answer.

c. All other factors being equal, in which of the two products is quality more important to customer satisfaction?

PROBLEM **13-4** **Target Costing**

Obj. 3

Seridan Enterprises has developed an amazing new egg-beating gizmo that it calls the Rooster Rotor. The company plans to sell the Rooster Rotor via direct television advertising and infomercials. Based on preliminary market research, the company has determined that customers would be willing to pay $19.95 for the item. The prototypes used in the market research cost $34 to produce. The company believes that it can cut cost from the product by substituting less expensive materials and reduce other costs by achieving economies of scale through mass production.

Required

a. Explain how target costing would help management determine the amount of cost that can be incurred in manufacturing the product.

b. If management desires a 25% profit margin on this product, how much cost must be eliminated from the cost of the original prototypes?

PROBLEM **13-5** **Cost Management Systems and Information Flow**

Obj. 3

Rip Tide Manufacturing produces a line of power boats that are popular with water skiers. The engineering department at Rip Tide is constantly developing new hull designs and other features intended to make the boats faster, safer, or more aerodynamic. One of Rip Tide's boats, an 18-foot inboard ski boat, recently underwent a dozen modifications in the engineering department. These adjustments included a new hull design, changes in material specifications, and increased seating capacity. Upon receiving the new product drawings in the production department, Leslie Houghton, the production manager, complained that producing the new designs would require an extensive upgrade of the manufacturing line. Adam Leigh, the purchasing manager, also complained that the materials needed to meet the new specifications would add significant cost to the product and might be difficult to obtain. Isaac Levine, the sales manager, noted that the new changes would result in a higher product cost which most customers might not find acceptable.

Required

a.   Explain why information sharing between organizational functions is important in developing new product designs.

b.   What elements of cost and function should the company consider when implementing new product designs? What areas of the company should have input into product design changes?

PROBLEM 13-6   Product Design and Value Engineering

Objs. 1, 2, 3

The Custom Mattress Factory manufactures a wide variety of quality custom mattresses. Each mattress is manufactured to last 25 years and is made with high-quality materials and painstaking attention to detail. The manufacturing process utilized at Custom Mattress Factory results in a very high product cost. The company emphasizes its high quality in its advertising promotions, and it relies on its reputation for quality to attract new buyers. While most of the mattresses produced conform to industry standards with respect to size and dimensions, the company also promotes its ability to manufacture mattresses that are not of standard dimensions. For example, in its advertising, the company notes its ability to manufacture round and extra long mattresses. The company also advertises that it will manufacture, within five business days, a mattress of any size or dimensions required by a customer.

Required

a.   Explain how the company utilizes a confrontation strategy with respect to its competition.

b.   How does value engineering affect the products offered by Custom Mattress Factory?

PROBLEM 13-7   Continuous Improvement

Obj. 4

Royal Power Equipment, Inc., has manufactured power tools for 54 years. During that time, the company has made numerous changes in its products that have caused them to be safer and easier to handle. For example, the company has switched to magnesium from steel for its most popular power saw, thereby eliminating 40% of the weight. It also has improved the saw's electrical wiring systems, thereby reducing the risk of shock to users. Similar advances have been incorporated in almost every other power tool that Royal produces. The cost of these enhancements has resulted in an 80% price increase on each tool, yet Royal remains one of the most popular brands of power tools on the market, and Royal tools are often the tool of choice in the construction industry.

Required

a.   Explain why the changes Royal made to its product specifications would add value to the product.

b.   What factors should Royal consider when making product improvements or enhancements? Why?

PROBLEM 13-8   Service Costs

Obj. 5

Marla's Maid Service provides cleaning services for commercial and residential customers. Each of Marla's customers is serviced by at least a two-person crew, with some commercial customers requiring as many as eight people to provide the service. Services are performed on a regular basis for 20 commercial customers and 15 residential customers. Most commercial customers receive daily cleaning that includes trash removal, bathroom cleaning, vacuuming, and dusting. Residential customers receive similar services, but providing them requires much less time, and these customers often are serviced only once a week or on a biweekly basis. Marla Pickens, owner of Marla's Maid Service, is thinking of expanding services to include window cleaning. She is aware that window cleaning will require significant time on the part of her crews, and she is unsure whether customers would be willing to pay the cost associated with this service. She also knows that this service is not offered by other cleaning services in her area.

Required

a. How would the addition of window cleaning differentiate Marla from her competitors?
b. Could Marla use target costing to help her decide whether to offer window cleaning services? Why or why not?

PROBLEM 13-9   Multiple-Choice Overview of the Chapter

1. After developing a product, a company surveys customers to determine whether they are willing to pay an established price. Based on this feedback from potential customers, the company redesigns aspects of the product to eliminate costs associated with certain features and benefits. This procedure would best be described as:
   a. continuous improvement.
   b. target costing.
   c. Kaizen.
   d. value engineering.

2. The three elements of the survival triplet are
   a. cost, quality, and profit margin.
   b. quality, design, and customer satisfaction.
   c. cost, functionality, and selling price.
   d. cost, quality, and functionality.

3. Which of the following statements best summarizes the Japanese perspective on manufacturing?
   a. Customers generally will be willing to pay any price for a quality product.
   b. A low-cost strategy will result in the most efficient production.
   c. Success depends on lean manufacturing with high quality and efficient production.
   d. Direct competition is avoided through product differentiation.

4. Which of the following would not be a reason for adopting a confrontation strategy?
   a. A company is unable to generate a sustainable competitive advantage.
   b. A company is able to generate a temporary competitive advantage.
   c. Head-to-head competition is unavoidable.
   d. Product differentiation creates a barrier to competition.

5. An alliance across organizational boundaries for sharing information to develop an efficient supply chain is known as:
   a. an interorganizational cost management system.
   b. the survival triplet.
   c. the Japanese cost management philosophy.
   d. Kaizen.

6. Which of the following is a benefit of prototype development?
   a. Manufacturing problems can be discovered before full production is initiated.
   b. Different materials can be tested for product compatibility.
   c. Prototypes can be shown to potential customers, and feedback can be obtained.
   d. All of the above.

7. Value engineering is an approach that is based on:
   a. representatives from numerous disciplines within the organization working together to eliminate product cost prior to manufacturing.
   b. the concept that quality and function can be enhanced by product design.

c.   customer expectations of functionality.

d.   continuous improvement resulting in greater levels of quality with lower product cost.

8. When a company cannot sustain a price advantage over competitors and cannot sufficiently differentiate its product from those of its competitors, the company should:
    a.   rely on increased product quality to attract customers.
    b.   search for any temporary advantages that would attract customers.
    c.   reduce its selling price and rely on other products to generate positive profit margins.
    d.   reengineer its product to better meet customer demands for functionality.

9. A pseudo-profit center:
    a.   is a profit center that sells products to outside customers.
    b.   is any profit center that is evaluated based on traditional variance analysis.
    c.   generates profits by transferring to internal customers at cost plus a markup.
    d.   holds managers responsible only for controlling costs of production.

10. Which of the following is true with respect to the conceptual design phase of a product?
    a.   Prototype products are manufactured.
    b.   Manufacturing processes are redesigned to more efficiently produce a product.
    c.   New forms of functionality are explored, and value engineering is used to reduce costs.
    d.   Pseudo-profit centers are identified or designed.

C A S E S

CASE 13-1   Competitive Strategies

Objs. 2, 3

Energy Resources of America, Inc. (ERA), produces geothermal sounding devices used by oil companies to determine the best locations for oil wells. The cost of each device is in excess of $1 million. Therefore, only the largest oil companies typically can afford to purchase ERA's equipment. The cost of developing the geothermal technology was very high, and it took ERA almost 12 years to perfect its device. Many of the parts used in ERA's devices are protected by patents. ERA customers have been very pleased with the product because the devices are extremely accurate at locating oil deposits. One customer commented that his company estimates that it saves 10 times the cost of each device when accurate well placement is obtained.

There are currently no other devices on the market that can perform the same service as ERA. In addition, ERA offers 100 hours of free geologist time with the purchase of every machine. The geologist will assist the customer in the initial use of the device and will teach the customer's personnel how to read the device's output. After the initial 100 hours of geologist assistance, customers may hire ERA personnel to assist in geological surveys at the price of $400 per hour.

Required

a.   Explain how the survival triplet relates to the ERA sounding devices. What are the elements of functionality and quality that customers are most likely to use to evaluate the sounding devices?

b.   Assume that ERA makes only one type of device (i.e., there can be no customization for particular customers). Does the fact that all devices are identical eliminate the need for value engineering in the organization? How could an interorganizational cost management system help make ERA more profitable?

c.   A major oil company recently purchased a sounding device from ERA and subsequently contracted for additional geologist help with field surveys. Since there is no competition for the sounding device, does the sale of in-house geologist time provide any form of product differentiation? Why or why not?

P R O J E C T S

PROJECT 13-1   Product Design

Objs. 2, 3

Select a product with which you are familiar that has undergone design changes over the past 20 years or so. The changes can be directed toward improved product performance, enhanced safety, or expanded functionality. Write a brief narrative explaining the changes and describing how these changes would affect the survival triplet from a customer's point of view.

PROJECT 13-2   Survival Strategy, Value Engineering, and Kaizen

Objs. 2, 3, 4, 5

Locate an article in a business periodical such as *The Wall Street Journal* that describes changes a company has made to a product. Write a short narrative briefly describing the changes, focusing on how the product changes affect the company's survival strategy and reflect value engineering and the concept of continuous product improvement.

PROJECT 13-3   Confrontation Strategy

Objs. 1, 2, 5

Browse the Internet for information on a particular company, product, or service that is differentiated from its competition by either cost or quality. Capture and print the information that is disclosed at this Web site. Prepare a short report on your findings. Explain how this company, product, or service uses a confrontation strategy as a competitive advantage.

APPENDIX

FUTURE AND PRESENT VALUE

Present and future value concepts are based on the simple idea that a dollar received today is worth more than a dollar received at some future time. If you received a dollar today, you could invest it in a savings account or other investment to earn interest. At the end of a month, a year, or five years, the value of the investment would be larger than it is today because you would have earned interest for the period of investment.

Future Value of a Single Amount

As an example, if you invested $100 on January 1, 1998 in a savings account that earns 6% interest, your investment will be worth $106 on December 31, 1998. The value of the investment on January 1 is the **present value** of the investment. The value of the investment on December 31 is the **future value** of the investment. Thus, we can express the relationship as:

Future Value = Present Value $\times$ (1 + R)
$106 = $100 $\times$ 1.06,

where R is the rate of return earned on the investment.

If an investment is made for more than one period in which interest is paid and the interest is not withdrawn, the investment earns compound interest. For example, if you leave your money in the savings account for a second year and it earns 6% in the second year, your investment will be worth $112.36 at the end of two years:

Future Value = Present Value $\times$ (1 + R) $\times$ (1 + R)
$112.36 = $100 $\times$ 1.06 $\times$ 1.06
$112.36 = $100 $\times$ $(1.06)^2$

Then, we can write the general equation for the future value of an investment as:

Future Value = Present Value $\times$ $(1 + R)^t$

where t is the number of periods of the investment.

The last term in this equation, $(1 + R)^t$, is referred to as an interest factor. Tables are available that provide the interest factor for various interest rates (R) and time periods (t). Table 3 on the back inside cover of this book provides this type of table. For example, the interest factor for 6% interest and two periods is 1.12360. Therefore, the future value of an investment of $100 that earns 6% for two periods is $112.36 = $100 $\times$ 1.12360. You can use the table rather than calculating the interest factor.

Present Value of a Single Amount

If we know the future value of an investment, we can solve for the present value using the same approach as in the previous section. For example, if we know an investment is worth $112.36 at the end of two years and earns 6% interest, we can solve for the present value as follows:

$$\text{Present Value} = \text{Future Value} \times \frac{1}{(1 + R)^t}$$

$$\$100 = \$112.36 \times \frac{1}{(1.06)^2}$$

Again, the last term in this equation is referred to as an interest factor. Table 1 on the front inside cover of this book contains this type of table. For example, the interest factor for 6% and two periods is 0.89000. Therefore, the present value of $112.36 received at the end of two years at 6% interest is $100 = $112.36 × 0.89000.

Future Value of an Annuity

In some situations, an investment consists of a series of payments. For example, you might invest $100 each year for three years in a savings account that earns 6%. This type of investment is an annuity because it consists of an equal payment ($100) during each period for a fixed number of periods (3) at a constant rate of return (6%). To calculate the future value of this series of payments, you could calculate the future value of each payment and add these amounts together:

$$\text{Future Value of Annuity} = \$100 \times [(1.06)^3 + (1.06)^2 + (1.06)^1] = \$337.46$$

Or, you could substitute the interest factors from Table 3:

$$\text{Future Value of Annuity} = \$100 \times (1.19102 + 1.12360 + 1.06000) = \$337.46$$

Another option is to use the interest factor from a table like Table 4 on the back inside cover of this book. This table provides interest factors for computing the future value of an annuity. For example, the interest factor for an annuity of three periods at 6% is 3.37462. Therefore, the future value of an annuity of $100 per period for three periods at 6% is $337.462 = $100 × 3.37462.

Present Value of an Annuity

We can use the same procedure as in the previous section to determine the present value of an annuity. For example, if you made an investment that paid you $100 at the end of each year for three years and earned a 6% rate of return, how much would the investment be worth at the beginning of the three year period? You could solve for the present value of the annuity by determining the present value of each payment:

$$\text{Present Value of Annuity} = \$100 \left[\frac{1}{(1.06)^3} + \frac{1}{(1.06)^2} + \frac{1}{(1.06)^1} \right] = \$267.30$$

Or, you could substitute interest factors from Table 1 in the equation:

$$\text{Present Value of Annuity} = \$100 (0.83962 + 0.89000 + 0.94340) = \$267.30$$

Another alternative is to use the interest factor from a present value of an annuity table such as Table 2 on the front inside cover of this book. The interest factor for three periods at 6% is 2.67301 from Table 2. Therefore,

$$\text{Present Value of Annuity} = \$100 \times 2.67301 = \$267.301$$

Future and present value calculations are common in business decisions. Interest factor tables can make these calculations simpler. To use the tables you must determine whether you are calculating a future or present value and whether you are dealing with a simple (one) amount or a series of equal amounts (an annuity). Also, you must know the number of periods and interest rate for the investment.

Glossary

A

accounting rate of return (ARR) The average accounting income a project generates per period divided by the amount of the investment in the project./10

activity-based costing (ABC) A decision-making tool that links the activities performed to create products with the costs of these activities./1

activity-based management (ABM) A decision-making tool emphasizing a company's ability to measure activities that create costs as the key to performance improvement./1

agents People hired by owners who are expected to manage the company in a way consistent with the owner's interests./9

B

balanced scorecard An approach to evaluation that uses key performance criteria in four categories: financial, customer satisfaction, innovation and learning, and internal business./9

bottlenecks Processes that produce at slow rates and restrict the flow of goods or services./8

bottom-up budget A budget that involves all levels of an organization working to achieve the organization's goals./6

budget A detailed plan describing the use of financial and operating resources over a specific period./6

C

capital budgeting The process of making capital investment decisions./10

capital investment decision A decision to invest in long-term assets such as plant and equipment./10

cash budget A budget that describes cash requirements for the budget period./6

common cause variation A variation that is the result of randomness inherent in a process./7

confrontation strategy A management approach that creates numerous temporary competitive advantages when a sustainable competitive advantage is not possible./13

cost-based transfer pricing policy A policy that uses either full cost or variable cost as a basis for determining a transfer price./9

cost center A division of an organization that consumes resources while performing its responsibilities, yet has no direct involvement in generating sales or acquiring property./9

cost driver analysis A decision-making tool that considers that costs are created or driven by many interrelated factors./1

cost drivers Activities that create costs./1

cost of capital The cost of funds that can be used to finance a project./10

critical path The steps need to complete a process./12

cycle time The number of minutes that pass between units leaving the final assembly area./8

D

direct labor budget A budget that identifies the labor resources required to meet production needs./6

direct materials budget A budget that identifies the amount of materials that will be required to support a company's total production needs./6

discounting The translation of future dollars into current dollars./10

discounting methods Methods of evaluating capital investments that rely on the time value of money./10

F

favorable variance A variance that results when the actual price (or quantity) is less than the standard price (or quantity) for materials or labor./7

financial budget A budget describing cash flows and financial position, including assets, liabilities, and owner's equity./6

flexible budget A budget that enables a company to examine projected income over a *range* of sales levels./6

flexible manufacturing The ability to change from manufacturing one product to manufacturing a different product without incurring significant delays or costs./1

H

hurdle rate The rate that must be earned before an investment is made; also called required rate of return./10

I

internal auditing An independent evaluation function in an organization designed to assess various activities of the organization to help the organization meet its objectives./11

internal control The methods a company uses to protect its assets and promote their efficient use, to ensure accurate and reliable information, and to encourage adherence to laws and regulations./11

internal rate of return (IRR) The interest rate that results in the present value of cash outflows being equal to the present value of cash inflows from an investment./10

interorganizational cost management systems Alliances across organizational boundaries for sharing cost information to develop an efficient supply chain./13

investment center A level within an organization that has the strategic responsibility for generating profits and managing assets./9

J

just-in-time (JIT) A manufacturing philosophy that attempts to eliminate activities that do not add value by reducing inventory levels./1

just-in-time manufacturing A production system that pulls products through the manufacturing process on the basis of market demand./8

K

Kaizen costing Continuous improvements resulting in greater levels of quality and lower costs./13

L

lead time The amount of time it takes to process, move, store, and inspect inventory./1

M

management accountant An accountant who produces managerial accounting information for a specific company./1

manufacturing cell A group of related machines, typically arranged in the shape of a U./8

manufacturing lead time The total time required to move a unit from raw materials inventory to finished goods inventory./8

manufacturing overhead budget A budget that provides a schedule of all costs of production other than direct materials and direct labor./6

margin For ROI, operating income expressed as a percentage of sales./9

market-based transfer pricing policy A policy that requires buyers and sellers to transfer goods based on externally verifiable market prices./9

master budget A one-year financial plan for a company./1 A collection of related operating budgets covering sales, production, purchasing, labor, manufacturing overhead, administrative expenses, and financing activities./6

milestones Major decision points in a capital investment project./10

moving baseline concept The assumption that cash flows will decrease because of the competition's superior quality if the investment is not made./10

N

negotiated transfer pricing policies Policies that permit managers to consider factors such as cost and external market prices when negotiating a mutually acceptable transfer price between two business units./9

net present value (NPV) The difference between the present value of expected future cash inflows from the investment and the present value of expected cash outflows invested./10

nondiscounting methods Methods of evaluating capital investments that ignore the time value of money./10

O

operating assets Those assets controlled by the division; they include investments in cash, accounts receivable, inventory, and plant assets used in production./9

operating budget A budget describing revenues, production costs, or general and administrative costs./6

operating income Sales − (cost of goods sold + other operating expenses)./9

operational audits Evaluations by internal auditors of the performance of various departments or divisions of a company./11

operational capital investment decision A capital investment decision that affects only part of a company's operations, has an easily predictable life, and represents a relatively small capital outlay for a business./10

operational planning Identifying objectives for day-to-day activities./1

operations restructuring A complete evaluation of the relationships among multiple processes, conducted to improve the quality and efficiency of services provided to customers./12

opportunity costs Costs associated with not taking a particular course of action./10

outcomes data dissemination The practice of sharing process and outcomes information with those who make resource decisions./12

P

participative budgeting A process that allows individuals at various levels of a company to participate in determining the company's goals and the plans for achieving those goals./6

payback period The time required to recover an initial investment from expected future cash flows./10

process-oriented plant layout A plant arranged according to machine function, with machines that perform similar functions placed together./8

production budget A budget that identifies the amount of a product that must be produced to meet the company's needs for sales and inventory./6

product-oriented plant layout A plant based on manufacturing cells that meet the production requirements of products or product families (products that have similar characteristics)./8

profit center A division of an organization that is responsible for both generating sales and controlling costs and expenses./9

Q

quality costs Costs incurred because poor quality can or does exist in a particular product, function, or business./7

quality loss function A measure of the loss to society from a product that does not perform satisfactorily./7

R

reciprocal service arrangement An arrangement whereby support departments exchange services./12

required rate of return The rate that must be earned before an investment is made; also called hurdle rate./10

residual value The market value of an investment at the end of its useful life to a company, or service life./10

responsibility accounting Assigning responsibility for the performance of a company's departments to department managers./6

return on investment (ROI) A performance indicator calculated by dividing operating income by operating assets./9

revenue center A division of an organization that has responsibility for generating sales./9

S

sales budget A budget that projects revenues from sales of a company's products or services./6

selling and administrative expense budget A budget containing a list of anticipated expenses for the period for activities other than manufacturing./6

service life The period during which an investment is expected to be used./10

special cause variation A variation with an identifiable source, such as faulty equipment or processes./7

standard costs The cost of the material and labor that should have been used to achieve actual production levels./7

standards The quantity and cost of inputs, such as materials and labor, expected for a single unit of product./6

static budget A budget that identifies the income that would be earned at a predetermined level of sales activity./6

strategic capital investment decision A capital investment decision that affects all or a considerable part of a company's operations, has an uncertain life, and requires a large investment./10

strategic cost management (SCM) The development of a sustainable competitive advantage through understanding a company's costs./1

strategic planning Identifying a company's long-run goals and developing plans for achieving these goals./1

strategic positioning analysis Analysis considering the information needs of different competitive strategies./1

sunk costs Costs associated with decisions that have already been made./10

survival triplet The three crucial success factors for a firm using a confrontational strategy: cost/price, quality, and functionality./13

T

target costing The technique used to determine the cost at which a new product must be manufactured to achieve desired profitability./13

theory of constraints (TOC) A theory that states that by identifying a constraint, such as a bottleneck, that exists in the processing of a good or service and taking corrective steps, the process will be improved./8

throughput The number of units completed by a process in a given period of time./8

time-based competition A management philosophy that focuses on reducing the length of time it takes to develop, manufacture, and deliver a product./1

top-down budget A budget that is established by management and then provided to lower levels of an organization for compliance./6

total quality management (TQM) A management philosophy that attempts to eliminate all waste, defects, and activities that do not add value to a company's products./1 A management system that seeks continued improvement by asking everyone in an organization to understand, meet, and exceed the needs of customers./8

turnover For ROI, sales divided by average operating assets employed./9

U

unfavorable variance A variance that results when the actual price (or quantity) exceeds the standard./7

V

value chain The set of value-creating activities that extends from the production of raw materials to the sale and servicing of finished goods./1

value engineering An engineering approach in which techniques are applied during a product's design phase by a multidisciplinary team; representatives from design engineering, manufacturing, and purchasing work together to find ways to trim costs from a product before the manufacturing stage./13

Index

Students: South-Western College Publishing values your feedback. Tell us what you think about Ingram/Albright/Hill's *Managerial Accounting: Information for Decisions*. We are committed to producing the highest quality books and learning resources, and your input will help us reach this goal. Please take a few moments and fill out this student review form. When you are finished, please mail or fax this form to us at (513) 527–6467. We appreciate your help.

(1) What was your favorite part of the book?

(2) What were three topics or chapters that you had a hard time understanding?

(3) Why were those areas hard to understand?

(4) What did you think of the writing style and readability of the book?

(5) Did you use any classroom aids such as a study guide?

(6) What sort of classroom aids would you be willing to purchase?

(7) Will you keep this book, or will you sell it? Why?

(8) May South-Western quote you in any of our advertising or marketing material?

Optional: Name _____

                     Major _____

                     School _____

TABLE 3
FUTURE VALUE OF SINGLE AMOUNT

Interest Rate

Period	0.01	0.02	0.03	0.04	0.05	0.06	0.07	0.08	0.09	0.10	0.11	0.12
1	1.01000	1.02000	1.03000	1.04000	1.05000	1.06000	1.07000	1.08000	1.09000	1.10000	1.11000	1.12000
2	1.02010	1.04040	1.06090	1.08160	1.10250	1.12360	1.14490	1.16640	1.18810	1.21000	1.23210	1.25440
3	1.03030	1.06121	1.09273	1.12486	1.15763	1.19102	1.22504	1.25971	1.29503	1.33100	1.36763	1.40493
4	1.04060	1.08243	1.12551	1.16986	1.21551	1.26248	1.31080	1.36049	1.41158	1.46410	1.51807	1.57352
5	1.05101	1.10408	1.15927	1.21665	1.27628	1.33823	1.40255	1.46933	1.53862	1.61051	1.68506	1.76234
6	1.06152	1.12616	1.19405	1.26532	1.34010	1.41852	1.50073	1.58687	1.67710	1.77156	1.87041	1.97382
7	1.07214	1.14869	1.22987	1.31593	1.40710	1.50363	1.60578	1.71382	1.82804	1.94872	2.07616	2.21068
8	1.08286	1.17166	1.26677	1.36857	1.47746	1.59385	1.71819	1.85093	1.99256	2.14359	2.30454	2.47596
9	1.09369	1.19509	1.30477	1.42331	1.55133	1.68948	1.83846	1.99900	2.17189	2.35795	2.55804	2.77308
10	1.10462	1.21899	1.34392	1.48024	1.62889	1.79085	1.96715	2.15892	2.36736	2.59374	2.83942	3.10585
11	1.11567	1.24337	1.38423	1.53945	1.71034	1.89830	2.10485	2.33164	2.58043	2.85312	3.15176	3.47855
12	1.12683	1.26824	1.42576	1.60103	1.79586	2.01220	2.25219	2.51817	2.81266	3.13843	3.49845	3.89598
13	1.13809	1.29361	1.46853	1.66507	1.88565	2.13293	2.40985	2.71962	3.06580	3.45227	3.88328	4.36349
14	1.14947	1.31948	1.51259	1.73168	1.97993	2.26090	2.57853	2.93719	3.34173	3.79750	4.31044	4.88711
15	1.16097	1.34587	1.55797	1.80094	2.07893	2.39656	2.75903	3.17217	3.64248	4.17725	4.78459	5.47357
16	1.17258	1.37279	1.60471	1.87298	2.18287	2.54035	2.95216	3.42594	3.97031	4.59497	5.31089	6.13039
17	1.18430	1.40024	1.65285	1.94790	2.29202	2.69277	3.15882	3.70002	4.32763	5.05447	5.89509	6.86604
18	1.19615	1.42825	1.70243	2.02582	2.40662	2.85434	3.37993	3.99602	4.71712	5.55992	6.54355	7.68997
19	1.20811	1.45681	1.75351	2.10685	2.52695	3.02560	3.61653	4.31570	5.14166	6.11591	7.26334	8.61276
20	1.22019	1.48595	1.80611	2.19112	2.65330	3.20714	3.86968	4.66096	5.60441	6.72750	8.06231	9.64629
21	1.23239	1.51567	1.86029	2.27877	2.78596	3.39956	4.14056	5.03383	6.10881	7.40025	8.94917	10.80385
22	1.24472	1.54598	1.91610	2.36992	2.92526	3.60354	4.43040	5.43654	6.65860	8.14027	9.93357	12.10031
23	1.25716	1.57690	1.97359	2.46472	3.07152	3.81975	4.74053	5.87146	7.25787	8.95430	11.02627	13.55235
24	1.26973	1.60844	2.03279	2.56330	3.22510	4.04893	5.07237	6.34118	7.91108	9.84973	12.23916	15.17863
25	1.28243	1.64061	2.09378	2.66584	3.38635	4.29187	5.42743	6.84848	8.62308	10.83471	13.58546	17.00006